The Columbia History
of Jews and Judaism in America

Edited by Marc Lee Raphael

The Columbia History
of Jews and Judaism in America

COLUMBIA UNIVERSITY PRESS

NEW YORK

Columbia University Press
Publishers Since 1893
New York   Chichester, West Sussex
Copyright © 2008 Columbia University Press

Library of Congress Cataloging-in-Publication Data

The Columbia history of Jews and Judaism in America / edited by Marc Lee Raphael.
   p. cm.
  Includes bibliographical references and index.
  ISBN 978–0–231–13222–0 (cloth : alk. paper)
  1. Jews—United States—History.   2. Judaism—United States—History.
  3. Jews—Cultural assimilation—United States.   I. Raphael, Marc Lee.
  II. Title: History of Jews and Judaism in America.

  E184.35.C65 2007
  973'.04924—dc22   2007024758

Casebound editions of Columbia University Press books are printed
on permanent and durable acid-free paper.
Printed in the United States of America
c 10 9 8 7 6 5 4 3 2 1

CONTENTS

Topical Essays

The Columbia History
of Jews and Judaism in America

Jewish parent enough? Must the person affirm a Jewish (if not Judaic, i.e., religious) identity? What if a person has two Jewish parents, has not converted to another religion, but denies any interest in American Jewish culture, any intent on its serving an ethnic purpose? What we do know is this: less than half the Jews in America are involved in the religion Judaism—they may be called secular Jews, cultural Jews (for the difference between these, see the essay by Jeffrey A. Shandler), or just plain Jews. But they are not Judaic, not involved in the religion Judaism. These folks—those that affiliate with Conservative, Orthodox, Reconstructionist, Reform, Renewal, or unaffiliated synagogues—are the material for the study of Judaism.

The choice of which word to use in the title will often suggest an emphasis on either religious or secular life, and this was true of the many volumes cited above. To take but one example: Sachar has little interest in Judaism, but devotes considerable space—at the expense of the rich life of synagogue communities, which receive about one page, total, out of one thousand plus—to elegant biographical sketches of Jews who have no connection to American Judaism. He appropriately uses the word *Jews* in the title, and there are no boundaries for identification as *Jewish*.

Thus the reader who sought a history of the Jews (e.g., Jewish culture) and a history of Judaism would have had to read more than one book. And no single work explored the full geographic experience of Jews and Judaism in America. Little scholarly work existed on the Jewish experience in the South, only slightly more on the Jews of the West (for example, there is still no history of San Francisco Jewry); important, large Jewish communities such as Atlanta (after World War I), Chicago, Dallas, Houston, Los Angeles (after 1960), Miami, Minneapolis-St. Paul, New York City (after World War I), Pittsburgh, and Seattle (among others) had not yet (and still have not) found a historian to write the history of its Jews and of its Judaism, and almost all the work of sociology and history encompassing this secular/religious community had been centered in the urban experience.

That has been remedied, to some extent, by numerous monographs of the past two decades, including studies of Jews in the Sun Belt, Jews in small towns, Jews in places of importance previously ignored (e.g., Boston), and Judaism everywhere. The best histories move far from New York/New Jersey and encompass institutions and individuals in all parts of the country. But no one person can do it all. Jonathan D. Sarna's fine history of Judaism ignores the South. He has more than a dozen references to Boston, but there is not a single reference to any city in Alabama, Arkansas, Florida, Georgia, Louisiana, Mississippi, Tennessee, or Texas.

For many decades American Jewish history was not only biographies of elite Jews (Sachar continues this tradition: Jacob Schiff is mentioned on at least seventy pages), but historical studies of New York organizations and institutions and sociological studies of New York Jews (and, occasionally, another large or medium-sized city, e.g., Chicago or Providence). When historians turned from the "top" to the "bottom," they noticed that many of the objectives and programs of the national organizations were reshaped on the local level, that Jews in smaller towns and Jews in the Midwest, South, and West, often behaved differently than in New York/New Jersey and even from Jews in Philadelphia and Baltimore. German Jewish and Russian Jewish (to use the old terminology) relations were different; the degree and kind of antisemitism was different; the Jewish residential density and thus the boundaries of the ethnic community (e.g., intermarriage) were different.

Whether we focus on New York City and the other large metropolitan areas or expand our breadth of interest in the Jewish and Judaic experience, the most unique aspect of the Jewish experience in the United States has been the minimal impact of antisemitism, whether measured in terms relative to other places where Jewish life has unfolded or in absolute terms. While it is true that some elite colleges and universities, undergraduate (e.g., Harvard and Columbia) as well as professional schools, set Jewish quotas in the 1920s, which continued, in some cases, for several decades, that Yale, Princeton, Johns Hopkins, and the University of Chicago employed only one Jewish faculty member as late as 1927, and that some demagogues, such as Father Coughlin and Gerald L. K. Smith, delivered antisemitic rants in the 1930s and 1940s, these were merely tiny bumps in the road on which American Jews traveled. There were plenty of other fine undergraduate institutions of higher learning as well as law schools and medical schools that welcomed Jews, and very few Americans, even among the millions who heard the antisemitic messages, translated these screeds into serious discrimination. Far more telling is the fact that there are hardly any Jews born since the 1970s who are able to offer personal examples of antisemitism. I will return to this theme.

Colonial America was certainly not free of prejudice and discrimination against Jews—their arrival in New Amsterdam from northeastern Brazil in 1654 was greeted with disgust ("a deceitful race . . . hateful enemies and blasphemers of the name of Christ") by the clergy, council, and governor, Peter Stuyvesant. But the images from the Hebrew Bible (the Zion metaphor) that guided the Puritans to the New English Canaan set in place not only an idealized "Jewish" community in biblical times (such as that in John Winthrop's 1630 sermon, "A Model of Christianity, who is certain that the 'God of Israel is among us'"), and a fondness for the ancient and holy language of these people, but also a friendliness to contemporary Jews. The president of Yale University, Ezra Stiles, studied Hebrew with the most famous of Newport, Rhode Island Jews, Aaron Lopez, and, together with William and Mary and Harvard, Yale required this language of students in the eighteenth century. Some Christians even went so far as to suggest that Hebrew be the official language of the new nation, while Benjamin Franklin proposed, as the motto for the seal of the United States, a verse from Leviticus: Rebellion to Tyrants is Obedience to God. These were but a few of the many symbols of the commitment the founding fathers had to religious toleration.

Individuals and governments, for the most part, left Jews to develop their religious and communal (early on, one and the same) institutions without interference. They could care less who the Jews hired as rabbis, or how and where they conducted their worship (in the eighteenth century the ritual style in all American synagogues was that of the Spanish-Portuguese Jews who had left Spain [1492] and Portugal [1497] hundreds of years earlier). Nobody told them where to erect their synagogues (in contast to most European communities, at the same time, where synagogues had to be built off a main street in an inconspicuous area), which architectural style to choose for their houses of worship, and to whom they should distribute their modest philanthropic dollars.

This toleration, of course, was forever inscribed in the Constitution, with the Bill of Rights (1789) and its First Amendment: "Congress shall make no law respecting an establishment of religion or prohibiting the free exercise thereof." As many have demonstrated, this meant both freedom of religion and freedom from religion. It encouraged Jews to compete for followers (voluntarism) with the many other religious communities in a generally pluralistic commonwealth, and it guaranteed the freedom of each American to be free of church and synagogue as well. And at least two groups—Catholics and Jews—did the latter so successfully that the categories of lapsed Catholics and secular Jews became large segments of the community. Members of each group answer affirmatively when asked if they are Catholic or Jewish, but simultaneously deny any attachment to rituals or worship. Thus the First Amendment has led some Americans to create the categories of lapsed Catholics, religious Catholics, secular or cultural Jews, and religious Jews.

Catholics and Jews are distinct from Protestants in this way, as few Presbyterians would affirm their Presbyterianness but concomitantly say that they do not attend church. Presbyterianism is, for the most part, bound up with a Presbyterian church. But millions of Catholics and hundreds of thousands (a million or more?) of Jews affirm that they are Catholic or Jewish but do not attend church or synagogue. So there is a story to be told about American Jews who have been involved with the synagogue or religious community and its primary institution and about American Jews who have been uninterested in the religion Judaism yet affirm their cultural or secular Jewishness by identifying with klezmer music, Jewish art, Jewish food, Jewish film festivals, Jewish periodicals, Jewish community centers, Jewish books, Jewish philanthropy, the Holocaust, Israel, the Jewish people wherever they might be, and who react strongly to antisemitism but do not visit a temple or synagogue (the terms are interchangeable—a Jewish house of worship). This book then is about both the history of Jews in America and the history of Judaism in America.

The unusual division of American Jewry into secular and religious highlights the difficulty of defining Jews. Some are religious, but, since many are not, *Jewish* is not simply a religious term. To call Jews an ethnic or national group like the Greeks or Poles is to ignore the religious community, and they are certainly not a race in any meaningful sense, as Jews come in all colors and varieties. We will call them a people (the Hebrew phrase is *am yisrael*)—a people that in the United States in 2000 numbered more than 5.5 million and has a large group of members active in synagogues and/or temples and a large group of members who identify in ways other than what Americans generally call religious.

Naturally, there are countless Jews for whom a cultural identity *and* a religious identity are important. These Jews not only join a synagogue but a Jewish community center as well, refusing to choose only one identity. Even when the mass exodus of eastern European Jews in the late nineteenth and early twentieth centuries brought huge numbers of immigrants to North and South America as well as Europe, commentators noted the tension between religious and secular identity. Some wondered whether the secular Jewish immigrants who attended Yiddish theater on Friday evening when the Sabbath day of rest began and then worked on Saturday mornings as the day of rest continued "lost their religion" in the Old World before they migrated or whether it was America that destroyed it. Was it the struggle to "make it" in America, to achieve success, that gave them no time for the synagogue, and would they return (if they ever had been connected) when the pressure to feed the family decreased? These immigrants affirmed their Jewish identity, even as they, for the most part, deserted the immigrant synagogues. Would they, or would their children, join later? For, if not, Judaism as a religion might fade and die. This tension between a religious and a secular identity continues to occupy the American Jewish community as the new century unfolds.

For those who chose to identify with the religious community, Orthodoxy (though not called that yet) was the only choice until the middle of the nineteenth century. Almost all congregations in America were traditional (the terms *Conservative, Orthodox, Reconstructionist,* and *Reform* had not yet emerged), which meant they used a liturgy mostly unchanged for centuries, and communal needs (burial, circumcisions, education, philanthropy, ritual slaughtering of animals) centered in the synagogue. The synagogue usually held the deed to the Jewish cemetery; kosher meat, when available, was distributed at the synagogue; and Jewish fraternal and cultural organizations usually met there. With the emergence, in the second half of the nineteenth century, of congregations that would clearly identify themselves as Reform and, in the first decades of the twentieth century, congregations that called themselves Orthodox and Conservative (even if the differences were not always obvious), many of these activities began to move outside the synagogue into the home as well as into communal institutions. The synagogue would soon become one of many American Jewish institutions, and the distinction between religious Jews (connected to the synagogue) and secular Jews (connected to social and cultural institutions exclusively or to none at all) more clearly defined.

Another way of noting this development is to point out that this period—the last decades of the nineteenth century and the opening decades of the twentieth century—was all about sorting out issues of American Jewish identity. Whether in immigrant fiction, journalism, or theater, as well as the observations of "native" American Jews, the issue of the relationship between one's Jewishness and/or Judaism and their Americanness was central.

Among the most discussed issues was that of the American Dream (largely a material one) and the price that one pays, in achieving this dream, as parts of a Jewish or Judaic identity are left behind. For some who worked on the Sabbath to fulfill this dream, it was often the loss of their religious identity with which they struggled. For others, it was the conflict between Old World parents and New World children and the (sometimes) emptiness of the children as they achieved, unhappily, their dream. The price was often loneliness, for the pursuit of success frequently meant isolating oneself from the immigrant community that was left behind. In Anzia Yezierska's semiautobiographical novel, *Bread Givers* (1925), Sara Smolinsky's "burning ambition to rise in the world" (171) is more important than seeing her "old mother," and she goes on with her solitary struggle without visiting her mother for six years.

When Sara finally decides to visit after this long absence, she wonders "would they understand that my silent aloofness for so long had been a necessity and not selfish indifference?" (242). The reader cannot help wonder, "Why should they understand this?" She chose middle-class values over close family ties, and the novel forces the reader to reflect on the tension between the American Dream, her individual, lonely "success" story, her "precious privacy" (241), her "beautiful aloneness" (241), and the price she pays, her uneasiness in America. It is a Jewish immigrant lament, as are so many immigrant memoirs, best summed up when Sara looks at the people left behind, those still in the ghetto, still poor, still suffering, and thinks, "as I walked along through Hester Street towards the Third Avenue L, my joy hurt like guilt." There is plenty of loss within the success as she ponders "the generations who made my father whose weight was still upon me" (297).[1]

Yekl, the protagonist in the staunch secularist and socialist Abraham Cahan's 1893 Yiddish novella by the same name (he published a slightly different version in English two years later, after it was rejected by *Harper's Weekly* and other major magazines), wrestled with similar issues of Jewish identity and the meaning of Jewishness for a secular Jew. Like Sara, he is a "defeated victor" (*Yekl: A Tale of the New York Ghetto*, 1896, 1970, 87), although he achieves freedom from his Old World wife through a divorce. Once again the reader knows all too well that Yekl (now Jake, "a *regely* Yankee," 8) has been fooled by his pursuit of the American Dream, that much has been lost as he substitutes shaving his beard" (35) and "a Yankee wink" (3) for the "mysterious light of two tallow candles rising from freshly burnished candlesticks" (30), the "Hebrew words of the Sanctification of the Sabbath" (30), and "his old home and old days" (31). Jake loses both his family and his freedom, and the question of the meaning of Jewishness is left unanswered.[2]

At the same time as issues of identity emerged into the discussion of what constitutes American Judaism and American Jewishness, the issue of regionalism became a topic of discussion. Commentators began to speak about a southern Jewish, a western Jewish, a New York Jewish experience, partitioning the American Jewish experience into patterns of regional distinctiveness and uniqueness. With the hindsight of a century of reflection on this topic, we are better able to judge the worthiness of such claims. It seems clear that regionalism is not a meaningful category for discussion of the past; Mark Bauman argues for "patterns across regional boundaries" and William Toll notes that young Jewish men on the Pacific Coast "pursued economic opportunities similar to their colleagues elsewhere in America." And precious little is left of it today.

The South in which Jews live in the new century looks pretty much like the West, Midwest, and East in which the Jews also reside. The sprawl surrounding Columbia, South Carolina looks just like the rest of America. Out by the interstate, the chain hotels all huddle together near Office Depot and Walgreens and RadioShack. In town the businesses sell the same unnecessary pretty things and boutique comestibles to the prosperous. There are fancy French soaps and artisan glass vases, antique Oriental rugs and massive four-poster canopied beds, tapas and microbrews and cosmopolitans: one nation, one commerce, indivisible, with the same cable channels for all. A political science professor at the University of South Carolina summed this up nicely, "there ain't no South anymore." Being a southerner, or a southern Jew, is what happens to those born and raised in the South. Not much more.

If it remains true, echoing Faulkner, that no one can comfortably dismiss the past in the South, it is no less true in, say, California. In 1865 General Sherman burned Columbia and its old state house, and his artillery hit the stone wall of the new statehouse under construction. The six pocks are still there, albeit covered by six bronze stars on the side wall of the capital building. But such historical consciousness is not uniquely (or even distinctly) southern. There is a romantic notion of moonlight and magnolias and mint juleps and graciousness and bubbas and 'bamas and stereotypical backward southerners. But California Jews speak of Left Coast and smog and sun-drenched, artificially enhanced starlet wannabees and wheatgrass, regular grass, and illegal grass. Hundreds of thousands of them cannot forget the concentration camps where the government placed American citizens of Japanese ancestry during World War II. As Randy Newman (a Jewish American) said, best of all, "Look at those mountains, look at them trees, look at that bum over there he's down on his knees, look at those women, ain't nothing like 'em nowhere." As the editors (Ava F. Kahn and Marc Dollinger) of a recent book on California Jews (*California Jews*, 2003) put it, "California Jews struggled with the same issues faced by Jews in other parts of the country." And William Toll sums it up nicely when he concludes that "provincial Jewish communities everywhere were not shaped by the unique history of the region in which they were located, but by the economic trajectory of commercial cities."

This reminds the student of American Jewish history that identification with a region exists irrespective of place of residence. Some Jews who lived in the South insisted on their nonsouthern identity. They had little identification with the regional group we call southerners, little feeling of closeness to them and their ways. Surely, everyone has a south (west? east?) of their own, and only when this is carefully delineated are we able to understand the Jewish part of the southern or western or eastern Jewish experience. Until this is done, we can talk only about *American* Jews in a meaningful way.

So this is a history of American Jews and American Judaism, with the caveat that though there are some regional differences, they are so minor as to make it possible to speak of a national Jewry. If one attends a Conservative synagogue in Atlanta, Boston, Chicago, Dallas, Denver, Pittsburgh, Queens, or Richmond on a Saturday morning, the experience is virtually identical (not quite; the rabbi in Richmond sometimes refers to the congregation as "y'all"). Just as the same shops tend to appear in shopping malls all over the country, American Jews are far more alike than different from place to place, as Mark Bauman demonstrates.

This does not mean that the local Jewish story is unimportant. Quite the contrary. The only way to provide details, color, and real people is to move from the American Jewish experience to that of Jews in Danville (VA), Fort Wayne, Indianapolis, Memphis, Portland, San Francisco, Savannah, and Wilkes-Barre . These are the places where Jews live, where they pray at synagogues, swim in Jewish community center pools, attend Israel Independence Day celebrations and Shoah memorial events, and read fiction by other Jews. But it rarely matters whether we discuss the Passover seder in Tacoma or in Charleston. Passover is Passover everywhere.

In the middle decades of the nineteenth century, as a result of Jewish emigration from central Europe, the Jewish population at last became statistically significant in the United States (there were only about two thousand Jews in the country at the time of the American Revolution—less than 1 percent of the population). The available evidence suggests that a significant majority of Jews identified with the synagogue. In large part this was because the secular communal, cultural, social, and philanthropic institutions, which later would become separate, were still intimately connected to the synagogue; typically, a congregation would advertise for a lecturer, hazan (cantor), reader, slaughterer, and teacher—all in one person! Dianne Ashton argues that this paralleled the role of the Protestant minister, as churches hired him to preach, teach, and comfort. She also reminds us of the role of women in maintaining these synagogues and, even more, the larger American Jewish community. So, in Baltimore, Chicago, Cincinnati, Louisville, Philadelphia, Richmond, and elsewhere, most Jews in the community identified with the synagogue.

This began to change significantly with the mass migration of Jews from eastern Europe in the final decades of the nineteenth and early decades of the twentieth century, as cultural, philanthropic, and social institutions (Yiddish theater, benevolent societies, YMHAs, immigrant aid organizations [Hebrew Immigrant Aid Society, Immigration Removal Office], B'nai B'rith, Jewish philanthropies, and the like) moved into their own offices.

At the same time, synagogues that were just known by their name throughout the eighteenth and nineteenth centuries began to attach a denominational label. First came those that adopted *The Union Prayer-Book [for the High Holy Days]* (1894) and *The Union Prayer-Book [for the Sabbath]* (1895), liturgies with a minimum of Hebrew (the Afternoon Service for the Day of Atonement begins on p. 205 and has no Hebrew until p. 225; the Evening Service for the Sabbath has eighteen pages of English and eight pages of Hebrew), and, more serious, abridged prayers. They were called Reform congregations, and by this same decade the umbrella organization that united them (Union of American Hebrew Congregations—today the Union of Reform Judaism) included exclusively synagogues that identified with the Reform movement.

This adoption of a prayer book radically different from that with which Jews had prayed for centuries led to the establishment of two more branches, Conservative and Orthodox, both emerging in the period of mass migration from eastern Europe. There was much confusion between these two sectors of American Judaism for many decades. Rabbis trained at the seminary of the Conservative movement, the Jewish Theological Seminary (JTS), served congregations affiliated with the Union of Orthodox Congregations of America (OU), the Orthodox movement umbrella organization, and rabbis trained at the seminary of the Orthodox movement, the Rabbi Isaac Elchanan Theological Seminary (RIETS), served congregations (notwithstanding some with mixed seating) affiliated with the United Synagogue of America, the Conservative movement's umbrella organization. By the 1930s most Conservative and most Orthodox synagogues were distinct from each other, and by the 1940s the seminaries sent recently ordained rabbis almost exclusively to synagogues from the seminary's "denomination." Whether the confusion was greater or less in a particular decade, in the first half of the twentieth century Conservative and Orthodox synagogues were far more clearly distinguished from Reform synagogues than from each other. All liturgies, to cite but two examples, in Conservative and Orthodox synagogues were predominately in Hebrew, several chapters of the Torah were read in Hebrew every Saturday morning, and all male worshippers (in contrast to the Reform synagogues where few males would do so) wore head covering during worship.

Riv-Ellen Prell reminds us that "people orient their lives in spaces," and she discusses "Jewish spaces," arguing, quite correctly, that the preeminent Jewish space of the 1950s was the synagogue. It was not just a "sacred space" of Judaic activities, but a space where secular Jewish (and non-Jewish) organizations met, including the Boy Scouts, Israel Bond committees, Big Brother groups, Hadassah, Council of Jewish Women, and, like the council, other organizations that the "remarkable cadre of educated and committed volunteers" (mothers with pre-K children) joined. Perhaps we could conclude that the concept of sacred space began to expand greatly in this decade.

With this expanded idea of sacred space came a greater interest in place. Not just the place of American Jews, as the question of what constituted a good Jew and what constituted a good American became more troubling in the 1960s with civil rights and Vietnam, and, again, with the war in Iraq, and charges that those who did not support the war were less patriotic than Americans who did support it, in the early 2000s. But in the past few decades Jewish writers have thought a lot about the place where their fiction is set (see the essay by Linda S. Raphael), as well as investigating the meaning of the "place from which one thinks about American Jewry." Indeed, the study of American Jewry has expanded far beyond the physical borders of America—in 2005 American historians of the Jewish experience gathered outside Munich with a group of German historians of the American Jewish experience to compare and contrast the role of place in one's interpretation of Judaica Americana. Is it possible for (mostly) non-Jewish German historians to have greater objectivity from afar than do the (exclusively) Jewish American historians? Much in the way several generations of American expatriates argued that they could write about America better from France or elsewhere, European historians, sociologists, and literary scholars defended their work, despite the distance.

Jeffrey S. Gurock argues that "Jewish religious life," from approximately 1925–1945, was "mired in a state of crisis and decline." We might differ over how to define "crisis and decline": this was a time when the number of Conservative, Orthodox, and Reform synagogues continued to grow, sometimes rapidly; the United Synagogue (officially, Conservative) grew from 130 congregations in 1920 to 229 by the end of the 1920s. But there can be no doubt that large numbers of children (and soon grandchildren) of immigrant parents, despite considerable residential propinquity everywhere, demonstrated disinterest and even indifference to traditional synagogue life. Large numbers took American voluntarism quite literally; freedom of religion also included freedom *from* religion. And in such a society, where competition among religious institutions is the norm, Jews "shopped" for rabbis, cantors, religious education programs, small dues and (the lack of) synagogue mortgages. Reform congregations were the most substantial beneficiary. As Reform rabbis and synagogue leaders began to reach out to a wider spectrum of Jews, significant numbers of these east European Jewish children and grandchildren joined Reform synagogues.

They brought with them, even if they had been previously unaffiliated with a synagogue (but often members of a Jewish community center), customs and rituals that had never been a part of Reform Judaism. These included the Hebrew

language, Zionism, head covering during prayer, and other observances and ceremonies that had been an intimate part of the east European community but
never experienced in the United States. Reform congregations vigorously recruited these indifferent Jews, and in the process the most radical branch (services stripped of Hebrew and heads stripped of hats) became, little by little, a bit
more comfortable with tradition.

Despite this severe hemorrhaging, the "ever dying denomination," as Kimmy
Caplan calls American Orthodoxy (Riv-Ellen Prell, in contrast, prefers to see orthodoxy as an "umbrella term" for diverse groups rather than as a movement in
the sense of the other denominations), experienced a resurgence beginning in the
1970s. Although it continually decreased in numbers (from 10 percent in 1990 to
9 percent in 2000), Caplan concludes his essay on the period through 1965 with
the claim that Orthodoxy would become "vibrant, thriving, and flourishing in
many ways." He of course has the advantage of observing the past several decades,
so this is not a prophetic statement but a description that is quite accurate. And
among the most vibrant (and changing) areas of Orthodox vitality in the decades
since 1970 are day schools, college campus life, resistors supplanting accommodators, and the increasing role for women.

There are day schools, to be sure, not affiliated with Orthodox Judaism, including those sponsored by Reform and Conservative Jewish associations and those
that are independent. In 2005, approximately 205,000 students were enrolled in
760 schools (elementary and secondary)—about two-thirds in New Jersey and
New York—an increase of more than 10 percent in the past five years. Of these
students, however, more than 80 percent are affiliated with Orthodox institutions,
and Orthodox-affiliated schools are growing at a slightly faster rate than the non-
Orthodox schools. This is in part the result of an insistence in most Orthodox
synagogues today that boys and girls attend Jewish day schools as well as of a
higher fertility rate among the Orthodox. The latter ensures enrollment growth
when the mandate to attend such schools is taken seriously.

One of the most dramatic changes in Orthodoxy in the past two decades or
so is the matriculation of observant Orthodox young men and women to nonsectarian universities. The result has been that colleges and universities committed to diversity—all over the country—welcomed these students, and adapted
to them. Kosher eating facilities, single sex dorms, careful awareness of, and accommodation to, Jewish holidays and observances are some of the ways in
which institutions of higher learning have responded to this influx and made it
possible for Orthodox Jewish students to populate even such unlikely choices
for Orthodox students as the College of Charleston and Muhlenberg College.
In 2005 the former president of Yeshiva University acknowledged this phenomenon when he came to Ithaca, New York to speak to an Orthodox-sponsored
assembly of hundreds of young men and women who had enrolled at Cornell
University.

Orthodoxy has moved right in the past few decades, and not just within the Hasidic dynasties and courts dominated by charismatic leaders, or rebbes, as the children of Orthodox parents and grandparents who were much less observant than their children support, in large numbers, the increased rigor of this generation's observance of ceremonies, customs, and rituals. A generation ago, parking lots at Orthodox synagogues were full on the Sabbath; today these same lots are much more likely to be closed to Sabbath parking and only a small percentage of worshippers come in automobiles, which they park out of sight a few blocks away. A generation ago most of these accommodating parents ate (albeit carefully) at nonkosher restaurants; today their children, in increasing numbers, resist the temptation to even enter nonkosher restaurants. In the 1950s and 1960s Orthodox Jews called their head covering an "indoor garment"; today they are worn by many everywhere. In the 1950s few Orthodox Jews attended Jewish day schools; today, as noted, it is de rigueur in the Orthodox community.

Caplan quite correctly mentions the virtual numerical explosion of Orthodox Jewish women who have recently begun to study sacred texts, an activity in previous generations reserved almost exclusively for men. There are now Orthodox Jewish women academics who study and teach Hebrew Bible, rabbinic literature, Jewish thought, and even Jewish mysticism, and there are many more nonacademic Orthodox Jewish women engaged in serious text study in their synagogue and adult education programs. Orthodox women are increasingly serving on synagogue ritual committees, creating Hebrew naming ceremonies to parallel the bris, experimenting with bat mitzvah ceremonies to correspond to the bar mitzvah for boys, participating in Sabbath worship women's minyanim (sing. minyan) or prayer groups, many of which include women reading from the Torah scroll, with women's *megillah* (e.g., the books of Esther and Ruth) readings, women's Simchat Torah (rejoicing with the Torah scroll) celebrations, and in a few synagogues—with separate seating for men and women—participating in the Sabbath service from the pulpit. In at least one New York City and Los Angeles Orthodox synagogue men are now called to the Torah using the Hebrew name of their father *and* their mother.

Use of the *mikveh* (ritual bath) has become a marker in the Orthodox community. When Rabbi Emanuel Feldman came to his Atlanta Orthodox congregation in 1952, he found not one Sabbath observer in the entire city and "perhaps two or three courageous women [who] used the *mikveh*."[3] And, when Rabbi David J. Radinsky arrived in Charleston twenty years later, he found "no more than three women who used the *mikveh*.[4] But, in Orthodox congregations all over the country, monthly immersion in the *mikveh* after menstruating has become a marker of piety. Indeed, even in a "modern" Orthodox synagogue in a suburb of Boston, "95 percent of the women use the *mikveh* on a regular basis."[5] It is one of the clearest boundary areas—for women—in the Orthodox community today.

When Kimmy Caplan writes of vibrant, thriving, and flourishing, and Stephen Whitfield notes that significant antisemitism has virtually disappeared in the forty years or so that have passed since the year that Caplan ends his discussion, they might be describing the entire history of Jews and Judaism in the United States. College-age Jews in the past few decades have trouble providing examples of antisemitism in their own lives (of course they have read about the occasional defacing of a synagogue or the like). Previous periods of heightened antisemitism were, with the hindsight of a historian, merely a minor nuisance. Jews are demographically overrepresented among the most affluent, the most politically powerful, the most cultural important, and the most intellectually accomplished of Americans. And they came to this position because of their resiliency in the face of earlier periods of discrimination and exclusion.

We noted earlier that significant antisemitism did not register in the United States until the late nineteenth century, and it began with exclusion from resorts, hotels, and watering holes. From there, in the 1920s, 1930s, and 1940s, it spread to college and professional school admission quotas in elite private schools, fraternities and sororities, city clubs and country clubs, prestigious law firms in a few large cities, the rantings of a handful of preachers and demagogues, and the exclusion of Jews from some residential neighborhoods. What is important about this antisemitism, from the late nineteenth century until just after World War II (with the awareness of what the Nazis did to Europe's Jews it became tacky for Americans to discriminate openly), is that it was unlike antisemitism in other places that Jews lived, for it left plenty of viable options for Jews who were excluded from this or that area or domain.

Jews who were denied admission to Dartmouth College or Harvard Law School went to other private colleges, fine public universities, and professional schools where no quotas existed. Jews started their own sororities and fraternities, city clubs and country clubs, law firms and businesses, moved to neighborhoods where they were welcome, founded and developed large synagogues everywhere, and, truth be told, often felt more comfortable surrounded by Jews than they would have been working in an overwhelmingly gentile environment. The result? The Jewish experience since the end of World War II may be the most dramatic single case in all of American history in which a group facing discrimination (nearly everywhere quite legal) suddenly emerged as overrepresented many times over in precisely those areas where it had been previously excluded. Several Ivy League colleges that had installed quota systems in the 1920s to dramatically curtail Jewish admission found themselves in the first decade of the new century with entering classes one-third to two-fifths Jewish!

Thus, as Jews wrote themselves into the history of America, so carefully delineated by Beth Wenger, they had grown to be so much a part of the postwar landscape that intermarriage and assimilation became a much more serious problem than discrimination. Jews were more likely to be loved to death than hated, so Friday night football, Saturday morning soccer, non-Jews who swamped online services such as JDate looking for a Jewish man or woman, and the general enthusiasm that a culturally and religiously pluralistic America demonstrated for Jews and Judaism were the threats, not residential, economic, or social discrimination.

A very large percentage of Jews active in Jewish (more precisely, Judaic) religious organizations—synagogue youth groups, synagogue worship—have at least one member of their close family who is married to a non-Jew. Among the Orthodox, such family members are not always embraced, but there is little difference in non-Orthodox families between their acceptance of relatives married to a Jew or a non-Jew. This is but the latest challenge in American Jewish life; how to embrace the religion and the people who practice that religion when the religion is not Judaism and the family members are not Jews.

Synagogue leaders face this same challenge in every non-Orthodox congregation: where to draw the boundary when one member of a unit that joins the congregation is not Jewish. Frequently, when it is the woman (and/or mother), she may be the person driving a child to and from synagogue activities, and the current challenge for rabbis and lay leaders is to figure out how to integrate a non-Jew into Judaic rituals and practices. What is the role of the nominally Christian parent, whether he or she attends church or not, in a bat or bar mitzvah ceremony where, everywhere, parents participate in the ceremony involving reading from the Torah (Scripture) scroll? May he or she join a committee? If so, may it be the Rabbinic Search Committee, or are there some committees permitted (serving refreshments after worship services), some not (nominating the slate of officers)? All of this is the result of an America so open that Jews welcome non-Jews into the worshipping community and are then forced to make decisions about boundaries.

The Conservative movement, at the time of this writing, is wrestling with numerous boundary issues. The most widely discussed, at least among member of Conservative synagogues after Saturday morning worship, is the ordination of gay and lesbian rabbis. Adopting the Reform and Reconstructionist positions—sexual preference is not a criterion for ordination—would move the movement even further from the Orthodox (who do not condone homosexuality), and if and when the movement should take this position is a burning issue.

The boundaries between religious and secular are not always clear either. Jeffrey Shandler notes that "a sizable number of people" (=Jews) who attend Jewish film festivals liken the experience to "attending synagogue," or they say that watching a Jewish film "has replaced congregational worship." This reminds us that when someone like Elliott Abrams contrasts "religion" (=Judaism) to "culture" (=Jewish), or when a Jew would describe herself (in previous generations) as a "secular Jew" or (more contemporaneously) a "cultural Jew," she usually means that she has little or nothing to do with the *Judaic* or synagogue community. For the most part, as we have seen, American Jews divide into those who are involved in the religious community (for Judaism *is* community) or those who define themselves as Jewish in secular or cultural ways.

With hardly an exception, as Shandler notes, when scholars write about Jewish culture they rarely write about Conservative, Orthodox, Reconstructionist, and Reform Judaism, but about Jewishness in art, film, food, humor, literature, music, and the like. Even the widely quoted sociologist of American Jews Nathan Glazer was generally uninterested in Judaism and distinguished between ethnic identity (without Judaism) and religious identity or Jewishness versus Judaism.

What makes this somewhat artificial distinction disturbing is that more than seven decades ago Mordecai Kaplan, in his brilliant book, *Judaism as a Civilization* (1934), warned against precisely this mistake. He emphasized that Jewish culture, Jewish civilization, Jewishness, or whatever one wishes to call it, is "arts, literature, laws, *religion* and philosophies" (my emphasis)—that is, Jewishness and Judaism are not, in Shandler's words, "inherently conflicted" but are complimentary parts of the American Jewish/Judaic experience.

And that experience, sadly, has generally been reconstructed with little attention to gender. Pamela Nadell notes not only the familiar names from the "constellation Jewish feminism" that resulted from feminism confronting Judaism during the second wave of American feminism in the 1960s and 1970s but also reminds us of the numerous "lively characters" who "pushed from within their establishment settings to raise feminist consciousness." Carrie Simon, the founder of the National Federation of Temple Sisterhoods in 1913, was surely such a woman. She traveled the land in the 1910s and 1920s speaking at synagogues and urging the male leaders to permit women to sit on the boards of directors and to permit women (and not just their husbands) to be voting members of synagogues. Today Jewish women synagogue and communal leaders are as common as women rabbis and women cantors—they are everywhere (less so in the Orthodox religious communities)—and they are surrounded by new religious rituals (private and public), a new vocabulary of prayer, and, in so many ways, reconfigured synagogues that have become egalitarian institutions. Nadell is right on target when she notes that "all the movements of American Judaism fall within the constellation Jewish feminism" and that the intersection of American feminism and Judaism has "transformed American Jewish life."

Another important intersection has been public advocacy and Jews, or the growing awareness in the American Jewish community of how to use the political process. True, as Rafael Medoff notes, Jews in America have a "long history of public protest rallies and behind-the-scenes lobbying to bring about government intercessions on behalf of Jews persecuted abroad." But these decades of experience in the art of public advocacy proved of limited avail in the 1930s and 1940s because of deep divisions among Jewish leaders on how to respond to what was happening in Europe, even when there was finally a consensus about what precisely *was* happening.

To give but one example. By the time the Allies had the capability of flying deep inside Poland and returning safely with good odds, most of Europe's Jews were dead. Flights from England across Europe and back were virtually impossible, even if one could have imagined the precision bombing of an underground gas chamber inside the Auschwitz-Birkenau complex or hitting some train tracks (quickly rebuilt) leading to a death camp. When the Allies secured Italian bases, and flights to this Polish area were possible (Medoff notes the bombing of industrial sites close to Auschwitz-Birkenau), there were Hungarian Jews still alive—the last Jewish community of Europe to be slaughtered (1944).

But American Jewish leaders never figured out how to convince American leaders to risk American lives and Allied aircraft on missions to bomb in or near Auschwitz-Birkenau. There were, as Medoff reminds us, "numerous and complex dilemmas faced by the American Jewish community in deciding how to respond to the Nazi persecutions," and this community—despite public protests and rallies and letters everywhere—failed to save very many Jews. It was still, in Eric Goldstein's words, a community that "remained divided by cultural, ideological and religious differences."

Jewish communal leaders learned an important lesson from their studies of what went wrong in the 1930s and 1940s, and, when the fate of Soviet Jews emerged into public consciousness in the mid-1960s, Jewish communal leaders spoke over and over about the need for a unified response. Jews in America had mostly ignored the two to three million Soviet Jews in the first two decades after World War II, assuming that they had virtually disappeared as Jews after a half century of communism. But by the late 1960s American Jews presented a unified appeal to political leaders for government intercession on behalf of a fundamental human right, exodus, and demanded that the Jews be permitted to leave the Soviet Union. Jewish leaders were determined not to be another generation of American Jews incapable of trying to save a doomed overseas community, and their efforts helped make it possible for more than one hundred thousand Soviet Jews to come to the United Sates in less than two decades. And the glow of success from this operation has not diminished at all as the new century unfolds.

Although eventually reunited with an extraordinary senior manuscript editor, Susan Pensak, and finding a talented indexer, Celeste Newbrough, together with James Warren, my first editor, I conceived this book at the Hungarian Pastry Shop in New York City, and we agreed upon the arrangement that follows. I would find eighteen scholars—experts in their field of either Jews or Judaism or both—and they would create a series of six comprehensive chronological essays, each with a different focus, covering the period 1654 to 2000. These would be followed by twelve topical essays, some covering a long period, some a very short period, delineating nearly every theme of significance in the history of Jews and Judaism in America. In all cases the authors would weave into their notes the "state of the field"—thus encouraging a reader to pursue any of the grand essays, or more limited topics, with the works noted by each author.

And, most unusually, many of the authors came together in Williamsburg, Virginia, to discuss their theses. Even more, numerous authors read the essays of other authors, and this resulted in considerable intertextuality—authors in conversation with one another. And, in imitation of the final editor of the Torah, where there were different interpretations of the same phenomenon, they have not been reconciled.

NOTES

1. Renny Christopher, "Rags to Riches to Suicide: Unhappy Narratives of Upward Mobility: *Martin Eden, Bread Givers, Delia's Song,* and *Hunger of Memory,*" *College Literature* 29.4 (Fall 2002): 79–107; Gay Wilentz, "Cultural Mediation and the Immigrant's Daughter: Anzia Yezierska's *Bread Givers,*" *MELUS* 17.3 (Fall 1991): 32–41.

2. On *Yekl,* see Matthew Frye Jacobson, " 'The Quintessence of the Jew': Polemics of Nationalism and Peoplehood in Turn-of-the-Century Fiction," in *Multilingual America: Transnationalism, Ethnicity, and the Languages of America Literature,* ed. Werner Sollors (New York, 1998), 103–11.

3. Emanuel Feldman, *Telling Tales Out of Shul: The Unorthodox Journal of an Orthodox Rabbi* (Brooklyn, 1996), 18.

4. Rabbi David J. Radinsky, lecture, Brith Sholom Beth Israel Congregation, Charleston, SC, November 2004.

5. Sylvia Barack Fishman, personal communication, August 11, 2005.

Chronological Essays

1

AMERICA'S EARLIEST JEWISH SETTLERS, 1654–1820

ELI FABER

THE GEOGRAPHY OF JEWISH SETTLEMENT IN EARLY AMERICA

The history of the Jewish people in America is dated by common agreement to early September 1654, when a small French vessel arrived in the harbor of New Amsterdam at the southern tip of Manhattan Island, carrying among its passengers twenty-three Jewish men, women, and children who were fleeing from Brazil. They were primarily Sephardic, tracing their origins to ancestors who had resided on the Iberian peninsula, but there may also have been several Ashkenazim from central and eastern Europe.[1]

The quest for the origins of a Jewish presence in colonial America leads back to Holland in the late 1500s, when Jews began to leave Portugal to resettle in Amsterdam. These migrants were New Christians, people whose ancestors had been forced to convert to Christianity as much as a century before, beginning in the year 1497, in order to be permitted to remain in Portugal. Many of the forced converts secretly adhered to Judaism, much as in Spain, where a large number of New Christians, the Marranos, covertly remained loyal to Judaism. As in Spain, the papacy authorized an Inquisition for Portugal to ferret out all heresy, especially the heresy of clandestine adherence to Judaism. Life for New Christians in Portugal was fraught therefore with tension and anxiety because of the ever looming possibility that one could be denounced to the Inquisition as an underground Jew, with dire consequences and penalties that followed if one were found guilty.[2]

The perils of such an existence increased dramatically for the New Christian population in the 1580s, for Portugal and Spain were joined under a single monarchy at that juncture, and they remained united for several decades. With unification under one crown, the aggressiveness of the Inquisition in Portugal increased, thanks to the influence of the Spanish Inquisition. New Christians who resided in Portugal consequently began to emigrate to Holland in the 1590s, finding a large measure of safety and toleration in Amsterdam, although it would take them almost half a century to receive the right to construct synagogues and thereby worship in public. Holland made sense as a destination, for the Dutch were struggling to win their independence from Spain—and Portugal was now a part of Spain. Accordingly, New Christians who sought to escape from an Inquisition that had become more intent upon unearthing heresy sought haven in the emerging nation that was the enemy of the combined crown of the two Iberian nations.

Once safely in Amsterdam, many of the New Christians began to practice Judaism openly. Some outwardly maintained their Christian identities for purposes of trade with commercial correspondents in Portugal and Spain while, at the same time, quietly reverting to Judaism. A flourishing Jewish community developed by the middle of the 1600s in the Netherlands; by mid-century Dutch Jews numbered two or three thousand, and Amsterdam Jewry created a major center of Jewish life, referred to by contemporaries as the Dutch Jerusalem.[3]

Its emergence and its significance made the Amsterdam Jewish community a destination not only for refugees from the Portuguese Inquisition but also from the Spanish Inquisition, so that New Christian emigration from the two countries to Holland during the 1600s reflected the cyclical campaigns that both Inquisitions periodically unleashed. In addition, by the middle of the 1600s Amsterdam began to attract Ashkenazic Jews, whether from the German states or Poland. Economic discrimination in the German states, as well as limits upon the number of Jews who could reside in many of them, drove some from central Europe. Farther to the east, the widespread attacks upon Jewish communities that began in 1648 under the leadership of Chmielnicki propelled still more to the west.[4]

At the same time that a dynamic Jewish community was developing in Holland during the first half of the seventeenth century, the Dutch embarked upon a program of overseas expansion. Simultaneously with their struggle for independence, they sought to become a commercially powerful nation, and to that end the Netherlanders challenged the Portuguese in both hemispheres. Though a small nation, Portugal had established a mighty empire in both halves of the globe, with colonies in Africa, India, the East Indies, and Brazil and lucrative trading connections between the mother country and the colonies. The small, emerging nation of the Netherlands daringly confronted the Portuguese on the high seas and in their colonies. A significant portion of the growing Jewish community in Holland chose to affiliate with their new homeland's ambitious effort against a nation they had their own reasons to oppose. Doing so thereby put them on the road that ultimately led a handful to New Amsterdam in 1654.

As part of Holland's program of expansion during the 1620s, the Dutch West Indies Company, a private stock corporation, established the colony of New Netherland along the Hudson River, stretching from Manhattan Island northward beyond the modern city of Albany. The Dutch West Indies Company's goals included not only earning profits and paying dividends to its shareholders but also serving as the engine of Holland's design to supplant the Portuguese in the Western hemisphere. Accordingly, at about the same time in 1624, it launched an expedition to seize Brazil, though it failed to capture that huge, profitable, sugar-producing colony. The Company tried again in 1630, this time succeeding, with Jewish soldiers, including one with the rank of colonel, among the personnel in its hired army. The Dutch remained in Brazil for the next twenty-four years until 1654, when the Portuguese successfully counterattacked and retook the colony.

During the period of Dutch West India Company rule in Brazil, Jewish settlers from Amsterdam established a sizable presence in the colony; by 1645 approximately 1,450 Jewish inhabitants resided in northeastern Brazil. Inasmuch as the Jewish population of Holland around 1650 was estimated at 2,000 or 3,000 individuals, the number of Dutch Jews who chose to migrate to Brazil represented a substantial proportion of Dutch Jewry. Once established in Brazil, the Jewish population participated in a wide array of economic enterprises ranging from artisan crafts to overseas trade and, in a few instances, to the ownership of sugar plantations. Their involvement in the sugar industry, however, largely took the form of purchasing and otherwise handling sugar for export; Jewish merchants, in other words, served as brokers and middlemen, thereby playing a significant role in what was Brazil's most important commodity. Furthermore, Brazil's Jewish inhabitants established two synagogues and employed a *haham* (the Sephardic term for rabbi) from Amsterdam, Isaac Aboab da Fonseca, who was thus the first Jewish religious authority in the New World.[5]

All this collapsed between 1645 and 1654. In the mid-1640s, Brazil's Portuguese inhabitants launched a brutal guerrilla war against their Dutch occupiers. It quickly took its toll on the Jewish population, primarily by inducing great unease, for, if the Portuguese staged a comeback, all Jews would be required to leave what would once again become part of the Portuguese realm. Worse, any who had originally been New Christians who had emigrated to Holland and then to Brazil would be targets for the Inquisition, which would of course be reintroduced in the wake of a Portuguese victory. The population of approximately 1,450 consequently began to decline, and by 1654 only 600 or so remained. In that year an overseas expedition launched by Portugal and aided by Portuguese guerrilla forces in Brazil successfully recaptured the colony, forcing the Dutch West India Company to relinquish its presence there. All Dutch settlers, including the Jews among them, were given three months to depart.[6]

Most of Brazil's Jews returned to Amsterdam, but some decided to head instead for the British colony of Barbados and the French colony of Martinique, logical destinations because of their extensive sugar cultivation, a commodity with which Brazilian Jews had developed considerable expertise.[7] But for reasons that remain unknown, twenty-three of them set sail for New Netherland, where they disembarked at New Amsterdam in time to observe Rosh Hashana (the Jewish new year festival).

Why the small band chose New Amsterdam is problematic. Economically, New Netherland was hardly a flourishing place. The climate, of course, precluded sugar production. Nor were there many attractions for merchants who wished to trade internationally, the ambition that most characterized Jews who settled in the American colonies. Population growth during New Netherland's first quarter century was meager, limiting prospects for shopkeepers and artisans at the local level. After 1640 four merchant houses in Amsterdam dominated trade between Holland and New Netherland, none of which was Jewish. This, alone, hampered opportunities for Jewish merchants, for membership in a transatlantic ethnic or religious network was crucial to success in international commerce. For that matter, the hold exerted by the four non-Jewish Amsterdam houses impeded even non-Jewish merchants who resided in the colony.[8]

The reasons a small number of the Brazilian refugees headed for New Amsterdam must remain speculative; contemporary explanations for this poor choice have never come to light. An answer may lie, though, in a remarkable pattern of activity that existed among Dutch Sephardic Jews during the 1650s. In a burst of enterprise that commenced in 1651, they demonstrated an interest in colonization and settlement in the New World in many locations other than Brazil. At Curaçao they made several efforts during the decade to establish a colony, at length succeeding in 1659. In 1654, as already indicated, some of the Jews in Brazil headed for Barbados and Martinique. In 1657 Jewish settlers established a colony on the Wild Coast, a region along the Atlantic Ocean north of Brazil. A year later, around fifteen Jewish families settled in Newport, Rhode Island, emigrating there either from Curaçao or Barbados, perhaps even from Holland. In 1659, David Nassy, who had led earlier colonizing efforts in Curaçao and at the Wild Coast, established a colony at Cayenne, an island in the Atlantic near the latter. He did so with 150 Jews from Livorno, Italy. Finally, when the French conquered Cayenne in 1664, he led his Jewish colonists to the mainland, where they successfully settled in Suriname, or Dutch Guiana. This remarkable record of Dutch Jewish overseas activity can even be said to have included the effort launched by the Amsterdam Jewish community in 1655 for the right of Jews to settle in England, an undertaking that came to fruition a year later when the British government quietly assented, permitting Jews to settle in Britain for the first time in 365 years.[9]

When placed in the context of this extraordinary record of activity, the decision by the small group of Jewish exiles from Brazil to head for an otherwise unpromising New Amsterdam appears credible. New Netherland was yet one more colonial outpost for exploration by a Jewish population that was expressing avid interest in colonial projects. In that context, New Amsterdam made as much sense as the recurrent interest during the 1650s in Curaçao, a hot, barren island with little in the way of natural resources, save for its proximity to the coast of South America and its consequent potential as a trading post through which goods could be shipped to and from the Spanish Empire.

The twenty-three refugees who arrived in New Amsterdam encountered two Jewish merchants who had arrived only several weeks before. Perhaps other Jewish traders from the Netherlands had previously visited the colony, but, in contrast to transient merchants, the Brazilians gave every indication they intended to stay. They did so by resisting the efforts of the colony's hostile leader, Director-General Peter Stuyvesant, to deport them. Joined by several other Jewish settlers who perhaps came directly from Amsterdam, the twenty-three appealed over Stuyvesant's head to the Dutch West India Company's officers, going through the small community of the Company's Jewish stockholders in Amsterdam. In response, Company officials ordered Stuyvesant to allow them to remain, for new settlers, they explained, were what colonies needed, and these newcomers, moreover, had risked their lives and fortunes in Brazil for the Company's benefit. Although forced to permit them to stay, Stuyvesant continued to place every obstacle he could in their path, forcing the Jewish colonists to appeal again and again to Amsterdam. Over the course of the next three years, they won the right to trade at any location in the colony, to purchase homes, to serve in the militia instead of being forced to pay a tax, and at last, in 1657, to enjoy the same civic rights that Jews exercised in Amsterdam.[10]

Despite their political achievements in New Amsterdam, nearly every one of its Jewish inhabitants subsequently left not long after the victory in 1657. Virtually all were gone before Britain's surprise attack and conquest of the colony in 1664 (renaming it New York), when only one or two Jews are known to have remained.[11] Apparently New Amsterdam proved too unpromising, but not because of Stuyvesant's attempts to impose restrictions upon the Jewish settlers; he had been forced repeatedly by the Company to give way. Instead, New Amsterdam's economic limitations seem more likely to have been the cause. Indeed, other Jews coming to North America in the 1650s went instead to Newport, Rhode Island. As mentioned previously, around fifteen families arrived there in 1658. This choice has often been attributed to Rhode Island's embrace of religious toleration; and perhaps this did play a role in the settlers' decision. On the other hand, the Dutch West India Company had rebuffed all of Stuyvesant's obstructionism. Choosing to settle in Newport in preference to New Amsterdam may well have had as much to do with New Amsterdam's lack of economic opportunity for Jewish traders as with Rhode Island's policy of tolerating Jews, along with Protestants of all stripes.

Almost nothing is known of Newport's mid-seventeenth-century Jewish settlers, and in fact one authority dates their first arrival not to 1658 but to the mid-1670s, when the Jews there purchased land for a cemetery in 1677.[12] (Significantly, Jewish immigrants at that date still avoided New York.) As was true wherever they settled in colonial America, Rhode Island's Jewish settlers turned to transatlantic commerce, as may be inferred by two prosecutions of Jewish merchants in the mid-1680s for suspected violations of England's Navigation Acts. In the early 1690s the Jewish population may have grown with the arrival of approximately ninety individuals from Curaçao. But thereafter, until the 1740s, traces of a Jewish presence in Newport are slim, suggesting that whatever Jewish community existed in Rhode Island at the end of the seventeenth century largely disappeared until the middle of the eighteenth.[13]

In New York, however, a new Jewish community began to form during the 1680s, and this time it was a permanent one; it is to this decade, therefore, that the beginnings of American Jewish history can be dated unequivocally. Jewish settlers were not attracted to New York after the English seized it in their sudden attack in 1664, despite the fact that Britain established religious toleration there following the conquest. When they contemplated settling in Britain's overseas possessions during the 1660s and 1670s, Jews preferred Barbados and Jamaica in the Caribbean.[14] Both specialized in plantation agriculture and therefore did not grow their own food supplies or produce manufactured goods, depending instead upon imports from North America for the former, England for the latter. Hence, a small number of Jews made their way to New York by the beginning of the 1680s, no doubt because of the commerce between it and the two important Caribbean islands. That a new Jewish community was indeed establishing itself in New York is evident from the purchase of land in 1682 for a cemetery. By 1700 the town's Jewish population stood at between 100 and 150 individuals, out of a total population of 5,000. At length in 1728 New York's Jews were sufficient in number and resources to organize a congregation and to construct a synagogue, the first on the North American mainland.[15]

Shortly after the New Yorkers organized their community, a second permanent Jewish settlement appeared in Savannah, Georgia. The colony was established in 1732 to provide a refuge for impoverished debtors, who otherwise would have been incarcerated in prison to work off what they owed their creditors. The Sephardic community in London was at that juncture faced by an influx of New Christians fleeing from the Portuguese Inquisition, and it found its resources stretched thin. Its leaders received permission to send Jewish settlers to the newly established colony, and in 1733 they sent over forty-two settlers to Savannah.[16]

Unfortunately, the newcomers soon quarreled, for they were split between Sephardim (thirty-four in number) and Ashkenzim. They may have actually established a synagogue in 1735, but they soon separated, much in keeping with the conflict that usually characterized relations between these two branches of the Jewish people wherever they encountered one another.[17] Five years later, most of the Sephardic population left the colony when Britain and Spain found themselves once again at war; the prospect of a Spanish victory did not bode well for Jews. Only three Jewish families remained in Savannah, and while others later settled there in the 1760s, the number remained minute, with as few as six families by the early 1770s. Despite an effort in 1774 to meet as a congregation in a private house, the Jewish population was unable to organize a community until the 1790s and did not construct a synagogue until 1820.[18]

The departure of Savannah's Sephardic Jews contributed to the formation of a new Jewish community in Charleston, South Carolina. Jews had been present at that location before, for as many as fifteen Jewish men are known to have appeared in Charleston between 1697 and 1740, attracted no doubt by the opportunities for Atlantic commerce that it afforded. By mid-century the Jewish population there was able to form a congregation as well as to establish a cemetery. Charleston proved attractive as a destination; by the 1790s its Jewish population began to exceed New York's, and it was able to maintain its lead until 1820.[19]

Jews also began to settle in Philadelphia and again at Newport by the middle of the eighteenth century, where the possibilities for Atlantic commerce proved the attraction, as they had in New York and Charleston. Settlement in Philadelphia began with the sons of two New York merchant families, in 1737 and 1738, who migrated there so that they could establish branches of their families' businesses. Other Jewish settlers soon appeared in Philadelphia thanks to its flourishing port, which funneled large numbers of immigrants from Northern Ireland and the German states into the American interior and great quantities of the hinterland's produce abroad. There may have been as many as a hundred Jews in the town by the eve of the American Revolution. The Jewish presence in Philadelphia soared during the Revolution, for a majority of the Jews of New York, Charleston, and Savannah fled there when the British captured those cities and remained for the duration of the struggle. The influx enabled the Philadelphians to construct their first synagogue in 1782.[20]

Newport's new Jewish community formed during the 1740, and by the late 1750s it was feasible for it to erect what is the oldest synagogue building in the United States. Newport's evolution as a port is what drew Jewish settlers, for the town's commercial reach had expanded since the end of the 1600s from trade along the coasts of North America to extensive traffic with England, the Caribbean, and Africa. Jewish merchants began to settle in Newport by 1746, and by the eve of the Revolution there may have been as many as twenty-two Jewish families there. The settlers included Aaron Lopez, a refugee from the Portuguese Inquisition who arrived at Newport in the early 1750s, where he began to practice Judaism publicly and where he proceeded to establish a commercial empire that spanned the Atlantic trading world. Lopez grew to become one of Newport's most prosperous inhabitants, although he lost his fortune with the outbreak of the Revolution. Indeed, Newport as a whole declined as a result of the conflict and ultimately sank into obscurity as a commercial center. By 1800, therefore, Newport disappeared as a center of Jewish settlement in early America.[21]

While Newport faded away, new Jewish communities arose in Baltimore and Richmond during the late 1700s and early 1800s, so that by 1820 there were six centers of Jewish life in the early United States, five of them seaports (New York, Savannah, Charleston, Philadelphia, and Baltimore).[22] Small numbers of Jews were also to be found during the eighteenth and early nineteenth centuries in locations that did not function as ports, ranging from eastern Long Island and Westchester County in New York, to New Jersey and Lancaster in Pennsylvania.[23] In all, the Jewish population of early America comprised a minute part of the entire American population, amounting in 1790 to between 1,300 and 1,500 in a total population that approached 4 million. In 1820 there were between 2,650 and 2,750 Jewish inhabitants, a mere three one-hundredths of 1 percent of the nation's entire population.[24]

ETHNIC AND ECONOMIC BASES

Most Jews who established themselves in early America were of Ashkenazic descent, despite the fact that the period between 1654 and 1820 is routinely known as the Sephardic era in American Jewish history. It carries this name because it was the Sephardic ritual that everywhere governed the community's religious life. Judaism was first introduced in North America in 1654 by refugees from Brazil who were almost all of Sephardic origin; the majority of the Newport community established in 1658 was undoubtedly Sephardic; and the new Jewish community in New York in the early 1680s was largely Sephardic. According to an important principle of traditional Jewish religious law, the custom established in a place becomes the law of that place, so long as it conforms to established traditional Jewish law. Hence, the Sephardic rite as the one that was originally established in the colonies remained the norm, even after Ashkenazic immigrants had become the majority, a position they achieved by 1720 and maintained for the next century.[25]

Whether Sephardic or Ashkenazic, Jewish immigrants between 1654 and 1820 came for the most part from London and Amsterdam. Even if born in Spain or Portugal or in central or eastern Europe, they generally went first to England or the Netherlands, only to relocate to the American colonies. For all the attractions of London and Amsterdam—"the great city of Amsterdam . . . [and] a very populous city, more highly praised and more glorious than all others, London," as the hazan of New York's community reminisced in 1759[26]—the Jewish communities in both localities were afflicted by a considerable amount of poverty among their members. To be sure, wealthy Jewish merchants were present in the two cities, but they were comparatively few in number. Much larger in number were the impoverished eastern and central European Jews called *beteljuden* (beggar Jews), who often subsisted by selling rags and castoff clothes. From Portugal and Spain émigrés fleeing increased levels of inquisitional activity arrived periodically, draining community resources. In Amsterdam the number of families requiring poor relief between 1725 and 1750 rose from 450 to more than 750, but contributors in the Sephardic congregation fell from almost 630 to 610. In London it was the prevalence of poverty that impelled the Sephardic leadership to send both Sephardim and Ashkenazim to Georgia and later to examine a similar plan to send another contingent of the poor to Charleston.

At the same time that poverty among the Jews of London and Amsterdam grew and contributed to settlement in the colonies, some among the well-to-do Jewish merchants of London and Amsterdam began to disengage from the Jewish community—and, by implication, from a sense of religious obligation for the less fortunate. In London's case some of the wealthy either converted to Christianity or took Christian spouses, thereby ultimately distancing themselves from the Jewish community and weakening the ability of communal institutions to extend assistance to those at the lower end of the Jewish social order. In Amsterdam the problem had different origins. Well-to-do Sephardic Jews in eighteenth-century Amsterdam, as one historian has argued, exhibited less economic initiative and creativity than in previous eras. Though they were still people of means, "stagnation and loss of dynamism were unmistakable . . . [and] the picture was one of slow eclipse." Ultimately, therefore, the community's ability to care for its growing poor population diminished.[27]

On the other hand, not all Jews who left Amsterdam and London for North America were impoverished. Some came from prosperous merchant families, which, while not of immense wealth, enjoyed comfortable circumstances. In these cases the impulse to migrate to the colonies arose from an elemental condition of commercial life in the seventeenth- and eighteenth-century Atlantic trading orbit, namely, the fact that a great deal of commerce was conducted within international networks that were religious and ethnic in origin. French Huguenots relied on other French Huguenots, Quakers traded with Quakers, and Jewish merchants did business with other Jewish merchants. Furthermore, religious and ethnic networks were even more solidly established when they encompassed family connections. Accordingly, Jewish merchants in London and Amsterdam sent brothers, sons, uncles, and cousins abroad to serve as commercial representatives in ports around the Atlantic basin. Rather, therefore, than poverty as the sole driving force, a significant number of the Jews who settled in early America did so in order to establish commercial outposts for their families' enterprises.

Sephardic and Ashkenazic merchants in the American colonies dealt in a wide array of merchandise: sugar from the Caribbean, wine from the Canary Islands and Madeira, slaves from Africa and the Caribbean,[28] English manufactured goods like guns, wallpaper, carriages, musical instruments, tools and other hardware, and fine clothing, as well as the commodities that the American colonies exported to Europe and the Caribbean, such as furs, wood staves, planks, barrels, wheat, rice, indigo, naval stores, whale oil candles, and fish. In other words, they dealt readily with any and all of the products that were exported and imported throughout the length and breadth of the Atlantic world, for this was an era in which businessmen did not specialize. In this respect the Jewish merchants of eighteenth-century America resembled their non-Jewish counterparts, among whom they resided and worked and with whom they often formed successful partnerships, for the early American environment was tolerant of and welcoming toward its Jewish inhabitants. Antisemitism did not throw up the barriers that it did in contemporary Europe, where legal restrictions impeded Jewish mercantile and financial enterprise in many jurisdictions. To the contrary: rather than economic restrictions, Jews in the American colonies enjoyed the same access to economic opportunity as their non-Jewish counterparts.

Not all Jewish immigrants could immediately become merchants who participated in the Atlantic export and import trade. One might begin as a shopkeeper rather than a merchant, but the aspiration was always to be known as the latter. That the transition could be made was apparent in Lancaster, Pennsylvania, a center for the exchange of furs and wheat from the interior in return for manufactured goods from England. Jews there (and non-Jews, too) who were listed as shopkeepers around 1760 succeeded over the course of the next two decades to the point where they could be listed as merchants. In Charleston Joseph Tobias described himself a "shopkeeper" in newspaper advertisements in the late 1730s, but by 1743 he had become a "merchant." Similarly, Isaac Da Costa of Charleston, known as a shopkeeper in 1751, was called a merchant by 1759. To underscore the preferability of being able to identify oneself as a merchant, members of the Jewish community of New York made certain to call themselves that in their wills. The authors of nineteen of the twenty-three wills written by Jewish men that were filed in probate between 1704 and 1774 used the term. Some also identified the Jewish executors and witnesses of their wills as merchants—but, curiously, not the non-Jewish friends whom they designated.[29]

Many important aspects of the lives of early America's Jews derived directly from their involvement in transatlantic commerce, beginning with settlement primarily in the seaport communities of New York, Newport, Philadelphia, Charleston, Savannah, and Baltimore. So, too, did their remarkable proclivity for travel, particularly during the eighteenth century. Although they were linked in trading networks based upon religion and family, personal familiarity bestowed even greater advantages. Accordingly, they traveled frequently and widely among North America's ports, the Caribbean, the dangers of travel on the high seas notwithstanding. Their journeys provided knowledge of market conditions abroad, familiarity with the products of a variety of lands, and, probably above all else, personal contact with their commercial counterparts in distant ports.[30] An impending journey logically became the occasion to write or update one's will. As one New Yorker explained in his will in 1725, "the Dangers of the Sea And the Uncertainty of this Mortal Life" impelled him to draw it up on the eve of his departure for Jamaica. Four years later, another invoked "the danger & hazards unto which I am Likely to be Exposed," prior to sailing for the Caribbean. A third, bound for England in 1743, explained that, "Considering the Dangers of the Seas," the time had come to write his last will and testament.[31]

Mercantile aspirations also had a profound effect on family life, and this in at least two decisive ways. First, it broke up families because of the need for commercial representatives in other locations. Just as a merchant family in England would send a son to New York as its commercial representative, that same son eventually would send one or more of his offspring out into the world to act as *his* commercial representative. That, in fact, was the origin of the permanent Jewish presence in Philadelphia during the 1730s mentioned before. More poignantly, families would send their children to settle in the Caribbean or in England, often never to see them again.

Second, the centrality of personal connections to commerce extended to marriage. By joining families that resided in distant locations around the Atlantic, marriage solidified commercial networks. Again, therefore, parents sent off a son or daughter to marry in a distant port, never to see him or her again. This practice served, of course, to perpetuate Judaism by preventing intermarriage, but its commercially advantageous side also played a vital part in these significant life decisions.[32]

The disruptive effects upon the family of the practices necessary for success in Atlantic commerce was a fact of life that deeply pained at least one Jewish woman in early America, Abigail Franks, née Levy. Abigail Levy married Jacob Franks, one of the New York Jewish community's most prosperous Ashkenzic member during the first half of the 1700s. Jacob Franks had come to New York early in the 1700s as the commercial representative of his merchant family in London. In New York he prospered, married Abigail, daughter of another of the town's Jewish merchants, and the two proceeded to raise a large family. At the beginning of the 1740s, Jacob sent two of their sons to Philadelphia to serve as the family's commercial representatives there, but he also sent a third son, Naphtali, back to London, there to rejoin the original merchant family. Abigail, suspecting that she would never see Naphtali again, corresponded with him regularly for the remainder of her life, and in 1741 she wrote, in a passage that reflected the price the early American Jewish family paid for its mercantile aspirations,

I wish but for the happyness of Seeing you wich I begin to fear I never Shall for I don't wish you here And I am Sure there is Little porbability of My Goeing to England. If parents would Give themselves Leave to Consider the many Difficulties that attends the bringing up of Childeren there would not be such Imoderate Joy att there birtth I dont mean the Care of there infancy thats the Least but its affter they are grown Up and behave in Such a maner As to Give Sattisfaction then to be bereaved of them in the Decline of Life when the injoying of them would be Our Greatest happyness for the Cares of giting a Liveing Disperses Them Up and down the world and the Only pleasure wee injoy (and thats intermixt with Anxiety) is to hear they doe well Wich is A pleasure I hope to have.[33]

JUDAISM IN EARLY AMERICA

The overseas networks to which they belonged enveloped the Jews of early America in a web of relationships and practices that nurtured their capacity to maintain Judaism in the English colonies. If family dispersal for commercial purposes meant that Abigail Franks and her contemporaries might never see some of their children again, it also guaranteed marriage within the faith for a great many individuals, despite the minute size of the early American Jewish population. Nuclear families paid a severe price, but at the same time they assured the perpetuation of the Jewish religion in America.

The larger Atlantic world contributed even more to Judaism's stability in the colonies, and later the young United States of America, by assisting with funds for the construction of synagogues and the acquisition of Torah scrolls. For example, when New York's congregation began to build its first synagogue in 1728, it received a large donation from Curaçao's Jewish community as well as contributions from the Jewish inhabitants of London, Jamaica, and Barbados. A generation later in 1761 the New Yorkers in turn provided a Torah scroll to the small Jewish population in Philadelphia, who at that time still worshiped in a private home. The New York community also provided money and a Torah to the Jews of Newport when they began to construct their synagogue in the late 1750s; and the Newporters also received financial contributions from the communities in London, Curaçao, Jamaica, and Suriname, along with Torah scrolls from London and Amsterdam.[34]

Religious functionaries—kosher meat slaughterers, teachers, and hazanim, the cantors who led services in the synagogue and chanted the text of the Torah on Sabbaths, holidays, and during Monday and Thursday morning services— were also drawn from the larger Atlantic world. When possible, such personnel came from within the local congregation, as in Charleston, where Isaac Da Costa served as hazan between 1750 and 1775, or as in New York before the Revolution when Gershom Mendes Seixas became the first native-born American to become a hazan. The rule of thumb, however, was to advertise for religious officiants in foreign ports, as in Newport, where the community lured Judah Touro away from the Caribbean in 1759. Touro served as Newport's hazan until 1779, when he went to New York because of his adherence to the British side during the Revolution, and ultimately returned to Jamaica when England finally lost the mainland colonies.[35]

Unlike cantors, slaughterers, and teachers, the early American Jewish population did not conduct searches for rabbis. Judaism in America had no rabbinic expertise or leadership at the helm until the mid-nineteenth century, when the first rabbi in North America settled in Baltimore in 1840. In marked contrast, the congregations at Jamaica employed rabbis beginning in the early 1680s and had ordained rabbinic leadership throughout the course of the eighteenth century.[36] In the absence of trained rabbinic experts in the North American communities, knowledge of the intricacies of traditional religious law inevitably suffered,[37] although the congregations could and did on occasion turn for religious rulings to rabbinic authorities in London and Amsterdam.[38]

Left to their own devices, the lay leaders of the congregations in North America did what they could to enforce religious norms, even in the private lives of their members, by resorting to several disciplinary devices. The mildest of these was admonition, but if that failed then the honor of being called to the Torah while it was read during services was the next step. The congregations could then move on to expulsion from membership in the community, a stringent form of punishment in that one who had been expelled could not be buried in the community's cemetery. Finally, there was *herem*, or excommunication, an even more severe penalty, inasmuch as there could be no contact whatsoever, neither inside the synagogue nor outside it socially or commercially, with an individual who had been excommunicated.[39]

Because there was as yet no movement to reform Jewish law and practices, what the Jewish communities of the eighteenth and early nineteenth centuries sought to maintain were the requirements of traditional rabbinic Judaism, or what today is called Orthodoxy. The community's governing principles were those of the Sephardic ritual, but Ashkenazim in the privacy of their homes no doubt perpetuated many of their own variations of the prayers, ritual ceremonies, and customs, although the sources that have come down to us do not elucidate this point. What is striking, however, is that the Ashkenazim, though they were in the majority after 1720, accepted the primacy of the Sephardic rite in the synagogue; they neither sought to change it nor withdraw to establish their own congregations and cemeteries, for, with the exception of the rancor between the two groups in Georgia during the 1730s, Ashkenazim and Sephardim achieved a unique degree of unification in the English mainland colonies.

Not so anywhere else they encountered one another. Sephardim viewed themselves as in every way superior to Ashkenazim, whom they regarded as uncouth, backward, unrefined, and uneducated. Claiming descent for themselves from the aristocrats of ancient Israel, the Sephardim alleged that the Ashkenazim were descended from its lower classes. The Ashenazim, for their part, indicted the Sephardim as insufficiently religious, as wanting in their adherence to orthodox requirements. Mutual recrimination and ill-will led in England, Holland, and their respective colonies in the Caribbean and Suriname to separate synagogues, separate cemeteries, separate business firms—and to separate marriages. The occasional Sephardic man who defied convention and married an Ashkenazic women forfeited the privileges of membership in the synagogue, and his wife was referred to in the community's marriage register not by her name but impersonally as "Tudesca," the Sephardic term for "German woman."[40]

In contrast to the discord and contempt that characterized relations between these two great subdivisions within Judaism, the Ashenazim and Sephardim in North America achieved an unheard-of record of cooperation, which could have had no other effect than to buttress their small communities. They were buried in the same cemeteries, the first religious institution that was established in each new Jewish community.[41] They joined hands to build their synagogues. In New York and Newport, for example, the community's leading Sephardic and Ashkenazic members served on the committees responsible for erecting the structures, in New York's case defying advice received from Curaçao's haham to keep the Ashkenazim in their place. To the contrary, Ashkenazim served as presidents of the Sephardic-rite community of New York more frequently than Sephardim.[42] Finally, contrary to what was undoubtedly the greatest taboo of all, marriages between Ashkenazic and Sephardic partners were more common in America than elsewhere, despite a raucous split within Sephardic ranks in New York that broke out in 1740 over the issue.[43]

Judaism in early America was thus strengthened not only by the imposition of communal discipline but also by the rare degree of integration achieved by Ashkenazim and Sephardim. Nevertheless, while many early American Jews adhered to tradition—often rigorously so—many did not. For every Abigail Franks in New York who would not write a letter on a holiday and who pleaded with her son in London to observe the dietary laws and to pray every morning as the law required, there were others, also in New York, who had to be warned publicly in 1757 on the solemn Day of Atonement that they risked expulsion from membership and noninterment in the cemetery for having engaged in "Trading on the Sabath, Eating of forbidden Meats & other Heinous Crimes."[44] If Massachusetts inhabitants during the American Revolution were impressed by the Sabbath scrupulousness of Jewish refugees from Newport, non-Jewish Americans in all of the thirteen original states were aware that their male Jewish neighbors did not cover their heads and had abandoned the practice of wearing beards.[45] And if Philadelphia's community constructed a ritual bath in the 1780s, an extremely important requirement under the religious laws of family purity, two members of that same community could report in 1785 to a leading rabbi in Amsterdam that there was a "great lack of discipline that prevails in our generation," complaining of declension in religious observance.[46] Above all, a small percentage of the Jewish population married out of the faith. While the numbers were small when compared with the rate of intermarriage at present, they suggest that, in early America, Judaism already confronted the challenges to its continuity that it would have to face in later eras as a consequence of its encounters with modernity. Between 1790 and 1820, references to intermarriage were included in the communities' constitutions and regulations; contemporaries perceived they faced a growing problem.[47]

EARLY AMERICAN JEWS AND THEIR POLITICAL LEGACY

Whatever the scope of the disenchantment Judaism faced in early America may have been, no initiatives to address the sources of disaffection emerged prior to 1820. The band of reformers in Charleston in 1824 who issued a call for change in the synagogue ritual, citing the high rate of synagogue absenteeism, the lack of decorum during services, and "the apathy and neglect which have been manifested towards our holy religion," had no precedent during the lengthy Sephardic period of American Jewish history.[48] In marked contrast, however, early America's Jews in the wake of the American Revolution daringly pursued change in quite another area, namely, the right to vote and to hold public office. They sought, in other words, equality of citizenship, and to achieve it they were willing to speak out openly and forcefully to their contemporary non-Jewish neighbors.

Throughout the colonial era the condition of the Jewish population in England's colonies differed markedly from conditions endured in much of Europe, to the benefit of the Jews who settled in America. Antisemitism, while it certainly existed in the colonies in the form of traditional stereotypes and a few rare, but minor, outbursts, did not take the violent forms it frequently did in Europe, nor did it encompass the kinds of economic restrictions and legal disabilities that prevailed in many European jurisdictions.[49] Jews could reside anywhere: they could own land, engage in retail trade, and become artisans and craftsmen. Because the general environment was one in which toleration prevailed, Jews and Christians in the American colonies established business partnerships, formed personal friendships, summered together, and even on occasion married one another. Furthermore, colonial legislatures bestowed commercial privileges upon Jews. In Rhode Island during the 1750s, for example, the legislature conferred a ten-year monopoly upon a Jewish merchant who had petitioned for the right to produce potash using a secret process. In South Carolina a Jewish inhabitant held the vitally important position of inspector general of indigo for a decade, an appointment that gave him an edge for his own investments in indigo.[50]

There was, however, one area to which toleration and acceptance did not extend: the political. Jews in the British colonies could neither vote nor serve in public office; they had no civic existence. Their exclusion from public life extended to the possibility of informal influence, as well, for there is no evidence to suggest that they served as advisers to public officials or participated in public debates on political issues. Even in America, therefore, the prevailing contemporary European theory that Jews comprised a separate nation applied. As members of an eternally separate people, they could never be incorporated into the body politic of the host nation. Public policy, office in government, and political activity was the one sector in which early American Jews did not mix with other colonial Americans. As the Reverend Ezra Stiles of Newport, a clergymen who was quite friendly toward Jews, remarked in 1761, "Providence seems to make everything to work for mortification of the Jews, and to prevent their incorporating into any nation; that thus they may continue a distinct people. . . . The opposition it has met with in Rhode Island, forebodes that the Jews will never become incorporated with the people of America any more than in Europe, Asia, and Africa."[51]

One exception, New York City, did exist, but apparently the Reverend Stiles was not aware of it. The city admitted Jews to freemanship by not imposing religious requirements for it. Freemanship permitted one to vote in municipal elections; and between 1688 and 1770, fifty-seven Jewish New Yorkers became freemen and voted. In addition, they voted for seats in the colony's legislature, until barred on grounds of religion by a statute enacted in 1737 as a result of a disputed election that year, but they continued to vote thereafter in municipal elections. Astonishingly, they served as city constables, a post that placed them in positions of authority over New Yorkers who were Christian, for constables served warrants, made arrests, kept the peace, walked the night watch, and were responsible for controlling vice, profanation of the Sabbath, and excessive drinking in taverns.[52]

Everywhere else in England's mainland colonies, however, the concept that Jews could not participate in the community's public life prevailed. Nor did colonial American Jews challenge the status quo. No doubt they knew that any attempt to do so would be rebuffed decisively. That is what occurred in 1750 in Jamaica, England's most important Caribbean colony, which had a larger Jewish population than that in any of the mainland colonies, when Abraham Sanches petitioned the island's legislature for the right to vote on the grounds that he owned a large tract of land and had been naturalized. The reaction was swift, and it was uncompromising. Kingston's inhabitants counterpetitioned that the Jews had "renounced their right of government to the governor, Pontius Pilate, in favour of the Roman emperors, in order to destroy, and put to the most cruel and ignominious death, Jesus Christ, the lord and saviour of mankind." In another petition the residents of the parish of St. Catherine, where the island's capital was located, cited another well-established truism: that Jews were not loyal to the societies in which they resided. Invoking the familiar concept that they permanently comprised a separate nation, the petitioners wrote: "The Jews are a foreign nation . . . and pay no voluntary obedience to our laws; but on the contrary, abhor both them and our religion. . . . To admit a nation, under such circumstances, to exercise a share in the legislature . . . might be destructive to our religion and constitution." Faced with such opposition, Sanches's petition failed.[53] In view of the fact that the Jews in the mainland colonies were in frequent contact with the Jews of Jamaica as part of their Atlantic trading and family networks, it is entirely likely that they knew about this abortive attempt to enter the political order.

With the advent of the American Revolution, however, Jews in America began to behave in a strikingly different manner: they began to comport themselves as if they actually had a role to play in public life. The change occurred everywhere, not just in New York City, where they had already enjoyed political inclusion for several decades, even if only on the municipal level. In Philadelphia the new assertiveness was apparent as early as 1765, when several Jewish merchants joined with non-Jewish merchants to sign the nonimportation agreement to protest against the Stamp Act by boycotting all English merchandise. In Savannah the city's committee for revolutionary activities included two Jews who played highly visible roles, one of whom served as chairman of the committee. In Charleston Francis Salvador was elected to the colony's first and second provincial congresses between 1773 and 1776—despite the fact that Jews had not yet been "incorporated." Salvador's participation was much in evidence, for he served on several of the congresses' committees, helped to draft South Carolina's first state constitution (which required a Christian oath to vote and serve in office), sat in the new state legislature after independence had been declared, and lost his life in battle against a Tory force.[54]

These declarations of political choice were not limited to just a few. Throughout the new nation most Jews took sides in the struggle, in a majority of cases declaring themselves for the American side, but in some cases for the British. If for the American cause, then many, if not most, abandoned their homes and businesses when their towns fell under British control and crossed over behind American lines, a choice that amounted to an overt statement of political affiliation. Conversely, those Jews in smaller numbers who remained behind in localities under British control indicated thereby their support for the British side in the conflict. Jews who supported the American cause demonstrated their commitment even more vividly by volunteering for military service. Approximately one hundred, a sizable proportion of the adult male Jewish population, are known to have fought in the Continental Army or in the state militias.[55]

The American Revolution, therefore, was a decisive turning point when examined in the context of Jewish exclusion from the political realm. It proved to be a milestone in the shift from the status of outsider to that of participant in the civic order. Moreover, it provided ammunition for the struggle that yet lay ahead for equality of citizenship. For despite the heady talk before and during the Revolution about natural rights and the equality of all men, as well as the definition of the struggle with England as one to secure civil rights and liberties, twelve of the thirteen state constitutions adopted during the course of the conflict prescribed religious tests for voting and serving in office that continued to bar Jews. Again there was only one exception: New York State's constitution, adopted in 1777, eliminated religion as a prerequisite for political participation. In all remaining twelve states, on the other hand, the new constitutions (and in Connecticut and Rhode Island, where the colonial charters remained in effect) included Christianity among the requirements for political participation.[56] The country's Jewish population responded by speaking out assertively, even confrontationally. When the officers of the Jewish community in Philadelphia protested in 1783 against the clause in the Pennsylvania constitution that required members of the state legislature to swear that both the Old and New Testaments were divinely inspired, a requirement that obviously disbarred Jews, they did not invoke the doctrine of natural rights but concentrated instead on their affiliation with the American cause during the recent struggle. As they wrote to the state's officials,

> The conduct and behaviour of the Jews in this and the neighboring states has always tallied with the great design of the revolution; the Jews of Charleston, New York, Newport, and other posts occupied by the British troops, have distinguishedly suffered for their attachment to the revolution principles . . . [and] the Jews of Pennsylvania in proportion to the number of their members, can count with any religious society, whatsoever the Whigs [supporters of the American side] among either of them; they have served some of them, in the continental army; some went out in the militia to fight the common enemy.[57]

Pennsylvania's officials did not respond to this representation on behalf of equal citizenship. But a major breakthrough occurred a little more than a year later in Virginia. With the way charted by Thomas Jefferson, the Virginia legislature in 1785 proclaimed religious freedom, disestablished the Episcopalian Church, and abolished all religious tests for participation in public life. Virginia thereby jointed New York in extending equality of citizenship to Jews who might settle in the state. Jewish spokesmen did not play a part in this vitally important development—only a handful as yet resided in Virginia—underscoring that the acquisition of political equality hardly occurred solely because of Jewish initiative; the ideology and principles that emanated from the Revolution, after all, did count too. But, following this development, the nation's Jews continued as earlier in Pennsylvania to make the case for inclusion, again basing it upon their contributions to the Revolution. Thus, a year after Virginia's statute for religious freedom went into effect, one of Philadelphia's Jewish leaders undertook to contact the men who were meeting behind closed doors in Philadelphia during the summer of 1787 to create a better form of government for the nation, in order to press the case for ending the political disabilities the Jewish population faced. Although he appealed to the doctrine of natural rights, he also firmly asserted of the Jews that "during the late Contest with England they have been foremost in aiding and assisting the states with their lifes [*sic*] and fortunes, they have supported the cause, have bravely fought and bled for liberty which they can not enjoy."[58]

An unparalleled opportunity to raise the issue of civic equality presented itself in 1790, when George Washington embarked on a tour of the nation. As he traveled, community organizations and institutions wrote to welcome him to their towns, and Washington would write back with his thanks. It was for this reason that the small Jewish community that yet remained in Newport, Rhode Island, wrote to him in the summer of 1790, initiating what is the most important exchange of letters in American Jewish history between a president and the Jewish population. The incident's fame stems from Washington's well-known assertion that the government of the United States "to bigotry gives no sanction, to persecution no assistance," a ringing line the president took from the congregation's letter to him. Less familiar, however, is another statement that had also appeared earlier in the congregation's letter, which Washington also incorporated in his response, and which in effect put him on the side of equal citizenship for America's Jewish inhabitants. In their letter to the president, the Newport Jews had introduced the issue of political equality, writing that, throughout the course of history, Jews had been denied "the invaluable rights of free citizens," but that there now fortunately existed "a [federal] Government deeming every one, of whatever nation, tongue or language equal parts of the great governmental machine." It was a government under which "All [have] liberty of conscience and immunities of citizenship." In his reply Washington closely repeated that last phrase, writing that "all possess alike liberty of conscience and immunities of citizenship," thereby suggesting that he accepted Jews as members of the political order. For the Jewish population of early America, this endorsement of their aspirations for incorporation, coming as it did from the Revolution's hero and the symbolic father of the nation, represented the culmination of their campaign to turn the corner on the view that they belonged permanently to a separate (and not equal) nation. The Jews of Newport had indeed acted shrewdly when they included their references to the issue in their letter to the president.[59]

As yet, however, eleven states excluded Jews from political participation. The barriers there began to fall, however, first in South Carolina and Pennsylvania in 1790, in Delaware in 1792, and in Georgia in 1798. Inasmuch as this still left seven of the original states with religious requirements for civic incorporation, Jewish spokesmen continued to press their case openly. In Maryland, for example, where

Jews were beginning to settle in Baltimore, merchant Reuben Etting repeatedly submitted petitions for civic rights to the legislature in the late 1790s and early 1800s, although inclusion would not come until 1826, and only after a lengthy, bitter struggle that began in 1818 and continued for eight years, a battle initiated and fought out in the state's legislature by sympathetic non-Jews.[60] In North Carolina a Jewish spokesman again took a bold stand. There in 1809 Jacob Henry was elected to the legislature, but was challenged when he sought to take his seat on the grounds that the state's constitution required that he take an oath affirming the New Testament's divinity. Henry argued successfully that he supported the principle that officeholders had to subscribe to religious beliefs but specific beliefs could not be made mandatory.[61] Even more eloquently, in Charleston in 1816 Isaac Harby protested in a letter to Secretary of State James Monroe against barring anyone on the basis of religion from appointment to a position in government, in the course of which he envisioned a society in which religious pluralism and political inclusion prevailed. Harby formulated his challenge to religious tests for government service after Monroe recalled the country's Jewish consul to Tunis because of his religion. Harby wrote to the secretary of state that Jews were "by no means to be considered as a *Religious sect*, tolerated by the government; they constitute a portion of *the People*. They are, in every respect, woven in and compacted with the citizens of the Republic. Quakers and Catholics, Episcopalians and Presbyterians, Baptists and Jews, all constitute one great political family."[62]

While Harby's eloquent words did not sway the secretary of state, their significance lies in the mere fact that they could be uttered at all—that in America members of the Jewish faith could and did speak directly to power and lay claim to the right to express political power. In doing so, they, as others, contributed to the evolution of equality and democracy in the United States. This, together with their creation of a permanent Jewish presence in America, is a central feature of the legacy that the Jews of early America bequeathed to their successors.

NOTES

1. For varying accounts of the arrival in 1654 and the composition of the population, see Arnold Wiznitzer, "The Exodus from Brazil and Arrival in New Amsterdam of the Jewish Pilgrim Fathers, 1654," in Martin A. Cohen, ed., *The Jewish Experience in Latin America: Selected Studies from the Publications of the American Jewish Historical Society*, 2 vols. (Waltham, MA, 1971), 2:320–27; and Egon Wolff and Frieda Wolff, "The Problem of the First Jewish Settlers in New Amsterdam, 1654," *Studia Rosenthaliana* 15 (1981): 169–77.

2. The hazards of arrest by the Inquisition included forfeiture of one's property, torture, going mad in its dungeons, and being handed over to the civil authorities for death by burning during a grand public spectacle. For the Portuguese Inquisition, see Alexandre Herculano, *History of the Origin and Establishment of the Inquisition in Portugal*,

trans. John C. Branner (New York, 1968 [1926]); for Spain's: Yitzhak Baer, *A History of the Jews in Christian Spain*, 2 vols. (Philadelphia, 1966), especially volume 2; and Henry Kamen, *The Spanish Inquisition: A Historical Revision* (New Haven, 1997). For a brief description of public executions of allegedly heretical New Christians in Portugal in 1739, one may consult Stanley F. Chyet, *Lopez of Newport: Colonial American Merchant Prince* (Detroit, 1970), 15.

3. For accounts of the Dutch Jewish community's development, see volume 15 of Salo Wittmayer Baron's *A Social and Religious History of the Jews*, 2d ed., 17 vols. (New York, 1952–1980); Jonathan I. Israel, "The Economic Contribution of Dutch Sephardi Jewry to Holland's Golden Age, 1595–1713," *Tijdschrift voor Geschiedenis* 96 (1983): 505, 513, and his *The Dutch Republic: Its Rise, Greatness, and Fall, 1477–1806* (Oxford, 1995), passim. Violet Barbour, *Capitalism in Amsterdam in the Seventeenth Century* (Ann Arbor, 1976 [1950]), 25, places the number of Jews at three thousand around 1650.

4. On the movement of Ashkenzic Jews westward, see generally Moses A. Shulvass, *From East to West: The Westward Migration of Jews from Eastern Europe During the Seventeenth and Eighteenth Centuries* (Detroit, 1971).

5. The authoritative account of the Jews of Brazil, 1630–1654, is Arnold Wiznitzer's *Jews in Colonial Brazil* (New York, 1960). For the information in this and the preceding paragraph, see 12–41, 46, 51–54, 59, 65–66, 71–72, 74, 81, 86, 130–35.

6. On the effort by the Portuguese to retake Brazil and the impact upon the Dutch (including Jewish) population, see C. R. Boxer, *The Dutch in Brazil, 1624–1654* (Oxford, 1957), 159–245.

7. Our knowledge that some went to Barbados and Martinique is from a petition the twenty-three refugees in New Amsterdam sent to the officers of the Dutch West India Company after they arrived on Manhattan Island; Morris U. Schappes, ed., *A Documentary History of the Jews in the United States, 1654–1875*, 3d ed. (New York, n.d.), 3.

8. Oliver A. Rink, *Holland on the Hudson: An Economic and Social History of Dutch New York* (Ithaca, 1986), 62, 67–68, 115–16, 134–35, 156, 158, 169, 171, 172, 175–77, 206, 212–13.

9. Robert Cohen, "The Egerton Manuscript," *American Jewish Historical Quarterly* 62 (1972–1973): 334–35; Jacob R. Marcus and Stanley F. Chyet, eds., Simon Cohen, trans., *Historical Essay on the Colony of Surinam, 1788* (Cincinnati, 1974), 183–88; Isaac S. and Suzanne A. Emmanuel, *History of the Jews of the Netherlands Antilles*, 2 vols. (Cincinnati, 1970), 1:38, 42, 45; Morris A. Gutstein, *The Story of the Jews of Newport: Two and a Half Centuries of Judaism, 1658–1908* (New York, 1936), 340–42; Leon Huhner, *The Life of Judah Touro (1775–1854)* (Philadelphia, 1946), 10, 145, note 5.

10. The ongoing struggle involving the Jews of New Amsterdam, Stuyvesant, and the Company may be followed in the documents assembled by Schappes, *A Documentary History*, 1–13.

11. The two were Jacob de Lucena and Asser Levy. The former is known to have been present in New York as late as 1678, as per Samuel Oppenheim, *The Early History of the Jews in New York, 1654–1664: Some New Matter on the Subject* (New York, 1909), 23, 60. Levy resided in the town until his death in 1683; see Leo Hershkowitz, "Original Inventories of Early New York Jews," *American Jewish History* 90 (2002): 251–52.

12. Jacob Rader Marcus, *The Colonial American Jew, 1492–1776*, 3 vols. (Detroit, 1970), 1:216.

13. Gutstein, *The Story of the Jews of Newport*, 36–38, 40–43, 46, 81–82, 113–14; Emmanuel and Emmanuel, *History of the Jews of the Netherlands Antilles*, 1:90; and "Items Relating to the Jews of Newport," *Publications of the American Jewish Historical Society* 27 (1920): 175–76.

14. That Jewish settlement in Barbados grew in the 1660s and 1670s is evident from customhouse records and the existence of a synagogue by 1664: Wilfred S. Samuel, "A Review of the Jewish Colonists in Barbados in the Year 1680," *Transactions of the Jewish Historical Society of England* 13 (1932–1935): 95; "Quaker Records," *Journal of the Barbados Museum and Historical Society* 15 (1947–48): 82; Hispanic Society of America, New York City, A Coppie Journall of Entries Made in the Custom House of Barbados Beginning August ye 10th 1665 continued in two distinct accotts to ye 24th Aprl [*sic*] 1667 & containes Ye accott Currant of 2 yeares 8½ months, passim, for Jewish merchants like Luis Dias, Abraham Burgos, David Namias, David Gabay, Anthony Rodrigues, Samuel De Leon, among others. In Jamaica the governor reported in 1672 that twenty-nine Jews resided there; Public Record Office, Kew, CO 1/28, no. 27, 57.

15. David de Sola Pool and Tamar de Sola Pool, *An Old Faith in the New World: Portrait of Shearith Israel, 1654–1954* (New York, 1955), 303; for Jews in New York in the 1680s: David de Sola Pool, *Portraits Etched in Stone: Early Jewish Settlers, 1682–1831* (New York, 1952); population data are in Marcus, *The Colonial American Jew*, 1:256, 258, 308, 390–91; and the construction of the synagogue may be followed in the opening pages of the New York community's records: "The Earliest Extant Minute Books of the Spanish and Portuguese Congregation Shearith Israel in New York, 1728–1786," *Publications of the American Jewish Historical Society* 21 (1913): 3ff.

16. Saul Jacob Rubin, *Third to None: The Saga of Savannah Jewry, 1733–1983* (N.p., 1983), 1–3, 10.

17. For the conflicts between Ashkenazim and Sephardim in general, see the discussion infra. For the possibility of a synagogue (as well as their quarrels): Rubin, *Third to None*, 3–5. For an eyewitness to their contentiousness, the Reverend Martin Bolzius, see R. D. Barnett, "Dr. Samuel Nunes Ribeiro and the Settlement of Georgia," *Migration and Settlement: Proceedings of the Anglo-American Jewish Historical Conference Held in London Jointly by the Jewish Historical Society of England and the American Jewish Historical Society, July 1970* (London, 1971), 87, 94.

18. Rubin, *Third to None*, 16–21, 25.

19. Barnett A. Elzas, *The Jews of South Carolina from the Earliest Times to the Present Day* (Philadelphia, 1905), 19–20, 23–30, 32–35, 120–21. In 1790 Charleston had 200 Jewish inhabitants, New York 242; in 1820 Charleston had around 700, New York 550. See Ira Rosenswaike, "An Estimate and Analysis of the Jewish Population of the United States in 1790," in Abraham J. Karp, ed., *The Jewish Experience in America: Selected Studies from the Publications of the American Jewish Historical Society*, 5 vols. (Waltham, MA, 1969), 1:395, 400; and Ira Rosenswaike, "The Jewish Population of the United States as Estimated from the Census of 1820," *American Jewish Historical Quarterly* 53 (1963–64): 152.

20. Edwin Wolf II and Maxwell Whiteman, *The History of the Jews of Philadelphia from Colonial Times to the Age of Jackson* (Philadelphia, 1965), 23, 26, 30–32, 41–42, 53, 58–59, 114–21.

21. The evolution of Newport's Jewish community as well as Lopez's history can be followed in Chyet, *Lopez of Newport*, but the date of 1746 is derived from the documents in the Court of Chancery of Jamaica, located at the Jamaica Archives in Spanish Town; see 1A/3/17, 30–31, for a case that involved Naphtali Hart, who resided in Newport but was involved in a privateering matter that came before chancery in Jamaica. The population figure on the eve of the revolution has been derived from the colony's 1774 census: *Census of the Inhabitants of the Colony of Rhode Island and Providence Plantations, Taken by Order of the General Assembly in the Year 1774* (Providence, 1858).

22. See Ira Rosenswaike, "The Jews of Baltimore to 1810," *American Jewish Historical Quarterly* 64 (1974–1975): 291–320; and Ira Rosenswaike, "The Jews of Baltimore: 1810 to 1820," *American Jewish Historical Quarterly* 67 (1977–1978): 101–24. For Richmond, consult Herbert T. Ezekiel and Gaston Lichtenstein, *The History of the Jews of Richmond from 1769 to 1917* (Richmond, 1917); and Myron Berman, *Richmond's Jewry, 1769–1976* (Charlottesville, 1979).

23. For these localities, see Marcus, *The Colonial American Jew*, vol. 1, passim.

24. Rosenswaike, "Jewish Population of the United States in 1790," and Rosenswaike, "Jewish Population from the Census of 1820."

25. Jacob Rader Marcus, the premiere historian of the Jews of early America, determined that Ashkenazim were in the majority by 1720; see Jacob R. Marcus, *Studies in American Jewish History: Studies and Addresses* (Cincinnati, 1969), 52.

26. Items Relating to Congregation Shearith Israel, New York," *Publications of the American Jewish Historical Society* 27 (1920): 15–16.

27. Todd Endelman, *The Jews of Georgian England, 1714–1830: Tradition and Change in a Liberal Society* (Philadelphia, 1979), 266; Jonathan I. Israel, *European Jewry in the Age of Mercantilism* (Oxford, 1985), 246–47.

28. During the 1990s, allegations that Jews financed, dominated, and controlled the slave trade captured wide attention and were widely accepted in the African American community (on the latter point, see Henry Louis Gates Jr., "Black Demagogues and Pseudo-Scholars," *New York Times*, July 20, 1992, A15). Subsequent extensive research demonstrated that this was not the case, for which see, for example, David Brion Davis, "Jews in the Slave Trade," *Culturefront* (Fall 1992): 42–45; Seymour Drescher, "The Role of Jews in the Transatlantic Slave Trade," *Immigrants and Minorities* 12 (1993): 113–25; Eli Faber, *Jews, Slaves, and the Slave Trade: Setting the Record Straight* (New York, 1998); and Saul S. Friedman, *Jews and the American Slave Trade* (New Brunswick, NJ, 1998). For numerical data demonstrating the minute role played by mainland colonial Jews in the importation of slaves from Africa and the Caribbean and their marginal role as slave sellers, see Faber, *Jews, Slaves, and the Slave Trade*, 131–42.

29. Leo Hershkowitz, ed., *Wills of Early New York Jews (1704–1799)* (New York, 1967), passim; Jerome H. Wood Jr., *Conestoga Crossroads: Lancaster, Pennsylvania, 1730–1790* (Harrisburg, 1979), 97; Thomas J. Tobias, "Joseph Tobias of Charles Town: Linguister," *Publications of the American Jewish Historical Society* 49 (1959–1960): 36; and Charles Reznikoff and Uriah Z. Engelman, *The Jews of Charleston: A History of an American Jewish Community* (Philadelphia, 1950), 15.

30. For examples, see Eli Faber, *A Time for Planting: The First Migration, 1654–1820* (Baltimore, 1992), 154*n*39.

31. Hershkowitz, *Wills of Early New York Jews*, 33, 44, 65.

32. For examples of such long-distance marriages, see Faber, *A Time for Planting*, 42, 47–48.

33. Leo Hershkowitz and Isidore S. Meyer, eds., *The Lee Max Friedman Collection of American Jewish Colonial Correspondence: Letters of the Franks Family (1733–1748)* (Waltham, MA, 1968); for the lives of members of the Franks family, see the introduction, for Abigail Franks's pained reflection, see p. 93.

34. "The Earliest Extant Minute Books," 19, 20, 22, 23, 24, 81; Gutstein, *The Story of the Jews of Newport*, 88, 94, 105–6.

35. "The Earliest Extant Minute Books," 73, 84–85, 92, 100–1; Gutstein, *The Story of the Jews of Newport*, 72–73, 82, 116.

36. Jamaica's first rabbi came from Curaçao as early as 1683; M. Kayserling, "The Jews in Jamaica and Daniel Israel Lopez Laguna," *Jewish Quarterly Review* 12 (1900): 711.

37. In 1779, when Solomon Myers-Cohen and Belle Simon married, the bride's father served as a witness when he signed their otherwise traditional marriage contract. Jewish religious law, however, does not permit a relative to serve as a witness. The *ketubah* (contract) was written in an elegant hand, suggesting that, while knowledge of the law suffered in early America, Hebrew calligraphy was alive and well. The contract is in the Gratz Family papers, American Jewish Historical Society (New York).

38. For a general discussion of the consultations between the English congregations in the Americas and London, see R. D. Barnett, "The Correspondence of the Mahamad of the Spanish and Portuguese Congregation of London during the Seventeenth and Eighteenth Centuries," in *Transactions of the Jewish Historical Society of England* 20 (1959–61): 1–50. For a case in 1785 in which a faction within the Philadelphia community turned to a major rabbinic authority in Amsterdam for a ruling, see Jacob Rader Marcus, ed., *American Jewry—Documents—Eighteenth Century* (Cincinnati, 1959), 139–41.

39. For examples of these techniques in New York, see "The Earliest Extant Minute Books," 71, 74–75, 81. For withholding religious honors in Philadelphia in 1770 for violations of the Sabbath: Marcus, *American Jewry*, 96. For efforts to maintain communal discipline between 1790 and 1820 in New York, Charleston, and Savannah: ibid., 166, 179–81; and Joseph L. Blau and Salo W. Baron, eds., *The Jews of the United States, 1790–1840: A Documentary History*, 3 vols. (New York, 1963), 2:552.

40. In addition to the article by R. D. Barnett cited in note 17 above, see Cecil Roth, *The Great Synagogue, London, 1690–1940* (London, 1950), 2–3, 7–8, 12–13, 16–17, 59–60, 73; H. J. Zimmels, *Ashkenazim and Sephardim: Their Relations, Differences, and Problems as Reflected in Their Rabbinical Responsa* (London, 1958), 85–87, 99–102, 108, 110, 113–14, 165–66, 182, 188, 194, 241, 279–83; Albert M. Hyamson, *The Sephardim of England: A History of the Spanish and Portuguese Community, 1492–1951* (London, 1952), 170–71; and Lee M. Friedman, *Rabbi Haim Issac Carigal: His Newport Sermon and His Yale Portrait* (Boston, 1940), 18.

41. Jewish law requires interment in a Jewish cemetery surrounded by a wall, while worship can take place anywhere. Accordingly, cemeteries came first, synagogues later. In New York the earliest settlers acquired cemetery property in 1656, while the first permanent settlers did so in 1682; the first synagogue did not rise until 1728. The dates for the first cemeteries and synagogues in the remaining colonial-era communities are, respectively, 1677 and 1759 in Newport; 1738 and 1782 in Philadelphia; by 1773 and 1820 in Savannah; and by 1764 and 1794 in Charleston.

42. Data for the New York community, the only one whose records have survived, indicate that, of the forty-six persons who served as president or assistant between 1728 and 1760, 35 percent were definitely Ashkenazic and another 19 percent probably were. Those who were definitely Sephardic comprised only 33 percent of the total. These computations are based upon a close reading of the annual elections for officers in "The Earliest Extant Minute Books." For the haham's advice: David de Sola Pool, *The Mill Street Synagogue (1730–1817) of the Congregation Shearith Israel* (New York, 1930), 49. The building committee in New York was comprised of Sephardics Luis Moses Gomez, Mordecai Gomez, and Benjamin Mendes Pacheco, and Ashkenazic Jacob Franks, as recorded in "The Earliest Extant Minute Books," 43. According to Malcolm Stern's findings of 942 American Jewish marriages between 1686 and 1840, 16.4 percent involved Ashkenazim and Sephardim, exceeding the 10.7 percent of Sephardim who wed Sephardim. In the Caribbean, on the other hand, the number of marriages that united representatives of the two groups was lower. Malcolm H. Stern, "The Function of Genealogy in American Jewish History," *Essays in American Jewish History to Commemorate the Tenth Anniversary of the Founding of the American Jewish Archives Under the Direction of Jacob Rader Marcus* (Cincinnati, 1958), 74–81. In 1740, in New York, the Sephardic Isaac Mendes Seixas wed Ashkenazic Rachel Levy. His fellow Sephardim vociferously disapproved, but Seixas, persisting, married Levy and retaliated by not inviting any of the Sephardim to the wedding. The incident was recounted by Abigail Franks in letters to her son in London; Hershkowitz and Meyer, *Letters of the Franks Family*, 66–67, 76.

44. Hershkowitz and Meyer, *Letters of the Franks Family*, 7–8, 69; "The Earliest Extant Minute Books," 74–75.

45. Gutstein, *The Story of the Jews of Newport*, 132; Abram Vossen Goodman, "A German Mercenary Observes American Jews During the Revolution," *American Jewish Historical Quarterly* 59 (1969–70): 227; and the many contemporary portraits in Richard Brilliant, *Facing the New World: Jewish Portraits in Colonial and Federal America* (Munich, 1997), in which early American Jews had themselves depicted without beards or head covering.

46. Marcus, *American Jewry*, 134–36, 141.

47. Stern, "The Function of Genealogy," passim, for the numbers involved. For references in the constitutions and regulations of New York in 1790, Savannah in 1791, Philadelphia in 1798, and Charleston in 1820 as to how members who married non-Jews were to be dealt with, see Marcus, *American Jewry*, 129, 150, 160–61, 179–80, and Blau and Baron, *The Jews of the United States*, 2:551.

48. See Schappes, *A Documentary History*, 171–77, for the petition of the first group to suggest a course of reform for American Judaism.

49. For a catalogue of antisemitic incidents and remarks during the colonial era, see Marcus, *The Colonial American Jew*, 3:1117–34. For incidents between 1780 and 1820, see Rubin, *Third to None*, 96–97; Nathan M. Kaganoff, "An Early American Synagogue Desecration," *American Jewish Historical Quarterly* 58 (1968–1969): 136; Wolf and Whiteman, *The History of the Jews of Philadelphia*, 110–13; Isaac Kramnick, "The 'Great National Discussion': The Discourse of Politics in 1787," *William and Mary Quarterly* 45 (1988; 3d ser.): 10–11; Jacob Rader Marcus, *Memoirs of American Jews, 1775–1865*, 3 vols. (Philadelphia, 1955–1956), 1:85–86; and Schappes, *A Documentary History*, 92–96.

50. Abram Vossen Goodman, *American Overture: Jewish Rights in Colonial Times* (Philadelphia, 1947), 51; and Reznikoff and Engelman, *The Jews of Charleston*, 23–33.

51. Stiles's comment is cited in Chyet, *Lopez of Newport*, 37–38.

52. Leo Hershkowitz, "Some Aspects of the New York Jewish Merchant and Community, 1654–1820," *American Jewish Historical Quarterly* 66 (1976–1977): 13, 16–18; Beverly McAnear, "The Place of the Freeman in Old New York," *New York History* 21 (1940): 419, 425; Goodman, *American Overture*, 111–12, 114. For Jews who served as constables, or who declined to do so even when elected, see Hershkowitz, *Wills of Early New York Jews*, 36, 56, 65, 75, 99, 118, 140.

53. Assembly of Jamaica, *Journals of the Assembly of Jamaica*, 14 vols. (Jamaica, 1811–1829), 4:238, 246–47, 249.

54. Goodman, *American Overture*, 165–66, 199; Jacob R. Marcus, "Jews and the American Revolution: A Bicentennial Documentary," *American Jewish Archives* 27 (1975): 116–19, 124–25, 128–29; Samuel Rezneck, *Unrecognized Patriots: The Jews in the American Revolution* (Westport, CT, 1975), 23–24; Miriam K. Freund, *Jewish Merchants in Colonial America* (New York, 1939), 40; and William V. Byars, *B. and M. Gratz, Merchants in Philadelphia, 1754–1798* (Jefferson City, MO, 1916), 14.

55. Rezneck, *Unrecognized Patriots*, 21–66; Chyet, *Lopez of Newport*, 156–62; Byars, *B. and M. Gratz*, 20, 158; Wolf and Whiteman, *The Jews of Philadelphia*, 84; de Sola Pool, *The Mill Street Synagogue*, 56; Gutstein, *The Story of the Jews of Newport*, 182; and Reznikoff and Engleman, *The Jews of Charleston*, 50.

56. Stanley F. Chyet, "The Political Rights of Jews in the United States: 1776–1840," in Jacob R. Marcus, ed., *Critical Studies in American Jewish History: Selected Articles from American Jewish Archives*, 3 vols. (Cincinnati, 1971), 2:35–62.

57. Schappes, *A Documentary History*, 65.

58. Ibid., 68–69.

59. The exchange of letters can be followed in ibid., 79–81.

60. Chyet, "The Political Rights," 53–62. On the struggle in Maryland, see Edward Eitches, "Maryland's 'Jew Bill,'" *American Jewish Historical Quarterly* 60 (1970–1971): 258–79. Documents in the Maryland controversy are in Blau and Baron, *The Jews of the United States*, 1:33–55.

61. Schappes, *A Documentary History*, 122–25.

62. Blau and Baron, *The Jews of the United States*, 2:318–23; and Jonathan Sarna, *Jacksonian Jew: The Two Worlds of Modecai Noah* (New York, 1981), 27–28.

2

EXPANDING JEWISH LIFE IN AMERICA, 1826–1901

DIANNE ASHTON

"If thou art one . . . whose pilgrimage from Palestine we trace, Brave the Atlantic . . . a Western Sun will gild thy future day," wrote Charleston, South Carolina's Penina Moise in 1826.[1] Her poem expressed the promise of freedom and good fortune in America that convinced over 250,000 European Jews to leave their towns and villages for the United States between 1820 and 1880.[2] Few of those who left could have read her work, written in English and published in a periodical in South Carolina, but many of Europe's Jews had already heard promises of a better life in the United States. They read similar thoughts expressed in Yiddish, the language most commonly used by Jews in central and eastern Europe, as well as in German. In newspapers, magazines, and, most convincingly, in letters sent by relations and friends who had already made the trek to America, opportunity and freedom beckoned.[3] Yet, for Jews who cared deeply that their religious lives continue to be shaped by trusted religious leaders and reliable religious resources, America, where in 1820 no properly ordained rabbi could be found, appeared a wild place, unfit for them. Only the combined force of worsening economic dislocation and political and legal oppression pushed Jews to leave central and eastern Europe. The Napoleonic wars of the early nineteenth century effectively blocked emigration, but by 1820 that barrier had dropped. They were attracted to America with promises of a better life, undertaking an ocean voyage of over two months by sailboat in the early days of the migration, less than two weeks by steamboat toward its close.

Their immigration transformed the American Jewish population from the approximately twenty-five hundred individuals mostly clustered along the Atlantic
seaboard at the start of the century. They continued to come during the much
larger migration of Jews from further east in Europe who lifted the American Jewish population to almost one million by 1900.[4] Most arrived as young adults, and
their ideas and energy gave new vibrancy to American Jewish life. They supported
new congregations, charitable organizations, schools, fraternities, women's clubs,
and literary associations. At the century's end American Jews provided the intellectual and financial support for a Jewish encyclopedia that marked the emergence of Jewish scholarship in America.[5] This essay will explore nineteenth-century
Jewish immigrants' integration into American life and the politics, charitable activities, religion, and associations they created. In order to explain those developments, we need first to understand their reasons for coming to America.

Julius Brooks's story is typical. An adventurous young man from a small village
near Breslau with few prospects as an apprentice weaver, Brooks changed careers
after meeting "a peddler who told him what fun it was to travel . . . the many beautiful places to be seen; . . . also what a lot of money he made." In 1847, when Brooks
was twenty-two, he came to America, but returned to Europe after five years to see
his family again and to marry. In 1853 he and his new wife, Fanny, traveled by ship
and wagon train to California and, after some years, settled in Salt Lake City.[6] Peddling provided Brooks and hundreds of Jewish immigrant young men with a way to
thrive in many regions of the United States, as Mark Bauman explains about the
South in his essay in this volume. A majority of newcomers like Brooks came from
small towns across Galicia and Posen, Lithuania and Bohemia, Alsace, Baden,
Bavaria, and Hesse, and other towns and villages of the Rhine Valley and eastward
in Poznan and Silesia.[7]

European Jews peddled because they rarely were permitted to own land and
usually were restricted from more remunerative crafts. In some areas of Europe
Jews were forbidden to trade with non-Jews, but Jewish traders most often provided the necessary links in a larger economy. From the late eighteenth through
the early twentieth centuries, when various areas of Europe shifted from subsis-
tence farming and small craft shops to commercial agriculture and industrial labor, traditional economies were transformed and more than five million uprooted
immigrants left their European homelands for the United States. When railroads
and other improvements in transportation made it possible to move goods to distant markets, Jews who had previously peddled the countryside to bring goods to
farmers lost their familiar place in Europe's economy.[8]

Many Jewish immigrants brought skills in weaving, shoemaking, tailoring,
baking, and butchering, but, as historian Hasia Diner has explained, in nineteenth-
century America most Jewish men began as peddlers, small shopkeepers, and
agents who mediated between farmers and the larger markets and manufacturers,
usually trading in dry goods as agents for more established Jewish businessmen in

urban centers.[9] Some Jewish women peddled in urban areas. Peddling brought many nineteenth-century Jewish immigrants to smaller towns and rural areas in the South, Midwest, and West.[10] As nineteenth-century America opened new land to farmers and developed its manufacturing base, Jews who had peddled the countryside in central Europe found that rural Americans also sought their services. Some peddlers developed new products to answer their customers' needs. After Baltimorean Rosanna Dyer married Joseph Osterman, the couple moved to Galveston, Texas, where they sold cornmeal biscuits that remained edible in a saddlebag for days, made according to Rosanna's own recipe.[11] In Sacramento, California, Bavarian-born Levi Strauss and his partner, Jacob Davis, patented denim pants with metal rivets to provide California's silver and gold miners with sturdier trousers, and denim jeans were born.[12]

Peddlers often began their labors tramping the countryside carrying a pack of fifty or more pounds filled with items to sell. They hoped to succeed to a wagon and ultimately to a small general store where a wife and other family members would share duties. Jewish communities grew in these small towns as peddlers returned each Sabbath to the local "hubs" of Jewish life. Through peddling, Jewish settlements sprang up in new small towns and then, as small shopkeepers found the means to relocate to larger "regional" centers like Cincinnati, Chicago, and San Francisco, peddling expanded Jewish populations in midsized cities. The Civil War's unprecedented economic demands spurred upward mobility in the North. By 1870 Jews owned 1,750 businesses in New York City, which had become a major Jewish population center and one of the country's largest mercantile centers. By the century's last decades, bankers Schiff, Seligman, Lehman, Kuhn, and Loeb and department store magnates Strauss, Bloomingdale, Gimbel, and Altman comprised a Jewish elite.[13]

These settlements transformed the American Jewish map. The century's opening years found the largest Jewish settlement gathered in Charleston, South Carolina, whose state constitution assured free exercise of religion and whose bustling trade with England offered economic opportunity that supported a lively cultural life.[14] Charleston was one of the five original port cities where colonial Jews gathered in sufficient numbers to support a synagogue. Jewish immigration from 1830 to 1870 caught the rush of western migration in the United States, and by 1877 Jews comprised nearly 8 percent of California's population.[15] By century's close, synagogues thrived across the continent, in larger centers like San Francisco, Cincinnati, St. Louis, Chicago, New Orleans, Philadelphia, and Boston and in smaller towns like Albany, Oregon, Trinidad, Colorado, and Tucson, Arizona.[16] Most individuals in those communities were immigrants who arrived first in eastern ports in New York, Boston, Philadelphia, and Baltimore. New York City, with the largest immigration center and a booming economy, far outdistanced all other Jewish communities in America in its size and its array of Jewish resources. By 1887 New York City was home to the largest Jewish community in the world.

Jews in nineteenth-century America, whether native or foreign born, fully participated in American society yet experienced the trials of minority existence. Numbering less than 1 percent of the American population, they enjoyed far greater freedom and acceptance in America than they had experienced in Europe, but antisemitism lived here too. Historian John Higham remarked that "alone among European immigrant groups . . . Jews . . . lost in reputation as they gained in social and economic status."[17] Stereotypes of Jews gaining enormous wealth by illegal means had long been part of European folklore and non-Jewish settlers from Europe brought that folklore with them to America. Newspaper editors occasionally published anti-Jewish diatribes when a local economy faltered. Forty years before Penina Moise encouraged Europe's Jews to relocate, a Charleston newspaper accused Jews arriving there from Savannah of bringing "ill-got wealth."[18] During the Civil War's economic upheavals those accusations became common. When the South's economy weakened because of manpower losses, Union blockades, and scorched earth military practices, Southerners responded with anger and fear. Some accused Jewish shopkeepers of hoarding goods to drive up prices when most items were simply no longer available at prewar prices, if at all. Northerners reacted similarly to the war's upheavals. In 1862 Union general Ulysses S. Grant evicted all Jews from a territory under his command that included Tennessee, Kentucky, and Mississippi for presumed violations of wartime trade regulations, an order soon rescinded by President Lincoln after Jewish protest. Later in the century, as Reconstruction—the country's first attempt at racial integration—ended with laws establishing racial segregation, other outsiders also felt the sting of prejudice. Increasing numbers of hotels, schools, and resorts banned Jews along with African Americans and Asians. By the century's close a self-defined "white" Anglo-Saxon Protestant social elite had placed its schools, businesses, and clubs beyond the reach of Jews and others it deemed outsiders. Despite those difficulties, Jews felt themselves to be part of America. Historian Jonathan Sarna noted that in the first six decades after the revolution "some 28.7 percent of all marriages involving Jews . . . were intermarriages."[19] Since colonial days Jews had served in America's civic associations, militias, and armed services. Nineteenth-century Jewish men voted in elections and contributed to political parties. Jews joined local Masonic lodges, fire companies, militias, athletic clubs, relief associations, and helped to establish libraries, schools, and orphanages.[20] One Jewish Freemason explained that, like Judaism, Masonry taught of "One Supreme Architect . . . of the Universe" and that it "teaches us to live together in peace and . . . brotherly love."[21] Some Jews were elected to political office. In 1841 Florida's David Levy Yulee became the first Jew to serve in the United States Congress; he later served as senator. At mid-century between eight and ten thousand Jews fought in the Civil War, most for the North where the majority lived; only about twenty thousand Jews resided in the South.[22] Many Jewish soldiers were recent immigrants, like Marcus Spiegel who enlisted in the Ohio Volunteers.

After arriving in America in 1849, Spiegel married Quaker Caroline Hamlin, who converted to Judaism, and fathered three children before joining the armed services in 1861. By the time he died from battle wounds three years later he had attained the rank of colonel.[23] Other young men fought for the Union near their birthplaces, like Kentuckian Cary Gist Gratz, killed at the Battle of Wilson's Creek.[24] During the war at least three Union officers of Jewish origin were breveted generals. Northern Jewish women often worked with local groups to provide bandages and clothing for soldiers. Louisiana senator Judah Benjamin later served the Confederacy as attorney general, secretary of state, and secretary of war. Phoebe Yates Levy Pember, a widow from Marietta, Georgia, became the first woman to oversee a branch of the Confederacy's Chimborazo Hospital, which became the largest hospital in the Western world by war's end. Some Jewish Southerners refused to fight for either side. Major Alfred Mordecai, a Virginian who had received his military training at West Point, spent the war years among his wife's family in Philadelphia. South Carolina judge Solomon Heydenfeldt relocated to California after publishing his condemnations of slavery in the 1840s.[25]

In the American far West, Jewish immigrants lived more easily amid diverse local populations made up of migrants from around the country, immigrants from Europe and Asia, and indigenous Mexicans. Marc Lee Raphael has suggested that by the time Jewish immigrants reached the West they had learned American language and customs.[26] By the century's close, citizens in Los Angeles, San Francisco, Portland, and Tucson had elected Jewish mayors.[27] Across the country nineteenth-century Jewish immigrants embraced integration into the gentile world.

DEFENDING THEIR RIGHTS

The United States Constitution made it possible for Jews to defend their rights in American law courts, and many Jews believed that American principles echoed Judaism's values.[28] The Bill of Rights, ratified with the Constitution in 1789, prohibited the United States government from both establishing a national religion or inhibiting religion's free exercise, but individual states worked out their own versions of religious rights at a slower pace. In Maryland nearly thirty years of struggle to allow non-Christians to serve in public office culminated in an 1825 ruling that Jews could take the oath of office on their Bible only if they also signed a document "declaring their belief in an afterlife of rewards and punishment."[29] New Hampshire finally granted its Jews full equal rights in 1877, the last state to do so.

Jews also joined other American religious minorities to defeat measures that restricted their rights as citizens. Throughout the century Sabbatarian Christian groups and politicians took measures to ban labor on Sunday. Such laws were first upheld most strictly in New England and in some southern towns, but soon also were implemented in the West. These laws pressured Jews to labor on their own Saturday Sabbath in order to be employed by gentiles or to keep the patronage of their Christian customers. Economic need forced Jews who did not work on their Saturday Sabbath to labor on Sunday. In 1833 Alexander Marks was prosecuted by the town council of Columbia, South Carolina for keeping his store open on Sunday. The court rejected his argument that he observed a Saturday Sabbath by closing his store on that day and ruled that the Sunday Sabbath was to be enforced universally.[30] As these cases arose in various states, Jews, along with Seventh Day Adventists, Unitarians, and others, fought for their rights to observe their own—or no—Sabbath.

Jews also prevailed upon American legislative bodies to assist their coreligionists facing crises abroad. Like Penina Moise, Jews in the United States often viewed America as the solution to the oppression Jews faced elsewhere. But while Moise imagined Jews integrating into American society, statesman, journalist, and playwright Mordecai Manuel Noah imagined a colony for Jews situated on Grand Island in the Niagara River near Buffalo, New York. In 1825, after purchasing the land and gaining the support of members of the New York state legislature, Noah announced the opening of this colony, named Ararat after the site where Noah's ark was said to have landed, and placed a marker on the island in the course of an elaborate dedication ceremony. Yet no Jews came. Russian and Austro-Hungarian political leaders may have suppressed news of Ararat, and many European religious leaders distanced themselves from it.[31] American Jews preferred to live among other Americans in towns and cities rather than in a Jewish agricultural colony. Yet, Noah's Ararat indicates early America's readiness to accept Jews as well as American Jews' dawning awareness that Jewish life in Europe was growing untenable.

At mid-century American Jews tried to engage the United States government in assisting coreligionists overseas. When a Capuchin monk and his servant disappeared from Damascus, Syria in 1840, that city's Jews were accused of killing them in order to use their blood in making Passover matzo—a falsehood called the blood libel. The incident culminated in the torture and sentencing to death of seventy-two Jews; thirty-two thousand more Jews were suspected of complicity. The United States government registered its outrage even before American Jews spoke out, but Jews in many American cities soon organized protest meetings where non-Jewish politicians and clergymen urged the United States government to try to secure a fair trial for those arrested. Yet international outcry from United States and European political and Protestant religious leaders had little effect.

American Jews in 1858 again tried to intervene on behalf of coreligionists abroad. In Bologna an eight-year-old Jewish boy, Edgardo Mortara, fell ill and was secretly baptized by a servant in his household. Catholic authorities deemed the boy a Christian and took him from his home to be raised by the Roman Catholic Church. American Jews and Protestants joined in organizing protests, which, like those fifteen years earlier, failed to achieve their goal.[32]

Those failures motivated American Jews to organize the Board of Delegates of American Israelites in 1859, their first attempt to create a national Jewish organization. Officers of the BDAI were lay leaders, not clergy, and, although the organization originally hoped to focus on both religious education and charitable efforts, it proved able to mobilize widespread support only when working to assist coreligionists abroad and when fighting for equal rights. When the United States government established a Christian chaplaincy to serve Union soldiers during the Civil War, the BDAI helped to obtain approval for Jewish chaplains two years later. Yet, representing less than 1 percent of the American population and with only half of America's Jewish congregations choosing to participate in its projects, the BDAI never became a powerful organization. Its efforts to convince the United States government to secure for its Jewish citizens treatment equal to that of United States Christian citizens when traveling in Switzerland achieved some success in 1866, but the same effort in Russia came to naught.[33] Success there was not achieved until 1911. Ultimately, by century's close, another organization, the Union of American Hebrew Congregations, absorbed the BDAI's goals and responsibilities.[34]

DIVERSIFYING AND DESIGNING
NEW CHARITABLE VENTURES

In the colonial era Jews provided charity as individuals or through their congregations. But three factors motivated Jews to find new ways to care for poor men and women. Repeated economic downturns impoverished many Americans, and as the number of immigrants outnumbered native-born Jews, congregations often found themselves unable to care for the increasing number of indigents. By 1801 Charleston's Jews had organized a society to arrange foster care for orphans. Second, few states granted married women property rights, and many charitable societies hesitated to assist a married woman who might be subject to an irresponsible husband. Most important, Christian charitable societies usually required their petitioners to hear evangelical instruction. More prosperous Jews often shouldered exceptional duties in solving those problems. In 1819 Philadelphia's wealthy Rebecca Gratz (1781–1869) organized women from her congregation to form the Female Hebrew Benevolent Society, the first nonsynagogal Jewish agency in America. Because the FHBS offered charity only to Jewish women, who were not counted as members of any congregation, it created bonds that bridged congregational and ethnic differences among Jewish families. Thus needy Jewish women around the country as far as Mobile, Alabama appealed to the FHBS. Only one

year after the FHBS formed, New York's oldest congregation, Shearith Israel, organized its own FHBS.[35] The FHBS remained an independent women's organization and provided a base for new Jewish women's agencies in Philadelphia.
Expecting that Jewish women would be "foremost in the work of charity," Gratz
rallied them to provide charity, religious education, and foster care.[36] By the end
of her life Gratz had organized the FHBS (1819), the first Sunday school for
Jewish children (1838), and one of the earliest foster homes for Jewish orphans
(1855) in America. Soon women's benevolent societies were among the first
organizations created in new American Jewish communities. In 1883, one year
after the Tucson *Citizen* noted the presence of Jews in that city, its Hebrew Ladies
Benevolent Society and a men's fraternity, B'nai B'rith (Sons of the Covenant)
had formed.[37]

By the 1820s Jewish men also organized local mutual aid and charitable associations like Philadelphia's United Hebrew Benevolent Society, in which both
immigrant and native-born Jewish men took active roles. These organizations
also spanned congregational loyalties and often required their members to fulfill
certain Jewish laws they deemed fundamental, such as circumcising their male
children and marrying according to Jewish law. Because needy Jews might not
join congregations, these charitable societies strived to maintain what they
deemed minimal Jewish obligations. Like the women's charitable societies, these
small men's charities also proliferated. By 1860 twenty-three different charitable
societies served Jews in Philadelphia, and thirty-five assisted Jews in New York
City.[38]

The needs of injured Civil War soldiers exacerbated the problems Jews faced
in hospitals where they were subject to evangelical efforts, where they could not
obtain kosher food, and where Jewish doctors could not find employment. In New
York, where a hospital for Jews existed since 1852, an entire ward was given over to
military needs.[39] Elsewhere, however, hospitals required a far greater financial
commitment than many smaller communities could muster. Ultimately, Jewish
hospitals emerged in very different ways, as the case of Pennsylvania can illustrate. Jewish soldiers received medical aid at any one of Philadelphia's several
military hospitals. When local Jews learned that a number of their coreligionists
had died without any attention by Jewish clergymen, they opened a Jews' hospital
in 1866 largely because of the energy of local B'nai B'rith lodges. But in Pittsburgh, a smaller community in the western part of the state, the scene was very
different. There Jews took the first steps toward a Jewish hospital in 1898, when
the Hebrew Ladies Hospital Aid, religious female immigrants from Lithuania
who provided kosher meals for Jewish patients, petitioned the Pennsylvania state
legislature for permission to establish a hospital for Jews.[40]

Civil War and immigration needs moved larger Jewish communities to bring
their diverse charitable societies under a more efficient umbrella, like St. Louis's
United Hebrew Relief Association. Yet all the charitable efforts made in mid-century

were dwarfed by the needs of more than seven hundred thousand Jews who arrived in the United States between 1881 and 1900. Most of these newcomers were impoverished Jews from eastern Europe, escaping severe economic and legal disabilities as well as violence organized against the myriad small Jewish towns clustered in the western area of Russia, Poland, and Ukraine. Most new immigrants settled in the industrial centers of America's cities, especially the garment industry near New York's port of entry and the cigar-making factories in Philadelphia and Boston. These factories demanded both skilled and unskilled labor but required little knowledge of the English language. Many of the immigrants spoke Yiddish, a language rooted in Hebrew, German, and Polish that had become the lingua franca of European Jews. American-born Jews and mid-century immigrants alike believed that these newcomers needed guidance in American ways as well as charitable assistance and set out to meet those goals.

New organizations, small and large, soon took shape. Sisterhoods of Personal Service, organized by New York's Reform Temple Emanu-El, became popular among Reform women in cities like New York and Chicago where many impoverished Jewish immigrants from eastern Europe lived. Such sisterhoods promised both sensitive care and discipline in apportioning their largesse.[41] Yet the newcomers soon overwhelmed local resources such as these, and in 1899 American Jews established the National Conference of Jewish Charities to efficiently marshal charitable resources nationwide.

DIVERSIFYING RELIGIOUS LIFE

With mid-nineteenth-century immigrants from central Europe, a "diverse and pluralistic" Judaism developed in America.[42] The United States Constitution guaranteed unprecedented levels of religious freedom, and both Christians and Jews revived and reformed their religions, with many Americans changing religious affiliations.[43] Soon after the Constitution was ratified, in 1795, the first Ashkenazic (central and eastern European) congregation formed in Philadelphia, breaking away from Mikveh Israel. Like many new congregations, it began as a separate prayer group within the larger congregation, when individuals met to worship according to customs familiar to them from their European homeland. Calling itself Rodeph Shalom (Seekers of Peace) it was only the first of such ethnic congregations organized in many towns by new immigrants. By mid-century Philadelphia boasted five separate congregations, each with its own distinctive melodies, Hebrew dialects, and customs. In New York the first central European Ashkenazic congregation did not organize until 1825, but by 1860 that city's Jews supported twenty-seven different congregations.[44] By then "every major Jewish community had at least two synagogues."[45] Even within congregations, as Jonathan Sarna points out, disputes about what constituted appropriate religious behavior were common, made all the more difficult to solve by the fact that individuals disagreed about which religious authority ought to settle their arguments.[46] As Jewish population centers grew and the numbers of congregations multiplied, religious diversity expanded and religious authority lost its power.

While nineteenth-century Jews diversified Jewish practice, they also articulated a new religious philosophy. Those leading the push for change drew on Enlightenment ideals of reason and universalism, focusing on Jewish ethics and faith. New periodicals reached local, regional, and national readers, and each religious innovation sparked discussions, retorts, reactions, and evaluations that were published in these periodicals, defining Jewish life in new ways. These exchanges expressed Jews' varied understanding of both Judaism and America. Different factions in American Judaism came to champion liberalism, biblical authority, or the pull of tradition. Although Philadelphia's Rodeph Shalom emerged peacefully from Mikveh Israel, other congregations were marked by strife. In Charleston, South Carolina some Jews began to urge more revolutionary changes in religious practices. Many traditional Jewish practices, like obtaining kosher meat, were difficult to maintain. Frontier conditions sometimes made regular travel to public worship impossible. Feeling compelled to labor on Saturday, many Jewish men chose the workplace over worship. Synagogue worship itself came under scrutiny since an increasing number of congregants lacked mastery of the Hebrew prayers and sought to bring English into the historically Hebrew worship service. Isaac Harby, a leader among those in Charleston seeking changes, explained that for prayer to "proceed from the heart . . . it must proceed from understanding."[47] Organized Judaism became a collection of voluntary associations, and the rabbi's vocation, which historically consisted largely of teaching and adjudicating matters of Jewish law, became more like that of a Protestant minister, delivering sermons at worship, overseeing religious education, and performing pastoral duties to congregants in crisis. The changes Jews made to their religious and communal lives reflected their participation in their local American economies and regional cultures as much as it did their understandings of the meaning of Jewish life and faith. Embracing both American and Jewish ideals, they transformed their Judaism into something that looked very much like some varieties of Protestantism.

The first effort to reform an American Jewish congregation occurred in Charleston in 1824. Challenged by the religious ferment among their Christian neighbors, by the ideas of individualism and liberality that marked the postrevolutionary era, and by the growing religious apathy among Jews in their community, some of Charleston's Jews petitioned the synagogue board for changes. Historian Marc Lee Raphael explained that their petition's rhetoric suggests that they understood the similar transformations taking place among Jewish congregations in Amsterdam, Westphalia, Berlin, and Hamburg, all European cities where newly emancipated Jews were modifying Jewish worship in an effort to adapt Judaism to the demands of Christian society. Like those Europeans, Charleston's reformers requested a weekly sermon along with commentary on the Torah reading, some vernacular (in this case, English) prayers, and greater solemnity and dignity at services. Rebuffed by fellow congregants at Beth Elohim (House of God), reformers in Charleston formed the Reformed Society of Israelites, the first significantly reforming congregation in the country. Although the society disbanded within a decade, its members rejoined the synagogue, Beth Elohim, where their influence grew. After 1841, when Gustavus Poznanski became its minister, Beth Elohim implemented the changes the reformers had sought.[48]

Penina Moise wrote most of the 1842 English language hymnal compiled for Beth Elohim's new worship services, which included organ music. Instrumental music had been banned from Jewish worship for centuries as a sign of mourning for the ancient temple in Jerusalem. But English language hymns sung to organ music helped more American Jews to participate in worship, as many of them, especially women, had little understanding of Hebrew. English language hymns became a centerpiece in worship services conducted by other reforming congregations later in the century. Thirteen of Moise's hymns were so well received that they were included in the hymnal used by Reform Jews as late as 1932.[49] Yet, in 1824, Charleston stood alone among reforming synagogues, and a larger movement to reform Judaism waited two decades for its influence to spread.

From 1825 through 1868 Isaac Leeser (1806–1868), an immigrant from Wesphalia, led efforts to revive and reinvigorate traditional Judaism. Becoming religious leader of Philadelphia's Mikveh Israel in 1824, Leeser so shaped his era through his dedication and skill that historians have referred to it as the Age of Leeser. He came to the United States with a good Jewish religious education—far more than all but a handful of American Jewish men had obtained—although he was not trained for the rabbinate. Perhaps because he lacked mastery of rabbinic texts, historians have seen Leeser's theology as bibliocentric, focusing on the Hebrew Bible rather than later rabbinic work.[50] However, his biblical focus suited the American environment that was dominated by Protestant Christianity, itself bibliocentric. Although he was expected to do little more than to lead prayers at worship, prepare boys for their bar mitzvah, supervise a kosher butcher, and represent Mikveh Israel in civic parades and on school boards, he moved well beyond those routine duties. Soon after he began his tenure at Mikveh Israel, women of the congregation requested that he deliver sermons in English, which he offered at the close of the standard worship service. Leeser collected and published those sermons in ten volumes, making them available to a wide reading circle. Many American rabbis followed this example. Because most American Jews had little grasp of Hebrew, Leeser translated the Hebrew Bible into English, compiled a new prayer book with updated translations for his congregants at Mikveh Israel, and translated Jewish textbooks used in Germany for American children. He established the first school of higher Jewish education in America, Maimonides

College, in 1867, which graduated only three students before it was forced to close its doors at his death.

Perhaps the most influential of Leeser's creations was the *Occident and American Jewish Advocate*, an English language periodical that he edited and published from 1843 to 1868. Circulated to Jews in the eastern and southern United States, the *Occident* carried Leeser's editorials on many issues of interest to Jews, such as reports on legal battles over Sunday Sabbath laws and instructions for celebrating upcoming holidays. It also featured articles by Leeser and other knowledgeable Jews on the meanings of weekly Torah readings. It conveyed news from European towns where many of the families of American Jews still resided and showcased original inspirational poems and short stories by Jewish women. Finally, the *Occident* published annual reports and news from Jewish congregations and charitable societies around the United States in order to encourage more American Jews to engage in similar activities. American Jewish congregations, like Protestant congregations, hired, supervised, and fired their clergy through a board of lay leaders, and men like Leeser turned to print media to expand their authority and provide national leadership.[51]

Women who contributed to the *Occident* provided readers with Jewish versions of the sort of women's religious literature that abounded in English language magazines and fictional volumes. Leeser had been raised by his grandmother, and he believed women's devotion to Judaism to be vital to a thriving Jewish life in America. Jewish women often were approached by female evangelists who urged them to convert, asserting that Christianity valued and respected women to a greater degree than did Judaism. To counter those assertions, Leeser felt that Jewish women needed to be inspired by Jewish heroines and instructed by knowledgeable Jewish women. To that end, Leeser edited Englishwoman Grace Aguilar's important theological volume, *The Spirit of Judaism*, first published in 1842, which was reprinted twenty times and continued to be sold in the United States into the twentieth century. Along with *Spirit*, Leeser saw to it that most of Aguilar's works, fiction as well as didactic literature, found an American audience. Her poetry, often based on biblical characters and themes, encouraged Pennsylvanian Rebekah Hyneman to compose poems also featured in the *Occident*. British sisters Marian Moss Hartog and Celia Moss Levetus contributed short stories depicting women in scenes from ancient Jewish history as well as contemporary life.[52] Those British writers found a ready audience among American Jewish women.

American Jewish women attended worship in larger numbers and on a more regular basis than was common in the congregations of Europe, where synagogues were nearly entirely a male arena. American women's galleries featured lower balustrades with more openwork in their design so that women could more easily view and participate in the service led from below. New synagogues in New York and Philadelphia enlarged the seating space allotted to women who joined in synagogue worship on a regular basis.[53] Jewish women may have been influenced by the values of the larger American society whose values, drawn from Christianity, linked religiosity with attendance at a house of worship.

Both American and Jewish values strongly encouraged women to participate in charitable activities and religious education and the relationships formed in women's galleries proved a foundation for early charitable and educational endeavors. Deeply felt religious faith motivated many Jewish women to take on the duties of religious educators. Assuring her sister charitable society coworkers that "our labor will not be lost to that Allseeing Eye that searches out the smallest . . . good and (helps it grow)"[54] in 1838, Rebecca Gratz and other Mikveh Israel women organized a Sunday school for Jewish youth, called the Hebrew Sunday School. American Jews developed Sunday schools because they suited the American parameters of Jewish life. In most states laws prohibiting Sunday labor made Sunday available for religious instruction. Often Protestant schools conducted "sweeps" that ushered nearby children into their classrooms, and the HSS women sought to keep Jewish children from such entrapments. Working without pay, Gratz joined Simha Peixotto and Rachel Peixotto Pyke, two sisters who conducted a secular school in their home, to open the Hebrew Sunday School. Initially, they adapted Protestant textbooks, but, with Leeser's assistance, the women soon wrote their own catechisms and graded primers and studied Judaism in order to instruct their pupils. Many other women volunteers gave their time to both teaching on Sunday mornings and to their own education in Judaism.

The HSS provided the only formal Jewish education available to Jewish girls, and, as educators, to American Jewish women. It offered coeducational classes where Jewish boys and girls from all parts of the city could meet, a benefit of the school the founders hoped would contribute to the formation of Jewish marriages. Its small classes encouraged emotional bonds between student and instructor and among classmates. Seeking to further religious practice, curriculum concentrated on the basic principles of Jewish belief and explanations of Jewish holidays. Students earned rewards for attending any of they city's synagogues. Informally, HSS instructors would alert FHBS members to needy children they met in Sunday school and arrange for older children to find positions with Jewish employers who would allow them to attend synagogue on Saturdays. By 1900 Philadelphia's HSS served over 4,000 students in several branches. It continued to serve Philadelphia's children over 150 years after its founding.

Limited to two hours of instruction each week, Sunday schools attained limited academic results. Yet the HSS women dramatically advanced American Jewish education. Outside of New York City resources for Jewish education were severely limited. In most towns Jewish boys received training for bar mitzvah and little else. So successful was the HSS that within two years similar schools were organized by women in Baltimore and Charleston. Women of Shearth Israel in New York organized a similar short-lived school.[55] By the late nineteenth century

Jewish Sunday schools became standard for small communities with limited resources as well as for most Reform Jewish congregations. Jewish Sunday schools in West Coast towns focused on Bible stories and holidays.[56] Through these schools the image of the Sunday school teacher became one of female intelligence, respectability, and leadership among both Christians and Jews.

In 1854 a new periodical advocated a new vision of what Jewish life could be. The *Israelite*, later renamed the *American Israelite*, was edited by Isaac Mayer Wise (1819–1900), who, over the next few decades, shaped the nascent efforts in reforming Judaism into a full-fledged Reform movement, complete with its own union of affiliated congregations (Union of American Hebrew Congregations, founded 1873), seminary (Hebrew Union College, founded 1875), and professional rabbinic association (Central Conference of American Rabbis, founded 1889). Based in Cincinnati, Wise had arrived in the United States from Bohemia in 1846 and first served as rabbi in a congregation in Albany, New York. His flamboyant personality brought him into conflict with his congregants, and he soon departed for an Ohio congregation, Bene Jeshurun, where he remained. His program for liberalizing Judaism sparked keen interest, especially among the Jewish immigrants struggling to make their way in a new country, among American-born Jews in towns with few Jewish resources, and among Jews who worried that their children might abandon Judaism entirely if not given an alternative to the traditions they found too restrictive. By 1860 the *Israelite* was the most popular Jewish magazine in the country, spreading Wise's influence far and wide.[57]

The Reform program Wise advocated urged simplifying Jewish practice, shortening worship services, and altering the traditional prayer book to emphasize ethics drawn from the Hebrew prophets and faith in God. It rejected dietary laws and some traditional customs—such as praying with heads covered. The worship service featured mixed male and female seating, choirs of men and women, a sermon in the vernacular delivered by the rabbi along with vernacular prayers. These changes were part of a larger movement begun in Germany in the early part of the nineteenth century. But in America Reform's popularity largely rested on its fit with American culture shaped by Protestantism's bibliocentric outlook and suspicion of ritual, the real lack of Jewish resources in many parts of the country, and the demanding pace of American life. Many Jews embraced Reform. Led by lay leaders like Moritz Loth, in 1876 the UAHC created Educational Aid Societies to raise funds for indigent rabbinical students at HUC and especially asked women to participate. By 1879 fifty-two societies, including those in Omaha, Galveston, Kalamazoo, Winona, Mississippi, and Wheeling, West Virginia raised $1,353. They continued to support HUC in this manner into the twentieth century.[58]

Wise urged UAHC congregations to greater equality for women and many Reform congregations replaced the women's gallery with mixed seating. Female readers of his *Die Deborah*, a German-language newspaper primarily for women readers, conveyed their perspectives. In 1857, two years after circulation began, one female Detroit reader argued that women ought to receive full emancipation in the synagogue and that the morning prayer said by men that thanks God for not creating them female ought to be stricken from "all prayer books." She explained that in her experience American Jewish communities began when Jewish women insisted that their husbands band together to hire a butcher who could assure their households kosher meat. "The glorious tree of Judaism . . . would have toppled . . . if its roots were not buried so deeply in the hearts of pious female Israelites," she explained.[59] Such letters alerted Wise to potential allies for change he would find among women.

By 1885 the UAHC stood as the sole organization of Jewish congregations. Yet less than half of American synagogues affiliated and congregational practices varied. Most UAHC congregations demanded the solemnity during religious services that their Protestant neighbors deemed appropriate for worship, despite the fact that such behavior ended the polyphonic chant, individualized pacing, and informal chatting familiar to traditional synagogues.[60] But different UAHC congregations prayed in Hebrew, English, or German, conducted Sabbath worship on Saturday or Sunday, maintained some or none of Judaism's dietary laws, and read from an array of different prayer books. Many but not all Reform congregations eliminated the bar mitzvah ceremony for boys, providing their children instead with coeducational Sunday school instruction that culminated in a newly designed confirmation ceremony. By allowing local congregations autonomy, UAHC thrived and Reformers achieved some unity.

Unlike Wise, David Einhorn (1809–1879), a more intellectual and radical reformer based in Baltimore, insisted that Jewish Reform must be more fully grounded in philosophy and that the rabbi's primary role was to instruct his congregants in a sophisticated Jewish theology that blended Judaism with German idealism. For Einhorn, religious practices should proceed from philosophy. Einhorn's approach seemed destined to fail in America's pragmatic-culture, but when his brilliant and erudite son-in-law, Kauffmann Kohler (1843–1926), a graduate of Hebrew Union College, rose to lead Reform at the century's close, lengthy and sophisticated sermons delivered by rabbis became the centerpiece in many Reform religious services. In 1885 American Reform clergy attempted to bring order to their movement by outlining a set of principles they hoped would unite them. Yet leaders were unsure if that agreement, later referred to as the Pittsburgh Platform, would succeed in inspiring their laity. Kohler, who called for the meeting, admitted that the greater problem facing Reform was not disagreement among congregations but the "appalling indifference . . . among the masses."[61]

Some among the masses saw things differently. Galveston, Texas B'nai B'rith leader Leo Napoleon Levi (1856–1904) condemned reform rabbis for concerning themselves too much with oratory and too little with the practical guidance congregants needed to raise their children as Jews.[62] Benjamin Franklin Peixotto (1834–1890), editor of B'nai B'rith's journal, the *Menorah Monthly*, refuted Reform's claim that Judaism was only morality and argued that "ritual, too, was needed to express man's feelings and emotions."[63] More tradition-minded leaders like Leeser, his successor at Mikveh Israel, Sabato Morais (1823–1897), an ordained rabbi from Livorno, Italy, and Henry Pereira Mendes (1852–1937), rabbi at New York's Sheareth Israel, believed that Reform encouraged Jews to apathy by jettisoning facets of Jewish practice that would enrich their religious lives. In the 1880s Morais began organizing a rabbinic seminary to train American rabbis in traditional Judaism after attending the 1883 graduation at Hebrew Union College of the first rabbis trained in United States. Wise had invited all of the major Jewish religious leaders to celebrate the important event. Wise hoped ultimately to unite all American Jewish congregations, but the graduation banquet made that dream impossible. The menu included shellfish, a food forbidden to Jews by both rabbinic directives and biblical law. Ultimately, the dinner convinced some that Reform had gone too far and that traditional Judaism needed new advocates. Forever after referred to as "the *treyfe* (unkosher) banquet," it proved a pivotal moment. Ironically, the Reform movement that had jettisoned dietary laws was thwarted in its attempt to unite all American Jews—by a dinner.

In 1886 Sabato Morais led efforts to establish the Jewish Theological Seminary Association, a more traditional rabbinical school, which accepted students the following year. A coalition of New Yorkers and Philadelphians worked together to keep the seminary on its feet, but it foundered until New York financier Jacob Schiff lent the venture his considerable support. Schiff's family worshiped in a Reform synagogue, but he hoped that an American-style traditional seminary would train rabbis who could help the many observant Jews among the eastern European newcomers adjust to American culture. Morais and Mendes agreed that the new seminary ought to be located in New York City, where most new immigrants resided. After 1900, as the children of those new immigrants sought formal Jewish education, JTSA ultimately became the centerpiece of the Conservative Movement in American Judaism. A decade later, east European immigrants themselves organized America's first European-style rabbinical school, the Rabbi Isaac Elchanan Theological School, in New York. Their Union of Orthodox Jewish Congregations of America formed shortly after century's close. Thus the century that began with the first Ashkenazic prayer group forming in Philadelphia closed with American Judaism divided into two distinct religious styles, Reform and traditionalist. At the dawn of the twentieth century American Judaism boasted three seminaries that each perpetuated its own religious style.

NEW ASSOCIATIONS CREATE
AND SUSTAIN JEWISH BONDS

Mid-nineteenth-century Jewish associational life often grew out of familial bonds. Frequently, the young immigrants made new marriages between others like themselves making the same journey. It was not uncommon for a family of brothers to marry a family of sisters, settle in the same region, form business partnerships, and found local Jewish associations together. Creating a familiar base of strength and mutual support, they helped one another to succeed in the new land. Many of these families felt an emotional attachment to German culture and language and to the ideal of *bildung*—or self-cultivation expressed through reading clubs, lectures, and social activities that brought families together. The organizational records kept by many of these groups evidence their commitment to the twin goals of practical usefulness and cultural development. Larger Jewish associations staged banquets and balls for festive Jewish holidays like Hanukkah and Purim and other occasions. Thus Jewish fraternities created social bonds that could unite communities otherwise divided by worship style.

American fraternal associations like the Freemasons had enjoyed widespread popularity from the colonial era through the nineteenth century, and Jewish men also formed fraternities. The most successful Jewish fraternity was the B'nai B'rith, begun in New York in 1843 by young men from Germany. Like other fraternities, secret rituals marked initiation and progress through its ranks, but B'nai B'rith's rituals and symbols derived from synagogue structure and Jewish religious sancta. Historian Deborah Dash Moore has suggested that, through them, B'nai B'rith translated a "religious past into a secular future" and circumvented religious disputes then raging across the American Jewish landscape.[64] By 1851 it counted seven hundred members in six lodges in New York City alone, one of which was already conducting its affairs in English. By 1860 more than fifty local lodges operated around the country.[65] In smaller towns the B'nai B'rith lodge was sometimes the first Jewish organization to be established, with congregations later growing from its base. Local lodges also provided the organizing momentum for Jewish hospitals, old age homes, libraries, and Jewish schools. Following the Civil War, B'nai B'rith rededicated itself to serving the "highest interest of humanity."[66] It commissioned sculptor Moses Ezekiel to create his famous statue *Religious Liberty* and donated it to Philadelphia's Centennial Exposition commemorating one hundred years since the Declaration of Independence. Today the sculpture can be seen on that city's Independence Mall. Despite its universalist perspective, B'nai B'rith remained a Jewish organization, and by the 1890s the *Menorah Monthly* provided a national forum to discuss issues concerning Jewish life. Because B'nai B'rith members reshaped their organization to answer their changing needs, it remains a vibrant organization today.[67]

Three years after B'nai B'rith began, members' wives organized a comparable women's organization, the United Order of True Sisters. According to historian Cornelia Wilhelm, the True Sisters, originally called Unabhangiger Orden Treuer Schwestern, was an entirely independent organization. By 1870 it boasted seven lodges from Philadelphia to New Haven, Connecticut. Through the order women hoped for both mutual aid and "refinement of the heart and mind and moral im-provement."[68] Yet these women sought more than *bildung*; they hoped to "fulfill their part of the Jewish mission" of morally advancing the larger society.[69] True Sisters passed through four degrees, each named for a biblical heroine—Miriam, Ruth, Esther, and Hannah. Passage was understood to entail expanding piety, leading from service (Miriam), through friendship and loyalty to sisterhood (Ruth), fidelity and self-sacrifice (Esther), and ultimately fortitude and true faith (Hannah). At the end of the century the True Sisters published their own newspa-per, which promoted political discussions among Jewish women, first in German and later in English, who were not affiliated with their group. By then they sup-ported Jewish hospitals, manual training schools, residences for women, and set-tlement houses around the country. As the order inevitably switched from German to English, many of its members, now American-born, interested themselves in what was to become a far larger women's group, the National Council of Jewish Women, formed at century's close.

The National Council of Jewish Women, the first truly national Jewish wom-en's organization, took shape after Chicago's Columbian Exhibition in 1893. Its World Parliament of Religion provided the setting for a Jewish Women's Congress where leading American Jewish women discussed their view of Judaism and its meaning for women. Female lay preacher Ray Frank delivered the opening prayer and spoke about women in the synagogue, journalist Mary M. Cohen explained her view of Judaism's importance to domestic life, while seven more women ex-plored the importance of charitable work in Judaism and the particular needs, as they saw them, of eastern European immigrant Jews. Congress convener Hannah Greenebaum Solomon along with Sadie American presented their idea for a na-tional Jewish women's organization, and within a year lodges had formed in New York, Pittsburgh, Chicago, and elsewhere. The NCJW aimed to provide a forum for the education and cultural development of its members and to offer charitable assistance to needy Jews. Three years later the NCJW counted fifty lodges pro-pelled by women's desire for educational uplift and a shared sense of urgency to assist new immigrants.[70] To Solomon the organization's success proved that "wom-en's sphere is the whole wide world without limits."[71] Like B'nai B'rith, NCJW continued to thrive throughout the twentieth century.

B'nai B'rith reflected the broad center of American Jewish men, but, for all its interest in *bildung*, it did little to advance intellectual life. Morais and Mendes, like Leeser before them, believed that without an educated laity Judaism would disap-pear. In their view nineteenth-century American Judaism needed well-trained educators, communal workers, and parents. By 1880 Morais had reorganized a Philadelphia Hebrew Literary Society into a chapter of the Young Men's Hebrew Association, with chapters in New York and, soon, Baltimore, Cincinnati, and other towns. The YMHA chapters provided a meeting place for literary, political, and religious discussions, meetings, concerts, and a library. Members often viewed the YMHA as a vehicle for revitalizing American Jewish life.

A small cadre of young YMHA men in New York and Philadelphia felt personally inspired to revitalize Judaism in America and provided much of the energy for two important projects launched in 1879. In December New York YMHA members staged a pageant—"The Grand Revival of the National Holiday of Chanucka"— hoping to trigger renewed interest in that holiday, which they believed was neglected in America. The gala YMHA event featured a series of *tableaux vivants*, comprising several hundred costumed men and women, followed by social dancing. Many American Jews anticipated annual social gatherings at Hanukkah, but these tableaux depicted episodes from Hanukkah's history in a manner designed to inspire the participants and audience to take up this celebration—along with other facets of Jewish life—with new spirit. Depicting the Maccabees dressed in battle armor triumphantly reclaiming the Temple in Jerusalem, cleansing it of Greek gods and sacrificial objects, and rededicating it to the God of the Jews by lighting the sacred candles, it was a dramatic assertion that Jewish religious life was a manly and exciting endeavor. It refuted the Victorian trend toward female domestic religion and religious apathy. The following year Jews in Baltimore and Philadelphia staged similar events, and New Yorkers repeated their pageant.

Some American Jews read about that pageant in a new periodical, the *American Hebrew*, which began weekly publication under the editorship of Philip Cowen (1853–1943), perhaps the most diplomatic of that small group who first organized the pageant. Published in New York, the *American Hebrew* refused to take sides on the politics of religious organizations, but guided its readers to appreciate Jewish traditions, literature, customs, and to commit themselves to answering the needs of Jews in crisis in the United States and abroad. Many of its original editorial board adamantly opposed reform, yet Kaufmann Kohler often published his ideas in its pages. Like Leeser's *Occident* decades earlier, the *American Hebrew* published reports from Jewish charitable and educational organizations along with occasional poems, essays, and stories by both women and men. Emma Lazarus (1849–1887), the most talented of American Jewish writers, often published there. A New Yorker who died from Hodgkins disease at only thirty-six, Lazarus had achieved national fame before the plight of Jews in eastern Europe stirred her to pen dramatic poems urging Jewish defense and uplift. Her most famous poem, "The New Colossus," can be found today on the base of the Statue of Liberty in New York harbor.

The *American Hebrew, Occident,* and *Israelite* were only three of more than sixty nineteenth-century American Jewish periodicals published in German,

English, Yiddish, or Hebrew. The last two conveyed the views of their editors, Leeser and Wise, while the *American Hebrew* editors provided a forum for wide debate. Other periodicals, like the *Menorah Monthly*, served members of a particular organization. The *American Jewess*, published in the 1890s by Rosa Sonneschein (1847–1932), first in Chicago and then in New York, sought readers among Jewish women, especially club women like members of the NCJW. Many more periodicals, like New York's *Asmonean*, San Francisco's the *Hebrew*, Chicago's *Jewish Advance*, and Baltimore's *Jewish Chronicle*, were edited by local rabbis and served local readers. Together they created a lively forum for Jewish news, politics, and creative works that encouraged many individuals to take up their pens. Yet by and large their content remained practical news, serialized fiction, or sermonlike essays on religion. For more intellectual works American Jews looked to Europe.

In the 1870s a handful of talented young Philadelphians—some linked to the *American Hebrew*—determined to resurrect the Jewish Publication Society formed many years earlier by Leeser but destroyed by a fire in 1851. Judge Mayer Sulzberger (1843–1923), Leeser's protégé, Semitics scholar Cyrus Adler (1863–1940), physician and poet Solomon Solis-Cohen (1857–1948), journalist Mary M. Cohen (1854–1911), businessman Morris Newburger (1834–1917), and Reform rabbi Joseph Krauskopf (1858–1923) led the effort. Ultimately organizing with lay control, JPS opened in 1888 determined to revitalize American Jewish life by publishing high-quality works on Jewish history and literature that would be truthful, free of prejudices, and geared to the general reader.[72] It began by adapting admired histories published abroad, but by the end of the century it had published twenty important volumes including Heinrich Graetz's seven-volume *History of the Jews*, newly indexed and translated, a translation of the Talmud, Israel Zangwill's dramatic novel, *Children of the Ghetto*, and high-quality children's books. The *American Hebrew*, the Hanukkah pageants, and JPS were part of a movement to revitalize American Jewish life by inspiring ordinary Jews to greater Jewish practice, Jewish learning, and Jewish culture.

The success of JPS signaled American Jewry's maturity, and in 1895 Moravian-born Isidore Singer, an editor and prolific author in French, German, and English, came to America with a new publication in mind. Deeply moved by the groundless conviction of Alfred Dreyfus in France and the antisemitic sentiment it unleashed there, Singer hoped that a comprehensive collection of Jewish history, literature, philosophy, rituals, sociology, and biology would combat popular misunderstandings about Jews that seemed to feed hatred. The work's historian, Shuly Rubin Schwartz, explained that Isaac Funk, a Lutheran minister and chairman of Funk & Wagnalls , agreed to publish the work, and several leading Jewish scholars, including many on JPS's board, comprised its editorial board. Hundreds of leading scholars wrote essays. Called the *Jewish Encyclopedia*, and published in twelve volumes between 1901 and 1906, this effort played a major role in transferring Jewish scholarship from Europe to America, promoting Jewish scholarship in English, and endowing American Jewry with new respectability.[73]

Those fin de siècle efforts, which also included an American Jewish historical society, an independent college of Jewish studies (Gratz College), and annual published analyses of the state of American Jewry, advanced Jewish culture immeasurably. American Jewish associations became more creative and ambitious at the same time that new immigrants from eastern Europe pushed American Jews to greater heights of charitable innovation and giving. New national organizations knit together American Jews of every region and educational materials instructed children and adults. Magazines and literature informed and provoked American Jews to redouble their Jewish commitments and consider new ideas. Jews depended upon these resources as they tackled new challenges in the twentieth century.

NOTES

1. Hasia R Diner and Beryl Leif Benderly, *Her Works Praise Her: A History of Jewish Women in America* (New York, 2002), 43.

2. Hasia R. Diner, *The Jews of the United States* (Berkeley, 2004), 79.

3. Hasia R. Diner, *A Time for Gathering* (Baltimore, 1992), 37–40.

4. Jonathan D. Sarna, *American Judaism: A History* (New Haven, 2004), 375.

5. Shuly Rubin Schwartz, *The Emergence of Jewish Scholarship in America: The Publication of the Jewish Encyclopedia* (Cincinnati, 1991).

6. Ava F. Kahn, *Jewish Voices of the California Gold Rush: A Documentary History, 1849–1880* (Detroit, 2002), 111.

7. Diner, *A Time for Gathering*, 9.

8. John Bodnar, *The Transplanted: A History of Immigrants in Urban America* (Bloomington, 1985).

9. Ibid, 11.

10. Hasia R. Diner, "Entering the Mainstream of Modern Jewish History: Peddlers and the American Jewish South" *Southern Jewish History* 8 (2005): 1–30.

11. Diner and Benderly, *Her Works Praise Her*, 93.

12. Kahn, *Jewish Voices of the California Gold Rush*, 245.

13. Deborah Dash Moore, *B'nai B'rith and the Challenge of Ethnic Leadership* (Albany, 1981), 25.

14. Gary Philip Zola, *Isaac Harby of Charleston, 1788–1828, Jewish Reformer and Intellectual* (Tuscaloosa, 1994), 1–10.

15. Moses Rischin, "The Jewish Experience in America: The View from the West," in Moses Rischin and John Livingston, eds., *Jews of the American West* (Detroit, 1991), 32.

16. William Toll, "From Domestic Judaism to Public Ritual: Women and Religious Identity in the American West," in Pamela S. Nadell and Jonathan D. Sarna, eds., *Women and American Judaism: Historical Perspectives* (Hanover, 2001), 128–34.

17. Moore, *B'nai B'rith and the Challenge of Ethnic Leadership*, 37.

18. Zola, *Isaac Harby of Charleston*, 3.

19. Sarna, *American Judaism*, 45.

20. Diner, *A Time for Gathering*, 161–162.

21. Anonymous, "Freemasonry and Religion: A Concise View of the Origin, Progress, and Ultimate Aim of the Masonic Institution," San Francisco, September 8, 1865 (Hebrew), quoted in Kahn, *Jewish Voices of the California Gold Rush*, p. 426–27.

22. Sarna, *American Judaism*, 113.

23. Jean Powers Soman and Frank L. Byrne, eds., *A Jewish Colonel in the Civil War: Marcus M. Spiegel of the Ohio Volunteers* (Omaha, 1985), 1–13.

24. Sarna, *American Judaism*, 114, Dianne Ashton, *Rebecca Gratz: Women and Judaism in Antebellum America* (Detroit, 1997), 227.

25. Anita Libman Lebeson, *Pilgrim People* (New York, 1975), 248.

26. Marc Lee Raphael, "Beyond New York: The Challenge to Local History," in Rischin and Livingston, *Jews of the American West*, 58.

27. Leonard Dinnerstein. "From Desert Oasis to Desert Caucus: The Jews of Tucson," 140, in Rischin and Livingston, *Jews of the American West*; and Earl Pomeroy, "On Becoming a Westerner," in Rischin and Livingston, *Jews of the American West*, 196.

28. Jonathan Sarna, *The American Jewish Experience*, 2d ed. (New York, 1997), xiv.

29. Stanley Feldstein, *The Land That I Show You* (New York, 1975), 35.

30. Egal Feldman, *Dual Destinies* (Urbana, 1990), 66–67.

31. Jonathan Sarna, *Jacksonian Jew: The Two Worlds of Mordecai Manuel Noah* (New York, 1981); Sarna, *American Judaism*, 63; Feldstein, *The Land That I Show You*, 57–60; Diner, *A Time for Gathering*, 153.

32. Diner, *A Time for Gathering*, 154.

33. Feldstein, *The Land That I Show You*, 94.

34. Steven A. Fox, "On the Road to Unity: The Union of American Hebrew Congregations in America, 1873–1903," *American Jewish Archives* 32.2 (November 1980): 166.

35. Hyman Grinstein, *The Rise of the Jewish Community of New York* (Philadelphia, 1947), 152.

36. See for example, Gratz's Annual Report to the Female Hebrew Benevolent Society, 1835, American Philosophical Society, Gratz Family Papers , box 17; Ashton, *Rebecca Gratz*.

37. Dinnerstein, "Desert Oasis to Desert Caucus," 140.

38. Bertram Korn, *American Jewry and the Civil War* (New York, 1970), 3.

39. Ibid., 105.

40. Dianne Ashton. *Jewish Life in Pennsylvania* (Harrisburg, 1998), 42–43.

41. Felicia Herman. "From Priestess to Hostess: Sisterhoods of Personal Service in New York City, 1887–1936," in Nadell and Sarna, *Women and American Judaism*, 148.

42. Sarna, *American Judaism*, 60.

43. Roger Finke and Rodney Stark, *The Churching of America, 1776–1990: Winners and Losers in Our Religious Economy* (New Brunswick, NJ, 2000), 54–199.

44. Grinstein, *The Rise of the Jewish Community of New York*, 49–50.

45. Sarna, *American Judaism*, 59.

46. Ibid., 44–45.

47. Zola, *Isaac Harby of Charleston*, 125.

48. Marc Lee Raphael, *Judaism in America* (New York, 2003), 48.

49. Jay M. Eidelman, "Penina Moise," in Paula E. Hyman and Deborah Dash Moore, eds., *Jewish Women in America*, 2 vols. (New York, 1997), 2:932–33.

50. Feldman, *Dual Destinies*, 84–87.

51. Lance Sussman, *Isaac Leeser and the Making of American Judaism* (Detroit, 1995).

52. Ashton, *Rebecca Gratz*, 162–66 and 186–194; Ashton, "Grace Aguilar and the Matriarchal Theme in Jewish Women's Spirituality," in Maurie Sacks, *Active Voices: Women in Jewish Culture* (Urbana, 1995), 79–92.

53. Karla Goldman, *Beyond the Synagogue Gallery: Finding a Place for Women in America* (Cambridge, 2000), 36–39.

54. Gratz's Annual Report to the Female Hebrew Benevolent Society, 1835, American Philosophical Society, Gratz Family Papers, box 17.

55. Grinstein, *The Rise of the Jewish Community of New York*, 152.

56. William Toll. "From Domestic Judaism to Public Ritual," in Nadell and Sarna, *Women and American Judaism*, 138.

57. Rudolph Glanz, "Where the Jewish Press Was Distributed in Pre–Civil War America," *Western States Jewish History Quarterly* 5 (1972–1973): 1–14.

58. Fox, "On the Road to Unity."

59. *Chasanlein* [little eagle], letter to the editor, *Die Deborah* 2.24 (January 30, 1857): 187, translated by Heidi Thumlert. One wonders if this letter might have been written by Wise.

60. Raphael, *Judaism in America*, 49–50.

61. Goldman, *Beyond the Synagogue Gallery*, 161.

62. Leo N. Levi, "Judaism in America from the Standpoint of a Layman," lecture to the Regular Council of UAHC, New Orleans, Louisiana, December 4, 1894, American Jewish Archives, MS collection no. 72, box 72, folder 5.

63. Moore, *B'nai B'rith and the Challenge of Ethnic Leadership*, 48.

64. Ibid., 7.

65. Korn, *American Jewry and the Civil War*, 4

66. Moore, *B'nai B'rith and the Challenge of Ethnic Leadership*, 28–29.

67. Ibid., 10.

68. Cornelia Wilhelm, "The Independent Order of True Sisters: Friendship, Fraternity, and a Model of Modernity for Nineteenth-Century American Jewish Womanhood," *American Jewish Archives Journal* 54.1 (2002): 43.

69. Ibid., 45.

70. Faith Rogow. *Gone to Another Meeting: The National Council of Jewish Women, 1893–1993* (Tuscaloosa, 1993), 26.

71. Mary McCune, *"The Whole Wide World Without Limits": International Relief, Gender Politics, and American Jewish Women, 1893–1930* (Detroit, 2005), 1.

72. Jonathan D. Sarna, *JPS: The Americanization of Jewish Culture, 1888–1998* (Philadelphia, 1998), 25.

73. Schwartz, *The Emergence of Jewish Scholarship in America*.

3

THE GREAT WAVE: EASTERN EUROPEAN JEWISH IMMIGRATION TO THE UNITED STATES, 1880–1924

ERIC L. GOLDSTEIN

Jewish life in the United States was constantly reshaped by the flow of immigrants from 1654 until Congress all but closed the doors to foreign immigration in 1924. No group of arrivals, however, altered the face of American Jewry quite as dramatically as those who came from eastern Europe after 1880 as part of what Yiddish journalist Peter Wiernik called "the greatest Jewish migration since the exodus from Egypt."[1] Encompassing nearly 2.5 million immigrants from the Russian Pale of Settlement, the Kingdom of Poland, Hapsburg Galicia and Romania, the post-1880 immigration transformed a middle-class, acculturated, and politically conservative Jewish community into one largely working-class, Yiddish-speaking, and committed to a mix of ideologies including socialism, Zionism, and religious orthodoxy. "The change," writes historian Morris Schappes, "was one of body, face, tone of voice, heart and soul."[2]

What most distinguished the "great wave" of Jewish immigrants from eastern Europe was how its size and force exacerbated and extended the problems of social, cultural, and religious adjustment experienced by previous arrivals. The roughly three hundred thousand Jews who lived in the United States in 1880 had certainly struggled to gain an economic foothold, adapt to the values of the larger society, and find models of Jewishness that fit their new surroundings. Yet their path to acculturation had been much less tumultuous than the one now faced by the newcomers. As the swelling stream of immigrants from eastern Europe pushed the Jewish population beyond the million mark by the turn of the century, Jews for the first time crowded into thickly Jewish neighborhoods where poor material conditions threatened their economic rise and where the encumbrances of family and tradition significantly complicated their embrace of American culture.

In facing these many challenges, eastern European Jews in America transformed the significance of American Jewry as surely as they changed its tone and texture. Though previous generations of American Jews experimented with the implications of living in a free environment, their experience remained a relatively marginal one in the larger Jewish world. As eastern European immigrants began to explore both the rewards and difficulties of Jewish life in the *goldene medine* ("golden land"), the United States not only became one of the world's major Jewish population centers, but American Jewry emerged as a major symbol of the modern Jewish condition.

CONTINUITY AND CHANGE IN JEWISH IMMIGRATION

Despite the enormous changes introduced to American Jewish life by the post-1880 stream of arrivals, the migration was in many ways a continuation of patterns already in place. Eastern European Jews had been crossing the ocean since the very beginning of Jewish settlement in America. Asser Levy, one of the original Jews to arrive in New Amsterdam in 1654, was born in Vilna (now Vilnius), Lithuania, and the eighteenth-century Philadelphia broker and revolutionary Haym Salomon hailed from Lissa (now Leźno), Poland.[3] As Hasia Diner has pointed out, the Jewish immigrants who came to the United States between 1820 and 1880 included many Lithuanians, Hungarians, Poseners, and Russians, in addition to Bavarians, Hessians, and Wurttembergers, a diversity that makes it improper to see the period as solely "German."[4]

And even if the geographical focus of Jewish immigration shifted more exclusively to eastern Europe after 1880, the newer immigrants were not significantly different in cultural background than those who had come before. While the cultural gap between the post-1880 arrivals and the more acculturated community of American Jews seemed wide at the time, many of the more settled group—even those from German lands—had themselves been raised in traditional, Yiddish-speaking homes and had not been significantly affected by integration and secularization before arriving in America.[5] Nor were the post-1880 arrivals totally sheltered from the forces of modernization as is usually assumed. Far from the stagnant and tradition-bound society often depicted in popular culture, the world of eastern European Jews was increasingly fluid and dynamic during the nineteenth century. While change came at a slower pace than in the West, the traditional Jewish communal structure in Russia—the point of origin for about 75 percent of the post-1880 arrivals—had been slowly crumbling since the 1820s as new forms of political activism emerged and new leaders, many of them endowed with secular knowledge, began to challenge the rabbinate and communal oligarchy.[6]

Moreover, as the nineteenth century progressed, a process of urbanization and internal migration took hold that brought many former shtetl Jews to larger centers like Warsaw, Kovno, and Odessa, a city so distant from traditional mores that detractors claimed the fires of hell burned for seven miles around its limits.[7] Statistical reports indicate that the eastern European Jews who arrived in the United States between 1899 and 1914 were more skilled and literate than the general Russian Jewish population, an indication that many had already been exposed to urban living. Finally, during the decades in which immigration to America was at its highest, movements like socialism, Zionism, and Bundism grew in influence and continued to reshape Jewish identity.[8] Overseas immigration was itself a reflection of the much larger set of social and demographic revolutions that were transforming the face of eastern European Jewry.

Eastern European Jewish immigrants in the post-1880 period were also motivated by many of the same forces that had brought Jews of the earlier period to these shores. Overcrowding due to rampant Jewish population growth (a fivefold increase in the Russian Empire between 1800 and 1897 and a roughly threefold increase in Galicia and Romania during the same period), economic and residential restrictions that limited the ability of Jews to make a decent living, and fear of military conscription were factors that convinced immigrants of both periods to leave home. Pogroms were a unique feature of Russian Jewish life after 1881, but they played a much smaller role in encouraging emigration than is normally assumed and were far less significant than the chronic economic and social problems already mentioned.[9]

Despite some important similarities and continuities between the pre-1880 and post-1880 periods, however, there were several major differences. Strong evidence exists that immigrants of the post-1880 era were leaving behind more dire circumstances than earlier immigrants and that they often saw immigration as a necessity rather than a choice. While Jews who arrived in the United States in the mid-nineteenth century were mainly unmarried youth who came to America looking for a better future, the later immigrants more often came as whole family units, indicating that even those already well rooted in eastern European Jewish society found the mounting social and economic crisis unbearable. In fact, it was not unheard of during this period for families spanning three generations to arrive together. The comparatively desperate circumstances from which the post-1880 immigrants escaped were also reflected in the sheer size of the human movement, which dwarfed all previous migrations of Jews to America.

The most important distinctions between the pre- and post-1880 migrations, however, have less to do with the immigrants' origins abroad than with the dramatic changes in the America they found upon arrival. Jews arriving in the 1840s and 1850s found a country still in the beginning stages of industrialization, with vast stretches of territory open for settlement and the development of commercial enterprises. This environment encouraged those with modest capital to head west or south with packs on their backs and fan out to areas in need of goods. While ultimately most Jewish immigrants of this period ended up in one of the country's larger cities, a significant number spent at least some time in smaller, more remote locations where economic opportunities abounded and contact with the non-Jewish population was extensive. Even as they moved on to places like New York and Chicago, the limited advance of industrialization meant that they usually found work in the retail world and had an easier path to advancement than subsequent Jewish arrivals. American cities of these years also tended to be less segregated on the basis of ethnic background, so that even in the largest Jewish communities Jews were far from isolated.

By the end of the nineteenth century, however, America was emerging as a major industrial power. As a result, cities began to offer new kinds of work and poorer, more segregated living conditions for Jewish immigrants, who were now overwhelmingly choosing the largest urban centers as their first, and often permanent, places of settlement. This shift did not mean that the Jewish presence outside the major population centers dwindled during this period. Jews continued to sink roots in all parts of the United States after 1880, and in every section of the country the Jewish population increased dramatically. Historian Ewa Morawska estimates that between 20 and 25 percent of Jewish immigrants from eastern Europe settled in small towns and cities whose populations were under one hundred thousand.[10] Still, compared with earlier trends, an even greater proportion of Jewish immigrants were now settling in New York or one of the other major industrial cities—Chicago, Philadelphia, Boston, Baltimore—where factory jobs were plentiful and huge Jewish enclaves were emerging. This new environment combined with the large size of the "great wave" to create a much different set of circumstances for Jewish life than had existed for previous waves of Jewish immigrants.

OVERCOMING INITIAL CHALLENGES

Jewish immigrants en route to America from eastern Europe firmly believed that they were headed for a better place, a conviction widely supported by popular lore in their homelands. By the end of the nineteenth century, tales of America's freedoms and riches were commonplace in cities and *shtetlekh* (small towns) across the region. Some read of the fabled *goldene medine* in popular novels by Ayzik Meyer Dik, who spun stories of wealthy Jewish plantation owners and hailed America as the land that had set its slaves free.[11] Harry Fischel, who later became a successful builder in New York, first learned about the opportunities in America from letters sent back to his town of Meretz (now Merkinę), Lithuania, by those who had already crossed the ocean. "These letters," Fischel recalled, "told of fabulous earnings to be made, of a prosperity and freedom wholly foreign to [our] little town, and of a mode of living that could only be regarded as luxurious, compared with anything that [we] had known before."[12] Many immigrants were particularly attracted by persistent assurances that they could attain great standing in America despite their humble origins. "A man with a brain and a ready hand can make something of himself there," Galician immigrant Louis Borgenicht was told as a young man.[13] Mary Antin, who left the Belorussian town of Polotsk (now Polatsk) for Boston in 1882, had heard that in America, "education would be ours for the asking, and economic independence also, as soon as we were prepared."[14]

Upon arrival in the United States, however, Jewish immigrants often discovered that the realities of life there were less dazzling than they had imagined in eastern Europe. Disappointment stemmed mainly from the economic privation experienced by the immigrants and the abysmal conditions many encountered in the urban centers where they settled. In Baltimore, according to one account, the Jewish immigrant quarter was "a crowded place of tenement houses, saloons, filthy shops, foul odors [and] hideous noises."[15] Similar conclusions were drawn about Boston's North End, which was described by settlement workers as a place of "much squalor" and "little real beauty."[16] For a young immigrant like Hilda Satt, who had grown up in Poland tending her family's vegetable garden and playing near the shores of the Vistula River, the atmosphere of West Chicago came as quite a shock. "The streets were paved with wooden blocks and after a heavy rainfall the blocks would become loose and float about in the street," she recalled. "During the drying process the stench was nauseating."[17]

Urban conditions in America were even challenging for those immigrants who had already experienced city life in Europe. On the Lower East Side of New York, home to the largest concentration of immigrant Jews in the country, tenement dwellers had to contend with crumbling walls, insects, and poor ventilation. Many structures had no plumbing and let in little sunlight. Worst of all, cramped conditions facilitated the easy transmission of diseases like tuberculosis and diphtheria. Decades earlier, reformers had tried to improve living conditions in New York City by introducing the "dumbbell tenement," an innovation that mainly succeeded in creating additional health and safety hazards. Chief among these was a central airshaft, intended to provide ventilation, which instead became a garbage receptacle and helped to spread noise, odors, and fires throughout the building. Although construction of these tenements ceased after 1901, they remained the dominant type of housing in the Jewish immigrant quarter for many years.[18]

This poor living environment was only exacerbated by the meager incomes and unsanitary conditions offered to new arrivals as workers in the clothing, tobacco, and building industries. Many immigrants, for example, found their first job in the cramped sweatshops that dotted the immigrant quarters of industrial cities. These shops owed their existence to the notorious contracting system, which allowed garment manufacturers to avoid a large investment of capital by engaging subcontractors to produce garments for them at their own expense. Subcontractors were often eastern European Jewish immigrants who had been in the country for a number of years and wished to better themselves economically. To maximize their profit, they hired workers who were willing to accept low wages and endure poor conditions in return for the ability to work among fellow Yiddish speakers and to observe the Sabbath and Jewish festivals. By 1910 a majority of Jewish immigrants had worked their way out of the sweatshops, but hazardous working conditions often remained a concern in the larger factories as well. One of the most egregious offenders was the Triangle Waist Company, where management kept emergency exits bolted to prevent theft, resulting in the death of 146 employees during a devastating fire in 1911.[19]

Sometimes, the struggle to survive economic hardship and to cope with poor living and working conditions could become overwhelming. Family desertion became so chronic among eastern European Jewish immigrants that one of the leading Yiddish newspapers, the *Forverts* (Jewish daily forward), began to publish a "gallery of missing husbands."[20] While some fled their obligations, others turned to crime as a means of escaping desperate circumstances.[21] Overall, however, eastern European Jews in America were usually better able than other immigrant groups to overcome their problems. In fact, their distinctive socioeconomic profile made them particularly well situated to recognize and appreciate the promise of American life. Unlike many other immigrants who had been peasants and farmers in Europe, Jews arrived in America with experience as urban dwellers and with skills that suited them well for trade and industrial life. Despite the initial setbacks they experienced working in sweatshops and in other low-paying jobs, Jews still entered the occupational pool at a higher level than most of their fellow immigrants and were able to use their skills to rise on the social and economic ladder.[22]

Jews also had an advantage over other immigrant groups because their history as a persecuted minority in eastern Europe made them especially adept at forging ethnic networks and evolving strategies for mutual aid, skills that many other immigrants had to learn for the first time after arriving in America. Jewish peddlers and small merchants knew they could turn to other Jews for assistance when trying to gain a foothold in the business world or when they needed merchandise or credit later on.[23] The same strong group ties allowed Jews working in industrial occupations to create a cohesive and successful labor movement. The United Hebrew Trades was founded in 1888 to help organize Yiddish-speaking workers and within two years represented twenty-two unions with six thousand members. During the early twentieth century the International Ladies' Garment Workers' Union and the Amalgamated Clothing Workers of America emerged as the two most influential "Jewish" unions (although both had a minority of non-Jewish, mainly Italian, members). All these ethnic networking activities allowed Jews to overcome obstacles and better their social and economic position much more effectively than if they had only been able to rely on the kindness of the non-Jewish population for support and sustenance.[24]

Jews' relative success not only allowed them to quickly improve their standard of living but also positioned them to embrace some of the most central symbols of American freedom and opportunity. Although the need to work and support their families prevented many young Jews from undertaking extensive courses of study, their rising fortunes helped to lighten these burdens, allowing them to attend the public schools in greater numbers than their Italian or Slavic counterparts.[25] Because of their advantageous economic position, Jews were also able to participate more fully than other immigrants in America's vibrant commercial culture, becoming enthusiastic consumers of ready-made clothing, packaged foodstuffs, and manufactured goods as well as regular attendees at dance palaces, nickelodeons, and other commercial places of amusement.[26] Whether Jewish immigrants were behind school desks or shopping carts, their exceptional ability to realize these symbolic opportunities helped encourage faith in their adopted homeland.

Finally, Jewish immigrants also tended to persevere in America because they understood their immigration as a permanent one. While a small percentage of Jewish arrivals did return to eastern Europe, overall, Jews stood apart from Italian "birds of passage" and other immigrants who arrived in the United States with plans to return home once they had accumulated sufficient capital. Because they were committed to staying, Jews often idealized the American experience more than other groups, seeing it as an antidote to the tyranny of oppressive eastern European regimes. As a result, when they recognized a deficiency in American society, they often felt the urge to correct it. This in part explains why Jews in the garment industry tended to participate more actively than their Italian and native-born coworkers in strike movements like the 1909–1910 "uprisings" of the shirtwaist and cloak makers.[27] It also explains why Jewish socialists, with their agenda for social reform, enjoyed a particularly influential role among Jewish immigrants as educators and shapers of public opinion. While only a minority of Jewish immigrants subscribed to the official platform of the Socialist Party, many admired the socialists' unbending insistence on fair treatment and equality of opportunity, values they understood as central to the American enterprise.[28]

Although initially shocked by the gap between their expectations of the *goldene medine* and the real world they found upon arrival, eastern European Jewish immigrants were eventually able to overcome material setbacks and affirm their faith in America as a land of promise. In their continued quest for acculturation, however, the immigrants discovered that material deficiencies were the least challenging aspect of their adaptation to American life. As a group that pursued economic and social mobility with special vigor, immigrant Jews would soon discover the difficulty of squaring the values and priorities of their new surroundings with some of their most deeply held commitments as Jews.

BETWEEN TWO WORLDS

Memories of poverty and oppression harbored by Jewish immigrants from eastern Europe as well as the difficulties they encountered during their first years in America all contributed to feelings of exhilaration as they took increasing advantage of opportunities for advancement. Yet while America's free environment offered Jews unlimited possibilities to transform themselves as individuals, it also helped to undermine many of the traditions and community standards Jews had brought with them from their homelands. Compared to the abundance of modern American culture, which allowed Jews and other immigrants to enjoy luxuries on a regular basis, the special pleasures of the Sabbath and holidays seemed much less significant.[29] In their scramble to achieve status in America, many Jews prioritized the accumulation of wealth and material goods over the observance of time-honored rituals and customs. Similarly, as immigrants became increasingly focused on individual self-fulfillment, their commitments to family and community often faltered. While immigrants tried their best to navigate between conflicting interests and loyalties, they were rarely able to synthesize the values of the Old World with those of the new.

Those most sensitive to the tendency of American values and priorities to undermine tradition were immigrant rabbis and religious scholars, who experienced a significant loss of status in the American setting. The decline of traditional religious authority here meant that leaders who had been honored and respected in Europe often sunk to a particularly low station in life, becoming what journalist Hutchins Hapgood called "prophets without honor." Less prepared than most other Jewish immigrants to succeed in the struggle for economic survival, the "submerged scholar" eked out his living as a peddler, a printer, or as a tutor of young boys. Yet even more debilitating than his poor material circumstances, explained Hapgood, was the difficult realization that his "moral capital [was] unrecognized by the people among whom he lives."[30]

Hapgood portrayed the typical religious scholar as a sad figure that languished in obscurity and despair, but many immigrant rabbis took a more activist stand, railing against what they considered the unwholesome influences of American life and proposing methods to combat them. Hungarian rabbi Moses Weinberger, writing in 1887, urged New York Jews to "create a chief rabbinate or Jewish Supreme Court, and [thereby] raise the dignity of and concern with Torah, its investigation, and its study." Until such measures were taken, he suggested, it was better for pious Jews to remain in Europe.[31] Later the same year, however, a group of prominent Orthodox lay leaders took up Weinberger's challenge and decided to bring a renowned religious scholar to New York to help improve the standing of traditional Judaism. Within months, they had installed Rabbi Jacob Joseph, formerly of Vilna, as the city's chief rabbi.[32]

Despite the great hopes of his patrons, Jacob Joseph was unable to signifi-cantly reinvigorate Orthodoxy in America or even to assert his control over exist-ing religious institutions. In fact, his rabbinate clearly illustrated the extent to which traditional religious authority had eroded under the influence of American democracy. When the rabbi imposed his supervision on the kosher meat industry and increased prices to cover the costs, he faced a wave of protest by Jews who likened the additional fee to the despised *korobka*, a tax exacted from poor Jews by the Russian government. This incident, followed by similar controversies regard-ing the regulation of matzo and wine for Passover and by several challenges from rabbinic rivals, weakened the rabbi's authority beyond repair. He remained in New York until his death in 1902, but wielded little influence over the Jews he was supposed to guide.[33]

If immigrant rabbis suffered most directly from the clash of values presented by the American setting, average Jews also shared in their struggles. As enthusi-astic as most immigrants were about adopting American ways, many also felt uneasy about departing from tradition. In fact, despite the powerful lure of secu-larization, immigrant Jews maintained a remarkable number of Orthodox reli-gious institutions. According to one study, the Lower East Side boasted more ritual baths (*mikvehs*) per capita than almost any eastern European Jewish com-munity.[34] Religious Jews also supported several daily newspapers in Yiddish—the *Yidishes tageblat* (Jewish daily news) and *Morgn zhurnal* (Jewish morning jour-nal) in New York and the *Yidisher kurier* (Jewish courier) in Chicago—that com-peted vigorously with the Yiddish socialist press.[35] By the early twentieth century there were hundreds of Orthodox congregations in New York City, many of which perpetuated styles of Jewish worship brought from particular Old World locales.[36] Even in small cities and towns across the country, eastern European Jews frequently maintained Orthodox synagogues and in some cases engaged noted religious scholars as their rabbis. Rabbi Tobias Geffen, who arrived in Atlanta in 1910, made his mark nationally when he certified Coca-Cola as both kosher and kosher for Passover.[37] As forcefully as immigrant Jews threw off rab-binical authority, they often harbored respect for religious leaders. Despite the contempt in which Rabbi Jacob Joseph was often held during his tenure as New York's chief rabbi, upon his death he was tendered the largest funeral procession the city's Jews had ever seen.[38]

Viewed against this backdrop, immigrants' encounter with American culture is more appropriately described as a struggle with competing values and priorities than as a wholesale abandonment of Jewish practice. This fact struck Hutchins Hapgood in 1902, when he paid a visit to one of New York's Yiddish theaters for a Friday night performance. Although the members of the audience had chosen to spend their evening at a theater in violation of the Sabbath, they chastised the ac-tors who transgressed Jewish law by smoking cigarettes on stage.[39] Examples abound of immigrants who threw off tradition in their drive for freedom and success but occasionally turned back to their old ways when they required the structure and support of a religious framework. Yekl, the title character in Abraham Cahan's 1896 novella, serves as a case in point. After changing his name to Jake, he shaves his beard, eschews religious observance, and becomes sexually promiscuous. When a letter arrives from the old country bearing news of his father's death, however, he borrows his landlady's prayer book and recites the evening service.[40] As long as the stream of new immigrants continued unabated during the early twentieth century, immigrants like Jake were unable to find a clear middle ground between traditional religious culture and the values of America. Instead, eastern European Jews often functioned as best they could in a world of sharp contrasts and frequent contradictions.

YIDDISH: A GUIDE

Although never quite able to overcome the dissonance between their old setting and the new world around them, eastern European Jewish immigrants in the United States were successful in creating cultural institutions that helped them navigate the tumultuous currents of immigrant life. The lodge, the union, and the benevolent society provided a means for immigrants to explore and imbibe the values and standards of American society in friendly and supportive settings.[41] Perhaps even more important in mediating the tensions of acculturation, however, were the Yiddish-language cultural institutions—the press, publishing houses, and the theater—that entertained and educated the newcomers. These institutions both extended the processes of Americanization and democratization and helped immigrant Jews retain their ties to the old country and to each other. While they never unified an immigrant population that remained divided by cultural, ideological, and religious differences, they did fashion them into a public by bringing them into conversation with one another about the challenges they shared.

In eastern Europe at the end of the nineteenth century the only Jewish daily press was in Hebrew and was read by the few intellectuals who had sufficient knowledge of the language. Yiddish weeklies had been published sporadically since 1862, but czarist censorship prevented any mass dissemination of literature in the "people's tongue" until after the turn of the century. The first Yiddish daily in Russia, the St. Petersburg *Fraynd*, did not appear until 1903.[42] In America, however, a daily Yiddish press had existed since the mid-1880s, when Kasriel Sarasohn, a rabbi and *maskil* (adherent of the Jewish Enlightenment), founded the *Yidishes tageblat*. By the 1890s Sarasohn's Orthodox organ was joined by several other weekly and daily Yiddish publications, many of which promoted a socialist or anarchist political agenda. The largest of these was the *Forverts*, a social-democratic paper founded in 1897 by Abraham Cahan. By 1900 six different Yiddish dailies were issued in the United States, far outstripping Yiddish cultural production in the eastern European homeland.[43]

For Yiddish-speaking immigrants, the Yiddish newspaper served a much different purpose than the English newspaper did for native-born Americans. In addition to news, it published novels, sketches, short stories, and articles on popular science. Advice columns like the *Forverts*'s Bintel Brief (a bundle of letters) and features that taught readers how to dress appropriately or to play baseball were typical of Yiddish journalism. Having read comparatively little secular literature before their arrival in America, Jewish immigrants looked to the Yiddish newspaper as one of their chief sources of education. By 1914 the daily Yiddish press alone had a circulation of over five hundred thousand.[44]

Yiddish books and pamphlets in America reached a smaller audience than the Yiddish press, but the strength of Yiddish commercial publishing on these shores was still remarkable by European standards in the period before World War I. Immigrant publishers initially focused on prayer books and rabbinic works, but after 1892 they grew increasingly aware of the large market for popular literature among immigrant Jews and started to issue cheap novels in installments that sold from newsstands and soda water carts. In addition to romantic thrillers, the publishers also found a ready market for loose translations of world literature, and soon Yiddish adaptations of Tolstoy, Zola, Swift, and many other European authors appeared.[45] Among the favorites of Jewish readers were the works of Jules Verne, which popularizer Abner Tanenbaum adapted for immigrants as a means of teaching them about science. Some entrepreneurs, like Chicago publisher Jacob Lidsky, found success selling sheet music and penny songs from the Yiddish stage. Finally, immigrants eagerly consumed a host of Americanization texts and how-to manuals compiled by tireless figures such as Alexander Harkavy, whose renowned Yiddish-English dictionary had already gone through several printings by the turn of the century.[46]

Theater was the third area in which Yiddish culture blossomed in America. Like Yiddish newspapers, Yiddish drama had been banned in Russia, a development that encouraged both writers and actors to establish themselves in the United States by the early 1880s. For the next two decades comedies, melodramas, and historical romances by Joseph Latteiner and "Professor" Moshe Horowitz dominated the stage, along with translations of Shakespeare and other non-Jewish classics. As the twentieth century dawned, however, more realistic offerings, supplied by writers like Jacob Gordin and Leon Kobrin, began to vie for supremacy in the Yiddish dramatic world.[47] By 1902, when Hutchins Hapgood surveyed New York's Yiddish theater scene in *The Spirit of the Ghetto*, there were between seventy and eighty professional Yiddish actors, among them well-known figures like Jacob Adler, who achieved star status in Gordin's *Jewish King Lear*, matinee idol Boris Thomashefsky, dramatic heavyweight David Kessler, and "Madam" Keni Liptzen. The three principal Yiddish theaters in New York, in addition to a number of smaller concert saloons and vaudeville houses, had helped launch Yiddish theater as a mass phenomenon. "Into these buildings," wrote Hapgood, "crowd the Jews of all Ghetto classes—the seat-shop woman with her baby, the day laborer, the small Hester Street shopkeeper, the Russian-Jewish anarchist and socialist, the Ghetto rabbi and scholar, the poet, the journalist."[48]

In whatever form it took, Yiddish culture as it developed in America exemplified the ability of Jewish immigrants to reinvent themselves through the exploration of ideas and attitudes that had previously been beyond their reach. Introducing them not only to science, art, and literature but also to fashion, sexual mores, and social etiquette, these media allowed Jews to conceive of themselves not as humble immigrants but as citizens of the wider world. Moreover, by making what had previously been the preserve of a scholarly elite available to the masses, Yiddish cultural institutions contributed to the leveling of social distinctions that was typical of American culture more broadly. What immigrant tailor Bernard Fenster recalled about the Yiddish press could be said equally of the publishing industry and theater: it provided him with "new words and a new way of thinking . . . and this breathed a new life into me, a new desire to progress and to make myself into a *mentsh*."[49] That immigrants were able to experience these dramatic changes within the somewhat sheltered environment of their own linguistic culture makes this passage a particularly significant one in the annals of American Jewish history.

As Yiddish writers and dramatists strove to educate their immigrant audiences and forge their native language into a vehicle for lofty thoughts and expressions, some of them began to harbor the dream that they might be able to preserve Yiddish as a distinctive culture in America. During the World War I era, immigrant intellectuals helped promote the growth of highbrow drama and literature in Yiddish, launching new ventures like Maurice Schwartz's Yiddish Art Theater and a whole string of literary publishing houses. While such enterprises asserted that Yiddish culture was on par with the cultural treasures of other peoples, however, most Yiddish-speaking Jews in America demonstrated little enthusiasm for such elitist fare and continued to consume the popular offerings that had been dubbed *shund* (trash) by the intelligentsia.[50]

Average Jewish immigrants were also much less interested than Yiddish-speaking intellectuals in constructing a wall around Yiddish culture and stressing its independence from English. Yiddishists like Khayim Zhitlovski decried the hybrid Yiddish-English dialect spoken by many Jewish immigrants, calling it "kitchen-chicken-potato" language for its reliance on English vocabulary.[51] Yet most eastern European Jews in America remained committed to moving toward English and saw little wisdom in preserving the autonomy of Yiddish at the expense of their efforts at Americanization. Certainly, they retained strong emotional ties to their *mameloshn* (mother tongue), often enshrining is as an object of nostalgia. But, by the close of the immigrant period in 1924, many were already conscious of the fact that Yiddish was a declining influence in American Jewish life. Despite its former utility, the language was ceasing to play the mediating role it long performed in the lives of Jewish immigrants.[52]

"GERMANS" AND "RUSSIANS"

The Yiddish-language culture that blossomed on New York's Lower East Side and in other urban neighborhoods across the country often betrayed a strong desire for Americanization among eastern European Jewish immigrants, but it also marked the social and cultural distance that remained between most of the newcomers and the American society that surrounded them. While there were certainly a few immigrant Jews who had embarked early on the path to social integration, before World War I most were still getting an economic and cultural foothold and had little hope of attending a university, working outside the established Jewish trades, or making friends or associates beyond immigrant circles. Thus, despite their intense interest in all things American, their day-to-day experience was not strongly shaped by regular social contact with non-Jews.

In this regard, the immigrants differed dramatically from the more acculturated portion of the American Jewish population. Mainly of central European origin, the acculturated Jews had either been in the United States for decades or were themselves native-born Americans. Their overwhelming embrace of Reform Judaism and their tendency to eschew a distinct national or cultural identity for the Jews reflected the extent to which they had been able to integrate into non-Jewish social spheres.[53] As immigrants from eastern Europe began to arrive in large numbers after 1880, however, members of the established Jewish community began to worry that the newcomers might threaten their hard-won acceptance in American society.

To a large extent, the fears harbored by the American Jewish establishment concerning the eastern European arrivals were encouraged by their own struggles with social discrimination and antisemitic sentiment within American society. In the decades after the Civil War an increasing number of hotels, clubs, and other private organizations began to restrict Jewish entry, slowing the strides central European Jews were making toward social integration. By the time immigration from eastern Europe was in full swing, anti-Jewish rhetoric had become much more common in the mainstream media and in public discourse. While Jews remained highly regarded in many quarters and most native-born Americans were ambivalent, rather than wholly negative, about them, the increased pressure on the Jewish establishment was enough to make them worry that the foreign appearance and distinctive social and religious behavior of the new immigrants would further soil their reputation among non-Jews.[54]

As a result of such fears, Jews of central European background—styling themselves as "Germans"—voiced their disapproval of the "Russian" newcomers with special intensity during the first decade of immigration from eastern Europe. Often Jewish officials would try to intervene with foreign aid societies and forestall their attempts to send over further groups of immigrants. In 1881 the governors of the Russian Emigrant Relief Fund of New York complained to the officers of the Alliance Israélite Universelle that further arrivals would render their burden "absolutely intolerable."[55] In some cases acculturated Jews of the period went so far as to advocate the legal restriction of all immigration into the country. The language and imagery that they sometimes used in the Jewish press suggested an urgent need to disassociate themselves from the eastern European newcomers. The *Hebrew Standard*, an organ of establishment Jewry, declared the "thoroughly acclimated American Jew" to be "closer to the Christian sentiment around him than to the Judaism of these miserable darkened Hebrews."[56]

For two major reasons, however, this uncompromising attitude of the Jewish establishment toward the new immigrants did not last long. First, by the 1890s it became clear that Jewish community leaders did not have the power to stop the flow of new arrivals from eastern Europe. As this reality set in, acculturated Jews realized that in order to protect their own image in American society they now needed to shift their energies toward aiding the immigrants and Americanizing them as soon as possible.[57] Faced with a growing immigrant population that already far outnumbered them, central European Jews in America became determined to assert their hegemony over immigrant affairs and to thereby project the "proper" image of *all* Jews to the non-Jewish public.

Second, and perhaps more significantly, central European Jews found it hard to maintain their initial antagonism toward the eastern Europeans because of feelings of kinship and responsibility that were not easily suppressed. The older immigrants liked to think of themselves as having come from a more sophisticated and worldly background than the newcomers, but, in truth, many of them had been just as traditional and just as unaware of the norms of non-Jewish society when they arrived on American shores. In fact, some of the "Germans" actually stemmed from the exact regions that were supplying a great share of the post-1880 arrivals.[58] Although these similarities bred anxiety among the established Jews who wished to obscure their own humble origins, they also reminded acculturated Jews of their ties to the eastern Europeans and encouraged concern and sympathy for them.

Identification with the immigrants was particularly pronounced among a small group of acculturated Jews who found American Jewish religious and cultural life to be severely lacking. Activists like Henrietta Szold, Stephen S. Wise, and Judah L. Magnes saw the newcomers as authentic Jews from whom they had much to learn.[59] To Szold, the daughter of a Baltimore rabbi, the members of her father's middle-class congregation had "the souls of bookkeepers," while the immigrants "had the souls of Jews."[60] Members of this group were drawn to Zionism through their contact with the eastern Europeans and took a leading role in the founding of the Federation of American Zionists in 1898. Most acculturated Jews did not share such deep bonds with the immigrants, but, when viewed alongside more negative interactions, the existence of these relationships demonstrates the rather complex emotions the post-1880 immigration inspired in their ranks.

These varying motivations—feelings of kinship and identification with immigrant Jews and a desire to control the Jewish image—often combined uneasily in establishment Jewry's efforts to aid the newcomers. Central European Jews built settlement houses, libraries, and night schools that provided immigrants with vocational training, a knowledge of the English language, and an introduction to American culture. They created charitable institutions where immigrants could apply for financial assistance and where they could seek medical care that was otherwise unavailable. Yet while these undertakings doubtlessly conveyed the deep concern of acculturated Jews for the eastern Europeans, the efforts of the established community were also infused with expressions of condescension and the suggestion that the immigrants still had far to go to achieve a desirable social and cultural station. Money was provided to hungry Jews at the United Hebrew Charities in New York, but recipients had to wait in line for hours and were often subjected to humiliating treatment.[61] While immigrants benefited greatly from the instruction given to them in community-sponsored schools and settlement houses, these institutions were sometimes heavy-handed in their attempts to eradicate what were seen as "extreme" ideological tendencies among the eastern European population, like socialism and Zionism. Similarly, the establishment in 1886 of the Jewish Theological Seminary of America, founded by a group of religiously traditional central European Jews in response to the growing strength of Reform Judaism, was also intended to combat the "old-style orthodoxy" that prevailed among many eastern European Jewish immigrants.[62]

The deep ambivalence of the Jewish establishment toward eastern European immigrants was nowhere more palpable than in the Galveston movement, an experiment carried out between 1907 and 1914 that hoped to redirect the flow of Jewish immigration away from New York and other major Jewish population centers toward the southern port of Galveston, Texas. The brainchild of prominent banker and Jewish communal leader Jacob H. Schiff, the plan claimed to address the chronic problems of overcrowding, poverty, and unsanitary conditions among urban Jews by helping to disperse new arrivals throughout the less crowded southern and western regions of the country. It also promised to forestall calls among American politicians for immigration restriction by ameliorating the social ills to which restrictionists pointed in making their case. Yet while the Galveston movement was ostensibly an attempt to help immigrants gain a solid footing in the United States and realize the American Dream more quickly, many eastern Europeans saw it as a self-serving public relations move on the part of the communal elite that had few real benefits for the immigrants themselves. A large number of those diverted to Galveston failed to realize the great opportunities predicted for them and were drawn back to Chicago or New York by the sense of cultural isolation they felt in the remote areas where they had been directed.[63]

The Galveston movement demonstrated just how determined acculturated Jews of central European background were to hold on to the reigns of Jewish communal leadership in the wake of the eastern European immigration to America. With impressive financial resources and a greater familiarity with the larger culture, they remained through the years of World War I an important force in influencing the policy and direction of American Jewry. Ultimately, however, the Galveston episode also made clear that establishment Jews could not control the actions of the much larger group of eastern European Jewish immigrants, who had managed to vote with their feet and undermine the objectives of Schiff and his colleagues. As the eastern European Jews further embraced American ways and grew in power and influence, members of the Jewish establishment would increasingly have to confront their own shrinking role as the arbiters of American Jewish life.

THE PROBLEM OF "COMMUNITY"

The challenges posed by eastern European Jewish immigrants to the leadership of acculturated central European Jews during the early twentieth century marked the passage of American Jewry into a new kind of Jewish communal structure, one characterized by a level of diversity and pluralism that had no historical precedent or parallel in any other world Jewish community. While no Jewish community was totally unified, in other countries communal cohesiveness was facilitated by either a rigid system of social stratification, in which elites controlled communal affairs, or by a homogeneity of background that provided a clear basis for group action. In the wake of eastern European Jewish immigration to the United States, however, neither of these conditions obtained. Not only did the country's democratic ethos work against a top-down model of communal governance, but the mix of immigrant groups resulted in a jumble of conflicting goals and priorities among the Jewish population. While American Jewry had been a relatively homogeneous and unified community through the late nineteenth century, the arrival of the new immigrants had transformed it into an unwieldy composite of various national, religious, political, and ideological groupings.

It was not only the differences between eastern European and central European Jews but also the internal divisions among the eastern European immigrants that gave American Jewry its pluralistic character during these years. Unlike their central European predecessors whose small numbers obviated the preservation of their diverse regional identities on these shores, Jews from Russia, Hungary,

Galicia, and Romania arriving after 1880 often remained sharply distinguished from one another. On the Lower East Side, the center of Jewish immigrant settlement in New York, each of these groups carved out their own defined territory where they could live among their compatriots from the old country.[64] Even within the various national groupings immigrants divided into individual *landsmanshaftn*, or hometown societies, where they carried out religious, social, and philanthropic activities.[65] In many cases Jews from different towns or regions developed rivalries, like the storied antagonism between the "Litvak" and "Galitsyaner"—Lithuanian and Galician Jews—who were said to embody opposite personality types.[66] According to one account, particular cafés on New York's Lower East Side were frequented by different groups of *landslayt* (countrymen), who jealously excluded outsiders from their company and posted banners in the windows asserting the superiority of their national cuisines.[67]

Aside from national and regional distinctions, the immigrants were also hopelessly divided on matters of religion and politics. Rifts between Orthodox and secular Jews, radicals and conservatives, socialists and anarchists, and Zionists and cosmopolitans were all regular features of immigrant Jewish life. Such disputes were often played out in the Yiddish press, where almost every shade of belief was represented. Radical journalists like Abraham Cahan wielded political power and literary influence in the immigrant quarter of New York, but so did spokesmen like Jacob Saphirstein, whose successful *Morgn zhurnal* supported the Republican Party and promoted an Orthodox lifestyle.[68] Occasionally immigrant political battles spilled out onto the streets, as they often did on Yom Kippur when Jewish anarchists paraded through the East Side smoking cigarettes and eating pork.[69]

Like many aspects of American culture, pluralism had both positive and negative implications for Jewish life. On the one hand, it represented the democratic promise of America, where each individual was free to determine his or her own beliefs and priorities and to balance individual and collective identities in whatever way seen fit. When even religious Jews refused to submit to the authority of Chief Rabbi Jacob Joseph after his arrival from Vilna in 1887, or when Jewish immigrant women staged a massive consumer boycott against kosher butchers in 1902 to protest the price of kosher meat, they were affirming the egalitarian ideals of a nation where one need not be limited by the dictates of traditional authority figures.[70] On the other hand, the lack of unity among American Jews could sometimes become debilitating, preventing them from effectively addressing challenges and problems of mutual concern.

American Jews became particularly aware of the challenges of maintaining a cohesive community structure in 1908, when New York police commissioner Theodore Bingham accused Jews of being the chief purveyors of crime in the city. Sensitized by Bingham's charges to the need for unified community action, a diverse array of groups, ranging from acculturated central European Jews to eastern

European immigrants and including almost every shade of belief and ideology, came together after much wrangling to form the New York Kehilla. Though based loosely on the traditional Jewish communal structure that had guided Jewish affairs in the preemancipation period, the Kehilla embraced a pluralistic model that provided for cooperation and prevented any one interest group from dominating its agenda. In this manner leaders of the various factions felt that they could address issues such as crime, education, and philanthropy.[71]

The Kehilla functioned smoothly for about a decade, but eventually began to deteriorate as the interests of its constituent groups began to diverge. Ultimately, even with its pluralist orientation, it presented too monolithic a structure to suit the diversity inherent in American Jewish affairs.[72] From the dissolution of the Kehilla in 1922, American Jews of every background and outlook would have to struggle with a world in which freedom and unity were often in tension.

FROM IMMIGRANTS TO AMERICAN JEWS

The problems and tensions surrounding immigrant adjustment continued to dominate the agenda of American Jewry from the 1880s through the early 1920s, as long as the foreign born remained the largest element in American Jewish society. The texture of American Jewish life finally began to change, however, as three related shifts took place in the wake of World War I.

First and foremost, Jewish immigration from eastern Europe declined dramatically. Beginning with the outbreak of hostilities in Europe in 1914, the journey to America from the disintegrating Russian and Austrian Empires became much more difficult and fewer potential immigrants were able to leave their homes. Between 1908 and 1914 almost ninety-four thousand Jewish immigrants were arriving on American shores each year, but during the war this number slipped to only about thirteen thousand arrivals annually.[73]

Immigration picked up slightly after the war, but the stream returned to only a trickle after 1924, this time due to restrictive legislation passed by the United States Congress. Influenced by a growing climate of nativism and xenophobia brought on by the rapid social changes of the postwar years, lawmakers passed the Johnson-Reed Act, which drastically restricted the entry of European groups and took special aim at those who had not been well represented in the United States before 1890.[74] In the years after the act's passage, the foreign born lost their numerical dominance among American Jews, who now became an increasingly native-born group.

The second major shift of the 1920s was the cultural realignment that accompanied demographic change. The rise of a younger generation thoroughly conversant with American ways meant that some of the cultural dissonance of the immigrant period began to vanish. Jews not only became major consumers of popular culture but also took an important role in crafting the American music and entertainment industries. They constructed middle-class ethnic neighborhoods that reflected their acculturated sensibilities and built "synagogue-centers" that combined worship facilities with space for American-style recreation. All these trends made clear that Jews were finding new ways of bringing their Jewish and American outlooks together.[75] Although certain immigrant institutions like the Yiddish press and theater survived intact, they now became only supplements to a much more active participation by Jews in English-language culture.[76]

Finally, both the ongoing acculturation of the immigrants and the direction of world events conspired to launch Jews of eastern European background into the forefront of American Jewish leadership. Increasingly, the children of the immigrants not only came to dominate the Orthodox and Conservative movements but began to strongly influence the Reform movement as well. Moreover, the voice of eastern European Jews began to grow in importance as issues like the Jewish refugee problem, the recognition of Jewish rights in postwar Europe, and attempts to create a Jewish homeland in Palestine all gained world attention. No longer content to allow the older establishment to speak for all of American Jewry, they founded new organizations like the American Jewish Congress and the American Jewish Joint Distribution Committee to pursue their agenda. These organizations not only rivaled established agencies like the American Jewish Committee but also forced the older leadership to recognize the newer guard of eastern European activists. Jews of eastern European background also seized control of the American Zionist movement, which had long been dominated by American-born Jews like Richard Gottheil, Stephen S. Wise, and Louis D. Brandeis.[77] While many of these leaders remained towering figures in American Jewish life, from the 1920s they increasing shared their power and influence with the eastern European Jews and their children.

The changes of the 1920s marked a definite passage to a new era in American Jewish history, but it did not resolve all the challenges of identity faced by American Jews. The immigrants and their children may have now seen themselves as full Americans, but it would be another two decades before the non-Jewish society around them would allow them to participate fully in the central institutions of American life. This new social and cultural configuration presented challenges that were different, but no less daunting, for American Jews.

NOTES

1. Peter Wiernik, *History of the Jews in America* (New York, 1912), 262.

2. Morris U. Schappes, *The Jews in the United States: A Pictorial History, 1654 to Present* (New York, 1958), 218.

3. Jacob Rader Marcus, *United States Jewry, 1776–1985* (Detroit, 1993), 4:10.

4. Hasia R. Diner, *A Time for Gathering: The Second Migration, 1820–1880* (Baltimore, 1992), 49–56.

5. Ibid., 8–35; Steven M. Lowenstein, *The Mechanics of Change: Essays in the Social History of German Jewry* (Atlanta, 1992), chapters 1, 5, and 7.

6. Michael Stanislawski, *Tsar Nicholas I and the Jews: The Transformation of Jewish Society in Russia, 1825–1855* (Philadelphia, 1983); Eli Lederhendler, *The Road to Modern Jewish Politics: Political Tradition and Political Reconstruction in the Jewish Community of Tsarist Russia* (New York, 1989).

7. Steven J. Zipperstein, *The Jews of Odessa: A Cultural History, 1794–1881* (Stanford, 1986), especially p. 1. See also Eli Lederhendler, "Modernity Without Emancipation or Assimilation? The Case of Russian Jewry," in Jonathan Frankel and Steven J. Zipperstein, eds., *Assimilation and Community: The Jews in Nineteenth-Century Europe* (Cambridge, 1992), 324–43.

8. Jonathan Frankel, *Prophecy and Politics: Socialism, Nationalism, and the Russian Jews, 1862–1917* (Cambridge, 1981).

9. Diner, *A Time for Gathering*, 42–9; Lloyd Gartner, "Jewish Migrants en Route from Europe to North America: Traditions and Realities," *Jewish History* 1 (Fall 1986): 50–51.

10. Ewa Morawska, *Insecure Prosperity: Small-Town Jews in Industrial America, 1890–1940* (Princeton, 1990), xiv.

11. S. Niger Charney, "America in the Works of I. M. Dick," *YIVO Annual of Jewish Social Science* 9 (1954): 63–71.

12. Harry Fischel, *Forty Years of Struggle for a Principle*, ed. Herbert S. Goldstein (New York, 1928), 6.

13. Louis Borgenicht, *The Happiest Man: The Life of Louis Borgenicht* (New York, 1942), 178.

14. Mary Antin, *The Promised Land* (Boston, 1912), 148.

15. Isaac M. Fein, *The Making of an American Jewish Community: The History of Baltimore Jewry from 1773 to 1920* (Philadelphia, 1973), 159.

16. Gerald H. Gamm, "In Search of Suburbs: Boston's Jewish District, 1843–1994," in Jonathan D. Sarna and Ellen Smith, eds., *The Jews of Boston* (Boston, 1995), 136.

17. Hilda Satt Polacheck, *I Came Here a Stranger: The Story of a Hull-House Girl* (Urbana, IL, 1989), 30.

18. Moses Rischin, *The Promised City: New York's Jews, 1870–1914* (New York, 1964), 81-89; Deborah Dwork, "Immigrant Jews on the Lower East Side of New York: 1880–1914," in Jonathan D. Sarna, ed., *The American Jewish Experience*, 2d ed. (New York, 1986), 125–30.

19. Dwork, "Immigrant Jews," 130–35.

20. Jenna Weissman Joselit, *The Wonders of America: Reinventing Jewish Culture, 1880–1950* (Bloomington, 1994), 38–39.

21. Jenna Weissman Joselit, *Our Gang: Jewish Crime and the New York Jewish Community, 1900–1940* (Bloomington, 1983).

22. Thomas Kessner, *The Golden Door: Italian and Jewish Immigrant Mobility in New York City, 1880–1915* (New York, 1977); Stephen Steinberg, *The Ethnic Myth: Race, Ethnicity, and Class in America* (Boston, 1989), chapters 3 and 6.

23. Eric L. Goldstein, "Beyond Lombard Street: Jewish Life in Maryland's Small Towns," in Karen Falk and Avi Y. Decter, eds., *They Call This Place Home: Jewish Life in Maryland's Small Towns* (Baltimore, 2002), 39–40.

24. Frankel, *Prophecy and Politics*, 117; Benjamin Stolberg, *Tailor's Progress: The Story of a Famous Union and the Men Who Made It* (Garden City, NY, 1944); Steve Fraser, *Labor Will Rule: Sidney Hillman and the Rise of American Labor* (New York, 1991).

25. See Selma Berrol, "Public School and Immigrants: The New York City Experience," in Bernard J. Weiss, ed., *American Education and the European Immigrant, 1840–1940* (Urbana, IL, 1982), 38–39.

26. Andrew Heinze, *Adapting to Abundance: Jewish Immigrants, Mass Consumption, and the Search for American Identity* (New York, 1990); Elizabeth Ewen, *Immigrant Women in the Land of Dollars: Life and Culture on the Lower East Side, 1890–1925* (New York, 1985).

27. Susan Glenn, *Daughters of the Shtetl: Life and Labor in the Immigrant Generation* (Ithaca, 1990), 191–94.

28. See Tony E. Michels, *A Fire in Their Hearts: Yiddish Socialists in New York* (Cambridge, 2005).

29. Heinze, *Adapting to Abundance*, chapters 3 and 4.

30. Hutchins Hapgood, *Spirit of the Ghetto* (New York, 1902), 53–54.

31. Moses Weinberger, *People Walk on Their Heads: Moses Weinberger's Jews and Judaism in New York*, ed. and trans. Jonathan D. Sarna (New York, 1982), 5–6, 114.

32. Abraham J. Karp, *Jewish Continuity in America: Creative Survival in a Free Society* (Tuscaloosa, 1998), 145–58.

33. Ibid., 170–85.

34. Heinze, *Adapting to Abundance*, 57-58.

35. Kenneth Rossett, *Sarasohn and Son: A Scrapbook*, 2d ed. (New York, 1984); Moshe Starkman, "Itonut yidish be-Shikago (1877–1955)," in Simon Rawidowicz, ed., *The Chicago Pinkas* (Chicago, 1952), 69–78; Arthur A. Goren, *The Politics and Public Culture of American Jews* (Bloomington, 1999), 100–9.

36. David Kaufman, *Shul with a Pool: The "Synagogue-Center" in American Jewish History* (Hanover, NH, 1999), 166–74.

37. Lee Shai Weissbach, "East European Immigrants and the Image of Jews in the Small-Town South," *American Jewish History* 85 (1997): 231–62. On Geffen, see Joel Ziff, ed., *Lev Tuviah: On the Life and Work of Rabbi Tobias Geffen* (Newton, MA, 1988).

38. Karp, *Jewish Continuity in America*, 185–86.

39. Hapgood, *Spirit of the Ghetto*, 126.

40. Abraham Cahan, *Yekl and the Imported Bridegroom and Other Stories of the New York Ghetto* (New York, 1970), 32–33.

41. Daniel Soyer, *Jewish Immigrant Associations and American Identity in New York, 1880–1939* (Cambridge, 1997); Glenn, *Daughters of the Shtetl*, 203–6.

42. On *Der fraynd*, see Sarah Abrevaya Stein, *Making Jews Modern: The Yiddish and Ladino Press in the Russian and Ottoman Empires* (Bloomington, 2004).

43. Hapgood, *Spirit of the Ghetto*, 176–98; Robert E. Parke, *The Immigrant Press and Its Control* (New York, 1922), 95–110.

44. See Isaac Metzker, ed., *A Bintel Brief: Sixty Years of Letters from the Lower East Side to the Jewish Daily Forward* (New York, 1971). Circulation figures for the Yiddish dailies are recorded in Nathan Goldberg, "Decline of the Yiddish Press," *Chicago Jewish Forum* (Fall 1944): 17.

45. Charles Madison, *Jewish Publishing in America* (New York, 1976), 80.

46. On Tanenbaum, see Zalmen Reyzen, *Leksikon fun der yidisher literatur, prese un filologye* (Vilna, 1926), 1:1159–64. On Lidsky (also known as Lidskin), see ibid., 2:128–9; and Robert Singerman, *Judaica Americana: A Bibliography of Publications to 1900* (New York, 1990), 656, 788–89, 812, 838. On Harkavy, see Dovid Katz's introduction to the reprint edition of Harkavy's *Yidish-English-Hebreisher verterbukh* (New York, 1987), vi–xxiii.

47. See Bettina Warnke, "Reforming the New York Yiddish Theater: The Cultural Politics of Immigrant Intellectuals and the Yiddish Press, 1887–1910," Ph.D. diss., Columbia University, 2001.

48. Hapgood, *Spirit of the Ghetto*, chapter 5 (the quote is from p. 118). When Yiddish theater was finally permitted in Russia in the years after 1905, theater directors there often turned to America for plays to perform and for dramatic talent. See Nina Warnke, "Going East: The Impact of American Yiddish Plays and Players on the Yiddish Stage in Czarist Russia, 1890–1914," in *American Jewish History* 92 (2005): 1–29.

49. Fenster quoted in Michels, *A Fire in Their Hearts*, 78–79.

50. Warnke, "Reforming the New York Yiddish Theater," chapter 6.

51. George Wolfe, "Notes on American Yiddish," *American Mercury* 29 (Aug 1933): 473.

52. See Uriah Zevi Engelman, "The Fate of Yiddish in America," *Menorah Journal* 15 (July 1928): 22–32.

53. Naomi W. Cohen, *Encounter with Emancipation: The German Jews in the United States, 1830–1914* (Philadelphia, 1984), chapters 3 and 4.

54. See Leonard Dinnerstein, *Antisemitism in America* (New York, 1994), chapters 3 and 4; and Eric L. Goldstein, "The Unstable Other: Locating Jewishness in Progressive Era American Racial Discourse," *American Jewish History* 89 (December 2001): 383–409.

55. Quoted in Evyatar Friesel, "The Age of Optimism in American Jewish History, 1900–1920," in Bertram W. Korn, ed., *Bicentennial Festschrift for Jacob Rader Marcus* (Waltham, MA, 1976), 136.

56. Quoted in Rischin, *The Promised City*, 97.

57. Friesel, "The Age of Optimism," 148–49.

58. Diner, *A Time for Gathering*, 49–56.

59. Norman Bentwich, *For Zion's Sake: A Biography of Judah L. Magnes* (Philadelphia, 1954), 30–31; Stephen S. Wise, *Challenging Years: The Autobiography of Stephen Wise* (New York, 1949), 27.

60. Joan Dash, *Summoned to Jerusalem: The Life of Henrietta Szold* (New York, 1979), 22.

61. See Rose Cohen, *Out of the Shadow: A Russian Jewish Girlhood on the Lower East Side* (Ithaca, 1995), 168–69.

62. Hasia Diner, "Like the Antelope and the Badger: The Founding and Early Years of the Jewish Theological Seminary, 1886–1902," in Jack Wertheimer, ed., *Tradition*

Renewed: A History of the Jewish Theological Seminary of America, 2 vols. (New York, 1997), 1:14.

63. Bernard Marinbach, *Galveston: Ellis Island of the West* (Albany, 1983).

64. Rischin, *The Promised City*, 76–78.

65. Soyer, *Jewish Immigrant Associations*.

66. This antagonism is discussed in Metzker, *A Bintel Brief*, 58–59.

67. *Forverts*, January 17, 1914, 4.

68. Goren, *The Politics and Public Culture of American Jews*, 100–9.

69. Elias Tcherikower, *The Early Jewish Labor Movement in the United States*, ed. and trans. Aaron Antonovsky (New York, 1961), 260.

70. Karp, *Jewish Continuity in America*, 172–74; Paula Hyman, "Immigrant Women and Consumer Protest: The New York City Kosher Meat Boycott of 1902," *American Jewish History* 70 (September 1980): 91–105.

71. Arthur A. Goren, *New York Jews and the Quest for Community: The Kehilla Experiment, 1908–1922* (New York, 1968), chapter 2.

72. Ibid., chapter 11.

73. These figures are drawn from Sarna, *American Jewish Experience*, 360.

74. See John Higham, *Strangers in the Land: Patterns of American Nativism, 1860–1925*, 2d ed. (New York, 1963), chapter 11.

75. Deborah Dash Moore, *At Home in America: Second Generation New York Jews* (New York, 1981); Peter Levine, *Ellis Island to Ebbet's Field: Sport and the American Jewish Experience* (New York, 1992); Andrea Most, *Making Americans: Jews and the Broadway Musical* (Cambridge, 2004); Kaufman, *Shul with a Pool*.

76. On Yiddish culture as an increasingly supplemental one in the 1920s, see Mordecai Soltes, *The Yiddish Press: An Americanizing Agency* (New York, 1925), 35, 39–42, 44.

77. Judd Teller, *Strangers and Natives: The Evolution of the American Jew from 1921 to the Present* (New York, 1968), chapter 1.

4

AMERICAN JUDAISM BETWEEN
THE TWO WORLD WARS

JEFFREY S. GUROCK

In 1924 the editors of the *American Hebrew*, a "National Jewish Weekly," were very worried about the impact upon their community of the congressional legislation passed that year, which effectively ended a century or more of constant Jewish immigration to this country. "Up to this time," these journalists observed, the "accretion of our numbers has been like a river which fructifies and blesses the land." But now, the "landlocked" Jews of America, "virtually isolated from the Jews of the rest of the world" and no longer the beneficiaries of "diverse infiltration of European Jewish culture, religion or language," were on their own. Would the indigenous community, these writers wondered, "adjust" and "adapt" itself to these new conditions? Might it draw upon "American sources" and its own "spiritual springs" to "survive environmental assimilation" as its "cultural contact and social commingling with the Gentile" inevitably increased? Could those born in the United States prove that "the ghetto ideal" was not "essential to the perpetuation of Judaism?"

The future that the editors hoped for, a "foretelling" they said required "only a little imagination," was a new American Judaism devoid of "every vestige of the Old World distinctiveness," but vibrant and progressive. While American Jews would "dispense with those externalities which constitute the heritage of ghetto days"—certainly "extreme East European orthodoxy" would be cast off—the next generation of that community, comfortable with the world around it, would remain "staunch" Jews and would "accept Judaism and practice it as a noble code of living." The exact details of what that religious world would look like were also left to the imagination.[1]

Possibly, to allay whatever doubts they may have harbored about their community's destiny, the *American Hebrew* turned to "the three heads of the three leading institutions of Jewish learning in America" for their predictions on what lay ahead for American Jewry. The trio of respondents, Dr. Julian Morgenstern of the long-standing Reform Hebrew Union College, Dr. Stephen S. Wise of the newly established Reform Jewish Institute of Religion, and Dr. Cyrus Adler of the Conservative Jewish Theological Seminary all rested assured that their community had good days ahead of it. (For the record, Dr. Bernard Revel, of the Orthodox Rabbi Isaac Elchanan Theological Seminary, aka the Yeshiva, was not approached for his opinion.)

Unqualifiedly the optimist, Dr. Morgenstern was unconvinced, to begin with, that it was "the Jewish immigrants to America during the last forty years who have kept Judaism alive here," and that without them and their spirit "Judaism in America would either have disappeared already or be well on the road thither." What he was certain of was that just as Judaism had "lived on through all the ages and in all the lands," it would survive and indeed prosper here, whether or not America's portals were ajar. He prophesied that "this American Judaism of tomorrow will not be the mere continuation of any one single, present day movement . . . neither of Reform nor Orthodoxy." Rather, the faith of the future would rest upon an adroit blending of "the old, eternal foundation of Jewish principles, history and tradition," adapted well to "the peculiar life we Jews must live here as American citizens."

For Morgenstern, his vision was neither a "prediction," a "hope," nor a "dream," as "the beginning has already been made; the process is well under way." He was heartened that "all over the land, new congregations are springing up so rapidly that their demand for rabbis and trained spiritual leaders cannot be satisfied." To meet the demand, "new departments and schools are being organized and planned for the training of professional Jewish workers of all kinds." As the rabbi saw it, a renaissance was underway, as American Judaism, "astir with activities," was "vigorously and earnestly alive."[2]

Dr. Wise was not nearly as sanguine about the future as he acknowledged that it was inevitable that "American Israel will slough off the faint-hearted whose spiritual standards seem to derive from chaos, from topsyturvyism." Still, the "thinning of the ranks" in the land of freedom, with no new large cohorts coming in to America, would not leave "Israel desolate." Rather, as this rabbi looked ahead to coming decades, even to as distant a year as 2000, Wise was confident that American Jews would demonstrate their continued affinity "for spiritual values," distinguish themselves through their valuing of "the treasures of Jewish tradition, intellectual, ethical, [and] spiritual," and be remarkable in their "passionate insistence" in "bear[ing] the torch as makes [them] the maintainer of the tradition, the utterer of the Jewish truth." Indeed, he believed that, at the present moment, in the 1920s, "we are in a new era in Jewish education," spurred on by those "Jews who will remain Jews" who comprehend "that they must repossess themselves of their Jewish spiritual treasures."[3]

Unlike his colleagues, Dr. Adler did not deign to offer an extensive response to the interrogatory. Still, in his terse, eighteen-line statement, he opined that he did not believe the immigration laws would "in the least injure Judaism in America." Ultimately upbeat in his estimation, he wrote, "I have a firm faith in the maintenance and normal development of traditional Judaism in America." Nonetheless, Adler did temper his optimistic prediction with a troubling admonition that "if the three million and a half of Jews in America cannot maintain Judaism without a constant stream of immigrants, they are unworthy of Judaism."[4]

These affirmative prognostications proved essentially incorrect. In the decades that immediately followed this 1924 symposium, American Judaism did not live up to these hopes and expectations. The community did not do all that well on its own in its landlocked environment. Quite the contrary, the years that bridged the two world wars did not witness an American Judaism engaged in an "onward march," to borrow a phrase from an *American Hebrew* headline.[5] Instead, devoid of that vibrant immigrant cohort of staunch Jewish identities rooted in a European past, even if these new Americans did not always practice what their traditional faith preached, Jewish religious life became mired in a state of crisis and decline. If anything, Cyrus Adler's dark bottom line may have been substantially true.

For example, disinterest in synagogue life—of any denominational sort—was rampant among the masses of second-generation east European Jews, who then constituted the largest individual cohort of American Jews. Unlike their parents, they were manifestly disinclined to identify formally with their people's religious past and showed little enthusiasm for charting its future. So disposed, they approximated, in their religious values and commitment to Jewish observances, the level of dissociation that earlier groups of this country's Jews had sunk to some generations earlier.

Arguably, what kept interwar communities from complete disintegration, at least within this country's larger cities, where most Jews lived, had much to do with the residential propinquity of Jews to one another in their urban neighborhoods. While 1920s–1930s Jews at home on their own turfs might never set foot in their local synagogues or open a prayer book after learning enough Hebrew to recite a bar mitzvah portion by rote on that memorable day, they still spent their lives among other Jews. Housing discrimination played a part in keeping Jews together as did, for that matter, the evident desire of other ethnic groups to live in their own largely homogeneous groupings. This was an era when social antisemitism restricted Jewish integration in education and occupational realms. America's best schools were often off-limits to aspiring Jewish students. Barriers in employment opportunities kept them from access to elite professions, like medicine or prestigious law partnerships. Accordingly, Jews found each other, on an ongoing basis, in their own ethnic-based industries. Or, to put it another way, "the environmental assimilation," born of the "cultural contact and the commingling with the Gentile" that so concerned the *American Hebrew* people, did not take place on a grand scale. Given this set of social circumstances, even a Jew who never found his or her path from outside a synagogue to inside the sanctuary might end up in a sacred space on one special occasion. He or she would be in a shul or temple when marrying a fellow Jew who had also grown up in that predominately Jewish neighborhood, attended the same school, or worked in the same job.[6]

Jews in smaller town and cities had a more difficult job avoiding ongoing "commingling" and keeping their Judaism afloat in places where they were truly a minority group. Memoirists of that time and those places where there was no "Jewish street" have suggested that to survive "in the small towns of America, Jews organized weekly, monthly and yearly visits, tying one family or a few Jewish families in a small town to Jewish families in another small town." In some cases a communal barbecue was the way "you get to know other Jewish kids [as] Jewish families made their own Jewish life, because there wasn't enough in any one town." Elsewhere, creative parents organized dances for youngsters in their region. They would, "pick up whole groups of Jewish kids" from neighboring towns, and afterward the youngsters "would stay in the house of the [host] people there." One historian who has closely studied this social nexus has argued that "in a sense, the Jews of America's smaller communities . . . developed a sort of New World *landsmanshaft* [special relationship among people from the same shtetl] mentality in the interwar decades." The concern people had "for each other's welfare" cemented enduring relationships.[7]

Lee Shai Weissbach has also argued that in these environments "the establishment of congregations" was far more important than in the "larger communities in this country [where] Jews could interact with each other, as Jews, in a variety of settings. . . . If they felt the need for any specifically Jewish connections, even Jews who did not have strongly held religious convictions were inclined to affiliate with the local congregations." Meanwhile, social antisemitism here too also played its role in keeping these Jews together. As a Jew who grew up in the 1930s in Danville, Virginia has remembered, "We did not mix with the Christian community socially. In business affairs, in club work—very few Jews were ever taken into the Kiwanis. No Jews could join the country club, and there was only one country club." Or, as Weissbach has put it, "even though antisemitism never dominated Jewish life in small-town America . . . few members of small Jewish communities felt completely comfortable. Every interaction between Jews and non-Jews had a certain edge." Just like the big cities, prejudice of all sorts undermined the commingling that was anticipated.[8]

There was, however, one dimension to interwar American Judaism about which prognosticators were right on target. As the two decades proceeded, increasingly the religion widely practiced in this country's synagogues and the faith preached from its pulpits looked neither like the transplanted Orthodoxy of the prior generation nor the deritualized Reform Judaism of the late nineteenth century. Rather, a new American Judaism evolved that defied easy denominational labeling. A blending of traditions, ideas, and practices was palpable in the land. As one observer of the 1930s scene put it: "Orthodoxy, Conservatism and Reform are gradually coming together, flowing down different streams into a river yet to be, whose depth and reach will comprise them all."[9] But, notwithstanding this confluence of movements, the Jewish religion in this country proved to be somewhat less than "astir with activity" and "vigorously and earnestly alive."

Only one community in America differed substantially from this pessimistic pattern and possessed a robust and highly visible core of staunchly committed second-generation Jews, youngsters whose lives revolved around Jewish schools, clubs, synagogues, and other forms of religious institutional life. Though many of the Jews of Brooklyn between the two wars contributed their share to this national pattern of religious decline, within specific local neighborhoods, like Williamsburg, Brownsville, East New York, and Bensonhurst, there were groups of youths born in the United States who kept alive forms of that "extreme East European orthodoxy" that the *American Hebrew*'s editors believed was destined to be cast off as an unwanted "heritage of ghetto days."

Not incidentally, noticeable cohorts of very Orthodox immigrants to this country contributed more than their share to this pious polity. Notwithstanding the discriminatory laws of 1924, some east European Jews did get into this country in the 1920s through the 1940s. The most religious types often found their way to Brooklyn. But this pattern of dissociation from America's way of life with which the newcomers were most comfortable and that the next generation sustained in that outer borough was hardly approximated elsewhere in this country. Not even the Lower East Side, which during this era lost much of its Jewish population, carried as many of the "vestiges of Old World distinctiveness."[10]

Only toward the end of this era the larger American Jewish community began to arise from its stupor. Indeed, Jonathan D. Sarna has suggested that in the years immediately preceding the Second World War "significant changes" took place in "American Jewish education, religion, and culture as well as in American Zionism." Furthermore, he has contended that these positive circumstances constituted a veritable renaissance in Jewish life, which "set the stage" for even greater growth and expansion in the postwar era. While positive change started to take place in locales both near and nowhere near Brooklyn, this outer borough's neighborhood youth and their families—particularly in Flatbush, Crown Heights, and Borough Park—contributed more than their share to the beginnings of this reversal of Jewish fortunes. But, whatever the dimensions and early impact of these innovations, as we will presently see, the revivalists of the late 1930s had their jobs cut out for them as they sought to change American Judaism's direction.[11]

Sociological studies conducted during this era of crisis and decline had to have provided little comfort and encouragement to those concerned with Judaism's future. Every investigation revealed how profoundly disaffected so many American Jewish young people were with religious life. For example, those who looked into the lives and attitudes of Jewish college students, from upstate New York to New England to as far west as North Dakota, found only a negligible minority feeling that synagogue attendance was essential to their lives. Everywhere the younger generation was shown to be less interested than their elders in the "preservation of existing religious organizations."[12]

And, from "Easttown," an un-named city situated some sixty miles from New York City, came a similar word, in 1931–32, that "religion played a relatively small part in the life of the Jewish family as compared to the aspects of making a living, marrying and educating one's children," secularly. Meanwhile, another on-the-scene reporter in Stamford, Connecticut made it known that "only three times a year [did] the synagogue fill all its pews." Then it was a combination of nostalgia, awe over the Days of Judgment, and the desire to be among, and to be seen by, fellow Jews that brought families near the shul.[13]

Striking a comparably discordant note, a rabbi in Wilkes-Barre, Pennsylvania of just about the same time lamented that even those Jews who might attend Sabbath morning services on a somewhat regular basis did not stay around long. In order to attract "a considerable number of men to Sabbath services," he had to make sure that all religious activities were ended by 11 AM. "In the whole congregation of about 250 families," he explained, "there are not one half-dozen men who are not compelled to go to business on Saturday."[14]

By the way, Brooklyn and its synagogues did not do much better than the rest of the country, except, that is, in its circumscribed, Orthodox hotbeds. Memoirists who grew up in Brownsville have related that even though that community could boast of "eighty-three synagogues . . . and dozens of Hebrew and Yiddish schools" in a "less than two square mile" section of that neighborhood, few young men "continued their Jewish education or frequented synagogue with any regularity." A 1940 sociological survey revealed, along these same lines, that "only about nine percent of adult males in Brownsville attended synagogue with any regularity." Even on the High Holidays there were more people standing on the Jewish street outside the synagogue than praying within the sanctuary.[15]

Clearly, all through this country, the tenuous holds traditional folk religion had maintained over immigrants who lived in inner city hubs were broken as those born and raised in America resided in those new neighborhoods situated toward the outskirts of the city. And, as the next generation moved away both physically and spiritually from "downtown," relatively few new arrivals came off the boats to replace them. In "Medurbia," that city locale situated somewhere between the immigrant hubs of the past and suburbia of the future, acculturated Jews continued their efforts to advance in America, leaving behind them most commitments to the demands of Judaism. And during the Depression decade many of those who might have liked to be more observant found the pressure to work at a job—any job, even on the Sabbath—unavoidable. As one young man who grew up in the 1930s has recalled, "with the Depression, things changed with my father even in religious practice. Before, he never failed to take us to the synagogue every single Saturday. After the crash, he didn't seem to care anymore." Meanwhile, the synagogues that they now attended less and less "struggled under heavy financial burdens and mortgage debts."[16]

Significantly, this dilemma of religious decline afflicted all Jewish religious expressions, and almost to an equal degree. Rabbi Henry P. Mendes, president of the Orthodox Union said as much when he surveyed an unhappy national scene at the very beginning of this era. "It is perfectly true," he admitted, "that Sabbath desecration is painfully noticeable in the Middle-West, the West and the South, where Reform Judaism is so powerful. But it is also true in the east, where Orthodox Judaism has its strongholds." Some twenty years later, Orthodox Union lay leader Bert Lewkowitz took an even more jaundiced viewed of his own movement when he toured the country. He reported, with an angrier tone, that "Jews who do not observe the Sabbath, who do not take their children to any Hebrew school and do not give them a Jewish home atmosphere consider themselves Orthodox Jews because they have a seat on the High Holidays." These people surely evinced no commitment to sustaining the forms of Orthodoxy the older generation harbored.[17]

If matters were not bad enough, interwar religious life also suffered at the hands of other nominally Jewish institutions that competed with synagogues and Jewish schools for the allegiances of Jewish youngsters. In many Jewish communities nationwide the local YMHA or Jewish Community Center (JCC) was the neighborhood's central congregating place. These were places where Jews came to play, or to dance, or to do artwork, or to perform in theater troupes, all with folks of their own ethnic background. Its national leaders asserted that the young men and women who were its devotees also imbibed "the rich cultural heritage of the Jewish group" and were "prepar[ing]" themselves for "Jewish living in America." But, reportedly, "in many associations the Jewish phase of the program is made a side issue, and too little attention is paid to the development of the religious side." Critics charged, with much evidence to support their claims, that at most YMHAs "the term, Hebrew, seems to play a more important part in the name [of the organization] than in the work" of the Ys. The worst offenders were those centers that kept their "general offices, gymnasium, pool, lunch-counters, restaurants etc." open on the Sabbath day in an epoch where a canvass of some fifty-nine JCCs revealed that "develop[ment] in Jewish atmosphere" ranked at the bottom of the list of institutional objectives.[18]

For rabbis and other concerned religious Jews, who were often bedeviled by their inability to attract youngsters to their precincts, the JCCs were tarred as among the last places Jewish kids should go to if they were interested in Jewish content in their lives. Indeed, by 1936 Reform rabbi Louis I. Newman of Manhattan's Rodeph Shalom would characterize "the [Jewish] cultural and educational activities . . . of the Center" as "in a sense a side show to adorn the circus" of its "central aim," social and athletic activities. In 1939 Rabbi Simon Greenberg of Philadelphia went even further as he called upon his fellow Conservative rabbis— and his Orthodox and Reform counterparts too—to "display some leadership and get together" to "remove the non-religious Jewish Center . . . this palpable evil from our midst."[19]

These rabbis had weapons at their disposal to battle back against these offending institutions. Many Conservative and American Orthodox congregations offered Synagogue Center programs—a few Reform synagogues had Temple Center institutions that dated back to the late nineteenth century—predicated upon the "translation" of Jewish sacred space into a place "where all the members of the family would feel at home during the seven days of the week. There they could sing and dance and play," just like they could at a JCC. But here they would be congregating in a religious Jewish environment. Such, at least, was the viewpoint of Rabbi Mordecai M. Kaplan, the seer most closely associated with the concept and strategy that those who came to play, and to recreate, might be moved, over the long haul, to stay to pray.[20]

But, did the "magic" that Kaplan disciple Rabbi Israel Herbert Levinthal spoke of when he predicted that "many [who] will come for other purposes than to meet God . . . will be won from outside the door into the portals of the Synagogue proper" really work? Many contemporary rabbinical colleagues were unconvinced that Judaism ultimately gained from having sports and games on holy premises. Brooklyn's Rabbi Harry Weiss argued that the layman "has only a certain amount of energy at his command, and when, during the week, one attends a card party, one feels that one's duty towards the Congregation is fully performed and the Friday night and Saturday morning services are of necessity neglected."[21]

Some contemporaneous and troubling statistics on "synagogue attendance" seemed to bear out his reservations. A 1928 survey within United Synagogue congregations revealed that the "majority of [reporting] rabbis having experience with synagogue centers indicate that the results thus far have been negative or very slight . . . in augmenting attendance at the religious services." Still, Synagogue Center advocates persevered.[22]

In the meantime, leaders of each of America's Jewish expressions found common cause in developing other schemes to battle back the tide of religious indifference. The Synagogue Council of America was one such venue for cooperative efforts among Jewish denominations that ostensibly were competitors and antagonists. Although this national umbrella organization eventually devoted almost all its energies to speaking out "on social and international issues" that worried the Jewish people in America, when formed in 1926, it had Reform, Conservative, and Orthodox leaders working together to further common *religious* concerns.[23]

For example, in 1934 Rabbi David de Sola Pool of the Orthodox Union took the lead as chair of the Synagogue Council's Committee on Community Planning in fostering the building of local councils coast to coast to combat "isolation or competition" among the several movements engaged in outreach work. Along these same lines, from 1933–35 some of these same individuals worked together, both within and without the council, in an interdenominational Back to the Synagogue movement. The plan that officials of the Reform Union of American Hebrew Congregations, the Conservative United Synagogue, and the Orthodox Union hatched in "synagogue drive" conferences was to call the Sabbath of Return (*Shabbat Shuvah* of 1935) a "Loyalty Sabbath" (October 1935). The idea was to have "every Jew present and accounted for" in their houses of worship, just as Christians were then rallying their communicants to "reaffirm . . . faith in God and their fellow men" during the depths of the Great Depression.[24]

Orthodox enthusiasts for "a movement to unite all the forces of Jewry to combat religious indifference wherever it may exist" were sure to assert that they stood "with the first rank against all compromise that might undermine the principle and unalterable truth of the Torah." But clearly that stance did not preclude them from working with their theological opponents. Such a swipe at liberal Judaism was also of no concern to those Reform rabbis who appreciated any, and all, help they could get with their own flocks. It was within that cooperative spirit that Rabbi Samuel H. Markowitz of Fort Wayne, Indiana observed trenchantly in 1935 that "Orthodoxy, Conservatism and Reform are coming together, not because they are recognizing themselves in agreement, but because they face a common enemy, assimilation." An increasingly united Jewish front was on the rise since "the main current in Jewish thought and life today is assimilation."[25]

Jewish religious leaders of this era could resonate to calls for common cause because, notwithstanding their affiliation with often antagonistic movements, so many Conservative, American Orthodox, and even some Reform rabbis then ministered in congregations that, as the two decades proceeded, were starting to resemble each other in ritual and orientation. There was, in fact, a new American Judaism in progress in the land that defied easy denominational labeling. Certainly, the lines of demarcation setting off Orthodox Union from United Synagogue congregations were difficult to discern.

On this point Rabbi de Sola Pool was particularly candid when, in 1942, he observed that "American Orthodoxy no longer mirrors east European life. It is adapting itself to the American environment." (His words were similar to those of the *American Hebrew* editorialists who had predicted a decade or so earlier that a new American Judaism would be free of "every vestige of Old World distinctiveness.") De Sola Pool noted specifically that "innovations like the late Friday night evening service or the removal of the women's gallery, or the confirmation of girls or a community seder . . . would have shocked worshippers of a generation ago. Today such practices are accepted in numerous congregations." As he surveyed the national scene it was clear that "today it is increasingly difficult to discern any essential organic differences between Orthodoxy and Conservatism."[26]

Indeed, had he looked at the practices at Orthodox Union congregation Ahavath Achim of Atlanta, Georgia, he would have witnessed a Friday night service held not at sundown but at a time that permitted members to "attend the synagogue after work or before the theatre," where women were allowed to come down from the balcony and sit across the aisle from men. They took part in a service that featured "a choir, songs prayers, English readings and, of course, an English language sermon."[27]

Mixed seating and late Friday night services could also be found within the Orthodox Union's New York hub. Interestingly enough, at the Mosholu Jewish Center, in the North-East Bronx, congregants were comfortable during the year with seating patterns where men and women sat across an aisle from each other. But on the High Holidays men and women prayed together in the main sanctuary. The large number of Jews who attended the synagogue only on Rosh Hashanah and Yom Kippur, liked, or maybe demanded, this mode of operation.[28]

At the same time that Orthodox Union congregations were playing loose and fast with Orthodox strictures, there were United Synagogue associates, like Manhattan's the Jewish Center or, for that matter, the Young Israel of Brooklyn (both were affiliates until at least 1929), where religious activities did not deviate at all from halakhic norms. These so-called Modern Orthodox synagogues did not change the basic structure or timing of the prayers while they campaigned for the unaffiliated with a panoply of American-style social activities conducted before and after services.[29]

On balance, however, at most Orthodox Union synagogues, coast to coast, the rituals and observances that were proffered did not raise the eyebrows of its lay and rabbinic leaders in the New York home office. And, for that matter, when it came to their religious practices and outlooks, the clear majority of United Synagogue congregations were incipient Conservative affiliates. Still, there was a general fluidity in the land among all traditional-leaning Jewish religious groups that worked so hard—and often unsuccessfully—to create forms of services that might be attractive within their local communities or neighborhood.[30]

Initiatives within some Reform temples during the 1920s–1940s designed to bring some adored past synagogue practices back into their services also contributed to this sense of ongoing religious homogenization. Leaders of that Jewish movement also sought out formulas for attracting those second-generation Jews of east European descent who had left their parent's immigrant Orthodox shuls and had yet to find a modern synagogue to which they could relate. Even the most traditionally minded Reform congregations of this era had a long way to go in in-tegrating the most popular features of old-time liturgy and behavior into their rit-uals. Still, in those temples where boys celebrated their bar mitzvahs or where kiddush was recited or where congregations sang "traditional Jewish hymns" or where a rabbi blew the shofar on Rosh Hashanah (sometimes with the help of a "trumpet mouthpiece"), these Reform Jews unabashedly linked themselves with the most fondly remembered aspects of their family's Orthodox past. In so doing they started, said one of its supporters, to move "[Jewish religious] liberalism" away from its "purely intellectual or logical formulae," which would not "grip the hearts" of lay people who described themselves as "born of orthodox [*sic*] parents and raised in an orthodox [*sic*] atmosphere."[31]

Such advocates certainly had many battles ahead of them against those from within their own movement who early on were already carping that Reform Juda-ism was "as now indistinguishable from Conservatism." These critics openly feared that "the entire American Jewish community was becoming homogenized" and they were "apprehensive for their identity." Sometimes discord led Reform forces in the same city or neighborhood to harbor two or more Union of American Hebrew Congregations affiliates, each with a very different liturgy, ideological orientation, and appeal to varyious types of potential worshippers.[32]

The commonality of backgrounds—and sometimes long-standing friendships—among young rabbis who came on the scene in the 1920s–1940s likewise added to this perception of a new, all-inclusive American Judaism in the making. And their personal linkages arguably played a role in increasing the possibilities for common cause among those who struggled to rouse a somnam-bulant Jewish population. Like the flocks to whom they sought to minister, the majority of these leaders were second-generation east European Jews. Com-menting on who were the change makers in his movement, Rabbi B. Benedict Glazer of Detroit, the son of an immigrant Orthodox rabbi, observed that "the complexion of Reform Judaism" has been altered "in recent years" because of a "Reform rabbinate [that] is almost exclusively composed of the offspring of East European immigrants." Glazer was on target in his estimate of the presence of those of his Jewish ethnic background within his movement. A 1933 study of Hebrew Union College students revealed that over the prior quarter-century— actually from 1904–1929—more than seven out of every ten Reform rabbis in training in Cincinnati had parents who hailed from east Europe. "Twenty-eight percent had themselves been born there" and very likely came as youngsters, with their elders, to these shores. The Russian Jewish majority was undoubtedly even greater at the new Reform rabbinical school, the Jewish Institute of Reli-gion, which Rabbi Stephen S. Wise organized in New York in 1922. The latter group would also have much to say about the directions Reform would increas-ingly take.[33]

Conservative and American Orthodox rabbis, most of whom were also children of Russian and Polish newcomers, shared even more than their ethnic roots. Many of them grew up in the same neighborhoods—like the Lower East Side or that interwar Brooklyn Orthodox hotbed to which we will return presently. These future leaders received their early and secondary intensive Jewish education at the same schools. Moreover, the Rabbi Isaac Elchanan Theological Seminary, much to the dismay of Dr. Revel, served as the prime "feeder school" of students who eventually would be ordained at the Jewish Theological Seminary. Basically, every time the Orthodox institution showed signs of instability or impermanence, students, desirous of careers as American rabbis—not necessarily as Conservative rabbis—left Yeshiva and enrolled at the Jewish Theological Seminary. For Orthodoxy, this talent drain was particularly acute in the years 1940–1943 when, after Revel's death and no successor was quickly appointed, the word on Washington Heights streets was that the school's days were numbered. The classmates that stayed behind and weathered Yeshiva's financial and leadership crisis would enter the Modern Orthodox rabbinate. But they frequently kept close contact with Jewish Theological Seminary men when they entered the American Jewish communal field.

As significant, more than a few erstwhile Yeshiva men did more than just relate well to their Seminary brethren. In search of sustainable pulpit careers, they joined them in United Synagogue or Orthodox Union pulpits that featured mixed seating, late Friday night services, and other characteristics that fell outside the pale of religious strictures that Yeshiva faithful hoped to maintain.[34]

The truly fluid American Jewish religious scene of this era can be, thus, inventoried as follows: immigrant-generation Orthodox rabbis and their faith communities were dying out, except, as we will presently see, in some places in Brooklyn. And relatively few staunchly observant newcomers were taking their place. At the other extreme of the religious spectrum, the hegemonic days within their own movement of old-line Reform rabbis and their temples were beginning to be numbered. The countdown started in 1937. Then, that movement's Columbus Platform affirmed—albeit by the smallest of majorities among the rabbis at its annual conference—the importance of "the retention and development of such customs, symbols and ceremonies as possess inspirational value . . . in our worship and instruction," even as it spoke loudly of the need for Reform to support the Zionist endeavor and the Jewish national presence in Palestine.[35] Meanwhile, nominally Orthodox and Conservative congregations nationwide displayed comparable forms of ritual behavior with the goal of reaching the many children of east European immigrants who cared little for synagogue life. Graduates of both the Jewish Theological Seminary and the Rabbi Isaac Elchanan Theological Seminary led this uphill battle with Yeshiva men often in "Conservative" pulpits while Seminary ordainees served "Orthodox" constituencies. Fledgling Reform rabbis emerging from the new Jewish Institute of Religion and their groups added to this indistinct mix that made up the struggling American Judaism of the 1920s to the mid-1940s.

For Mordecai M. Kaplan, philosopher and leader of the incipient Reconstructionist movement, this lack of rigidity to Jewish religious life made it possible to dream of a future ideal situation where "one may be a Reconstructionist-Orthodox Jew, Reform Jew or Conservative Jew [with] the Reconstructionist part of the hyphen [representing] those goals that all Jews have in common." A united and engaged Jewish community was possible, if thoughtful leaders, freed from long-standing denominational fragmentation, would only seize the opportunity to be creative. "The so-called enlightened Orthodox or Conservative" amalgam held out unique promise "of evolving as complete a Jewish life as we can hope for in this country" addressing "Jewish life as a problem in social and spiritual adjustment." But, even this most optimistic and peripatetic Jewish thinker of his era, who traveled the country and mediated among Jews who sought to create synagogue environments attractive to young people, also knew that much needed to be done to reverse the endemic religious malaise that he observed in his peregrinations.[36]

There was, however, during this era of crisis and decline, a unique, deeply committed Orthodox community in Brooklyn that lived a religious existence fundamentally different from almost all other Jews then in the United States.[37] For the families that supported old-line yeshivas like Williamsburg's Mesifta Torah Vodaath—or its distaff counterpart, Bais Yaakov, ensconced in that same neighborhood—or Yeshiva Chaim Berlin of Brownsville, the 1920s through the mid-1940s was a time where faith commitments and levels of practice intensified rather than ossified. For these individuals strict observance of the Sabbath and the other demands of Jewish law were a given. And when they chose to pray publicly—and they did so quite often—they offered their devotions with great regard for past traditions. Old-world-style *shtibls* (storefront houses of worship) were common fare in those locales.[38] While Jews like these had great concerns that the "Torah is increasingly being forgotten by our youth and the best of our young people," they did not view Conservative, Reform, or even accommodating Americanized Orthodox congregations as in any way legitimate partners, worthy of emulation or common cause as colleagues addressing these troubling trends.[39]

Most important, when parents in these neighborhoods sent their youngsters to their local yeshivas or Orthodox schools for girls, they committed themselves and the next American-born generation to a religious culture and movement that aspired to sustain the religious civilization of eastern Europe on foreign American soil. These Jews were part of a transplanted civilization dedicated to the survival of "extreme East European orthodoxy" and possessed of the "heritage of ghetto days," to again quote the *American Hebrew*, that had largely died out elsewhere on this continent. In these schools the highest premium was placed on the transmission of Torah and Talmud learning while students were discouraged, as much as possible, from pursuing secular studies beyond the years prescribed by state law.

In an era when most American Jewish kids were taught, in public schools, to embrace American culture—and often did so without any Jewish education in their lives—in Brooklyn every effort was made to inculcate a studied separatism from the American way of life.

As fate would have it, the arrival on these shores, and the settlement in Brooklyn during the 1930s, of the first refugees from the terrors of Hitlerism strengthened the resolve and deepened the constituency for old-world-style institutions on American shores. These founders of the incipient so-called yeshiva world and Hasidic communities in America would pave the way for the emergence of an even more strident and separatist Orthodoxy in the post–World War II period.

If these early refugee communities presaged one new dimension of American Judaism after 1945, the interwar period, especially the latter years of the 1930s, also witnessed some discernible movement within the indigenous community—the "creativity" Kaplan called for—that augured better days for the faith in this country. Amidst an era of religious aridity and dissolution, some initial actions were taken to build new forms of communal life that could potentially attract the next generation's interest in its ancestral identity. For example, Jewish educational camping found its first firm footing with its formula of round-the-clock summer exposure for youngsters to the practices and ethos of Judaism in a fun-filled environment. Nationally based congregational youth movements also started to spring up, providing creative ideas, programs, and events for youngsters during the school year. However, the most impressive of these innovations was the Jewish day school movement. This system granted youngsters diversified Jewish learning, often with a cultural Zionist flavor, and a general studies curriculum that approximated, and, more important, rivaled the assimilatory public schools.[40]

At their core these institutions, argued one of their earliest proponents, were "Jewish Public School[s] . . . in contradistinction to Jewish Parochial Schools [like Torah Vodaath] which to the average Jewish mind savors of sectarianism." Rather, the system he believed in would raise "our sons"—and we will say also our daughters—"to be good Americans . . . [and] good and loyal and enlightened Jews." Max Kufeld, who for many years served simultaneously as general studies principal of Borough Park's Hebrew Institute (aka Etz Chayim Yeshiva), Flatbush Yeshivah, and Shulamith School for Girls articulated this mission statement in 1924. Similar sentiments informed activities at the Crown Heights Yeshiva, which from its start in the 1920s also offered this innovative dual curriculum education. These efforts set the stage—if they did not offer models—for several comparable initiatives in the 1930s. An early banner year for this movement was 1937 when in Manhattan, in Far Rockaway, New York, and in Brookline, Massachusetts the Ramaz School, the Hebrew Institute of Long Island, and the Maimonides School were founded.[41]

What these schools ultimately represented was a communal recognition that, even at its best, the Jewish supplementary school system was ultimately unsuccessful in keeping many Jewish youths close to their religion. The Talmud Torah's afternoon and weekend hours were, in the end, no match for the week-long hold that public schools, those temples of Americanization, maintained on Jewish youngsters. And, although fewer than eight thousand students would be enrolled in day schools as of 1940, a new tradition in Jewish education was estab-lished before World War II that would be an all-important component in the quest for the survival of Jewish identity after 1945.[42]

The calculus of American Jewish religious life changed dramatically after the Second World War. The arrival of refugee and survivor cohorts added both num-bers and, often, an uncommon level of dynamism to Judaism's life in this country. Although not all these newcomers were observant or Orthodox, those who were practiced what the faith preached fervently and with great stridency. The intensity of their commitments—and their not so subtle criticism of all Jews who came be-fore them—was predicated upon their vision that they were the bearers of the only authentic Orthodoxy and were thus alone the preservers and perpetuators of Juda-ism. Ultimately their uncompromising positions would permeate the existent ac-commodating Orthodox camp and undermine its willingness to find common cause with other Jewish religious groups on communitywide issues.[43]

Essentially, those so-called right-wing Orthodox elements embraced more than just the "vestiges of the Old World distinctiveness." They hallowed those "externalities which constitute the heritage of ghetto days," those elements of the "extreme East European orthodoxy" that the *American Hebrew*'s writers, back in 1924, predicted and hoped would not be part of the future American scene.

Meanwhile the indigenous- communities—those of east European extraction who were well into their third generation—suburbanized. Along the "crabgrass frontier," affiliation with the synagogue of their choice became an American value that many Jews wanted to uphold. As parents of baby boomers reacted to the large-scale commingling that took place among their kids in their religiously di-verse new hometowns, it became essential for them to identify with that touch-stone institution, the synagogue. Jews joined suburban Conservative, Modern Orthodox, and Reform congregations en masse, with the United Synagogue expe-riencing the most dramatic growth.[44]

The youth-oriented institutions that made their early appearances in the de-cades before the Second World War—like camps, synagogue youth groups, and, of course, day schools—were also called upon to play major roles in stemming the tide of assimilation in an ever more accepting American society. But, even as rab-bis and concerned lay leaders of all Jewish expressions battled against common social and cultural foes, they also started to struggle—much more than before—against each other for primacy among post–World War II Jews. After 1945 the beginning of the ideological rigidity and competition that would characterize the last years of the twentieth century increasingly became a communal reality. The story of this disengagement and the end of possibilities for an all-inclusive

American Judaism would form an important chapter in the contemporary history of Jewish life in the United States.

NOTES

1. "Landlocked in America," *American Hebrew,* September 26, 1924, 521.

2. Julian Morgenstern, "American Judaism in the Year 2,000," *American Hebrew,* September 26, 1924, 524, 560.

3. Stephen S. Wise, "The Bond of Jewish Oneness," *American Hebrew,* September 26, 1924, 520, 583.

4. Cyrus Adler, "Not Concerned Over Future," *American Hebrew,* September 26, 1924, 520.

5. "The Onward March of Judaism," *American Hebrew,* October 10, 1924, 673, 676.

6. On informal neighborhood associations preserving Jewish identities in interwar New York, see Deborah Dash Moore, *At Home in America: Second Generation New York Jews* (New York, 1981), especially 19–60. On the tensions between Jews and other ethnic groups in that city's neighborhoods, see Ronald Bayor, *Neighbors in Conflict: The Irish, Germans, Jews, and Italians of New York City, 1929–1941* (Baltimore, 1978), especially 150–63. On the varying forms of social antisemitism that limited Jewish integration, see Digby Baltzell, *The Protestant Establishment: Aristocracy and Caste in America* (New York, 1964).

7. Howard Simons, *Jewish Times: Voices of the American Jewish Experience* (Boston, 1988), especially 4–5, 207–9, 225. See also Lee Shai Weissbach, *Jewish Life in Small-Town America: A History* (New Haven, 2005), 279.

8. Simons, *Jewish Times,* 225; Weissbach, *Jewish Life in Small-Town America,* 157, 278.

9. Samuel M. Gup, "Currents in Jewish Religious Thought and Life in America in the Twentieth Century," *Central Conference of American Rabbis Yearbook* (hereafter *CCARYB*) 41 (1931): 301.

10. On the impact the interwar new arrivals made upon the indigenous Orthodox community in Brooklyn, see George Kranzler, *Williamsburg : A Jewish Community in Transition* (New York, 1961), 18–19 and passim. For statistics on how the new Brooklyn neighborhoods superseded the Lower East Side as a hub of Orthodox Jewish life, see Jeffrey S. Gurock, "Jewish Continuity and Commitment in Interwar Brooklyn," in Ilana Abramovitch and Sean Galvin, eds., *Jews of Brooklyn* (Hanover, 2001), 240, note 8.

11. Jonathan D. Sarna, "Reimagining American Judaism: From Declension to Revival," paper delivered at the conference "Imagining the American Jewish Community," Jewish Theological Seminary, March 23, 2004, 5.

12. Nathan Goldberg, "Religious and Social Attitudes of Jewish Youth in the U.S.A.," *Jewish Review* 1 (1943): 146–49.

13. Langer, "The Jewish Community of Easttown, 1931–1932," unpublished abstract of thesis written at the Graduate School for Jewish Social Work, New York, 1932, on file at the Library of the American Jewish Historical Society; Samuel Koenig, "The Socio-economic Structure of an American Jewish Community," in Isacque Graeber and

Stuart Henderson Brit, eds., *Jews in a Gentile World: The Problem of Anti-Semitism* (New York, 1942), 227, 229.

14. Louis M. Levitsky," The Story of an Awakened Community," *Reconstructionist* 1, no. 20 (February 7, 1936): 9.

15. Gerald Sorin, *The Nurturing Neighborhood: The Brownsville Boys Club and Jewish Community in Urban America, 1940–1990* (New York, 1990), 15–16.

16. On the so-called Spiritual Depression, see Beth S. Wenger, *New York Jews and the Great Depression* (New Haven, 1996), 166–73. For the young man's recollections, see Joseph A. D. Sutton, *Magic Carpet: Aleppo-in-Flatbush, the Story of a Unique Ethnic Community* (New York, 1979), 124, quoted ibid., 173–74.

17. Henry Pereira Mendes, "Orthodox Judaism (the Present)," *Jewish Forum* 3.1 (January 1920): 35; Bert Lewkowitz, "The Future of Judaism as a Layman Visions It," *Jewish Forum* 23.10 (December 1940): 177.

18. On the great growth of JCCs in the 1920s–1930s, see the *Jewish Center* (hereafter *JC*) (September 1942): 6. On the vision articulated by its national leadership about the JCC's Jewish mission, see Louis Kraft, *A Century of the Jewish Community Center (1854–1954)* (New York, 1954), 20–21. For criticism of what actually went on in these institutions, see Tobias Roth, "Jewish and Religious Elements," *JC* (October 1922): 29; Mordecai Soltes, "A Program of Jewish Activities for Jewish Community Centers," *JC* (September 1925): 42–45; and Samuel Leff, "Health and Physical Education in Jewish Community Centers," *JC* (September 1930): 14, 18.

19. Louis I. Newman," The Organization of American Jewry," *CCARYB* 46 (1936): 242; Simon Greenberg, "President's Message," *Proceedings of the Rabbinical Assembly of the Jewish Theological Seminary of America* (1939): 33.

20. The idea of a synagogue center dates back to the incipient Temple Center movement that began under Reform Jewish auspices in America. See David Kaufman, *Shul with a Pool:The Synagogue Center in American Jewish History* (Hanover, 1999), 10–49. On the Kaplan version of the "seven day a week synagogue" metaphor as it was instituted in his Jewish Center synagogue on New York's West Side in the late 1910s to early 1920s, see Jacob J. Schacter, "A Rich Man's Club?: The Founding of the Jewish Center," in Yaakov Elman and Jeffrey S. Gurock, eds., *Hazon Nahum: Studies in Jewish Law, Thought and History Presented to Dr. Norman Lamm on the Occasion of His Seventieth Birthday* (New York, 1997), 693, 713.

21. Israel Herbert Levinthal, "The Value of the Center to the Synagogue," *United Synagogue Recorder* (June 1926): 19; Harry Weiss, "The Synagogue Center," *Problems of the Jewish Ministry* (New York, 1927), 131–33.

22. Alter F. Landesman, "Synagogue Attendance (A Statistical Survey)," *Proceedings of the Twenty-Eighth Annual Conference of the Rabbinical Assembly of the Jewish Theological Seminary* (1928): 439.

23. On how the functions of the Synagogue Council of America has been remembered, especially the omission of its decidedly religious work among denominational groups, see Sidney L. Regner, "Synagogue Council of America," *Encyclopaedia Judaica* (CD Rom edition).

24. For reports on Synagogue Council activities, see *CCARYB* 44 (1934): 48–50. See also, on the "Sabbath of Return" idea, *Orthodox Union* (August 1935): 1, 7; and Minutes

of the Administrative Council [Orthodox Union], January 11, 1934, 1, files at the Library of the American Jewish Historical Society.

25. On the Orthodox Jewish mixed message on the question of cooperation with liberal Judaism's leaders, see *Orthodox Union* (April 1935): 14 and (February 1935): 1. On a Reform rabbi's view of the situation, see Samuel M. Markowitz, "Discussion," *CCA-RYB* 41 (1931): 336–37.

26. David de Sola Pool, "Judaism and the Synagogue," in Oscar Janowsky, ed., *The American Jew: A Composite Portrait* (New York, 1942), 50–54.

27. On the history of Atlanta's Ahavath Achim, including the religious behavior patterns of its members, see Michael J. Safra, "America's Challenge to Traditional Jewish Worship: Changes in Atlanta's Synagogues, 1867–1972," , 64–65, Honors Thesis, University of Michigan, 1997; Kenneth Stein, *A History of Ahavath Achim* (Atlanta, 1978), 44.

28. On the nature of synagogue life at the Mosholu synagogue, see Gurock interview with Rabbi Herschel Schacter, July 22, 1997, noted in Gurock, *From Fluidity to Rigidity: The Religious Worlds of Conservative and Orthodox Jews in Twentieth-Century America,* David W. Belin Lecture in American Jewish Affairs, the Frankel Center for Judaic Studies, University of Michigan, 1998, 28.

29. On early Jewish Center involvement with the United Synagogue and its self-definition as Orthodox, see Jeffrey S. Gurock and Jacob J. Schacter, *A Modern Heretic and a Traditional Community: Mordecai M. Kaplan, Orthodoxy, and American Judaism* (New York, 1998). On the Young Israel of Brooklyn's affiliation, see National Council of Young Israel, *Annual Convention:5694/1934* (brochure on file at the Library of the American Jewish Historical Society), 48. See also *United Synagogue Recorder* 3.2 (April 1923): 11.

30. For a full discussion of the ritual patterns of congregations affiliated with both national Jewish religious organizations, see Gurock, *From Fluidity to Rigidity,* 16–32.

31. On the introduction of traditional forms of worship into Reform congregations during this period, see *CCARYB* 36 (1926): 314; 50 (1940): 172–74; 51 (1941): 102–4. See also Leon Jick, "The Reform Synagogue," in Jack Wertheimer, ed., *The American Synagogue: A Sanctuary Transformed* (Cambridge, 1987), 100–1. For a statement reflective of what potential congregants, born of east European Jewish stock, wanted out of Reform synagogue life, see Meyer Jacobstein, "Mobilizing the Laymen," *CCARYB* 32 (1922): 243–50.

32. For sources on criticisms within the Reform camp that worried about an all-embracing "native American Judaism," see Samuel Cauman, *Jonah Bondi Wise* (New York, 1959), 175; and Felix Levy, "President's Message," *CCARYB* 46 (1936): 163–64, where a supporter of changes within Reform Judaism toward traditionalism identifies his opponents' allegations that he and his compatriots were rendering Reform "indistinguishable" from Conservatism. For an example of a community where Reform forces were split, see these studies of 1930s Detroit: Sidney Bolkovsky, *Harmony and Dissonance: Voices of Jewish Identity in Detroit, 1914–1967* (Detroit, 1991), 225–29; and Leon Fram, "The Saga of Rabbi Leon Fram, Dean of the Michigan Rabbinate: An Interview on His Seventy-fifth Birthday," *Michigan Jewish History* 11.2 (November 1970): 12–28.

Additionally, the capture by traditionalists with the Reform camp of the hearts and minds of its movement's Jews was gradual. See, for a study that points out the lack of observance of traditional rituals in Reform Jewish households in the 1930s, Union of American Hebrew Congregations, Commission on Research, *Reform Judaism in the Large Cities: A Survey* (New York, 1931), 10, 47–51.

33. B. Benedict Glazer, "The Spirit and Character of the American Jewish Community," *CCARYB* 50 (1940): 326. For a brief biographical sketch of Glazer, see *New York Times,* May 16, 1952, 23. On the background of Glazer's Orthodox rabbi father, Simon, see *Encyclopaedia Judaica* 7:618. For a statistical study of the ethnic background of Reform rabbinical students at Hebrew Union College, see Abraham N. Franzblau, "A Quarter-Century of Rabbinical Training at the Hebrew Union College," mimeograph (Cincinnati, 1933). No comparable study of the then fledgling New York Reform rabbinical school exists.

34. On the commonality of neighborhood and educational background of Yeshiva and Seminary students during this era, see Gurock, "Jewish Continuity and Commitment in Interwar Brooklyn," 236–39. On Yeshiva as a "feeder school" for the Jewish Theological Seminary, see Jeffrey S. Gurock, "Yeshiva Students at the Jewish Theological Seminary," in Jack Wertheimer, ed., *Tradition Renewed: A History of the Jewish Theological Seminary* (New York: Jewish Theological Seminary, 1997), 473–513.

35. It may be noted, with reference to the pace of the more traditional form of Reform taking over from its classical Reform predecessor, that on the ideological issue of Zionism, which won out in Columbus, the position triumphed by one vote. It would take time for that position to win out totally within the denomination. Still, arguably, the momentum was in that direction. See *CCARYB* 48 (1937): 418–22.

36. For a discussion of Kaplan's ideas on what we might today call transdenominationalism, see Deborah Musher, "Reconstructionist Judaism in the Mind of Mordecai M. Kaplan: The Transformation from a Philosophy to a Religious Denomination," *American Jewish History* 86.4 (December 1998): 415, which contains the quote from Kaplan's *Journal,* vol. 24, April 29, 1968. I am suggesting that this unrealized hope was closest to reality during the 1920s–1940s. On Kaplan's frequent tours of the United States and his advice to those who would abide by his words, see his accounts in his *Journal,* vols. 3, 4, and 10 (1925, 1928, 1929, 1942).

37. While pockets of profound observance and strict religious ideology could be found in some other parts of the metropolis and in places like Baltimore and New Haven, no American community possessed such an intense Orthodox presence as Brooklyn communities. Using commitment to old-line yeshiva education as a barometer to east European ways, Brooklyn was home in the 1920s–1940s to five such schools, with Torah Vodaath being the largest and most comprehensive. As of 1933, over 1,350 boys were attending such elementary schools in that borough as opposed to less than 900 in Manhattan's Lower East Side. Also, as of 1940, some 1,000 students attended Torah Vodaath at a time when nationally only 7,700 students received any sort of Orthodox yeshiva education. During this time period, Baltimore and New Haven also had yeshivas whose approach to American life corresponded to that of the Brooklyn Orthodox epicenter. For studies of this group of intensely committed Jews, see Kranzler, *Williamsburg,* 141; William Helmreich, *The World of the Yeshiva: An Intimate Portrait of Orthodox*

Jewry (New York, 1982), 26–37, which also notes the yeshivas outside of Brooklyn; Meir Kimmel, "The History of Yeshivat Rabbi Chaim Berlin," *Shevely Hahinuch* (Fall 1948): 51–54; Alter Landesman, *Brownsville: The Birth, Development, and Passing of a Jewish Community in New York* (New York, 1969), 234–35; Jacob I. Hartstein, "Jewish Community Elementary Parochial Schools," unpublished thesis, circa 1934, Yeshiva University Archives, table 1, 14; and Alvin Irwin Schiff, *The Jewish Day School in America* (New York, 1966), 39, 69.

38. For the best study of Williamsburg, an idiosyncratic community for the interwar period by virtue of its high level of Orthodox practice, see Kranzler, *Williamsburg,* especially 17–18, 164–67, 214–17.

39. For an example from the 1930s of a staunchly committed Orthodox Jew's attitude toward noncooperation with Conservative and Reform Jews and their problems with accommodationist Orthodox activities like late Friday night forums that seemed to emulate what liberal Jews were doing, see *Ha-Pardes* (December 1930): 6.

40. Sarna has argued forcefully for the recognition of camping, youth movements, adult educational initiatives, Jewish publishing, etc., in addition to the growth in popularity of Jewish day school education as among the signs of an incipient "revival" of American Judaism during an era of declension. See Jonathan D. Sarna, *American Judaism: A History* (New Haven, 2004), 267–71.

41. Max Kufeld, "The Jewish Institute of Boro Park," *Jewish Forum* (April 1924): 268–69. See also, on the founding of these modern schools, Moses I. Shulman, "The Yeshivath Etz Hayim–Hebrew Institute of Boro Park," *Jewish Education* (Fall 1948): 47; Noah Nardi, "A Survey of Jewish Day Schools in America," *Jewish Education* (September 1944): 22–23; *Yeshiva of Flatbush Golden Jubilee Commemorative Volume, 1917–1977* (Brooklyn, 1977), 31, which notes Kufeld's role in a number of local schools; Jeffrey S. Gurock, ed., *Ramaz: School, Community, Scholarship, and Orthodoxy* (Hoboken, 1989), 40–82; Seth Farber, *An American Orthodox Dreamer: Rabbi Joseph B. Soloveitchik and Boston's Maimonides School* (Hanover, 2004), 46–57.

42. The estimated figure of seventy-seven hundred students—mostly boys enrolled in thirty-five day schools and yeshivas in the United States and Canada—utilized by Schiff, *The Jewish Day School in America,* 49, runs the educational gamut from Torah Vodaath-type schools to the day school institutions. It is impossible to determine the precise percentages among school-types.

43. For the best analysis of the arrival and progress of those who fled the terrors of Hitlerism, which notes the diversity of their religious identities and affiliations, see Helmreich, *Against All Odds: Holocaust Survivors and the Successful Lives They Made in America* (New York, 1992). For a study that takes significant note of the impact of the arrival of these highly Orthodox newcomers upon the indigenous community, see Haym Soloveitchik, "Rupture and Rapture: the Transformation of Contemporary Orthodoxy," *Tradition* 28.4 (1994): 63–120. For a discussion of a turning point moment in Orthodoxy Judaism's move away from common cause with other Jewish expression, the 1956 demand from right-wing circles that the Orthodox Union and other Modern Orthodox organizations leave the Synagogue Council of America, which then dealt only with nonreligious issues, see Jack Wertheimer, *A People Divided: Judaism in Contemporary America* (New York, 1992), 12, 178.

44. For contemporaneous accounts of the so-called Jewish revival in suburbia, see Nathan Glazer, *American Judaism* (Chicago, 1957), 107–28; Will Herberg, *Protestant-Catholic-Jew: An Essay in American Jewish Sociology* (Garden City, NY, 1955); and Marshall Sklare, *Conservative Judaism: An American Religious Movement* (Glencoe, IL, 1955).

5

TRIUMPH, ACCOMMODATION, AND RESISTANCE: AMERICAN JEWISH LIFE FROM THE END OF WORLD WAR II TO THE SIX-DAY WAR

RIV-ELLEN PRELL

Following World War II, American culture was strikingly different from the one in which Americans lived during the 1930s and the war years of the early 1940s. This emerging culture was both more urban and suburban than in previous decades. New media, television in particular, shaped Americans' understanding of the world around them. The parents of baby boom children turned increasingly to "experts" in magazines and on television to learn how to live happier lives, and how to raise better "adjusted" boys and girls. Religion and spirituality became a matter of far greater concern to adults than in the previous decades. A new generation of young writers and social scientists wrote for wider audiences about the problems that beset an increasingly affluent society. Virtually every one of these cultural transformations not only affected Jews as well as Christians, but Jews were among the key actors in these cultural changes. Television comics of the 1950s marveled at the fact that what they regarded as a sense of humor that was uniquely Jewish spoke to millions of Americans on popular variety shows like *Ed Sullivan* or *Your Show of Shows*.[1] The most influential spiritual writer of the 1950s was a young rabbi who merged religion and psychology to guide people on the path to "peace of mind."[2] And Jewish characters were central to some of the most praised and popular novels of the 1950s written by Jewish children of immigrants.[3]

The United States was changing not only because of the economic success that followed its wartime victory, but because it was an increasingly diverse nation.

Racial discrimination and civil rights activism both persisted and grew. However, the descendants of immigrants once thought of as unfit for citizenship because they were not Protestant, Jews among them, were moving to the center of American life. Jews were changing too. The majority of them were now native born and members of the middle class; their primary language was English, and many felt that to be a good Jew was equivalent to being a good American.

Many scholars look back upon the period from 1945 to 1967 as one of strong consensus among American Jews who appeared to share similar views on aspirations for their families, on their responsibility to Jews both within and outside the United States, and on politics. They appeared to be increasingly confident of their place in America and the waning of antisemitism that had shaped the consciousness of immigrants and their children in the 1930s.

These scholars then are certainly correct that many Jews shared a particular view of their lives in America. However, there are other stories to tell about American Jewish life after World War II. The crucial twenty year period from 1945 to 1967 was in fact one of remarkable realignment in American Jewish culture. Virtually every domain of Jewish life underwent changes with far-reaching consequences. American Jews' religion, politics, social class, occupations, family, and where and how they lived changed during these decades. These new modes of life generated the cultural transformation that became only truly apparent in the 1970s. The postwar period, then, is best understood as a dynamic moment when the fundamental definitions of what it meant to be an American Jew were worked out in the new synagogues, living rooms, organizations, and political debates of the time. How Jews emerged from the devastations of World War II in the 1940s to enter a utopian moment in 1967, which led to a reshaping of American Jewish life, is a more complex story than most scholars have assumed.

POSTWAR OPTIMISM

The triumphant optimism not only for American Jews, but for a great swath of the American people, marked the uniqueness of this era. Arthur Goren, an American Jewish historian, was hardly alone in claiming that this period was "a golden era" for American Jewry who shared in the triumph of their country conquering German fascism. In addition, between 1946 and 1948 they raised more than $330 million to resettle European Jews and to direct those efforts to the newly declared State of Israel.[4] With the war barely over, American Jews demonstrated their ability and willingness to meet the needs of Jews in many corners of the world.

Jews, in addition, found themselves moving ever closer to the mainstream of American life through economic mobility by joining the middle class in great numbers following the war. After the war Judaism was included in what Will Herberg, a scholar of religion, called America's "triple melting pot" of Catholics,

Protestants, and Jews.[5] This degree of inclusion was unprecedented in American Jewish history.

Jews' optimism might also have been evident in their moving into new and different areas. Most Jews lived in the Northeast in urban neighborhoods surrounded by other Jews and a little more distant from Catholic neighbors before World War II. After the war they began to move to the West and the South of the United States as well as to suburbs in the Northeast and Midwest. In their new neighborhoods, now surrounded by Protestants, they built and joined synagogues in numbers no one would have previously predicted.

Despite these shared attitudes, social class, and patterns of Jewish life, the postwar period was as much about difference and conflict among Jews as it was about a shared consensus. A closer look at Jewish life certainly reveals optimism but also anxiety about an American Jewish future. Debates over how to shape that future are key to understanding Jewish life in America after the war. With Europe no longer the anchor of Jewish life, antisemitism no longer perceived as the ultimate barrier to acculturation, and the urban neighborhood no longer the primary address for Jewish life, what and who would be Jewish was at the center of a developing American Jewish culture. Jews disagreed as much as they agreed; their consensus was real, but at best partial.

THE CENTER OF GRAVITY

Before the war Europe provided the center of gravity of Jewish experience. The majority of America's Jews were of eastern European descent (Ashkenazim). Europe was, therefore, the center from which they and their family had originally hailed. It was the source of their language, music, food, Jewish practices, and other "authentically" Jewish cultural features. Though immigrants and their children rejected many of those practices, none doubted their authenticity.

For American Jewish leaders—educators, rabbis, scholars, writers, and political activists—eastern Europe was all the more so the source of all things Jewish. European academies of Jewish learning (yeshivot) were the best training ground for rabbis and teachers, some of whom led American Jewish institutions. For centuries they viewed American Jewry, in contrast to European Jewry, as immature because of the absence of such institutions.

While some European Jewish leaders and scholars escaped the Nazi death machine, with the destruction of one-third of world Jewry the Jewish center of gravity for American Jews was forever altered. At the end of the war, Palestine's future as a Jewish nation was very much in question. Therefore the Jewish world's axis was shifting in only one direction, toward North America.

In the midst of World War II the significance of this change was becoming part of the consciousness of American Jewish leaders. Harry Schneiderman, editor of the *American Jewish Year Book*, noted what lay ahead in addition to the needs of the war's survivors:

> In the United States, the only important Jewish community of the world left unscathed by the direct effects of the Hitler war, there were indications . . . of a growing awareness of both the challenge and the opportunity presented by the community's . . . immunity from the plague which has virtually destroyed Jewish life in Europe. American Jews are realizing that they have been spared for a sacred task—to preserve Judaism and its cultural, social and moral values."[6]

Robert Gordis, the editor of *Conservative Judaism*, observed in its first issue, in January 1945, the more direct implications for American Jewry. The war, he noted, had "catapulted American Jewry into a position of leadership and responsibility undreamt of twenty-five years ago, for which we are far from adequately prepared."[7]

At the same time, Jews felt triumphant about America's victory and appreciative to be part of it. Arthur Hertzberg, a young rabbi at the time, captured the complex position of many American Jews at the war's end.

> We wanted to be thought of as part of the brave, undaunted, victorious America. We were saying Kaddish as Jews, and we were glad for the condolences from the rest of America, but we wanted our neighbors to think of us as wrapped, together with them, in an American flag, preferably with the slogan Don't Tread on Me written over it.[8]

American Jews, in Hertzberg's memory, felt more American as a result of a war in which five hundred thousand Jews served in a victorious military that defeated the enemy of the Jews and Americans.[9]

Ordinary Jews accepted responsibility for America as a new center of Jewish life. Their Jewish communities throughout the United States raised funds for world Jewry, including the resettlement of displaced persons, those who were left homeless by the war in Europe. In 1945 these campaigns produced $57.3 million. In 1948 that amount totaled $205 million, 80 percent of which went directly to refugee resettlement in Israel.[10]

By the early 1950s American Jews' contributions to overseas efforts significantly dwindled. Jewish philanthropy in part shifted to building synagogues, religious schools, and hospitals, all institutions that addressed the needs of Jews. For many decades that followed American Jews debated what were the most important needs of a viable and growing community.

URBAN AND SUBURBAN

If Europe had been the center of the Jewish world for American, Ashkenazic Jews, then urban life was its American center. For at last six decades prior to World War II most of America's Jews lived in a handful of northeastern states. More than 46 percent of them lived in the state of New York. Another 28 percent lived in Massachusetts, Pennsylvania, New Jersey, and Illinois.[11]

The largely Jewish and predominantly working-class neighborhoods of these states were the destination for immigrant Jews who once lived in their ghettos. Though Jews lived among other ethnic and minority groups (e.g., Italians and African Americans), in their neighborhoods, it was the predominance of other Jews that most residents recalled. Stores that catered to Jewish needs became a version of a Jewish civic square along with synagogues and other establishments.

For example, Boston's Jewish neighborhoods, particularly Roxbury and Dorchester, counted about seventy thousand Jews as residents in the 1940s and 1950s. They had forty synagogues, only two of which were non-Orthodox. Sixty kosher butchers and shops, bakeries, pharmacies, and stores lined Blue Hill Avenue, a main thoroughfare. A memoirist recalled the local G&G Delicatessen as the center of life on the avenue. He wrote, "On the tables of the cafeteria Talmudic jurisprudence sorted out racing results, politics, the stock market and the student could look up from his 'desk' to leer at young girls sipping cream soda under the immense wings of their mother."[12] Mark Mirsky captured this Jewish neighborhood space by linking "secular" topics like politics and racing to sharp "Talmudic logic." He glossed the delicatessen table as the *shtendar*, or the study desk. If the study hall was no longer the primary gathering spot for Jewish men, the delicatessen was a social substitute.

Brownsville, a neighborhood of Brooklyn, New York was 95 percent Jewish. No wonder that Orthodox inhabitants dubbed it and its eighty-three synagogues the "Jerusalem of America." A 1940 survey revealed that only about 9 percent of men attended those synagogues with any regularity, and no young men between the ages of sixteen and twenty-four admitted to having spent any time in a synagogue.[13] Therefore urban Jewish neighborhoods before the war were paradoxically very "religious" for older men and still quite Jewish, if secular, for others.

Because of the density of Jewish neighborhoods, a Jew was no less Jewish for joining or not joining a particular organization, whether it was a synagogue or a women's group. In 1954 a social worker captured that sensibility. "The places we lived were ghettos, no matter how well concealed. . . . In those days we were the majority in our community and we reacted as a majority. We were not hyperconscious of our Jewishness. Things Jewish were ingrained in our lives."[14]

Not surprisingly, then, Jewish neighborhood life was as likely to be cast as nurturing as it was prisonlike for the younger generation who led an exodus away from Jewish neighborhoods. One writer for the popular Jewish magazine

Commentary wrote candidly on her feelings about the Bronx when she was a student at Hunter College in 1942. "Everything I thought and did was part of an effort to get away from the family, the neighborhood, the whole city if such a thing was possible."[15] That flight was to fundamentally change American Jewish life.

SUBURBANIZATION AND A NEW JEWISH GEOGRAPHY

American Jews began living in suburbia in the early part of the twentieth century. However, the pace of suburbanization increased for them, as it did for most Americans, following World War II. The GI Bill and other federal loans made the purchase of housing affordable in specified residential areas in the United States. In the 1950s America's Jewish suburban population doubled, with Jews suburbanizing at four times the rate of non-Jewish Americans.[16] Young Jewish families moved into different types of suburbs, some long established and others that were built in the postwar housing boom. New York was the first site of Levittown, a new housing development that made affordable suburban life for a generation of young white families. However, its developers spun off clones in Philadelphia, New Jersey, and beyond where, by the late 1950s, about 14 percent of residents were Jews at a time when they constituted 3 percent of the nation's population.[17] Highland Park, Illinois, a suburb of Chicago, developed in the 1850s, became a desirable suburb by the 1920s for a small number of affluent Jews. In the 1940s Highland Park became attractive to Chicago's young middle-class residents, and by the 1950s one of every three families who lived there was Jewish.[18]

Jews moved not only to suburbs, but from the Northeast to the West and the South.[19] Los Angeles and Miami and their suburbs developed an American Jewish culture that was less dominated by a Jewish establishment than New York or Chicago.

The city in which Jews suburbanized the most slowly was Manhattan, where the Jewish population remained stable throughout the 1950s, likely because occupations and industries that Jews pursued tended to be in the city. In the 1960s the Jewish population declined by 41 percent. Jews left Manhattan for suburbs and other regions of the country, but by the 1970s it stabilized again.[20]

Jews unquestionably lost a sense of comfort by leaving an area where neighbors, kin, shop owners, and coworkers were all Jewish. Many, however, also believed they were encountering America in a new way. Sam Gordon, the subject of a study of postwar family life, left the Bronx and purchased his first home on Long Island in 1952. He recalled looking across the sand at his new lot and thinking that he "was seeing democracy for the first time, democracy un-tempered as it was meant to be."[21] For Gordon, this new frontier away from the city constituted a freedom he had never before experienced.

Some suburban realtors and developers also insidiously insisted on Jewish "difference" in the way they managed the suburban housing market. Suburbs were racially segregated; at the same time many also were religiously divided. Realtors urged people identified and identifiable as Jewish to live near synagogues as a code to enforce "ethnic" or "religious" boundaries. Many suburban neighborhoods then became religiously homogeneous, a choice some embraced and others resisted. In 1958 Alan Wood (a pseudonym), for example, recounted his attempt to sell his family home in a new suburb of Long Island, New York. He discovered that despite the efforts of local ministers and rabbis to encourage their congregants to live near one another, some buyers who were Christians were not shown homes in neighborhoods that had a majority of Jewish home owners and that other areas remained "restricted" to Jewish buyers to ensure Christian dominance.[22] The unvarnished democracy that Gordon imagined was an unrealized ideal.

Jewish suburbanites and pioneers of new Jewish neighborhoods of Miami and Los Angeles did not experience life as Jewish urbanites did. They were not a majority, and they did not want to nor could they recreate Brooklyn and Brownsville. *Self-consciousness* was a term that they regularly applied to their new lives. They responded to their difference and self-consciousness by behaving quite differently than they had in cities. Jews began to create and join organizations, many of them Jewish. Suburbs were the center of an active and, to some commentators of the time, coercive organizational life. *Commentary* noted the significance of this shift from city to suburb by featuring articles on suburbanization as part of its marking of the three hundredth anniversary of Jewish immigration to the United States. The editors compared the move from city to suburb to the journey from the Old World to the New World.

At the beginning of the postwar period both men and women flocked to religious, fraternal, philanthropic, welfare, Zionist, and educational organizations, which counted a membership of two million Jews, although the number reflected overlapping memberships. While American Jews joined organizations throughout their history, all but fifteen of those catalogued in 1946 were founded in the twentieth century, and the single greatest increase, forty-seven new organizations, occurred between 1940 and 1946. The devastations of the war, the uncharted areas of new suburbs, and Americans' interest in organizational life created a culture of joiners for Jewish Americans. Organizational life became a source of friendship, peer relationships, and communal commitments.[23]

No address for Jews was more prominent than the synagogue. The well-known Jewish neighborhoods of America—Brooklyn, for example—did not have as great a level of synagogue affiliation as suburbanites did. At any one point in time during the 1950s and early 1960s synagogue membership stood at about 51 percent of American Jews, which is the highest rate of affiliation in American Jewish history. However, over the lifetime of a family in suburbia, it is generally estimated that a far greater percentage of Jews joined and then left synagogues; some commentators suggest as many as 80 percent of suburbia's Jews.

The postwar period, particularly 1940–1965, was a time of institution building. The large denominations of American Judaism, Reform, Orthodox, and Conservative, expanded in response to the new demand from suburbanites to build synagogues. At the end of World War II, 350 synagogues were affiliated with the United Synagogue of America, the umbrella organization of Conservative Judaism. In 1965 it counted 800 congregations as affiliates with over 100 congregations joining in a two-year period in the 1950s.[24]

Conservative Judaism emerged as the dominant denomination in America's suburbs because of its high rate of affiliation. It was perceived as the middle road between the "extremes" of Reform and Orthodox Judaism. It accommodated the expectations of younger Jews by integrating men and women in worship in family pews. However, it maintained the use of Hebrew and other familiar traditions. One Conservative Jewish activist said at a 1948 gathering of synagogue leadership, "Conservative Judaism maintains dignity in Judaism. . . . After all, why did we drift away from the so-called Orthodox point of view? Because we recognize that . . . [it] is obsolete in America. We want to create a service that should be applicable to our children and to future generations."[25] Jews who had gone to a small neighborhood shul led by a European-born rabbi, Jewish women who had rarely been included in synagogues, and Jewish veterans who had found Judaism meaningful for the first time in the military appeared to find common ground in what was most likely the Conservative synagogues newly built in suburbs.

The Conservative movement's Committee on Jewish Law and Standards, a centralized body that was empowered by the denomination's rabbis to render decisions in response to traditional Jewish law, halacha, took bold steps to accommodate the sensibilities of postwar Jews and loosen various prohibitions. They ruled in 1950 that driving was permitted for the purpose of attending synagogue on the Sabbath. Mixed seating of men and women together was the norm in suburban synagogues. In 1954 the Conservative Rabbinical Assembly voted in principle for the equalization of the status of women in Jewish law. These rulings and resolutions signaled Conservative Jewish leaders' confidence that they could make traditional Judaism relevant to the children of immigrants who may have left the city and their parents, but not Judaism. Like other Jewish reformers of the past, they understood themselves to be keeping Judaism alive by adapting it to contemporary life.[26]

Reform Judaism did not have as large a following in the suburbs as Conservative Judaism did, however its congregations grew in numbers. After the war 520 Reform temples served 255,000 families, and the movement began to reenvision its mission.[27] Once the bastion of a well-articulated platform of beliefs and principles that put it in opposition to traditional Judaism, Reform also began to reach out to a wider spectrum of Jews, including the children of east European immigrants.

The suburban synagogue was a center of communal activity. It housed religious school, youth groups, men's and women's organizations, and the meetings of such secular Jewish groups as Hadassah or B'nai B'rith. Its members, like its rabbis, were initially young, and it lacked longtime members and a small group who controlled the congregation. Rabbis were often optimistic because they believed they had the opportunity to teach their congregants about Jewish life and to demonstrate that Judaism could be attractive to young Americans.[28] Balancing that optimism were the pessimistic voices of a steady stream of commentators who condemned suburban synagogues.

RELIGIOUS REVIVAL: AMERICAN CONFORMISM OR RITUALIZED ETHNICITY?

The synagogue came to dominate suburbs as the preeminent space of suburban Jewish life. In contrast to urban neighborhoods, it had no real competition from political or cultural Jewish organizations as a primary way to affiliate with the community. Paradoxically, the new spaces where Judaism flourished were frequently accused of failure. Many writers, professionals, and lay people asserted that suburban synagogues did not offer an authentic Jewish religious life. Some of the common epithets of the day summarized those concerns. The synagogue was ridiculed as purveying "country club Judaism" or "pediatric Judaism." The first charge implied that there was little difference between what happened at social gatherings and what happened in synagogues, and the latter that it was a place to drop off children rather than to participate. Certainly critics were correct that suburban Jews did not attend Sabbath services frequently, nor did surveys reveal that they observed Jewish law more than the immigrant generation.

Suburban Jews' religious behaviors resembled that of most American Jews of their generation. The difference seemed to be their memberships in Jewish groups and their strong commitment to send their children to after-school programs for Jewish education. Even that commitment seemed ambiguous however. In 1959 the first national study of American Jewish education revealed that parents were less concerned with the content of what their children learned than the location of the school. They had difficulty articulating why education was important for their children, although most felt that it was.[29]

Suburbanites were commended at the same time for the very attitudes that received condemnation. Oscar Handlin, for example, a well-known American historian, praised Jews' participation in synagogue life precisely because it was "empty of meaning."[30] Handlin claimed that American Jews did not trouble themselves about the "Jewish content" or the "American environment" that "moved them" to their involvement in adult education or synagogue benefit card parties, dances, or brotherhoods. Rather, they found "peace of mind" in the company of their fellows and emotional satisfaction for the whole personality.[31] His only explanation for the pleasure and tranquillity that resulted was the failure of any prior vision such as Zionism, universalism, political radicalism, or liberalism.[32] The blandness of the synagogue, its offer of a social life and friendship, commended it to cultural analysts who were leery of the commitments and movements of the 1930s and 1940s.

After World War II, with suburbanization and upward mobility, Jewish families joined synagogues both to be like their Christian neighbors and to be different from them. Their self-consciousness as a minority, the experience of antisemitism in the 1930s, the defeat of Nazism, attachment to memories, and a host of other reasons all played a role in suburban synagogue membership. These parents wanted their children to feel some attachment to Judaism even if they found it difficult to explain why.

So extreme was the split between adults' lack of participation in Judaism and their enrolling children in religious schools that the sociologist Herbert Gans, who studied a new suburb of Chicago in the 1940s, coined the term *child oriented* for the synagogue. Indeed, children were now, according to the sociologist Gans, the primary participants in suburban Jewish religious life.[33]

Approximately 590,000 children nationwide enrolled in synagogue schools by the early 1960s, up from more than 230,000 in 1940, which was an increase from the Depression and war years of the 1930s. Not only had the number of children enrolled in Jewish schooling increased, the site of their education had shifted from the community schools of the interwar years to the congregation, and with it to denominations. New York's Jewish student population provides an interesting example of who opted for education. More than 40 percent of suburban Jewish youth were enrolled in some form of religious education, while 28 percent were enrolled in the city.[34]

Jews in suburbs, then, had reformulated a new liberal Judaism in the two decades following World War II. The parents who had come of age in the Depression sought a Judaism that was compatible with America and that would instill in their children a sense of pride and knowledge of being a Jew, something many of them believed they lacked themselves. It would be a mistake to overlook the fact that many adults participated in suburban synagogue life. The presence of adult education classes and a variety of men's and women's organizations within the synagogue demonstrates that there was a strong adult presence in the synagogue, even if it did not include worship services.

Social scientists of this period astutely described the "religion" of the majority of America's Jews. They wished to mark their difference from the larger, Christian society by maintaining a sense of a shared Jewish past and future. Family and communal loyalty were central. Jewish observance was not commanded (as it had not been for most American Jews in the interwar years) as much as chosen, and only those rituals that were the least demanding persisted, for example, a Passover seder or a Hanukkah celebration. In additions, rituals that marked life passages that brought extended family together flourished and became occasions for celebration and display.[35]

Charles Liebman,a political scientists, argued that the authority of American Jewish life was not Jewish law but what he variously termed "personalism" and "familism." Jews participated in holidays and Jewish life out of loyalty to family traditions and a felt connection to other Jews. Those important commitments made many Jews generous contributors to Jewish philanthropies and to Israel over these decades, but it also underlined the question of what being a Jew meant in America.[36] Were Jews simply transferring the behaviors of an ethnic rather than religious group into the synagogue building, as one sociologist contended?

ORTHODOX JUDAISM

Few of the patterns of the suburban synagogue applied to Orthodox Judaism. Indeed, the persistence of Orthodox Judaism, following the war, was largely viewed as an anomaly in the eyes of the majority of American Jews. Its minimal suburban presence created the illusion that it was not a significant contender for American Jews' loyalty. Although Orthodox Judaism did not follow a path similar to other denominations it was in the midst of consolidating strength and its own revival.

The number of communities and groups labeled *orthodox* makes apparent that it is not a movement in the sense of other denominations. Rather, *orthodoxy* became an umbrella term for groups as diverse as Modern Orthodox Judaism and Hasidic courts from Europe that did not recognize the legitimacy of other Jewish practices. Orthodox Judaism became associated with a variety of interpretations of Jewish tradition.

Historian Jeffrey Gurock divided the leadership of American Orthodox Judaism between those who were "accommodators" and those who were "resisters" to American culture.[37] While many of the rabbis who shaped American Orthodoxy engaged in both types of organizations and commitments, unquestionably their real ideological differences around Jews' relationship to America and the secular world created a substantial divide between them. Following World War II those differences intensified.

The history of Orthodox Judaism is often written through the religious institutions and leaders who shaped it. The needs of observant Jews, in contrast to followers of "liberal" Judaism, were addressed by their rabbis' decisions regarding religious education, synagogue worship, and particularly the proper butchering of kosher meat. Thus the regulation of religious life lent itself more readily to institutionalization and control, albeit among competing groups who made competing claims to legitimacy. Discussions of Orthodox Judaism, therefore, focus on leadership and institutions.

Paradoxically, following World War II Orthodox Jews became both better integrated into American life, and their movement grew increasingly less committed to accommodation to its demands. How and why this happened effectively illuminates postwar American Jewish life in ways that parallel and diverge from the experiences of other Jews.

The great boom in Conservative Judaism certainly drew on men and women raised by immigrant parents who thought of themselves as Orthodox. Hundreds of small shuls closed after the war as Jews moved away from the cities, often abandoning small groups of Jewish immigrants who stayed behind. Many American Jews were convinced that Americanization and mobility would lead Jews to abandon orthodoxy. They were wrong.

While Orthodox Jews continued to count in its ranks the foreign born, their children and grandchildren did successfully Americanize. They invested their resources in an expanding Jewish day school movement, which provided access to a far more advanced Jewish education than would be available in after-school programs. By the mid-1950s twenty thousand children were enrolled in Orthodox day schools, a more than sixfold increase from the mid-1930s.[38] In addition, Modern Orthodox Jews also invested in a denominational mode of organizing Jewish life. The Orthodox Union created youth groups, summer camps, and women's and men's leagues that provided opportunities for community and activities within a traditional milieu.

The most striking change of postwar life for Orthodox Jews was the arrival of Holocaust survivors who recreated the rigorous traditionalism found only among European Jews. Almost a third of a million Jews who survived the Holocaust immigrated to the United States between 1933 and 1950. Among those refugees and displaced persons were scholars and teachers who would help to shape all Judaism's major movements. However, many of them radically altered the norms of American Judaism by rejecting modernity as an ideological component of their Jewish practices.

Brooklyn's neighborhoods of Crown Heights and Williamsburg, as well as Borough Park, became home to competing Hasidic dynasties and courts dominated by charismatic leaders, or rebbes. The courts of the Satmar rebbe (originally from Hungary) and the Lubavitch rebbe (originally from Belorussia) flourished. Lubavitch became the more well-known of the two because of its commitment to "outreach" in the United States and ultimately throughout the world, while Satmar worked to transplant and recreate the practices and institutions of the world destroyed by Nazism. The Skverer rebbe (originally from Hungary) left the urban center of New York to create New Square, an entirely Hassidic community. The area ultimately attracted followers of Satmar as well.[39]

In addition to leaders of Hassidic Orthodox Judaism, other followers of Orthodox Judaism came to the United States. New York was by no means the only location of a postwar traditionalist Judaism. Other scholars moved to Boston, Baltimore, New Jersey, and Cleveland to develop communities and schools of higher learning. In contrast to the rabbis who came to the United States from Europe in the nineteenth and early twentieth centuries and found Jews often hostile or indifferent to their authority, the post-Holocaust rabbis came with followers intent on rebuilding a traditional Jewish life in the New World.

The authority of "right-wing" Orthodox leaders influenced Modern Orthodox Judaism, often by taking leadership positions from American-born rabbis and refusing to cooperate with many Orthodox rabbis or rabbis from other denominations. They had no interest in Zionism and viewed support of the secular state of Israel as an act of heresy. Their policies acted as a brake on accommodation to Americanization. In addition, they supported an alternative system of schools and activities that further helped to insulate a stable group of committed Orthodox Jews.

The 1950s and 1960s created new Jewish spaces for the Jews of the United States. Many Jews came into synagogues for the first time just as those sacred spaces were changing. For some the changes signaled an entirely new era for American Jews. For others, synagogues reflected American Jews' conformity created by their new social class and neighbors in the boom years following the war. For some Judaism provided a critique of American life and for others it was a medium to embrace it. Certainly, the practice of Judaism in America in this period was one of the most significant changes from the Depression era.

POSTWAR FAMILIES:
THE CHALLENGES OF SUCCESS

Jewish families' postwar mobility created the need for new neighborhoods and new institutions. The same growing affluence that made it possible for Jews to send their children to day schools also expanded liberal Judaism. Affluence did not determine attitudes toward traditionalism, but it did affect them.

Many Americans' lives improved economically during the economic boom of the postwar period. However, the economy did not solely determine mobility. For Jews, family patterns also were an important contribution. For the majority of America's Jews, Jewish men were the primary breadwinners. Over the course of two generations Jewish men left behind manual labor and became, particularly after the war, increasingly engaged in white collar work.

Surveys taken between 1948 and 1953 in fourteen Jewish communities in the United States demonstrated that only 4 percent of Jews were engaged in manual occupations, that is, were members of the working class. In merely five years that represented a drop of more than 20 percent. In that same period almost 20 percent of Jewish men were professionals, a gain of 4 percent.[40] By the 1980s, the decade when children raised in the postwar period became adults, 43 percent of Jewish respondents to a national survey identified themselves as professionals.[41] Jews were twice as likely to be in a white collar occupation as other whites in the United States during this period. In the 1950s and 1960s families clearly encouraged their sons to prolong their educations in order to hold prestigious jobs. They invested in their educations.[42] However, personal choice was not the only explanation for success. Inexpensive public education during both the Depression and the postwar years made mobility possible for Jews. At the same time, the American economy was becoming far more service oriented. The professions that Jews valued, teaching, law, medicine, and management, all were central to postwar life.[43]

Jewish women's aspirations and achievements differed from men's in important ways. In the 1950s nearly 60 percent of Jewish women between the ages of eighteen to twenty-four participated in the workforce, but only slightly over 20 percent of Jewish women of childbearing ages, twenty-five to thirty-four, worked outside the home. The fact that the number rose to 40 percent for women between the ages of forty-five and sixty-four suggests that Jewish women valued work. They simply delayed their careers to support both their children's and husband's needs. Economic mobility then resulted from the contributions of both parents—men to earning and women to family managing.

Jewish women's commitment to leave the workforce until their children entered school created a remarkable cadre of educated and committed volunteers in the Jewish community. Jewish women's organizations were a major force in American Jewish life, supporting both Israeli and American causes. Their members were the backbone of suburban synagogue life both as fund-raisers and as students of adult education. They worked actively in public schools not only through the PTA but also through programs created by the National Council of Jewish Women to tutor and support poor children. Though often ridiculed by Jewish writers and even rabbis for assuming male roles, by any measure their contributions were enormous.[44]

As men changed the type of work they did, their families had changing expectations for their lives. Jews were no different from other Americans in this regard. What was unique about Jews was that in contrast to the children of Italians or Irish immigrants, Jewish mobility occurred more quickly and for most Jews simultaneously. Being Jewish and being a member of the middle class, therefore, became closely bound up with one another in new ways following the war.

The most important outcome of Jews' mobility and growing economic comfort was that it led directly to lowering the boundaries between Jewish and non-Jewish spaces in America. Though restrictions on housing, country clubs, and admission to Ivy League colleges persisted through the 1960s, most Jews had ready access to the mainstream of American life. The majority of America's Jews most likely believed what sociologists found in their study of suburban Jewry, that being a good American, being a good Jew, and being a good person were virtually synonymous.[45]

The strong overlap between being middle class and being Jewish created a culture for most American Jews that made them both like and unlike Christian Americans. Though Jews attended synagogue far less than their Protestant counterparts went to church, they did all agree to fairly general definitions of religion as belief in God and to behave ethically. Like other religious groups, the majority of American Jews believed that it was important for Jews to continue to marry one another and not outside of Judaism. Fewer than 5 percent of American Jews were intermarried at the close of the 1950s. The first discussions of intermarriage began in the Jewish community in the early 1960s. What alarmed American Jews about intermarriage was their fear, if Judaism was a family matter centered more in the home than the synagogue, over what would become of their shared culture. For American Jews of the time, memories of Christian antisemitism remained vivid, and their children's marriages to non-Jews felt like bringing outsiders into the intimate circle of family and community. The greatest fear of religious and communal leaders, as well as ordinary men and women, was that intermarried couples would not raise their children as Jews. That likelihood would be disappointing to any group, but, a mere decade after the destruction of six million Jews in Europe, its consequences were particularly devastating.

What often set Jews apart from others of their class was their view of both national and international politics. They voted far more liberally than their economic class might dictate. And in retrospect it is probable that they experienced the world differently as a result of antisemitism and the events of World War II.

AMERICAN JEWS AND POLITICS

If American Jews shared a consensus about anything, it appeared to be United States politics. Jews overwhelmingly voted for the Democratic candidate for president, from Franklin Delano Roosevelt in the 1930s to the unsuccessful Hubert H. Humphrey in 1968. The "Jewish vote" for Democratic candidates was as high as 90 percent for Roosevelt and, with the exception of the popular Republican candidate, the war hero Dwight D. Eisenhower, never less than 81 percent.[46] In this period Jews were thought of as liberals.

However, American Jewish political life was in fact more complicated and more contested than it appears. If one were to think of the postwar period in terms other than presidential elections, some of these conflicts become apparent. The three American political issues that dominated 1945–1967 were the cold war and with that the threat of nuclear war, the civil rights movement, and the war in Vietnam. They overlapped one another and affected American's responses to each. In this same period Israel became a state and fought a series of wars culminating in the Six-Day War. American Jews experienced those events in ways that were also shaped by the dominant American political issues of the time.

Rather than American Jews being united in their response to the key political issues of American life, they were, in fact, divided from one another. This era ended with its single most unifying event for American Jews, the Six-Day War. But what that unity underlined was how vulnerable American Jews felt in the very country where they had become successfully integrated. The possibility that Israel might well be facing destruction at the hands of Arab neighbors led a huge percentage of American Jews to experience a deep and shattering fear for their future and to launch changes in American Jewish politics and culture.

The Holocaust continued to shape American Jews' experiences and debates even during the decades that it appeared to remain in the shadows of Jewish public life. Despite the triumphs of the postwar era that brought Jews to the center of American life and their own remarkable successes, most scholars and commentators agree that American Jews continued to worry about antisemitism and their own vulnerability throughout the second half of the twentieth century. Whether or not that anxiety was grounded in "reality" is less important than the ways it shaped American Jewish politics.[47]

The cold war began at the end of World War II and transformed the wartime allies, the Soviet Union and the United States, into global enemies competing for influence and control. In an atmosphere of anxiety about Soviet influence the administration of President Harry Truman initiated a public program to review the loyalty of federal employees in 1947. This program was followed by legislation that required communist organizations to register with the government. In turn, the United States Senate Permanent Subcommittee on Investigations, under the leadership of a Wisconsin senator, Joseph McCarthy, from 1953–1954, searched out communists and former communists who its staff and members claimed posed a danger to American security. Virtually no one was immune from hearings that demanded people confess or implicate others or face imprisonment.

American Jews were affected in unique and powerful ways during this period of intensive pursuit of communists because the American right wing, both in Congress and the Senate, as well as its demagogic political leaders and organizations like the John Birch Society, systematically equated Jews with communism. This long time antisemitic slur was used in Nazi Germany, throughout Europe, and in the United States for half a century. When Jews encountered it at the same moment they were entering America's mainstream it created a charged atmosphere within American Jewish life that precipitated deep conflicts.

American Jews did have a unique relationship with the American Communist Party. Though the vast majority of American Jews were not communists, a considerable number of communists were Jews. Often idealistic, usually products of the workers movement and committed to dreams of justice and equality, eastern European immigrants looked to the socialism and communism of their youth as a hopeful answer to antisemitism and universal oppression. These men and women joined leftist organizations, which included the Communist Party, but also unions, artists' collectives, and groups committed to international friendship and racial justice who counted among their numbers members of the party. During the 1930s and 1940s these groups stood for basic principles of freedom and democracy and opposed fascism. They epitomized American values. In the period of cold war fear those same organizations were cast as sources of subversion. Many American Jews disavowed their membership in those groups because of their own disapproval of communism as well as anxiety for their jobs. Many American Jews did not, and this created bitter conflicts among Jews.

One of the important staging grounds of these conflicts was within the communal organizations that claimed to speak for American Jews. Like all other minority and religious groups, Jews created a variety of organizations throughout the twentieth century whose purpose was to speak against attacks on them and to defend their legal rights. After World War II these groups were drawn into the cold war conflicts that defined American politics. The Anti-Defamation League, the American Jewish Committee, and the American Jewish Congress were powerful advocates for the view that what was good for America was good for American Jews. They also consistently defended Jews against accusations of communism by emphasizing that the Soviet Union under Stalin was antisemitic.

On the one hand, they worked with Christian and minority groups to advocate for "tolerance," and equal legal rights for all groups. They used film, the new medium of television, and radio to attack prejudice as un-American. On the other hand, they embraced anticommunism whole heartedly, often firing their own employees who might be thought of as subversive, just as government agencies did.[48] As a result, Jews made claims and counterclaims about who was or was not a good Jew, who deserved the appreciation of the community, and who had no place in it. Former squabbles among Jewish organizations with different political agendas began to take on national significance. For example, in 1958 an article appeared in the Los Angeles publication of B'nai B'rith, a popular Jewish men's organization, which supported a Jewish defense organization, the Anti-Defamation League. It praised a local couple for their patriotism and concluded, "The Millers are Jews—good Jews—and I, as a Jew, am as proud of them as I am of (Albert) Einstein."

The deed that the writer took pride in was the couple's willing spying for the FBI from 1950–1955. The organization that was their target was the Los Angeles Committee for the Protection of the Foreign Born. It was founded in Los Angeles in Boyle Heights, one of the city's oldest Jewish neighborhoods. After the war older Jewish residents remained while most of the younger families moved away, many to suburban areas. The group was a multiracial, multiethnic association that initially protected European immigrants who lacked proper documentation to remain in the United States. Jews led the organization, and many were certainly left wing.[49] When a Jewish journalist equated Jews who were willing to spy on their former neighbors with an icon of Jewish genius, it is clear that the cold war created powerful new divisions among Jews as well as among all Americans.

Though McCarthyism and its excesses were defeated by1954, the right wing continued to equate communism, progressive causes, and Jews for many more decades. That was particularly the case in the civil rights movement, which was without question one of the most significant American political causes for Jews and many Jewish organizations. Jews participated in many ways in the civil rights movement. They were generous financial contributors to organizations engaged in the struggle and especially to Dr. Martin Luther King's organization, the Southern Christian Leadership Conference. Many Jews were activists at the national and local levels in integrating housing, neighborhoods, and schools. Jewish students participated in Mississippi Summer when northern white students went south to help register African American voters.

Many of these Jews have explained and written over the years that they were motivated to act because of what happened to Jews during the Holocaust or because of their families' commitment to justice.[50] Many were indifferent to their Judaism or were raised with little connection to Judaism or Jewish life. At the same time, there was tremendous support for civil rights from Jewish organizations, individual synagogues and temples, and from rabbinical organizations. Despite the extreme right's accusations of communism or Jewish disloyalty, American Jews could not be intimidated out of their support.

Southern Jews, by contrast, were often caught in what they experienced as an impossible situation. White racists unleashed a campaign of terror in the South to protest the Supreme Court's order to desegregate schools in 1954. Of the attacks on houses of worship and private homes of clergy and activists from 1954 to 1959, 10 percent were directed against synagogues, rabbis' homes, and Jewish community centers. The other 90 percent took the lives and property of African Americans. Jewish communities were attacked in Charlotte, Miami, Gastonia, North Carolina, Jacksonville, and, most surprisingly, Atlanta, Georgia, among other towns and cities.[51]

Several southern rabbis were eloquent spokespeople for the support of civil rights. However, most southern Jews were not strong advocates for equality. Many had reservations about the treatment of African Americans and many did not. Jewish institutions often called on northern Jews to express compassion for southern Jews rather than work so energetically for African American rights. Rabbi Abraham Ruderman, a northern-born Greenville, Mississippi rabbi, noted in his diary in 1968, "Identifying with Negroes is not a popular pastime in Mississippi." Ruderman faced bitter criticism from many congregants for organizing a nationwide drive to gather used clothing for impoverished African Americans in his city. He left the congregation in 1970 after four years in his pulpit.[52]

In 1963 the march on Washington was one of the high points of civil rights activism. Before Dr. King delivered his eloquent "I Have a Dream" speech, Rabbi Joachim Prinz, a Berlin Reform rabbi who was expelled by the Nazis, addressed the massive crowd and compared racism to Nazism. In 1965 Rabbi Abraham Joshua Heschel marched with Dr. Martin Luther King Jr. from Selma to Montgomery, Alabama to protest the denial of voting rights to African Americans, an action that was not supported by many rabbis because of its "radicalism." Rabbi Heschel, also a refugee of Nazism who taught at the Jewish Theological Seminary of America, wrote about his activism in explicitly "religious" terms. He termed it a "mitzvah," a religious requirement that was linked to the biblical prophets' call for justice. Jewish summer camps in the 1960s as well as religious schools and youth groups included the events of the civil rights movement in their curriculum, consistently underlining the demands for justice within Jewish law and life.

The civil rights movement changed dramatically during the 1960s; ultimately many Jews began to distance themselves from it for many predictable if unfortunate reasons. In the last half of the decade of the 1960s a series of violent confrontations—some called them riots, others called them uprisings—occurred in Cincinnati, Minneapolis, Chicago, Los Angeles, and other cities in urban areas, or "ghettos," most Jews left when they began their exodus to the suburbs. However, many Jewish merchants continued to maintain businesses there, and some older Jews still lived in these urban neighborhoods and sometimes were among the targets of these explosions of rage and frustration at the racism and problems in the urban core. In the face of these and other events, some activists among Jews and African Americans began increasingly to talk and write about "Black antisemitism" and "Jewish racism."

The city was a logical site for such conflicts. New York city schools, the demand for integrated housing in northern areas, and bussing as a means to integrate schools were among issues that divided longtime Jewish activists and African American activists as well as younger and older Jewish activists. Though Jews and Jewish organizations in many cities worked for integrated housing and bussing, others did not.[53]

The civil rights movement itself splintered among the many organizations that worked to change the United States. Not all embraced nonviolence, and some ultimately asked their white members to leave and work in their own communities rather than among southern African Americans. The end of what some called the black-Jewish alliance coincided with condemnations of Israel by African American nationalists in 1967. Jewish communal institutions and defense organizations condemned rising radicalism. The situation grew more explosive precisely as the war in Vietnam became a highly divisive issue among Americans and Jews. Dr. King, a lifelong advocate of nonviolence, condemned the war in Vietnam and further alienated some of his white supporters.

The steady condemnation of Israel and the American Jewish community by some African American leaders, and Jewish criticism of a few African American leaders and movements, led a number of journalists and scholars to assert that a once steady alliance was now broken. Scholars agree that this alliance was primarily one of elites—lawyers, clergy, and leaders of large organizations—rather than a grassroots movement. In fact, a civil rights campaign like Mississippi Summer, of 1964, when African American students were joined by about eight hundred northern white students, many of whom were Jewish, to provide voter education and help register African American voters, was exceptional in the history of American Jews and African Americans precisely because it was a grassroots effort.[54]

The Vietnam War moved the center of student activism to opposing American participation in the war and the draft. Some Jewish organizations took stands against that war by the mid-1960s, but far fewer than had supported civil rights. The most liberal among them, the American Jewish Congress, the Union of American Hebrew Congregations, and the National Council of Jewish Women, were among the most prominent. Around issues of American political life the confident equation of the 1950s no longer carried the illusion of consensus. If Jews continued to believe that being a good American and a good Jew was the same thing, there was little agreement any longer about what either assertion meant. Being a good American certainly no longer implied supporting the president and the government for those American Jews who opposed Vietnam, including some who argued that their opposition was grounded in Jewish principles and values.

However, opposing American policies concerned many congregational rabbis, associations, and organizations that believed their colleagues and friends had lost their way. Progressive Jewish activists, they claimed, had no regard for the needs of other Jews or Jewish concerns. Community leaders, with reason, feared that Jews opposing the war in Vietnam might well lead the administration of President Lyndon Baines Johnson to withdraw his support for Israel. They believed that American Jewish youth were bent on assimilation. It appeared that nothing could draw together American Jewry. All of that was to change in June of 1967.

"DUAL LOYALTY": AMERICAN JEWS AND ISRAEL

The Six-Day War in Israel briefly created an unprecedented consensus among American Jews. It did not, alone, alter the anxieties and conflicts that beset American Jews, but it did serve as a boundary of sorts that marked a new focus on their own cultural and organizational life and on Israel. Jewish communal concerns after that became increasingly taken up with "assimilation," intermarriage, Jewish education, and the memory of the Holocaust, and United States support for the State of Israel.

Postwar American Jewish life was marked by the establishment of the State of Israel in 1948, an event that was central to the optimism of the period. In the two decades following the end of World War II, Israel realized its greatest support among American Jews. In turn, American Judaism came to be deeply influenced by the existence of a State of Israel. In the twists and turns of American Jews' responses to Zionism and to Israel, Jews remained fully rooted in America, even as Israel came to dominate the agenda of Jewish communal life and the concerns and passions of many American Jews.

In 1945 Palestine's Jewish populations' aspirations for statehood hardly seemed assured. Debates persisted among the leadership of the Yishuv (the Jewish settlement under British control) about the most effective political program to advance. Some leaders advocated continued cooperation with British control of the region. A militant right-wing group, the Irgun, advocated violence as a tactic to force the British to leave in order to declare statehood. Others sought compromises. What all parties agreed upon was that they demand the right to bring to Palestine those European Jews displaced by Nazi fascism.[55]

In 1939, during what would become World War II, the British issued a White Paper declaring that all Jewish immigration to Palestine would be halted in five years. Only small numbers of European Jewish refugees would be admitted in the interim. The British sided with Arabs against Jews for many reasons, the most obvious to obtain their support against the Axis forces. However, the end of the war did not lead to rescinding the White Paper, nor did it end Britain's inconsistencies and double promises to all sides in the struggle for Palestine.

The Zionist leadership demanded one hundred thousand certificates for Jewish immigration to Palestine, which Britain and the Arab leadership opposed but Truman supported as a result of a report made by Earl Harrison, who was sent to Europe to investigate the refugee problem. He found an intolerable situation and learned of their overwhelming desire to go to Palestine. The near destruction of European Jewry brought American sympathy, both Jewish and non-Jewish, to the Zionist cause for the first time in its long struggles. President Harry S. Truman inherited from Franklin Delano Roosevelt a contradictory foreign policy toward Palestine with inconsistent promises made to all parties, Arab and Jewish. President Truman would also change position on Palestine several times.

Various attempts at compromise offered by an Anglo-American commission failed. In 1946 Winston Churchill, now prime minister of England, urged the United Nations to come up with a solution for Arab and Jewish demands for Palestine. The British, worn down by the war effort and persistent attacks against them by both Jews and Arabs, wanted to escape the unsolvable problems created by their policies. In May of 1947 the United Nation appointed a commission, UNSCOP (United Nations Special Committee on Palestine), to draw up a plan for Palestine. Their final recommendation was for its partition.

The British, all Arab, and most Asian nations opposed the plan. The United States held back its support, waiting to see if a consensus would develop. There were divided opinions in the Truman administration. Truman weighed the American Jewish Democratic vote, particularly in New York and California, as well as alienating Arab interests, because of their control over oil, in his ultimate decision. In the end, over the opposition of the Department of State, Truman did support partition and the creation of a Jewish state in November of 1947. By May of 1948, when Israel declared its statehood, the United States was the first country to grant it recognition. Israel engaged in continual war with its Arab neighbors for the next thirty years. Many American Jews saw Israel's statehood as a joyful and even redemptive response to the devastations of the Holocaust. For them it was the fulfillment of a longtime dream of Jewish statehood, and Jews' public celebrations in New York City and other urban centers are remembered as truly extraordinary. For a minority of American Jews, the Jewish state was a nightmare because of their opposition to the idea that any place other than America could be a true "homeland" for Jews.

The heated environment of postwar American politics put Jews on the defensive around issues of loyalty to the nation, despite United States support for Israel. American Jews did feel the need to negotiate the terrain of American politics differently than most other ethnic groups as they presented themselves as loyal citizens of the United States and advocates for a Jewish state in Israel.

Because American Zionist leaders were reluctant to call for the creation of a nation that would serve as the "sole" homeland of the Jewish people, American Zionism never became a movement comparable to those in Europe and North Africa. Indeed, in August of 1950 this issue was dramatized in a meeting between David Ben-Gurion, Israel's prime minister, and Jacob Blaustein, president of the American Jewish Committee, one of the most influential Jewish organizations in the United States.

Blaustein threatened to withdraw the support of his organization for Israel if the Jewish state's leaders did not stop calling for worldwide immigration of Jews to Israel, Zionism's central tenet. Ben-Gurion backed down and publicly stated that the primary political attachment of United States Jews was to their own nation.[56] While Zionism did not capture the interest of most American Jews until after statehood, virtually no leaders, rabbis, or intellectuals were neutral about it. Zionist organizations and their leaders were important participants in American Jewish politics.

Those who supported Zionism are often characterized as following one of two paths. The first, "the secular and political," focused on creating a state and developing strategies necessary for its realization. The "spiritual and religious" approach supported a Jewish presence in Palestine, but for a variety of reasons opposed statehood.[57] Following World War II those strands of American Zionism took on new and compelling forms and meanings and merged by the mid-1960s.

In the years after World War II leading up to statehood and those following, spiritual and religious Zionism was considered the more American of the two strands. Its most forceful spokespersons were rabbis and scholars who saw in Zionism a religious worldview. Mordecai Kaplan was one of the members of the rabbinical circle who embraced Zionism as a religious and spiritual vision. He was the founder of Reconstructionist Judaism and one of the twentieth century's most influential Jewish thinkers and teachers at the Conservative movement's rabbinical school, the Jewish Theological Seminary of America. Kaplan argued that American Jews would languish without a spiritual and cultural center, which was what Palestine, a truly Jewish civilization, represented to him in the 1940s. While it need not serve as a "home" to all Jews, it had a central role to play in Jewish life.

Jewish and Christian leaders in the years immediately following the war frequently advocated for peace and internationalism as a response to the two world wars of the century. Many rabbis opposed Israel becoming a nation because they were leery of nationalism and feared that the nation-state was itself the source of war. For those, such as Louis Finkelstein, president of the Jewish Theological Seminary, who believed that Israel had a moral and ethical role to play in the world as the embodiment of Judaism, nationhood was unnecessary and even dangerous. The religious and spiritual rationales for a homeland for some, if not all Jews, frequently linked those Jewish aspirations to American ones.[58] American rabbis, in their sermons and writings, noted that the prophetic tradition of the Bible provided justification for both America and a Jewish homeland. They compared Jewish pioneers of Palestine to pilgrims and to revolutionary patriots and portrayed the democratic aspirations of the Jewish state as a parallel to those of the United States. Israel's role as home to refugees, they asserted, was similarly evocative of a shared destiny with America, which had harbored generations of immigrants.

Rabbis and intellectuals were not the only ones taken up with issues related to statehood and interpreting the meaning of the existence of Israel in light of the genocidal war against the Jews. Jewish organizations' boards made support for Israel a key tenet of life in America. The single most effective Zionist organization in the United States, both prior to and following Israel's statehood, was the women's organization Hadassah. Founded in 1912, it served both educationally and philanthropically to promote women's leadership. Hadassah actively worked to establish a state through political ends. At the same time, its national membership was particularly effective at fund-raising to support its two key projects in Israel, support for young immigrants, often orphaned during World War II, and health care.

Following World War II, the founding of Israel, and American Jews' suburbanization, Hadassah became one of the most popular Jewish women's organizations in the United States. Members were recruited to work on two fronts: as Zionists, for the welfare of the Jewish people in Israel, and as Americans for a democratic America and a democratic world. Like the religious and spiritual Zionists, their support did not demand an ideological commitment to Israel as a unique homeland of the Jewish people. Unlike religious and spiritual Zionists, they were uncompromising advocates for Israel's statehood as a political entity.

Once Israel became a state, its spiritual and religious significance became more central to Jewish life in America. Celebrations of Israel's statehood were incorporated into the holiday cycle, and prayers for the nation became part of the Jewish liturgy for all denominations. Modern Hebrew using Israeli pronunciation became the norm of religious education taught by Conservative and Reform schools. And Israeli music, dance, arts and crafts were integrated into summer camps and schools that were not even explicitly Zionist. In the 1960s the Reform movement began sending teenagers on organized trips to Israel and Conservative Judaism followed suit.

Without question, however, in 1967 the Six-Day War waged between Israel and its Arab neighbors had an unexpected effect on American Jewry. Arthur Hertzberg, the young rabbi who wrote about Jewish identification with Americans after World War II, saw a radically different outlook take hold in June of 1967. He wrote, "As soon as the Arab armies began to mass on the borders of Israel, the mood of the American Jewish community underwent an abrupt, radical and possibly . . . permanent change far more intense and widespread than anyone could have foreseen."[59] Jews with little interest in Israel and American Jewish organizations that did not rank Israel high on their agenda of issues were transformed by the six days in June when it was initially unclear if Israel could withstand the Arab military assault. When a successful and swift military victory followed, the impact was enormous.

As a result of the war, Jerusalem was under Israel's control for the first time, furthering what appeared to many Jews as the "divine," or "redemptive" significance of the war. The one-time distinctions between political and spiritual Zionism were not only erased but actually reversed. A new American Jewish consensus emerged that placed Israel and Jerusalem at the center of American Jewish life.

The postwar period of American Jewish life is best understood as a realignment of American Jewish culture and a transformation in the social patterns of the majority of American Jews. What primarily drove those changes was American Jews' entry into the middle class and with that their access to the center of American culture. Israel's victory in the Six-Day War coincided with a deep political and cultural polarization in the larger nation in which Jews were active participants.

The decades that preceded those changes appear on the surface to have been stable and conformist for many American Jews. In fact, the debates that this chapter featured about American Jewish life and what constituted an authentic Judaism anticipated the more dramatic changes that lay ahead.

The debates over the nature of American Judaism and the synagogue were not idle chatter. By the end of the 1960s, alternatives to the synagogue were appearing in New York, Boston, Chicago, Los Angeles, Denver, and elsewhere. Influenced by the American counterculture, havurot (fellowships), and small minyanim (prayer groups) eschewed rabbis, buildings, and complex organizations to create alternatives to the synagogue that featured communal singing over cantorial music and potlucks over elaborate dinners in social halls. Though a minority of affiliated Jews, these challenges to synagogue life had far-reaching effects on the mainstream of Judaism, across its denominations, leading to a loosely constituted "movement" for synagogue transformation.

The first stirrings of Jewish feminism grew out of the commitment to Jewish education for girls and boys that marked the baby boom generation's wide exposure to Hebrew school, summer camps and youth groups. As the larger culture raised issues about gender equality, Jewish women responded as Jews demanding greater equality and ultimately ordination.

These examples can be multiplied many times over. The "renaissance" in American Jewish life focused on learning, observance, experimentation, and commitments among a wide range of Jews was radical departure from the Judaism of the immediate postwar period. However, none of these changes are intelligible apart from the key debates and institutions that dominated the 1950s and 1960s.

The parents of the baby boom have often been blamed for the failures of American Judaism. Their "superficial" Jewish life, their inadequate suburban synagogues, their emphasis on success, and their eager conformism were attacked not only by "experts," but by their children as well. Did their desire for acculturation and success "cause" the rise in intermarriage from 5 percent in 1960 to 48 percent by the 1990s? Did the overall drop in synagogue affiliation and the religious educations of their grandchildren grow out of the experiences of the suburban synagogues that they built for themselves and their children? Do these men and women who dominated the postwar period deserve credit for some of their children's efforts at pioneering Jewish studies as an academic field, creating new institutions in Jewish life committed to the Jewish arts, and the increase in Jewish day schools?

This generation, in fact, pioneered American Judaism just as the immigrant generation who preceded them. They lacked moorings in Europe or easy childhoods in America. They lived through the worst antisemitism in American history and the terrors of Nazism, which many of them fought in Europe in order to defeat. Three-quarters of them received no Jewish educations in the United States.

Their fears, anxieties, and dreams set the course of a complex and often contradictory vision for American postwar Jewry.

NOTES

1. Interview in *"Next Time Dear God, Please Choose Someone Else,"* British Broadcasting Company, 1990.

2. Andrew Heinze, *Jews and the American Soul: Human Nature in the Twentieth Century* (Princeton, 2004), 195–216.

3. For example, Herman Wouk's *Marjorie Morningstar* (New York, 1955) was one of the top-ten-selling books in America that year. Wouk appeared on the cover of *Time* magazine as well. Philip Roth's critically acclaimed debut collection of short stories, *Goodbye Columbus* (New York, 1959), largely focused on the lives of newly suburbanized Jews.

4. Arthur Goren, "A Golden Decade for American Jews: 1945–1955," in Jonathan Sarna, ed., *The American Jewish Experience*, 2d ed. (New York, 1997), 296. Hasia Diner challenges the notion of a golden age in *The Jews of the United States* (Berkeley, 2004), 259–304.

5. Will Herberg. *Protestant, Catholic, Jew: An Essay in American Religious Sociology,* rev. ed. (Garden City, NY, 1960).

6. Harry Scheniderman. *American Jewish Year Book* 43 (1941–1942): 28.

7. Robert Gordis, "Editorial," *Conservative Judaism* 42, no. 1 (1945): 33.

8. Arthur Hertzberg, *A Jew in America* (New York, 2002), 148.

9. Deborah Dash Moore, *GI Jews: How World War II Changed a Generation* (Cambridge, 2004), 9.

10. Goren, "A Golden Decade," 296.

11. H. S. Infeld, "The Jewish Population of the United States," *American Jewish Yearbook* 47 (1946–47): 605. The data was drawn on the last major population survey taken in 1937.

12. Cited in Gerald Gamm, *Urban Exodus: Why the Jews Left Boston and the Catholics Stayed* (Cambridge, 1999), 198–99 (from a 1971 article in the Sunday *Boston Globe*).

13. Gerald Sorin, *The Nurturing Neighborhood: The Brownsville Boys Club and Jewish Community in Urban America, 1940–1990* (New York, 1990), 14–17.

14. Harry Gersh, "The New Suburbanites of the 50's," *Commentary* 17 (March 1954): 211–12.

15. Evelyn Rossman, "The Community and I: Belonging, Its Satisfactions and Dissatisfactions," *Commentary* 18.5 (November 1954): 393–405.

16. Jonathan D. Sarna, *American Judaism: A History* (New Haven, 2004), 282.

17. Herbert J. Gans, *The Levittowners: Ways of Life and Politics in a New Suburban Community* (New York, 1982 [1967]), 23.

18. Marshall Sklare and Joseph Greenblum, *Jewish Identity on the Suburban Frontier: A Study of Group Survival in the Open Society*, 2d ed. (Chicago, 1979 [1967]), 11–14.

19. See Deborah Dash Moore, *To the Golden Cities: Pursuing the American Jewish Dream in Miami and L.A.* (New York, 1994).

20. Eli Lederhendler, *New York Jews and the Decline of Urban Ethnicity, 1950–1970* (Syracuse, 2001), 148–53.

21. Donald Katz, *Home Fires: An Intimate Portrait of One Middle Class Family in Postwar America* (New York, 1992), 62.

22. Alan Wood, "I Sell My House: One Man's Experience with Suburban Segregation." *Commentary* 26.5 (November 1958): 383–89.

23. "Jewish National Organizations," *American Jewish Yearbook* 47 (1945–1946): 549.

24. Jack Wertheimer, *A People Divided: Judaism in Contemporary America* (New York, 1993), 5.

25. Marshall Sklare, *Conservative Judaism: An American Religious Movement* (New York, 1972), 96.

26. Sarna, *American Judaism*, 286–87.

27. Nathan Glazer, *American Judaism*, 2d ed. (Chicago, 1972), 108–9.

28. Many generations of rabbis and lay leaders made similar claims for American synagogues throughout the United States. See Marc Lee Raphael, *Judaism in America* (New York, 2003); Leon Jick, *The Americanization of the Synagogue: 1820–1870* (Hanover, 1976).

29. Alexander M. Dushkin and Uriah Z. Engleman, *Jewish Education in the United States: Report of the Commission for the Study of Jewish Education in the United States,* vol. 1 (New York, 1959), 84.

30. Oscar Handlin, "The American Jewish Pattern, After Three Hundred Years," *Commentary* 18.4 (October 1954): 303.

31. Handlin is clearly addressing pre- and postwar Jewish enclaves in this description, particularly in the 1940s and as part of what he described as "the religious redefinition" that Jews underwent. "The American Jewish Pattern," 304–5.

32. Handlin, "The American Jewish Pattern," 302.

33. Herbert J. Gans. "The Origin and Growth of a Jewish Community in the Suburbs: A Study of the Jews of Park Forest," in Marshall Sklare, ed., *The Jews: Social Patterns of an American Group* (New York, 1958), 205–48.

34. Jack Wertheimer. "Jewish Education in the United States: Recent Trends and Issues." *American Jewish Yearbook* 99 (New York, 1999).

35. Sklare and Greenblum, *Jewish Identity on the Suburban Frontier.*

36. Charles Liebman, "Ritual, Ceremony, and the Reconstruction of Judaism in the United States," in Ezra Mendelsohn, ed., *Studies in Contemporary Judaism: An Annual* 6 (New York, 1990).

37. Jeffrey Gurock, *American Jewish Orthodoxy in Historical Perspective* (Hoboken, 1996), 47–58.

38. Glazer, *American Judaism*, 110.

39. A fuller discussion of these developments appears in Sarna, *American Judaism*, 296–301.

40. Glazer, *American Judaism*, 107–8.

41. Riv-Ellen Prell, *Fighting to Become Americans: Jews, Gender and the Anxiety of Assimilation* (Boston, 1999), 171–72.

42. Calvin Goldscheider and Alvin Zuckerman, *The Transformation of the Jews* (Chicago, 1984), 182.

43. Ira Katznelson. "Strangers No Longer: Jews and Postwar American Political Culture," in Deborah Dash Moore and S. Ilan Toren, eds., *Divergent Jewish Cultures: Israel and America* (New Haven. 2001), 313.

44. See Prell, *Fighting to Become Americans*; and Hasia R Diner and Beryl Lieff Benderly, *Her Works Praise Her: A History of Jewish Women in America from Colonial Times to the Present* (New York, 2002).

45. Sklare and Greenblum, *Jewish Identity on the Suburban Frontier.*

46. Stephen D. Isaacs, *Jews and American Politics* (New York, 1974), 152

47. Stuart Svonkin makes this point effectively in his discussion of the political work of American Jewish defense organizations. *Jews Against Prejudice: American Jews and the Fight for Civil Liberties* (New York, 2001), 8.

48. Ibid.

49. George J. Sanchez, "What's Good for Boyle Heights Is Good for the Jews: Creating Multiculturalism on the Eastside During the 1950s,"*American Quarterly* 56.3 (September 2004): 633–63.

50. See Debra Schultz, *Going South: Jewish Women in the Civil Rights Movement* (New York, 2000); Paul Cowan, *An Orphan in History: Retrieving a Jewish Legacy* (Garden City, NY, 1982).

51. Melissa Fay Greene, *The Temple Bombing* (New York, 1996), 4–6.

52. David B. Ruderman, "Greenville Diary: A Northern Rabbi Confronts the Deep South, 1966–1970," *Jewish Quarterly Review* 94.4 (Fall 2004): 651.

53. See Diner, *The Jews of the United States*, 265–74.

54. Schultz, *Going South*, and Diner, *The Jews of the United States* both recount the details of Mississippi summer and Jewish involvement. An analysis of immigrant Jewish attitudes toward African Americans may be found in Hasia Diner, *In the Almost Promised Land: American Jews and Blacks, 1915–1935* (Baltimore, 1995 [1977]). A discussion of the history of the alliance may be found in David Levering Lewis, "Parallels and Divergences: Assimilationist Strategies of Afro-Americans and Jewish American Elites from 1910 to the Early 1930s," *Journal of American History* 71 (December 1984): 543–64. A useful source on these issues in the 1990s is Paul Berman, ed., *Blacks and Jews: Alliances and Arguments* (New York, 1994).

55. The following narrative of Israel statehood is derived from Walter Laquer, *A History of Zionism* (New York, 1976), 564–86.

56. Edward Shapiro, *A Time for Healing: American Jewry Since World War II* (Baltimore, 1992), 205.

57. Arthur Goren, "Spiritual Zionists and Jewish Sovereignty," in Robert M. Seltzer and Norman J. Cohen, eds., *The Americanization of the Jews* (New York, 1995).

58. David Ellenson, "Zion in the Mind of the American Rabbinate," in Robert M. Seltzer and Norman J. Cohen, eds., *The Americanization of the Jews* (New York, 1995).

59. Arthur Hertzberg, "Israel and American Jewry," *Commentary* (August 1967): 69.

6

INFLUENCE AND AFFLUENCE, 1967–2000

STEPHEN J. WHITFIELD

In the nineteenth century a "whig interpretation" of the national experience was the fashion among American historians. They claimed that the present was better than the past and that the future would be even better than the present. The line of ascent was presumed to be straight and progressive. *Change* was a synonym for *improvement*; historical study would justify a spirit of optimism. A poet put it most succinctly: "America was promises," according Archibald MacLeish,[1] and in this country pledges were honored and dreams realized. From the chastened perspective of the early twenty-first century, the whig paradigm has ceased to attract scholarly adherents, for obvious reasons. The atrocities that inflicted so much suffering and death in the past century—global wars, the Holocaust, genocide in the Third World, torture, totalitarianism, and terrorism—long ago discredited the positive thinking that once animated the American historical profession.

One sliver of the American past nevertheless warrants a revival of the whig interpretation. The last third of the twentieth century vindicates all the hopes—and then some—that Jewish refugees and immigrants had invested from 1654 onward in their adopted land. This most recent phase of American Jewish history deserves to be appreciated as ratification of the often extravagant expectations that the newcomers had held. Such, at any rate, is the argument of this essay.

THE ECLIPSE OF ANTISEMITISM

In 1790 President George Washington had assured the Jews of Newport, Rhode Island (and, in effect, the Jews who hovered along the coast of the new nation) that the government would endorse neither bigotry nor persecution. That promise was almost fully honored thereafter . The faith in a democratic nation that would offer opportunity even to skeptics on the subject of Christ was vindicated. Of course no president could compel his fellow citizens to discard their prejudices in their social interactions, or their private lives; but for nearly the entire span of American history neither federal nor state government posed an obstacle to opportunity in the economy. Antagonism marked the attitudes of many citizens, however, even during the war against Nazism. "Popular opposition to Hitler did little to stave off domestic antisemitism," historian Marc Dollinger noted, "which took a turn for the worse during the war years." In the aftermath of the Holocaust, however, the consequences of Judeophobia became so evident that its decline in the United States was noticeable. In 1965 even the *American Jewish Year Book* abandoned the editorial policy that had characterized the reference work from its birth and stopped listing in a separate section instances of antisemitism in the United States. Such episodes were too eccentric to be stretched into such an entry.[2] The editorial change was a bit premature—but only a bit.

One dramatic blow against antisemitism was struck in 1967 when the self-styled *Führer* of the Nazi movement, George Lincoln Rockwell, was murdered by a disgruntled acolyte. In that same year portions of a novel began to appear, portraying a Jew, according to one critic, as a "sexual defiler" of gentile women, as relishing the opportunity to get even with the ancient oppressors of the Jewish people through sexual transgression. Literary critic Marie Syrkin compared the fantasies and acts of the protagonist of Philip Roth's *Portnoy's Complaint* to "the Goebbels-Streicher script" and read the novel as a continuation of "the antisemitic indictment straight through Hitler."[3] The Israeli scholar Gershom Scholem warned that, for the imaginative excess of this "perverted artist," Jewry would someday pay a high price. "Woe to us on that day of reckoning!" Scholem added.[4] Nothing even remotely adverse happened that could be traced to Roth's satiric novel, suggesting that Jewish fears of hostility were wildly inflated. To be sure, pockets of antisemitism remained. One such site was the Oval Office when Richard M. Nixon occupied it, spewing rancid cracks about "Jew-boys." The bias of one of his speechwriters, Patrick Buchanan, became more vocal in the 1990s, when he served as a media commentator and ran for the presidency. A fellow conservative, William F. Buckley, found "it impossible to defend Pat Buchanan against the charge" of antisemitism.[5] Yet no evidence surfaced that any Jewish interests—much less any actual Jews—were harmed by the outbursts that Nixon could not suppress in private and that Buchanan expressed in public.

The conventional measurement of polls pointed to a sharp decline in antisemitic attitudes since the 1930s. But in 1979—exactly a century after Wilhelm Marr coined the term *der Antisemitismus* in the Second Reich—a Louis Harris poll revealed that a third to a half of the black population subscribed to negative stereotypes of Jews. Younger and better-educated blacks were more likely to harbor such attitudes than the general black population.[6] This represented the only—and the most glaring—exception to the general trend. Whites who openly signaled their animus to Jews were discredited. But two key figures in black America were not so scrupulous. The Reverend Jesse Jackson was the most viable black political candidate of the era, running for the Democratic nomination for the presidency in 1984 and 1988. He managed to get the Democratic National Convention to scuttle a denunciation of antisemitism, because his followers suspected that the plank was aimed at him. Louis Farrakhan, a minister of the Nation of Islam, was far more demagogic in expressing hostility to Jews and even called Judaism "a gutter religion."[7]

In the summer of 1991 the appeal of such prejudice was reflected in the most serious outbreak of violence against Jews since 1913, when a riot erupted in the Crown Heights section of Brooklyn. A Lubavitch Hasidic driver, part of the entourage of Rabbi Menachem M. Schneerson, accidentally ran over and killed a black seven year old, Gavin Cato. During the ensuing riot a gang of blacks attacked Hasidim and stabbed to death a student from Australia, Yankel Rosenbaum. Such violence was a terrifying aberration during an era when bigotry had never been so widely stigmatized or so remote from respectability.

THE ACHIEVEMENT OF UPWARD MOBILITY

Much of the comfort and security that American Jews enjoyed stemmed from the high economic status that they had achieved in the last third of the century. When Americans meet a stranger, Benjamin Franklin remarked in 1782, they do not ask, "What is he?" Instead they wonder: "What can he do?"[8] Talent was supposed to matter more than ancestry, and the hierarchical structure of Europe could not be easily duplicated because the alluring ubiquity of individualism trumped the receding pedigree of family.

Relief from political persecution and religious bigotry did not alone hurtle Jews across the Atlantic; an even more important factor was economic deprivation and aspiration. Most of the Jews who fled to the New World probably anticipated that their economic status might be improved, that confinement to poverty need not be permanent. By the last three decades of the century, the material ease that Jews enjoyed in the United States was undoubtedly more widespread than any time since Abram left Ur of the Chaldees. With the partial exception of New York City, the Jewish working class had largely vanished. "What is the difference between the

International Ladies' Garment Workers Union and the American Psychiatric Association?" goes one riddle. The answer—one generation—resonated in countless lives. The title of Communist *littérateur* Mike Gold's novel of the Lower East Side—*Jews Without Money* (1930)—fit only a fraction of the Jewish elderly. From the dense pressure of such impoverished neighborhoods, the overwhelming majority of the children and grandchildren had propelled themselves; the injunction drummed in the barrios—*sal si puedes* (leave if you can)—was obeyed by Jews, who extended their geographical horizons to include the booming economy of the Sunbelt in particular. The environs of Los Angeles and Miami became home to the second and third largest concentrations of Jews in the metropolitan statistical areas of the United States. After the Supreme Court outlawed residential discrimination in 1948, Jews could opt to live anywhere and often had the financial resources to share the glee of satirist Tom Lehrer, "spending Chanukah in Santa Monica."

Members of the Church of England had been decisive in the formation of colonial America. By the last third of the twentieth century their descendants—the Episcopalians—ranked sixth in average household incomes among ethnic and religious groups. Ranking first were the Jews (in 1974 dollars: $13,340), according to the National Opinion Research Center. In the same period "the socioeconomic gap between Jews and Christians" had widened more dramatically "than the gap between blacks and whites," according to two scholars of race relations. By the 1920s, when Congress imposed immigration quotas that discouraged the influx of many more Jews, they were showing up in *Who's Who* in proportions greater than their percentage of the population—beating out all other ethnic groups except for Anglo-Saxons. Half a century later Jews had even jumped ahead of the descendants of the colonial founders in *Who's Who*. During the last four decades, Jews were estimated to be 40 percent of the partners of top law firms in New York City and in Washington and to be over a quarter of the reporters, editors, and executives of the most prominent media.[9]

The Jews' occupational structure did not replicate the rest of the population. By 1930, for example, they had constituted a quarter of New Yorkers. But 55 percent of the city's physicians were Jews, as were 64 percent of its dentists and 65 percent of its attorneys. So pronounced a professional proclivity would constitute a dilemma six or seven decades later, when textbook publishers felt compelled to ensure that their young readers would not eventually exclude themselves from the variety of jobs the nation offered its citizens. Holt, Rinehart and Winston, for example, formulated guidelines urging writers and illustrators to show Jews in other than "stereotypical occupations" such as medicine, dentistry and law.[10] Left unexplained was how textbooks should depict the jobs in which Jews have excelled. Perhaps they should be portrayed as migrant workers, as rodeo bronco busters, as baton twirlers, as oil rig maintenance personnel, or as automobile welders (despite comedian Jackie Mason's ethnographic axiom that "you never see a Jew under a car").

To be sure, neither the occupational structure nor the accumulation of wealth of the Jews was uniquely American. In the Western world in the nineteenth century, probably no family was richer than the Rothschilds of Frankfurt, Vienna, London, Paris, and Naples. In 1992 the family that had amassed the world's largest collection of real estate was Canadian—the Reichmanns. But by any standard the economic success of American Jewry was impressive. By 1988 this minority enjoyed a per capita income double that of non-Jews—a ratio that may have been skewed by the striking number of extremely rich Jews. In 1982, when *Forbes* magazine identified the forty wealthiest Americans, sixteen were Jews. Of the wealthiest four hundred Americans, slightly under a quarter of them were Jews. A 1986 study of senior executives of the largest businesses revealed that 7.4 percent were Jews (more than double their proportion of the general population), as were 13 percent of the senior executives under the age of forty. That year a New York real estate developer named Gerald Guterman threw a bar mitzvah party in honor of his son Jason and six hundred guests, renting the *Queen Elizabeth 2* (and two of its orchestras) for an overnight cruise. *Boston Magazine*, published in the city where Benjamin Franklin was born, inadvertently validated his faith that ability outweighs ancestry. In May 2004 the monthly identified the "fifty families that run this town." Absent were Cabots or Lodges or Lowells or Forbeses. But distinctly non-Brahmin families like the Epsteins, Leventhals, Finebergs, and Rappaports had joined the inner circle; and ranking first—ahead even of Kennedys—were the Krafts.[11] Many other cities reflected similar patterns of elite transformation.

Such occupants of the very upper brackets seemed to soar above even the traditional upper class. An exemplar was the Hungarian-born George Schwartz, whose family name his parents changed during his childhood to Soros. The word means "soar" (in the future tense) in Esperanto, the artificial language that a Yiddish-speaking Jew, Ludwig Lazar Zamenhof, had invented to unite a humanity otherwise torn by national animosities.[12] Based in London and then New York, the billionaire George Soros became the most famous hedge fund manager in the world, "the man who broke the Bank of England" in 1992. So formidable was his reputation for currency manipulation that in 1997 the prime minister of Malaysia blamed Soros for a precipitous drop in its currency. "The Jews robbed the Palestinians of everything, but in Malaysia they could not do so," Mahathir Mohamad opined. "Hence they do this—depress the ringgit."[13] Such speculators and financiers no doubt inspired the Reverend Jerry Falwell to inform his followers in the Moral Majority in 1979 that Jews aroused hostility because they "can make more money accidentally than you can on purpose." (This diagnosis of prejudice, he later averred, was made "in jest.") Two years later the director of the Moral Majority in New York, the Reverend Dan T. Fore, insisted that "Jews have a God-given ability to make money, almost a supernatural ability to make money."[14]

THE AUTHORITY OF EDUCATION

Another clergyman, Father Andrew M. Greeley, offered a more plausible explanation: "overthrust" among striving groups, which he defined as "the sheer raw power of their elemental drive for respectability and success." If Jews did better than most other ethnic and racial minorities, credit the advantages that formal education bestows in an economy that is increasingly dependent upon knowledge. It cannot be mere coincidence that Jews have spent more time in school (fourteen years) than other whites (11.1 years). Nearly nine out of every ten Jews of college age could be found at institutions of higher learning—twice the percentage of college-age Americans in general. Jews were also disproportionately represented at colleges and universities with the most demanding academic standards. When the American Council on Education surveyed first-year students, it discovered that those with Jewish parents had significantly better high school grades than their gentile peers, even though a far greater proportion of all Jews were attending college. Jews continued to excel in higher education and were by striking disproportions likely to be elected to Phi Beta Kappa.[15]

The history of higher education ratifies a whiggish view because the most prestigious private colleges and universities had earlier in the century lifted the gangplank to keep Jews out. "To hurt the Negro and avoid the Jew / Is the curriculum" is the beginning of Karl Shapiro's poem "University"; for the male Ivy League and the female Seven Sisters colleges, he did not take poetic license. In 1921 Jews constituted a fifth of the freshman class admitted to Harvard, prompting an effort to impose informal but severe quotas upon qualified Jews seeking admission. Between 1933 and 1942 the college cut in half the proportion of Jews in the student body. Yale allowed only slightly above 10 percent,[16] due to Dean Frederick S. Jones's complaint that "a few years ago every single scholarship of any value was won by a Jew. . . . We cannot allow that to go on." He peppered Yale's director of admissions with queries about an incoming class, as follows:"How many Jews among them? And are there any coons?"[17]

The discrimination that Dartmouth imposed, President Ernest Martin Hopkins cheerfully announced in 1933, meant that "life is so much pleasanter in Hanover . . . and friends of the college visiting us are so much happier with the decreased quota of the Hebraic element." In 1935, despite Richard Feynman's outstanding high school grades and his intellectual promise, Columbia College rejected him. Its Jewish quota had filled up, leaving no room for the future Nobel laureate (and possibly the greatest physicist of the second half of the twentieth century).[18] Only after the Second World War, when the genocidal policy of the Third Reich had made discrimination against American Jewish adolescents look a bit tacky, did the academy move toward greater meritocracy. So far did it move that, by 1998, the student body at Harvard College had become one-fifth Asian and close to one-third Jewish, provoking Pat Buchanan to call upon "ethnic

Catholics and Christians" to get "their fair share of the slots at Harvard," according to their proportion of the population.[19]

The faculty also diversified in the postwar era. During the Great Depression perhaps fewer than five hundred Jews were teaching in departments in the arts and sciences in institutions of higher learning.[20] Letters of recommendation betrayed the scope of academic bias. Daniel J. Boorstin "is a Jew, though not the kind to which one takes exception" (1934). Oscar Handlin was praised for having "none of the offensive traits which some people associate with his race" (1935). Both historians would later join the inner circle of the most influential scholars of the national past. Before 1940 no Jew had ever received tenure at Yale College, and in 1946, when its Department of Philosophy considered appointing one, its chairman asked a colleague to make allowances, given the "difficult[y] for men who like [Paul] Weiss have been brought out of the lowliest social condition to know how to behave in a society of genuine equality where it is not necessary to assert oneself."[21]

Half a century later no excuses were made when Yale selected Richard C. Levin as its president, and his coreligionists were heading so many other Ivy League institutions (James O. Freedman at Dartmouth, Harold Shapiro at Princeton, Michael I. Sovern at Columbia, Lawrence H. Summers at Harvard) that reminders were needed that the newly designated "Oy-vey League" was once otherwise. By the end of the century even Dartmouth was building a kosher kitchen on campus.[22] The downtrodden immigrants who arrived by the end of the nineteenth century were pitied by the MIT economist Francis I. Walker. He called them "the beaten races." But one of their progeny, Jerome Wiesner, would serve as president of MIT from 1971 until 1980. Though the number of Jewish teachers in higher education has been triple their proportion in the general population in the past four decades, Jews have constituted one-fifth to one-third of the faculty at prestigious colleges and universities.[23]

The rise of such academically gifted Jews despite the obstacles that had once defied the promise of American life is one conspicuous feature of the general pattern of upward mobility. H. L. Mencken offered this explanation:

> The majority of non-Anglo-Saxon immigrants since the Revolution, like the majority of Anglo-Saxon immigrants before the Revolution, have been, not the superior men of their native lands, but the botched and unfit: Irishmen starving to death in Ireland, Germans unable to weather the *Sturm und Drang* of the post-Napoleonic reorganization, Italians weed-grown on exhausted soil, Scandinavians run all to bone and no brain, Jews too incompetent to swindle even the barbarous peasants of Russia, Poland and Rumania.

But even the caustic Mencken accounted for the Jews' success by pointing to their superior acuity. "Some of the most intelligent people in America are Jewish," he noted. "Jews average much higher than [other] Americans." Empirical support comes from the controversial study of mental testing in comparative perspective, *The Bell Curve*, which claims that "Ashkenazic Jews of European origins test higher than any other ethnic group." In Great Britain as well as the United States "Jews . . . have an overall IQ mean somewhere between a half and a full standard deviation above the mean, with the source of the difference concentrated in the verbal component."[24] Such testimony undermined a prophecy of the Nazi minister of culture, Josef Goebbels. While encouraging the book burning in Berlin in May 1933, he predicted that "an age of exaggerated Jewish intellectualism" was over.[25] He was wrong.

INFLUENCE IN THE CULTURE

The prominence of one tiny minority as creative shapers and arbiters of the nation's culture was slyly revealed in September 1992, when presidential candidate Bill Clinton went to Hollywood for a million dollar fund-raiser. A routine featuring Mike Nichols and Elaine May began with director Nichols addressing the crowd of celebrities: "We can drop the Republican code for 'cultural elite'—good evening, fellow Jews."[26]

They were able to operate in a culture so fluid and so dynamic that their artistic and intellectual aspirations could be fulfilled not simply as Americans but also—if they chose—as Jews. The era began with dread, prior to the Six-Day War. "Any real catastrophe in Israel would affect me more deeply than almost anything else," the political theorist Hannah Arendt wrote; and her sentiment was shared by many other American Jews.[27] The spectacular triumph of the Israel Defense Forces stimulated not only the pride of many American Jews but also encouraged a return to ethnic "roots" that had the effect of tempering the venerable Diaspora yearning for inclusion. The civil rights movement was increasingly dominated by blacks who fostered an appreciation for their own versions of identity politics and cultural retrieval associated with Africa. That served as a model for younger Jews, many of whom became avid readers of translated Israeli novelists such as Amos Oz, A. B. Yehoshua, and Aharon Appelfeld. By the end of the 1960s a distinctive subculture emerged alongside the popular culture that was remarkably receptive to Jewish input.

The year 1976 marked the publication of *World of Our Fathers*, an effort to analyze and evoke the entire fabric of the Yiddishkeit of the eastern European Jewish immigrants who had lived primarily in New York. Author Irving Howe was not a professional historian, though his book may be the most monumental single achievement in American Jewish historiography; and he was careful to distinguish his interpretation from the easy temptations of nostalgia and from the perils of ethnic particularism. Howe believed that the community that had shaped the lives of his own parents could not be perpetuated or resuscitated; its passing could only be mourned. He could not have envisioned that, even as the Yiddish-inflected, proletarian-tinctured, progressively charged sensibility honored in *World of Our Fathers* was vanishing, Jewish culture was recharging its batteries. Mothers had lived in that world too, though Howe had manifestly neglected them and displayed scant interest in the gender divisions of the Lower East Side and Brooklyn and the Bronx. One rectification of such omissions came that very year. *Lilith*, the first Jewish feminist magazine, began publishing in 1976 under the leadership of editor in chief Susan Weidman Schneider.

That year the first klezmer record of the modern era was cut, by the Klez-morim, in Berkeley. Though Howe's book devotes sections to novelists and paint-ers and sculptors, musicians are ignored. Yet no signet of Yiddishkeit would prove to be so famous and so widespread as klezmer music—as though phantoms had been reborn and were transforming themselves in bewildering ways beyond the Pale. The most popular klezmer bands could sell as many as forty to fifty thou-sand albums. Probably the favorite, however, was violinist Itzhak Perlman's first klezmer CD, which sold over two hundred thousand. By the end of the era no self-respecting Jewish community—indeed, barely any synagogue—seemed to be without a klezmer band. Its foot-stomping power exerted an impact not confined to American Jewry. By the end of the century, more than a hundred klezmer bands were entertaining audiences in Germany alone.[28]

Nineteen seventy-six was also the year the Nobel Prize for Literature was awarded to Saul Bellow. A winner of the Pulitzer Prize and the National Book Award (three times) as well, he enjoyed so fluent a command of Yiddish as to be the catalyst for the transformation of Isaac Bashevis Singer into an American writer. In 1952, the very year that leading Yiddish writers were executed in the Soviet Union, Howe read Singer's "Gimpl Tam" (1945) and realized its liter-ary significance. With the aid of Eliezer Greenberg, with whom Howe co-edited *A Treasury of Yiddish Stories* (1953), Bellow translated what became "Gimpel the Fool" for the readers of *Partisan Review*. Two years after Bellow had journeyed to Stockholm, Singer followed him there; and though Singer paid tribute on that occasion to the Yiddish language and literature that had formed him, his work could not be reduced to the category of Yiddish fiction,[29] since his nearly two hundred short stories and eighteen novels, plus children's books, were widely known only in translation. (The huge number of articles, essays, sketches, and reviews that Singer published in the *Forverts* remain bur-ied in obscurity.) A life that had begun in his father's rabbinical court in Poland and shifted to New York's Upper West Side would end in Surfside, Florida. Singer thus personified the historical span of twentieth-century Jewry, from *shtetl* to Sunbelt.

The Yiddish language itself was supposed to be, in the indelible phrase of Casey Stengel, "dead at the present time." Its writers were the victims of the actuarial tables; and the *Forverts*, once the most widely read foreign language newspaper in the nation (in the era of the First World War), was losing its readers as well. In 1980 Aaron Lansky founded the National Yiddish Book Center and nurtured it into a powerhouse with an annual budget of $3 million, eighteen full-time staffers, and thirty-one thousand members. Its emergence needs to be put in a certain context, since some younger writers were turning from the problem of social adjustment to the spiritual problem of recovering tradition. While conceding that only "a small percentage of contemporary Jews will learn Yiddish," Lansky feared that "if we lose our bookishness, we lose the nuance of Judaism."[30] Yet the National Yiddish Book Center signified in itself a remarkable reclamation of Jewish literature within American culture.

Since 1992 only aerospace has topped entertainment on the list of the nation's exports. Jewish creativity is encased within and has helped to nourish the first global culture, which is more American than it is anything else. To be sure, the birth certificate had been registered as far back as the 1920s, when the United States was producing 90 percent of the world's films and was establishing a system of distributing them: Planet Hollywood. The studio bosses, who were mostly Jews, determined which movies would be made, characteristically on the basis of instinct. "If my fanny squirms" during the screening of a film, Harry Cohn of Columbia Pictures once claimed, "it's bad. If my fanny doesn't squirm, it's good. It's as simple as that." When a scenarist, Herman Mankiewicz, interjected, "Imagine—the whole world wired to Harry Cohn's ass!"[31] he was fired—but the writer's inference was not entirely wrong. Because American culture has been so enormously popular, wired to the whole world, Jews in the arts differed from the poets and philosophers who helped shape the multireligious, multicultural literature of Spain in the High Middle Ages or even the avant-garde sophistication of fin de siècle Austria and of Weimar Germany.

To the mass culture that formed in the United States, with its best-sellers and its box office blockbusters and hit television shows, Jews have been pivotal. After Communism collapsed in Czechoslovakia, the first novel to be translated into Czech was *Portnoy's Complaint*; Roth's extended in-joke had surmounted national borders as well as any ethnic enclave to which it might otherwise have been consigned. The first post-Communist ambassador whom Czechoslovakia assigned to the United States, Michael Zantovsky, was also the author of a book on Woody Allen.[32] Three months after the terrorist attack upon the World Trade Center, a reporter interviewed an Iranian teacher living in North Tehran, where echoes of *Marg bar Amrika* (death to America) had reverberated through the streets. She recalled the news of September 11 vividly: "Do you want to know what I was really worried about?" She paused. "Woody Allen. I didn't want him to die. I wanted to know that he was all right. I love his films."[33] A 1995 poll taken in Bangkok disclosed that more of its teenagers could identify Steven Spielberg than could name the mayor of their city. During the Golden Age of Spanish

Jewry, its most eminent figures wrote in Arabic. German had been the lingua franca of the Zionist congresses as well other international organizations in which Jews were nearly as well represented: the socialists' Second International and the International Psychoanalytic Association. But, by the end of the century, English—sometimes with a Yiddish inflection—was unrivaled as the lingo of global culture.

The replete opportunities the United States offered included fields that were not historically attractive to Jews. A century ago, who could have predicted that the profession of architecture would be dominated by practitioners and visionaries whose ancestors were wanderers, expecting only instability and eviction? Yet, in the era after 1967, any list of the nation's most admired architects would have included Louis Kahn, Frank Gehry, and Daniel Libeskind, plus the Israeli-born, Boston-based Moshe Safdie. Libeskind designed the Jewish Museum in Berlin and won the commission to design the "master plan" to replace the World Trade Center. Richard Meier designed not only the Getty Center in Los Angeles, but won the commission to design a new Vatican church in a suburb of Rome. Meier wanted Pope John Paul II to inspect the model only when properly lit. "It's just my *mishegoss*, I know," Meier recalled, "but the Pope should not see the model in the dark. . . . He was very gracious." As befits an eclectic and heterogeneous national culture, the synagogue in the United States has flaunted so many architectural styles—from Romanesque to Gothic, from Moorish to Modern—that when the actor Walter Matthau asked the director Billy Wilder, while driving past the Wilshire Boulevard Temple in Los Angeles, what to call its style, he replied, "Mishegothic."[34] The painter Anselm Kiefer once explained why the tonalities in his paintings were so dark: he was German.[35] So severe a limitation would have struck American Jewish artists—and American Jews in general—as arbitrary. Their palette need not be restricted; they have been free to wear a coat of many colors.

THE RESPECT FOR DIVERSITY

Opportunities for the cultivation of the imagination are therefore greater than a century earlier. What has changed is the framework within which Jews and other minorities operate. In the era of the First World War, nativism was a force to be reckoned with, while racism was even more pervasive. The champions of Christianity did not recognize other faiths as equals, and the ideal of American-ism put Jews at a disadvantage. They did at least enjoy the status of membership in the white race when no group was more despised, shunned, and persecuted than black Americans. They sought equality of opportunity in the economy and equality of treatment in public life, according to polls, which revealed white suspicion that the chief goal of civil rights agitation was instead to smash the taboo against intermarriage.[36] The last third of the century therefore began, quite aptly, with *Loving v. Virginia*, in 1967, when the Supreme Court invalidated state statutes prohibiting wedlock across the racial divide. Like all other states, Virginia was now for lovers. Race would no longer legally trump romance, and the deepest anxieties buttressing white supremacy had been faced (if not exorcised). With racial exclusivity decisively repudiated, diversity would henceforth be legitimated as a public ideal that would affect private life as well. The balance would be struck between the right to be equal and the freedom to be different.

By the dawn of the twenty-first century, nativism had been so thoroughly buried, and the notion of a society hospitable to immigrants has become so enchanting, that President George W. Bush, visiting Dakar, Senegal in 2003, gave the impression that all Americans had come voluntarily: "It's very interesting when you think about it, the slaves who left here to go to America, because of their steadfast [*sic*] and their religion and their belief in freedom, helped change America."[37] Among their descendants were Bush's two choices of secretary of state. That Colin Powell and Condoleezza Rice would occupy such a post—in a very conservative Republican administration—would have been unimaginable when the decade of the 1960s began and symbolized how thoroughly racism had been discredited.

The challenge of religious diversity remained. In the history of the Constitution, religion and the state were separated at birth. The First Amendment stipulated that the government was not supposed to support one faith, or some denominations, or all denominations; Congress was blocked from even *considering* legislation pertaining to the establishment of religion. But the amendment also vouchsafed freedom of worship, and the yearning of believers to exercise that right (by mandating prayers and reading the Bible in public schools or by teaching the book of Genesis instead of the Darwinian case for natural selection in biology classes or by building creches on town squares) often threatened to lower the wall of separation that the Framers had erected for the sake of civic peace. An uneasy truce was achieved in 1971, when the Supreme Court ruled in *Lemon v. Kurtzman* that a law pertaining to faith must have a secular purpose, that the primary consequence of such a law must neither advance nor inhibit religion, and that government would not thereby be entangled excessively in religion.[38]

Despite the upsurge in evangelical and fundamentalist Protestantism and its willingness to engage in political action, the religious status of the Jewish minority did not suffer; in the ceremonies of public life Judaism was generally accepted as more than merely a junior partner of Christianity. Group relations among Jews and other religious groups were generally conducted without friction. The 1992 riots in Los Angeles—in the wake of the arrest and beating of motorist Rodney King—left fifty-five dead and about $1 billion in property damage. But,

for religious minorities, the plea that he issued ("Can't we all get along?") produced an answer in the affirmative.

THE ALLURE OF POLITICS

The first Jew whom gentiles ever elected anywhere to public office was Francis
Salvador, a delegate to the First and Second Provincial Congresses of South
Carolina in the eighteenth century. When the Framers of the Constitution stipulated that no religious test would be imposed upon any public official, they could
hardly have foreseen that an Orthodox Jew would be selected as the vice presidential nominee by the most continuous of American political parties. In 2000
the candidacy of Senator Joseph Lieberman (D-CT) confirmed the absence of a
religious test, and, though the Democratic ticket received half a million more
popular votes than the GOP but was denied the White House, no observer
blamed the defeat upon Lieberman or his religion. In 1815, when Secretary of
State James Monroe fired Mordecai M. Noah as consul in Tunis, the rationale
was simple: "At the time of your appointment, it was not known that the religion
which you profess would form any obstacle" to performing his diplomatic duties.[39] One of Monroe's successors was Henry A. Kissinger, a German refugee
born to Orthodox parents. His religion was no obstacle to the conduct of negotiations between Israel and Egypt, nor to representing his adopted country (or
President Nixon) in Moscow and Beijing during some of the most delicate diplomatic moments of the cold war.

In the fall of 1975 Uganda's despotic Idi Amin addressed the General Assembly of the United Nations and asserted that "the United States of America
has been colonized by the Zionists who hold all the tools of development and
power." He called upon Americans to "rid their society of the Zionists." But,
though the delegates gave Amin a standing ovation,[40] the United States ignored his advice. If anything, the momentum that had begun with Francis
Salvador seemed to accelerate in the period after 1967. Wisconsinites voted to
be represented in the United States Senate only by Jews (Russell Feingold and
Herb Kohl) and both of California's senators also belong to Hadassah (Barbara
Boxer and Dianne Feinstein). In 1968 President Lyndon B. Johnson nominated
Abe Fortas to serve as chief justice of the Supreme Court, an effort undermined by ethical lapses on the bench that required his resignation the follow-
ing year.

Johnson's successor was asked by his attorney general: "When are you going
to fill that Jewish seat on the Supreme Court?" The answer was unenthusiastic.
"Well, how about after I die?" Nixon snorted, provoking John Mitchell to laugh.
In any event the president resented having his choices graded by the American

Bar Association, "with all those kikes on that."[41] But the last of the twentieth-century presidents lacked Nixon's bigotry; Bill Clinton's only appointments to the Supreme Court were both Jews: Ruth Bader Ginsburg and Stephen Breyer. The two terms of the Clinton administration also ignited the biggest boom in American economic history, and, on February 15, 1999, when *Time* magazine put on its cover "the Three Marketeers" hailed for orchestrating the prosperity, Federal Reserve chairperson Alan Greenspan, Secretary of the Treasury Robert Rubin, and his deputy and successor Lawrence Summers belonged to "The Committee to Save the World." (Christians might beg to differ: only one Jew is needed to save the world.) Summers (whose uncle is Paul Samuelson) also praised United States Trade Representative Charlene Barshefsky as crucial to Clinton's "economic leadership team." Its "very heavily Jewish" (that is, entirely Jewish) composition "passed without comment or notice," which, Summers added, "was something that would have been inconceivable a generation or two ago."[42]

The habit of Jews to vote mostly for progressive or leftist candidates was hard to break. In 2002 the Hillel Foundation surveyed the political attitudes of Jewish college freshmen. Even those whose grandparents had voted for Franklin D. Roosevelt (whose New Deal set the groove within which Jews have voted with such predictability thereafter) remained on the left side of the political spectrum: 50.9 percent of the first-year students labeled themselves "liberal" or "far left," 39.5 percent "middle of the road," and only 9.5 percent "conservative" or "far right." Like their parents and grandparents, younger Jews still tended to be about "20 to 30 percentage points more liberal than the general population," according to political analyst Leonard Fein, and even "as the general population moves rightward, the Jews move too, but the margin of difference remains the same." No wonder then that the idealist young Chinese American who is the protagonist of Gish Jen's novel, *Mona in the Promised Land*, looks up to the Jews not merely as a model minority, not merely as successful enough to be mainstream, but also because of their politics, "with their booming belief in doing right, with their calling and their crying out *Justice!*"[43]

THE IMPACT OF FEMINISM

No demand for justice was more reverberant during this era than the cry for gender equality. The most successful appellate attorney on behalf of women's rights was Ruth Bader Ginsburg, who served as general counsel of the Women's Rights Project of the American Civil Liberties Union, winning five of her first six cases before the Supreme Court on which she would begin serving in 1993. When her father died in Brooklyn, kaddish was recited in the family's home. But the mourners had trouble collecting the sufficient number of ten. She recalled: "They kept counting the men, and my mother and I were there, and they looked right past us, as if my mother and I were not there." Justice Ginsburg traced her opposition to gender discrimination to that night, when she was excluded from the circle entitled to say the kaddish.[44] She personified the struggle of feminism to end the overt sexism on which Judaism had long been based.

Modern feminism began with one book, *The Feminine Mystique* (1963). Its author, Betty Friedan, became president of the National Organization for Women, which she cofounded, from 1966 until 1969. Friedan was also Jewish, as were a striking number of the most prominent feminists, both liberal and radical: Bella Abzug, Phyllis Chesler, Andrea Dworkin, Shulamith Firestone, Vivian Gornick, Robin Morgan, Letty Cottin Pogrebin, Meredith Tax, and Naomi Weisstein. Their energy and dedication (and rage) was often intensified by encounters with the patriarchal norms of Jewish marriages and families.[45] These activists not only mobilized others to challenge male chauvinism in law and policy but also inspired others to enlarge the narrow roles to which traditional Judaism had confined women. The result was a transformation as dramatic as any in the saga of American Jewry.

When the era began, no woman in history had been an ordained rabbi. Nor did any woman in Jewish public and institutional life in the nation identify herself as a lesbian. Nor did any rabbi acknowledge himself to be gay. The Reform movement ordained Sally Priesand in 1972; Reconstructionist Sandy Eisenberg Sasso joined her the following year. By 1980 there were enough of their colleagues to form a Women's Rabbinic Network, and five years later the Conservative movement ordained a woman for the first time, Amy Eilberg, who graduated from the Jewish Theological Seminary. Scarcely eight decades earlier, it had accepted for admission Henrietta Szold, the editorial sparkplug of the Jewish Publication Society of America and of the *American Jewish Year Book*, precisely with the understanding that she would *not* want to become a rabbi (as her father had been).[46] By the end of the century Orthodox and Conservative seminaries refused to ordain openly gay and lesbian candidates for the rabbinate. But rabbis with such an orientation were no longer invisible; and some of their straight colleagues joined them in devising commitment ceremonies for lesbians and gay men in states depriving such couples of the right to marry. Nothing more soundly validated the whig angle on the Jewish past than the opportunity afforded to all members of the non-Orthodox community—regardless of gender or sexual orientation—to engage as rabbis in the biblical and postbiblical texts and in the durable mysteries of theology.

In 1975, when Priesand published her revised rabbinic thesis of three years earlier, *Judaism and the New Woman*, she called for changes that would soon pervade Jewish worship: the principle of equality for men and women and for sons and daughters, the right to be counted in the minyan, the right to read from the Torah, the revision of liturgical language so that it would henceforth be gender sensitive. Soon there would be even more changes, as historian Pamela S. Nadell has noted: adult bat mitzvah ceremonies for women who had not done so as teenagers; women's communal seders; new prayers for healing after rape and after divorce and for remaining single; meditations after miscarriage; feminist midrashim; covenantal birth ceremonies for daughters as the equivalent of the *brit milah* (rite of circumcision); readings and prayers for stillbirth, for infertility, for adoption, for marital separation. *Rosh Chodesh*—the new moon—has been reclaimed as a feminist holiday. The emergence of feminism has probably affected liturgy, rituals, theology, and institutional practices more strikingly than any ideological change within American Judaism since the birth of Reform in the mid-nineteenth century. Such innovations also reflected the values that were amplified as never before. In 1988, when American Jews were invited to name which attribute was most salient to their Jewish identity, "equality" ranked first, easily beating support of Israel and adherence to Judaism itself.[47]

THE PERSISTENCE OF RELIGION

The contours of the ancient religion that trailed behind the prestige Jews accorded to the American principle of equality were altered in ways that could not have been anticipated earlier in the century. The varieties of religious experience would have bewildered earlier generations of Jews. Here the author's own testimony cannot be atypical: he has been invited to a gay commitment ceremony in a synagogue, participated in a sabbath dinner that concluded with the traditional blessings and also with marijuana, attended weddings conducted by a rabbi who recited Navajo prayers. The whig interpretation is therefore compatible with the Yiddish adage: "Oib men lebt lang genug, vet men alles derleben" (If you live long enough, you'll live to see everything). In 1922 the first bat mitzvah ceremony in history guaranteed that honorees henceforth did not have to be boys. Eight decades later they didn't have to be Jewish—because envious gentile friends wanted to stage their own increasingly popular "bar mitzvah parties." One pubescent Methodist in Dallas told her parents that she "wanted to be Jewish," and was willing to study Hebrew, "so that I could have a bat mitzvah." Madonna got into the act as well, wearing a T-shirt during her Re-Invention World Tour that proclaimed "Kabbalists Do It Better." Indeed satirists in the employ of *Mad* magazine targeted the transformation of the Material Girl into the Meshuggeneh Girl and wondered if her identification with Jewishness included culinary markers such as gefilte fish ("Like a Sturgeon").[48]

The surprise that most practitioners of Judaism pulled by embracing feminism was nearly matched by the resilience of Orthodoxy, which exerted a disproportionate influence in the Jewish community. No longer an immigrant phenomenon, Orthodoxy violated expectations of a mere half-life in a republic that was devoted only to those truths that are self-evident. American public life is also marked by more than just a trace of don't-tread-on-me antinomianism. Of the nearly 3 percent of the American populace that was Jewish in this era, the very observant remained a very small minority (about 10 percent). But the overwhelming majority of children enrolled in Jewish day schools are Orthodox, and the observant have managed to create institutions and social networks that are likely to endure. The varieties of religious experience also characterize the Orthodox themselves—ranging from Modern Orthodox to assorted Hasidic groups, of which the most prominent was Lubavitch, most recently known as Chabad-Lubavitch. Its ardent messianism entailed outreach to far less observant coreligionists and divergence from the rest of the community, for example, in sponsoring huge candle-lighting ceremonies during Hanukkah on public property.[49]

The openness with which this holiday of Jewish national liberation was conducted reflected the expansiveness of freedom of worship by the end of the twentieth century. It also suggested a renegotiation of the way that Jews celebrated the religious calendar every December. Beginning in the 1940s, Jewish songwriters gave their Christian neighbors a wider repertory with which to commemorate the birth of the Savior. Irving Berlin's "White Christmas" (1942) became the most recorded song in history; even Barbra Streisand cut a version. But other Jews are credited with composing or helping to write such yuletide standards as "Rudolph the Red-Nosed Reindeer" (1949), "Let It Snow! Let It Snow! Let It Snow!" (1946), "Silver Bells" (1951), and "The Christmas Song" (1946), which begins, "Chestnuts roasting on an open fire, / Jack Frost nipping at your nose." Hanukkah songs were also composed in the 1940s. Some, ironically, were written by the "Okie" troubadour Woody Guthrie, whose mother-in-law was the Yiddish poet Aliza Greenblatt. His oeuvre included "Honeyky Hanukkah"—songs that his daughter Nora Guthrie later classified as "culturally Jewish" and that diverge from the tumbleweed-tossed ballads that made him famous; Guthrie's musical tributes to Hanukkah were unrecorded before his death in 1967.[50]

But, during the era that opened that year, the claims of a festival that is virtually synchronous with Christmas could be more directly honored. Folksinger Peter Yarrow had little formal Jewish education and grew up believing that religion meant ethics, not ritual. After a rabbi assured him that being a good Jew entailed living decently (and consistently with Judaic values), rather than synagogue attendance, Yarrow got the point. Only in 1983, when Peter, Paul and Mary were scheduled to perform a "Holiday Celebration" at Carnegie Hall, modeled upon the Weavers' Christmas concert, did Yarrow reach toward the Judaism he had abandoned. Because the concert coincided with the third night of Hanukkah, he decided to write "a kind of manifesto of my own Jewishness." The result was "Light One Candle": "Light one candle for the Maccabee children / With thanks that their light didn't die / Light one candle for the pain they endured / When their right to exist was denied." He asked listeners to "Light one candle for the terrible sacrifice / Justice and freedom demand / But light one candle for the wisdom to know / When the peacemaker's time is at hand." The chorus of the song enjoins listeners not to "let the light go out! / It's lasted for so many years! Don't let the light go out! / Let it shine through our love and our tears."[51] Such sentiments echoed the 1960s ideals of seeking social justice and opposing war, repackaged as an explicitly Jewish song in which only the opening line refers to a distinctive religious heritage or to the holiday itself. "Light One Candle" manages to be both Jewish and universal.

Aging devotees of the sun might well share Tom Lehrer's yearning to observe that festival in southern California, "wearing sandals, / Lighting candles / By the sea," and hailing "Judas Maccabeus / Boy, if he could only see us!" (1990). But for children feeling bereft during the yuletide season because of their parents' denial of the divinity of Christ, solace arrived in the form of "The Chanukah Song" (1995). Comedian Adam Sandler gave that holiday a series of celebrity endorsements: "When you feel like the only kid in town without a Christmas tree, / Here's a list of people who are Jewish, just like you and me." The list from show business was a little padded, however ("Paul Newman's half Jewish; Goldie Hawn's half too, / Put them together—what a fine lookin' Jew"). When it premiered on the Christmas show of *Saturday Night Live*, "The Chanukah Song" generated such enthusiasm that Sandler did two sequels. The concept was expanded into an animated film, Sony Pictures' *Eight Crazy Nights* (2002), the first movie dedicated to this holiday to emerge from Hollywood. "I Have a Little Dreidel" never exploded into mass culture. But in 1999, when West Point installed a Hillel Foundation, Jewish cadets sang "The Chanukah Song."[52] Half a century earlier, Jewish celebrities tended to mute their ethnic origins. Sandler pushed in the opposite direction, by exaggerating piety: "Melissa Gilbert and Michael Landon never mix meat with dairy / Maybe they shoulda called that show *Little Kosher House on the Prairie*." Sandler's effort to pump *tam* (soul) into the holiday season had its analogue in *Mamaloshen* (1998), in which Mandy Patinkin dreams of a "White Christmas" in Irving Berlin's first language: Yiddish.

The capacity of Judaism to renew itself, to assume new forms, to erupt in the most unpredictable places is a reminder of the persistence of faith among a people that has also harbored more than its share of unobservant "coreligionists," of secularists and freethinkers. Indeed they have been numerous enough to stir doubt whether this minority constitutes a community at all, so fragmented does it appear to be. Such multifariousness may not be a source of strength, but is surely a sign of life. Whether religion itself can serve as a force cohesive enough and compelling enough to sustain this people through a new century, or whether some other resource will need to be summoned to sustain American Jews, is not the sort of knowledge to which the historian is privy. But, having made the United States their home, they can sit under their own vines and fig trees, with no one to make them afraid. Complete citizens of a modern republic, American Jews are also unabashed legatees of an ancient faith and a richly textured past.

NOTES

1. Archibald MacLeish, "America Was Promises" (1939), in Collected Poems, 1917–1952 (Boston, 1952), 333–41.

2. Marc Dollinger, Quest for Inclusion: Jews and Liberalism in Modern America (Princeton, 2000), 78; John Higham, Send These to Me: Jews and Other Immigrants in Urban America (New York, 1975), 193.

3. Marie Syrkin, "About Philip Roth," Commentary 55 (March 1973): 12; Philip Roth, "Imagining Jews" (1974), in Reading Myself and Others (New York, 1975), 243–45.

4. Quoted in Hillel Halkin, "The Trajectory from Portnoy to Sabbath," Forward, August 23, 1996, 21.

5. William F. Buckley Jr., In Search of Anti-Semitism (New York, 1992), 44; Edward S. Shapiro, We Are Many: Reflections on American Jewish History and Identity (Syracuse, 2005), 208–17.

6. Murray Friedman, "Intergroup Relations," in Milton Himmelfarb and David Singer, eds., American Jewish Year Book 81 (Philadelphia, 1980): 121.

7. Murray Friedman, with Peter Binzen, What Went Wrong? The Creation and Collapse of the Black-Jewish Alliance (New York, 1995), 323, 328–342; Stephen J. Whitfield, "An Anatomy of Black Antisemitism," Judaism 43 (Fall 1994): 342–43, 345, 351–55.

8. Benjamin Franklin, "Information to Those Who Would Remove to America" (1782), in Ralph Ketcham, ed., The Political Thought of Benjamin Franklin (Indianapolis, 1965), 338.

9. Stephan Thernstrom and Abigail Thernstrom, America in Black and White: One Nation, Indivisible (New York, 1997), 541; Seymour Martin Lipset and Earl Raab, Jews and the New American Scene (Cambridge, 1995), 26–27.

10. Lipset and Raab, Jews and the New American Scene, 22–23; Diane Ravitch, The Language Police: How Pressure Groups Restrict What Students Learn (New York, 2003), 192.

11. Edward S. Shapiro, "Jews with Money," Judaism 36 (Winter 1987): 7–8, 11–12, 13–15; "Wiping the Joneses Off the Map," New York Times, August 27, 1995, F6; "The Fifty Families," Boston Magazine 42 (May 2004): 190, 192–93.

12. Joshua Muravchik, "The Mind of George Soros," Commentary 117 (March 2004): 48.

13. Quoted in Timothy L. O'Brien, "He's Seen the Enemy. It Looks Like Him," *New York Times*, December 6, 1998, 3:1, 11.

14. Quoted in Alan Crawford, *Thunder on the Right: The "New Right" and the Politics of Resentment* (New York, 1980), 160, and in Joyce Purnick, "Moral Majority Establishes Beachhead in New York," *New York Times*, February 5, 1981, B4.

15. Andrew M. Greeley, *Ethnicity, Denomination, and Inequality* (Beverly Hills, 1976), 18–19, 21, 24, 39, 70, 76; Seymour M. Lipset, "The Political Profile of American Jewry," in Robert S. Wistrich, ed., *Terms of Survival: The Jewish World Since 1945* (New York, 1995), 157; Lipset and Raab, *Jews and the New American Scene*, 27.

16. Karl Shapiro, *Selected Poems* (New York, 1968), 8; Laurence Veysey, "The History of University Admissions," *Reviews in American History* 8 (March 1980): 117–18.

17. Quoted in Marcia Graham Synnott, *The Half-Opened Door: Discrimination and Admissions at Harvard, Yale, and Princeton, 1900–1970* (Westport, CT, 1979), 17, 141.

18. Quoted in James O. Freedman, "Ghosts of the Past: Anti-Semitism at Elite Colleges," *Chronicle of Higher Education*, December 1, 2000, B9; John Gribben and Mary Gribben, *Richard Feynman: A Life in Science* (London, 1998), 22.

19. Quoted in Blake Eskin, "The Featherman File," *Forward*, December 4, 1998, 2.

20. Lewis S. Feuer, "The Stages in the Social History of Jewish Professors in American Colleges and Universities," *American Jewish History* 71 (June 1982): 462.

21. Quoted in Peter Novick, *That Noble Dream: The "Objectivity Question" and the American Historical Profession* (New York, 1988), 172–73, in Dan A. Oren, *Joining the Club: A History of Jews and Yale* (New Haven, 1985), 261–67, and in Susanne Klingenstein, *Jews in the American Academy, 1900–1940: The Dynamics of Intellectual Assimilation* (New Haven, 1991), 3–4.

22. "Dartmouth OKs Kosher Dining," *Forward*, December 8, 2000, 14.

23. Quoted in Ann Douglas, *Terrible Honesty: Mongrel Manhattan in the 1920s* (New York, 1995), 306; Lipset and Raab, *Jews and the New American Scene*, 27; Lipset, "Political Profile of American Jewry," in Wistrich, *Terms of Survival*, 157; Marshall I. Goldman, "Disputing Auerbach's View of Wellesley," *Sh'ma* 15 (November 16, 1984): 5.

24. H. L. Mencken, "On Being an American" (1922), in *Prejudices: A Selection*, ed. James T. Farrell (New York, 1958), 99; H. L. Mencken to Roscoe Peacock, April 30, 1931, in Guy J. Forgue, ed., *Letters of H. L. Mencken* (Boston, 1981), 328–29; Richard J. Herrnstein and Charles Murray, *The Bell Curve: Intelligence and Class Structure in American Life* (New York, 1994), 275.

25. Quoted in Sander L. Gilman, *Smart Jews: The Construction of the Image of Jewish Superior Intelligence* (Lincoln, 1996), 84.

26. Quoted in Alan Schroeder, *Celebrity-in-Chief: How Show Business Took Over the White House* (Boulder, 2004), 135.

27. Quoted in Elisabeth Young-Bruehl, *Hannah Arendt: For Love of the World* (New Haven, 1982), 455.

28. Hankus Netsky, "American Klezmer: A Brief History," in Mark Slobin, ed., *American Klezmer: Its Roots and Offshoots* (Berkeley, 2002), 21; Mark Slobin, *Fiddler on the Move: Exploring the Klezmer World* (New York, 2000), 38; Jeremy Eichler, "Klezmer's Final Frontier," *New York Times*, August 29, 2004, 2:1.

29. Janet Hadda, *Isaac Bashevis Singer: A Life* (New York, 1997), 130; Sidra DeKoven Ezrahi, *Booking Passage: Exile and Homecoming in the Modern Jewish Imagination* (Berkeley, 2000), 200–8.

30. Zackary Sholem Berger, "Man Who Saved a Million Books Writes One of His Own," *Forward*, September 17, 2004, 2.

31. Quoted in Bob Thomas, *King Cohn: The Life and Times of Hollywood Mogul Harry Cohn* (Beverly Hills, 2000), 137–38.

32. David Remnick, "Exit Havel: The King Leaves the Castle," *New Yorker* 79 (February 17 and 24, 2003): 91.

33. Quoted in Joe Klein, "Shadow Land: Who's Winning the Fight for Iran's Future?" *New Yorker* 78 (February 18 and 25, 2002): 66–67.

34. Quoted in "Heaven's Window," *New Yorker* 74 (April 27 and May 4, 1998): 116; Maurice Zolotow, *Billy Wilder in Hollywood* (New York, 1977), 230.

35. Mark Rosenthal, *Anselm Kiefer* (Munich, 1987), 32.

36. Gunnar Myrdal, *An American Dilemma: The Negro Problem and Modern Democracy* (New York, 1944), 54–61.

37. Jacob Weisberg, ed., *Still More George W. Bushisms* (New York, 2003), 49.

38. Leonard W. Levy, *The Establishment Clause: Religion and the First Amendment* (New York, 1986), 129–32.

39. Quoted in Jonathan D. Sarna, *Jacksonian Jew: The Two Worlds of Mordecai Noah* (New York, 1981), 26.

40. Quoted in Daniel Patrick Moynihan, with Suzanne Weaver, *A Dangerous Place* (Boston, 1978), 152–54.

41. Quoted in John W. Dean, *The Rehnquist Choice: The Untold Story of the Nixon Appointment That Redefined the Supreme Court* (New York, 2001), 73, 206.

42. Lawrence H. Summers, "Harvard President Denounces Anti-Semitism," FrontPageMagazine.com, November 17, 2003.

43. Leonard Fein, "A Generational Shift That Isn't," *Forward*, January 16, 2004, 10; Gish Jen, *Mona in the Promised Land* (New York, 1997), 254.

44. Quoted in Leon Wieseltier, *Kaddish* (New York, 1998), 189.

45. Joyce Antler, *The Journey Home: Jewish Women and the American Century* (New York, 1997), 260.

46. Michael E. Staub, *Torn at the Roots: The Crisis of Jewish Liberalism in Postwar America* (New York, 2002), 247–49; Pamela S. Nadell, *Women Who Would Be Rabbis: A History of Women's Ordination, 1889–1985* (Boston, 1998), 54, 56–59, 151–53, 188–89.

47. Pamela S. Nadell, "Bridges to 'A Judaism Transformed by Women's Wisdom,'" 1, 3, 11, 12–14, in MS; Lipset and Raab, *Jews and the New American Scene*, 134.

48. Quoted in Elizabeth Bernstein, "You Don't Have to Be Jewish to Want a *Bar Mitzvah*," *Wall Street Journal*, January 14, 2004, A1; Ruth La Ferla, "Front Row," *New York Times*, June 29, 2004, B7; "The Dumbest People, Events, and Things of 2004," *Mad*, no. 449 (January 2005): 38.

49. Jonathan D. Sarna, *American Judaism: A History* (New Haven, 2004), 290–91, 296–306, 326–327.

50. Jody Rosen, *White Christmas: The Story of an American Song* (New York, 2002), 163–64; Larry Katz, "Oy Vey, Look Who's Writing Christmas Favorites," *Boston*

Herald, December 24, 2003, 37, 44; Jon Moskowitz, "Holy Folk," *Forward*, December 12, 2003, 14.

51. Peter Yarrow in Judea and Ruth Pearl, eds., *I Am Jewish: Personal Reflections Inspired by the Last Words of Daniel Pearl* (Woodstock, VT, 2004), 217–20.

52. Jennifer Fishbein-Gold, "Playing Sweetheart to West Point Cadets—At Least for a Night," *Forward*, December 31, 1999, 18.

Topical Essays

7

THE EVER DYING DENOMINATION

American Jewish Orthodoxy, 1824–1965

KIMMY CAPLAN

In a newspaper interview in 1912, Rabbi Leon Harrison (1866–1928) of the Reform congregation Temple Israel in St. Louis, declared that "Reform Judaism holds the future of American Judaism in its hands. . . . Under the conditions that prevail, orthodoxy [in America] is impossible."[1] Several Orthodox rabbis and lay leaders of the mass immigration period, such as Rabbi Zalman J. Friederman (1865/66–1936) of Boston, shared a similar grim view regarding the future of Orthodoxy in America, although for different reasons.[2] This pessimistic outlook prevailed over several decades. For example, in a sermon published in 1946, Orthodox Rabbi Jacob D. Gordon wondered whether "there will, God forbid, come a time in which one will see the type of a real [i.e., Orthodox] Jew in a picture in chronicles or in an antique house."[3]

The future of American Judaism and American Jews in general, and that of the Orthodox community in particular, has been and remains an issue of primary concern and interest for Jewish religious leaders, intellectuals, and scholars of American Judaism and Jewish life, and, although much less documented, rank-and-file Jews. This topic has been continuously discussed for over a century in various lectures, presentations, and sermons, as well as in texts, in both religious and nonreligious contexts and has been used as a platform for ongoing fund-raising among numerous Jewish organizations for several decades.[4]

As far as the mostly pessimistic scenarios regarding the future of American Jewish Orthodoxy are concerned, this ongoing discussion is obviously tied to the ideological opinions of those relating to this topic, but also to the scholarly interest in American Orthodoxy, both directly and indirectly. These pessimistic scenarios are common among various Orthodox leaders no less than among their opponents and observers. The origins of this Orthodox self-perception regarding its uncertain survival in the future lay in this camp's widespread historical outlook, according to which all Jews were traditional (i.e., in according to their understanding Orthodox) until the second half of the eighteenth century, and, within half a century (1800–1850), that number shrinking considerably. As a result of this quick and consequently most threatening development, Orthodoxy perceives itself as being in an ongoing struggle for its existence, and in order to exist its leaders developed various and at times different counterculture and enclave-culture strategies in order to survive.[5]

This chapter provides an overview of certain stages in the development of American Jewish Orthodoxy between 1824 and 1965, emphasizing several crossroads in which the perceived threat was that Orthodoxy is in a battle for its very survival. This discussion begins in 1824, the year in which Isaac Leeser (1806–1868) immigrated to America and the Reformed Society of Israelites was founded in Charleston, South Carolina—both landmark events in the history of Orthodoxy in America. Toward the mid-1960s it became evident that Orthodoxy survived all the pessimistic predictions, wishes, and prophecies regarding its probable disappearance, notwithstanding additional grim forecasts regarding its future that have appeared in later years, and therefore 1965 ends an era insofar as this article's main theme in concerned.

I will highlight certain major themes and processes in the history of American Jewish Orthodoxy and the connections between these processes, including Orthodox perceptions of and attitudes toward America, the shift from Orthodoxy in America to American Orthodoxy, changing levels of openness and closeness, inclusion and seclusion, within Orthodoxy toward the surrounding Jewish and non-Jewish societies, as well as the development of certain subgroups within American Orthodoxy such as the Haredi (ultra-Orthodox) community. In addition, this essay indirectly addresses certain Orthodox perceptions and images regarding American society, culture, and religion and the strategies of survival Orthodox leaders created and implemented in this distinctive Jewish Diaspora. Understanding these perceptions, images, and strategies would shed light on why, despite all the aforementioned predictions, American Jewish Orthodoxy has not disappeared but rather emerged as a vibrant community within contemporary American Judaism.

JEWISH ORTHODOXY SETS FOOT IN AMERICA

During the colonial period strictly observant Jews settled in America. The Spanish-Portuguese congregations were traditional in nature and demanded adherence to certain publicly noticeable aspects of religious observance, such as Sabbath observance in the public sphere. However, conservative religious practice is not identical with Orthodoxy. Neither these congregations nor their members were Orthodox. Rather they were traditional. Another expression of their traditional outlook is the fact that they did not consciously recognize definitions, such as religious and secular, and certainly had no sense of denominational-theological differences within Judaism, which did not seem to exist in their worldview.[6] This is in complete contrast to later developments within American Jewish religious trends, which were self-conscious of these definitions as well as the differences between them and other religious denominations.

Ethnic differences between Sephardi and Ashkenazi Jews in America created tensions in many congregations, some of which did result in a split into two congregations as early as the second decade of the eighteenth century. These splits were not ideologically or theologically motivated, but rather related to different customs, liturgy, and pronunciation of prayers that Jews wished to maintain.[7] In sum, ethnic differences, just as strict observance, may characterize a group or a congregation as Orthodox only when it is accompanied by a self-conscious traditionalizing approach.

Isaac Leeser is arguably the first self-conscious Orthodox Jew in the New World who left a notable mark on American Jewish history.[8] Leeser immigrated to America from a village in Westphalia in 1824 and settled in Richmond, Virginia. In 1829 he began to serve as a hazan at Congregation Mikveh Israel of Philadelphia and thus embarked upon a career as a preacher, educator, scholar, and author of numerous publications.[9] Leeser, who was influenced by German Orthodox rabbis and leaders prior to his arrival in America, strongly advocated religious observance, devoted time to improve what he perceived as the low level of Jewish education in America, as well as communal activities such as charity and battling Christian missionaries' efforts, and, most important, began to set forth the grounds for the future organized Orthodox response to Reform Judaism, which, at the time, was not yet an organized movement.[10]

A portion of Leeser's response to acts of reform within American congregations and their dangers to the future of Judaism in America was directed at an unprecedented development, which took place toward the end of 1824, just a few months after Leeser immigrated. The Reformed Society of Israelites, formed in Charleston, South Carolina, in December 1824, represented the first ideologically motivated split within an American Jewish congregation. Led by Isaac Harby, a group of young members of Congregation K.K. Beth Elohim decided to set up the Reformed Society, which developed into another congregation, after leaders rejected their petition requesting certain changes within the synagogue service. This society disintegrated toward the end of the 1830s, nevertheless, it influenced the religious atmosphere in Beth Elohim and ultimately was a strong force in the reforms that took place at Beth Elohim during the early 1840s.[11] In a sermon at

Philadelphia's Shearith Israel Congregation in February 1841, Leeser denounced Reform Judaism and its potential danger to the future of the Jewish people.[12]

While the debates around the split in Charleston waned gradually after Beth Elohim became the Reform congregation and Shearith Israel the Orthodox split-off alternative, the first ordained rabbi arrived in America. Rabbi Abraham J. Rice (1802–1862), originally of Bavaria, an observant and staunch Orthodox Jew who studied at Orthodox academies in Fuerth and Wuerzburg and was ordained by Rabbis Abraham Bing (1752–1841) and Abraham B. Hamburger (1770–1850), immigrated in 1840 and settled in Baltimore.[13]

There are several similarities between Rice and Leeser. For example, they both targeted reforms as a major problem for the future of Judaism in general and in America specifically, and both understood the pressing need for weekly sermons in the English language, although for different reasons than contemporary Reform rabbis.[14] But unlike Leeser, Rice chose a much stronger anti-Reform strategy. Furthermore, Rice opposed any association with Reform rabbis, such as Leeser's idea in 1848 to establish, together with Rabbi Isaac M. Wise (1819–1900), a national assembly of rabbis. By 1849 Leeser and Wise understood that this idea would not materialize and blamed each other for this failure.[15]

The basic difference between Rice and Leeser lays in the fact that whereas the former "gloomily predicted the demise of Judaism in the United States and stressed the absolute incompatibility of the faith of Israel with the spirit of America," Leeser, like another of his Orthodox contemporaries, Rabbi Morris Raphall (1798–1868), was willing to recognize the need to address the conditions of Jewish life in America with an understanding that certain modifications must be made within Orthodoxy for it to survive.[16]

Leeser and Rice were not the only Orthodox rabbis in mid-nineteenth-century America who perceived the religious reforms as a major threat to Judaism and had a pessimistic outlook on the future of "true" Judaism (i.e., Orthodoxy) in America. Another example is Rabbi Dr. Bernard Illowy (1812–1871), who immigrated to America in the early 1850s and for the next two decades served as a teacher, preacher, and rabbi in New York, Philadelphia, St. Louis, Syracuse, Baltimore, New Orleans, and Cincinnati.[17]

It is important to keep in mind the Jewish religious communal-congregational scene in order to understand these rabbis' fears. They observed rapid changes in synagogue rituals within several congregations in the 1840s and 1850s, all of them leaning toward Reform.[18] In addition, they experienced the arrival from Europe of several Reform rabbis and personalities associated with European Reform during these years, including Leo Merzbacher (1809–1856) between 1841 and 1843, Max Lilienthal (1815–1882) in 1845, Isaac M. Wise in 1846, and David Einhorn (1809–1879) in 1855, all of whom ultimately contributed, although primarily Wise, to the founding of the institutions of the Reform movement in America. As a result of this influx of Reform rabbis, local observers as well as others who visited

America and were not part of the local scene, such as Israel J. Benjamin (1818–1864), predicted "that in the next generation Reform will gain the upper hand and that Judaism will be transformed."[19]

This pessimistic outlook was shared by several leading European Orthodox rabbis, although for a slightly different reason. Upon receiving information about Jewish life in America in the 1840s–1860s, they concluded that a "true-believing" Orthodox Jew cannot conduct a religiously observant life in America, and therefore should not cross the Atlantic Ocean. These Orthodox rabbis pointed, in addition, to the potentially bad influences life in America would have on Orthodox Jews.[20]

However, several additional Orthodox congregations developed in America starting in the mid-nineteenth century, such as Beth Hamedrash of New York, later known as Beth Hamedrash Hagadol, in 1852,[21] and additional Orthodox rabbis arrived during these years. They created a small but firm stronghold for the Orthodox camp for a few decades, until new challenges arose, which, once again, led certain American rabbis and lay leaders to predict the possible demise of true Judaism in the New World.

AMERICAN JEWISH ORTHODOXY FACES THE CHALLENGES OF THE MASS IMMIGRATION

As we have seen, various American Jewish personalities and observers in the mid-nineteenth century were pessimistic about the future of Orthodoxy in this land because of the expansion of Reform, the relatively small numbers of Orthodox Jews and congregations, and the fact that Orthodoxy was not organized as a movement. This outlook should have changed in the wake of the mass immigration from eastern and central Europe to America. But Orthodoxy faced new challenges, such as a new overflow of immigrants, and contemporary rabbis and lay leaders perceived this mass immigration as threatening Orthodoxy's very existence. If one of the main fears of American Orthodoxy in the mid-nineteenth century was the small numbers of Orthodox Jews in America, during the mass immigration era these fears were replaced by contrasting ones that related to the massive numbers of Orthodox Jews in America.

A combination of limited economic opportunities, significant demographic growth throughout the nineteenth century, and changing political circumstances worsened the situation of Jews in central and eastern Europe. The economic-demographic problem, i.e., the struggle to make a living and to feed more mouths with the same resources, was the main and constant cause for immigration of around two and a half million Jews from central and eastern Europe to America between 1870 and 1924. Antisemitism and political circumstances served as a catalyst that advanced immigration on a local or state level. For example, the

Kishinev pogroms in 1903 and 1905, and the internal economic crisis and persecutions in Romania in 1900, followed by the 1907 revolt of peasants in Romania,
enhanced immigration from these areas.[22]

The vast majority of east European Jews who left central and eastern Europe—
over 80 percent—ended their long journey, which at times took several months, in
America, and a significant portion of them settled in New York's Lower East Side.
Although this influx of Jewish immigrants began in 1870, it grew in vast numbers
every year, starting in the second half of 1881. Similar to the immigration experience in general, these Jewish immigrants held strongly to certain ties of identity
with their homelands, and, since many of them were Orthodox to some extent,
their identity had a religious component. This religious identity served the immigrants as one of the only stable aspects while struggling for survival in a new,
unknown, and therefore seemingly threatening environment and society.

The immigrants' urge for homeland ties of identity expressed itself in the
founding of hundreds of congregations (six hundred in 1910) based upon the immigrants' local geographical origins,[23] similar in nature to the establishment of
thousands (over two thousand in 1910) of aid and other societies, known as *landsmanshaftn*, which represented more than nine hundred European cities, towns,
and villages that had a Jewish population.[24] This massive founding of congregations led to and was enhanced by the immigration of hundreds of Orthodox rabbis
to America in general and specifically to New York.[25] Another expression of this
identity was the hiring of renown cantors, such as Pinchas Minkovsky (1859–1924),
Israel Michaelovsky, Yosele Rosenblatt (1880–1933), and, slightly later, Gershon
Sirota (1874–1943), by affluent congregations for extremely high salaries, in relative terms.[26]

However, unlike the Reform movement, which established itself organization-
ally in the 1870s—the Union of American Hebrew Congregations (1873) and the
Hebrew Union College (1875)—the Orthodox were not organized in any way;
numerous Orthodox Jews and congregations were established in New York, where
the bulk of Orthodox Jews lived, but no general Orthodox movement or organization existed.

Several Orthodox rabbis and lay leaders who were already well situated in
America saw this complete chaos as a serious threat to the future of Orthodoxy
and sought to organize New York's Orthodox congregations. They focused their
initial efforts on trying to establish a central religious leadership that would unite
New York's Orthodox Jews, and then, while doing so, turned also to influence the
religious-educational arena by creating a few institutions for the sake of the
younger generations. These actions, they believed, would secure the future of
Orthodoxy in America.

The first attempt of this organization was to appoint a chief rabbi for New
York's Orthodox Jews. This idea was raised toward the end of the 1870s, after
Rabbi Abraham J. Ash (1813–1887) resigned as rabbi of the Beth Hamedrash

Hagadol Congregation in New York. The leaders of Beth Hamedrash Hagadol approached Rabbi Meir L. Malbim (1809–1879), then in Odessa, but he declined. At the same time, several leading Orthodox congregations in New York set up the United Hebrew Orthodox Congregations, an organization that was to take a major role in future developments within New York's Orthodoxy. Following Malbim's refusal, this organization did not do much until the spring of 1887, when Rabbi Ash died. The United Hebrew Orthodox Congregations proceeded to approach several leading east European Orthodox rabbis offering them the job, but all of them rejected it. At the end of this process, which took a few months, they were left with two candidates, Rabbi Zvi H. Rabinovitch (circa 1847–1910), son of Rabbi Isaac E. Spektor (1817–1896) of Kovno, and Rabbi Jacob Joseph (1840/1–1902), who, since 1883, had served as an official preacher in Vilna's Jewish community. Notwithstanding Rabinovitch's clear advantage due to the massive support he received from leading east European rabbis, New York's Orthodox congregations chose Rabbi Joseph.[27]

The expectations of Rabbi Joseph were high and focused primarily on his centrality to organizing New York's Orthodox Jewry. Ironically, the peak of Rabbi Joseph's career in New York was within the first few months of his arrival, on July 7, 1888. A few weeks after his arrival, Joseph preached his first Sabbath sermon at Beth Hamedrash Hagadol, and Judah D. Eisenstein reported that thousands of people attended, way beyond the capacity of this synagogue; New York's police had to intervene to maintain order. In October 1888 Rabbi Joseph announced new regulations for the Jewish poultry business in New York, attempting to standardize it in accordance with Orthodox requirements.[28] This organizational effort was to be funded by raising the price of meat and chickens. However, those involved in this business, as well as consumers who were requested to pay more for their meat and chickens, refused to abide by Joseph's regulations and organized a mass meeting in January 1889 against "the imported rabbi."

Ultimately, Rabbi Joseph failed to organize the kosher meat business, but this is not the only issue that explains his failure. In addition, his lack of success can be understood to issue from his sermons, which, although initially arousing nostalgic sentiments among New York's immigrants, ceased over time to appeal to them, his illness, the fact that he was not the ideal choice for the position to begin with, internal criticism and the lack of acceptance of his authority by local Orthodox rabbis, external criticism by Jews representing other groups and ideologies, and the separation of church and state, all left Joseph without the means to force the implementation of his plans.[29]

Joseph spent his last years as a sick man, and his family lived in growing poverty since they did not have any source of income. Rabbi Joseph died on July 28, 1902, and the riots that occurred during his funeral, attended by tens of thousands of Jews, clouded the guilt-driven attempt of New York's Orthodox Jews to honor him for the last time, as partial compensation for the way they treated him during his life.[30]

Other efforts were directed at the religious-educational sphere, under the assumption that if the Orthodox did not preserve Torah studies or produce leaders for the younger generations it would gradually disappear. In 1886 two Orthodox-oriented educational institutions were founded in New York: the Etz Hayim Yeshiva and the Jewish Theological Seminary of America. Although both associated with the Orthodox, they represented two contrasting approaches. The founders of Etz Hayim intended to create a religious enclave for younger children until the age of twelve or thirteen, based upon their perceived ideal models of yeshivas in eastern Europe. This model included only religious studies and a conscious attempt to block any possible influences of the surrounding American culture as well as any process of Americanization. For example, they excluded secular studies as well as learning the English language. They believed that this curriculum would save Orthodox children from assimilation in American society and thus save Orthodoxy. However, this institution remained marginal, and at the most hosted between one and two hundred pupils, which were a drop in the sea of thousands of immigrants' children who opted for public schools or no schools at all.[31]

The Jewish Theological Seminary opened its doors in early January 1887. The main drive of the founders was to create a traditional institution for training rabbis, an alternative to the Reform movement and its rabbinical school in Cincinnati, the only one of its kind up until then in America. This act came in response to the famous nonkosher dinner in honor of the first graduates of the Hebrew Union College, known as the *"treyfe* banquet," which took place in Cincinnati in July 1883, as well as the Pittsburgh Platform of the Reform movement, which was formulated in November 1885.[32]

Unlike the Etz Hayim Yeshiva, the founders of the Jewish Theological Seminary had a much more favorable outlook regarding Jewish life in America. Overall, they recognized the potential advantages that America could offer and saw the problems of the Americanization process that Jewish youth was undergoing as an issue that needed to be addressed. The way to do so was to produce rabbis who were familiar with the immigrant's challenges and experiences, were fluent in English, and yet abiding by Orthodox beliefs and ritual observance.[33]

Notwithstanding the relatively liberal approach of the seminary in Orthodox terms, it was not banned by Orthodox Jews and rabbis. Rabbi Joseph supported this institution, and Rabbi Israel Kaplan (circa 1848–1917) sent his son Mordechai (1881–1983) to study at the seminary in 1893. In other words, it was accepted by many as a legitimate institution for Orthodox students who sought a rabbinic career, without disregarding the voices of some of its opponents in New York during the last decade of the nineteenth century.[34] This institution did not attract scores of students in its first fifteen years, and those few who graduated did so after studying for many more years than the original program anticipated. However, some of the rabbinical students at the seminary did attempt to create new religious attractions for the younger generation and founded temporary prayer gatherings on Sabbath. But these activities could not accommodate the massive numbers of youngsters living in the Lower East Side. Overall, the seminary was not a great success story during its first fifteen years and was, in fact, facing serious financial problems as the nineteenth century came to an end.

In 1897 a group of immigrant Orthodox rabbis and lay leaders founded the Rabbi Isaac Elhanan Yeshiva, later renamed the Rabbi Isaac Elchanan Theological Seminary (RIETS), thus presenting another religious-educational institution that would solve the perceived serious problems Orthodoxy was facing. This yeshiva, designed for teenagers, those who completed their studies at Etz Hayim, and others, continued the anti-Americanization attitude of Etz Hayim. These rabbis and lay leaders wished to establish "an East European Yeshiva in American Soil."[35] The founders and leaders of this institution made every effort to isolate secular and "American" influences, but the student body demanded certain secular studies and English classes. These demands resulted in ongoing tensions and clashes between the students and heads of RIETS in the first decade of the twentieth century, which harmed this institution's reputation, drove some students to relocate to the Jewish Theological Seminary, and led to serious financial and other problems.[36]

The existence of two quite different rabbinical seminaries within Orthodoxy, the seminary and RIETS, did not last for many years. A meeting of immigrant Orthodox rabbis that was scheduled, months in advance, for the end of July 1902, found them all attending Rabbi Joseph's funeral, following which they convened and founded the "Union of Orthodox Rabbis of the United States and Canada," known as Agudat Harabanim.[37]

One of the first steps of this union, which took place in June 1904, was to publicly exclude graduates of the Jewish Theological Seminary as unfit to serve as Orthodox rabbis and to promote RIETS as the only legitimate institution for the training of Orthodox rabbis in America. However, this did not prevent a few Orthodox rabbis from sending their children to the seminary. For example, Rabbi Bernard Levinthal (1865–1952), one of the leaders of Agudat Harabanim and a leading protester against the seminary, allowed his son, Israel (1888–1982), to attend this institution a year or two later, met with Professor Solomon Schecter (1847–1915), then its president, and attended his son's graduation ceremony.[38] It therefore seems as though this exclusion of the seminary was a political-organizational act more than one based upon ideological motives.

Both the seminary and RIETS underwent significant changes within the first twenty years of their establishment. In April 1902 Professor Solomon Schecter, a renown scholar of rabbinics who had, since 1890, taught talmudics and rabbinics at Cambridge University and became, in 1899, a professor at University College in

London as well, arrived in New York and shortly thereafter assumed the role of president of the seminary. The expectations were very high,[39] some of them reminders of the expectations for Rabbi Joseph. Schecter changed the direction of this institution in various dimensions, primarily toward academization of Jewish studies. He replaced some the old-time teachers at the seminary with several personalities who held academic degrees, had gained reputations as scholars, and had undergone rabbinic training at yeshivas in Europe. Examples include Israel Friedlander (1876–1920), Louis Ginzberg (1873–1953), and Alexander Marx (1878–1953).[40] Although Schecter aimed to set a middle-of-the-road Judaism, the seminary remained Orthodox-oriented, and the only criticism that observant Jews could find with regard to Schecter's observance was the fact that he carried an umbrella on rainy Sabbath days. The best proof for the seminary being acceptable to many Orthodox Jews was the fact that Orthodox students continued to enroll and attend this institution during Schecter's years, and well beyond them,[41] and that graduates of the seminary served as rabbis in Orthodox congregations.[42] It should be noted that the unclear borders between Orthodoxy and Conservatism transcended these movements' flagship educational institutions and existed among rank-and-file Orthodox and Conservative Jews until the mid-twentieth century.[43]

The change in RIETS took place in 1915, following the appointment of Rabbi Dr. Bernard Revel (1885–1940) as its president.[44] Notwithstanding their hesitations and suspicions, several Agudat Harabanim rabbis understood that if this institution did not undergo a change, thus acknowledging that their segregationist approach could not sustain itself, it would cease to exist. Revel indeed made considerable changes within this institution and lived to be criticized for them by Agudat Harabanim in general and a few leading Orthodox rabbis in particular.[45]

Notwithstanding the significant differences between these two institutions, they ultimately appeared to be close enough to consider merging. Two such attempts occurred: the first initiated by the Travis family, whom Revel married into toward the end of the second decade of the twentieth century, and the second in the mid-1920s.[46] Both ended unsuccessfully, but the discussions were serious. To be sure, all those involved were well aware of the differences between the two institutions, but the overall assumption was that they had much in common, enough to combine them and create one strong institution.

In addition to the institutional struggle and communal challenges, American Orthodoxy gradually found itself under a new theological attack, this time from within. Upon their arrival, immigrant Orthodox rabbis in America exerted considerable energies to delegitimize the Reform movement and followed in the footsteps of their predecessors Leeser and Rice in doing so. However, they were either unaware or unconscious of the rising status of a "modern heretic" from within, Mordecai Kaplan.

Kaplan grew up in an Orthodox family and studied at the Jewish Theological Seminary. In 1903, shortly after graduating, he accepted a six-year contract as a rabbi at Congregation Kehilath Jeshurun in the Yorkville neighborhood of New York City. During these years he developed severe criticisms of Orthodoxy in both the realms of beliefs and ritual practice. In 1909 Kaplan was relieved to leave the pulpit rabbinate and was therefore most grateful for Schecter's offer that he serve as the head of the newly established Teacher's Institute at the seminary. What is more important to our discussion is that during the mid-1910s Kaplan began to publicly voice his "heretical" opinions (from an Orthodox point of view) regarding Orthodoxy, at first verbally and later in written form as well.[47] Kaplan gradually disqualified much of what Orthodoxy stood for, and the ultimate expression of this act appears in his *Judaism as a Civilization*, which appeared in 1934.[48]

The response of Orthodoxy's religious leadership to this development was for years primarily one of denial in varying degrees.[49] Only in 1945, following the publication of a *Sabbath Prayer Book* by Kaplan, did they excommunicate him religiously, after defining him as a heretic.[50] However, even this act had no long-standing effect and was not honored even by some of those who participated in the ceremony.[51] This ongoing lack of and finally weak and indecisive response to Kaplan further illustrates, from a different standpoint, American Orthodoxy's situation in the mid-twentieth century.

The perceived challenges, problems, and threats that Orthodoxy was facing were reflected not only within its leadership. They were part and parcel of Jewish day-to-day life in America. Heavily populated areas of Jewish immigrants in New York, Chicago, and other major cities were exposed to various activities of Christian missionaries. Even though their success was rather limited in absolute numbers, their existence posed a threat and was perceived as a danger to the future of Jewish society in America. This is especially true within Orthodox circles, since the missionaries had a special interest in converting Orthodox Jews for various reasons.[52] Orthodox leaders did not succeed in joining forces and agreeing on the nature of the threat, let alone the appropriate response to it.[53]

In their attempt to survive in New York, immigrants were forced to choose between a job and certain aspects of religious observance. For example, the Jewish Sabbath was a working day, and a Jew who wished to observe it would find it hard if not impossible to find an employer, Jew or non-Jew, in the garment or textile business who would employ him while allowing this worker to be absent on Saturdays. Many observant or partially observant Jews did not want to work on the Sabbath, but they had no choice.[54] During these years many synagogues and congregations introduced a "working men's minyan"—early prayer services on Saturday mornings—that would enable the attendees to get to work on time. This situation was one of the forces that led to the establishment of the Jewish Sabbath movement in the early twentieth century.[55]

However, not all situations were such that observant Jews were forced to make a choice. In many other areas of life they chose out of free will to adopt a low level of observance, since they perceived it as contradicting the process of Americanization. In other words, strict observance and Americanization were polarized forces, and most immigrants favored Americanization. To be sure, this contradiction was not always a result of the reality, but rather of the immigrants' perception of it, as well as their understanding of American society and culture. Finally, the separation of church and state had further implications regarding various aspects of Jewish religious observance, such as the religious status of men and women who married in civil ceremonies.[56]

The decline in religious practice among Orthodox or Orthodox-oriented immigrants, which extended to areas such as the observance of dietary and family purity laws, was significant to the point that one scholar went so far as to doubt their very definition as Orthodox Jews.[57] Notwithstanding the resentment of Orthodox rabbis, this widespread phenomenon of nonobservant Orthodox Jews continued to prevail for several decades, long after the mass immigration ended, and continued as Jews relocated from the downtown neighborhoods to the surrounding boroughs and later to the suburbs.[58]

As the mass immigration era came to a close, the conservative educational line of Agudat Harabanim and their vision regarding the way to preserve Orthodox Judaism in America did not prove successful. As we shall see, they were challenged from within by some of their contemporaries and their views did not gain popularity in many Orthodox congregations or among their congregants. In addition, the various existing practical versions of "flexible" Orthodoxy did not seem to have any guidelines, clear visions, or strategies that would help the rank-and-file Orthodox Jew successfully combine life in America with a committed version of Orthodox Judaism.

When considering all the processes and developments within American Orthodoxy during the mass immigration period, it is not surprising to find a host of Orthodox rabbis and observers who, in newspaper articles and rabbinic writings, predicted the demise of Orthodoxy in America. While these writers agreed about the future, they disagreed as to how quickly it would happen. One example is Gershon Miller, who as early as November 1888 argued that Orthodox Judaism in America continued to exist thanks only to the ongoing influx of immigrants, and "if the immigration should stop, Orthodox Judaism would cease [to exist] as well." Ten years later he predicted that the Jewish nation in America would die a "moral death, the soul will burn and the body will continue to exist." Additionally, Rabbis Gedalya Silverstone (1871/72–1944) and Zalman Friederman both expressed similar views based primarily upon the decline in observance among the immigrants' children and the lack of locally trained Orthodox leaders.[59]

ALIVE AGAINST ALL ODDS: ORTHODOXY
BETWEEN THE WORLD WARS

Notwithstanding pessimistic predictions regarding the future of Orthodoxy in America, which should be seen within the context of a host of unfavorable contemporary accounts of the Reform and Conservative movements,[60] Orthodoxy did not disappear between the two world wars. During these years the bulk of American Orthodox Jews strove for what has been defined as "The 'Reasonable' Orthodox."[61] This trend was characterized by an ongoing attempt to settle the perceived tensions between Orthodoxy and life in America as well as to be part of mainstream American society. In the religious realm of life, these attempts were noticeable among rank-and-file Orthodox Jews who, like many other Jews, held a more flexible attitude toward certain aspects of Orthodox rituals: Some they changed and others they ceased to observe or observed to a far lesser degree.[62]

In addition, during the interwar years Orthodox Jews strove to change certain religious institutions, such as the synagogue. These changes were perceived by contemporary Orthodox Jews as a necessity for Orthodox survival, without which Orthodoxy's future in America might be in jeopardy. For example, New York's Orthodox Jews built new synagogues during the interwar period. These included sanctuaries quite different from those of the Lower East Side, and prayers were conducted in a decorous manner. This followed the belief "that the typically un-decorous service threatened the future of an American Orthodoxy." They were convinced that the indecorous manner of prayers in downtown synagogues drove the younger generation away from synagogue life.[63] Completely contradicting the view of many immigrant Orthodox rabbis, who saw great potential danger in "Americanizing" Orthodoxy's institutions, these interwar Orthodox Jews understood "Americanizing" the synagogue to be the only hope for Orthodoxy in America.

Some of these changes were led by Orthodox rabbis including Leo Jung (1892–1987) and Joseph H. Lookstein (1902–1979), who added an ideological and theological framework according to which "Torah-true" Judaism and American values would not be perceived as counterforces, but rather as complementary, and that compromises in "nonessential customs" must be made "in order to maintain the essence of the laws."[64]

Jung, and those of his contemporaries with whom he saw eye to eye, were part of a major change that occurred within the American Orthodox rabbinate during the interwar years, which began with the founding of the Rabbinical Council of the Union of Orthodox Jewish Congregations in America in 1926 and ended with the establishment of the Rabbinical Council of America in 1935. These rabbis, mostly American born, raised, and educated, concluded that the approach of

Agudat Harabanim was doomed to fail and that significant change was required. One major issue was the language of the sermons. As we have seen, Leeser promoted preaching in English as early as the mid-nineteenth century, and several Orthodox rabbis during this period and slightly after, such as Henry P. Mendes (1852–1937) and Bernard Drachman (1861–1945), adopted this approach.[65] However, during the mass immigration period they were outnumbered by immigrant Orthodox rabbis who opposed preaching in English and demanded that Orthodox rabbis preach in Yiddish. In the interwar years these older rabbis were joined by a new and forceful young generation who promoted a generational conflict within the immigrant Orthodox rabbinate.[66]

This internal pressing need for change and reevaluation, accompanied by a feeling that Orthodoxy had no future in America, also expressed itself in Orthodox rabbis, such as Harry H. Epstein of Atlanta (1903–2003), who led their congregations to leave the Orthodox fold and join the Conservative movement.[67]

These changes and tensions within American Orthodoxy, in addition to the ongoing lack of observance among Orthodox Jews, did not offer an optimistic future for American Orthodoxy. Furthermore, the Great Depression had a devastating effect on the Jewish community in general, and Orthodoxy was no exception. Synagogues, educational institutions, and other arenas of Jewish religious life all suffered from the drastic decrease of income of their consumers as well their changing patterns of consuming religious services.[68]

Within this rather complex situation, which did not leave much optimism for the future, an alternative and rather conservative, demanding, exclusive, and segregating Orthodoxy arose gradually between the early 1920s and the mid-1940s. This new trend is best represented by four developments that occurred during these years, some simultaneously:

1. Lithuanian-oriented yeshivas, the first of which was founded in the early 1920s. Examples include the Hebrew Theological Seminary of Chicago (1922), Torah Vada'at of New York (1926–1929), Ner Israel of Baltimore (1933), and Chaim Berlin of New York (1939). In the early 1940s another "wave" of opening and reopening yeshivas in America occurred, including the Telz Yeshiva in Cleveland (1941) and the Beth Medrash Govoha at Lakewood (1943), a wave that continued after the Second World War.[69] Some of the leaders of this institutional development, most notably Rabbi Aaron Kotler (1892–1962), were instrumental in setting forth the new tone and direction within American Orthodoxy.

2. Certain charismatic Hassidic leaders and some of their followers, who arrived on American shores in the 1930s, and more so during the Second World War period and immediately after. For example, Chabad, led by Rabbi Joseph I. Schneerson (1880–1950), who escaped Europe in 1940, and Satmar, which reestablished its court in 1946 under the leadership of Rabbi Yoel Teitelbaum (1888–1979).[70]

3. German Orthodox refugees who escaped in the late 1930s and immediately after the Second World War, a considerable number of whom settled in Washington Heights.[71]

4. Finally, Torah Umesorah, the National Society for Hebrew Day Schools, founded in 1944 by Rabbi Shraga F. Mendlowitz (1886–1948).[72]

Although all four developed primarily within the greater New York area, and the personalities behind them shared certain common views regarding the changes that must be made within American Orthodoxy to ensure its survival, these institutions and individuals began to change the face of the movement starting in the second half of the 1940s, upon realizing the devastation of the Holocaust.

One such change in communal life was that leaders of segregating Orthodoxy called upon Orthodox rabbis, rank-and-file Jews, and congregations to stop accepting nonobservance or partial religious observance as legitimate. They voiced a clear demand that Orthodox Jews be devoted and consistent. This, they argued, was the only strategy that would secure the future of "Torah-true" Judaism in America.

Alongside their attempts to draw clear lines between Orthodoxy and Conservatism and minimize or possibly eliminate cooperation with either Conservative or Reform Jews, certain leaders of segregating Orthodoxy devoted considerable energy to setting clear internal-Orthodox boundaries between Haredim(=ultra-Orthodoxy) and Modern Orthodoxy.

Modern Orthodoxy developed gradually during the 1940s and 1950s and has since been associated with its then partially recognized leader, Rabbi Joseph B. Soloveitchik (1903–1993).[73] While Haredim and Modern Orthodoxy share some values and beliefs, they differ significantly on others. For example, while agreeing with Haredi groups overall that Orthodoxy must maintain and insist on certain standards of observance, Modern Orthodoxy's leadership differed ideologically by embracing secular studies and holding a more favorable outlook regarding the prospects of Jewish life in America.[74]

Ironically, while this resurgence was happening within American Orthodoxy, several scholars of contemporary American Jewry, most notably Nathan Glazer (1923–) and Marshall Sklare (1921–1992), neglected Orthodoxy, assuming that its role in American Judaism had ended and its years were numbered.[75] This assertion was supported by statistical data from the mid-twentieth century, which pointed to the decline in numbers within Orthodoxy.[76]

However, during the 1950s and early 1960s the resurgence and its impact on the character of American Orthodoxy gradually became apparent. The various components of the Haredi camp in America gained self-confidence, and their representatives did not hesitate to voice their beliefs, demands, and aspirations assertively and publicly. The appearance of the *Jewish Observer* in September

1963, sponsored by Agudath Israel of America, represents much of this process insofar as it voiced a clear, unfavorable opinion regarding Modern Orthodoxy—primarily Yeshiva University and its leaders, as well as Conservative and Reform Judaism.

That, in the mid-twentieth century, certain observers were sure the ever dying denomination was finally dead best explains their astonishment and insecure feelings in the mid-1960s when some of them realized the exact opposite had happened.[77] For example, in 1965 Rabbi Max Jonah Routtenberg (1909–1987), then the president of the Rabbinical Assembly of the Conservative movement, spoke about the unanticipated resurgence of Orthodoxy as a threat to Conservative Judaism in America. This helps explain why the morale in the Conservative movement was in decline in the mid-1960s, whereas its achievements and future prospects pointed to the contrary.[78] The aforementioned contrast between the decline of Orthodoxy on the one hand and its resurgence on the other hand exists also in the pioneering studies of Hasidic groups and neighborhoods, which appeared in the 1960s and early 1970s.[79] This resurgence also explains, as least in part, the rising scholarly attention that American Orthodoxy received starting in the mid-1960s.[80]

Rabbi Stuart Rosenberg (1922–1990) of Toronto noted that "in a very real sense, the 'fall and rise of Orthodoxy' in this century has been one of the most spectacular phenomena of recent Jewish history."[81] The underlying assumption of his amazement regarding Orthodoxy and American Orthodoxy was that, by all accounts, it should have long since disappeared. It seems as though scholars of nineteenth- and twentieth-century American Judaism do not express the same sense of surprise when writing about the Conservative or Reform movements.

In clinical terms, death is an irreversible process. This process has certain indicators, and when they are traced the individual's death is just a question of time, depending on access to medical technology that could prolong life as well as the will to do so. It seems as though several scholars of American Jewish history and life in the twentieth century, as well as non- or anti-Orthodox Jews, and many Orthodox rank-and-file Jews, religious or lay leaders, starting with Issac Leeser, had this clinical outlook with regard to Orthodox Judaism in America. In other words, they were convinced that the existence of certain indicators led to an irreversible process. As we have seen, in certain periods American Orthodoxy was characterized by a low level of observance, theological weakness, and a perceived absence of authoritative leadership, but it nevertheless did not disappear.

Some of these pessimistic predictions were based upon the wishes of Orthodoxy's opponents, the rhetoric created by Orthodoxy, or an understanding that the existence of certain characteristics of Orthodoxy and Orthodox life are crucial to the point of life and death. But, the world is full of individuals who throughout their lives are in consistent fear of what they perceive as their impending death. Returning to the opening part of this essay, I argue that Orthodoxy's survival is built in its very definition as an ever dying denomination. A denomination that has such a strong self-perception of being in an ongoing battle for survival would be bound to live under constant threat and consequently almost always feel its existence in the future to be uncertain. This is one of its primary driving forces to exist.

Be it as it may, since the mid-1960s there are many indications that American Orthodoxy is vibrant, thriving, and flourishing in both heavily Jewish populated areas such as greater New York and communities situated in America's Jewish periphery, even though its actual size is not rising, and some say that it decreased in the last decade of the twentieth century. This is evident in various areas of religious life, such as the rising numbers of Jewish day schools, Chabad's noticeable presence on academic campuses, and the growing involvement of Orthodox women in learning sacred texts, in congregational life, and their ongoing demands for greater recognition and legitimacy regarding their share in the religious experience.[82] Nevertheless, almost all of Orthodoxy's subgroups continue to carry the ethos of being in a consistent battle over their existence, even though they seem to be more secure than ever before in the New World.

NOTES

I thank Richelle Budd Caplan, Jeffrey S. Gurock, Marc L. Raphael, Jonathan D. Sarna, and Chaim I. Waxman for their criticism, comments, and suggestions on earlier versions of this essay, as well as those participants in this project who were kind enough to share with me their knowledge and wisdom. Two essays served as a source of inspiration for both the title of this chapter and some of its observations. See Simon Rawidowicz's (1897–1957) posthumously published article, "Israel: The Ever-Dying People," *Judaism* 16.4 (1967): 423–33 (reprinted in Nahum N. Glatzer, ed., *Studies in Jewish Thought* [Philadelphia, 1974], 210–24, and in Simon Rawidowicz [Benjamin C. I. Ravid, ed.], *State of Israel, Diaspora, and Jewish Continuity: Essays on the "Ever-Dying People"* [Hanover, 1986], 53–64); Marshall Sklare (1921–1992), *Observing America's Jews*, Jonathan D. Sarna, ed. (Hanover, 1993), 262–75.

1. "The American Judaism of the Future," *American Hebrew* 91.13 (July 26, 1912): 338.

2. See, for example, Zalman J. Friederman, "She'erit Yisrael," *Haivri* 7.39 (July 2, 1897): 2–3; first in a series of articles, reprinted in his *Minhat Ya'acov* (New York, 1901), starting 119 (in Hebrew).

3. Jacob D. Gordon, *Dor Vedorshav* (New York, 1946), 32 (Hebrew pagination).

4. Examples include Steven Bayme, ed., *Facing the Future: Essays on Contemporary Jewish Life* (Hoboken, 1989); Eugene Kohn, *The Future of Judaism in America* (New

Rochelle, 1934); Jacob R. Marcus, *The Future of American Jewry* (Cincinnati, 1956); Marc L. Raphael, *Judaism in America* (New York, 2003), 115–135; David Sidorsky, ed., *The Future of the Jewish Community in America* (Philadelphia, 1973); Sklare, *Observing America's Jews*, 262–75; Milton Steinberg, *A Believing Jew* (New York, 1951), 77–85.

5. See Jacob Katz, "Orthodoxy in Historical Perspective," *Studies in Contemporary Jewry* 2 (1986): 3–17; Jacob Katz, *Halacha in Straits: Obstacles to Orthodoxy at Its Inception* (Jerusalem, 1992; Hebrew), especially 9–21; Moshe Samet, "The Beginnings of Orthodoxy," *Modern Judaism* 8.3 (1988): 249–70; Emmanuel Sivan, "The Enclave Culture," in Martin E. Marty and R. Scott Appleby, eds., *Fundamentalisms Comprehended* (Chicago, 1995), 1–69.

6. See Eli Faber, *A Time for Planting: The First Migration, 1654–1820* (Baltimore, 1992), 66–70; Jacob R. Marcus, *United States Jewry, 1776–1985*, 4 vols. (Detroit, 1989), 1:265–72; Jacob R. Marcus, *An Introduction to Early American Jewish History* (Jerusalem, 1971; Hebrew), 60–82.

7. Faber, *A Time for Planting*, 58–66; Marcus, *United States Jewry*, 1:220–32.

8. To be sure, Leeser was not the first Orthodox Jew in America. Earlier examples include Jacob Mordecai, who devoted time to defend Orthodoxy from perceived dangers from within and without. See Emily Bingham, *Mordecai: An Early American Family* (New York, 2003), 110.

9. On his life and activities, see Lance J. Sussman, *Isaac Leeser and the Making of American Judaism* (Detroit, 1995).

10. See Jonathan D. Sarna, *American Judaism: A History* (New Haven, 2004), 76–82.

11. For a detailed account of this episode, see Michael A. Meyer, *Response to Modernity: A History of the Reform Movement in Judaism* (New York, 1988), 228–35.

12. Sussman, *Isaac Leeser and the Making of American Judaism*, 122.

13. On Rice, see I. Harold Shrafman, *The First Rabbi: Origins of the Conflict Between Orthodox and Reform* (Malibu, 1988); Israel Tabak, "Rabbi Abraham Rice of Baltimore," *Tradition* 7.2 (1965): 100–21.

14. See Sharfman, *The First Rabbi*, 175–80; Sussman, *Isaac Leeser and the Making of American Judaism*, 51–80.

15. Sussman, *Isaac Leeser and the Making of American Judaism*, 169–70.

16. Hasia R. Diner, *A Time for Gathering: The Second Migration, 1820–1880* (Baltimore, 1992), 122; Arthur Hertzberg, "'Treifene Medina': Learned Opposition to Emigration to the United States," *Proceedings of the Eighth World Congress of Jewish Studies* (Jerusalem, 1984), 5.

17. Diner, *A Time for Gathering*, 122. On Illowy, see Irwin Lachoff, "Rabbi Bernard Illowy: Counter Reformer," *Southern Jewish History* 5 (2002): 43–68; Moshe D. Sherman, "Bernard Illowy and Nineteenth-Century American Orthodoxy," Ph.D. diss., Yeshiva University, 1991.

18. Although it should be noted that the differences between Reform and Orthodox congregations were unclear, and remained so, until the late 1870s. See, for example, Marc L. Raphael, "'Our treasury is empty and our bank account is overdrawn': Washington Hebrew Congregation, 1855–1872," *American Jewish History* 84.2 (1996): 91–96.

19. Meyer, *Response to Modernity*, 252; Sarna, *American Judaism*, 101.

20. See Hertzberg, "Treifene Medina," 2–5; Kimmy Caplan, *Orthodoxy in the New World: Immigrant Rabbis and Preaching in America, 1881–1924* (Jerusalem, 2002; Hebrew), 83.

21. See Alfred A. Greenbaum, "The Early 'Russian' Congregation in America and Its Ethnic and Religious Setting," *American Jewish Historical Quarterly* 62.2 (1972): 162–71.

22. See Salo W. Baron, *The Russian Jew Under Tsars and Soviets* (New York, 1987), 63–99, 205–25; Uriah Z. Engelman, *The Rise of the Jew in the Western World: A Social and Economic History of the Jewish People of Europe* (New York, 1944), 130–210; Simon Kuznets, "Immigration of Russian Jews to the United States: Background and Structure," *Perspectives in American History* 9 (1975): 35–124; Gerald Sorin, *A Time for Building: The Third Migration, 1880–1920* (Baltimore, 1992), 12–38; Shaul Stampfer, "The Geographic Background of East European Jewish Migration to the United States Before World War I," in Ira A. Glazier and Luigi De Rosa, eds., *Migration Across Time and Nations: Population Mobility in Historical Contexts* (New York, 1986), 220–31.

23. The best source of information remains *The Jewish Communal Register of New York City, 1917–1918* (New York, 1918). See also Sorin, *A Time for Building*, 97, 175–76.

24. See Nathan M. Kaganoff, "The Jewish Landsmanshaftn in New York City Before World War I," *American Jewish History* 76.1 (1986): 56–67; Daniel Soyer, *Jewish Immigrant Associations and American Identity in New York, 1880–1939* (Cambridge, 1997); Michael R. Weisser, *A Brotherhood of Memory: Jewish Landsmanshaftn in the New World* (New York, 1985).

25. The numbers vary between three and seven hundred. See Charles S. Bernheimer, "The American Jewish Minister and His Work," *Godey's Magazine* (1898): 311–14; Menachem Blondheim, "The Orthodox Rabbinate Discovers America: The Geography of the Mind," in Miriam Eliav-Feldon, ed., *Following Columbus: America, 1492–1992* (Jerusalem, 1996; Hebrew), 507; Arthur A. Goren, "Preaching American Jewish History: A Review Essay," *American Jewish History* 79.4 (1990): 544–45.

26. See Kimmy Caplan, "In God We Trust: Salaries and Income of American Orthodox Rabbis, 1881–1924," *American Jewish History* 86.1 (1998): 89–93; Jeffrey S. Gurock, *American Jewish Orthodoxy in Historical Perspective* (Hoboken, 1996), 78–79; Mark Slobin, *Chosen Voices: The Story of the American Cantorate* (Urbana, 1989), 51–77.

27. The best account of this episode remains Abraham J. Karp, "New York Chooses a Chief Rabbi," *Publications of the American Jewish Historical Society* 44.3 (1955): 129–99. Additional aspects are raised in Kimmy Caplan, "Rabbi Jacob Joseph, New York's Chief Rabbi: New Perspectives," *Hebrew Union College Annual* 67 (1996; Hebrew section): 1–43.

28. On this business and its vast monetary turnover, see Harold P. Gastwirt, *Fraud, Corruption, and Holiness: The Controversy Over the Supervision of Jewish Dietary Practice in New York City, 1881–1940* (Port Washington, 1974).

29. See Karp, "New York Chooses a Chief Rabbi," 182–88; Caplan, "Rabbi Jacob Joseph," 33–38.

30. See Leonard Dinnerstein, "The Funeral of Rabbi Jacob Joseph," in David A. Gerber, ed., *Antisemitism in American History* (Urbana, 1986), 275–305. It should be noted that other cities, such as Kansas City, Philadelphia, Pittsburgh, and St. Louis, had chief rabbis, some of them for extended periods.

31. See Jeffrey S. Gurock, *The Men and Women of Yeshiva: Higher Education, Orthodoxy, and American Judaism* (New York, 1988), 8–18.

32. On these two events, see Meyer, *Response to Modernity*, 263–70; Sarna, *American Judaism*, 144–50.

33. See Hasia Diner, "Like the Antelope and the Badger: The Founding and Early Years of the Jewish Theological Seminary, 1886–1902," in Jack Wertheimer, ed., *Tradition Renewed: A History of the Jewish Theological Seminary of America*, 2 vols. (New York, 1997), 1:1–43.

34. See Gurock, *American Jewish Orthodoxy in Historical Perspective*, 103–17; Jeffrey S. Gurock and Jacob J. Schacter, *A Modern Heretic and a Traditional Community: Mordecai M. Kaplan, Orthodoxy, and American Judaism* (New York, 1997), 18–31; David Weinberg, "JTS and the 'Dowtown' Jews of New York at the Turn of the Century," in Wertheimer, *Tradition Renewed*, 2:1–53.

35. Gurock, *The Men and Women of Yeshiva*, 18–43.

36. Ibid.

37. For a recent outline, see Moshe D. Sherman, *Orthodox Judaism in America: A Biographical Dictionary and Sourcebook* (Westport, 1996), 225–36.

38. See Kimmy Caplan, "The Life and Sermons of Rabbi Israel Herbert Levinthal (1888–1982)," *American Jewish History* 87.1 (1999): 5–6; Weinberg, "JTS and the 'Downtown' Jews," 37–38.

39. Sarna, *American Judaism*, 187–88.

40. See Jonathan D. Sarna, "Two Traditions of Seminary Scholarship," in Wertheimer, *Tradition Renewed*, 2:53–81; Mel Scult, "Schecter's Seminary," ibid., 1:45–103.

41. Aryeh Davidson, "Seminary Rabbinical Students: Who Attended and Why," Wertheimer, *Tradition Renewed*, 1:447–50; Jeffrey S. Gurock, "Yeshiva Students at JTS," ibid., 1:471–515.

42. See, for example, Jeffrey S. Gurock, *When Harlem Was Jewish, 1870–1930* (New York, 1979), 134–35, 165–66.

43. Jeffrey S. Gurock, *From Fluidity to Rigidity: The Religious Worlds of Conservative and Orthodox Jews in Twentieth-Century America* (Ann Arbor, 1998).

44. The only biographical account of Revel remains Aaron Rothkoff, *Bernard Revel: Builder of American Jewish Orthodoxy* (Philadelphia, 1972).

45. Ibid., 135–58.

46. See Jeffrey S. Gurock, "Another Look at the Proposed Merger: Lay Perspectives on Yeshiva-Jewish Theological Seminary Relations in the 1920s," in Yaakov Elman and Jeffrey S. Gurock, eds., *Hazon Nahum: Studies in Jewish Law, Thought, and History Presented to Dr. Norman Lamm* (New York, 1997), 729–43, and "An Orthodox Conspiracy Theory: The Travis Family, Bernard Revel, and the Jewish Theological Seminary," *Modern Judaism* 19.3 (1999): 241–54; Aaron Rakeffet-Rothkoff, "The Attempt to Merge the Jewish Theological Seminary and Yeshiva College, 1926–27," *Michael* 3 (1975): 254–81.

47. For a detailed account, see Gurock and Schacter, *A Modern Heretic and a Traditional Community*, 31–135.

48. Mordecai M. Kaplan, *Judaism as a Civilization: Toward a Reconstruction of American-Jewish Life* (New York, 1934), 133–70. In the first part of this book, Kaplan

systematically analyzes the theological foundations of Reform, Orthodox, and Conservative Judaism and attempts to prove that all three approaches are inconsistent or illogical.

49. For the only attempt of the Jewish Theological Seminary's faculty to fire Kaplan, which did not materialize, see Jack Wertheimer, "Kaplan vs. 'the Great Do-Nothings': The Inconclusive Battle over the New Haggadah," *Conservative Judaism* 45.4 (1993): 20–38.

50. Religious excommunication consists of a series of socioreligious sanctions that the community is obliged to keep, such as not to include the one excommunicated in communal social and religious activities and not to eat in his or her home.

51. Gurock and Schacter, *A Modern Heretic and a Traditional Community*, 139–54.

52. See Yaakov Ariel, *Evangelizing the Chosen People: Missions to the Jews in America, 1880–2000* (Chapel Hill, 2000), 9–77.

53. Gurock, *American Jewish Orthodoxy in Historical Perspective*, 135–81.

54. See, for example, Sorin, *A Time for Building*, 180; Chaim I. Waxman, "From Institutional Decay to Primary Day: American Orthodox Jewry Since World War II," *American Jewish History* 91.3 (2005): 407–8.

55. Benjamin K. Hunnicutt, "The Jewish Sabbath Movement in the Early Twentieth Century," *American Jewish History* 69.2 (1979): 196–226.

56. See Rod Glogower, "The Impact of the American Experience Upon Responsa Literature," *American Jewish History* 69.2 (1979): 257–70.

57. See Charles S. Liebman, "Religion, Class, and Culture in American Jewish History," *Jewish Journal of Sociology* 9.2 (1967): 227–32, and "Studying Orthodox Judaism in the United States: A Review Essay," *American Jewish History* 80.3 (1990): 415–18. See also Sorin, *A Time for Building*, 180–81.

58. See Jeffrey S. Gurock, "Twentieth-Century American Orthodoxy's Era of Non-Observance, 1900–1960," *Torah U-Madda Journal* 9 (2000): 87–108.

59. See Gershon Miller, "Mikhtav MeZinzinati," *Hapisgah* 1.9 (November 23, 1888; Hebrew): 3, and "Atidot Benei Yisrael Beamerikah," *Hapisgah* 5.18 (February 18, 1898; Hebrew): 2–3, continuing in the following issues; Gedalya Silverstone, *Meirat Einayim* (Washington, DC, 1924; Hebrew), 19, and *Peninim Yekarim*, 3 vols. (Baltimore, 1915; Hebrew), 1:18–19; Friederman, "She'erit Yisrael."

60. See Jeffrey S. Gurock's "American Judaism Between the Two World Wars," this volume.

61. Jenna Weissman Joselit, *New York's Jewish Jews: The Orthodox Community in the Interwar Years* (Bloomington, 1990), 1–25.

62. See, among others, Gurock, *From Fluidity to Rigidity*, and "Twentieth-Century American Orthodoxy's Era of Non-Observance"; Henry L. Feingold, *A Time for Searching: Entering the Mainstream, 1920–1945* (Baltimore, 1992), 106–7; Jenna Weissman Joselit, *The Wonders of America: Reinventing Jewish Culture, 1880–1950* (New York, 1994), 9–55.

63. Joselit, *New York's Jewish Jews*, 36–37.

64. Ibid., 68–71; Mark K. Bauman, *Harry H. Epstein and the Rabbinate as Conduit of Change* (London, 1994), 47–48, 51.

65. See Gurock, *American Jewish Orthodoxy in Historical Perspective*, 201–33.

66. See Louis Bernstein, *Challenge and Mission: The Emergence of the English-Speaking Orthodox Rabbinate* (New York, 1982).

67. See Bauman, *Harry H. Epstein*, 43–58, 106–12.

68. See Beth S. Wenger, *New York Jews and the Great Depression: Uncertain Promise* (New Haven, 1996), 88–9, 177–8, 184–5, 188.

69. See William B. Helmreich, *The World of the Yeshiva: An Intimate Portrait of Orthodox Jewry*, augmented ed. (Hoboken, 2000), 18–52; Yoel Finkelman, "Haredi Isolation in Changing Environments: A Case Study in Yeshiva Immigration," *Modern Judaism* 22.1 (2002): 61–83.

70. See Sarna, *American Judaism*, 293–300. Others include Bobov, Skver, Talin, and Zanz.

71. See Steven M. Lowenstein, *Frankfurt on the Hudson: The German-Jewish Community of Washington Heights, 1933–1983: Its Structure and Culture* (Detroit, 1989), 22–57.

72. See Sarna, *American Judaism*, 228–30.

73. On his early years in America, see Seth Farber, *An American Orthodox Dreamer: Rabbi Joseph B. Soloveitchik and Boston's Maimonides School* (Hanover, 2004).

74. On the differences between them, see Charles Liebman, "Orthodoxy in American Jewish Life," *American Jewish Year Book* 66 (1965): 48–84; Marc L. Raphael, *Profiles in American Judaism: The Reform, Conservative, Orthodox, and Reconstructionist Traditions in Historical Perspective* (San Francisco, 1984), 155–65, and *Judaism in America*, 133–34.

75. See Benny Kraut, "*American Judaism*: An Appreciative Critical Appraisal," *American Jewish History* 77.2 (1987): 220–25; Marshall Sklare, *Conservative Judaism: An American Religious Movement* (Glencoe, IL, 1955), 43, 73.

76. See Sarna, *American Judaism*, 278.

77. See Raphael, *Judaism in America*, 67.

78. See Abraham J. Karp, "The Conservative Rabbi—'Dissatisfied But Not Unhappy,'" *American Jewish Archives* 35.2 (1983): 241.

79. See Gershon Kranzler, *Williamsburg: A Jewish Community in Transition* (New York, 1961); Solomon Poll, *The Hasidic Community of Williamsburg* (New York, 1962); Israel Rubin, *Satmar: An Island in the City* (Chicago, 1972).

80. Most notably a series of articles by Charles Liebman. See, in chronological order, "Orthodoxy in Nineteenth Century America," *Tradition* 7.2 (1964): 132–41; "A Sociological Analysis of Contemporary Orthodoxy," *Judaism* 13.3 (1964): 285–305; "Orthodoxy in American Jewish Life," 21–99; "Religion, Class, and Culture in American Jewish History."

81. Stuart E. Rosenberg, *The Real Jewish World: A Rabbi's Second Thoughts* (New York, 1984), 93.

82. See Raphael, *Judaism in America*, 67–68; Sarna, *American Judaism*, 326–28, 343–55; Waxman, "From Institutional Decay to Primary Day," 405–22.

8

THE HISTORY OF JEWISH EDUCATION
IN AMERICA, 1700–2000

MELISSA R. KLAPPER

From the earliest days of Jewish settlement in the Atlantic colonies to the modern-day presence of Jews in every corner of the United States, religious education has been a communal concern. No single model of American Jewish education ever cohered, and, indeed, at any given moment, many Jews in America probably did not have access to or even interest in sustained religious education. Still, Jewish education in one form or another has existed in America for centuries and deserves closer examination. This essay will focus on three major themes in the history of Jewish education in America: the debates about the form, content, and results of Jewish education, the steady expansion of student populations, and the use of Jewish education as a means of formulating American Jewish identity. There are, of course, many other angles from which to view American Jewish education, but these themes resonate particularly well with both historical and contemporary perspectives.

THE DEBATES ABOUT THE FORM, CONTENT,
AND RESULTS OF JEWISH EDUCATION

Before the emergence of the common school movement of the 1820s and 1830s that brought free public education to ever increasing numbers of American children, Jewish children typically attended pay schools in their communities. Many of these private institutions were affiliated with local congregations. From at least 1700 forward, Jewish parents made a concerted effort to provide their children with some form of religious education. Small colonial Jewish communities found that including girls in student bodies helped ensure the schools' viability. At the time, the observably high intermarriage rates of the tiny numbers of Jews in America provided all the rationale needed. Furthermore, most schools in colonial and early national America were essentially religious schools operated by denominations or churches for the children of their adherents. Jewish schools developed no differently.

Education was thus a concern of many Jewish families during the colonial period but was rarely seen as a formal communal function. Community development in the coastal cities of New York and Newport, and, later, Baltimore and Philadelphia, among others, generally followed a pattern that proceeded from cemetery to congregation to synagogue building to ritual bath and only then—if at all—to religious school. Unlike many European congregations, the duties of ritual leaders did not automatically include teaching the members' children. Early synagogue constitutions, such as that of New York's Shearith Israel in 1728, made no mention of religious education. Newport's Congregation Jeshuat Israel, however, solicited for funds to start a school, appealing, "How unhappy the positions must be of the children and their parents, who are through necessity educated in a place where they must remain almost totally uninstructed in our most Holy and Divine Law, our Rites and Ceremonies."[1] Although a few congregations did make some attempts to provide religious education, there were not enough teachers or students to stabilize schools prior to 1800. Private instruction in the home of some families remained an important source of religious education for Jewish children.

In 1803 Shearith Israel opened the Polonies Talmud Torah to boys and girls, an educational gambit that achieved only tentative success. The new school constitution included in its mission both moral schooling in general and Jewish education in particular. Even at this early stage, direct religious instruction was not the only goal of the community in providing Jewish education. The school opened and closed and changed formats for the next few decades. A group of concerned congregation members eventually formed a society for educating children that contributed to the breakaway of Congregation B'nai Jeshurun in 1825.

With the advent of public schools during the mid-nineteenth century, American education changed fundamentally. Although public schools were almost always Protestant in nature, they were still less sectarian than the denominational pay schools of the past because they aimed to educate all American children as a necessary public service and fundamental common good. Most Jewish parents did not want their children to be excluded from this vision of a unifying childhood experience for all American citizens. The free tuition supplied an additional incentive. As the American Jewish community began to develop after the

American Revolution and then explode in population during the mid-nineteenth-century immigration of Jews from central and western Europe, the desire to integrate into American society grew stronger. The theory of public education for all children seemed to promise Jewish parents a path directly toward safe and natural acculturation.

Two major problems persisted. One was the undeniably Protestant, even missionary, nature of most early American public schools. The other was the continuing concern with Jewish education, which obviously would not be provided by the public school system. These two issues became the central concerns of nineteenth-century Jewish education in America and led to ongoing debate in Jewish communities throughout the country. Jewish parents were faced with a choice between what historian Jonathan D. Sarna has called the "Catholic model" or the "Protestant model."[2] Recognizing that they shared with Catholics grave reservations about the mission of the public schools as either godless or Protestant, some American Jews opted to continue sustaining separate schools for Jewish children. Like the Catholic schools whose model they followed, these Jewish schools received some state funding through most of the nineteenth century.

The Jewish schools featured all the fundamentals of a public school education but included religious instruction as a part of daily lessons. The religious environment would protect Jewish children from evangelizing public schools and help them sustain deeply ingrained commitments to living as Jews in America. Given the already fractured nature of Jewish religious communities in the United States, there was little hope of developing semicentralized educational systems along the same lines as Catholic parish schools, but communities and synagogues all over the United States did sponsor Jewish alternatives to public schools. Jews of all religious persuasions who immigrated from central and western Europe brought with them the idea of private day schools and sometimes attached such schools to their congregations.

Jewish schools achieved limited success. At Cincinnati's Talmud Yeladim, founded in 1849 and led by Reform leader Isaac Mayer Wise for many years, the school day was long enough to accommodate both religious and secular subjects, but the school closed in 1867 due to high rates of teacher turnover and lack of students. Some private Jewish institutions, such as Max Lilienthal's school in New York during the 1840s and 1850s, thrived free of congregational control. The religious education at these schools was tenuous at best. Joseph Sachs demonstrated his priorities during the 1870s by removing Hebrew from the English, French, and German curricula in the private Jewish school he had founded in 1859. During the mid-nineteenth century the apparent success of Christian missionaries in appealing to poor Jewish children in New York led to the founding of the Hebrew Free School. An examination of the pupils revealed that they were learning Hebrew, prayers, holidays, law, and rituals at satisfactory levels. Similar institutions appeared in other urban areas with sizable Jewish populations.

However, the absentee rate was high, and the opposition of some Jews to the all-day format led to financial problems. The day school division closed in 1872, leaving only branch afternoon schools behind.[3]

Despite the continued presence of such Jewish schools, the Protestant model of education appealed to much larger numbers of American Jews. According to this model, public schools taught secular subjects and left religious education up to the family and home. In theory, at least, public schools would provide common training for (white) children of all backgrounds, and particularist education of any kind would not come under their purview. American Jews seized enthusiastically on the assurance that the rapidly expanding public schools were not religious schools. They believed the promise of social integration for their children outweighed any other risks. They feared segregation in Jewish schools was short-sighted and bound to cause needless division and resentment in their local communities. The majority of Jews in nineteenth-century America opted for the Protestant model, cementing the foundation of a century-long love affair between Jews and public education. By the mid-1800s, important precedents in American Jewish education had been set: a divide between secular and religious education, the solution of supplementary religious education, and the low status of Jewish educators.[4]

Once they decided to send their children to public schools, Jewish parents then had to determine how and whether to provide religious training. When Rebecca Gratz started the Hebrew Sunday School Society in Philadelphia in 1838, she understood that most American Jews did care about religious education, but in a subordinate role. Gratz also noted a decrease in home observance. If children were not going to get religious training at school and did not learn about their religion organically through home-based observance, some supplementary form of Jewish education was critical to the survival of Judaism in America. The Protestant Sunday schools provided an obvious model for structuring American Jewish education. However, the inherently supplementary nature of all children's Jewish education that took place outside the Jewish schools run on the Catholic model spoke volumes about the place Jewish parents accorded religious education. It was necessary and important, but not central.

As Gratz and her supporters intended, Jewish Sunday schools, or Sabbath schools, would provide a basic knowledge of Judaism to students otherwise ignorant of all but the most elementary home-based rituals. Weekly attendance at a religious school would also provide a social space for Jewish children who were otherwise so outnumbered in their public schools. When Gratz and others put the plan for the Hebrew Sunday School Society into action in Philadelphia, the relatively small Jewish population of the United States found the chance to meet and mingle provided by religious classes a major benefit. Another benefit of the religious system accrued to the women whom Gratz insisted would run the program and, even more significantly, teach the classes. This feature of Sabbath school education marked the first time in America that women had systematically been given a formal religious role as community educators. Women remained the primary instructors in Jewish Sabbath schools for more than 150 years.[5]

Criticism abounded in spite of the popularity of Sabbath schools for both the practical reason of providing systematic religious education to more children and the ideological reason of doing so within a supplementary framework. One to two hours of instruction once a week, critics charged, was hopelessly inadequate for the task of teaching Jewish children about their centuries-old religious tradition, culture, and heritage. Even those who applauded the attendance rates of both boys and girls expressed concern over the Sabbath schools' exclusive focus on young children. Gratz's decision to make the Hebrew Sunday School Society an independent body with no congregational ties, a precedent not followed in every locale, provoked hostility and confusion in an American Jewish community gradually dividing along lines of traditionalism and reform. Congregations responded by creating their own Sabbath school programs, many of which included confirmation as a ritual acknowledgment of the coming of age of their adolescent members.

Sabbath schools functioned as the primary form of Jewish education in America for most of the nineteenth century. However, another system of religious education also achieved prominence by providing remedies for the weaknesses of its predecessor. Talmud Torahs appeared several decades after the Jewish Sabbath school movement began. They owed their development in part to the post–Civil War revival of interest in Jewish learning among a cadre of influential American-born Jews centered in Philadelphia and New York.[6] Talmud Torahs also grew in number and size in response to the immigrants arriving in America after 1880, many of whom were determined to provide their children with a more intensive Jewish education than was available in even the best Sabbath schools.[7]

Talmud Torahs required more of students and of teachers alike. They were often affiliated with local community bodies and therefore lent themselves to greater centralized control, a larger student body drawn from the broader community, and a curriculum that would satisfy a more demanding group of parents and local leaders. Whether they were centralized local institutions or affiliated with specific congregations, Talmud Torahs typically met weekday afternoons and on weekends. They offered classes for older students as well as grade school children, automatically increasing the number of students in attendance. In the largest, most successful networks of Talmud Torahs, such as those run by the Board of Jewish Education (BJE) in New York, the teachers were professionally trained and knowledgeable about both Judaism and modern educational theory.

Talmud Torahs resembled the Sunday schools in their inherently supplementary nature. Samson Benderly, the most influential American Jewish educator of the first half of the twentieth century, maintained his support for public education. However, he also believed in major investments of time and community resources to serious Jewish education.[8] In the Talmud Torahs Benderly ran through the New York BJE, students met every day for several hours after public school ended and then again on weekends. He made a particular point of attracting adolescents, especially girls who might later become teachers themselves. The students who stayed in Talmud Torahs throughout their school lives emerged with a firm knowledge of Jewish history, texts, literature, customs, and rituals. The Talmud Torahs also incorporated a significant amount of Hebrew into their curricula, unlike most of the Sabbath schools. Benderly and other leaders in the Talmud Torah system, many of them Zionists, believed that knowledge of the holy and historic language of Judaism was critical to all religious education. At the Indianapolis Talmud Torah in 1912, for instance, the school was in operation four afternoons a week and on Sunday morning. Hebrew was the language of instruction for all subjects, including Bible with commentary, Prophets, Jewish history, and laws and customs.[9] The professionally run Talmud Torahs of New York and other large Jewish cities like Baltimore, Cleveland, and Chicago provided a model for other communities. As Frieda Gass recalled her busy childhood schedule in Portland, Oregon, "We would go to school, come home from school, go to Hebrew School and come home from Hebrew School, from Monday through Thursday, never on Fridays, and again on Sunday."[10]

Advances in religious education notwithstanding, resistance remained. Institutional backing was by no means assured for Jewish education. Sabbath schools during the 1800s were usually poorly funded, and communities were slow to establish organized support for Jewish education. Regardless of denomination, the success of congregational schools depended heavily on the whims of the affiliated synagogue members. The early twentieth-century debate over communities' responsibility for Jewish education illustrated the issues involved. After 1900, Jewish communal bodies in American cities began to affiliate formally with each other. The federation movement, as this was known, brought a variety of Jewish organizations under one umbrella, with each city's federation acting as a central coordinating and funding institution while leaving daily administrative functions to the individual agencies. In cities like Baltimore, the Associated Jewish Charities, founded in 1921, included the Hebrew Sheltering Home, Hebrew Free Loan Society, Hebrew Burial Societies, and other community organizations. All these agencies had their counterparts in other federations around the country and were included as a matter of course.

Whether Jewish education should be encompassed in federations of Jewish charities was a more contentious issue, one that was decided variously in Jewish communities. Baltimore's federation leader Louis Levin consulted with a number of prominent Jewish citizens. Some, like educator Henry Berkowitz of Philadelphia, believed that Jewish education, even if not a charity by definition, was a communal responsibility and should therefore be included. As Berkowitz wrote, charitable functions "should not be limited to meeting physical needs alone—but those of the whole man—mind, heart, and soul as well." Others, like Ludwig B. Bernstein, the executive director of Pittsburgh's federation, argued that Jewish education was vitally important but as a religious matter did not fit the definition of need served by other agencies. In the end, Baltimore's federation, unlike most other cities' central Jewish organization, did include an educational agency.[11] The question of community funding for Jewish education persisted over the twentieth century. In many cities, even those with large, thriving federations, Jewish education still received only limited funding from central communal organizations.

Another form of resistance came from the most traditionally observant parents, who often viewed Jewish education outside the home as either unnecessary, especially for girls, or wholly inadequate, especially for boys. Sons of some eastern European immigrants continued to attend private cheders run by individual melamdim. Benderly and other professional Jewish educators condemned cheders, deploring the practice of one teacher per forty or fifty students paying lip service to studying Bible, Mishnah, and sometimes Talmud in dank, crowded rooms. Daughters frequently received no formal Jewish education at all, on the assumption that they would learn what they needed to know at home from their mothers. These attitudes led to structural differentiation in boys' and girls' education, sometimes even within the same family. What was good enough for girls was not always adequate for boys. By the turn of the century Jewish educators in New Jersey acknowledged the discrepancy, reporting that parents, "being less particular about the education of girls are willing to send them to the community school but entrust their boys' education primarily to the Yiddish-speaking melamed."[12] The same dynamic affected the Hebraic curriculum so favored by most professional Jewish educators of the pre–World War II period. Schools with Hebrew curricula usually enrolled more girls because, as the BJE's Alexander Dushkin pointed out, "it was easier to get Jewish parents to permit the teaching of these modern 'fads' to girls than to boys."[13]

Except for a few boys attending yeshiva-type schools in New York, immigrant children from observant families generally attended public schools. It might have been expected that the sometimes more traditional Jewish immigrants pouring into the United States from the 1880s through the 1920s would start their own Jewish schools, but they rarely did during that period. They may have grumbled about the vapid lessons of Sabbath schools or the inattention of the Hebraic curriculum at Talmud Torahs to Talmud itself, but the children went to these schools anyway. Religious education as supplementary education reigned supreme.

Supplementary religious education carried its own dangers. The most pernicious problem faced by Jewish education was apathy. Especially for middle-class children, Jewish education became just one of many competing extracurricular activities. Jewish educators from the mid-nineteenth century on found it difficult to convince parents that religious education was as important as piano lessons or athletic activities. At most, fifteen thousand out of nearly fifty thousand Jewish children got any kind of formal religious education in 1880.[14] The preference of many parents and children for developing nonsectarian interests reflected the overriding concern for social integration. As one Chicago Jewish educator wrote in 1914 of her failed plan to start a religious school, "Money can be had for everything; for music and dancing; but when it comes to Jewish education only excuses are offered. How cheap Judaism has become to many of our parents."[15]

This complaint resounded throughout the twentieth century. Despite the BJE's best efforts, in 1921 only 25 percent of the Jewish children of school age in New York received any form of religious instruction.[16] A 1932 study found that of the 45 percent of Jewish children in Philadelphia who attended Jewish schools, the majority of those students received less than one hundred hours of religious instruction per year.[17] In 1936 a study of Jewish school enrollment in Cleveland found that overall numbers of students had dropped and that even those students who remained attended the congregational Sabbath schools rather than the community Talmud Torah schools.[18] The Depression made it difficult for religious educators to convince a financially strapped and sometimes fundamentally disinterested American Jewish public that religious education was important. In part because of the expenses associated with religious education and in part because of a growing trend of Jewish education as preparation for specific life cycle events, post–bar mitzvah dropout rates increased during the 1930s. It may have been the case that some American Jewish parents felt secure in the Jewishness of their home and family life and saw little need for formal religious instruction. It is more likely, however, that as most American Jews moved further away from traditional observance and retained Jewish identity largely through ethnic rituals, they simply did not consider religious education important enough to sacrifice anything else for.

In the wake of the post–World War II baby boom, Jewish education seemed to become associated with children alone, a development that later critics termed "pediatric Judaism."[19] The average student in a Sunday school stayed there four years, and the average student in a weekday afternoon school stayed there three years.[20] The post–bar and then bat mitzvah dropout rate was immense, and even synagogues that substituted or added confirmation classes for teenagers failed to keep adolescent students in religious schools. There were a number of factors involved, but one thing was clear. Jewish education in America was not only supplementary but temporary. Religious educators and synagogue leaders argued that adolescence was the most crucial period in identity formation, but to no avail. Even children in religious schools who, when questioned, had generally positive feelings about Jewish education still exhibited little interest in continuing into high school. There would be other priorities then.

Professional Jewish educators fought against these trends as best they could. In 1952 Emanuel Gamoran, a Samson Benderly protege then heading the Reform movement's Commission on Jewish Education, argued that most Jewish children between the ages of four and eight should go to foundation schools where they could be socialized into the Jewish community. After third grade they should supplement public schooling with religious education at least three times a week, preferably in two-hour sessions, and attend Jewish or Hebrew summer camps. The 10–15 percent most interested in and best suited for Jewish leadership should stay in a network of "liberal-cultural" day schools for advanced Jewish education.[21] Gamoran's plan never went into effect, but his concerns about the religious education of American Jewish leaders were well founded. A 1953 survey of Conservative lay leaders found that only 27 percent could understand most of a service conducted in Hebrew—13 percent could not follow the services in their own synagogues. A commentator on this survey tried to distinguish between "realistic goals" and "noble sentiments" in reference to Hebrew skills, but it was difficult to sustain optimism in the face of such numbers.[22]

Starting from the middle of the twentieth century, commissions on Jewish education attempted to respond to these systemic problems. New York's BJE became the Jewish Education Committee in 1939. Under the initial leadership of Alexander Dushkin, the Jewish Education Committee successfully provided professional services to Jewish educators and schools, but found it difficult to resolve the central question of how to define Jewish education in the modern world. Several new national commissions on Jewish education appeared during the 1940s in addition to the already existing Reform and Yiddishist commissions. These included the Lubavitch Merkos L'Yinyonie Chinuch (1941) and the Conservative movement's Commission on Jewish Education of the United Synagogue (1949). All the commissions published textbooks, established professional organizations for teachers, and sponsored journals for teachers, parents, and pupils. All agreed that intensification of religious education was necessary, but the required course of action was less certain. The Commission on Jewish Education of the United Synagogue tried to implement a plan by which Conservative synagogues would offer Sabbath school classes only to children under eight years of age, with all older children required to attend Talmud Torah-type classes three times a week. In some congregations this plan worked, but in others the number of students above eight years old who attended the religious schools dropped in response to the new requirements.[23]

It was hard to know how to gauge the results of Jewish education. Widespread disappointment among professional Jewish educators and some parents led to a declension model of Jewish education that has persisted ever since. The conviction that fewer students were receiving any kind of religious schooling and that the content of their Jewish education was diluted compared with past instruction became so prevalent that it dominated most thinking about American Jewish education from at least the mid-twentieth century forward. However, the situation was more complex than the mournful tones of the Jewish educational establishment would seem to indicate. In terms of sheer numbers and groups of people,

American Jewry actually achieved some success in expanding the reach and scope of American Jewish education.

THE EXPANSION OF STUDENT POPULATIONS

A relentlessly optimistic view of the history of Jewish education in America would be no more appropriate than a pessimistic one. Still, it was generally the case that the number of people receiving some form of religious education steadily increased. One critical factor explaining this increase was the inclusion of girls in nearly all models of Jewish education. The earliest confirmation classes in America, established by congregations like Baltimore's Har Sinai and Charleston's Beth Elohim, included both girls and boys from their inception as they prepared Jewish adolescents for ceremonies affirming their adult membership in the Jewish community.[24] Rebecca Gratz and her colleagues at the Hebrew Sunday School Society in Philadelphia took it for granted that girls as well as boys should participate in religious schooling. As Sabbath schools all over the country followed the Philadelphia model, they naturally ran coeducational classes. Samson Benderly, too, set the religious education of Jewish girls high on his agenda. Benderly's success at widening the female student base in all kinds of Jewish schools was the most immediately visible of his accomplishments. All the model Talmud Torahs operated by the BJE were for girls. These schools, known as Hebrew Preparatory Schools, served more than eleven hundred students between eleven and fifteen years old at three different locations in New York. The girls' schools offered Hebrew language, Bible, modern Hebrew literature, Jewish history, and Jewish activities in music, arts and crafts, dance, and drama.[25]

Confirmation classes, Sabbath schools, and Talmud Torahs faced a fundamental problem that eventually led to the further expansion of religious educational opportunities for girls and women. All forms of education shared the dilemma of a scarcity of trained teachers. Female Sabbath school teachers were especially likely to come under fire for ignorance and lack of preparation for taking charge of Jewish education, but the problem was not merely a function of gender. It had proven very difficult to launch higher Jewish education in America. Maimonides College was founded in Philadelphia in 1867 to train rabbis and teachers, but, despite a distinguished faculty, few students enrolled; the school closed in 1873. New York's Temple Emanu-el tried to start a theological school, beginning in 1865 with intermediate students who could then continue their studies in Europe. Future American Jewish leaders like Bernard Drachman and Felix Adler attended the Emanu-el Theological Seminary, which convened a national conference on Jewish education in 1876 and sparked some new interest in religious education in large Jewish communities. In its first incarnation in 1886, the Jewish Theological Seminary provided teacher training for traditional

Jews opposed to the Reform movement, but the school suffered from poor organization and finances.

The state of higher Jewish education remained poor. Hebrew Union College, the Reform rabbinical seminary founded in 1875, was less interested in producing classroom educators and administrators than pulpit rabbis and scholars. Yet in 1898 it did not limit admission to students able to read the Bible in the original Hebrew.[26] During the 1910s the recently reorganized Jewish Theological Seminary of America in New York became more open to the possibility of training Jewish educators, largely due to the influence of Mordecai Kaplan. With Kaplan's cooperation the BJE offered a particularly demanding yearlong course to young women between the ages of seventeen and twenty-one who had a high school education and some knowledge of Hebrew. Convinced that at least half the future teaching staff in religious schools should be women, Benderly expected these students to continue studying once they began to teach.[27]

New teachers colleges aimed to provide qualified religious educators. Gratz College in Philadelphia, Hebrew Teachers College in Boston, and the Teachers Institute of the Jewish Theological Seminary in New York: all were rooted in the turn-of-the-century call for more and better prepared Jewish educators. They were founded and staffed by a cadre of communal leaders and educators, including many early American Zionists, who believed in the importance of both a Hebraic curriculum and the cultural aspects of Judaism. Whether as teachers or as parents, the founders of these teachers colleges reasoned, knowledgeable men and women would be better able to sustain commitments to Judaism and Jewishness. However, the teachers colleges also helped deflect the possibility of a widespread push for women's rabbinic ordination, as for the first time women could obtain an intensive Jewish education at these institutions of higher learning.

Like the original Hebrew Sunday School Society in Philadelphia and many of the Talmud Torahs, most of the Hebrew teachers colleges were communally supported rather than denominational. New Hebrew teachers colleges appeared nearly every decade from the 1890s on. Most, such as Baltimore Hebrew College (now Baltimore Hebrew University) and the College of Jewish Studies in Chicago (now the Spertus Institute), still exist. The number of students rose steadily. A 1935 study counted 600 students in nine Hebrew teachers colleges. In 1949 a follow-up study found 705 students in eight schools. Nearly twenty years later, 1,800 students attended eleven institutions.[28]

Although the Hebrew teachers colleges were an important expression of the expansion of Jewish education to female and adult audiences, the majority of religious educators never attended Hebrew teachers colleges. For the many religious educators who taught at Sabbath schools, the primacy of Hebrew language and literature at the teachers colleges, though reflected in the curriculum of most weekday and day schools, was inappropriate and irrelevant to their primary tasks of teaching basic tenets of Jewish religion and culture, sometimes without much reference to any form of Hebrew.

Jewish education at teachers colleges was actually less supplementary in nature than the religious schooling offered to most children. Even students at Hebrew teachers colleges who pursued secular degrees concomitantly with their advanced Jewish education saw their two curricular tracks as complementary and devoted equal time to them. In New York Benderly urged Jewish girls to attend Teachers Institute instead of Hunter College, not as a weekly extracurricular activity but as their primary educational training center.[29] Even though relatively few people attended the Hebrew teachers colleges full time, the colleges' existence in a community usually guaranteed trained Jewish educators and professionally run Jewish schools. Women attended these centers for adult Jewish education with great enthusiasm and acceptance, although men typically took charge of community institutions of religious education.

The growth of religious education for both girls and women affected every segment of American Jewry, including the most traditionally observant. Formal religious education of girls was still controversial in parts of the Orthodox community, since many felt that learning from their mothers was all girls needed. Still, it seemed clear to parents and leaders that religiously educated girls would be better prepared to maintain Orthodoxy in America. Orthodox families watched with interest as in 1923 several giants of European Torah scholarship approved Sarah Schenirer's Bais Yaakov movement, which expanded into a network of religious girls' schools across Europe. The idea took off more slowly in America. Vichna Eisen Kaplan, a student of Schenirer's, started a Bais Yaakov in Williamsburg in 1937 with seven girls around her dining room table. Kaplan, like Schenirer, stressed the importance of training teachers to promulgate the Bais Yaakov movement and thus began her educational quest with older girls.[30] The first all-day Bais Yaakov opened in Williamsburg in 1944. The school grew very slowly. Suky Rosengarten, one of the twenty pupils present on opening day, looked askance at the poor physical facilities and unaccredited secular program and at first wanted to return to her public school class. Kaplan and others convinced all the girls that environment was as important as learning in their life journeys toward committed traditional Judaism, and surprisingly few students left. As word spread, Bais Yaakov opened a dormitory for out-of-town students and eventually a summer camp.[31] At the Bais Yaakov schools that eventually opened in communities from Baltimore to Denver, teaching toward traditional observance was always paramount. Even Orthodox girls' schools with no formal affiliation owed something to the Bais Yaakov movement, which irrevocably established the necessity of offering girls as rigorous a religious education as boys. By extending religious education to girls, Orthodoxy in America greatly expanded the student population of the most traditionally oriented Jewish schools.

The twentieth-century combination of denominationalism and suburbanization also contributed to the growth in numbers of students receiving some form of Jewish education. Congregational schools gradually made gains over communal Talmud Torahs. From 1917 to 1927 the total enrollment at congregational schools in New York increased 150 percent.[32] Perhaps in response to events overseas, religious schools expanded their reach during and after World War II. In 1941 60 percent of all Jewish children received some kind of religious education in New York, a percentage that might have been even higher if cheders and home tutors had been factored in.[33] As American Jews moved from the cities to the suburbs, they joined the synagogues mushrooming in the new areas of Jewish settlement. Conservative Judaism became the fastest growing denomination. Reform and Orthodox congregations, too, began to relocate. A mid-1950s study found that rising Jewish synagogue affiliation was linked to parents' interest in religious education for their children.[34] As a result, both the percentage of Jewish children receiving a religious education and the percentage of religious education obtained in congregational schools increased. From 200,000 in 1937, to 266,000 in 1950, to 533,600 in 1959, the total number of students rose steadily. Of the 1959 number, more than 90 percent of the students attended weekday afternoon and Sunday schools.[35]

The Jewish educational establishment applauded the rise in attendance but expressed concern about the community divisiveness that accompanied the denominationalism of congregational schools, believing that Jewish education should follow public education in consolidating resources and facilities to achieve the best results.[36] In some cities, such as Detroit, consolidated religious schools were already successfully in place, complete with communal busing.[37] Smaller Jewish communities, which would have benefited the most from such consolidation, sometimes had the most trouble achieving it. With suburbanization also came a hardening of denominationalism in American Judaism. A small community might well have three synagogues that offered distinctive approaches to Judaism. They were unlikely to agree on the form religious instruction should take and rarely joined forces to provide Jewish education. In larger communities it was more possible for all the Reform or all the Conservative synagogues to provide joint religious education to their members. As congregational affiliation became one of the primary expressions of religious identity for many American Jews, there was less incentive for individual congregations to give up their autonomy by acting in concert with others. The end result of the fragmentation of Jewish education along denominational lines, however, was noticeable growth in the number of students attending religious schools.

Denominational religious schools included the Orthodox day schools run under the auspices of Torah Umesorah, founded in 1944. Backed by influential lay leaders and a rabbinical council, Torah Umesorah set out to start new day schools all over the United States. The organization also trained qualified teachers for day

schools, provided funds to existing schools for expansion, and consulted with affiliate schools on curricular and managerial matters. By 1952, due largely to Torah
Umesorah efforts, thirty thousand boys and girls attended 157 day schools, half of
them in New York City. Torah Umesorah also served Jewish children who did not
attend day schools by publishing *Olomeinu*, a children's magazine with worldwide
circulation of ten thousand during the 1960s. From its inception, Torah Umesorah was created, staffed, planned, and rabbinically supervised by members of the
Orthodox community. However, it succeeded in part because it wanted day
schools to appeal to nonobservant parents and based levels of both secular and
religious education on local conditions. The organization extended rigorous Jewish schooling to thousands more children than had ever had access to such an
education before.[38]

As more American Jewish children had at least a minimal religious education,
the call for adult Jewish education also grew louder. Renewed interest in Jewish
education for growing numbers of adults resulted in the rise of Jewish studies at
the college level, which defined Jewish education more broadly than had previously been the case. As historian Arnold J. Band has explained, a number of factors during the 1960s and 1970s led to the growth of collegiate Jewish studies. One
was the more general expansion of racial and ethnic consciousness in the United
States, with Americans of all backgrounds reclaiming their particular heritage
without rejecting their American identities. Another was the academic development of area studies beyond languages and texts to culture, society, and history.
A third was a new confidence that American Jewry was the center of the Jewish
Diaspora. Finally, the emerging acceptance of academic religious studies as a
scholarly field helped to legitimate Jewish studies. The expansiveness of the field
was symbolized with the 1968 establishment of the Association of Jewish Studies,
which encompassed all time periods, all languages, and all disciplines of Jewish
studies.[39]

The same expansiveness that widened the modern field of Jewish studies, as
opposed to earlier permutations like Semitic philology or a *Wissenschaft* focus on
intellectual history and premodern Judaism, eventually displaced older traditions
of the study of Hebrew on campuses. Hebrew continued to be taught on campuses large and small all over the United States, with enrollments growing every
year (as they now do in Yiddish classes as well). However, earlier models that focused on Hebrew language and literature were subsumed into the broader rubric
of Jewish studies. At Rutgers University, for instance, the Bildner Center for the
Study of Jewish Life, established in 1996, over a transition period of a few years
replaced the department of Hebraic studies with a department of Jewish studies.
Faculty members were generally retained, but the focus and mission of academic
inquiry about Judaism on campus expanded markedly. Jewish students without
previous religious education often took Jewish studies courses while attending
college, comprising another growing audience for Jewish education.

Adult religious education became another factor in the expansion of American Jewish education. As the Jewish leaders of the late nineteenth century pointed out, childhood religious instruction guaranteed no identification with the Jewish community or knowledge of Jewish culture, tradition, rituals, and text. Maintenance was key, as campaigns for adolescent and adult Jewish education signified. One reason for confirmation's popularity as a rite of passage for Jewish adolescents was that it prolonged religious education beyond the tender years of bar mitzvah for boys and (later) bat mitzvah for girls. Because specialized programs of adult Jewish education were even less rooted in either American Jewish experience or Jewish tradition, they tended to take on the cast of "informal" education. The Jewish awakening of the late nineteenth century that Jonathan D. Sarna has described in part followed from the establishment of the Reform Hebrew Union College and contributed to the establishment of the Conservative Jewish Theological Seminary and even the Orthodox Rabbi Isaac Elchanan Theological Seminary.[40] These rabbinical seminaries unquestionably educated the elite (men) of the day. However, most adult Jews interested in religious learning found it in alternative venues, such as the National Council of Jewish Women or the Jewish Chautauqua Society. No wave of formal adult Jewish education appeared during the early 1900s, although alternative forms of Jewish learning were continuously available. The real expansion of adult Jewish education classes came later in the twentieth century, as symbolized by the founding of the University of Judaism in Los Angeles in 1947. Its mission was not only to educate Jewish professionals but also to offer higher education to American Jews.[41]

Hebrew teachers colleges continued to make Jewish education available to adults who sought it out. By the 1950s the Hebrew teachers colleges were already coming under fire for devoting more of their resources to postsecondary Jewish studies in general and less of their resources to explicit teacher training. Beyond even such common events as community lecture series and book clubs, adult Jewish education came to include ongoing learning opportunities. Synagogues established centers for adult learning and provided space for everything from traditional text study to informal classes in Jewish liturgy and life. Jewish community centers at the turn of the century had supplied facilities for other institutions' Hebrew schools for children. By the end of the twentieth century they were developing original programming. Large organizations like Hadassah created academies for their lay leadership to study Jewish subjects more intensively. Every major Jewish organization, from the Anti-Defamation League to the American Jewish Congress, boasted an education department. Melton Adult Mini-Schools and Me'ah programs required serious time commitments over two-year periods to interactive text study on the postgraduate level, with the Melton program focusing largely on life cycle events and the Me'ah program on Bible, rabbinics, and modern Jewish history. These formal programs of Jewish education and others like them represented another stage in the continuous growth of religious education in America, reaching groups not previously included.

Adult education efforts formed the basis of outreach, another important trend in contemporary American Jewish education. The Lubavitch community's unwavering commitment to outreach spurred the creation of thirty-three hundred Chabad centers all over the world, with an influence particularly felt on college campuses and areas with small Jewish populations.[42] The popularity of the National Jewish Outreach Project's (NJOP) crash courses in reading Hebrew, which NJOP claimed to have reached more than four hundred thousand adult learners, testified to growing interest in adult Jewish education at the end of the twentieth century.[43] The Internet provided further opportunities for a less formal but possibly even more common Jewish learning experience, with organizations like Aish HaTorah reporting a million hits on its Web site every month.[44] The concept of outreach was exemplified by these Orthodox institutions but was taken up by all denominations. Growing communal concern over the swiftly rising number of unaffiliated, uneducated American Jews made Jewish education seem more important than ever—indeed critical to the survival of American Judaism. Adults became a crucial target for Jewish educational outreach because only interested, knowledgeable adults were likely to affiliate with the believing Jewish community and provide religious education to their children. The Orthodox had long since operated on the model of family education in prioritizing lifelong study. The move away from youth-oriented Judaism was somewhat more recent a development for less traditionally observant American Jews.

The most traditional yeshivas began to establish kollels, centers for intensive Jewish learning, in communities across America. Much of the day for the men in the kollel consisted of studying Talmud and other Jewish texts with each other, but they also gave classes and formed study partnerships with individuals in the community. The men and women, generally husbands and wives, of the kollel also often taught in the local day schools, injecting a strictly Orthodox outlook into Jewish education where none might have existed locally before. In the Conservative movement, adult b'nai mitzvah classes, requiring one to two years of regular study before a public ceremony, grew popular. Conservative synagogues also established adult outreach programs of their own. Reform synagogues began Kallah programs that ran four-day adult educational workshops on particular topics and themes. The Reform movement also issued manuals suggesting ways to increase personal observance and distributed weekly Torah commentaries.[45] All these efforts demonstrated that the growth of outreach in the last quarter of the twentieth century transcended denominational bounds. Ideas about what it meant to be Jews in America shifted as knowledge of Jewish history, religion, and culture reclaimed its place next to ethnic ties.

THE USE OF JEWISH EDUCATION AS A MEANS
OF FORMULATING AMERICAN JEWISH IDENTITY

The steady expansion of numbers and programs of religious education is not really surprising, given that Jewish education in America always had at least two goals. One was the direct goal of religious instruction, though it was variously defined, developed, and delivered. The other, no less weighty, was the indirect goal of using religious education as a vehicle for adapting to American life. At times of crisis or intense feeling, such as mass Jewish migration during the late nineteenth and early twentieth centuries, the latter goal took priority. The general struggle of modern Jews to integrate into their host society and culture without forsaking religious tradition and ethnicity found expression in programs of Jewish education that promised to deliver the key to successful acculturation while staving off complete assimilation. In 1890, for example, 56 boys and 119 girls attended religious classes at the Hebrew Free and Industrial School Society of St. Louis. These students, the institutional report noted, not only "obtain[ed] an acquaintance with our sacred literature, but also receive[d] a fundamental knowledge of the language of this country."[46] The St. Louis classroom was a model of how to reach simultaneously the complementary goals of religious instruction and acculturation.

Educational materials for Jewish schools reflected commitments to an agenda of both social integration and religious identity. As historian Jonathan Krasner has argued, the main goal of American Jewish schoolbooks was always to socialize students. At the turn of the twentieth century the chapters on American Jewish history written by Cyrus Adler and Henrietta Szold and inserted into Lady Katie Magnus's *Outlines of Jewish History* for the American audience promoted religious harmony among all Jews. Since Talmud Torahs, in particular, theoretically served whole communities, supplementary Jewish schools found it practical to adopt a textbook that stressed the importance of Jewish unity in coming to terms with America. Magnus's book sold tens of thousands of copies. Samson Benderly worked closely with Mordecai Kaplan on the production of Jewish textbooks, although Kaplan favored more outright religious content. Among the results of BJE work on textbooks were Elma and Lee Levinger's 1928 *The Story of the Jews*, which tried to present a balanced view of all the denominations in America, and Dorothy Zeligs's 1938 *A History of Jewish Life in Modern Times*, which used two fictional characters arguing over joining a Reform temple to represent ongoing Jewish debates about assimilation, acculturation, and group loyalty.[47] Boys who drew on the 1931 English translation of Kalman Whiteman's prepared speeches for bar mitzvahs delivered perorations explaining, "Here we have found absolute security, and the best Americans acknowledge the benefits we bring to the country. . . . I will endeavor to know and cherish the laws and institutions of this country but never shall there be any weakening of my love for our religion, for our people, and for everything that Jews hold dear."[48] This explicit syncretization of values typified American Jewish educational materials.

Coeducation represented another adaptation of American educational values into Jewish education. At virtually all supplementary religious schools except a few Talmud Torahs in large cities, Jewish education was coeducational. Confirmation classes also tended to be coeducational and likewise resemble American secondary schooling. Coeducation offered another way in which Jewish education signified Americanization, as religious schooling intentionally emulated public schooling in its (theoretical) commitment to all children. This also helps explain why girls outnumbered boys in confirmation classes, as they did in public high schools. Boys still had the option of having bar mitzvah ceremonies in many congregations and then often stopped their Jewish education at age thirteen. Boys were also much more likely to be working full time by sixteen, the typical age of confirmation. It was certainly possible for a working boy to continue his religious education, but it was unlikely. Supplementary religious education marched in tandem with public education. When the latter came to an end, the former usually did too. Since girls, with fewer employment options, often stayed in high school for longer periods, they were also more likely to stay in religious school.

Adopting the "Protestant model" of supplementary religious education was the most obvious and structurally most significant statement that American values as inculcated in public schools would be of primary importance to Jews in America. But other values remained important as well, and the various types of Jewish education illuminated major philosophical debate over American Jewish identity. Language became one indication of this debate. At various times, Jewish schools offered education in German, English, Yiddish, Ladino, and Hebrew, illustrating the widely divergent backgrounds and interests of differentiated groups within American Jewry.

Yiddishist schools, for example, incorporated political and national values into Jewish education, which they took pains not to equate with religious instruction per se. Still, as one proponent of Yiddishist schools explained, "The rising Jewish generation should as a matter of course grow up as good American citizens, part and parcel of the great American nation [and] the Jewish children should not at the same time be strangers to the Jewish people throughout the world."[49] These goals of integration differed little from those of other kinds of religious schools. At least three different kinds of Yiddishist schools flourished briefly. The National-Radical schools, established in 1910 in New York, used Yiddish as the language of instruction for Jewish history, literature, customs, ceremonies, music, socialism, and, sometimes, Hebrew. From 1917 on, these schools were generally called *folkshuln*. Teachers trained at the Idisher-Lehrer Seminary treated religion ethnographically in *folkshuln*. Sholem Aleichem schools, founded in 1916 in the Bronx, claimed independence from labor affiliations and taught nationalism and

Zionism in Yiddish. The Sholem Aleichem Folk Institute and Camp Boiberek were supporting institutions. The Arbeter-Ring schools, emerging out of a 1918 convention, initially focused on fostering children's Jewish working-class consciousness rather than Jewish peoplehood. Eventually, class difference remained paramount largely in theory, as Jewish unity in the face of threats at home and abroad became increasingly important.[50]

The 1930s saw a major decline in secular Yiddish schooling, which persisted but was never again a significant factor in American Jewish education. Secular Yiddish schools decreased precipitously in enrollment and cultural power as Yiddish became the language of the Old World to the American-born children of immigrants. Even in the largest Jewish communities, independent Yiddish schools, despite their strong connections to labor activism and socialism, found it difficult to justify their cultural outlook when the culture they championed was disappearing into the iron maw of a melting pot most American Jews favored strongly. It proved impossible in the long run to separate Yiddish education from Judaism, and by the 1930s the *folkschuln* and other secular Yiddish institutions had largely succumbed to perceived irrelevance.

Yiddish still retained some force in the cheders and yeshivas functioning as educational centers for the most traditionally observant Jews in America. These schools provided Jewish education in the same language as the political radicals but to very different ends, arguing that religious training should innoculate Jewish children against the perils of secular Americanization. A few yeshivas, institutions of full time Talmudic study, were already in place in New York, including the Etz Chaim school for boys, founded in 1886, and the Rabbi Isaac Elchanan Theological Seminary, a yeshiva founded in 1897. Torah Vodaath expanded into a post–high school yeshiva in 1929. During the 1930s, as Orthodox rabbis and observant students fled to America, yeshivas began to proliferate. Ner Israel in Baltimore (1933), Telshe in Cleveland (1941), and others became important preservers of European-style Orthodoxy. At Torah Vodaath Yiddish replaced Hebrew as the language of instruction in Talmud, and at European-based yeshivas, like Beth Midrash Gavoha in Lakewood, New Jersey, secular study played no role in Talmudic learning grounded in Yiddish.[51] Enrollments in the Lakewood yeshiva went from one hundred young men in 1946 to two hundred in 1964 and approximately one thousand by the 1980s.[52] After World War II Hasidic refugees created communities in which Yiddish continued to be the native language and sign of separatism.

As these schools demonstrated, there were always those for whom Jewish education was central, not peripheral, to Jewish practice and observance. Still, few American Jews desired the stark separatism of the yeshivas and Hasidic schools. The great question became how to develop a comprehensive educational system that would integrate American and Jewish identity. To the most traditional Jews in America, often first- and second-generation immigrants before World War II and survivors and refugees after World War II, the model of supplementary Jewish education was anathema. Some Orthodox parents joined their less traditional Jewish neighbors in sending their children to public schools. Free tuition, after all, remained a draw, as did the promise of adjustment to American life. However, for the first time since the 1870s, a variety of day schools offered other options. From separate schools for boys and girls to coeducational, modern institutions, day schools slowly but steadily became schools of choice and then of necessity for the Orthodox community. Living as observant Jews required total immersion in Jewishness and deep knowledge of Judaism of a kind that even the best weekday afternoon schools found impossible to teach in such a limited time. The refugee and survivor communities of Orthodox and Hasidic Jews, wary of involvement with anything state sponsored, opened their own schools as soon as they arrived in the United Sates, although they could not compel attendance. Fears about perceived dangers inherent in the youth culture of the 1950s, with its juvenile delinquency and rock and roll music, also led parents to consider the possibility that separate schools might be the only way to transmit their values and preserve their knowledge and tradition. The existing day schools started to look like viable models of education, proving the best of both worlds in dual curriculum settings. The fundamental concern, as always, was not separation but appropriate integration. For Orthodox Jews, day schools supplied the central answer to the question of how to live as committed Jews and committed Americans in a rapidly changing world.

Day schools succeeded in large part because they claimed not to move Jewish students out of American society. The National Association of Hebrew Day School PTAs affiliated with Torah Umesorah stated in 1949 that its objectives included "equipping our children to live creatively as Jews and as Americans." At the Torah Umesorah annual dinner in 1954, day school students speaking about "What a Yeshiva Education Has Meant to Me" emphasized the congruence of American values and Jewish education. Solomon Braunstein explained that he enjoyed sports and hobbies like other American boys but that he believed only day school education would enable him to live a committed Jewish life. "I feel very lucky," his speech concluded, "to have been given this wonderful chance to grow up as a good Jew and a good American."[53] This rhetoric appealed to Jewish parents concerned with preserving Jewish culture and customs if not all forms of ritual observance. The high scholastic standards of most Torah Umesorah schools met with general approval, and the central organization knew how important it was to keep those standards high enough to attract parents with many educational options. Not all motives were so rosy; in some cities, particularly in the urban Northeast and the South, the schools also served the default function of alternative schools for parents unhappy with desegregated public school systems.[54]

Other schools also demonstrated the consonance of Jewish and American values. Defending Hasidic schools from accusations of a lack of patriotism, educator

Joseph Kaminetsky explained that "loyalty to America is not underplayed by any means," even while the major curricular emphasis was placed upon the religious studies.[55] A post–World War II description of the Talmudical Academy of Yeshiva University, founded in 1916 to provide secular secondary education to boys devoted to studying Talmud in a traditional setting, claimed that the school's goal was "to raise generations of American youth imbued with a love and respect for the country of their birth or adoption, and for its institutions."[56] Yeshiva University, which had its roots in both precollegiate and yeshiva education, offered the self-styled Modern Orthodox community a unique philosophy of *Torah Umadda,* or "Torah and Science." Students spent long days learning yeshiva-style at the Rabbi Isaac Elchanan Theological Seminary and attending college courses at Yeshiva College. Graduates might be rabbis, doctors, or both. When Stern College for Women opened in 1954, everything was in place for Yeshiva University to become the central address for the creation and maintenance of an American Orthodoxy that would blend the best of old and new worlds.

Many non-Orthodox Jews reacted with horror to the development of the day school movement, which seemed to them to counter a century of benefiting from the ethnically (if not racially) diverse classrooms of the American common school. A heated debate raged for much of the 1950s and 1960s, with the Reform movement, in particular, staunchly reaffirming its commitment to public education. Torah Umesorah schools sometimes managed to garner the support of local Conservative rabbis and congregants. Accusations flew back and forth, indictments of ghettoization and assimilation countering each other and changing few minds. During the 1950s nearly all day schools were under Orthodox auspices. By the 1960s Reform and Conservative Jews also worried that most of the highly qualified Jewish educators available to teach in their congregational schools were the products of Orthodox day schools and did not share their religious values. With such high stakes in play, tensions unsurprisingly continued to run high.

On one level no meeting ground seemed possible. Jewish education was either supplementary or central. However, the two sides may actually have had some effect on each other. The percentage of Jewish children receiving any kind of Jewish education grew during the course of this debate, particularly among Conservative Jews, possibly reflecting in part the impact of Orthodox arguments about the importance of Jewish education. By the late 1960s the Conservative movement had established twenty-eight Solomon Schechter day schools.[57] The day schools became more modern in outlook and tone, possibly reflecting in part the concerns Orthodox parents shared with Reform and Conservative parents about acculturation into American life.

As day school education became more prevalent among the Orthodox, for the first time in Jewish history intensive training in Jewish texts became the province of the laity and not just the elite, including girls. To be sure, the standards were mixed at these schools, and not all students in all schools learned the same thing.

But extensive knowledge beyond basic familiarity with liturgy and home-based rituals became the norm not just in yeshivas and Bais Yaakovs but also for average day school students. Most of the hundreds and then thousands of Orthodox day school graduates did not go into the rabbinate or Jewish education, and they represented many kinds of Judaism. They gradually constituted an expanding group with a significant knowledge of texts and ritual and a commitment to lifelong study within traditional communities. The widespread nature of this Orthodox Jewish learning transformed an important element of American Jewish life and helps explain why, contrary to sociologists' gloomy predictions of the 1960s, the Orthodox Jew never did vanish.

Ideological battles over day schools notwithstanding, by the 1960s there was one issue that American Jews across the denominations agreed on: support for Israel. American Jewish identity had not always incorporated Zionism. The Reform movement's Pittsburgh Platform of 1885 rejected Zionism, a position not officially changed until the Columbus Platform of 1937. The place of Zionism or even Hebraism in American Jewish education was not assured either. Zionism presented textbook writers with a difficult challenge, generally resolved by conveying the idea that the state of Israel would be a good solution to Jewish problems in Europe even if it was unnecessary for Jews in America. The syncretization of values was most evident in Elma and Lee Levinger's *The Story of the Jew*, which borrowed a phrase from Louis Brandeis to describe halutzim as "Jewish Pilgrim Fathers," neatly synthesizing American, Jewish, and Zionist identity.[58] By 1936 a study of Jewish education in Cleveland discovered that teaching about Zionism and Palestine was becoming more common. While approving of the renewed interest in Hebrew to which these subjects naturally led, the study observed that, given the time constraints of weekly religious schools, greater attention to current Jewish events meant less attention to religion, customs, and Jewish texts.[59] When detailing the curricular goals of Reform Sunday schools, one educator listed "acquiring Jewish knowledge" last, after "enjoyment of Jewish fellowship" and "the problems of present-day Jewish life," such as Zionism.[60] This new commitment to Zionism among even those who had previously disavowed it reflected the entire American Jewish community's great concern over the events unfolding in Europe.

Education connected to Israel and Hebrew found another venue in summer camps. From the early twentieth century on, various groups of Jews in America, including radical activists of many stripes, had operated summer camps for both adults and children to strengthen causes ranging from socialism to Zionism to secular Yiddish culture. Summer camps offered social benefits, religious learning opportunities, Hebrew literary development, and ethnic group bonding otherwise unavailable to Jewish students. In 1927 Samson Benderly started Camp Achvah for high school students. Although a firm proponent of supplementary religious education during the regular school year, Benderly and his colleagues placed tremendous importance on Hebraism and believed that summer immersion in

Hebrew-speaking environments would deepen students' attachment to Judaism, promote Hebrew literature, and support Zionism. In 1941 Camp Massad began to set the standard for other camps that adopted Hebrew as their official language. Some of its successors, such as the Conservative movement's Camp Ramah, foregrounded denominational concerns as well. By 1967 three hundred thousand children enrolled in Jewish camps. Another goal of Jewish camping, like other forms of religious education, was, as the chancellor of Jewish Theological Seminary later put it, "to create a native American elite for the Jewish community."[61] No matter what the venue, Jewish education kept this goal of integrating American and Jewish identity at the forefront.

After the Holocaust, Israel became a synechdocic form of Jewish identity to the point that, for some American Jews, no religious education was necessary as long as support for the state of Israel stayed strong and reflexive. The focus on Israel in religious schools received further support from an Israeli teacher exchange program set up by the umbrella commission of Jewish education in America, the American Association for Jewish Education. This venture worked so well that during the 1950s 25 percent of the teachers in weekday schools were Israeli.[62] Widespread support for Israel had a noticeable effect on Jewish education in America. Addressing the Central Conference of American Rabbis in 1955, Rabbi Barnett Brickner commented that Reform Jewish education had already gone through two phases. In the first the focus was largely on the Bible and ethics. In the second the curriculum expanded to include Israel, Zionism, and Hebrew language and literature. "We are now," he said, "in the third phase, where we realize that the American child must be conditioned to become a reverent and believing Jew, a praying Jew, an observant Jew, one who feels spiritually secure in America."[63] Despite Brickner's prescient concerns about American Jews placing too much emphasis on Israel, intense sympathy for and identification with Israel continued to have a major impact on religious education in America. Starting in the 1960s, more Jewish youth began spending summers or a semester in Israel, Israeli pronunciation became more common across the denominations, and Israel dominated most religious school curricula.[64] Symbolically, after 1970, Hebrew Union College students spent their first year of rabbinical training in Israel.[65]

Hebrew language acquisition grew in importance because of its connection to the modern state of Israel rather than to the entire history and culture of Judaism. For many Jewish children Hebrew school became just that—a language school with little religious content. Since it was very difficult to learn Hebrew fluently in a few hours (at most) a week over a few years, Jewish education focused on Hebrew but devoid of the other content of the pre–World War II years suffered from terrible retention and reputation. While generally lauding and supporting Israel across the denominations, religious educators bemoaned the substitution of "Israelism" for Judaism. At the other end of the spectrum, some Orthodox day schools downplayed Zionism except in its religious context.

Graduates of these schools tended to have a better command of the biblical Hebrew of their intensive study of Jewish texts and liturgy than the modern Hebrew of the state of Israel. What the focus on Israel did provide, especially after Israel's 1967 victory in the Six-Day War, was the basis for significant increases in community support for Jewish education, particularly adult education and outreach efforts.

The results of centuries of communal investment in Jewish education are mixed. Paradoxically, more opportunities for Jewish education for people of all ages exist than ever before, but there are also more American Jews today ignorant about their cultural and religious traditions than ever before. The growth of day school education, for example, has yielded an intensively educated cadre of knowledgeable Jewish students and leaders, but, relative to the entire American Jewish population, they form a small group indeed. In 2001 there were five hundred Orthodox, seventy Conservative, twenty Reform, and fifty nondenominational day schools with a total population of only two hundred thousand students.[66] The fact that the majority of them are Orthodox has contributed to the steady distancing of Jewish denominations from each other. It raises the question whether intensive Jewish education is only possible within the Catholic model of schooling rejected by most American Jews over 150 years ago. What would it mean for notions of American pluralism if American Jewry were to discover that religious, ethnic, and cultural continuity is not, after all, sustainable through supplementary education? The contemporary Jewish educational scene in America also reflects a secular trend of shifting responsibility from parents at home to teachers in school. Just as schools in the twentieth century increasingly performed socialization tasks previously carried out at home—vocational education, ethical training, etc.—so too did the burden of Jewish continuity fall on religious schools. As varieties of Judaism that did not require ritual observance achieved legitimacy in America, religious schools often served as the only sources for Jewish education in either theory or practice. Since religious instruction was entirely optional in civil society, it could not but fail to achieve either of the goals of religious education for Jewish children. In America, at least, voluntarism has been both a blessing and a curse for Jewishness. The blessings of living in a free society are too obvious to require recital, but the curse of "too much" freedom of choice is no less obvious to a minority community concerned with continuity.

There is a head versus hand issue at the core of modern Jewish education in America. What is the purpose of religious education now? Is it to know more or to do more? Most American Jews do not claim increasing Jewish practice as their goal. Yet turning Jewish education into only an intellectual endeavor, as academic

Jewish studies does as a discipline, will probably not attract many more American Jews than requiring ritual observance. Other primary forms of American Jewish identity, including Jewish culture and charitable work, do not necessarily require educational programs. This leaves modern Jewish education with a problem of emphasis and content delivery. New models of family religious education try to address the issue by offering integrated approaches to Jewish knowledge and practice, but it is not yet clear how effective this will be in fostering greater Jewish commitment.

American Jews have increasingly positioned religious education as central to Jewish continuity, thus raising the stakes even higher for the dual goals of Jewish education. The average nonobservant American Jew has the opportunity to become significantly more Jewishly educated than his nonobservant grandparents, but he must acquire that religious knowledge by choice. The average observant American Jew will almost inevitably be considerably more learned than her observant grandparents as a consequence of her education in the day school system. These generalizations obscure the huge variety within Jewish education across all denominations in contemporary American Jewish life, but they do underscore both the promise and the perils of the communal focus on education as the means to continuity in an environment where religious education remains voluntary.

NOTES

1. Quoted in Seymour Fromer, "In the Colonial Period," in Judah Pilch, ed., *A History of Jewish Education in America* (New York, 1969), 8.

2. Jonathan D. Sarna, "American Jewish Education in Historical Perspective," *Journal of Jewish Education* 64 (Winter/Spring 1998): 11.

3. Hyman B. Grinstein, "In the Course of the Nineteenth Century," in Pilch, *A History of Jewish Education in America*, 33, 37–39.

4. Fromer, "In the Colonial Period," 23.

5. See Dianne Ashton, *Rebecca Gratz: Women and Judaism in Antebellum America* (Detroit, 1997).

6. For more on this revival, see Jonathan D. Sarna, *A Great Awakening: The Transformation That Shaped Twentieth-Century American Judaism and Its Implications for Today* (New York, 1995).

7. Joseph Reimer, "Passionate Visions in Contest: On the History of Jewish Education in Boston," in Jonathan Sarna and Ellen Smith, eds., *The Jews of Boston: Essays on the Occasion of the Centenary (1895–1995) of the Combined Jewish Philanthropies of Greater Boston* (Boston, 1995), provides a clear picture of the distinctions between the two types of religious school systems in his Boston case study.

8. See, for example, Samson Benderly, "The Jewish Educational Problem," *Jewish Comment*, June 12, 1903.

9. Louis Hurwich, *Memoirs of a Jewish Educator*, ed. and trans. Aaron Darsa (Boston, 1999), 20–21.

10. Frieda Gass Cohen, quoted in Kenneth Libo and Irving Howe, *We Lived There Too: In Their Own Words and Pictures–Pioneer Jews and the Westward Movement of America, 1630–1930* (New York, 1984).

11. Melissa R. Klapper, "The Debate Over Jewish Education," *Generations: The Magazine of the Jewish Historical Society of Maryland* (Fall 1996): 17–18.

12. Quoted in Bernard Ducoff, "Seventy Years of Jewish Schooling in New Jersey," *Jewish Education* 51 (Fall 1983): 27.

13. Alexander M. Dushkin, *Jewish Education in New York City* (New York, 1918), 83.

14. Grinstein, "In the Course of the Nineteenth Century," 45.

15. Anna Goldberg quoted in Harold Korey, "The History of Jewish Education in Chicago," 79, M.A. thesis, University of Chicago, 1942.

16. "To Provide Every Child with Religious Education," *American Hebrew*, May 27, 1921.

17. Alexander Segel, "A Survey of One-Day-A-Week Jewish Education in Philadelphia," *Jewish Education* 4 (April-June 1932): 116.

18. Isaac B. Berkson and Ben Rosen, "1936 Jewish Educational Survey of Cleveland, Part I–Enrollment and Withdrawals," in Lloyd P. Gartner, ed., *Jewish Education in the United States: A Documentary History* (New York, 1969), 174–77.

19. See, for example, Eric H. Yoffie, "Remarks to the National Association of Temple Educators Convention, Clearwater, Florida, December 23, 1998," http://www.uahc.org/yoffie/nate.shtml (July 8, 2004).

20. Judah Pilch, "From the Early Forties to the Mid-Sixties," in Pilch, *A History of Jewish Education in America*, 123.

21. Emanuel Gamoran, "Jewish Education in a Changing Jewish Community," *Jewish Education* 23 (Fall 1952): 15–16.

22. Oscar I. Janowsky, "Jewish Education," in Janowsky, ed., *The American Jew: A Reappraisal* (Philadelphia, 1964), 154, 165.

23. Pilch, *A History of Jewish Education in America*, 121–23, 135–37.

24. Marc Lee Raphael, *Profiles in American Judaism: The Reform, Conservative, Orthodox, and Reconstructionist Traditions in Historical Perspective* (San Francisco, 1984), 11.

25. Samson Benderly, *Aims and Activities of the Bureau of Jewish Education of the Jewish Community (Kehillah) of New York City* (N.p., 1912), 36–37; Alexander M. Dushkin, *Living Bridges: Memoirs of an Educator* (Jerusalem, 1975), 11–12, 17.

26. Grinstein, "In the Course of the Nineteenth Century," 43–45.

27. Benderly, *Aims and Activities*, 25.

28. Walter Ackerman, "A World Apart: Hebrew Teachers Colleges and Hebrew-Speaking Camps," in Alan Mintz, ed., *Hebrew in America: Perspectives and Prospects* (Detroit, 1993), 114.

29. Benderly, *Aims and Activities*, 24–25.

30. Pearl Benisch, *Carry Me in Your Heart: The Life and Legacy of Sarah Schenirer* (New York, 2003), 437–38, 442, 447.

31. Sudy Rosengarten, *Worlds Apart: The Birth of Bais Yaakov in America* (Southfield, MI, 1992), 29, 188; Devora Rubin, ed., *Daughters of Destiny: Women Who Revolutionized Jewish Life and Torah Education* (New York, 1988), 218, 222.

32. Meir Ben-Horin, "From the Turn of the Century to the Late Thirties," in Pilch, *A History of Jewish Education in America*, 81–83.

33. Isaac B. Berkson, "Jewish Education: Achievement and Needs," in Oscar I. Janowsky, ed., *The American Jew: A Composite Portrait* (New York, 1942), 71.

34. Uriah Zevi Engelman, *Trends and Developments in American Jewish Education, 1956–1957* (New York, 1957).

35. Pilch, *A History of Jewish Education in America*, 121–23.

36. Engleman, *Trends and Developments in American Jewish Education*.

37. Daniel J. Elazar, "The National-Cultural Movement in Hebrew Education in the Mississippi Valley," in Mintz, *Hebrew in America*, 133.

38. Doniel Tzvi Kramer, *The Day Schools and Torah Umesorah: The Seeding of Traditional Judaism in America* (New York, 1984), 11, 38, 40, 66, 13, 36–37.

39. Arnold J. Band, "From Sacred Tongue to Foreign Language: Hebrew in the American University," in Mintz, *Hebrew in America*, 179–82.

40. Sarna, *A Great Awakening*.

41. Raphael, *Profiles in American Judaism*, 115–16.

42. See http://www.chabad.org (July 22, 2004).

43. See http://www.njop.org/html/stats.html (July 22, 2004).

44. See http://www.aish.org (July 22, 2004).

45. Marc Lee Raphael, *Judaism in America* (New York, 2003), 113, 81.

46. Report of the Hebrew Free and Industrial School Society of St. Louis to the Central Committee of the Baron de Hirsch Fund, December 17, 1890, Baron de Hirsch Fund Papers, I-80, American Jewish Historical Society.

47. Jonathan B. Krasner, "Representations of Self and Other in American Jewish History and Social Studies Textbooks: An Exploration of the Changing Shape of American Jewish Identity," 3, 70, 77, 113, 125, 150, 261, 316, Ph.D. diss., Brandeis University, 2002.

48. Kalman Whiteman, *Bar Mitzvah: Speeches Based on the Sidra and Haftarah of Every Sabbath in the Year*, trans. Maximilian Hurwitz (New York, 1931), 33–34.

49. A. Glanz, "The National Radical Schools," *American Hebrew*, June 16, 1916.

50. Ben-Horin, "From the Turn of the Century to the Late Thirties," 104–10.

51. For more on these institutions, see Moshe D. Sherman, *Orthodox Judaism in America: A Biographical Dictionary and Sourcebook* (Westport, 1996).

52. Raphael, *Profiles in American Judaism*, 167.

53. Solomon Braunstein and Judith Myrun, "The Children Speak," *Jewish Parent* 6 (February 1955): 18.

54. Kramer, *The Day Schools and Torah Umesorah*, 79–80, 68.

55. Joseph Kaminetsky, "The Program and Effectiveness of the All-Day School," *Jewish Education* 27 (Winter 1956–57): 41.

56. Shelly R. Saphire, "The Talmudical Academy of Yeshiva University," *Jewish Education* 20 (November 1948): 40.

57. Raphael, *Profiles in American Judaism*, 120–21.

58. Krasner, "Representations of Self and Other," 3, 70, 77, 113, 125, 150, 261, 316.

59. Berkson and Rosen, "1936 Jewish Educational Survey of Cleveland," 174–77.

60. Abraham N. Franzblau, "Toward the Reorientation of Jewish Religious Education," in Gartner, *Jewish Education in the United States*, 185–86.

61. Ackerman, "A World Apart," 115–25. Full treatment of Jewish and Hebrew summer camps is unfortunately beyond the scope of this essay.

62. Pilch, *A History of Jewish Education in America*, 153–57, 173.

63. Quoted in Krasner, "Representations of Self and Other," 224.

64. Jack Wertheimer, *A People Divided: Judaism in Contemporary America* (New York, 1993), 304.

65. Raphael, *Profiles in American Judaism*, 63.

66. Raphael, *Judaism in America*, 124.

9

A REGIONAL CONTEXT FOR PACIFIC JEWRY, 1880–1930

WILLIAM TOLL

WESTERN REGIONALISM AS AN INTERPRETIVE THEME

American Jewish historical writing includes many carefully researched studies of communities in specific cities. But Jewish communities may also acquire a social status, and political legacy, and their cohesiveness may be augmented because of their regional location. Regionalism has provided a major theme for describing the affects of geography and environmental influences on economic and political rivalries in nineteenth-century America. It has also been properly criticized because of the often vague definitions of *region* and because of the similarities that marked America's people as they migrated to bring newly settled territory into a national market economy.[1] For the concept of regionalism to hold broad interpretative power, it should explain how an economic base, social networks, and institutions tied communities to one another, how the iconography of region gave these communities a distinctive self-image, and how that image influenced behavior over time.

A growing literature on Jewish communities in the nineteenth and early twentieth century South, for example, illustrates how small town Jews, who were supplied from commercial cities like New Orleans, Atlanta, or Galveston, followed life patterns and created institutions different from those created by the Jews of New York, the nation's main port of entry and population center.[2] But as Mark Bauman quite correctly notes, southern social patterns seem to have differed little from those of Jews settling in commercial centers almost anywhere in America beyond the industrial Northeast.[3] Nevertheless, Jews entered America's various regions at different moments in the history of each, found themselves at varying distances from the influence of major population centers, encountered different ethnic and racial mixes and different political circumstances, and absorbed different regional lore. Jews constructing similar commercial roles and similar religious and philanthropic institutions in different regions could conceivably have developed a different sense of who they were becoming—as Americans and as Jews—in part because of their neighbors and because of their own relative prominence in defining regional political priorities.[4] Along the Pacific Coast, Jewish newcomers understood that they were traveling through vast landscapes far removed from the rest of the nation and facing unprecedented civic challenges as regional pioneers. As Jacob Nieto, an immigrant from England and rabbi at San Francisco's Reform Temple Sherith Israel, wrote ironically in 1911, "The Sierras perform the same kind of unkind office for California that the sea does for Great Britain—we are insular in our prejudices."[5]

On the Pacific Coast young Jewish men pursued economic opportunities similar to their colleagues elsewhere in America. But Jews who remained after the Gold Rush saw their adventure as part of America's most far-flung effort at pioneering. The extraordinary port at the Golden Gate made San Francisco, like Chicago in the Midwest, the central place and transforming node for an entire region.[6] It became an "instant city," where "the empty heights of society were occupied by men and women, regardless of background or creed, who were there early enough and were fortunate enough to become rich." And a disproportionate number of those who established the city's first commercial ventures were Jews.[7] As individual Jews reoriented their layered personalities to new homes, their religious identities were affected by their new geographic location and secular status.

A key date for measuring the status of Jews in the Pacific West is 1880, because by then Jewish families had become mercantile anchors of the region's new commercial towns. The most successful had established partnerships with gentiles in creating regional financial and transportation infrastructure, and their prominence as merchants made them visible pillars of the struggle for civic order.[8] They had endowed their sons and daughters with religious, fraternal, and philanthropic institutions to cement their own communities. Despite exclusion of Jews from city clubs established by the gentile elite, by the 1890s Jewish Concordia clubs, with a list of their members, were included in the elite social registers in San Francisco and Portland.[9]

Internally, between 1900 and the mid-1920s, western Jewish communities developed a sense of place that allowed their leaders to believe that their collective status was superior to that of Jewish communities in the East. The large contingents of east European and Sephardic immigrants then arriving moved into

Table 9.1. Jewish Population Estimates, Pacific West States

State	1877	1907	1917	1927	1937
Arizona	48	500	1,013	1,455	1,847
California	18,580	42,000	63,652	123,284	157,471
Nevada	780	300	503	264	379
Oregon	868	6,000	9,767	13,075	11,649
Washington	145	5,500	9,117	14,698	18,422

Sources: *American Jewish Yearbook, 5675 [1914–1915]* (Philadelphia, 1914), 352; *American Jewish Yearbook, 5701 [1940–1941]* (Philadelphia, 1941).

lower-income residential neighborhoods, where they created the West's first traditionally Jewish landscapes. But even these neighborhoods had open space for new homes. Their neighbors were not only familiar immigrants like Italians, but people from Mexico and Japan, whose homelands, places of worship, and public rituals tied Pacific Coast cities not to a receding Europe but to a beckoning Pacific Rim. In addition, descendants of Jewish pioneer families hoped to create an inclusive Jewish communal leadership through fraternal and philanthropic links. They recruited east European and Sephardic leaders into consolidated B'nai B'rith lodges, which became the largest in the country.[10] New federations for philanthropy included charities established by the Orthodox, Orthodox laymen served on federation boards, and columns by Orthodox rabbis and laymen were included in community newspapers.[11]

In the 1920s, as Los Angeles developed a heavy industrial sector, it surpassed San Francisco as the region's economic, demographic, and cultural hub. Oil refining, automobile assembly and rubber tire plants, and federal investment in the port at Long Beach created the Los Angeles boom. But, as in the Gold Rush, Jews pioneered in shaping consumer demands.[12] Those with extraordinary chutzpah created motion pictures, the region's most celebrated industry and the nation's fifth largest, while hundreds of others created a unique sportswear industry, which grew in the 1930s because of its link to motion picture costume design.[13] By 1930 Los Angeles had become the nation's fourth largest city, and its Jewish population, estimated at eighty-two thousand, had doubled that of San Francisco. Over half the Jews on the Pacific Coast, as over half in the Northeast, now lived in one city. All manner of Jewish organizations now held their conventions in southern California, and both religious and lay leaders emphasized an ideology of public service and brotherhood to integrate Jewish communities into regional civic life. The continued separation from the rest of the country, which drew communal leaders along the Pacific Coast together, the array of new Jewish architectural landmarks completed in the 1920s, and the immense respect that the gentile commercial elite afforded their Jewish counterparts, made Jews of the West believe that their status in this newest region of the new land remained unique.[14]

JEWISH PIONEERING: SAN FRANCISCO AND THE PROVINCES

From 1849 through World War I, commercial and social life for the Pacific region focused on San Francisco. Its sixteen thousand Jews in the 1870s comprised the second largest Jewish population in the country and 8 percent of the city's total.[15] Immigrants from Bavaria like Lewis Gerstle, his brother-in-law Louis Sloss, and Aaron Fleishacker, whose Sacramento stores had prospered by supplying gold miners, relocated to San Francisco, where they invested in whatever seemed inviting. Their ventures ranged from fur trading and salmon canning in Alaska to railroads in central California and to light industry and real estate in San Francisco.[16] As facilitators for a chain migration of aspiring Jewish merchants, Sloss and his colleagues provided merchandise on credit to young men who peddled to mining camps and moved on to extraordinary commercial and civic careers.[17] By 1880 not only did San Francisco hold 21 percent of the population of the Pacific region, but its merchants, including Jews, handled 99 percent of the region's imports. As the city became the region's manufacturing center, Jewish men like Levi Straus in clothing and Isadore Zellerbach in paper products helped it to produce more goods than the other twenty-four cities of the region combined.[18] In 1890, I. W. Hellman, a Bavarian immigrant merchant who had become the most influential banker in Los Angeles, was recruited by railroad barons to manage a major bank in San Francisco. By 1905 it had merged with the Wells Fargo Bank, and Hellman was the most respected and influential banker in the region. Even before his move from Los Angeles he had been appointed to the board of regents of the University of California, a position he held until his death in 1920.[19]

As Moses Rischin has argued, San Francisco Jews participated in an unprecedented expansion of culture as well as commerce. In 1880 four English-language Jewish newspapers were published there, as many as in New York. Young men a continent as well as an ocean away from their origins turned to one another for mutual support. San Francisco boasted several Jewish mutual aid societies, like the aptly named Eureka Benevolent Society, and by 1880 had five permanent synagogues as well as seven B'nai B'rith lodges. The merchants of Bavarian origins expressed their pride through Temple Emanu-El, erected in 1866 on Sutter Street as an instant civic landmark. Its twin domes were visible to all ships sailing through the passage known as "the Golden Gate." As Professor Rischin aptly

Table 9.2 Jewish Population of Selected Western Towns, 1880

Town	Total Population	Jewish Population		
		No.	% Jews	% Jews 0–16 years old
Portland, OR	17,577	508	2.9	43.9
Albany, OR	1,867	72	3.9	36.1
Seattle, WA	3,533	98	2.8	48.0
Los Angeles, CA	11,183	420	3.8	48.3
San Jose, CA	12,567	242	1.9	45.0
Virginia Ct, NV	10,917	146	1.3	46.6

Source: Data on Jews gathered from United States manuscript census returns.

notes, "Like no other building in the nation, the region's cathedral synagogue dramatically came to symbolize the freedom, equality, openness and fraternity of America and the West for Jews and others."[20] Emanu-El's entry in the 1879 city directory informs the public that the lot and building cost $185,000, more than the amount expended on all but one church.[21] When Congregation Sherith Israel, which welcomed men of varying geographic origins, completed a new edifice in 1905 at California and Webster Streets, its magnificent stained glass window depicted Moses bringing down the Ten Commandments, not from Mt. Sinai but from El Capitan to the Yosemite Valley.[22]

By 1880, in towns along the Pacific Coast, Jews had established themselves as "Main Street" merchants. Like the general population, Jews concentrated in northern California, though individuals and families scattered to most small towns, where they were often from 2 to 4 percent of the population. Through the early twentieth century Jewish men supplied farmers and ranchers on credit during the growing seasons and in exchange took gold nuggets, grain, cattle, wool, and hides after harvest. In Los Angeles the firm of Newmark and Kremer advertised in the 1872 city directory, "will exchange produce of all descriptions for hides, lumber, barley, beans, corn, potatoes, butter, eggs; our charge will be 5% on original invoice."[23] Harris Newmark, whose narrative of Los Angeles Jewry provides so many details about commercial and social life in general, shipped the hides and grain he bought from local farmers and ranchers to his brother in San Francisco.

As commercial farming, timber, and light industry came to dominate the region, the sons of immigrants coordinated their business careers with life cycle transitions and reinforced their image as pillars of civic stability. The chain of migration that had drawn their parents from Central European villages in the

1850s now launched them in the 1870s and 1880s on more complex mercantile apprenticeships around the region, from larger cities to smaller towns and back. City directories in the late 1870s carry engraved advertisements for hundreds of general merchandise houses owned by Jews. In Albany, Oregon in 1880 over two dozen Jewish storekeepers from half a dozen European states were interspersed with other businesses over the three blocks of the main business street. In such a small town, merchants lived within a few blocks of their stores and they and their families were known to everyone.

The image of Jewish mercantile cohesiveness persisted into the 1920s in a large city like Spokane, where forty-three Jewish-owned jewelry, clothing, and furniture stores clustered on six consecutive blocks of three parallel downtown business streets. Only four blocks to the south the Reform temple and the Orthodox synagogue stood a block apart, and the vast majority of Jewish families resided within walking distance of both structures. While Jews were not more numerous than other merchants, their narrow lines of merchandising, the close proximity of their stores and homes, as well as their cohesion in synagogues, fraternal lodges, and benefit societies created the image of an intense community integral to the city's commercial success.[24]

By the late 1850s the pioneer Jewish merchants felt sufficiently secure to start families. Most found wives through business or family ties either in German villages or in cities like San Francisco, Portland, or Los Angeles.[25] Most women were considerably younger than their husbands, started to have children shortly after marriage, and usually bore from four to eight, though many children died before reaching adulthood. Separated from their mothers and sisters by thousands of miles, Jewish women turned to one another to surmount family tragedies. While Jewish women throughout the Western world were adding public responsibilities to their family practices, in cities like San Francisco and Portland—in conjunction with Protestant and Catholic women—they built the social infrastructure.[26] From the founding of Pacific Coast cities, Catholic nuns and Protestant wives had provided medical, educational, and charitable services to sustain newly located families. Though most of their work was confined to their respective religious communities, women did cooperate across communal lines where broader civic interest required. All along the coast nuns from the Sisters of Charity, the Sisters of the Holy Name, or the Sisters of Providence started boarding schools and hospitals that served non-Catholics as well.[27] In most cities Protestant women from merchant families founded clinics, homes for unwed mothers, as well as Sunday Schools, and sponsored missions in the overwhelmingly male waterfront districts to combat alcoholism and violence and to promote Christian observance.

Jewish women began by forming benevolent societies, often connected informally to a synagogue, to assist their own families. By 1857 in San Francisco, 1870 in Los Angeles, and 1874 in Portland, the need to provide emergency services, including the ritual need to bury women and children, led the women to form

Jewish Ladies Relief Societies or Ladies Hebrew Benevolent Societies.[28] The organizations, while reflecting the patriarchal character of Jewish families, also enabled women to gain greater knowledge of their growing cities and some sense of gender autonomy. For example, in both Los Angeles and Portland several husbands of members served either as officers or advisers for organizing the meetings, dispensing funds, and creating an endowment by investing in real estate. By the early 1880s, however, male officers had been supplanted by women who raised large sums of money to pay off the temples' mortgages.

In the late 1880s when Reform rabbis were encouraged by Rabbi Kaufman Kohler to transform an abstract "Mission of Israel" into a concrete social gospel,[29] they recruited the wives and adult daughters of their members to provide assistance to the growing numbers of poor Jewish families. In San Francisco, a group called "The Helpers," whose members had performed "friendly visiting" under the auspices of the Eureka Benevolent Society, worked with the Associated Charities and at first dispensed provisions and medicine to as many gentile as Jewish cases. By the mid-1890s, when the number of immigrant Jews increased and the local economy declined, a much larger proportion of their services focused on Jewish families.[30] In a concerted effort to bring modern criteria of welfare assistance to Jewish communal services, Rabbi Jacob Voorsanger of Emanu-El borrowed from a model developed at New York's Temple Emanu-El to initiate a Sisterhood of Personal Service. The sisterhood created an employment service for adults, acquired a clubhouse in the mixed immigrant district "South of Market" to initiate recreation and vocational training for boys and girls, and soon started cooking, sewing, and child-rearing classes for immigrant mothers.[31]

The Council of Jewish Women was founded in 1893 in Chicago, and by 1896 a "section" in Portland became the first on the West Coast. By 1900 sections had been founded in San Francisco and in Seattle, though the section in Los Angeles was not founded until 1909. Council sections soon shifted their focus from study groups under rabbinical direction examining Jewish history and literature to the welfare of poor Jewish families proliferating around them. By 1906 the section in Portland rented a building to establish a Neighborhood House, while Seattle's section created a Council House, where members and their daughter and sons prepared immigrant children for American urban conditions. The women formed clubs for girls and boys, taught classes to prepare them to participate in Jewish ceremonies at Hanukkah, Purim, and Succoth, and established relief nurseries, educational meetings for immigrant mothers, and well baby clinics.

By 1910 council sections in Portland, Seattle, and San Francisco expanded their volunteer work to include more demanding intervention with public agencies. Volunteers in effect became social workers by going between immigrant households and neighborhood schools to arrange for medical and dental services and to establish after-school playgrounds. Even more ambitiously, several women became volunteer caseworkers for the new juvenile courts, where they gained supervisory powers over Jewish children placed in Jewish foster homes.[32] As late as 1924 in Los Angeles, the judge of the juvenile court commended the Case Committee of the local section of the National Council of Jewish Women for its work in finding foster homes, employment, and religious instruction for sixty-seven girls remanded to its care.[33]

The efficiency of the Jewish philanthropic network and the high status of Jews within the city of San Francisco was acknowledged by their collective response to the region's most horrifying disaster, the earthquake and firestorms of April 1906. The district south of Market Street was burned out, and many Jewish immigrant families relocated to the south and east along San Bruno Road. New synagogues were built there, as was a new settlement house that included rooms for Rabbi Nieto's Hebrew School. Emanu-El's building was badly damaged, but Sherith Israel's new building remained largely intact and was used by the city as a temporary courthouse. Rabbis Nieto and Voorsanger were appointed by the mayor to head emergency relief committees, while I. W. Hellman and a committee of Jewish businessmen raised funds to repair all damaged synagogues and to offer relief to displaced Jewish families. Synagogues and B'nai B'rith lodges along the coast sent relief funds, but when national Jewish charities sent investigators to determine the need for further relief, Rabbi Voorsanger and I. W. Hellman were so affronted by their findings that they refused to accept any funding from New York. The official survey of relief operations completed in 1909 was supervised by Professor Jessica Peixotto, the second woman to receive a doctorate from the University of California, and its first female professor. Professor Peixotto found that very few Jews were asking for relief from the city because the Jewish community had managed its own recovery.[34]

INTEGRATING NATIONAL PATTERNS

The tens of thousands of east European Jewish immigrants settling into the major cities of the Pacific West by 1910 created districts that seemed facsimiles of those in cities like New York. The many small synagogues, the kosher stores along a main business street, and the network of brothers and sisters who orchestrated the migration across the continent and settled as neighbors suggests the transit of an intense cultural world. Areas like South Portland, Seattle's Yesler Way, and Boyle Heights in Los Angeles have come to dominate the romantic lore of contemporary Jewish communities.[35] An article in the *B'nai B'rith Messenger* in 1928 lauded Boyle Heights, then housing an estimated thirty thousand Jews, as a haven for the Orthodox, with a large synagogue on Breed Street and several storefront synagogues, two Talmud Torahs, and two public libraries with collections of Yiddish books. A similar neighborly ambience existed in South Portland.[36] Before the earthquake in San Francisco, however, Jewish immigrants resided in a district "south of Market" dominated by male seasonal workers rather than immigrant families. Rabbi Nieto's recollection of the district was far from romantic. Parents, he wrote, neglected the religious instruction of their children "who were arrested by the police for pilfering in fruit stalls on Saturday and Sunday when they had no public school work to do."[37]

East European Jews may have created a neighborhood ambience, but, unlike on the Lower East Side, they never dominated any. And their children learned to socialize with immigrants unique to the Pacific Coast—Mexicans and Japanese. A photo of the eighth-grade class of Seattle's Pacific Elementary School in 1917 shows that twelve of the forty-two pupils were Asian, while school records for South Portland's Failing School in 1920 show 40 percent of the pupils were Jewish and 17 percent Italian.[38] As late as 1940 the WPA-sponsored guide to Los Angeles referred to Boyle Heights as "a section teeming with Jews and Mexicans."[39] After extensive interviewing, one scholar concluded that "Japanese, Armenian, Chinese, Mexicans and other immigrant groups lived in Boyle Heights after 1930, yet survey respondents reported few unpleasant experiences."[40]

In addition, by 1905, a growing number of Sephardic Jews from Rhodes and the Istanbul area settled in Seattle and sent relatives to Portland and Los Angeles, where they created a separate economic and social niche. Starting modestly, Sephardic men opened fish and vegetable stalls in the public markets and bootblack stands in the downtown areas. In Los Angeles many also sold flowers on street corners until they were able to open stores that grew into a network of over forty shops. Despite their similar economic base, families from different Ottoman cities at first formed separate clubs for religious worship, and individual men preferred to associate with immigrants from Greece, with whom they shared Mediterranean languages and cuisine, rather than with Ashkenazic Jews.

In Los Angeles Congregation Beth David Nusach Sephard was opened on Brooklyn Avenue in Boyle Heights, but most Sephardic families in the 1920s moved southwest to an area near 56th and Normandie.[41] Los Angeles in 1930 had at least five Sephardic congregations, stretching from Boyle Heights to West Adams.[42] Orthodox leaders were concerned at the factional divisions among the Sephardim, and in Los Angeles Rabbi Meyer Winkler of Conservative Sinai Congregation urged the Rhodeslis of the Peace and Progress Society to participate in the larger Jewish community. Rabbi David Essrig of Beth Israel led Talmudic discussions at Beth Israel Anshe Sephard, and Congregation Talmud Torah's Rabbi S. M. Neches, who had come to Los Angeles from Jerusalem, organized a club for Palestinian Jews that included several Sephardim.[43]

Scholars agree that east European Jews coming west, as well as the Sephardim, were generally intent on opening small businesses rather than seeking industrial labor.[44] By comparing the employment profiles of Seattle's Orthodox Congregation Bikur Cholim with that of Spokane's Reform Temple Emanu-el we can appreciate how the small business orientation of Pacific Coast Jewry extended across

Table 9.3 Occupational Profile, Bikur Cholim and Emanu-el

Occupations	Bikur Cholim, Seattle, 1910		Emanu-el, Spokane, 1920	
	Number	% Total	Number	% Total
Proprietors				
Clothing, jewelry	44	28.2	42	21.6
Grocers	10	6.4	4	3.0
Second hand, loans	16	10.3	6	4.5
Tailors, other propr	41	25.3	22	16.5
Employees (clerk)	10	6.4	22	16.6
Prof, business serv	11	7.0	18	13.5
No occupation	6	3.8	12	9.0
Not in city directory	14	9.1	0	0.0
Total	156	100.0	133	100.0

Sources: Membership lists of Bikur Cholim and Emanu-El, city directories.

denominational lines. Both synagogues date from 1892, but Bikur Cholim evolved from a friendship society that conducted prayer services, visited the sick, and buried the dead, while Emanu-el from its founding followed a Reform ritual and aspired to include the city's most prominent Jewish families.[45] Bikur Cholim's members in 1910 served Seattle's large working class, many as proprietors of junk and pawn shops, a few of whom even lived next to their waterfront businesses. In 1920 about 30 percent of Emanu-el's members were either clerks in large businesses or professionals in businesses services, while a few others had become woolen manufacturers or timber brokers. But what is most striking about the comparison is how similar were the work orientations of the two groups. Emanu-el's retailers might cluster on Spokane's primary business blocks, and Bikur Cholim's along Seattle's waterfront. But large contingents of both sold clothing, jewelry, and furniture, and neither group included industrial workers. In the most remote and last settled region of the country, the economic base of both Orthodox and Reform congregations was focused on the same narrow lines of entrepreneurship.

By the end of World War I, in each of the major cities, Jewish immigrant families were served by a network of social workers who gained broad public recognition for their expertise. In Portland Ida Loewenberg began as a volunteer with Neighborhood House and, after formal schooling in Chicago, returned as a full-time superintendent.[46] Seattle's section in 1908 brought Mrs. Hannah Schwartz from San Francisco to live in their newly rented Neighborhood House, and in the early 1920s the women of the Hebrew Benevolent Society recruited Miss May Goldsmith from Portland as their executive secretary.[47] The driving force in the Bay Area for the training of Jewish women for social work was Professor Jessica Peixotto, who had prepared the major study of San Francisco relief work after the earthquake and served as the secretary of child welfare under the Council of National Defense during World War I.[48] The most experienced social worker was Ethel Feineman, a graduate of Hull House and the resident head of the home for working girls erected by the Emanu-El Sisterhood in 1915.[49]

When Portland's juvenile court needed a child psychologist in 1918, it hired Samuel C. Kohs, whose career and contacts helped define the interlocking network of Jewish social work in the Pacific region. Originally from New York, Kohs earned a doctorate from Stanford and became a psychology professor at Reed College. He also taught at the University of Oregon's extension service in Portland, participated in the B'nai B'rith, and spoke throughout the region for Zionist organizations.[50] By 1924 Kohs had moved to the Bay Area as the superintendent of the Jewish Federation of Oakland, where he put into practice his view that Jewish social work required a strong infusion of cultural education.[51] Here he joined Irving Lipsitch, superintendent of both the Eureka Benevolent Society and of the San Francisco Federation, and Rabbi Rudolph Coffee of Temple Sinai of Oakland, who also headed the statewide Jewish Committee of Personal Service that ministered to Jews in state prisons. In January 1924 the governor appointed Coffee to the State Board of Charities and Corrections, with responsibility for supervising state prisons. In 1933 Coffee left the rabbinate to become chaplain at San Quentin.[52]

In 1926 Irving Lipsitch moved to Los Angeles to succeed the renowned Boris Bogen as director of the Federation of Jewish Social Welfare.[53] Lipsitch also became the manager of West Coast fund-raising for the Joint Distribution Committee and for the United Palestine Appeal.[54] Kohs then succeeded Lipsitch at the Eureka Benevolent Society and the San Francisco Federation of Jewish Charities.[55] Despite frequent conflicts between Kohs and Lipsitch over the best practices for Jewish social work, the recognition they received from local political leaders enhanced the sense within the Jewish elite that their communities were integral to professionalizing social welfare in the region.[56] By the late 1920s Jews were recognized in major cities because of their disproportionate charitable contributions. As Rabbi Louis Newman of San Francisco's Emanu-El noted, "The high standards of philanthropy in San Francisco are due in large measure to Jewish contributions of money and intelligence."[57]

As Jewish communities became more cohesive by constructing social and recreational centers, federating their charitable institutions, and participating in national fund-raising efforts, community leaders transmuted the pioneering heritage to mean that Jews must support nonpartisan civic activism. Reform rabbis, newspaper editors, and clubwomen honored Jewish public officials as exemplary citizens, not as spokesmen for an ethnic community. Paragons of Jewish political achievement were not "bosses" like Abe Ruff of San Francisco or Joseph Simon of Portland, who might appoint Jewish friends to public office. Instead true representatives of the Jewish community were "non-partisans," like David Solis Cohen, who served in the 1890s as Portland's police commissioner, San Francisco's long-time Republican Congressman Julius Kahn and his wife, Florence, who succeeded him, and Simon Lubin of Sacramento, who in 1912 was appointed by Governor Hiram Johnson to California's Immigration Commission.[58]

Between 1900 and 1910 several Jewish pioneer families created the commercial equivalent of progressive citizenship by turning their large retail businesses into sophisticated "department stores." The elite in the region's major cities could now identify sophisticated taste and architectural innovation with Jewish salesmanship. By apprenticing young relatives at eastern department stores like John Wanamaker and Macy's,[59] the new Pacific Coast emporia imported new techniques like set prices, window displays featuring expensive items rather than a clutter of all that the store had to offer, and amenities like tearooms and the free delivery of merchandise.[60] High-rise buildings for Lipman, Wolfe and Meier and Frank in Portland, the City of Paris in San Francisco, and Hamburgers in Los Angeles sprawled over entire blocks to realign the city's shopping core.[61] In San Francisco after the earthquake I. Magnin and Company and Raphael Weil and Company relocated from the old business center along Market Street to the intersection of Grant and Geary near Union Square, which became the new center of elegant shopping.[62] In Pacific Coast cities few other tall buildings housed a single firm, other than utilities or banks, so the Jewish department store symbolized not only sophisticated shopping but a modernized urban core.

Commensurate with a commercial elegance that consciously emulated national standards came a sophisticated cultural leadership from a new generation of Reform rabbis with whom elite Protestant ministers could "dialogue" over the ideology of Brotherhood. Jews were no longer represented by self-conscious foreigners claiming a stake in a new land, but by fellow Americans who eloquently expressed common values, whose rituals—conducted almost entirely in English— were fully comprehensible, and who were routinely invited to speak from Protestant pulpits and at university convocations. Rabbis Jacob Nieto, Samuel Koch, Jonah Wise, and Edgar Magnin spoke for decades to the gentile public and became Jewish partners in the quest for humanistic pluralism. When Rabbi Julius Liebert in Spokane spoke on the "Brotherhood of Man" to the Unitarians, when rabbis and social workers agreed to raise funds to save a Congregational Church in Los Angeles, or when Rabbi Edgar Magnin spoke to a joint meeting of the Knights of Columbus and the B'nai B'rith, Jewish community newspapers saw centuries of "misunderstanding" fading away.[63]

The generation of Reform rabbis in the American West from 1910 to 1930 integrated their pluralistic civic ideal into congregational life. When their activism

led them into strident conflict with prominent congregants, as occurred with Stephen Wise at Beth Israel in Portland in 1905 and with his protégé Louis Newman
at Emanu-El in San Francisco in the late 1920s, they left for New York. The more
diplomatic rabbis cultivated the enthusiasm of congregants by building contacts
with Protestant clergymen and gentile civic leaders. Rabbi Koch in Seattle belonged to so many organizations that his board asked him to "refrain from participation in political affairs in a public manner," a request with which he generally
complied.[64] But in June 1916 his congregants welcomed President Suzzalo of the
University of Washington as a guest speaker.[65] Jonah Wise, a son of the founder of
Hebrew Union College, was so admired as a pubic speaker that he was cultivated
for a decade by President Prince Lucien Campbell of the University of Oregon to
deliver lectures and even an introductory course on Judaism. In 1929 Wise's successor, Henry Berkowitz, delivered the baccalaureate address at the graduation
ceremony of Oregon Agricultural College in Corvallis.[66]

The initial wave of Orthodox Jews who arrived on the Pacific slope between
the 1880s and 1900 also appreciated the need to create a niche as Americans. Before their arrival virtually all had spent time elsewhere in America, where they
learned English as well as the ability to accommodate the secular demands of the
new life. The oldest consciously Orthodox synagogues, like Nevek Tzedek in
Portland and Beth Israel in Los Angeles that date from the early 1890s, were often
veering toward what would become the Conservative movement and support of
cultural Zionism. Some of their leaders were veterans of utopian farming communities in the Dakotas, northern California, and Oregon, who demonstrated
their virtuosity as pioneers by opening successful businesses once they moved to
the cities.[67] A new wave of Orthodox synagogues like Shaarei Torah in Portland,
Knesseth Israel in San Francisco, and Congregation Talmud Torah in Los Angeles that date from the 1910s had a more strictly religious focus. Their congregations were augmented by relatives coming directly from Russia who desired
Orthodox religious practices. Even they, however, absorbed the sense of congregational autonomy that marked the urban West. When some Orthodox laymen in
1918 tried to consolidate the Orthodox synagogues of San Francisco under the
leadership of a Rabbi Glazer of Montreal, dissenting congregations refused to relinquish control over ritual and Rabbi Glazer never relocated.[68]

In all major Pacific Coast cities during the 1920s, Orthodox communities
gained membership, constructed new buildings for worship, education, and sociability, and sponsored talks by visiting dignitaries like Gedalia Bublick.[69] Talmud Torahs were the pride of Bikur Cholim in Seattle, and itinerant Yiddish
theater companies played at local theaters and found a special reception in Los
Angeles. Yet Orthodox leaders expressed anxiety over the future of authentic Judaism, because their great distance from centers of religious study seemed to exacerbate the allure that American culture held out to their children. The same
issue of the Los Angeles *B'nai B'rith Messenger* that announced the construction

of a new building for Conservative Sinai Temple reported a meeting at Klein's Kosher Restaurant where Rabbi Winkler of Sinai, and Rabbis Neches, as well as several leading Orthodox laymen complained that only 16 percent of the local Jewish young people were enrolled in Jewish schools.[70]

How the content of a Jewish education should be altered to attract children in an overwhelmingly secular world remained a dilemma for lay and rabbinic leaders all along the coast. Despite the frustrations, the quality of educational leadership was surprisingly strong in a district so far removed from sources of traditional Judaism. Spokesmen for Orthodoxy agreed that they could not start Jewish day schools and that they wanted Jewish educators as professionally trained as were teachers in public schools, so they debated the content and pedagogy for a much reduced curriculum. Sam Prottas, a lay leader at Seattle's Bikur Cholim, said that his Talmud Torah, which enrolled over two hundred pupils, should teach about "Torah." But he did not explain what that might mean. Students graduating from the religious school at Congregation Talmud Torah of Boyle Heights gave brief speeches in Yiddish, not Hebrew, though all were to continue their Hebrew education at an afternoon "high school" recently established by the Jewish Education Association of Los Angeles.[71]

Several educational alternatives focused on Modern Hebrew as a cultural solvent that would perpetuate religious ritual while also revitalizing cultural nationalism. In San Francisco Rabbi Nieto's Jewish Education Society in 1918 hired a Moses Menuhin who had come from Palestine to introduce "modern Hebrew pedagogy."[72] The school met in an Orthodox synagogue until a new building was erected in 1925. A second Free Hebrew School was opened at the new Jewish Community Home along San Bruno Road, and by 1926 the two schools enrolled five hundred pupils who met on weekday afternoons. Its purpose, according to Menuhin, "is to give the children an intensive cultural and religious Jewish education, with due consideration to American Jewish conditions."[73]

In Portland, by 1905, members of Neveh Tzedeck founded the Portland Hebrew School to express their Zionist zeal. By the 1920s Bert Treiger, who also taught Modern Hebrew at the University of Oregon's extension program, became its principal. Dedicated to Hebrew teaching as a career, he introduced a pedagogy based on "Ivrit B'Ivrit," by which pupils learned to turn a language first encountered in religious ritual into a vehicle for expressing their own thoughts. As its enrollment slowly grew, Treiger remained enthusiastic about the school because he had persuaded colleges and universities in the Pacific Northwest to give his graduates credit for Hebrew as a foreign language.[74]

As Jewish communities in Los Angeles, San Francisco, and Seattle continued to grow, fears expressed by rabbis that young people would be snared by Christian Science or by the Unitarians seemed absurd. An editorial in the *B'nai B'rith Messenger* in 1928 pointed to the many new structures built by Jewish philanthropy and to the religious zeal exhibited at holidays to conclude, "American Jewish culture may assume a different form from that of other times and places, but it is JEWISH CULTURE just the same and bears no aspect of deterioration."[75] The attention that visitors to the region placed on exotic Protestant evangelists like Aime Semple McPherson or Bob Shuler seems exaggerated when compared with denominational statistics.[76] According to the federal *Census of Religious Bodies, 1926*, Jews were the second largest denomination in the region's cities, behind Roman Catholics. In San Francisco and Los Angeles in 1926, Jews outnumbered Methodists, Presbyterians, and Episcopalians combined. By not differentiating between Jewish denominations, the Bureau of the Census reinforced the image of a community that had unified its lodges, federated and rationalized its charities, and had a small group of rabbis, businessmen, and secular professionals as public spokesmen.[77]

Before 1920 the small number of young Pacific Coast Jews who attended college usually enrolled at schools on the East Coast, and through the 1920s young men from wealthy families still did.[78] But in the 1920s, as children of east European families were prepared to attend college, their less affluent families sent them to schools within the region. In 1910 young people from Portland, as well as those from Seattle, had been attending the University of Washington, but after 1915 dozens of young men and women in Portland enrolled at the new Reed College.[79] By the late 1920s contingents of twenty or more even attended the University of Oregon in Eugene, where sixteen of the male students had formed a fraternity as the first Jewish organization on campus. . In California most students were sent to Berkeley, with a few attending Stanford. In the mid-1920s the teachers college in Los Angeles was elevated to a branch of the state university and quickly attracted many Jewish students.[80]

During the 1920s Jewish college students along the coast were made to feel part of a regional community. Newspapers carried information about Jewish literary and fraternal societies, and, in keeping with the national valorization of sports, they featured stories about Jewish athletes excelling in football, swimming, tennis, or baseball at Berkeley, Washington, or Stanford. Male students aspired to organize their own social life through new fraternities, while Jewish faculty at most of these schools helped students found Menorah Societies. By 1927 the University of Washington had a chapter of ZBT, which the *Scribe* claimed was composed primarily of Portlanders.[81] Reed College's Menorah Society traveled several times to Seattle to debate with their counterparts at the University of Washington, and it soon expanded to a Portland Menorah that included students at the city's professional schools. The Menorah Society at UCLA began with essay contests, but soon hosted a regional convention.[82] Delegations attended from the University of Washington, the University of California, and UCLA, as did representatives from the University of Southern California, Stanford, Fresno State, and the University of Arizona.

A study of Jewish undergrads at Berkeley by Sol Silverman, a 1923 graduate, estimated an enrollment of about five hundred in 1926, with about five hundred

Table 9.4 Jews and Other Selected Denominations in Selected Pacific Coast Cities

Denomination	Los Angeles		San Francisco		Portland		Seattle	
	1926	1936	1926	1936	1926	1936	1926	1936
Jewish	65,000	82,000	35,000	40,900	12,000	10,700	10,000	14,500
Christian Science	3,920	7,069	1,570	2,150	1,695	2,188	1,899	2,842
Unitarian	612	485	400	400	484	566	?	170
Mormon	9,441	9,548	2,227	1,288	3,050	1,678	2,675	594
R. Catholic	114,2111	169,077	154,385	176,169	27,165	30,705	?	28,427
North Baptist	14,614	17,608	1,631	1,667	6,924	5,052	5,274	4,304
Meth Episcopal	18,290	20,264	3,983	2,490	9,779	8,478	9,269	6,862
Presbyt. Church	17,742	17,619	5,025	5,069	9,583	9,143	12,636	14,102
Prot Episcopal	10,137	15,502	6,808	6,616	3,515	3,718	?	4,907

Sources: Census of Religious Bodies: 1926, vol. 1 (Washington, DC, 1930), table 31; Census of Religious Bodies: 1936, vol. 1 (Washington, DC, 1941), table 31.

more at other West Coast colleges.[83] In 1927 the B'nai B'rith brought young Reform rabbi Benjamin Goldstein to Berkeley to found its fifth Hillel House. Rabbi Louis Newman, a former national president of the Inter-Collegiate Menorah Society, reported that Berkeley Hillel brought a large proportion of the Jewish students together to foster a sense of community that the more selective fraternities and the Menorah Society could not. Rabbi Goldstein told audiences along the coast that Hillel enabled students to organize their own Jewish group life so that after graduation they would be prepared to provide leadership in their home communities.[84] According to an editorial in the *Scribe*, Hillel work had created a new pride in Jewish identity among the growing contingents of Jewish students at state universities.[85]

THE PACIFIC WEST IN THE 1920s:
CENTERING LOS ANGELES

Los Angeles in the 1920s more than doubled its population to 1.2 million, with Jews perhaps 7 percent of the total. The diversity of their origins, their large Orthodox component, their wide geographical distribution, and their ability to support a great variety of institutions created a Jewish community new to the American West. As Los Angeles outstripped San Francisco in construction of new religious and philanthropic buildings, especially the Cedars of Lebanon Hospital, the new orphanage with its innovative cottage system at Del Mar, and the Wilshire Boulevard Temple, its new preeminence as the regional Jewish center became obvious.

The Jewish population grew, as it had during the Gold Rush, because it could provide unique services. During the 1920s, in Seattle and Portland, Jewish entrepreneurs created a cluster of small women's garment factories in downtown loft buildings, while San Francisco had an authentic clothing district between Chinatown and Market Street. The far more rapid expansion of Los Angeles, however, induced between one and two hundred small manufacturers to create the largest clothing district west of Chicago. A district emerged in loft buildings along Los Angeles Street and Broadway between Second and Tenth Streets. Unlike New York, however, the great majority of the workers were not Jews but Mexican women, though Russian Jews were among the more skilled cutters.[86]

The residential patterns of the Pacific Coast clothing manufacturers highlighted the internal migration of the Jewish population. In San Francisco they moved directly west of their small factories, following the car lines to the Western Addition and into newer homes in the Richmond district, north of Golden Gate Park. Emanu-El and Sherith Israel soon relocated there, in what became the new center of the city's Jewish community. In Portland clothing manufactures followed a car line on East Glisan Street, with the most affluent settling farthest

Table 9.5 Women's Clothing Production, Selected Cities, 1919, 1929

City	1919				1929			
	Estab	Officer	Worker	Value ($mil)	Estab	Officers	Worker	Value ($ mil)
N. York	5,089	11,750	95,842	$759.6	5,781	19,205	104,202	$1,313.5
Chicago	374	816	9,147	$42.9	373	1,261	11,590	$70.0
L.A.	80	178	1,938	$10.3	205	686	5,376	$29.2
S. Fran.	68	116	1,074	$6.2	82	192	1,459	$8.3

Sources: Fourteenth Census of the United States Taken in the Year 1920: Manufactures, 1919, vol. 9 (Washington: Government Printing Office, 1923); Fifteenth Census of the United States: Manufactures, 1929, Reports by States, vol. 3 (Washington, Government Printing Office, 1933).

out in the Laurelhurst neighborhood. In Los Angeles the larger numbers led to a wider dispersal, but if anything the clustering in specific neighborhoods was even more intense. The residences of the one hundred and fifteen manufacturers who could be located in the 1927 Los Angeles City Directory followed clear patterns. A contingent of twenty-one manufacturers had settled in Boyle Heights, where streetcars on Brooklyn Avenue could take them easily to the garment lofts downtown. But the residential trajectory of the majority of garment manufacturers illustrates how the industry promoted the social integration of upwardly mobile Jews into the wider city. Like the general population of Los Angeles, most Jewish clothing manufacturers were moving to the west side or to residential cities like Pasadena and Alhambra that lay north and east of Boyle Heights. A group of thirty-two men, for example, moved to an area that held not only the offices of the smaller motion picture producers, as well as Paramount Studios and Twentieth Century Fox, but new temples for Congregation B'nai B'rith and Emanu-El as well as Sinai Congregation, Temple Beth-El, Temple Israel, and the Hollywood Jewish Center. So prosperous had this region suddenly become that the owners of downtown department stores like Bullocks and the May Company built a new shopping district along Wilshire, where the anchor stores were even more glamorous than those in the central business core.[87] Another group of thirteen clothing manufacturers was scattered over the West Adams Street area, the site of the new West Adams Hebrew Congregation. Eight others, including the prominent manufacturer Joseph Zukin, settled near a fringe of the movie colony in far-off Venice, which boasted Congregation Mishcan Tephilo.[88]

The new affluence of the 1920s allowed clothing designed and manufactured in Los Angeles to gain unique exposure through the region's glamorous new industry, the motion pictures. The movie industry has been analyzed as a revolutionary cultural tool that transformed popular consciousness,[89] but its immigrant entrepreneurs saw it as a business for entertainment. By late 1926 an estimated seventy-five thousand people worked in some aspect of film production, distribution, and viewing in the Los Angeles area.[90] The arrival of the moguls and their many family members added a new layer of affluence, visibility, and cosmopolitanism to the region's Jewish life. Community newspapers chronicled their achievements, and the *B'nai B'rith Messenger* carried a biographical column on Jewish production professionals like casting directors, photographers, and directors. Though the moguls may have been snubbed in the 1920s by the Hellmans and the Newmarks at the Hillcrest Country Club, they were carefully courted for philanthropic causes.[91] In 1926 Louis B. Mayer, much to the delight of the descendants of the old merchant families, agreed to be the city chairman of the United Jewish Appeal and to host a dinner of Hollywood luminaries to raise funds for the United Jewish Campaign. When the Federation of Jewish Welfare Organizations in 1928 sought to replace the old Kaspare Cohn Hospital with a modern Cedars of Lebanon Hospital, the largest fund-raisers were Louis B. Mayer and Jack Warner, who headed the Motion Picture Division and who served on the hospital's board. When the City of Hope sanitarium at Duarte needed funds, the Warner brothers hosted a "mid-night gala" highlighted by Fanny Brice and Al Jolson.[92]

Relatives of the moguls and the studios' salaried workers supported a variety of Judaisms in the neighborhoods of West Los Angeles. Louis B. Mayer's father-in-law, Hyman Shenberg, came from Boston to become rabbi of Congregation Knesseth Israel, while B. P. Shulberg's father-in-law and the parents of other studio heads rented a Hollywood bungalow, which studio carpenters transformed into an Orthodox shul. The officers and board of directors of Temple Israel of Hollywood in 1928 consisted of executives of Fox and Universal Studios, including Sol Wurtzel, John Stone, E. D. Laemmle, and J. P. Fox.[93] Rabbis cultivated movie people to raise funds to create the largest and most diversified set of religious institutions west of Chicago, and city directories indicate that during the 1920s more new synagogues and community centers were built in Los Angeles than in the rest of the Pacific region combined.

The shifting authority of rabbinic personalities as well as the close ties within the regional rabbinate was dramatized in the late 1920s in successive temple dedications. As Samuel Hecht and Jacob Nieto died, as Jonah Wise and Louis Newman left for pulpits in New York, and as movie wealth transformed Congregation B'nai B'rith into the Wilshire Boulevard Temple, Edgar Magnin emerged as Jewry's regional spokesman. When Beth Israel in Portland dedicated its new building in April 1928, Magnin came as featured speaker to honor his former Hebrew Union College classmate and Beth Israel's new rabbi, Henry Berkowitz. Other speakers included former Rabbi Jonah Wise, Rabbi Samuel Koch of Seattle, and Cantor Reuben Rinder of Emanu-El.[94] When the Wilshire Boulevard temple was dedicated in June 1929. Rabbi Magnin summoned the regional rabbinic illuminati, including Rabbis Koch, Berkowitz, Coffee, Lissauer, and even Rabbi Louis

Newman. Berkowitz and Newman spoke on Friday evening, while the other rabbis shared time with moguls Louis B Mayer and Jack Warner and the banker Marco Hellman at the main event on Saturday. While San Francisco's Sherith Israel in the late 1920s proposed to raise $150,00 for a new athletic and social facility called a temple house, Congregation B'nai B'rith had pledged over $1.5 million to complete its three-building complex.[95] Louis Newman, though viewing Pacific Coast Jewry as "in a wilderness,"[96] nevertheless prophesied after visiting Los Angeles in 1927 that "in a few years there will be two major centers of Jewish creative effort in this land, New York and Los Angeles."[97]

Jewish regional prominence was formally recognized in 1928, when gentile business leaders in Seattle and those in Portland selected Nathan Eckstein and Ben Selling respectively as the first citizens of their cities.[98] In Los Angeles Louis H Cole, spokesman for the American Jewish Committee and the Masonic lodge officer given most credit for building the Shrine Auditorium, received similar recognition.[99] In San Francisco Milton Esberg, who had married into the Lilienthal banking family, was considered one of the city's four key figures in public life.[100] Louis Newman, always skeptical of the moral depth of western Jewry, nevertheless wrote in 1929, "The high rank of Western Jewry in the general commonwealth is taken for granted. . . . It is edifying to behold that the very leaders of prominence in the general community are at the same time the foremost Jewish spokesmen, communal workers, and philanthropists."[101]

The import of Jewish regional status was marked in San Francisco on March 31, 1930, when the Board of Supervisors began its meeting with a lengthy memorial to Rabbi Nieto, who had died five days before. Rabbi Nieto had been the clerical face of Jewish activism in the region's first metropolis since the mid-1890s. The Board of Supervisors, with Mayor Rolph presiding, passed a resolution that read in part "the said Rabbi Jacob Nieto was identified with the civic life of our community for nearly forty years . . . and by his passing San Francisco suffers an irreparable loss." But an equal tribute to Jewish leadership was provided by the presence of ex-supervisor Milton Marks and supervisors Jesse Colman (1921–1947) and Jefferson Peyser (1929–1933), who spoke as Nieto's Jewish comrades. Supervisor and future mayor Angelo Rossi, after noting Nieto's endearing personal traits, concluded that, above all, he "was democratic. He was a civic leader."[102] Such was the image that Pacific Coast Jewry believed it had earned for itself.

The proud and insular image that Pacific Coast Jewry projected as late as 1930 was eclipsed by the extraordinary growth of the region and of its Jewish population during and after World War II. As had been true in the past, individual Jews in unprecedented numbers quite selectively chose to join the national migration away from the industrial northeast to the new economy growing up in the West. Thousands of Jewish veterans who had passed through Los Angeles during the war returned between 1946 and the mid-1950s, partly because of the climate and certainly because of defense contracts, which were triggering immense regional growth.[103] The demand for new housing was met largely by Jewish builders like Larry Weinberg, Louis Boyer, and Eli Broad, while savings and loan institutions owned in part by Jews like Mark Taper provided mortgage money.[104] The growth of television increased demand for studios to produce new programs, and the sportswear industry grew steadily, until in the 1990s Los Angeles passed New York as the largest locale for clothing production in the nation.[105] By 1960 Los Angeles already held the second largest Jewish population in the nation, over half a million, and, with the concurrent growth of southeast Florida as a national retirement center, the central place of New York as the economic, cultural, and even demographic focus of American Jewry was seriously challenged.[106]

The legacy of the Jewish pioneer experience in the West had further resonance for a growing proportion of America's Jews. By the 1980s Western cities like Phoenix, San Diego, and Las Vegas were growing, at rates that matched that of Los Angeles in the 1940s and 1950s, to become among the nation's largest. Young well-educated Jews, many from eastern and midwestern cities, were disproportionately among those seeking opportunities.[107] In sprawling suburbs like Poway, Scottsdale, and Henderson, young families added to communities of eighty thousand or more Jews that eclipsed in size the declining Jewish communities of cities like Cleveland, Detroit, and Pittsburgh. In addition, perhaps as many as thirty thousand Jewish émigrés from Iran, most quite prosperous, have since 1979 created a unique community centered primarily in Beverley Hills.[108] As in Los Angeles in the 1920s and again in the 1950s, so in Phoenix, San Diego, and Las Vegas in the 1980s and 1990s, innovative entrepreneurs like Steve Wynn in the gaming industry and Irwin Jacobs, a professor of engineering at UC San Diego, have had a major impact on local economies and on Jewish philanthropy. Dozens of new synagogues have been built and revitalized federations have raised funds for Jewish community centers, day schools, and retirement homes.

Equally important, Los Angeles has become the regional center of Jewish politics and culture. Starting in the 1950s, representatives of predominantly Jewish districts for the first time placed issues of civil rights and the defense of Israel on local political agendas, and by the 1990s Westside congressmen and media moguls were the most prominent fund-raisers for the national Democratic Party. New institutions like the Skirball Museum and the Wiesenthal Center and Holocaust Museum in Los Angeles have brought Jewish culture and history to the attention of the larger community and have developed national reputations, while the retired insurance billionaire, Eli Broad, and the architect Frank Gehry have emerged as the leading sponsors of art collecting, philanthropy, and civic design in the region and well beyond.[109] Cedar-Sinai Hospital, in conjunction with the school of medicine at UCLA, has become the largest medical complex west of New York City and is supported largely by Jewish philanthropy and government grants. In a sign of an incipient struggle for national leadership, the seminary at the University of Judaism and local branches of the American Jewish Congress, the American Jewish Committee, and the Anti-Defamation League have each engaged in acrimonious conflicts with their national headquarters in New York. As younger Jews continue to seek careers in cities of the Pacific West, the national center of gravity continues to shift and the meaning of its founding will bulk larger in our reexamination of the national Jewish experience.[110] Perhaps the framework for an American Jewish history will shift, from a focus on the experience of immigrant communities painfully "assimilating" on the Atlantic seaboard to a more diffuse and regional experience of people creating and building on a pioneer legacy.[111]

NOTES

1. On "sectionalism" and its interpretive limitations in American historical writing, see, for example, Richard Hofstadter, *The Progressive Historians, Turner, Beard, Parrington* (New York, 1969), 94–99; Ray Allen Billington, *Frederick Jackson Turner, Historian, Scholar, Teacher* (New York, 1973), 210, 214, 230–31, 368–75.

2. Thomas D. Clark, "The Post–Civil War Economy in the South," in Leonard Dinnerstein and Mary Dale Paulson, eds, *Jews in the South* (Baton Rouge, 1973), 166–68; Harold Hyman, *Oleaner Odyssey: The Kempners of Galveston, Texas, 1854–1980* (College Station, 1990), 48, 63–64, 102; Leonard Rogoff, *Homelands: Southern Jewish Identity in Durham and Chapel Hill, North Carolina* (Tuscaloosa, 2001), 3, 20, 27, passim; Steven Hertzberg, *Strangers Within the Gate City: The Jews of Atlanta, 1845–1915* (Philadelphia, 1978).

3. Mark Bauman, *The Southerner as American: Jewish Style* (Cincinnati, 1996), 30, concludes, "the issues raised here point to the existence of patterns across regional boundaries. They assume that the factors in American and Jewish history affecting acculturation and tradition bred greater similarities both qualitatively and quantitatively than differences." See also Mark Bauman, "Southern Jewish Women and Their Social Service Organizations," *Journal of American Ethnic History* 22.3 (Spring, 2003): 34.

4. For the role of Jews, and negative perceptions of that role, on a very different mining frontier in the late nineteenth century, see Geoffrey Wheatcroft, *The Randlords* (New York, 1985), 197, 202–3; J. A. Hobson, *The War in South Africa: Its Causes and Effects* (New York, 1900), 11, 190–97.

5. Jacob Nieto, editorial in the *Jewish Times*, November 17, 1911, clipping in Jacob Nieto Papers, American Jewish Archives. While evidence abounds on Jewish attitudes toward being westerners, Bauman notes that "more needs to be done on atti-

tudes of Jews in the South toward the South." Bauman, *The Southerner as American*, 38, 22.

6. William Cronon, *Nature's Metropolis: Chicago and the Great West* (New York, 1991), 38–39, passim.

7. Gunther Barth, *Instant Cities: Urbanization and the Rise of San Francisco and Denver* (New York, 1975), 173; Peter Decker, "Jewish Merchants in San Francisco: Social Mobility on the Urban Frontier," in Moses Rischin, ed., *The Jews of the West: The Metropolitan Years* (Berkeley, 1979), 20; Robert E. Levinson, *The Jews in the California Gold Rush* (New York, 1978), 15–40.

8. Harriet Rochlin and Fred Rochlin, *Pioneer Jews: A New Life in the Far West* (Boston, 1984), 158–59.

9. Max Vorspan and Lloyd P. Gartner, *History of the Jews of Los Angeles* (San Marino, 1970), 104; William Toll, *The Making of an Ethnic Middle Class: Portland Jewry Over Four Generations* (Albany, 1982), 80–84; William Issell and Robert W Cherny, *San Francisco, 1865–1932: Politics, Power, and Urban Development* (Berkeley, 1986), 205–6.

10. William Toll, "Voluntarism and Modernization in Portland Jewry: The B'nai B'rith in the 1920s," *Western Historical Quarterly* 10.1 (January 1979): 30–37. *Scribe*, June 22, 1928, notes that the lodges in Portland and San Francisco numbered over twenty-five hundred.

11. Community newspapers in Seattle, Portland, and Los Angeles provided far better coverage to the Orthodox than did *Emanu-El* in San Francisco.

12. Robert Fogelson, *The Fragmented Metropolis: Los Angeles, 1850–1930* (Cambridge, 1967), 119–29.

13. "Los Angeles Becomes Style Center," *Business Week* (September 14, 1940), 42; "Los Angeles' Little Cutters," *Fortune* 31 (May 1945): 134.

14. Louis Newman, "Telling It in Gath," *Scribe*, February 1, 1929.

15. Moses Rischin, "The Jewish Experience in America: A View from the West," in M. Rischin and John Livingston, eds., *Jews of the American West* (Detroit: Wayne State University Press, 1991), 34–35.

16. Michael Zarchin, *Glimpses of Jewish Life in San Francisco* (Berkeley, 1964), 52–59.

17. Bernard Goldsmith interview, Portland (November 29, 1889), H. H. Bancroft Collection, Bancroft Library.

18. Issel and Cherny, *San Francisco*, 23–24. Goldsmith interview indicates he was mayor of Portland, built locks at Willamette Falls to enable shipping along the river, and lost $400,000 when a new railroad soon rendered river shipping obsolete.

19. Vorspan and Gartner, *History of the Jews of Los Angeles*, 41–42.

20. Rischin, "The Jewish Experience in America," 36; Currier and Ives elevation map of San Francisco (1878), Map Library, University of Oregon; an editorial in *Emanu-El*, January 29, 1926, referred to it as "once the chief architectural ornament of the city."

21. By contrast, the Howard Street Methodist Episcopal Church and parsonage were valued at $100,000, the First Presbyterian Church (1857), cost $60,000, and the First Methodist Episcopal Church(1871) cost $25,000. See the *San Francisco City Directory, 1879* (San Francisco, 1879), 1067, 1072–73, 1075.

22. Ava F. Kahn, "Looking at America from the West to the East, 1850–1920s," in Ava F. Kahn, ed., *Jewish Life in the American West* (Los Angeles, 2002), 25.

23. Quoted in Rudolf Glanz, *The Jews of California from the Discovery of Gold Until 1880* (Los Angeles: Southern California Jewish Historical Society, 1960), 83.

24. Data on Spokane's Jews has been gathered from a membership list for Temple Emanu-El, from Spokane city directories, and plotted on a street map of Spokane.

25. Social columns in Jewish newspapers for all cities in the 1920s are filled with accounts of families visiting back and forth with relatives in San Francisco or Los Angeles.

26. The extension of Jewish female nurture into the public realm in Western Europe and the United States is discussed in Paula Hyman, *Gender and Assimilation in Modern Jewish History* (Seattle, 1995), 31–34.

27. Harris Newmark, *Sixty Years in Southern Califrnia, 1853–1913*, Maurice H. Newmark and Marco R. Newmark, eds. (New York, 1916), 190. On January 5, 1856, the Sisters of Charity first appeared in Los Angeles and soon conducted a school, an institute, and orphan asylum. Sydney Clevenger, "St. Vincent's and the Sisters of Providence, Oregon's First Permanent Hospital," *Oregon Historical Quarterly* (Summer 2001): 210–21; Michael E. Engh, *Frontier Faiths, Church, Temple, and Synagogue in Los Angeles, 1846–1888* (Albuquerque, 1992), 13, 79, 83–84.

28. Jewish Ladies Relief Society, Forty-eighth Annual Report (1905), in Eureka Benevolent Society Papers, box 1, file 2, Western Jewish History Center. I thank Professor Ellen Eisenberg of Willamette University for this reference.

29. Jonathan D. Sarna, "New Light on the Pittsburgh Platform of 1885," *American Jewish History* 76.3 (March 1987): 358–68; Gilbert Rosenthal, *Contemporary Judaism: Patterns of Survival* (New York, 1986), 100–1.

30. "The Helpers," in box 1, file 2, Eureka Benevolent Society, Western Jewish History Center. I thank Professor Ellen Eisenberg for this reference.

31. "Temporary Relief Committee," "Employment Department," in *Third Annual Report of the Emanu-El Sisterhood for Fiscal Year 1896–97* (San Francisco, 1897), 11, 17; Rabbi Jacob Nieto, "The Charity Fad," undated typescript, Jacob Nieto Papers, Western Jewish History Archives, Berkeley, California; Felicia Herman, "Sisterhoods of Personal Service," in Paula E. Hyman and Deborah Dash Moore, eds., *Jewish Women in America: An Historical Encyclopedia* (New York, 1997), 1264–65.

32. William Toll, "Gender, Ethnicity and Jewish Settlement Work in the Urban West," in Jeffrey S. Gurock and Marc Lee Raphael, eds., *An Inventory of Promise: Essays on American Jewish History in Honor of Moses Rischin* (Brooklyn, 1995), 299–305.

33. *B'nai B'rith Messenger*, January 18, 1924.

34. [Jessica Peixotto], "Relief Work of the Associated Charities from June, 1907 to June, 1909," 281–317, copy in Jessica Peixotto Papers, Bancroft Library, University of California, Berkeley. Henry Rand Hatfield, "Jessica Blanche Peixotto," in *Essays in Social Economics in Honor of Jessica Blanche Peixotto* (Berkeley, 1935), 9.

35. *Seattle Jewish Transcript*, January 3, 1930, notes that the Women's Club of the Arbeiter Ring met on December 28 to install new officers and sent a delegation to Tacoma to meet with their club.

36. *B'nai B'rith Messenger*, March 9, 1928; interview with Gaulda Jermuloske Hahn, June 10 and December 17, 1979, Jewish Historical Society of Oregon.

37. Jacob Nieto, unnamed and undated typescript, Jacob Nieto papers, American Jewish Archives.

38. Molly Cone, Howard Droker, Jacqueline Williams, *Family of Strangers, Building a Jewish Community in Washington State* (Seattle, 2003), 147–48. Cone, *Family of Strangers*, 147–48; William Toll, "Ethnicity and Stability: The Italians and Jews of South Portland, 1900–1940," *Pacific Historical Review* 54.2 (May 1985): 175.

39. *Los Angeles: A Guide to the City and Its Environs* (New York, 1941), 169.

40. Wendy Elliott, "The Jews of Boyle Heights, 1900–1950: The Melting Pot of Los Angeles," *Southern California Quarterly* 78.1 (1996): 6–7.

41. Aron Hason, "The Sephardic Jews of Rhodes in Los Angeles," *Western States Jewish Historical Quarterly* (July 1974): 247–48, 252.

42. "Dr. Spivak Ends Visit to Seattle," *Jewish Transcript*, March 18, 1924; *Los Angeles City Directory, 1930* (Los Angeles, 1930), 2508.

43. *B'nai B'rith Messenger*, June 6, 1924, January 6, 1928, May 9, 1930; Hason, "The Sephardic Jews of Rhodes," 248.

44. Ben Selling to David Bressler, Portland File, Industrial Removal Office Papers, American Jewish Historical Society; Ellen Eisenberg, "The Transplanted to the Rose City: The Creation of East European Jewish Community in Portland, Oregon," *Journal of American Ethnic History* 19.3 (Spring 2000): 83–85.

45. Cone, *Family of Strangers*, 110, 120.

46. *Scribe*, October 15, 1920.

47. Mrs. Thornton Goldsby, "The History of the Seattle Section, National Council of Jewish Women, 1900–1927," manuscript in Seattle Section, NCJW Papers, Research Library, University of Washington.

48. [Peixoto], "Relief Work of the Associated Charities"; *Emanu-El*, January 11, 1918. Professor Peixotto was the second woman to receive a doctorate from the University of California. See "Peixotto, Jessica Blanche," in Hyman and Moore, *Jewish Women in America*, 1040.

49. *Emanu-El*, January 11, 1918; William Toll, "The Feminization of the Heroic: Ethel Feineman and Professional Nurture," in Menachim Mor, ed., *Crisis and Reaction: The Hero in Jewish History* (Omaha, 1995), 202–10.

50. *Scribe*, October 15, November 26, 1920, February 21, 1921, March 31, 1922.

51. See Samuel C. Kohs, *The Roots of Social Work* (New York, 1966), 132–34.

52. *B'nai B'rith Messenger*, January 11, 1924, reported that the Jewish Committee for Personal Service, a statewide body headed by Rabbi Coffee, visited Jews in state prisons. There were then sixty-three Jews incarcerated at San Quentin, and thirty-three at Folsom. A report in the *Scribe*, June 1, 1928, noted that Jews were about 2 percent of California's prison population, most being young men drifting through who broke the law. See also Fred Rosenbaum, *Free to Choose: The Making of a Jewish Community in the American West, the Jews of Oakland, California from the Gold Rush to the Present Day* (Berkeley, 1976), 91–93.

53. On Boris Bogin's prominence at the Los Angeles Jewish Welfare Federation and as a key figure in the Community Chest, see *B'nai B'rith Messenger*, October 17, 1924.

54. *Emanu-El*, February 5, March 5, March 12, 1926.

55. *B'nai B'rith Messenger*, January 4, 1924; *Emanu-El*, January, 15, 1926.

56. Samuel Kohs to M. J. Karpf, July 16, 1927, Samuel Kohs Papers, Western Jewish History Center. The first regional conference of Jewish social service workers was held in 1928, see the *Scribe*, June 1, 1928. *Scribe*, August 3, 1928, notes that Kohs had assumed directorship of the Brooklyn Federation of Jewish Charities.

57. *Scribe*, September 28, 1928.

58. *Emanu-El*, May 17, 1918, reports a "Julius Kahn Day" honoring the California congressman in New York city by two thousand master masons for pushing through the selective service bill; Hiram Johnson to Simon Lubin, August 20, 1912, September 13, 1913; Harry Miller (The Judeans of Oakland) to Lubin, May 29, 1914, Simon Lubin Papers, Bancroft Library, University of California, Berkeley; David G. Dalin, "Jewish and Non-Partisan Republicanism in San Francisco, 1911–1963," in Rischin, ed. *Jews of the West*, 110–17.

59. *Scribe*, February 24, 1922, carries a story on the new Macy's Building at 34th and Broadway.

60. The apprenticeship at Wanamakers is explained in Harold Hirsch interview, typescript, undated, Jewish Historical Society of Oregon. Susan Porter Benson, *Counter Cultures: Saleswomen, Managers and Customers in American Department Stores, 1890–1940* (Urbana, 1986), 14–20, explains innovations in sales techniques. Images of Meier and Frank, Lipman Wolfe, Bullocks Wilshire and the May Department Store can be found on the World Wide Web at pdx.history.com.tripod.com; www.swlaw.edu/bullock swilshire; www.you-are-here.com/building.

61. William Leach, *Land of Desire, Merchants, Power and the Rise of a New American Culture* (New York, 1993), 20–35.

62. Zarchin, *Glimpses of Jewish Life in San Francisco*, 67; Rosenbaum, *Free to Choose*, 26–31.

63. *Scribe*, October 29, 1920; *Emanu-El*, February 24, 1928; *B'nai B'rith Messenger*, February 17, May 18, 1928.

64. Cone, *Family of Strangers*, 109.

65. Minute Book, Seattle Section, National Council of Jewish Women, January 13, 1916, Research Library, University of Washington.

66. Jonah Wise to Prince Lucien Campbell, December 8, 1915, Campbell to Wise, December 9, 1915, October 9, 1917, Wise to Campbell, May 19, 1919, Campbell to Wise, November 10, 1919, Wise to Campbell, September 23, 1920, Campbell to Wise, October 3, 1921, Karl Onthank to Mrs. Campbell, March 6, 1925, President's Office Correspondence, University of Oregon Archives; *Scribe*, May 31, 1929.

67. Ellen Eisenberg, "From Cooperative Farming to Urban Leadership," in Kahn, *Jewish Life in the American West*, 113–31.

68. *Emanu-El*, January 4, 1918.

69. *B'nai B'rith Messenger*, January 3, 1930; *Seattle Jewish Transcript*, January 3, 1930; *Scribe*, January 3, 1930.

70. *B'nai B'rith Messenger*, January 29, 1926.

71. *B'nai B'rith Messenger*, March 9, 1928.

72. Menuhin was the father of the violin virtuoso, Yehudi Menuhin. See Moshe Menuhin, "Jewish Communal Education in San Francisco in 1926," in *Western States Jewish Historical Quarterly* 21.2 (January 1989): 99.

73. The expansion of Jewish education in San Francisco from 1897 through 1920 under the auspices of the Jewish Education Society is noted in an untitled and undated typescript in Jacob Nieto Papers, American Jewish Archives; *Emanu-El*, May 3, 1918. See also Menuhin, "Jewish Communal Education," 101–2.

74. *Scribe*, February 1, 1929.

75. "Beautiful Manifestations of Jewish Culture," *B'nai B'rith Messenger*, March 30, 1928.

76. See Robert Adamic, "Los Angeles! There She Blows!" *Outlook and Independent*, August 13, 1930, 596; Joseph Lilly, "Metropolis of the West," *North American Review* (September 1931), 244–45.

77. "Spokane," *Scribe*, October 29, 1920; *Emanu-El*, February 24, 1928.

78. Many oral histories describe education. Bernhard Goldsmith sent his sons to Lawrenceville School near Princeton; Mark Gerstle went to law school at Harvard; daughters were usually educated at local private schools and by tutors. See "Bernhard Goldsmith Interview," H. H. Bancroft Collection; Mark Gerstle memoirs, Alice Gerstle Levison interview, Lucile Hening Koshland interview, Bancroft Library.

79. *Scribe*, January 6, 1922: Jewish college students at Reed, 20; North Pacific Dental College, 8; University of Oregon Medical School, 6.

80. *Scribe*, November 4, December 9, December 16, 1927.

81. *Scribe*, April 19, 1929; *The Oregana 1928, University of Oregon Yearbook* (Eugene, 1928), 353, Division of Special Collections and University Archives, University of Oregon Library.

82. *B'nai B'rith Messenger*, January 27, 1928.

83. Sol Silverman, "Opportunities and Achievements of Jewish Students in the University," *Emanu-El*, April 6, 1928.

84. *Scribe*, September 23, October 28, December 23, 1927. In 1929 Rabbi Goldstein took a pulpit in Alabama and was succeeded by Rabbi Max Merritt, who came from a Hillel post at in the University of Illinois. *Scribe*, July 19, 1929

85. *Scribe*, June 14, 1929.

86. Rose Pesotta, *Bread Upon the Waters* (Ithaca, 1987), 19, estimated 75 percent of the workers were Mexican women. The rest were Italians, Russian Jews, and Americans.

87. Fogelson, *The Fragmented Metroplis*, 154.

88. For temple locations see *B'nai B'rith Messenger*, January 6, 1928, 20–21.

89. Steven J. Ross, *Working-Class Hollywood, Silent Film, and the Shaping of Class in America* (Princeton, 1998), 3–7, argues that, because the early movies were viewed primarily by immigrant workers, attendance could transform lives as personal problems were dramatized on the silver screen.

90. Thomas Schatz, *The Genius of the System: Hollywood Film Making in the Studio Era* (New York, 1988), 4–11, 21–28, 60, 80; Aubrey Solomon, *Twentieth Century Fox: A Corporate and Financial History* (Metuchen, NJ, 1988), 3–4, 9. The key role of the

distribution of films in cementing the studio system is emphasized in Vorspan and Gartner, *History of the Jews of Los Angeles*, 132. On land speculation see William C. DeMille, *Hollywood Saga* (New York, 1939), 87. For wage rates see Murray Ross, *Stars and Strikes: Unionization of Hollywood* (New York, 1935), 6–7. Leo B. Rosten, *Hollywood: The Movie Colony; The Movie Makers* (New York, 1941), 4, 107, estimates the studios in 1939 employed between 27,500 and 33,600 people each week producing films.

91. The social snobbery of the old Jewish elite is presented in Neil Gabler, *An Empire of Their Own: How the Jews Invented Hollywood* (New York, 1988), 275–77.

92. *B'nai B'rith Messenger*; March 26, April 2, 1926; June 15, 22, 1928; January 10, 24, February 7, 1930; *Scribe*, January 10, 1930.

93. *B'nai B'rith Messenger*, January 13, 1928; Charles Higham, *Merchant of Dreams, Louis B Mayer, M.G.M., and the Secret of Hollywood* (New York, 1994),78; Budd Shulberg, *Moving Pictures: Memories of a Hollywood Prince* (New York, 1981), 191.

94. See the account of Rabbi Magnin's triumphal appearance in Portland in *B'nai B'rith Messinger*, May 4, 1928.

95. *Scribe*, June 7, 1929; *Emanu-El*, February 10, March 16, 1928.

96. *B'nai B'rith Messenger*, October 17, 1924.

97. Louis Newman, "Telling It in Gath," *Scribe*, November 11, 1927; Newman, "Editorial," *Scribe*, December 23, 1927.

98. *Scribe*, November 9 and December 21, 1928.

99. See the editorial memorializing his death in a traffic accident in *B'nai B'rith Messinger*, October 3, 1930.

100. Issell and Cherny, *San Francisco*, 40–41.

101. Louis Newman, "Telling It in Gath," *Scribe*, February 1, 1929.

102. "Meeting of the Board of Supervisors of the City and County of San Francisco, Monday, March 31, 1930," typescript in Nieto Papers, American Jewish Archives.

103. Deborah Dash Moore, *To the Golden Cities: Pursuing the American Jewish Dream in Miami and Los Angeles* (New York, 1994), 23–24.

104. Mike Davis, *City of Quartz: Excavating the Future in Los Angeles* (New York, 1992), 124–25.

105. Jonathan Bowles, "The Empire Has No Clothes," *Center for an Urban Future* (February 2000): 3–4, 14–15, www.nycfuture.org/images_pdfs/pdfs/Empire%20No%20clothes%2000.pdf online.

106. Gary R. Mormino, *Land of Sunshine, State of Dreams: A Social History of Modern Florida* (Gainsville, 2005), 24, 128–38.

107. Bruce Phillips, "The Challenge of Family, Identity and Affiliation," in Ava F. Kahn and Marc Dollinger, eds., *California Jews* (Hanover, 2002), 20–21.

108. Saba Soomekh, "Tehrangeles: Capital, Culture, and Faith Among Iranian Jews," paper presented at Religious Pluralism in Southern California Conference, UC Santa Barbara (May 9, 2003), pdf available on internet at www.religion.ucsb.edu/projects/newpluralism/tehrangeles.doc.

109. Tom Tugend, "Rites Launch Israel Tolerance Museum," *Jewish Journal of Greater Los Angeles*, May 7, 2004; Bernard Weinraub, "Jewish History Museum Opening in Los Angeles," *New York Times*, April 21, 1996; Naomi Pfefferman, "Skirbal at

Five," *Jewish Journal of Greater Los Angeles*, April 13, 2001; Gene Lichtenstein, "L.A. Museums Saved by the Jews," *Jewish Journal of Greater Los Angeles*, August 16, 2002.

110. Joe Eskenazi, "Have Demographers Undercounted Jews in the West?" *Jewish News Weekly*, October 18, 2002, www.jewish.com/content/2–0-/module/displaystory/story_id/1908/format/html/edition_id/386/displaystory.html. Bob Colacello, "Eli Broad's Big Picture," *Vanity Fair* (December 2006), 324–30, 379–86.

111. See Rob Eshman, "A Fistful of Scholars," *Jewish Journal of Greater Los Angeles*, December 2, 2005, www.jewishjournal.com/home/preview.php?id = 15043.

10

FUN AND GAMES

The American Jewish Social Club

JENNA WEISSMAN JOSELIT

American Jews, the latter-day descendants of the people of the book, are no strangers to pleasure. Some have found it in Torah study, others in cooking and eating, and still others in pursuit of what William James called the gospel of relaxation. From the lavish Purim balls of the 1880s to the modest dance halls of the 1900s, from Chicago's stately Standard Club to its more humble cousin, the Aleph Beth Gymal Doled Club of Minneapolis, from lodges to *landsmanshaftn*, America's Jews made ample room in their lives for the social whirl of things—for card playing, convivial conversation, a good meal, a turn on the dance floor, and, on occasion, even a Swedish massage. In the process of having fun, America's Jews transformed sociability into one of the hallmarks of the modern Jewish experience, giving rise along the way to new forms of community such as the urban social club and its suburban offshoot, the Jewish country club, and to equally new forms of identity such as the club member.

It is to the history—and consequences—of sociability among late nineteenth- and early twentieth-century American Jews that this essay attends. Focusing on the Jewish social club, a little studied social phenomenon of the modern era, it looks at how the organized pursuit of sociability, especially among upwardly mobile Jewish men of the 1870s through the 1920s, affected American Jewish life. As much a part of the landscape as synagogues and charities, Jewish social clubs with decidedly non-Jewish names such as the Harmonie, the Phoenix, the Elysium, and the Concordia could be found in virtually every fair-sized metropolis by the waning years of the nineteenth century, offering their members a congenial venue in which to assuage their loneliness, hone their social skills, multiply their business contacts, or simply relax.

But then there was more—much more—to the Jewish social club than that. Central to the enterprise was the creation of a new kind of Jew or, more precisely still, a new kind of American Jewish male. The antithesis of the Old World Jew with his wariness, bookish ways, and demanding religion, the American Jewish club member was at home in the world, a congenial and affable fella whose Jewishness was unobtrusive and discreet at best. More to the point, the American Jewish club member was a consummate gentleman, the kind of man who, to paraphrase Maurice Samuel, modulated his manners as well as his ties.[1] Although gentlemanliness was never expressly described as the sine qua non of membership—nowhere—not in the charters, bylaws, minutes, or newsletters is this a stated objective—its pursuit and cultivation was the peg on which members hung their top hats and eventually their golf caps as well.

As much a collective goal as an individual one, gentlemanliness appealed handily to thousands of American Jewish men across the country. In Mobile they congregated at the Fidelia; in Cleveland, they dropped in for a nightcap or a hand of cards at the Excelsior; and in San Francisco they sought one another's company at the Concordia Club, reportedly "one of the best-known clubs on the coast."[2] Appealing to the "finest type of Jews"—middle-class men in their early twenties and thirties, virtually all of whom claimed German Jewish descent—Jewish social clubs grew steadily throughout the 1870s, 1880s, and 1890s from a handful of members to several hundred; some like the Harmonie in New York or the Phoenix in Baltimore also maintained a substantial waiting list.[3] Jewish by default, not design, they made a point of pursuing conviviality rather than *chesed* (good deeds), effecting a revolution in the process. In each instance the "aim and keyword" of these clubs was not the furtherance of Jewish tradition, the expression of religious devotion, or even the performance of charity—the customary elements of Jewish communal life—as much as it was "sociability" pure and simple, its very innocuousness a profound challenge, even an assault on, the established Jewish order.[4]

I

An artifact of the Gilded Age, the urban social club took hold in the years immediately following the Civil War. By the mid-1870s no American city was without one or two or possibly even three. "At no time, probably in the history of the metropolis, has there been a movement so marked in the direction of club-life," observed Francis Gerry Fairfield in 1873, charting its rapid development.[5] A number of factors accounted for the postbellum popularity of the urban social club. For one thing, the flush of prosperity that accompanied the postwar years led to an expansion in and growing appreciation of leisure time; for another, American men, having grown accustomed to one another's company during the Civil War, continued to seek out exclusively male forms of camaraderie in peacetime, too. At the same time, the growth of cities, increasingly inhabited by immigrants, also had much to do with the increasing popularity of the private social club, prompting the well-heeled to turn inward, away from the street.

Surely it is no coincidence that urban social clubs took off at the very same moment that cities grew larger, more ethnically diverse and economically stratified, prompting a heightened attentiveness to manners. "On crowded streets, in shops and hotels, on omnibuses, streetcars, trains, and steamboats, and in elevators, strangers were promiscuously amassed in intimate proximity," explains historian John Kasson. "Such scenes were ripe with potential obtrusions from which defense or escape could be difficult."[6] An exercise in social control, in keeping unwelcome exchanges at bay, etiquette helped tame the growing unruliness of the metropolis. So, too, did the urban social club. You might even say it was etiquette writ large.

"Club life is undoubtedly civilizing," gushed one of its fans, writer Charles Page Bryan, taking to the pages of the *Cosmopolitan* in 1889 to welcome the addition of the Chicago Club, the Union Club, the Calumet Club, and the Marquette Club to the Windy City.[7] Bryan applauded their dignified and occasionally "baronial" surroundings where a premium was placed on manners, discipline, and a fidelity to rules and regulations; even the waiters, it was said, behaved like gentlemen. Although still in their infancy, these clubs already had a salutary effect, especially on the younger generation. "A marked improvement has taken place in the morals and manners of the younger men," Bryan cheered. Where earlier generations of Chicago men, especially those who had jettisoned their "Puritan backgrounds," tended to "rush headlong down the toboggan-slides to destruction," contemporary gents practiced restraint, thanks in no small measure to the discipline exacted upon them by their club.[8]

After singing the praises of Chicago's social clubs in the most general of terms, Bryan went on to catalogue their respective attributes: which one set the finest table, which one was most enamored of sports or especially keen on politics. Among those inventoried in this manner was the Standard Club. But its claim to fame, its inclusion in the list of distinguished clubs, had little to do with its bill of fare or roster of activities as much as its clientele: "The Hebrews have recently completed a massive edifice for their Standard Club," Bryan noted. "It is built of granite, with an impressive, fortress-like exterior but containing the most luxurious appointments. It occupies a corner not far from the Calumet Club and is worthy in every respect of an intelligent and worthy membership."[9] With the exception of the revealing reference to the Standard Club's "fortress-like exterior"—surely not even Bryan was unmindful of the implications of alluding to a Jewish institution as a fortress—he registered the existence of a club that ca-tered exclusively to Hebrews with barely a hiccup. The need for a club peopled entirely by Jews occasioned no glum thoughts about the ills of discrimination or the perils of social segregation. By Bryan's lights, one club for the Jews and a dozen more for everyone else was a perfectly natural part of the social order. No intelligent and worthy Jewish membership, he insinuated, would have it any other way.

But then, the Jews of Chicago had little choice in the matter. As a group, they were not welcome at the Union Club or the Century Club or even the Calumet Club just around the corner. Things were not much better in Atlanta, Cleveland, and Kansas City, either. Throughout the nation, rare, indeed, was the urban social club that accepted American Jews as members. From time to time an occasional aspirant of Jewish origins might be granted admission, but, by and large, gentlemen's clubs were off-limits to those of the Mosaic persua-sion. When it came to admitting a Jewish member, blackball was the norm, ac-ceptance the exception. Put simply, the Jews were widely believed to lack a "clubbable disposition," that indefinable yet indispensable blend of grace and charm that came with good breeding and hoary ancestry.[10] Of course, clubba-bility was not the only thing American Jews seemed to be without. If the nation's leading hoteliers were to be believed, the American Jew had absolutely nothing going for him, not when it came to his public demeanor. "In the art of annoying others, he is a past-master," they said. "His favorite attitude is the ostentatious counting of yellow-backs; his secret whisper is vulgar loudness." Worse still, the American Jew was thought to be the very avatar of disagreeableness and, in some instances, even close kin to the devil, for as the *American Hebrew* related, hotel proprietors all agreed that the American Jew "has everything except horns and cloven hoofs."[11]

Not every late nineteenth-century American harbored such negative thoughts about the Jews or celebrated their exclusion from society. Some, like the editors of the *Nation*, rued this state of affairs but felt there was little one could do about it; prejudices were far too entrenched to be overcome. The exclusionary nature of the social club, it editorialized, "may be as sad and reprehensible as you please, but it is as notorious as the sun at noonday and is of long standing."[12] What's more, explained the well-regarded magazine, the social club is "simply an extension" of a man's home, giving him the prerogative to do as he pleases. "This right to select his guests and associate for reasons best known to himself is one which every man carries to his club." In the end, no good would come of protesting; the gentle-manly thing, in fact, was not to try. "The part of good taste and good manners is to avoid fighting one's way into clubs, private houses or society of any description in which one's presence would be for any reason objectionable to any part of the company," it counseled.

II

Much as they might bristle at the *Nation*'s advice, those American Jews eager for club life did not spend too much time nursing their wounds. Instead, they quickly formed a parallel universe of social clubs whose sensibility hardly differed from those institutions that had excluded them in the first place.[13] A defensive response to antisemitism, at least initially, the Jewish social club nevertheless modeled itself, from top to bottom, after its non-Jewish counterpart. Its handsome appointments as well as its calendar of events—card games and billiards, dinner dances, stag parties, singing contests, bowling tournaments, and other "doings"—varied not a whit from the norm.[14] So much did the Jewish club resemble its non-Jewish counterpart that one observer allowed how the "disciples of Confucius and the devotees of Buddha" would certainly feel at home there: nothing, apart from the names on the membership roster—all those Bernheimers and Loewensteins—distinguished it from a non-Jewish facility.[15] Even Purim balls and masquerades, high-spirited annual events that drew throngs of "ardent Terpsichoreans," held little appeal: their overt association with Jewish history and tradition rendered them far too Jewish for most club members.[16] More strikingly still, the Jewish social club was not above brandishing its own form of exclusion, looking down its nose at east European Jews. Despite having been on the receiving end of exclusionary practices, its members persisted in keeping to their own kind well into the postwar era, prompting affluent east European Jews, in turn, to establish yet another universe of social clubs.

Centrally located, in the very heart of the metropolis, the Jewish social club boasted its own multistory building, which typically featured a number of distinctive spaces: a palatial ballroom, a library, a billiard room, a dining room, card rooms, poolrooms, as well as a series of lounges outfitted with smokers' stands, small tables ("for a hundred club uses"), and cushy couches where members could comfortably recline while nursing their scotch.[17] Most institutions also maintained "incidental accomodations . . . for the ladies"—usually a separate lounge or parlor—where, on those occasions when the opposite sex was welcome in the building, its members could tend to their appearance or just set awhile before appearing on the arms of their husbands, fiancés, fathers, or brothers.[18] With the exception of this presumably feminine space, wood and leather abounded, as did the smoke from members' cigarettes and cigars. Just as inviting as their parlors at home but better—after all, at the clubhouse men could smoke and drink in peace, without the nagging of wives or sisters—the clubhouse interior, through and through, exuded the "smart, comfortable, enduring" affects of masculinity.[19]

Many Jewish clubhouses, determined to be up-to-date in every way, also boasted their very own bowling alley. At the time, bowling was especially popular among the sporting set. "Pleasing to the eye and mind," as well as a "healthy and invigorating exercise," the game took off during the closing years of the nineteenth century.[20]

As S. Karpf, secretary of the American Bowling Congress, put it in 1903, the growing popularity of ten pins over the past ten years was nothing short of "marvelous."[21] Some attributed bowling's newfound appeal to the standardization of its rules and the emergence of "regulation"-sized bowling alleys and bowling balls. Others attributed the game's growing popularity to changes in the construction industry, which, resulting in sturdier foundations, made it possible to remove bowling alleys from the basement, where they had languished in the murk, to a sunnier and airier second story, where conditions were far more congenial. All agreed that bowling benefited every part of the body. "I don't think medical skill can introduce any better elixir of life," gushed Mr. Karpf. "It will lengthen one's years to a certainty."[22]

Even women took to the sport, prompting A. E. Vogell, another enthusiast, to note as early as 1895 that bowling was no longer a "pastime dedicated to masculine monopoly."[23] In cities throughout the nation, "women seem to take as much interest and derive as much enjoyment mentally and physically as the "sterner sex.'" The popularity of bowling was so assured among both men and women that Vogell believed it was only a matter of time before weekly bowling clubs superseded weekly dancing clubs. *Spalding's Official Bowling Guide*, in turn, published a testimonial from one female bowler who acknowledged that, after bowling, "my blood tingles, my appetite is ravenous and I feel that it is good just to be alive."[24]

Subsequent generations of club members felt the same way about golf, which, by the 1920s, had superseded bowling as the sport *du jour*; by then countless Jewish club members had succumbed to what one eyewitness called "golf fever."[25] Where the metropolitan Jewish social club cultivated an urban form of gentlemanliness, the Jewish country club cultivated that other perquisite of the modern gent: sportmanship. With growing wealth and increased mobility, many members of the urban social club, often the children and grandchildren of the founding generation, expressed interest in acquiring property in the country where they could experience the great outdoors and its sporting traditions. These American Jews, heeding the "call of the open," took to the ways of the country club, to golf and tennis (and occasionally to riding as well), with such a vengeance that, during the early 1920s, major Jewish newspapers such as the *American Hebrew* routinely devoted an annual issue to "Country Clubs and Sports."[26] Within the past couple of years American Jews have taken to sport with great relish, related the weekly, explaining its decision to focus on the community's newfound penchant for outdoor recreation. "This characteristic may be adjectived as a virtue or a vice, depending upon your point of view. We state it here merely for the obvious fact that is."[27]

But then, the *American Hebrew* was being somewhat disingenuous. For implicit in its public discussion of American Jewry's "astonishing turn toward outdoor life" was a real sense of pride at the speed and ease with which its sons and daughters had transformed themselves from bookworms to sports hounds.[28] As much an occasion for celebration as an opportunity for sociologizing, the paper's coverage of the Jewish country club scene emphasized the extent to which this institution, much like its predecessor, successfully normalized the American Jew. "Given half a chance and shown the way, the Jew proves himself [as] human out of doors as other Americans," proclaimed the paper, noting that the "American love of sports, no less than the ardor for democracy, fair play and the square deal has entered the Jew's soul."[29] By playing golf, for instance, the American Jew absorbed "many of the habits, customs and social amenities of the American non-Jew."[30] By playing golf, he learned now only how to relax but how to tone down his characteristic competitive streak. Success, he discovered while out on the links, was "not necessarily the concomitant of winning the game."[31] And if that weren't enough to persuade thousands of American Jews across the country to wield a club, the American Hebrew insisted that the ancient Scottish game had the potential to put an end to what was often referred to euphemistically as clannishness, breaking down barriers between Jews and non-Jews. "Eighteen holes of leisurely, pleasant, sporting rivalry tends to promote mutual good feeling and the in-between chats that develop as [players] wander over the fairways always add to their good fellowship."[32] Of all America's institutions, the fairway, the paper concluded ringingly, offered the Jew and non-Jew common ground.[33]

Golf did wonders for intra-Jewish relations as well. By spending time together on the links or around the card table, Jewish club members created an exclusively male world that made little room for women. Now and then—at a ball, an occasional family dinner, a golf or tennis tournament, or during "Ladies' Day" when they had the run of the club for an afternoon—mothers, daughters, sisters, and wives were admitted on the premises, but only in the company of their menfolk. Otherwise, they were conspicuously—and deliberately—absent or, alternatively, segregated in the ladies lounge. To be sure, middle-class Jewish women did not want for social outlets. Between the demands of the synagogue sisterhood, whose combination of socializing and social welfare activities energized the American Jewish community at the tail end of the nineteenth century, or the press of logistical arrangements that characterized the opening and administration of sanitary fairs, another popular pastime of the Gilded Age, between the intellectual demands of a literary society and the physical demands of female bowling leagues and cycling clubs, those American Jewish women "dowered with leisure" could easily fill their calendars with a wealth of extradomestic pursuits.[34] There's also little evidence to suggest that at any point between the 1880s and the 1920s women begrudged their menfolk's club membership, let alone demanded that they be admitted to one; that would come later—much later. Though surely not above criticizing this aspect or that of the club ("Late again for dinner, darling?"), Jewish women seemed to have accepted the all-male Jewish social club as part of the established order of things much as Jewish men had made their peace with the all-Jewish roster.

Even so, not everyone within the American Jewish community of the late nineteenth century looked favorably upon it. On the contrary. The social club's very existence, especially during its formative years, gave rise to a spirited, even fierce public discussion about the limitations of club life and the moral short-comings of its members. Are club members "capable of advancing no cause save the dance and the card table?" wondered some of their critics as early as 1873, noting the social club's penchant for frivolous activities whose sole objective was fun and games.[35] More alarming still was the social club's determination to chart its own course, to hold itself aloof from communitywide affairs or, as the *Jewish Messenger* put it, to bid "good-bye to charity balls." Club members, the weekly explained, no longer "participate in stately or social balls or entertainments, whose delightful object was to aid the needy."[36] By absenting themselves from these events, the revenue from which helped to support American Jewry's net-work of charitable organizations, they limited the latter's effectiveness: the "cause of charity suffers."[37] And that was only the half of it. When, in 1881, Isaac Mayer Wise, for one, welcomed Jewish social clubs into the fold, claiming in a sermon delivered at the dedication of a new building on the campus of the Hebrew Union College that they were as vital to "self preservation" as the more tradi-tional institutions of Jewish communal life, his remarks kicked off a firestorm of protest. Said Wise in part (his speech took the better part of several pages in the *American Israelite*): "As a religious denomination we feel the duty of self-preservation. Therefore, our co-religionists all over this country, at very heavy expense, have organized and supported congregations, societies, lodges and even clubs; have erected temples, synagogues, schoolhouses."[38]

The rabbi's decision to include social clubs within the moral taxonomy of Jew-ish communal organizations infuriated a number of those who read of his speech in the paper. "We are not willing to believe that [Judaism in America] has fallen so low that cards and billiards are essential to its vitality," editorialized the *Ameri-can Hebrew*, responding quite negatively to Wise's endorsement. "The mere suggestion is an insult to every intelligent Hebrew."[39] One such intelligent He-brew expressed concern about the type of Jew the social club tended to produce, young men who "dabble in silly fashions, drink and gamble, swear and make bets . . . spend more money on clothing and jewelry for their own persons than their fathers would absorb in supporting a whole family and never entertain a thought of religion or duty, synagogue or God. Their days are spent in business speculation, their nights a succession of dissipations."[40] Fearful lest American Jewish men develop into feckless and dandified youths rather than solid citizens, he strongly encouraged them to look elsewhere for camaraderie. A third detractor, an "American Hebrew from Philadelphia," went even further, urging that Jewish social clubs be abolished completely. Having nothing to do with either faith or ritual, they offered American Jews little of value. "Pray, what is that religion which is to be preserved by clubs? It was certainly not Judaism."[41] Still other critics wondered about the club's impact on the family as more and more men seemed inclined to spend the better part of their evenings at the clubhouse, in the company of other men, instead of spending time with their loved ones. Club members are "weaned from home by the influence of the Club—How do the nights pass for their wives and children?"[42]

To be sure, Jewish social clubs were not the only target of sustained criticism; the Young Men's Hebrew Association (YMHA), another institution whose mandate was manifestly recreational rather than religious, was also tarred with the same brush. Time and again, throughout the early 1880s, the pages of the English-language Jewish press took the YMHA to task for "aping" its Christian counterpart, the YMCA, "without even the pretense of fostering any religion [and] reclaiming any sinners" or doing good works.[43] "The enterprise of the Harlem Y.M.H.A. is commendable; but how many of its members belong to the Harlem synagogue?" wondered the *Jewish Messenger*, hinting broadly that those who made use of the Y stayed clear of the sanctuary.[44] Echoing its competitor, the *American Israelite* also roundly criticized the Y and those who sought it out. If a member was asked to point out what he liked best about the institution, would he point to its reading room? Surely not, insisted the weekly. He would extol its facilities, sports programs, and annual dance instead. "Gymnastics, bowling and dancing are in their way excellent things, but their successful practice hardly requires a Young Men's Hebrew Association," it opined. "Why such an association should be called 'Hebrew,' we are unable to find out."[45]

Were things not bad enough, the press also gave voice to grave disappointment about the sort of men who, in Chicago, Buffalo, and San Francisco, formed the backbone of the social club or the Y, depicting them as callow and shallow dandies more familiar with the latest lingo than with the verities of the Torah. Chicago young men, it was said, "all know how to dance and can repeat minstrel jokes by heart. They have all the slang that permeates Tony Pastor's New York Theater at their fingers' ends and employ it on every conceivable occasion."[46] More damning still, these young men, many from upstanding Jewish families, had little use for Judaism, rarely, if ever, attending synagogue. Equally disturbing was their apparent disdain for *kultur*. "They go to the opera rarely and to minstrel or variety shows frequently. Of concerts and music as an art they know nothing. Our Jewish maidens are much better educated. Taken as a whole, there is much to improve in our Jewish young men."[47] In Buffalo, meanwhile, it was reported that the "absorbing history, the rich literature of Israel [were] neglected for dancing and fun." It is high time "that our youth lost sight of mere money making and adopted a profession in which they could soon push to the front. The ranks of business are overcrowded; the ranks of the literary army welcome every accession."[48] Things, it seemed, were no better in San Francisco or, for that matter, in the rest of the country. On the West Coast, related one eyewitness, Jewish social clubs contributed to a "state of mental stagnation which seems to have captivated the Jewish mind all over the United States."[49]

Fighting words, indeed. Were things really that bad? Were Jewish social clubs and the slang-spouting, fleet-footed men who frequented them truly a blight on the Jewish community? Might the fulminations against them simply reflect the views of an impatient older generation uncomfortable with change and the unfamiliar ways of the young? Reading these fiercely worded critiques more than a hundred years after they were first written, one can't help but wonder how to interpret them. Are they to be taken at face value, as an accurate reflection of a community gone wrong, or should they be seen as an expression of sour grapes, of bitter institutional competition? Complicating matters still further is that, apart from the press, the identities of those who publicly excoriated the Jewish social club—all those "intelligent Hebrews"—is elusive. Were they representing themselves or some larger affiliation? It's hard to say.

What is clear, though, is that the clubhouse and the sanctuary did not always hold one another at arm's length. As William Toll's research into the history of Portland, Oregon's Jews suggest, those who belonged to that city's leading Jewish social club, the Concordia Club, also made sure to contribute to the building fund of Congregation Beth Israel.[50] While they themselves may not have attended synagogue, Concordia's members were sufficiently galvanized either by peer pressure or by a strong sense of communal responsibility to lend their support. In this case at least, the clubhouse and the sanctuary were not mutually exclusive. Even so, cooperation between the two institutions may well have occurred only in smaller cities like Portland where, given a relatively contained Jewish population, face-to-face exchanges were common and, conversely, broader opportunities for social exchange were limited. But in the larger Jewish urban centers things developed differently. There the clubhouse and the sanctuary not only claimed different constituencies but, more important still, held out entirely divergent objectives.

By offering growing numbers of young Jewish men an alternative social realm, one in which the traditional restraints of communal and familial responsibility were cast off in favor of the brand-new rewards of pleasure and release, the convivial but undemanding regimen of the Jewish social club threatened the traditional scheme of things. Its mandate, after all, was not a Jewish one, certainly not as many American Jews would have it. Talk of good deeds, of social justice and of ritual performance, of the family and of Jewish history—all this was conspicuously absent, its place filled with "doings" and other gentlemanly pursuits that took place at considerable remove from the bosom of the family and the heart of the community. Even the club's leaders seemed to have been cut from different cloth, chosen not because of their standing as "representative Israelites but for their proficiency in bowling."[51] Under these circumstances, the Jewish community was right to worry. It wasn't just that the social club siphoned off new recruits to the "household of Israel," distracting them along the way with all manner of seductive, easy pleasures. That was bad enough. Worse still was how it stood the time-honored notion of inclusiveness, of the Jewish collective, on its head. An example of privatization at its most extreme, the Jewish social club of the late nineteenth and early twentieth centuries turned its back on the rest of the community, earning its opprobrium in the process.

III

Within a generation or so, the Jewish social club changed its stripes, opening its doors to all sorts of manifestly communal activities it had once shunned as unduly parochial. "Gone are the Friday night bowling clubs, the amateur shows, the billiard room and the German Bierstube, which the older members remember with nostalgic delight," wrote a historically minded member of the Harmonie Club. "In their place we have a Club that is modern, democratic, forward looking and above all else capable of change."[52] But then, in the aftermath of World War I, it was hard not to. For one thing, the challenges facing the American Jewish community both during and after the war's end were exigent and many; no responsible institution could afford to ignore them. For another thing, in the wake of the Great War an ethos of democratization had taken hold of the American body politic, rendering elitist enterprises like the Jewish social club increasingly suspect, if not out-of-date. What's more, east European Jews as a group had begun to enter the ranks of the middle class in growing numbers during the 1910s and 1920s, making the class-based animus of German Jews seem silly, if not downright irrelevant. Little by little, then, the universe of Jewish social clubs began to position itself within the American Jewish public square or at least to take note of it. Atlanta's Jewish Progressive Club, for one, became a veritable "boon to weary Jewish travellers," while Philadelphia's Mercantile Club lent its "handsome hall to shows" sponsored by the Jewish Welfare Board whose chaplains ministered to Jewish servicemen.[53] Brooklyn's Unity Club extended a "cordial welcome and its enthusiastic support to every worthy endeavor and undertaking in the field of Jewish charity and social welfare work."[54] Chicago, meanwhile, could boast the addition of a brand-new Jewish social club, the Covenant Club, whose charter spoke exuberantly of the "advancement of the social, cultural and physical well-being of its members, the fostering of ideals of American democracy, and the encouragement and stimulation of Jewish culture and tradition."[55]

The Covenant Club was first established in 1917 as a downtown meeting place for local members of B'nai B'rith. A few years later it opened its membership even wider to what it called "Jewish men of good character," among them the former members of a noontime card game who, picking up where the Aleph Beth Gymal

Doled Club in Minneapolis left off, had styled themselves the Hey Vov Club.[56] East European in origin, Covenant Club members prided themselves on their inclusive, democratic sense of fellowship. The "Covenant Club," they declared, "recognizes no caste, no aristocracy except for the fundamental aristocracy of the Jewish integrity."[57] Rejecting partisan politics and pedigree in equal measure, even as it thumbed its nose at the snobbish German Jewish establishment, the Covenant Club, as its name implied, sought to provide common ground for Chicago Jewry's growing middle class.

Much like its longstanding counterparts, this downtown clubhouse also radiated a sense of prosperity.[58] Likened to a "symphony in rich colors and gold," it contained a lounge, a library, a capacious ballroom that accommodated a thousand people as well as a series of smaller dining rooms and a bar known, tantalizingly enough, as the "Florida Palm Room." A euphemistically called "recreation room" where guests could "concentrate on the intricacies of pinochle or contract bridge," handball courts, pool tables, a fully equipped gym along with a pool or "natatorium," whose water, it was proudly said, was "cleaner and purer than Lake Michigan—filtered, irradiated with ultra-violet light, tempered and freed from germs"—such pleasures were placed at every member's disposal. Monday and Thursday mornings were set aside for their wives, sisters, and daughters, who were encouraged to take advantage of the splendid pool. The clubhouse also boasted a "Ladies Bath department," which, it was said, "permitted them to build up a strong, graceful, well-poised carriage."

Good posture and a supple spine were not the only concerns of the Covenant Club. Great pains were also taken to gratify the palate. Its (non-kosher) food, boasted a membership brochure from the late 1930s, is the "ultimate in cuisine and embellishment. Not merely cooks but Artists [*sic*] prepare it." The food was indeed "memorable," recalled a former member, citing the culinary magic of a Mrs. Maxfield whose creations ranged from a colorful cream cheese loaf, studded with olives and pimentos, to "squares of jello with floating pieces of fruit and a dollop of some mayonnaissy stuff on top," which, he confessed, "I always pushed aside."[59]

Jello and mayonnaise notwithstanding, the Covenant Club exuded a strong sense of Jewishness. Jewish books and magazines were available in the library while the artwork of known Jewish painters and sculptors, from that of Boris Schatz to Enrico Glicenstein, hung on the club's walls and stood on its pedestals. An annual Passover seder and Hanukkah party as well as frequent lectures on and noted appearances by celebrated Jewish personalities—the "great men of Israel," they were called—created a pronounced "Jewish spirit" in the clubhouse. Later still, during the post–World War II years, Jewish organizations, from the Jewish Book Council to those seeking to raise funds for Israel, routinely held meetings at the club while families, just as routinely, celebrated their children's bar and bat mitzvah receptions in one of its many dining rooms, firmly planting the Covenant

Club within the cultural geography—and social consciousness—of Chicago Jewish life.

Although the creation of the Covenant Club and other institutions like it led some observers of the 1920s to speak enthusiastically of a renaissance of Jewish club life, the reality was something else again. By then, many Jewish social clubs had lost their sparkle, becoming in effect little more than "lunch and card clubs," a place to socialize during business hours rather than the fulcrum of a varied and lively nocturnal culture.[60] The popularity of the country club had much to do with diminishing the importance of its urban counterpart, as did suburbanization more generally. In the first instance, the metropolitan club was increasingly supplanted by the likes of the Beresford Country Club and the Hollywood Golf Club, which offered a wider range of activities and a more spacious setting in which to pursue them than anything the Harmonie or the Excelsior could provide. Once the *dernier cri* in stylishness, the urban social club of the 1920s could no longer hold a candle to its country cousin. All but "doomed," it came alive only during the winter months when opportunities for swimming, golfing, and tennis were limited.[61] Even then, the social club functioned as a pale shadow of its former self, no thanks to suburbanization, which had an equally deleterious effect on its fortunes. As growing numbers of affluent American Jews forsook the city for the suburbs, the prospect of dropping by their club of an evening grew increasingly untenable. Scrambling to catch the 6:14 or anxiously contemplating the prospect of a long drive, they no longer had the time or the inclination to spend a leisurely hour or two nursing a drink before heading home; besides, the "club car," an amenity provided by the suburban commuter train, took care of all that. As for visiting the club on, say, a Sunday afternoon, perhaps for a dinner *en famille*, that, too, was increasingly a thing of the past. "One does not jump into one's automobile for a run into town," observed one eyewitness. "On the contrary, one takes his family and motors into the wide spaces of the country."[62]

And if that weren't enough to send the urban club into eclipse, its entire raison d'être—gentlemanliness as a social and cultural idea—no longer seemed quite as compelling or nearly as urgent as it had back at the turn of the century. Among the young, gentlemanliness, in fact, was held in ill repute. Long since attained by the members of the Harmonie Club and the Concordia Club and the Standard Club, the display of good manners and the practice of restraint in America of the Jazz Age, the era of "anything goes," were now seen by their children as old-fashioned virtues to be honored exclusively in the breach. Those who came of age during the 1920s were "making mincemeat" of the nation's moral code, observed Frederick Lewis Allen in his wryly detailed account of postwar America, *Only Yesterday*. As a result, "manners became not merely different, but—for a few years—unmannerly."[63] Standards had fallen so low that Allen even went so far as to propose that the 1920s might live on in the popular imagination as the "Decade of Bad Manners."[64]

That said, the strongest challenge to the Jewish social club came not from within but from without: the movies. Rendering the older rituals of sociability obsolete, the chance to see and immerse oneself in a feature film, especially when screened in a deluxe movie palace such as the Paramount or the Orpheum, represented the fullest and most unfettered expression of modern America, a place where imagination rather than pocketbook or pedigree held sway. With their marbled and velvet interiors, acres of seats and "swirl[s] of color and splendor," these grand theatres outdid even the most sumptuously appointed clubhouse.[65] More to the point, they offered a sense of life's possibilities that no social club or even country club could possibly ever duplicate. "In the isolation of this twilight palace," breathlessly related the *New Republic* in 1929, the audience abandons itself to "adventure with a freedom that is simply impossible [elsewhere]."[66] There, amid the flickering light of the silver screen, one could fantasize about being Cleopatra or the Sheik of Araby, not just chairman of the club's finance committee or coordinator of its annual dinner dance.

Offering an escape from the pressures of daily life, the movie palace also heralded a new form of democracy, one that cast the clubhouse even deeper into the shadows. Where the social club embraced distinctions of class, social background, and ethnic origin and institutionalized them, the movies stood these distinctions on their head, subverting them. Once inside the deluxe movie palace where ticket prices were the same for the banker and his barber, the "differences of cunning, charm and wealth that determine our lives outside are forgotten," related one enraptured moviegoer.[67] No wonder, then, that the clubhouse became increasingly marginal to the lives of so many American Jews or, for that matter, that the rituals of sociability became increasingly intertwined with those of commercial entertainment, of going to the cinema, which, by the 1940s, sold a hundred million tickets a week. In its appeal to the senses and its embodiment of democracy, the movies offered a vision of daily life that was hard to beat. What was fellowship, conviviality, politesse, and the occasional good deed when compared with the glories of Hollywood? Nothing the clubhouse might offer could come close to what the movies, that "temple of day dreams," had in store.[68]

NOTES

1. Maurice Samuel, *The Gentleman and the Jew* (New York, 1932), 10.
2. "Clubs Everywhere: Centers of Jewish Life from Coast to Coast," *American Hebrew*, February 1, 1924, 378.
3. Ibid., 373.
4. "New York City Clubs Where Gothamites Find Recreation and Entertainment," *American Hebrew*, February 1, 1924, 369. See especially Rudolph Glanz, "The Rise of the Jewish Club in America," *Jewish Social Studies* 31.2 (April 1969): 82–99, an invaluable source for the study of the Jewish club movement in nineteenth-century America.

For an imaginative and provocative look at the joys of sociability more generally, see Ray Oldenburg, *The Great Good Place: Cafes, Coffee Shops, Bookstores, Bars, Hair Salons, and Other Hangouts at the Heart of a Community* (New York, 1999).

5. Francis Gerry Fairfield, *The Clubs of New York* (New York, 1873), 8.

6. John Kasson, *Rudeness and Civility: Manners in Nineteenth-Century Urban America* (New York, 1990), 115.

7. Charles Page Bryan, "The Clubs of Chicago," *Cosmopolitan*, 7.3 (July 1889): 211.

8. Ibid.

9. Ibid., 224.

10. Fairfield, *The Clubs of New York*, 11.

11. Elias Lieberman, "That Summer Hotel Problem," *American Hebrew*, July 6, 1923, 156. See also Jenna Weissman Joselit, "Leisure and Recreation," in Paula E. Hyman and Deborah Dash Moore, eds., *Jewish Women in America: An Historical Encyclopedia*, 2 vols. (New York, 1998), 1:818–827.

12. What follows is drawn from "Club Candidates," *Nation* 56 (1893): 86.

13. Some Jewish social clubs such as the Harmonie were actually founded in the years prior to the Civil War to tend to the needs of German Jewish immigrants, many of them single men.

14. "New York City Clubs," 369.

15. "About Clubs," *Jewish Messenger* 33.10 (1873): 1.

16. "New York: The Purim Ball," *American Israelite*, March 25, 1881, 306.

17. "Furniture for Man's Club," *American Hebrew*, February 1, 1924, 350.

18. "New York City Clubs," 366.

19. "Furniture for Man's Club," 350.

20. S. Karpf, ed., *Spalding's Official Bowling Guide* (New York, 1903), 5.

21. Ibid.

22. Ibid., 25.

23. A. E. Vogell, *Bowling* (New York, 1895), 19.

24. Karpf, *Spalding's Official Bowling Guide*, 27.

25. "Clubs Everywhere," 373. On the relationship of American Jews to physical activity, see Jeffrey S. Gurock, *Judaism's Encounter with American Sports* (Bloomington, 2005).

26. Untitled editorial, *American Hebrew*, May 3, 1929, 955.

27. "Renaissance of the Town Club," *American Hebrew*, February 1, 1924, 352.

28. Ibid. See also Peter J. Levine, "The *American Hebrew* Looks at 'Our Crowd': The Jewish Country Club in the 1920s," *American Jewish History* 83.1 (1995): 27–49.

29. "The New Art of Recreation," *American Hebrew*, May 4, 1923, 789.

30. Gene Sarazen, "The Common Ground of Golf," *American Hebrew*, June 5, 1925, 135.

31. Ibid., 178.

32. Ibid., 135.

33. See also "Sports and Sportsmanship," *American Hebrew*, June 5, 1925, 133. "We believe that there should be no segregation or separatism under God's sky," editorialized the paper. "We hope for the advent of the day when men and women will be welcomed in a country club by virtue of their sportsmanship, not their religious affiliation."

34. Mrs. Enoch Rauh, "Women Suffrage and Jewish Women," *American Jewish Chronicle* 2.22 (April 6, 1917): 721. See also Jenna Weissman Joselit, "The Special Sphere of the Middle-Class American Jewish Woman: The Synagogue Sisterhood, 1890–1940," in Jack Wertheimer, ed., *The American Synagogue: A Sanctuary Transformed* (New York, 1987), 206–30.

35. "About Clubs," *Jewish Messenger* 33.10 (1873): 1.

36. Ibid.

37. Ibid.

38. Isaac Mayer Wise address, *American Israelite*, April 29, 1881, 337.

39. *American Hebrew*, May 20, 1881, 1.

40. "Clubs in Cincinnati," *Jewish Messenger*, January 24, 1873, 4.

41. "Clubs in Judaism," *American Hebrew*, May 20, 1881, 4.

42. "About Clubs."

43. "Correspondence: New York," *American Israelite*, June 3, 1881, 381.

44. *Jewish Messenger*, May 13, 1881, 4. For more on the Jews of Harlem, see Jeffrey S. Gurock, *When Harlem Was Jewish, 1870–1930* (New York, 1979).

45. "Correspondence: New York." Not to be outdone, the *Jewish Messenger* agreed, writing, "It should not be forgotten that the term Hebrew means Hebrew and not athletic, terpsichorean, dramatic, etc." *Jewish Messenger*, May 20, 1881, 4.

46. "Chicago," *American Israelite*, March 25, 1881, 306.

47. Ibid.

48. "Buffalo," *American Israelite*, June 10, 1881, 390.

49. *Hebrew* 16.2 (1878/79): 2.

50. William Toll, *The Making of an Ethnic Middle Class: Portland Jewry Over Four Generations* (Albany, 1982), 33–34.

51. Untitled editorial, *Jewish Messenger*, May 20, 1881, 4.

52. The Harmonie Club, *One Hundred Years, 1852–1952* (New York, 1952), 48.

53. "Clubs Everywhere," 355, 376.

54. "New York City Clubs," 369.

55. Information about the Covenant Club is drawn from "The Covenant Club, 1917–1986," an exhibition presented by the Spertus Institute of Jewish Studies, 2003. Its curator, Joy Kingsolver, generously provided me with the text of the exhibition's labels from which this quote is drawn.

56. See www.geocities.com/txsynvr/superior/covenantclub.html, 1.

57. Joy Kingsolver, "The Covenant Club," in *From the Chicago Jewish Archives*, 6 (2003), courtesy of Joy Kingsolver.

58. The citations that follow are drawn from "The Story of the Covenant Club," 1938, Chicago Jewish Archives. The text, a membership brochure, is unpaginated.

59. See www.geocities.com/txsynvr/superior/covenantclub.html.

60. "Clubs Everywhere," 374.

61. "Renaissance of the Town Club," 352.

62. Ibid.

63. Frederick Lewis Allen, *Only Yesterday: An Informal History of the Nineteen-Twenties* (New York, 1931), 89, 120.

64. Ibid., 120.

65. Lloyd Lewis, "The Deluxe Picture Palace," *New Republic* 58 (March 27, 1929): 175.

66. Ibid., 176.

67. Ibid.

68. Ibid.

11

A MULTITHEMATIC APPROACH TO
SOUTHERN JEWISH HISTORY

MARK K. BAUMAN

Various interpretations have been employed to explicate immigration and ethnic history, and American Jewish history in particular, many of which underwent challenge or modification. Oscar Handlin's *The Uprooted*, which emphasized the wrenching immigration experience with its destruction of Old World culture, has been replaced by John Bodnar's *The Transplanted*, with its greater recognition of continuity as well as change. Jacob Rader Marcus organized American Jewish history in terms of waves of immigration dominated by specific groups that placed their mark on an era. Now historians, particularly Hasia Diner, recognize overlap across waves, variations within them, and greater diversity. Did Jews find a *Haven and Home*, as Abraham J. Karp argued, or has the story of acceptance versus discrimination been more problematic? Discussions of degrees of acculturation in relation to the maintenance of tradition are normative. Cliometricians of the 1960s introduced analysis of statistical sources that helped plot, among many things, socioeconomic and geographic mobility patterns of ethnic groups in cities. In recent decades authors have emphasized changing and multiple identities and memory. Today historians debate "whiteness" studies and ask when, how, and why Jews became "white."

During the last thirty years the dominant theme in southern Jewish historiography has been regional distinctiveness. Frequently contrasting the story of central European Jews in the South with that of east European Jews in New York, historians have described the ways in which adaptation to a unique region and

circumstances shape divergent mores and behavior. From this perspective, southern Jewish life appears provincial and exotic. Yes, Jews resided in the South and
they were different.[1]

Since the early 1990s this interpretation has been challenged and remains a
bone of contention. Challengers maintain variations always exist, but the more
surprising phenomenon is the confluence of southern and American Jewish experiences. This essay describes how southern Jews provided leadership and participated in national Jewish affairs and, with few exceptions, followed national models
of Jewish institutional development, economic and civic advancement, and life
within a parallel social world. More important, it responds to the question, "Why
did Jews replicate the national patterns as much as they did given the seemingly
overwhelming local forces for assimilation?" Keys to the answer are family, business, and institutional ties, senses of peoplehood and religious identity, and the
constant flow of population. The picture that emerges is of dynamism and movement, repeated rejuvenation and transformation, and cross-regional, national,
and international networks. Much here is familiar to specialists and harks back to
the business and genealogical emphases of Jacob R. Marcus and his students Bertram W. Korn and Malcolm Stern. This essay breaks new ground by tracing the
patterns across periods and making them central to understanding.[2]

FROM THE COLONIAL TO THE
EARLY NATIONAL ERAS

Colonial ties of family, business, and religion spanned America, the Atlantic, and
the Caribbean. The Spanish and Portuguese congregations in London and Amsterdam served as centers for frontier, periphery communities. They encouraged
colonization, provided financing, credit, and brokerage functions, helped combat
antisemitism, and offered ritual items, assistance in congregation building, and
expertise in questions of halacha (Jewish law) and ritual. The first Jews in the
western hemisphere went to the Caribbean, South America, and future American
South, although in Spanish, Portuguese, and French territories they had to practice their religion secretly to avoid the Inquisition and French Code Noir, respectively. Scattered Jews like the Monsanto family moved freely along the coast of the
Gulf of Mexico and to the Caribbean for business and trade opportunities. Few in
number, highly mobile, and mostly men, their religious needs, if they perceived
any, were met by Sephardic congregations established on the islands.[3]

Leaders of London's Bevis Marks Congregation, two of whom were trustees,
ignored the orders of the trustees who controlled Georgia and sent Sephardim
and Ashkenazim to Savannah in 1733, only months after the colony began. The
inclusion of a physician and a Portuguese vintner among the immigrants, and the
fact that these people's financing was guaranteed in a colony partly settled as a

refuge for debtors, transformed colonial leader James Oglethorpe into a champion of toleration for the Jews against trustee protestations. Reflecting national identity, Jews from the Germanic states welcomed Lutherans from their homeland. The two Jewish subcommunities attempted to unite to form a congregation and other Jewish institutions partly in response to Christian proselytizing, but splintered into competing factions; one supporting the Portuguese and the other the Ashkenazic rite. Both struggled without a synagogue. Only two Ashkenazic families remained when others fled because of fear the Spanish would overtake the colony during the War of Jenkins Ear and impose the Inquisition on crypto-Jews who had practiced their religion openly in the British domain. Some may have also opposed trustee policy against slavery and traveled north to Charleston and other colonies for opportunity and religious security. The loss of Savannah's Sephardic population incapacitated K.K. Mikve Israel at the same time it nurtured Charleston, New York, and Philadelphia Jewry. Yet a reverse migration followed. Americanized and more observant Sephardim moved from Charleston to Savannah, and Old World differences lost their edge.[4]

London Jews who supported Georgia Jewry helped create the Charleston community to which most early Jews emigrated from London or the Caribbean. Thereafter the population mixture changed repeatedly and frequently. Reflecting identical centripetal and centrifugal forces, Charleston (originally Charles Town), like Savannah, temporarily supported two congregations. Incorporated in response to changes in state government policy in 1790, K.K. Mikve Israel and Charleston's K.K. Beth Elohim used the mother congregation's Sephardic rite although both had Ashkenazic members. Religious functionaries came from London or Amsterdam. Charleston Jews allied with Huguenots (French Protestants) for rights but limitations were more often de jure than de facto. Acumen in trade marked Jews as desirable residents, and, small in number, they posed little threat to authority. The latter remained true through the Revolution when most Jews joined patriot ranks.[5]

Multiple transcolonial and international ties stand out. Mordecai Sheftall chose trustees from Savannah, Charleston, New York, Newport, and London for the Savannah community's second cemetery. Many of Savannah's and Charleston's Jews, moving to avoid British occupation, resided in Philadelphia during and after the American Revolution. Several leaders of Philadelphia's congregation had roots in southern cities. The constitution of Savannah's Mikve Israel drew on the guidelines of its Philadelphia sister Mikveh Israel and New York's Shearith Israel. Savannah prayer leader Emanuel De la Motta helped develop Charleston's K.K. Beth Elohim. New York hazan Gershom Mendes Seixas's brother was a charter member of Mikve Israel. When Savannah's Levi Sheftall, representing the congregation, sent a letter to George Washington congratulating him on his inauguration, the four other extant congregations followed using similar language. Certainly variations from community to community reflected local circumstances, but the overwhelming similarities across colonies illustrated this constant movement of people and, with them, ideas and institutions, patterns replicated repeatedly over American Jewish history.

Business failure was routine, and some arrived with the lowly status as one of the hundred or so Jews who bound themselves to others as indentured servants in return for passage to colonial Maryland.[6] Nonetheless, the dominant economic story is of success. Such success can be attributed to Old World backgrounds in commerce that were easily applicable to colonial conditions, partnerships and other financial and trade dealings with friends and family, mobility, and relative tolerance, and because Jews fit into important niches. Most Jews in the colonies became merchants or factors who performed middleman services of buying and selling goods and offering credit. Some trade took place with Native Americans, and facility with foreign languages led a few Jews to become translators and work as Indian agents. In an area dominated by agriculture, some merchants purchased plantations usually as secondary sources of income. Such purchases symbolized upward mobility.

During the colonial era and thereafter, Jews mixed their merchandising expertise with agriculture and became innovators. Moses Lindo facilitated South Carolina indigo production. In Florida Moses Elias Levy experimented with sugar production as did the Kempner family in Texas. Raphael J. Moses introduced peach sales to the Georgia marketplace. The Levy and Kempner families also illustrate the roles of Jews in land development, railroads, and finance.[7]

1800 TO THE 1880s

Second- and third-generation Jews acculturated and aspired to upper-class status. Ashkenazim intermarried with Sephardim and, although in the majority, accepted Sephardic rites, with some even claiming the seemingly superior Sephardic lineage. Scions of early families attained a level of culture, education, and affluence that allowed many to become professionals. Jews became doctors and lawyers and ran private educational academies. In Charleston Isaac Harby achieved acclaim as a journalist and literary critic, and Penina Möise wrote as the first American Jewish woman poet.[8]

The ascension of these Jacksonian Jews had several ramifications. Few in number, scions of the colonial settlers chose between intermarriage, marriage within their group, or life as single individuals. In a tolerant society non-Jews of their class saw them as worthy partners, and many traveled the first path. Children of intermarriages were often raised as Christians and later generations were lost to the faith. Those marrying within the fold established the ranks of the first Jewish families of America. Transcending regional boundaries, these familial bonds were augmented during the 1850s with Jewish immigrants who had begun arriving in the 1820s but who had to acculturate and rise in status before being viewed as eligible partners.[9]

Newcomers came from the Germanic states and Alsace-Lorraine and, in lesser numbers, from Poland, England, and eastern Europe. Chain migration patterns replicated by later immigrants dominated so that Jewish communities in towns and small cities were typically composed of a few extended families and people from the same areas in Europe. National identity remained important as Jews from Alsace and Lorraine moved to Louisiana and the Mississippi Delta, where the French culture was strong, and those from the Germanic states interacted with fellow Germans, especially in Texas but really throughout the South. Germania societies proliferated, and Jews organized English-Hebrew-German academies.[10]

The webs of family and place of origin facilitated business and mobility. Starting as peddlers and small shopkeepers or arriving with sufficient resources and contacts to open larger businesses, Jews spread out with westward expansion. As exemplified by the Seligmans and Lehmans, they obtained credit from Jewish wholesalers in Baltimore, Cincinnati, New York, and New Orleans, became financiers, and formed partnerships, which included the creation of satellite stores in surrounding communities and across regions. Jews relocated frequently as some areas declined and others showed potential because of new land development, the building of railroads, or the opening of natural resources.[11]

Acculturation and economic mobility in a relatively tolerant environment facilitated participation in civic and political life. Jews joined others in charitable societies and won election as sheriffs, city councilmen, and in numerous other local offices. They worked prominently in state common councils during the American Revolution. Joseph Henry was even elected to the North Carolina legislature before restrictions were removed. David Levy Yulee, a pivotal figure in Florida statehood, became its first United States senator. Henry Hyams became lieutenant governor of Louisiana, and Judah P. Benjamin and Benjamin Franklin Jonas served that state in the United States Senate.

Although the newcomers brought a reinfusion of tradition, lacking powerful rabbinic authorities to either thwart or encourage their path, Jacksonian Jews sought change. Americanized, educated Jews on the rise encouraged Charleston's K.K. Beth Elohim to improve decorum in the service and undertake other reforms to align Jewish practices more closely with middle-class Protestant norms. Aware of similar reforms in Europe, Charlestonian changes paralleled these more than they were influenced by them. Rebuffed by the congregation, the reformers established the Reform Society of Israelites and composed the first Reform prayer book. Although women were not in positions of power, their participation was manifested in numerous decisions. Ultimately, the separate society dissolved and the congregation accepted reforms under Reverend Gustavus Poznanski. Yet reform was wrought with further division. The first traditional congregation to split from a reforming synagogue, Shearith Israel, formed when Beth Elohim installed an organ.[12]

From the 1820s Charleston gradually declined economically while Baltimore rose during the 1840s and 1850s. Its Jewish community followed the same trajectory. With a larger and more robust Jewish population, Baltimore succeeded Charleston as a center of Reform and innovation. The first ordained rabbi in America fought a rearguard battle for tradition and rabbinic authority in that border city, which housed the first congregation in America, started as what was perceived at the time as Reform. But Reform at Baltimore's Har Sinai Verein, like Reform under Poznanski, was transmitted from Hamburg, which became a model for both lay- and rabbinic-led change in American congregations. Radical reformer David Einhorn was welcomed to the congregation's pulpit until his abolitionist views brought him into danger. Baltimore, like New York and Philadelphia, continued to house Orthodox congregations and even a quasi-Conservative rabbi and congregation called the city home.[13]

In the decades before the Civil War, Charleston, Baltimore, Richmond, and New Orleans functioned as centers, as did Philadelphia and Cincinnati, in a complex matrix. With Charleston's decline, Jews moved to Columbia, South Carolina, New Orleans, Louisiana, Galveston, Texas, and San Francisco, California, and helped found peripheral congregations. Har Sinai Verein of Baltimore members transmitted their congregation's rites to Wheeling in western Virginia. Members of the Harby, Labatt, Dyer, and Hyams families from these cities crossed back and forth moving frontiers. North Carolina's Jewish enclaves "tended to be colonial outposts of . . . the places of first settlement." Peddlers and shopkeepers went to Baltimore, Cincinnati, Philadelphia, and New York for merchandise that nationalized southern tastes. They also returned with ideas of religious development and spouses who extended the family/business network.[14]

Organizations and rabbis/reverends acted as agents of the network. Leeser, Isaac M. Wise, and Rebecca Gratz, the most important institution builders of nineteenth-century Jewry, exemplify the national model for local events. Educational curriculum, prayer books, and personal newspapers with correspondents reporting on local events were but the most formal instruments of national communication, even in the absence of organized union in a factious land. Leeser and Wise traveled the South officiating at weddings and other events, and used the occasions to encourage the creation and expansion of congregations. Southern Jews actively participated in and followed the national conferences aimed to forge union that ultimately attempted to define Reform. They joined Wise's Union of American Hebrew Congregations and sent money to his rabbinical seminary, Hebrew Union College. Gratz's Sunday schools, curriculum materials, and Hebrew ladies benevolent societies spread to Charleston, Savannah, and Kentucky, through her family members and friends, and from those cities throughout the South. The sense of sisterhood engendered was a palpable tool for networking.

Like the men's benevolent societies, the women sent funds to the needy and to institutions throughout the country. Besides raising money for their own congregations, they routinely allocated donations to others building sanctuaries. Correspondence and visits fostered camaraderie and further overcame provincialism. B'nai B'rith lodges and other fraternities played similar roles besides reinforcing networks through national conferences. The first Jewish orphans' and widows' home in America was founded in New Orleans during the 1850s in response to yellow fever epidemics. The home and ultimately B'nai B'rith's district orphanages drew national support and clients from peripheral communities.[15]

Indeed philanthropy acted as a major tool of identity, unity, and organizational development. After accumulating wealth in New Orleans, Rhode Island-born Jacob Touro bequeathed his fortune to synagogues and other Jewish institutions in the United States and Palestine. Rosanna Dyer Osterman moved from Baltimore to Texas and conducted business so successfully after her husband's death that she was able to follow Touro's lead with major bequests to create new and support existing congregations and benevolent societies in far-flung communities.[16]

Rabbinic power and religious practices were in a muddled state during the middle decades of the nineteenth century. Lacking an ordained rabbinate, congregations had acclimated to lay governance. Congregations hired ordained and less formally trained religious leaders who frequently came into conflict with recalcitrant laymen. Friction over the nature and degree of Reform and tradition exacerbated tensions as one faction or the other wrestled control. Consequently a peripatetic clergy crossing sectional lines became the rule. A few rabbis and laymen also edited regional newspapers to supplement national Jewish media coverage. In 1885 rabbis in the South, emulating a New York-based organization, created a union that served as a precursor of the Central Conference of American Rabbis, the national organization of Reform rabbis. These happenings were made possible by communications across regional lines and, in turn, facilitated them.[17]

Compared to European communal control, American Judaism lacked formal unity and structure. Nonetheless national and international events precipitated significant interaction among Jews and a sense of identity as a people transcending national borders. Protestations against the Swiss Treaty, the Damascus incident, and the Mortara affair occurred haphazardly, but illustrated communications between individuals and congregations and the integral part played by Jews in the South. Scion of colonial businessmen of the Atlantic world and hazanim in New York, Philadelphia, and Richmond, Gershom Kursheedt, who had been influenced by Leeser and who, in turn, influenced Touro, represented American congregations in negotiations with the Vatican in the last incident along with Sir Moses Montefiore. As joint executors of Touro's bequests, Kursheedt and Montiore, tied by family bonds, also traveled to the Holy Land to distribute *tzedakah* (communal charity) and found a hospital. James K. Guttheim, a Reform rabbi for synagogues in Cincinnati and New York, worked with traditionalist Kursheedt in

New Orleans in the protest and in behalf of the New Orleans Jewish Widows and Orphans Home. Guttheim helped establish the Board of Delegates of American Israelites, a direct result of the ineffectiveness of the Mortara protest and the first long-term national American Jewish organization.[18]

The Board of Delegates began on the eve of the Civil War, and southerners attended the first meeting in New York in 1860. Although the organization did not unify all of American Jewry, it stands in stark contrast to the Methodist, Baptist, and Presbyterian denominations that had already divided along sectional lines. Yet differences existed. Most Jews shared opinions on slavery, secession, and the Civil War with other southerners, just as Jews in the North conformed to the positions of their adopted region. A few among an elite fought duels of honor, but a larger though still small group manumitted slaves and lived with African Americans in family relationships, practices not necessarily at variance with those of their gentile counterparts.[19]

However, adaptation typically had an ethnically Jewish slant. Although Jewish slave ownership reflected that of others in similar positions, the high percentage of Jews involved in commerce, uncharacteristic of their non-Jewish neighbors, meant that the majority of Jews who owned slaves did so in the cities rather than on small farms and plantations. Jews and those of Jewish descent prominent in politics, even as they supported the region and however much they had assimilated, had to defend themselves against antisemitic attacks. Robert Rosen finds that the typical Jewish Confederate was a recent German immigrant who peddled or worked in a dry goods store in Louisiana and who was better educated and more cosmopolitan than the usual private. Although Jews had served in the military and some even pursued military careers, as city dwellers employed in merchandising they were less likely to join the cavalry and more likely to become commissary officers than other southerners. Regardless of sectional divisions that rent some families apart, numerous stories are told of Jews helping Jews across regions or traveling to the North for safety. During Reconstruction and thereafter some Jewish women participated in Confederate memorial associations, even serving as officers. The few Jewish Republicans who participated in Reconstruction notwithstanding, congregations like Richmond's Beth Ahabah, which established Confederate burial memorial areas in their cemeteries, more closely reflected southern Jewish opinion. Yet after the war Hebrew benevolent societies, congregations, and other Jewish organizations concentrated on their missions and hardly otherwise mentioned Reconstruction and the Lost Cause.[20] None of these provisos negate the identity of Jews in the South with the South. Rather they place that identity in the perspective of Jewish history.

Indeed in many ways the war and its aftermath exerted a decidedly different impact on Jews than other southerners because of the disproportionate propensity of Jews to be urban merchants. Although Louisiana boasted numerous die-hard Jewish Confederates, in Tennessee and Texas the arrival of federal troops during the war led to the rapid resumption of business with prewar Jewish associates in the North. Jewish soldiers returned to clerk or run businesses. Although the southern economy was shattered, and this influenced trade and profit, resumption of the road to middle-class status for Jews appears to have been rapid. Jewish business and financial ties assisted the rebuilding of the southern credit system through the medium of Jewish storekeepers and wholesale houses. Northern Jewish financiers with ties to European Jewish banking firms and to fellow Jews in the South helped finance the rebuilding and expansion of the southern railroad system.[21]

The growth of cities and the economic initiative of Jewish merchants contributed to the transformation of the specialized dry goods store into the giant department store. Jewish, family-owned department stores with innovative merchandising techniques dominated retail streets in almost every small town and city. They were joined by Jewish-owned jewelry and hardware stores and, by the 1880s and 1890s, Jewish-owned factories like Fulton Bag and Cotton in Atlanta and Cone Mills in North Carolina. Like their non-Jewish counterparts, Jewish factory owners built company housing, stores, schools, and churches, employed spies to oversee employee actions, and opposed unionization. In Galveston and along the Mississippi River towns, Jews worked as cotton and sugar jobbers and factors, occupations dating to the antebellum era. In fact, diversity marked the Jewish businesses that epitomized the New South Creed.[22]

As successful businessmen who valued education, and efficient, ethical government, Jews helped establish and won election as officers of hospitals, school systems, chambers of commerce, and music associations. Jews served as progressive mayors of numerous southern cities, and Isaac Kempner fostered the Galveston managerial plan of government copied widely by many municipalities. Because Jews tended to reside in ethnic clusters, their concentrated voting strength and contributions led to "Jewish seats" on schools boards, city councils, and later draft boards in some locations, although they were a tiny minority of the general population. Besides civic improvements, they opposed Sunday blue laws, prayer in the public schools, and high school reading of the *Merchant of Venice* with its antisemitic caricature of Shylock, all illustrating identity as Jews.[23]

These Jews were not all old-time southerners and their descendents. Jews from other parts of the country, many because of exposure to the South during the war, flocked to southern cities after the war. They quickly and easily integrated into the Jewish business, social, and religious scene. The lack of Civil War or Reconstruction antagonism between old and new residents is remarkable until one recognizes the continuing impact of Jewish networks and the fact that they shared national background and other attributes.

With increased population, the size and number of B'nai B'rith lodges and benevolent societies increased dramatically. A wave of congregation creation and ultimately sanctuary building washed over the South from about 1868 through the 1890s. Although much of this represented rejuvenation of existing Jewish communities from in-migration, many congregations began in secondary areas of Jewish residence. Instead of going through the conflict-ridden stage of tradition versus Reform, these communities, from Anniston, Alabama to Dallas, Texas, started with Reform temples without debate. They had already learned their lessons the hard way in the core communities.[24]

Many women had worked side by side with their husbands in the small shops or ran businesses, if their husbands died before the war, and continued to do so in its aftermath. Yet upper- and middle-class status for Jewish and gentile women alike translated into limited roles and options within the household. Ladies benevolent societies provided an outlet that gradually pressed boundaries in the postbellum decades. This may have been especially true for southern Jewish women who did not want or have the outlets of missionary or temperance societies open to Protestant women. Male concentration on business also nurtured a tiny vacuum in many congregations, especially in small Jewish communities. Through their initiative or as a result of entreaties by their husbands, Jewish women became major fund-raisers for building and maintaining congregation structures and even pressured the men to act. Fund-raising acumen led to inroads in terms of influence and, occasionally, congregation decision making.[25]

The benevolent societies laid the groundwork for the later sisterhoods, the National Council of Jewish Women, and activism that belies the image of southern Jewish parochialism and hesitancy to challenge the status quo. Sections of the NCJW spread rapidly through the South as young rabbis trained at Hebrew Union College filled southern pulpits, solidified Reform, and encouraged the women's efforts. Rabbis from outside who married local women from established families gained acceptance and support by doing so. Marriage ties again forged alliances. The NCJW pressed women's boundaries further than the benevolent societies by expanding lobbying efforts, reaching out to others in need among newly arrived eastern European Jews and the general population, working with secular women's societies, and sponsoring conferences and educational programs for members. Free kindergartens and social settlements designed to Americanize immigrants and combat proselytizing typified activities. Jewish women in Atlanta, Memphis, and Goldsboro, North Carolina, as elsewhere, were committed leaders in the drive for passage of the women's suffrage constitutional amendment. Thereafter they actively participated in the League of Women Voters and the interwar women's league for peace and disarmament.

The women's activities fit in line with those of the rabbis who became ambassadors to the gentiles and emphasized the prophetic Jewish social gospel of the Pittsburgh Platform of 1885. Variations abounded. Max Heller of New Orleans fought urban corruption, opposed lynching, and supported Zionism. Preferring the title *doctor* to *rabbi*, most opposed Zionism, espoused social reforms including education and implementations of the findings of social work experts, and were moderates concerning black rights and unions. Morris Newfield of

Birmingham generally fit this profile but limited his support for workers' rights because of community and congregation pressures. From his Galveston pulpit, Henry Cohen became the major southern agent for immigrant relocation from New York into the heartland. Unlike their predecessors, these men usually held their pulpits—and power—for decades. They were also cosmopolitan, highly educated, well-read men of culture who traveled frequently, created and led local Jewish and secular organizations, remained cognizant of and active on behalf of national and international Jewish causes, and conducted extensive correspondence. Like Jewish club men and women in the South, their networks spanned the nation.[26]

The rabbis who held national positions in the Reform movement and helped found and lead organizations like the American Jewish Historical Society worked with laymen illustrated by Texan Leo N. Levi who presided over B'nai B'rith, and lobbied Washington on policies affecting Jews overseas. While the American Jewish Committee remained an elite, selective organization centered in New York and Philadelphia, it included southerners like Levi and later Coca-Cola lead attorney and Atlantan Harold Hirsch.

Although many Protestant churches in the region espoused evangelicalism, eschewed the social gospel, and maintained their patriarchy, Reform temples emphasized rationalism, social activism, and limited feminization of the synagogue, as they simultaneously rejected traditional ceremonies, customs, rituals, and what today would be called spirituality. The actions of Reform Jews in the South, reflecting the middle-/upper-class background and values of their members, were more aligned with their northern Jewish and Christian counterparts and the minority of Christians in the South who shared their urban/commercial values. Yet they still differed with the latter over such issues as temperance and Sunday blue laws.

Immigration of eastern European Jews into the region increased dramatically after 1881. Family and *landsleit* chain migration patterns dominated location choice even when agents of the Industrial Removal Office, Hebrew Immigrant Aid Society, and Galveston movement relocated people from New York into the heartland.[27] The experiences of this immigrant cohort reflected that of their counterparts throughout America in similar environments. Less educated, poorer, Orthodox, Zionist, Yiddish-speaking, and beginning the process of acculturation, they differed dramatically from their already established brethren. Shared religious identity and immigration background drew them together and almost everything else set the two apart.

The newcomers established a parallel infrastructure with variations between urban and small-town environments. Cities from Atlanta and Baltimore to New Orleans and Memphis, where the Jewish populations exceeded one thousand, housed ethnic clusters in which Yiddish culture, ethnic businesses, and multiple congregations and associated institutions flourished. Many congregations were formed by people from the same European locale, others by people who arrived in the early 1900s because members of synagogues formed during the 1880s and 1890s had already begun to acculturate and rise economically. Widespread Anshi S'fard synagogues, many of whose members came from Romania and surrounding areas, followed the mystical rite of Isaac Luria of Safed, Palestine. Split-off congregations and mergers were more the rule than the exception.[28]

Forces of movement and rejuvenation played out in the small towns as they had since the colonial era. The Columbia, South Carolina Jewish community virtually moved away with the Civil War but was reborn with new people in the war's aftermath. "German" Jews who had found success in small towns retired to larger Jewish communities in the decades around 1900, but the small communities were either reinvigorated or entirely reconstituted when east Europeans restarted the process. Constant in- and out-migration continued through the twentieth century, and ethnic population clusters even developed in smaller Orthodox enclaves like Knoxville. The single Orthodox congregations in small towns often relied on survival mechanisms. These included sharing facilities and even rabbis with Reform Jews whose congregation's existence was also precarious. Women again served as a driving force behind congregations, even providing Torah scrolls.[29]

Twentieth-century survival mechanisms for Reform and Orthodox Jews in far-flung areas included the use of circuit-riding rabbis, the creation of statewide Jewish federations, as in Arkansas where local communities could not support their own agencies, the Texas Kallal of Rabbis (an association that brought together rabbis regularly for intellectual stimulation and camaraderie),[30] and the North Carolina Association of Jewish Women (with laymen's and rabbinic offshoots) that claimed to be the first state institution of its kind to transcend denominational differences.

Peripheral communities also depended on larger centers. Orthodox rabbis like Tobias Geffen in Atlanta provided Talmudic decisions and kosher food, supervised religious courts, and conducted ceremonies for traditionalists across state lines. Reform and Orthodox congregations and auxiliary organizations including sisterhoods provided services and drew people from surrounding communities unable to support their own institutions.[31]

Eastern European Jews in the cities tended to live near African Americans. Their grocery stores, secondhand clothing, pawn, and liquor businesses served poor blacks and whites much as they had as peddlers. These people started their rise up the economic ladder using kin and *landsleit* ties, obtaining small loans from free loan associations, borrowing from Morris Plan banks where two character references substituted for collateral, and gradually investing in real estate. Socialism, communism, and labor unionism were topics of debate rather than actual pursuits, and the Arbeiter Ring/Workmen's Circle was known for Yiddish schools rather than overt activism, since few Jews in the South worked in factories and the capitalist marketplace provided an enticing lure.

Beginning in 1906, Ashkenazim were joined by Sephardim from the Ottoman Empire in Atlanta and Montgomery. Their Ladino language, music, liturgy, and even foodways were so different that other Jews questioned whether they were brethren. These immigrants, who lived near Greeks, opened grocery stores, fruit stands, delicatessens, and hat, shoe, and clothing businesses, besides their own Jewish institutions.[32]

Jewish benevolence had been geared to self-help for people with common national background. By the late nineteenth century demand among this group had declined in line with its economic rise. Now the needs of the newcomers were addressed by a myriad of agencies including Jewish education alliances. "German" Jewish aid typically stressed Americanization and was given in patronizing fashion. Following in Boston's steps, federations of Jewish social services formed in virtually every southern city during the first decades of the twentieth century. The established Jews attempted to centralize fund-raising, rationalize the delivery of services, and switch from direct volunteer intervention to professional service providers. Nonetheless, representatives of the different subgroups served on federation boards, and interaction, in spite of clashes, gradually eroded differences.[33]

An event that clearly shattered the image of Jewish acceptance in the South, and one of the most notorious episodes of antisemitism in American history, is the Leo Frank case. From the perspectives of this essay the case takes on new meaning. Born in Texas but raised in New York, Frank managed a relative's pencil factory in Atlanta. Married to a member of the Jewish establishment, Frank became president of the local B'nai B'rith shortly after his arrival. Thus his life illustrated both the movement of Jews across sectional lines and the impact of networks. When a young female employee was found murdered in the factory basement, Frank was falsely accused and convicted of the crime. Governor John Slaton commuted the sentence to life in prison, but Frank was subsequently kidnapped from the penitentiary and lynched. Frank symbolized a transplanted northern Jewish businessman out to exploit poor white womanhood to those who hated him. But, to the American Jewish community, he was one of their own, and his struggle for justice was theirs. Petitions and letters from throughout the country flooded the governor, and Jews in New York and Chicago provided direct aid. That the avalanche of support compounded the anger of southerners and likely even hurt his cause reinforces the fact that the sense of peoplehood made the reaction logical, and the networks made it possible. The Frank case led to the formation of the Anti-Defamation League and the reborn Ku Klux Klan, both representing the impact of events in the South on the national stage.[34]

Was it an aberration or just a dramatic manifestation of long term antisemitism? Undoubtedly, Jews in the South found a tolerant environment compared to Jews in Europe or African Americans. A small minority that made substantial contributions and did not compete with other groups economically, Jews found acceptance in business, government and civic affairs, and, with few exceptions until the late nineteenth century, society. Some argue that prejudice against blacks shielded Jews and that acceptance was purchased at the cost of acculturation to southern mores and silence in the face of social injustices. On the other hand, Jews had to fight for passage of the Maryland Jew Bill, and North Carolina did not grant full political rights until 1868, the next to last state to do so. Jews had to contend with antisemitic attacks on numerous occasions and were murdered in Florida and Tennessee during Reconstruction partly as a consequence of prejudice. Terms like *Jew store* were commonly used and, regardless of how completely individuals attempted to assimilate, they were still thought of as Jews. Radical fringe groups and individuals found ready audiences in the South. Jewish autobiographers and interviewees usually remark about the lack of antisemitism they experienced during much of the twentieth century but also comment about incidents of insensitivity and prejudice and living in a separate social world.[35] With all the exceptions and counteracting evidence and arguments, perhaps a nuanced conclusion that Jews were both relatively tolerated, if not accepted, and yet also often felt marginalized is as close as the historian can get. The Frank case thus stands out as an unusual manifestation of a dangerous, usually subdued undercurrent. It also showed that Jews of all persuasions could be lumped together in the gentile mind.

The decline of immigration with World War I and the exclusionary laws of the 1920s led to an era of acculturation. What were then called modern Orthodox rabbis, like Harry Epstein at Atlanta's Ahavath Achim, conducted Talmudic discourses for the traditionalists and gave English-language sermons for their children and the more Americanized first generation. These rabbis raised the interest in and quality of Jewish education for the youth and adults, led Zionist programs, and participated in ecumenical activities. Influenced by Rabbi Mordecai Kaplan, professor at the Jewish Theological Seminary, they viewed Judaism as a civilization and culture. From the late 1930s into the 1950s many such rabbis, including Epstein and Abraham J. Mesch of Birmingham's Beth-El, led their congregations into the Conservative movement. However much they may have followed Orthodoxy personally, these rabbis saw few practical differences between their programs and the observance of ritual among their congregants and the programs and practices of Conservative congregations and their members. Although the next decades proved them wrong, they believed that Orthodoxy was doomed. They did not want their congregants to depart too far from Judaism, so the rabbis eased their members' way into a branch of Judaism that seemed to fit better with their needs.[36]

Southern Jews moved to new suburbs and brought their institutions with them as ethnic clustering continued. They played cards and fielded sports teams as well as creating country clubs and mechanisms for Jewish youth to interact and find partners. The latter included summer camps, affiliation with national Jewish youth groups, the formation of Jewish college fraternity and sorority chapters, and the holding of Falcon, Jubilee, Hollyday, and Ballyhoo-type events in which young people socialized at dances and picnics.[37] Jews lived in a parallel social universe to their Christian counterparts and still divided among themselves. Scions of old and new immigrants maintained separate country clubs, Harmonie/Concordia/Standard Clubs were for the German Jews and Progressive Clubs for the east Europeans, and Zionist groups failed to attract many old timers. Hadassah proved the exception as Jewish women, regardless of background, were drawn to the organization's humanitarian mission in Palestine.

Economic success was marked by diversity during these and later decades. Jewish-owned department stores lined downtown streets. Jewish men attained national offices in professional associations and Jewish women worked as lawyers, teachers, and social workers. Family and religious ties remained the foundation of numerous enterprises as exemplified by Zale's jewelry stores, the *Chattanooga* and *New York Times* of the Ochs family, and twentieth-century conglomerate National Service Industries.[38]

The Depression and World War II only temporarily derailed gains. Void of a working class, perhaps Jews in the South weathered the Depression better than Jewish workers in industrial centers. Rabbis accepted salary cuts, pledge went unpaid, and Jewish building infrastructure was neglected. Charter members of community chests, during the 1930s successful Jewish institutions often shared their leaders with those charities. New Deal agencies freed Jewish social service organizations from the relief burden and mission. Following contemporary trends, foster care replaced Hebrew orphans' homes. Preparedness and entrance into the world war included the expansion of military facilities, which contributed to economic recovery. It also brought Jewish military personnel from elsewhere in the United States who were catered to by their Jewish hosts and returned as spouses and business partners after the war.

The rise of Hitler, the Third Reich persecution of European Jewry, and the creation of Israel directly impacted southern Jewish community structures and missions. Jewish social service federations reorganized, especially during the mid to late 1930s and again after the war. The first transformation occurred to unify fund-raising on behalf of European Jews and to concentrate efforts to combat antisemitism at home and abroad. The second reflected new realities and desire for community control. With the exception of assistance and Americanization for Holocaust survivors and refugees, charity for local Jews was now perceived as a minor need. Improvements in Jewish education for adults and children, rebuilding the long-neglected infrastructure, and moving from Jewish education alliances to community centers and from Hebrew orphans' homes to family and vocation services became core local missions. Homes for senior citizens also expanded dramatically as multigenerational family housing patterns changed. Nationally recognized experts were hired, and every move was analyzed and planned. Urban Jewish population studies and community calendars became normative.

Congregations built new facilities in almost every city. Overseas relief to Jews remaining in Europe was quickly overshadowed with support for Israel, and fundraising campaigns skyrocketed.

Structural and mission changes illustrated new and old patterns. Southern Jews held offices in virtually every national Jewish organization, participating in and hosting conventions. Centers like Atlanta housed state and regional headquarters of national groups and provided expertise to peripheral communities. Through these networks Jews in the South both followed and led national models. Whereas individual laypeople and Reform rabbis formerly dominated decision making, organization building, and spokesperson roles, now numerous individuals from the various subcommunities came forward, and federation executives solidified their hegemony. Although anti-Zionism remained strong within some Reform circles, as illustrated by support for the American Council for Judaism, Hitler's persecution of European Jewry, the entrance of Jews of east European descent into the Reform rabbinate, the Reform movement's acceptance of Zionism in the Columbus Platform (1937), and the rise of Israel lowered barriers between subcommunities. Differences over socioeconomic, education, and charity-giving levels and language disappeared, and marriages between children of the subcommunities further eroded former divisions.

Patterns in towns and smaller cities varied. Military spending and migration of northern Jews after the war translated into temporary renewal. But children who went away to college found economic opportunity and spouses in cities. Cities and suburbs also drew retirees who sought enhanced Jewish life and culture or moved to be nearer to children. The rise of national chain stores and federated department store ownership, suburban malls, credit card companies, and fallout from civil rights demonstrations marked the decline of small-town and, gradually too, inner-city Jewish life.

Nonetheless, counteracting forces were also at work. Internal migrations benefited suburban growth in southern and northern communities. During the last thirty-five years small Jewish communities succumbed to declining economic opportunity as suburbs flourished, but smaller communities also rose or expanded. South Florida proved the harbinger of future dynamics. With air conditioning and the end of discriminatory policies, Miami became a haven for northern vacationers and retirees. The Jewish population expanded exponentially along southeastern Florida, as it has in resort and retirement areas from the coastal islands to the Appalachians. The migrants both created a market for medical facilities manned by Jewish physicians and located where such facilities already existed. The North Carolina Research Triangle and the academic rise of southern universities drew Jewish academics with different ideas of Jewish community. The decline of the Snowbelt economy and rise of the Sunbelt coupled with the Americanization of Dixie brought young, educated northern Jews along the well-traveled path south.[39]

The civil rights movement exerted substantial impact on events. It engendered the movement of some Jews away from what they perceived as reactionary communities, the southern migration of northerners by making the South a more acceptable environment, and the creation of an egalitarian South more hospitable also to native southern Jews. The relationship between blacks and Jews in the region can best be described using historian Arnold Shankman's phrase, ambivalent friendship. Jews owned slaves and supported the Confederacy, but also conducted business with African Americans on a respectful basis. Divergence from the southern norm reflected a shared sense of historical prejudice, prophetic social justice, and generated profit as well. Rabbi Max Heller opposed lynching and segregation as early as the 1890s in New Orleans. Rabbi David Marx advocated reason, law, and order in the wake of the Atlanta race riot of 1906. During the 1920s and 1930s Jews joined the Urban League, and mayor Arnold Bernstein emphasized a policy of toleration and rights in Monroe, Louisiana. Dora Sterne in Montgomery and Morris Abram from Fitzgerald, Georgia exemplified those who opposed the poll tax and advocated equality. Harry Golden of the *Carolina Israelite*, Sylvan Meyer of the Gainesville [Georgia] *Times*, and Louis Jaffe of the Norfolk *Virginian-Pilot* won renown as crusading journalists. In Durham, North Carolina and Keystone, West Virginia blacks and Jews even formed close political and economic relationships on a relatively equitable basis. During the heyday of the civil rights movement, although some Jews accepted southern racial mores and even became ardent segregationists like Charles Bloch of Georgia and Solomon Blatt of South Carolina, the majority belonged to the moderate camp, and a minority openly advocated black rights.[40]

Jewish responses to the civil rights movement represented continuity of national networks and leadership as well as perhaps the greatest example of breakdown. Among the activists, many southern rabbis and especially Jewish women supported desegregation, equitable rights, and keeping open the schools. Some were smeared with the communist label, threats were made, and temples bombed. The fear was so palpable that rabbis were warned to remain silent, and some lost pulpits. The relationship between blacks and Jews from the mid-1960s into the 1970s was strained on the national and local level, but black-Jewish coalition organizations appeared by the early 1980s. Although influenced by southern mores and residence in the region and differing on tactics with northern Jews, southern Jewish opinion tended to be closer to the views of their coreligionists on civil rights and other cosmopolitan issues than typical southern whites. Rabbis, including Jacob Rothschild in Atlanta and Charles Mantinband in Mississippi, emerged as respected national leaders, but even they preferred working behind the scenes to marching and demonstrating and questioned the tactics of national Jewish organizations. A few congregations left national Jewish organizations, in protest of what they saw as outside agitation that could precipitate antisemitic repercussions, and many more cringed at what they perceived as a lack of understanding on the part of northern Jews for the precarious position of Jews in the South. For their part, northern Jews and national Jewish organizations found it difficult to comprehend the inaction and reactions of so many of their southern brethren.

Other events since the 1960s return the southern experience to the national mold. Immigrants from Cuba, Iran, Russia, South Africa, and Israel have joined northern migrants and southerners, creating diverse congregations and newly braided identities where economic opportunity and freedom beckoned.[41] Advocacy for Russian refuseniks and Israel's wars for survival illustrated continuing senses of peoplehood and comfort that Jews in America and the South have felt since the colonial era. Southern rabbis have headed each of the denominational rabbinic associations. Since the 1980s Jewish women have become presidents of congregations and federations, executives of Jewish institutions, rabbis, and cantors. Dramatic increases in day schools, *havurot*, Chabad centers, ritual observance even within Reform congregations, philanthropy, concern for Israel, and national and international networks have marked the last decades of southern Jewish history as have high rates of intermarriage and secularization and low rates of affiliation. With these trends and more, Jews in the South join Jews elsewhere.

When Jews from different areas meet, they play Jewish geography. Not unusually they identify common friends and relatives. The intricate networks of families, businesses, organizations, meetings, camps, social clubs, travel, and newspapers link people together. In the region perhaps most likely to divide Jew from Jew, the networks have also meant that Jewish life and experience frequently mirrored and led national norms to a remarkable extent.

NOTES

1. Eli N. Evans, *The Provincials: A Personal History of the Jews in the South* (New York, 1998 [1973]).

2. Lee Shai Weissbach, "Kentucky's Jewish History in National Perspective: The Era of Mass Migration," *Filson Club Historical Quarterly* 69 (July 1995): 255–74; Mark K. Bauman, *The Southerner as American, Jewish Style* (Cincinnati, 1996). Some themes expanded in this essay were outlined in Mark K. Bauman, "Perspectives: History from a Variety of Vantage Points," *American Jewish History* 90 (March 2002): 3–12. See also Mark K. Bauman, "The Flowering of Interest in Southern Jewish History," in Corrie E. Norman and Don S. Armentrout, eds., *Religion in the Contemporary South* (Knoxville, 2005), 159–90; Mark K. Bauman, ed, *Dixie Diaspora: An Anthology of Southern Jewish History* (Tuscaloosa, 2006). Presentations at the October 2003 conference of the Southern Jewish Historical Society by Micah Greenstein and at the April 2003 conference of the Organization of American Historians by Leonard Dinnerstein stimulated my thought concerning the rejuvenating force of migration from small towns to cities, and from North to South, respectively. I also benefited greatly from conversations with Leonard Rogoff concerning contemporary growth in small towns and cities and migrations.

3. Bertram Wallace Korn, *The Early Jews of New Orleans* (Waltham, MA, 1969), *The Jews of Mobile, Alabama, 1763–1841* (Cincinnati, 1970), and "Jews in Eighteenth-Century West Florida," in Samuel Proctor, ed., *Eighteenth-Century Florida: Life on the Frontier* (Gainesville, 1976), 50–59; Malvina W. Liebman, *Jewish Frontiersmen: Historical Highlights of Early South Florida Jewish Communities* (Miami Beach, 1979); Chris Monaco, *Moses Levy of Florida* (Baton Rouge, 2005); Natalie Ornish, *Pioneer Jewish Texans, 1590–1990* (Dallas, 1989); Samuel Proctor, "Pioneer Jewish Settlement in Florida, 1765–1900," *Proceedings of the Conference on the Writing of Regional History in the South* (Miami, 1956); Leo and Evelyn Turitz, *Jews in Early Mississippi* (Jackson, 1983); Ruthe Winegarten and Cathy Schecter, *Deep in the Heart: The Lives and Legends of Texas Jews* (Austin, 1990). Hollace Ava Weiner and Kenneth D. Roseman, eds., *Lone Stars of Texas: The Jews of Texas* (Hanover and London, 2007).

4. For this and following see Saul Jacob Rubin, *Third to None: The Saga of Savannah Jewry* (Savannah, 1983); Mark I. Greenberg, "A 'Haven for Benignity': Conflict and Cooperation Between Eighteenth-Century Savannah Jews," *Georgia Historical Quarterly* 86 (Winter 2002): 544–68.

5. For this and following see James William Hagy, *This Happy Land: The Jews of Colonial and Antebellum Charleston* (Tuscaloosa, 1993); Theodore Rosengarten and Dale Rosengarten, eds., *A Portion of the People: Three Hundred Years of Southern Jewish Life* (Columbia, SC, 2002); Solomon Breibart, "Two Jewish Congregations in Charleston, SC, before 1791: A New Conclusion," *Explorations in Charleston's Jewish History* (Charleston, 2005). Hagy's population tables in chapter 1 depict the varied and changing origins of the population. The largest number of native-born, early Charlestonian Jews hailed from New York, Georgia, Pennsylvania, and Virginia, respectively, but sixteen present and future states were represented including California. The foreign born originated in twenty-one countries and eight Caribbean islands.

6. Eric L. Goldstein, *Traders and Transports: The Jews of Colonial Maryland* (Baltimore, 1993).

7. For Lindo, see Hagy, *This Happy Land*; and Rosengarten and Rosengarten, *A Portion of the People*; Chris Monaco, "A Sugar Utopia on the Florida Frontier: Moses Elias Levy's Pilgrimage Plantation," *Southern Jewish History* 5 (2002): 103–40, *Moses Levy of Florida: Jewish Utopian and Antebellum Reformer* (Baton Rouge, 2005); Harold Hyman, *Oleander Odyssey: The Kempners of Galveston, Texas, 1854–1980s* (College Station, TX, 1990); for Moses, Raphael Jacob Moses, *Last Order of the Lost Cause: The Civil War Memoirs of a Jewish Family from the "Old South,"* ed. Mel Young (Lanham, MD, 1995). See also Gary R. Freeze, "Roots, Barks, Berries and Jews: The Herb Trade in Guilded-Age North Carolina," *Essays in Economic and Business History* 13 (1995): 107–27.

8. On this and following see Myron Berman, *The Last of the Jews?* (Lanham, MD, 1998); Kaye Kole, *The Minis Family of Georgia, 1733–1992* (Savannah, 1992); Emily Bingham, *Mordecai: An Early American Family* (New York, 2003); Jean E. Friedman, *Ways of Wisdom: Moral Education in the Early National Period* (Athens, 2001); Sheldon Hanft, "Mordecai's Female Academy," *American Jewish History* 79 (Autumn 1989): 72–93; Milton M. Gottesman, *Hoopskirts and Huppas: A Chronicle of the Early Years of the Garfunkel-Trager Family in America, 1856–1920* (New York, 1999); Gary Phillip Zola, *Isaac Harby of Charleston, 1788–1828: Jewish Reformer and Intellectual* (Tuscaloosa,

1994); Solomon Breibart, "Penina Möise: Southern Jewish Poetess," in Samuel Proctor and Louis Schmier with Malcolm Stern, eds., *Jews of the South* (Macon, 1984), 31–43. Bingham offers the unusual example of Jews who converted out of conviction. The following discussion of Jacksonian Jews is influenced by Zola and Jonathan D. Sarna, *Jacksonian Jew: The Two Worlds of Mordecai Noah* (New York, 1981). Herein I will use the term loosely and, in fact, Hagy points to the influence of Jeffersonian Republican values on Charleston reformers discussed below.

9. For the concept of the first Jewish families of America, with reference to the South, see Myron Berman, *Richmond's Jewry, 1769–1976: Shabbat in Shockoe* (Charlottesville, 1979); Louis Ginsburg, *History of the Jews of Petersburg, 1789–1950* (Petersburg, 1954).

10. Anny Bloch, "Mercy on Rude Streams: Jewish Immigrants from Alsace-Lorraine to the Lower Mississippi Region and the Concept of Fidelity," *Southern Jewish History* 2 (1999): 81–110; Hollace A. Weiner, *Jewish Stars in Texas: Rabbis and Their Work* (College Station, TX, 1999).

11. Elliott Ashkenazi, *The Business of Jews in Louisiana, 1840–1875* (Tuscaloosa, 1988), "Jewish Commercial Interests Between North and South: The Case of the Lehmans and Seligmans," *American Jewish Archives* 39 (Spring/Summer 1991): 25–39; Hasia Diner, "Entering the Mainstream of Modern Jewish History: Peddlers and the American Jewish South," *Southern Jewish History* 8 (2008): 1–30; Richard Hawkins, "Lynchburg's Swabian Jewish Entrepreneurs in War and Peace," *Southern Jewish History* 3 (2000): 45–82; Morton Rothstein, "Sugar and Secession: A New York Firm in Antebellum Louisiana," *Explorations in Entrepreneurial History* 5 (1968): 115–31; Louis Schmier, "Helloo! Peddler Man! Helloo!" in Jerrell H. Schofner, ed., *Ethnic Minorities in Gulf Coast Society* (Pensacola, 1979), 75–88.

12. Besides Zola, *Isaac Harby of Charleston*; Hagy, *This Happy Land*; and Rosengarten and Rosengarten, *A Portion of the People*, cited above, see Michael Meyer, *Response to Modernity: A History of the Reform Movement in American Judaism* (New York, 1988); Leon Jick, *The Americanization of the Synagogue: 1820–1870* (Hanover, 1992 [1976]); Zola, "The First Reform Prayer Book in America: The Liturgy of the Reform Society of Israelites," in Dana Evan Kaplan, ed., *Platforms and Prayer Books* (Lanham, MD, 2002): 99–118; Robert Liberles, "Conflict Over Reforms: The Case of Beth Elohim, Charleston, South Carolina," in Jack Wertheimer, ed., *The American Synagogue: A Sanctuary Transformed* (Cambridge, 1987), 274–96; Solomon Breibart, *The Rev. Mr. Gustavus Poznanski: First American Jewish Reform Minister* (Charleston, 1979); Allan Tarshish, "The Charleston Organ Case," *American Jewish Historical Quarterly* 54 (July 1965): 411–49.

13. Isaac M. Fein, *The Making of an American Jewish Community: The History of Baltimore Jewry from 1773 to 1920* (Philadelphia, 1971); Abraham Shusterman, *Legacy of a Liberal: The Miracle of Har Sinai Congregation* (Baltimore, 1967); I. Harold Sharfman, *The First Rabbi: Origins of Conflict Between Orthodox and Reform, Jewish Polemic Warfare in Pre–Civil War America* (N.p., 1988); Israel Tabak, "Rabbi Abraham Rice of Baltimore: Pioneer of Orthodox Judaism in America," *Tradition* 7 (Summer 1965): 100–20; Marsha Rozenblit, "Choosing a Synagogue," in Jack Wertheimer, ed., *The American Synagogue: A Sanctuary Transformed* (Cambridge, 1987): 327–63; Israel Goldman, "Henry W. Schneeberger: His Role in American Judaism," *American Jewish Historical Quarterly* 57

(December 1967): 153–90; Abraham J. Karp, "Simon Tuska Becomes a Rabbi," *Publications of the American Jewish Historical Society* 50 (December 1960): 79–97.

14. Leonard Rogoff, *Homelands: Southern Jewish Identity in Durham and Chapel Hill, North Carolina* (Tuscaloosa, 2001), 12, 32 (quotation); Amy Hill Shevitz, "Religious Reforms, the National Road, and the Dismemberment of Virginia: A Study in Cultural Transmission," Fourth Biennial Scholars' Conference on American Jewish History, Denver, June 5, 2000; Belinda Gergel and Richard Gergel, *In Pursuit of the Tree of Life: A History of the Early Jews of Columbia, South Carolina, and the Tree of Life Congregation* (Columbia, SC, 1996).

15. Lance Sussman, *Isaac Leeser and the Making of American Judaism* (Detroit, 1995); Dianne Ashton, *Rebecca Gratz: Woman and Judaism in Antebellum America* (Detroit, 1997); Mark K. Bauman, "Southern Jewish Women and Their Social Service Organizations," *Journal of American Ethnic History* 22 (Spring 2003): 34–78. Much of this and other material is gleaned from state and local histories. See, for example, Steven Hertzberg, *Strangers Within the Gate City: The Jews of Atlanta, 1845–1915* (Philadelphia, 1978); Medora Small Frank, *Five Families and Eight Young Men: Nashville and Her Jewry, 1850–1861* (Nashville, 1962), *Beginnings on Market Street: Nashville and Her Jewry, 1861–1901* (Nashville, 1976); Andrea Greenbaum, ed., *Jews of South Florida* (Waltham, 2005); Martin I. Hinchin, *Fourscore and Eleven: A History of the Jews of Rapides Parish, 1828–1919* (Alexandria, LA, 1984); Marsha Kass, "Jewish Life in Alabama, the Formative Stages," *Alabama Heritage* 36 (Spring 1995): 6–13; Carolyn Gray LeMaster, *A Corner of the Tapestry: A History of the Jewish Experience in Arkansas, 1820s–1990s* (Fayetteville, 1994); Gertrude Phillipsborn, *The History of the Jewish Community of Vicksburg from 1820 to 1968* (Vicksburg, 1969); Ira Rosenwaike, "The First Jewish Settlers in Louisville," *Filson Club Historical Quarterly* 53 (January 1979): 37–44; Melvin I. Urofsky, *Commonwealth and Community: The Jewish Experience in Virginia* (Richmond 1997); *The Story of the Jewish Orphans' Home of New Orleans* (New Orleans, 1905); Anne Rochell Konigsmark, *Isadore Newman School: One Hundred Years* (New Orleans, 2004); Wendy Besmann, "The 'Typical Home Kid Overachievers,'" *Southern Jewish History* 8 (2005): 121–60.

16. Henry Cohen, *One Hundred Years of Texas Jewry* (Dallas, 1936); Rosanna Dyer Osterman biography files, Jacob R. Marcus Center of the American Jewish Archives.

17. Janice R. Blumberg, "Rabbi Alphabet Browne: The Atlanta Years," *Southern Jewish History* 5 (2003): 1–42; Irwin Lachoff, "Rabbi Bernard Illowy: Counter Reformer," *Southern Jewish History* 5 (2003): 43–68; Dana Evan Kaplan, "The Determination of Jewish Identity Below the Mason-Dixon Line," *Journal of Jewish Studies* 52 (Spring 2001): 98–121; Scott M. Langston, "James K. Gutheim as Southern Reform Rabbi, Community Leader, and Symbol," *Southern Jewish History* 5 (2003): 69–102, "Interaction and Identity: Jews and Christians in Nineteenth-Century New Orleans," *Southern Jewish History* 3 (2000): 83–124; Karla Goldman, "The Path to Reform Judaism: An Examination of Religious Leadership in Cincinnati, 1841–1855," *American Jewish History* 90 (March 2002): 35–50 (both Gutheim and Jacob Rosenfeld of Charleston preceded Wise in the pulpit at Cincinnati's B'nai Yeshurun, and their actions in the congregation prepared the way for his acceptance and success); Bryan Stone, "Edgar Goldberg and the *Texas Jewish Herald*: Changing Coverage and Blended Identity," *Southern Jewish History*

7 (2004): 71–108; Louis Schmier, ed., *Reflections on Southern Jewry: The Letters of Charles Wessolowsky, 1878–1879* (Macon 1982); Gary P. Zola, "Southern Rabbis and the Founding of the First National Association of Rabbis," *American Jewish History* 85 (December 1997): 353–72.

18. Jonathan Frankel, *The Damascus Affair: "Ritual Murder," Politics, and the Jews in 1840* (New York, 1997); Bertram W. Korn, *The American Reaction to the Mortara Case, 1858–59* (Cincinnati, 1957); Mark K. Bauman, "Variations on the Mortara Case in Mid-Nineteenth-Century New Orleans," *American Jewish Archives Journal* 60 (2003): 43–58; Eliza R. R. McGraw, *Two Covenants: Representations of Southern Jewishness* (Baton Rouge, 2005); Kenneth Libo and Abigail Kursheedt Hoffman, *The Seixas-Kursheedts and the Rise of American Jewry* (N.p., 2001). The last illustrates the transnational and intercontinental ties of family, business, and religion discussed throughout this essay.

19. Joshua D. Rothman, *Notorious in the Neighborhood: Sex and Families Across the Color Line in Virginia, 1787–1861* (Chapel Hill, 2004); Mark I. Greenberg, "Becoming Southern: The Jews of Savannah, Georgia, 1830–1870," *American Jewish History* 86 (March 1998): 55–75.

20. Robert N. Rosen, *The Jewish Confederates* (Columbia, SC, 2002); Eli Evans, *Judah P. Benjamin, the Jewish Confederate* (New York, 1988); Bertram W. Korn, *American Jewry and the Civil War* (Philadelphia, 1951), *Jews and Negro Slavery in the Old South, 1789–1865* (Elkins Park, 1961); David T. Morgan, "Eugenia Levy Phillips: The Civil War Experiences of a Southern Jewish Woman," in Proctor and Schmier, *Jews of the South*, 95–106, "Philip Phillips, Jurist and Statesman," in Proctor and Schmier, *Jews of the South*, 107–20; Jason H. Silverman, "Stars, Bars, and Foreigners: The Immigrant and the Making of the Confederacy," *Journal of Confederate History* 1 (Fall 1988): 265–85, " 'The Law of the Land Is the Law,' Antebellum Jews, Slavery and the Old South," in Jack Salzman and Cornel West, eds., *Struggles in the Promised Land* (New York, 1997), 73–86, "Ashley Wilkes Revisited: The Immigrant as Slaveholder in the Old South," *Journal of Confederate History* 7 (1991): 123–35; Mel Young, *Where They Lie: A Story of the Jewish Soldiers of the North and South* (Lanham, MD, 1991); Joan M. Johnson, *Southern Ladies, New Women: Race, Region, and Clubwomen in South Carolina, 1890–1930* (Gainesville, 2004).

21. Richard E. Sapon-White, "A Polish Jew on the Florida Frontier and in Occupied Tennessee: Excerpts from the Memoirs of Max White," *Southern Jewish History* 4 (2001): 93–122; Thomas D. Clark, *Pills, Petticoats, and Plows* (Indianapolis, 1944), "The Post-Civil War Economy in the South," *American Jewish Historical Quarterly* 55 (1966); Michael Wayne, *The Reshaping of Plantation Society: The Natchez District, 1860–80* (Urbana, 1990); Rose G. Biderman, *They Came to Stay: The Story of the Jews of Dallas, 1870–1997* (Austin, 2002); Selma S. Lewis, *A Biblical People of the Bible Belt: The Jewish Community of Memphis, Tennessee, 1840s–1960s* (Macon, 1998). On kinship networks and Jews in banking, see Larry Schweikart, *Banking in the American South from the Age of Jackson to Reconstruction* (Baton Rouge, 1987), 213–17.

22. Leon Harris, *Merchant Princes: An Intimate History of the Jewish Families who Built Great Department Stores* (New York, 1979); Don M. Coever and Linda D. Hall, "Neiman-Marcus: Innovators in Fashion and Advertising," *American Jewish Historical Quarterly* 66 (September 1976): 123–36; Leon Joseph Rosenberg, *Sangers': Pioneer Texas*

Merchants (Austin, 1978); Leona Rostenberg, "Portrait from a Family Archive: Leon Dreyfus, 1842–1898," *Manuscripts* 37 (1985): 283–94 (a jeweler, an occupation in which southern Jews played a prominent role); Stephen J. Whitfield, "Commercial Passions: The Southern Jew as Businessman," *American Jewish History* 71 (March 1982): 342–57.

23. Ronald Bayor, "Ethnic Residential Patterns in Atlanta, 1880–1940," *Georgia Historical Quarterly* 63 (Winter 1979): 435–46; Margaret Armbrester, "Samuel Ullman [1840–1924]: Birmingham Progressive," *Alabama Review* 47 (January 1994): 29–43; Mark K. Bauman, "Factionalism and Ethnic Politics in Atlanta: German Jews from the Civil War through the Progressive Era," in Glenn Feldman, ed., *Politics and Religion in the White South* (Knoxville, 2005), 35–56; Canter Brown Jr., *Jewish Pioneers of the Tampa Bay* (Tampa, 1999), "Philip and Morris Dzialynski: Jewish Contributions to the Rebuilding of the New South," *American Jewish Archives* 39 (Spring/Summer 1992): 517–39; Mark I. Greenberg, "Tampa Mayor Herman Glogowski: Jewish Leadership in Gilded Age Florida," in Mark I. Greenberg and Canter Brown Jr., eds., *Florida's Heritage of Diversity: Essays in Honor of Samuel Proctor* (Tallahassee, 1997); Hyman, *Oleander Odyssey*; Gertrude Samet, "Harry Reyner: Individualism and Community in Newport News, Virginia," *Southern Jewish History* 1 (1998): 109–19; Patricia A. Smith, "Rhoda Kaufman: A Southern Progressive's Career, 1913–1956," *Atlanta Historical Bulletin* 18 (Spring/Summer 1973): 43–50; Arlene G. Rotter, "Climbing the Crystal Stair: Annie T. Wise's Success as an Immigrant in Atlanta's Public School System (1872–1925)," *Southern Jewish History* 4 (2001): 45–70; Susan Mayer, "Amelia Greenwald and Regina Kaplan: Jewish Nursing Pioneers," *Southern Jewish History* 1 (1998): 83–108. For southern distinctiveness, see Greenberg, "Becoming Southern"; Charles Joyner, "A Community of Memory; Assimiliation and Identity among the Jews of Georgetown," in *Shared Traditions: Southern History and Folk Culture* (Urbana, 1999), 177–92.

24. For this and following see, among other works, Gerry Cristol, *A Light on the Prairie: Temple Emanu-El of Dallas, 1872–1977* (Fort Worth, 1998); Marc Lee Raphael, *Towards a 'National Shrine': A Centennial History of Washington Hebrew Congregation, 1855–1955* (Williamsburg, 2005); Hollace A. Weiner, *Beth-El Congregation, Fort Worth: Centennial, 1902–2002* (Fort Worth, 2002); Sherry Blanton, "Lives of Quiet Affirmation: The Jewish Women of Early Anniston," *Southern Jewish History* 2 (1999): 25–54. Before the influx of east European Jews late in the nineteenth century, only one Texas congregation, Beth Israel of Houston, started as traditional. It was also the only one officially begun before the Civil War. The literature emphasizes fluid population movement related to the opening of railroads and economic expansion. Weiner discusses chain migration and familial ties at length.

25. Stanley R. Brav, "The Jewish Woman, 1861–1865," *American Jewish Archives* (April 1965): 34–75; Bauman, "Southern Jewish Women"; Janice R. Blumberg, "Sophie Weil Browne," *Southern Jewish History* 9 (2006): 1–33; Karla Goldman, *Beyond the Synagogue Gallery: Finding a Place for Women in American Judaism* (Cambridge, 2000); Mark I. Greenberg, "Savannah's Jewish Women and the Shaping of Ethnic and Gender Identity, 1830–1900," *Georgia Historical Quarterly* 82 (Winter 1998): 751–74; Beth Wenger, "Jewish Women and Voluntarism: Beyond the Myth of Enablers," *American Jewish History* 79 (Autumn 1989): 16–36, "Jewish Women of the Club: The Changing

Public Roles of Atlanta's Jewish Women (1870–1930)," *American Jewish History* 76 (March 1987): 311–33.

26. Myron Berman, "Rabbi Edward N. Calisch and the Debate over Zionism in Richmond, VA," *American Jewish Historical Quarterly* 62 (March 1973): 295–305; Mark Cowett, *Birmingham's Rabbi: Morris Newfield and Alabama, 1895–1940* (Tuscaloosa, 1986); A. Stanley Dreyfus, *Henry Cohen: Messenger of the Lord* (New York, 1963); Berkley Kalin, "Rabbi William Fineshriber: The Memphis Years," *West Tennessee Historical Society Papers* 25 (1971): 47–62; Bobbie S. Malone, *Rabbi Max Heller: Reformer, Zionist, Southerner* (Tuscaloosa, 1997); Karl Preuss, "Personality, Politics, and the Price of Justice: Ephraim Frisch, San Antonio's 'Radical' Rabbi," *American Jewish History* 85 (September 1997): 263–88; Marc Lee Raphael, " 'Training Men and Women in Dignity, in Civic Righteousness, and the Responsibilities of American Citizenship': The Thought of Rabbi Abram Simon, 1897–1938," *American Jewish Archives Journal* 49 (1997): 62–77; Gladys Rosen, "The Rabbi in Miami: A Case History," in Nathan M. Kaganoff and Melvin I. Urofsky, eds., *Turn to the South* (Charlottesville, 1979), 33–40; Bryan Sherwin, "Portrait of a Romantic Rebel: Bernard C. Ehrenreich (1876–1955)," in Kaganoff and Urofsky, *Turn to the South*, 1–12; Harold S. Wechsler, "Rabbi Bernard C. Ehrenreich: A Northern Progressive Goes South," in Proctor and Schmier, *Jews of the South*, 45–64; Malcolm S. Stern, "The Role of the Rabbi in the South," in Kaganoff and Urofsky, *Turn to the South*, 21–32; Mark K. Bauman and Arnold Shankman, "The Rabbi as Ethnic Broker: The Case of David Marx," *Journal of American Ethnic History* 3 (Spring 1983): 51–68; George Wilkes, "Rabbi Dr. David Marx and the Unity Club," *Southern Jewish History* 9 (2006): 35–68; Ellen M. Umansky, "Christian Science, Jewish Science, and Abraham Geiger Moses," *Southern Jewish History* 6 (2003): 1–36, *From Christian Science to Jewish Science* (New York, 2005).

27. Gary Dean Best, "Jacob H. Schiff's Galveston Movement: An Experiment in Immigrant Deflection, 1907–1914," *American Jewish Archives* 30 (April 1978): 43–79; Eugene Kaufmann, *Half a Century of HIAS in Baltimore, 1903–1953* (Baltimore, 1953); Bernard Marinbach, *Galveston: Ellis Island of the West* (Albany, 1983); Hollace A. Weiner, "Removal Approval: The Industrial Removal Office Experience in Fort Worth, Texas," *Southern Jewish History* 4 (2001): 1–44.

28. Mark K. Bauman, "Centripetal and Centrifugal Forces Facing the People of Many Communities: Atlanta Jewry from the Frank Case to the Great Depression," *Atlanta Historical Journal* 23 (Fall 1979): 25–54; Wendy Lowe Besmann, *A Separate Circle: Jewish Life in Knoxville, Tennessee* (Knoxville, 2001); Gilbert Sandler, *Jewish Baltimore: A Family Album* (Baltimore, 2000); Jessica Elfenbein, "Uptown and Traditional," *Southern Jewish History* 9 (2006): 69–102; Peggy Kronsberg Pearlstein, "Macey Kronsberg: Institution Builder of Conservative Judaism in Charleston, S.C. and the Southeast," *Southern Jewish History* 8 (2005): 161–204, "Israel Fine: Baltimore Businessman and Hebrew Poet," *Southern Jewish History* 9 (2006): 103–39; Kenneth W. Stein, *A History of Ahavath Achim Congregation, 1887–1977* (Atlanta, 1978). The name Anshi S'fard, or men of S'fard (often spelled in different ways even by the same congregation), implying Sephardic origin, is somewhat problematic. The acronym for Luria is actually ARI, or Ashkenazi Rabbi Isaac, although his mother was Sephardic. See Martin A. Cohen,

"The Sephardic Phenomenon: A Reappraisal," *American Jewish Archives* 44 (Spring/Summer 1992): 62–63.

29. Edward Cohen, *The Peddler's Grandson: Growing Up Jewish in Mississippi* (Jackson, 1999); Stanley E. Ely, *In Jewish Texas: A Family Memoir* (Fort Worth, 1998); Susan Gross, *Wings Toward the South: The First Hundred Years of Congregation Agudath Achim* (Shreveport, 1999); Abraham Landau, "First-Person History: American Ghetto," *Filson Club Historical Quarterly* 72 (1998): 193–98 (Louisville); Benjamin Kaplan, *The Eternal Stranger: A Study of Jewish Life in the Small Community* (New York, 1957; three towns in Louisiana); Richard L. Zweigenhaft, "Two Cities in North Carolina: A Comparative Study of Jews in the Upper Class," *Jewish Social Studies* 41 (1979); James Lebeau, "Profile of a Southern Jewish Community: Waycross, Georgia," *American Jewish Historical Quarterly* 58 (June 1969): 429–44; Theodore Lowi, "Southern Jews: The Two Communities," in Leonard Dinnerstein and Mary Dale Palsson, eds., *Jews in the South* (Baton Rouge, 1973), 264–82; Leonard Rogoff, "Synagogue and Jewish Church: A Congregational History of North Carolina," *Southern Jewish History* 1 (1998): 43–81, *Homelands*; Louis Schmier, "Jews and Gentiles in a South Georgia Towns," in Proctor and Schmier, *Jews of the South*, 1–16; Karen Falk and Avi Y. Dector, eds., *We Call This Place Home: Jewish Life in Maryland's Small Towns* (Baltimore, 2002); Deborah R. Weiner, "The Jews of Clarksburg: Community Adaptation and Survival, 1900–60," *West Virginia History* 54 (1995): 59–77, "Jewish Women of the Central Appalachian Coal Fields, 1880–1960: From Breadwinners to Community Builders," *American Jewish Archives Journal* 52 (2000): 10–33, "Middlemen of the Coalfields: The Role of Jews in the Economy of the Southern West Virginia Coal Towns, 1890–1950," *Journal of Appalachian Studies* 4 (Spring 1998): 29–56, *Coalfield Jews: An Appalachian History* (Urbana, 2006); Lee Shai Weissbach, "Stability and Mobility in the Small Jewish Community: Examples from Kentucky History," *American Jewish History* 79 (Spring 1990): 355–75, "Decline in an Age of Expansion: Disappearing Jewish Communities in the Era of Mass Migration," *American Jewish Archives Journal* 49 (1997): 39–61, *Jewish Life in Small-Town America* (New Haven, 2005).

30. For the derivation of the term *kallal*, see Hollace A. Weiner, "The Mixers: The Roles of Rabbis Deep in the Heart of Texas," *American Jewish History* 85 (September 1997): 292–93, note 13.

31. Joel Ziff, ed., *Lev Tuviah: On the Life and Work of Rabbi Tobias Geffen* (Newton, MA, 1988); David Geffen, "The Literary Legacy of Rabbi Tobias Geffen in Atlanta, 1910–1970," *Atlanta Historical Journal* 23 (Fall 1979): 85–90; Nathan M. Kaganoff, "An Orthodox Rabbinate in the South: Tobias Geffen, 1870–1970," *American Jewish History* 73 (September 1983): 56–70.

32. Sol Beton, *Sephardim and a History of Congregation OrVeShalom* (Atlanta, 1981), "Sephardim—Atlanta," *Atlanta Historical Journal* 23 (Fall 1979): 119–27; Miriam Cohen, ed., *Congregation Etz Ahayem: Tree of Life, 1912–1987* (Montgomery, 1987); Rubin M. Hanan, *The History of the Etz Ahayem Congregation, 1906–1912* (Montgomery, 1962); Yitzchak Kerem, "The Settlement of Rhodesian and Other Sephardic Jews in Montgomery and Atlanta in the Twentieth Century," *American Jewish History* 85 (December 1997): 373–91; Marcie Cohen Ferris, "From the Recipe File of Luba Cohen: A Study of Southern Jewish Foodways and Cultural Identity," *Southern Jewish History* 2

(1999): 129–64, "Feeding the Jewish Soul in the Delta Diaspora," *Southern Cultures* 10 (Fall 2004): 52–85, *Matzah Ball Gumbo* (Chapel Hill, 2005).

33. Peter K. Opper, *"Like a Giant Oak": A History of the Ladies Hebrew Benevolent Association and Jewish Family Services of Richmond, Virginia, 1849–1999* (Richmond, 1999); Max Gettinger, *Coming of Age: The Atlanta Jewish Federation, 1962–1982* (Hoboken, 1994); Mark K. Bauman, "The Emergence of Jewish Social Service Agencies in Atlanta," *Georgia Historical Quarterly* 69 (Winter 1985): 488–508, "The Transformation of Jewish Social Services in Atlanta, 1928–1948," *American Jewish Archives Journal* 53 (2001): 83–111, "Role Theory and History: Ethnic Brokerage in the Atlanta Jewish Community," *American Jewish History* 73 (September 1983): 71–96, "Victor H. Kriegshaber, Community Builder," *American Jewish History* 79 (Autumn 1989): 94–110.

34. Steve Oney, *And the Dead Shall Rise: The Murder of Mary Phagan and the Lynching of Leo Frank* (New York, 2003); Leonard Dinnerstein, *The Leo Frank Case* (New York, 1968); Jeffrey Melnick, *Black-Jewish Relations on Trial: Leo Frank and Jim Conley in the New South* (Jackson, MS, 2000); Nancy McLean, "The Leo Frank Case Reconsidered: Gender and Sexual Politics in the Making of Reactionary Populism," *Journal of American History* 78 (1991): 917–48; Harry Golden *A Little Girl is Dead* (New York, 1965); Stephen J. Goldfarb, "The Slaton Memorandum: A Governor Looks Back at His Decision to Commute the Death Sentence of Leo Frank," *American Jewish History* 88 (September 2000): 325–40; Mary Phagan Kean, *The Murder of Little Mary Phagan* (Far Hills, NJ, 1987); Eugene Levy, "'Is the Jew a White Man?': Press Reaction to the Leo Frank Case, 1913–1915" *Phylon* 35 (1974): 212–22; Robert Seitz Frey, "Christian Responses to the Trial and Lynching of Leo Frank," *Georgia Historical Quarterly* 71 (1987): 461–76; Cliff Kuhn, *Contesting the New South Order: The 1914–1915 Strike at Atlanta's Fulton Mills* (Chapel Hill, 2001).

35. Howard N. Rabinowitz, "Nativism, Bigotry, and Anti-Semitism in the South," *American Jewish History* 72 (March 1988): 437–51 summarizes the literature. See also Abraham J. Peck, "'That Other Peculiar Institution': Jews and Judaism in the Nineteenth Century South," *Modern Judaism* 7 (February 1987): 99–114; Rosen, *Jewish Confederates*, chapter 5; Bertram W. Korn, "American Judaeophobia: Confederate Version," in Dinnerstein and Palsson, *Jews in the South* , 135–56; Mark I. Greenberg, "Ambivalent Relations: Acceptance and Anti-Semitism in Confederate Thomasville," *American Jewish Archives* 65 (Spring/Summer 1993): 13–30; Richard McMurray, "Rebels, Extortioners, and Counterfeiters: A Note on Confederate Judaeophobia," *Atlanta Historical Journal* 22 (Fall-Winter 1978): 45–52; Louis Schmier, "An Unbecoming Act: Anti-Semitic Uprising in Thomas County, Georgia," *Civil War Times Illustrated* 23 (October 1984), "Notes and Documents on the 1862 Expulsion of Jews from Thomasville, Georgia," *American Jewish Archives* 32 (April 1980): 9–22; Lewis S. Feuer, "America's First Jewish Professor: James Joseph Sylvester at the University of Virginia," *American Jewish Archives* 36 (November 1984): 152–201; Morton Borden, *Jews, Turks, and Infidels* (Chapel Hill, 1984); Leonard Dinnerstein, *Uneasy at Home: Antisemitism and the American Jewish Experience* (New York, 1987); Leonard Rogoff, "Is the Jew White? The Racial Place of the Southern Jew," *American Jewish History* 85 (September 1997): 195–230; Carlton Moseley, "Latent Klanism in Georgia, 1890–1915," *Georgia Historical Quarterly* 56 (1972): 365–86; Rosalind Benjet, "The Ku Klux Klan and the Jewish Community of Dallas, 1921–23," *Southern Jewish*

History 6 (2003): 133–62; Till Van Rahden, "Beyond Ambivalence: Variations of Catholic Anti-Semitism in Turn-of-the-Century Baltimore," *American Jewish History* 82 (1994): 7–42; Edward C. Halperin, "Frank Porter Graham, Isaac Hall Manning, and the Jewish Quota at the University of North Carolina Medical School," *North Carolina Historical Review* 67 (1990): 385–410; Edward S. Shapiro, "Anti-Semitism Mississippi Style," in David A. Gerber, ed., *Anti-Semitism in American History* (Urbana, 1986), 129–51; Marcia Graham Synnott, "Anti-Semitism and American Universities: Did Quotas Follow the Jews?" in Gerber, *Anti-Semitism in American History*, 233–74; Beverly Williams, "Anti-Semitism and Shreveport, Louisiana: The Situation in the 1920s," *Louisiana History* 21 (Fall 1980): 387–98; Lawrence N. Powell, *Troubled Memory: Anne Levy, the Holocaust, and David Duke's Louisiana* (Chapel Hill, 2000); Tom Keating, *Saturday School: How One Town Kept out the "Jewish," 1902–1932* (Bloomington, 1999). On violence see Daniel R. Weinfield, "Samuel Fleishman: Tragedy in Reconstruction-Era Florida," *Southern Jewish History* 8 (2005): 31–76; Patrick Q. Mason, "Anti-Jewish Violence in the New South," *Southern Jewish History* 8 (2005): 77–120.

36. Mark K. Bauman, *Harry H. Epstein and the Rabbinate as Conduit for Change* (Rutherford, 1994), especially 52–57, including discussion of Mesch; Henry M. Green, *Gesher VaGesher/Bridges and Bonds: The Life of Leon Kronish* (Atlanta, 1996).

37. Carolyn Lipson-Walker, "Shalom Y'all: The Folklore and Culture of Southern Jews," Ph.D. diss., Indiana University, 1986.

38. Susan E. Tifft and Alex S. Jones, *The Trusts: The Private and Powerful Family Behind the New York Times* (Boston, 1999); Bernard Rapoport, as told to Don Carleton, *Being Rapoport, Capitalist with a Conscience* (Austin, 2002); Burton Alan Boxerman, "The Edison Brothers, Shoe Merchants: Their Georgia Years," *Georgia Historical Quarterly* 57 (Winter 1973): 511–25.

39. The end of discriminatory quotas in colleges and medical facilities served as a prerequisite for these changes. Deborah Dash Moore, *To the Golden Cities: Pursuing the American Dream in Los Angeles and Miami* (New York, 1994); Terry Barr, "A Shtetl Grew in Bessemer: Temple Beth-El and Jewish Life in Small Town Alabama," *Southern Jewish History* 3 (2000): 1–44; Gerald L. Gold, "A Tale of Two Communities: The Growth and Decline of Small-Town Jewish Communities in Northern Ontario and Southwestern Louisiana," in Moses Rischin, ed., *The Jews of North American* (Detroit, 1987), 224–34; Jacob Koch, "A Special Heritage: The Demopolis Jewish Community," in Jerry Elijah Brown, ed., *An Alabama Humanities Reader* (Macon, 1985), 137–45; Ira M. Sheskin, "The Dixie Diaspora: The 'Loss' of Small Southern Jewish Communities," *Southeastern Geographer* 40 (May 2000): 52–74; John Egerton, *The Americanization of Dixie: The Southernization of America* (New York, 1974).

40. On this and following, Phillip J. Johnson, "The Limits of Interracial Compromise: Louisiana, 1941," *Journal of Southern History* 69 (May 2003): 319–48; Sarah Wilkerson-Freeman, "The Second Battle for Woman Suffrage: Alabama White Women, the Poll Tax, and V. O. Key's Master Narrative of Southern Politics," *Journal of Southern History* 68 (May 2002): 333–74; Mark K. Bauman, "Morris B. Abram," in Jack Fischel and Sanford Pinsker, eds., *Jewish-American History and Culture: An Encyclopedia* (New York, 1991); Mark K. Bauman and Berkley Kalin, eds., *Quiet Voices: Southern Rabbis and Black Civil Rights* (Tuscaloosa, 1997); Clive Webb, *Fight Against Fear: Southern*

Jews and Black Civil Rights (Athens, 2001); Alexander S. Leidholdt, *The Life of Louis Jaffe: Editor for Justice* (Baton Rouge, 2002); Deborah R. Weiner, "The Jews of Keystone: Life in a Multicultural Boomtown," *Southern Jewish History* 2 (1999): 1–24; Raymond Arsenault, "Charles Jacobson of Arkansas: A Jewish Politician in the Land of the Razorbacks, 1891–1915," in Kaganoff and Urofsky, *Turn to the South*, 55–75; Karl Preuss, "Personality, Politics, and the Price of Justice: Ephraim Frisch, San Antonio's 'Radical' Rabbi," *American Jewish History* 85 (September 1997): 263–88; Debra L. Schultz, *Going South: Jewish Women in the Civil Rights Movement* (New York, 2001); Deborah Dash Moore, "Separate Paths: Blacks and Jews in the Twentieth-Century South," in Salzman and West, *Struggles in the Promised Land*, 275–93; Cheryl Lynn Greenberg, "Negotiating Coalitions: Black and Jewish Civil Rights Agencies in the Twentieth Century," in Salzman and West, *Struggles in the Promised Land*, "The Southern Jewish Community and the Struggle for Civil Rights," in V. P. Franklin, ed, *African Americans and Jews in the Twentieth Century* (Columbia, MO, 1998); Greenberg, *Troubling the Waters: Black-Jewish Relations in the American Century* (Princeton, 2006); Eric L. Goldstein, *The Price of Whiteness: Jews, Race, and American Identity* (Princeton, 2006); Herman Pollack, "A Forgotten Fighter for Justice: Ben Goldstein-Lowell," *Jewish Currents* 30 (June 1976): 14–18; Mary Stanton, "At One with the Majority," *Southern Jewish History* 9 (2006): 141–99; Jonathan Bass, *Blessed Are the Peacemakers: Martin Luther King, Jr., Eight White Religious Leaders, and the "Letter from Birmingham Jail"* (Tuscaloosa, 2001). Raymond A. Mohl, *South of the South: Jewish Activists and the Civil Rights Movement in Miami, 1945–1960* (Gainesville, 2003); Adam Mendelsohn, "Two Far South: Rabbinical Responses to Apartheid and Segregation in South Africa and the American South," *Southern Jewish History* 6 (2003): 63–132; Melissa Fay Greene, *The Temple Bombing* (Reading, MA, 1996).

41. Caroline Bettinger-Lopez, *Cuban-Jewish Journeys: Searching for Identity, Home, and History in Miami* (Knoxville, 2000).

12

AMERICAN JEWISH RESPONSES TO NAZISM AND THE HOLOCAUST

RAFAEL MEDOFF

"President [Roosevelt] has not by a single word or act intimated the faintest interest in what is going on" regarding the Jews in Germany, American Jewish Congress president Stephen Wise confided to a friend in April 1933, a month after Adolf Hitler rose to power in Germany. Despite numerous reports of Nazi mistreatment of German Jews, FDR had refrained from any public comment on their plight. Six months later, in another letter to the same friend, Wise again bemoaned Roosevelt's silence: "FDR has not lifted a finger on behalf of the Jews of Germany," he wrote. "We have had nothing but indifference and unconcern up to this time." Anxious for some gesture by which the president would at least indicate his sympathy for the suffering of Jews under Hitler, Wise arranged for an interlocutor to propose that Albert Einstein be invited to the White House. The administration rebuffed the suggestion, preferring to avoid any actions that might irritate U.S.-German relations.[1]

Likewise, when longtime Roosevelt friend Henry Morgenthau Jr. and New York judge Irving Lehman visited the White House that September to request a statement about Germany's Jews, FDR said he preferred to make a statement about human rights abuses in Germany in general, without focusing on the Jews. Ultimately, however, he made no such statement. In the eighty-two press conferences FDR held in 1933, the subject of the persecution of the Jews arose just once, and not at Roosevelt's initiative.[2]

While Roosevelt's silence in the early 1930s in many ways foreshadowed the U.S. response to the Nazi genocide a decade later, the response of Jewish leaders such as Wise in 1933 illustrated the numerous and complex dilemmas faced by the American Jewish community in deciding how to respond to the Nazi persecutions. Was there any way for U.S. Jews to influence government policy toward German Jewry? Was it politically wise for Jews to take issue with the president of the United States? How would the American public react to a Jewish outcry over a European matter at a time of isolationism and deepening economic depression at home?

American Jewish strategies for responding to the rise of Nazism reflected, in part, the cultural divide in the community between Jews of central European origin and those who traced their roots to eastern Europe. The first major waves of Jewish immigrants to the United States, numbering about two hundred thousand, came from Germany and elsewhere in central Europe in the mid and late 1800s. The newcomers came because of economic hardship, not persecution, typically chose acculturation over religious observance, felt little sympathy for Zionism, and tended to quickly climb the socioeconomic ladder. Wealthy German-born Jews established the first U.S. Jewish defense organization, the American Jewish Committee, in 1906. Its purpose was to serve as a respectable representative of the Jewish community in its dealings with the non-Jewish public and to ensure communal power would not fall into the hands of more nationalistic elements whose behavior, they feared, might stimulate antisemitism. The AJCommittee's preferred method of political action was backstairs diplomacy, or *shtadlanut*—quiet intercession with political figures and modest requests that would not ruffle feathers. This approach was endorsed by another major Jewish organization, B'nai B'rith, a fraternal order and advocacy group.

The next waves of Jewish immigration came from Russia and its environs: between 1891 and 1914 1.3 million east European Jews came to the United States to escape pogroms and discrimination. They were less eager than their German brethren to shed Old World ways and slower to achieve economic success in the new world. They spoke Yiddish, embraced Jewish folkways, and supported Zionism. Less Americanized and typically found in the lower economic strata, they were less concerned about how they were viewed by non-Jews and more inclined to advocate publicly for Jewish causes. Resenting the elitist, self-appointed leadership of the AJCommittee, east European immigrants in 1918 organized the rival American Jewish Congress, which embraced Zionism, spoke out more aggressively for Jewish interests at home and abroad, and claimed to represent the sentiments of grassroots American Jews.

Secure in the knowledge that public protests were consistent with the norms of American political culture, U.S. Jews generally have felt comfortable expressing their views in the public arena, even if they often have disagreed among themselves on tactics. As far back as the mid-nineteenth century, attempts were made, both through public protest rallies and behind-the-scenes lobbying, to bring about U.S. government intercession on behalf of Jews persecuted abroad, even when American interests were not clearly at stake. Jewish protesters secured U.S. intervention against a planned expulsion of two thousand Russian Jews from their homes in 1869 and against the mistreatment of Jews in Romania during the late 1800s and early 1900s. Jewish lobbying led to the U.S. abrogation of the Russo-American Commercial Treaty in response to the persecution of Russian Jews in the early 1900s. These efforts accustomed the Jewish community to speaking out against persecution overseas and helped cement the concept of Jewish advocacy as a legitimate part of American political life.

By the time of Hitler's rise to power in early 1933, the American Jewish community had the advantage of many decades of experience in the art of public advocacy. But it was also saddled with deep divisions, both substantive and stylistic, among its leaders as to how to respond to overseas crises. The differences between the AJCommittee's approach and that of the AJCongress were readily apparent in the weeks following Hitler's rise to power. The committee opposed public protests, fearing the non-Jewish public would be irritated by noisy Jewish demonstrations; the congress quickly organized an anti-Hitler rally at Madison Square Garden. The committee denounced calls for a boycott of German goods, fearing Jews would be accused of interfering in U.S.-German relations; the congress, after some initial hesitation, embraced boycotting.

Rabbi Wise, the longtime leader of the AJCongress, was outspoken on a variety of controversial social issues, including union rights, women's suffrage, and race relations. He was one of the founders of the American Civil Liberties Union and the National Association for the Advancement of Colored People. Wise was also a devoted Zionist amidst a Reform rabbinate that was overwhelmingly non-Zionist or anti-Zionist. But Wise's strong admiration for Franklin Roosevelt complicated his willingness to take issue with U.S. policy regarding the Jews under Hitler. As a lifelong social justice activist and supporter of the Democratic Party, Wise saw Roosevelt's New Deal as the embodiment of his own dreams for reforming American society.

Thus although Wise in private was deeply disappointed by FDR's refusal, in 1933, to criticize Nazi brutalities against the Jews, he said nothing publicly against Roosevelt and even opposed a plan by Utah senator William King in 1933 to introduce a resolution expressing sympathy with German Jewry. According to Wise, such a resolution would imply that the administration was not sympathetic to the Jews under Hitler. Wise's AJCongress did sponsor several large "Stop Hitler Now" rallies that year, although the speakers focused on condemning Hitler and avoided even implicit criticism of the Roosevelt administration's position. In the years to follow, the AJCongress scaled back such mass protests, typically holding at most one such rally in New York City each year, with smaller events in some other cities, depending on the initiative of local activists.

Shortly after Hitler became chancellor, grassroots American Jewish activists spontaneously initiated a boycott of German goods.[3] The AJCommittee and B'nai B'rith opposed the boycott, fearing it could arouse antisemitic accusations that American Jews were trying to drag the U.S. into a conflict with Germany. At Stephen Wise's insistence, the AJCongress declined to join the boycott movement during its first six months. He believed they needed to obtain "the sanction of our government" before doing so.[4] He also later recalled that "as a pacifist, I was hesitant about the boycott because it is an economic weapon." Pressure from the AJCongress membership compelled a reversal by August 1933, and the organization soon assumed the leadership of the boycott movement, with its women's division taking on a particularly active role. Boycotting, with its picket lines and letter writing, offered grassroots AJCongress members a concrete way to express their outrage over the treatment of Germany's Jews, although its actual impact on Germany was limited.[5]

Although many German Jews hoped to come to the United States, immigration was severely restricted. America's traditional open door immigration policy was reversed by the national origins immigration bill, the Johnson Immigration Act of 1921. Public and congressional support for immigration restriction was fueled by a combination of factors, including the spread of theories by prominent anthropologists that non-Caucasian races were corrupting Anglo-Saxon society; anxiety about Communism as a result of the Soviet revolution in Russia; and fear of foreigners in general, especially of Catholics and Jews. The law passed in 1921 stipulated that the number of immigrants from any single country during a given year could not exceed 3 percent of the number of immigrants from that country who had been living in the U.S. at the time of the 1910 national census. A strong indication of the antisemitic sentiment that helped motivate the legislation was the fact that the original version of the bill was submitted to Congress with a report by the chief of the United States Consular Service characterizing would-be Jewish immigrants from Poland as "filthy, un-American, and often dangerous in their habits . . . lacking any conception of patriotism or national spirit."[6] In 1924 the immigration regulations were tightened even further. The percentage was reduced from 3 percent to 2 percent and, instead of the 1910 census, the quota numbers would be based on an earlier census, the one taken in 1890. This sharply reduced the number of Jews and (predominantly Catholic) Italian Americans, since the bulk of Jewish and Italian immigrants in the U.S. had not arrived until after 1890.

As the Nazi persecution of Jews intensified during the middle and late 1930s, the U.S. quota system functioned precisely as its creators had intended. The annual quota for Germany and Austria, for example, was 27,370, and just 6,542 for Poland. Even those meager quota allotments were almost always underfilled, as zealous consular officials implemented the bureaucratic method that senior State Department official Breckinridge Long described in these blunt terms: "postpone and postpone and postpone the granting of the visas." A deliberately designed bureaucratic maze—a series of "paper walls," to borrow the title of

David S. Wyman's 1968 book—ensured most Jewish refugees would remain far from America's shores. During the period of the Nazi genocide, from late 1941 and until early 1945, only 10 percent of the already minuscule quotas from Axis-controlled European countries would be used—meaning that almost 190,000 quota places would be left unfilled.[7]

Strong congressional support for restrictionism, backed by polls showing overwhelming public opposition to immigration, intimidated American Jewry. During the 1930s no major Jewish organization called for liberalizing the quota system and few sought increases in Jewish refugee immigration even within the existing laws. Labor Secretary Frances Perkins, the only consistently pro-refugee voice within Roosevelt's cabinet, was willing, in 1933, to utilize a legal but little-known bond guarantee procedure that would have permitted more refugees to enter within the existing quotas, but Jewish organizations were reluctant to support the Perkins initiative, fearing the arrival of a large numbers of immigrants would stimulate antisemitism.[8] Jewish groups also feared that attempts to bring in more immigrants would provoke restrictionists to tighten the laws even further. Numerous such proposals were floated in Congress during the 1930s.

Another option was to seek the admission of refugees to an American territory, thereby avoiding the restrictions that limited entry to the mainland United States. In November 1939 the Legislative Assembly of the Virgin Islands offered haven to refugees from Hitler. The State Department vetoed the scheme, claiming "undesirables and spies" might use it as a way of sneaking into the United States, an argument FDR accepted. Dr. Wise declined to endorse the Virgin Islands as a haven on the grounds that "it might be used effectively against [Roosevelt]" in the 1940 presidential campaign. "Cruel as I may seem," Wise explained to a friend, "his election is much more important for everything that is worthwhile and that counts than the admission of a few people, however imminent be their peril."[9]

A comparable proposal floated at about the same time suggested utilizing Alaska (which was not yet a state) as a refuge. This idea attracted the support of some members of Congress, as well as the Department of Labor and the Department of the Interior, but no major American Jewish organizations. Rabbi Wise feared any plan to settle refugees in Alaska "makes a wrong and hurtful impression" among non-Jews "that Jews are taking over some part of the country for settlement." Poale Zion, the Labor Zionists of America, was the only American Jewish organization to publicly endorse the idea of opening Alaska to Jewish refugees. Although as a matter of principle the Labor Zionists regarded Palestine as the appropriate destination for European Jewish refugees, they endorsed the Alaska scheme as an opportunity to save lives.[10]

American Jewish attitudes toward the immigration issue were further complicated by the fact that the very concept of mass immigration troubled some Jewish leaders, because of its implications for the status of Jews around the world. In a 1936 essay Rabbi Wise warned against mass Jewish emigration from Poland on the grounds that it "might well become the 'locus classicus' for groups in all lands seeking to rid themselves of their Jewish populations . . . France, Czecho-Slovokia, or England might conceivably propose a conference on Jewish emigrants and refugees, without exciting suspicion with respect to their purpose."[11] During Wise's meeting with the Polish ambassador to the United States in April 1938, the ambassador repeatedly asserted Poland's interest in mass Jewish emigration, but Wise adamantly rejected the very concept.[12]

The possibility of British Mandatory Palestine serving as a haven for large numbers of European Jewish refugees presented its own unique dilemmas for American Jewish leaders. In response to Palestinian Arab violence, the British authorities began restricting Jewish immigration in 1936. American Jewish leaders would not support a public campaign against England's Palestine restrictions. The AJCommittee warned that "notoriety and over-conspicuousness" by Jews might provoke antisemitism, while Rabbi Wise refused to take part in "anti-British propaganda," arguing that everyone should "march shoulder to shoulder with England in the war against fascism, even if the Zionist cause suffered."[13]

Yet it was precisely in the area of Palestine policy that Wise had some impact. Shortly after the eruption of Palestinian Arab violence in mid-1936, the British government was poised to suspend all Jewish immigration to Palestine. Wise's plea to FDR for American intervention was well received by the president and his advisers, who thought a gesture regarding Palestine would help ensure Jewish support for the president's forthcoming reelection campaign. Seeing political gain and little risk, the administration opted to intervene. Anxious to keep Anglo-American relations in good order, London announced the planned suspension would be postponed until after the completion of a forthcoming Royal Commission study of the Palestine problem. During the lengthy delay, another fifty thousand Jews reached Palestine.[14]

The German annexation of Austria in March 1938, with its attendant brutalization of Austria's Jews, cast a fresh international spotlight on Nazi barbarism. Facing mounting criticism from liberal members of Congress and some of the media, the Roosevelt administration organized a conference in Evian, France in July 1938, which brought together delegates from thirty-three countries to discuss the Jewish refugee problem. But the attendees reaffirmed their unwillingness to liberalize their immigration quotas, and the British refused even to discuss Palestine. Some critics later pointed out that "Evian" was "Naive" spelled backwards. The problem, however, was not so much naïveté as it was calculated indifference. Internal State Department memoranda reveal that the U.S. convened the gathering largely for public relations purposes, to give the impression that the free world was taking action.

The persecution of German Jews intensified suddenly and dramatically when Nazi storm troopers carried out the nationwide Kristallnacht pogroms of November 9 and 10, 1938. About one hundred Jews were murdered and thirty thousand more were sent to concentration camps. Nearly two hundred synagogues were burned down, and more than seven thousand Jewish-owned businesses were destroyed. President Roosevelt responded to Kristallnacht with a sharp verbal condemnation and two gestures. He recalled the U.S. ambassador from Germany for "consultations" and he extended the visitors' visas of the twelve to fifteen thousand German Jewish refugees who were then in the United States. At the same time, FDR announced that liberalization of America's tight immigration quotas was "not in contemplation."[15]

American Jewish organizations hesitated to challenge either the administration's policy or the prevailing public mood, which, according to the polls, continued to oppose large-scale immigration. Three days after Kristallnacht, representatives of the General Jewish Council, the umbrella group for the four largest Jewish defense organizations, resolved "that there should be no parades, public demonstrations or protests by Jews" and that although "on humanitarian grounds, mass immigration of German Jews could not be opposed . . . at least for the time being, nothing should be done with regard to this matter." When FDR queried his closest Jewish adviser, Samuel Rosenman—a prominent member of the American Jewish Committee—as to whether he thought more Jewish refugees should be allowed to enter the U.S. in the wake of Kristallnacht, Rosenman opposed such a move because "it would create a Jewish problem in the U.S."[16]

In the wake of Kristallnacht, Senator Robert F. Wagner (D-NY) and Rep. Edith Rogers (R-MA) introduced legislation to admit twenty thousand German refugee children outside the quotas. Nativist and isolationist groups vociferously opposed the Wagner-Rogers bill. Typical of their perspective was a remark by FDR's cousin, Laura Delano Houghteling, who was the wife of the U.S. commissioner of immigration: she warned that "20,000 charming children would all too soon grow into 20,000 ugly adults." A private appeal to FDR by First Lady Eleanor Roosevelt for his support of the bill received a negative reply. He did tell the first lady that he would not object if she endorsed it, but she did not do so. An inquiry by a congresswoman as to the president's position was returned to his secretary marked "File No action FDR." Mindful of polls showing most Americans opposed to more immigration, Roosevelt preferred to follow public opinion rather than lead it. Without his support, the Wagner-Rogers bill was buried in committee. Ironically, when *Pets Magazine* the following year launched a campaign to have Americans take in pure-bred British puppies so they would not be harmed by German bombing raids, the magazine received several thousand offers of haven for the dogs.[17]

A dramatic demonstration of the refugee crisis was provided that May, when the German steamship SS *St. Louis*, carrying 930 Jewish refugees with entry visas to Cuba, was turned away by the Cuban authorities. Hoping for haven in the United States, the "saddest ship afloat" hovered off the coast of Florida, prevented by Coast Guard patrols from coming too close to the shore. "There was great excitement when the Florida coast was sighted and hope that we might be able to enter that beautiful land," a message from the passengers declared. But no asylum was offered by the Roosevelt administration. Eventually, a deal was brokered to send the passengers to a number of European countries which, tragically, lay in the path of the soon-to-be advancing German armies. Hitler's press scornfully highlighted the dramatic contrast between America's verbal criticism of German policy toward the Jews and its refusal to take in the refugees.

American public opinion during the 1930s strongly opposed any significant U.S. action against Nazi Germany. A 1937 poll found 71 percent of Americans thought America was wrong to have entered World War I; many believed the U.S. had been tricked into the conflict by greedy weapons manufacturers. The hardships of the Great Depression further intensified the view that domestic concerns required America's full attention and that the country could not spare any resources for overseas matters. While most Americans found Hitler's totalitarian ways distasteful, only about one-tenth were willing to go to war for any reason other than to fend off an invasion of the United States itself.[18]

Many American Jews felt differently. They hoped the U.S. would take action against Hitler, not only because of the Nazis' persecution of the Jews, but because they realized Hitler was a threat to the entire free world. At the same time, they feared being perceived as warmongers. In numerous public statements Jewish leaders tried to reassure the public of Jewish disinterest in military action against Nazi Germany. "No Jew on earth has asked any nation to take up arms against Hitler," Stephen Wise asserted in 1941. This was something of an exaggeration, since small numbers of American Jews were active in the Fight for Freedom movement, which advocated a preemptive U.S. war against Hitler. Still, Wise's statement did accurately reflect the fear among Jews before U.S. entry into World War II. Those concerns were exacerbated by the activities of extreme isolationists such as Charles Lindbergh, the widely admired aviator, who in September 1941 publicly accused "the Jews" of "pressing this country toward war" and complained about what he called "their large ownership and influence in our motion pictures, our press, our radio and our government." He also implicitly threatened American Jews, declaring, "Instead of agitating for war, the Jewish groups in this country should be opposing it in every possible way for they will be among the first to feel its consequences. Tolerance is a virtue that depends upon peace and strength. History shows that it cannot survive war and devastation."[19]

On the other hand, there were no such political or social dilemmas when it came to philanthropy, and American Jewish financial aid to beleaguered European Jews, consistent with the Jewish tradition of *tzedakah* (charity) to the less fortunate, increased steadily during the 1930s despite the hardships of the Depression. The Jewish community's major organizational vehicle for overseas relief aid, the American Jewish Joint Distribution Committee, known simply as the Joint, intensified its efforts in Europe as the persecution of Jews steadily worsened during the Hitler years. Its activities ranged from direct charitable assistance to endangered Jewish communities in the 1930s to financing the sheltering and emigration of Jews during the war period.[20]

The Joint periodically clashed with an American Orthodox relief group, the Vaad ha-Hatzala, which was established in 1939 to aid the thousands of Polish rabbis and students who fled to Lithuania after the German invasion. The conflicts between the two groups were partly rooted in the German-versus-Russian phenomenon that characterized much of early twentieth-century American Jewish history. The Joint, like the AJCommittee and other leading Jewish groups, was dominated by acculturated Jewish philanthropists of German origin or ancestry, whose attitudes and policies on various issues were often at odds with those in the community who represented the lower-income strata, the east European, or the Orthodox.[21]

Separatist grassroots fund-raising organizations such as the Vaad ha-Hatzala were perceived by the Joint as a threat by the east Europeans to the communal power and donor base of the German Jews. Joint leaders feared the Vaad's appeals for funds implied that the Joint was not properly fulfilling its mission. Vaad leaders, in turn, feared that the Reform Jews who ran the Joint did not recognize the importance of giving priority to the sustenance and rescue of rabbinical luminaries, whom the Vaad considered critical to the future of traditional Judaism. After 1942, when news of the Nazi mass murders was confirmed, both groups shifted their emphasis from relief work to facilitating rescue, within the limits of their capabilities and the difficult circumstances on the continent. The Joint's efforts were also sometimes hampered by its adherence to the U.S. government's ban on sending funds into enemy territory.[22]

Allied governments and American Jewish leaders received a steady flow of reports throughout 1942 about German massacres of Jewish civilians, climaxing with a telegram in August from the World Jewish Congress representative in Switzerland, Gerhart Riegner, reporting Hitler's intention to systematically annihilate all of Europe's Jews. At the State Department's request, Rabbi Wise refrained from publicizing the Riegner telegram while U.S. officials sought to authenticate the information. Three months later, the administration confirmed the accuracy of Riegner's report and Wise made it public. The British government, trying to deflect criticism by Jewish leaders and members of Parliament over London's cautious response to the mass murders, then proposed to the U.S. that the Allies issue an official statement condemning the killings. The first draft prepared by the British referred to "reports from Europe which leave no room for doubt" that systematic annihilation was underway, but the State Department objected to that phrase on the grounds that it would "expose [the Allies] to increased pressure from all sides to do something more specific in order to aid these people." The final statement, released on December 17, 1942, omitted the phrase "which leave no room for doubt."[23]

The Allied declaration strongly condemned the Nazis' "bestial policy of cold-blooded extermination," warned that the perpetrators would face postwar punishment, but refrained from pledging any specific steps to aid the Jews. A delegation of American Jewish leaders that met with FDR at the White House in early December came face to face with the gap between U.S. rhetoric and action. Rabbi Wise, presenting the president with a twenty-page memorandum detailing the mass murders, asked him "to do all in your power to make an effort to stop it." The president replied that he was already "very well acquainted with the Nazi annihilation of European Jewry, condemned Hitler as "insane," and joked about appointing the governor of New York, Herbert Lehman, a Jew, as postwar administrator in Germany in order to "see some Junkers on their knees, asking Lehman for bread." The meeting concluded without any presidential assurances of practical measures to aid the refugees.

For American Jewish leaders with minimalist expectations, FDR's verbal denunciation of the genocide was sufficient. The day after the meeting at the White House, Rabbi Wise wrote to presidential adviser David Niles: "We ought to distribute cards throughout the country bearing just four letters, TGFR (Thank God For Roosevelt), and as the Psalmist would have said, thank Him every day and every hour."[24] Some rumblings of dissatisfaction were apparent within the community, however. When the major Jewish organizations sponsored a community-wide day of fasting and prayer, in December 1942, in response to the confirmation of the genocide reports, the *Reconstructionist* published an editorial headlined "Fasting Is Not Enough." The following month the *Jewish Spectator* called on Jewish organizations to change their priorities to meet the crisis: "Who can bring themselves to sit down at banquet tables, resplendent in evening clothes, while at the very same evening hundreds of Jews expire in the agonies of hunger, gas poisoning, mass electrocution—and what other forms of death fiendish sadists can invent."

A different response came from Ben Hecht, the newspaper columnist and award-winning screenwriter. Early in 1943 he authored a dramatic pageant called "We Will Never Die" to publicize the Nazi slaughter of the Jews. Hecht was involved with a small Jewish activist group led by Peter Bergson (born Hillel Kook), a Zionist emissary from Palestine who had been lobbying for the creation of a Jewish army to fight the Nazis but changed his focus to the rescue issue after confirmation of the genocide reports. Hecht and Bergson believed "We Will Never Die" would have maximum impact if sponsored by a broad coalition of Jewish organizations, but mainstream Jewish groups declined to cooperate and in several cities actually attempted to prevent the show from being staged. Some Jewish leaders feared the Bergson group's vocal activism would usurp their own leadership role in the Jewish community. Other Jewish leaders worried that dramatic public activities such as Hecht's pageant might provoke antisemitism. Some would not work with Bergson because their particular factions in the Zionist movement regarded him as a political rival, since he had been a follower of the founder of Revisionist Zionism, Vladimir Ze'ev Jabotinsky.[25]

Personal, political, religious, and ideological rivalries were rampant within the Jewish organizational world. The major defense organizations, the AJCongress, AJCommittee, and B'nai B'rith, jockeyed fiercely to be seen as the community's preeminent representative. Zionists clashed with non-Zionists and anti-Zionists. Among American Zionists there was tension between factions aligned with the right-wing and left-wing parties in the world Zionist movement. Religious conflicts raged between the Orthodox, Conservative, Reform, and Reconstructionist movements. Viewed in the context of what was happening to Europe's Jews, such disputes "seem amazingly irrelevant today," Henry Feingold has written. "The organizations allowed themselves the luxury of fiddling while Jews burned."[26]

Despite the lack of cooperation, Bergson and Hecht went ahead with "We Will Never Die" on their own. Starring Edward G. Robinson and Paul Muni, and directed by Moss Hart with an original score by Kurt Weill, it played to audiences of more than forty thousand in two shows at Madison Square Garden in March 1943. It was subsequently staged in Philadelphia, Boston, Chicago, the Hollywood Bowl in Los Angeles, and Washington, DC, where the audience included First Lady Eleanor Roosevelt, six Supreme Court justices, numerous members of the international diplomatic corps, and an estimated three hundred members of Congress. In addition to the more than one hundred thousand people who viewed the shows, the performances received substantial media coverage, thus carrying Hecht's message to audiences well beyond those who actually attended the pageant. It was the first major effort to rouse America's conscience about the Holocaust.

Also in March 1943 eight major Jewish organizations established the Joint Emergency Committee on European Jewish Affairs, the first serious attempt at intraorganizational cooperation in response to the Nazi genocide. The members were the AJCommittee, AJCongress, B'nai B'rith, the socialist Jewish Labor Committee, the Synagogue Council of America, representing congregations from all streams of Judaism, two Orthodox groups, Agudath Israel and the Union of Orthodox Rabbis, and the American Emergency Committee for Zionist Affairs, an umbrella for the leading Zionist organizations. The upstart Bergson group was excluded.[27]

The Joint Emergency Committee got off to a promising start, organizing well-attended protest meetings in forty cities around the country in the spring of 1943. Subsequent efforts, however, met with frustration. Wise and AJCommittee president Joseph Proskauer held meetings with the undersecretary of state, Sumner Welles, and British foreign minister Anthony Eden in late March, but found both of them completely unreceptive to any suggestions of U.S. intervention on behalf of the Jews. Wise's attempts to arrange a meeting with the president in April were rebuffed.

The Roosevelt administration contended that the only practical means of aiding Hitler's victims was to attain military victory over the Nazis, at which point the Allies would ensure that Nazi war criminals faced appropriate "retribution." The major Jewish organizations hesitated to take issue with the president. Strongly supportive of the president's New Deal policies and grateful for his stance against the prewar isolationists, most Jews instinctively trusted FDR's judgment. In addition, some feared that taking issue with a popular president in the midst of a world war could provoke antisemitism. The difficulty of absorbing the shocking news from Europe further slowed the community's response. As a result, there were few visible signs of American Jewish protest activity beyond the proclamation of December 2 as a day of communitywide mourning and fasting for European Jewry. It would be left to three rabbinical students at Conservative Judaism's Jewish Theological Seminary (JTS) to challenge the conventional wisdom.

"Retribution Is Not Enough" was the title of a startling essay by the students, Noah Golinkin, Jerome Lipnick, and Moshe "Buddy" Sachs, that appeared in the March 5, 1943, issue of the *Reconstructionist*, a small but respected intellectual monthly. The U.S. should do much more than merely mete out postwar retribution to war criminals, they argued; ways had to be found to rescue Jews immediately. Taking Jewish leaders to task, the article also asked, "What have the rabbis and leaders . . . done to arouse themselves and their communities to the demands of the hour? What have they undertaken to awaken the conscience of the American people?"[28]

Shaken by reports of Nazi atrocities, the JTS trio had established their own student action committee to publicize the news from Europe and promote rescue. In early 1943 they organized a daylong Jewish-Christian interseminary conference, held at JTS and its Protestant counterpart, the nearby Union Theological Seminary. Hundreds of students and faculty listened to prominent Jewish and Christian leaders and an array of refugee and relief experts, among them Varian Fry, who in 1940–41 had defied the State Department and personally rescued refugees trapped in Vichy France.[29]

In the aftermath of the conference the students focused their attention on the Synagogue Council of America and persuaded the SCA to establish a committee to publicize the European catastrophe. At the students' suggestion, the new committee undertook a seven-week publicity campaign to coincide with the traditional *Sefira* period of semimourning between Pesach and Shavuot. The SCA urged its member synagogues to recite special prayers for European Jewry, limit "occasions of amusement," observe partial fast days and moments of silence, write letters to government officials and Christian leaders, and hold memorial rallies during which congregants would wear black armbands designed by Noah Golinkin three decades before Vietnam War protesters adopted a similar badge of mourning.[30]

The Sefira plan touched a responsive chord in the community. It took place at virtually the same time as the Warsaw Ghetto uprising and the failure of the Allies' Bermuda refugee conference, which both began on April 19. Thus rabbis across the country were receiving the Sefira project mailings, and synagogue boards were considering how to participate, during the very week they were reading about the desperate battle in Warsaw and the Allies' foot-dragging in Bermuda. The SCA's Sefira activities enabled ordinary Jews, even in remote communities, to participate in concrete protests against the Nazi atrocities, providing a way for individuals to feel they could do something meaningful in response to the news from Europe. A Jew in Tulsa or Charlotte could—as one Jewish weekly editorialized—take part in this "spiritual response" as a complement to the "mass rallies of protest, huge pageants, [and] full page advertisements" sponsored by the largest Jewish communities. The JTS students had brought to the Synagogue Council a keen intuitive feel for how to turn ancient Jewish rites into grassroots action for contemporary Jewish rights. The Sefira protest exemplified a creativity sometimes lacking in the older generation of Jewish leadership.[31]

Prayer-and-mourning rallies, in many cases jointly led by Reform, Conservative, and Orthodox rabbis in an uncommon display of unity, were held in numerous Jewish communities around the country during the Sefira weeks. At the conclusion of the Sefira period, five hundred Orthodox, Conservative, and Reform rabbis held a dramatic convocation in New York City.[32]

The SCA's simultaneous effort to increase Christian awareness of the Holocaust was less successful. It persuaded the Federal Council of Churches (the national coalition of major Protestant denominations) to designate May 2 a nationwide Day of Compassion for Europe's Jews, and in some communities Christian clergymen made guest speeches at Jewish gatherings or churches held prayer services for European Jewry. Overall, however, only a handful of America's many thousands of churches sponsored special services or otherwise participated in the memorial activities.[33] Jewish newspapers gave generous coverage to the church services. Christian participation in prayer and mourning for Hitler's Jewish victims provided American Jews with a psychological boost. For those who worried about adverse Christian reaction to Jewish appeals, evidence of any Christian concern about the Nazi genocide helped legitimize Jewish concern.[34]

The aforementioned Bermuda conference grew out of discussions between the British Foreign Office and the State Department in early 1943, fueled by increasing calls in the British parliament, media, and churches for Allied assistance to Jewish refugees. Like the Evian conference five years earlier, Bermuda was born of the Allies' desire to appear to be concerned about the refugees without taking concrete steps to alleviate the Jews' plight. The Joint Emergency Committee on European Jewry requested permission to send a delegation to the conference. It was rejected. The JEC then presented Undersecretary Welles with a list of proposals for rescue action. It was ignored. The U.S. delegates in Bermuda re-iterated America's refusal to take in more refugees and the English refused even to discuss Palestine.

The Bergson group responded to the conference with a large newspaper ad headlined "To 5,000,000 Jews in the Nazi Death-Trap, Bermuda was a Cruel Mockery." Mainstream Jewish leaders spoke similarly. Dr. Israel Goldstein of the Synagogue Council of America criticized the conference as "not only a failure, but a mockery," and even Stephen Wise characterized the Bermuda parley as "a woeful failure."[35] But strong words were not always followed by strong action. More than a month passed after Bermuda before the Joint Emergency Commit-tee met to draw up a letter of protest. A deep division of opinion soon emerged within the committee, with some officials proposing nationwide demonstrations, a march on Washington, and even threats to withhold Jewish votes, while others, such as Wise and Proskauer, strongly opposed such tactics. Appalled by what he called "all the wild people" in the JEC, Wise warned that public criticism of the president would be "morally and perhaps even physically suicidal." Wise patiently listened to his JEC colleagues' array of proposals, then referred them to subcom-mittees which took no further action. By the end of the summer, frustrated lead-ers of the Jewish Labor Committee went so far as to publicly condemn the JEC as a "do-nothing" body. Wise soon decided to dissolve the JEC altogether, breaking a four-to-four split on the issue by adding a close ally, Hadassah, to the JEC roster. In November 1943 the JEC dissolved itself by a five-to-four vote. The JEC's duties were officially turned over to the rescue committee of the American Jewish Con-ference, but that committee had no real staff or budget to implement significant programs.[36]

The Bergson group strove to fill the vacuum left by mainstream leaders. At a time when Jewish organizations seldom used the medium of newspaper advertise-ments to advance their causes, the Bergson group placed more than two hundred sharply worded newspaper ads, many of them authored by Ben Hecht, in newspa-pers around the country. They featured provocative headlines such as "How Well Are You Sleeping? Is There Something You Could Have Done to Save Millions of Innocent People—Men, Women, and Children—from Torture and Death?" and "Time Races Death: What Are We Waiting For? One ad, headlined "Ballad of the Doomed Jews of Europe," suggested that the world would enjoy a peaceful Christmas in 1943 because there would not be any Jews left alive. Bergson post-poned publication of the ad in deference to a plea by officials of the AJCommit-tee, who warned him that "such an anti-Christian attitude [as implied in the ad] could well bring on pogroms in the USA."[37]

The Bergson group proved particularly adept at recruiting the support of celeb-rities, a noteworthy accomplishment in an era when the stars of Hollywood and Broadway tended to shy away from political controversies. Thanks to the efforts of Ben Hecht and the actress Stella Adler, the group's newspaper ads frequently featured an array of well-known names whose endorsement brought luster to their cause and helped attract public interest.

One of the most important components of the Bergson group's rescue campaign was its weeklong Emergency Conference to Save the Jewish People of Europe, which attracted more than fifteen hundred delegates to the Hotel Commodore in New York City in July 1943. Determined to disprove the administration's "rescue through victory" claim, the Bergsonites' event featured panels of experts outlining ways to save Jews from Hitler. A panel on transportation focused on specific routes that could be used to take Jews out of Axis territory. Experts on relief outlined ways to organize food shipments to the Jews. The panel on international relations urged U.S. pressure on nonbelligerent countries to give temporary shelter to Jewish refugees. Military experts drew up a list of steps that could be taken without impairing the war effort, such as Allied warnings of immediate military reprisals for atrocities against the Jews. A panel of rabbis and Christian clergymen focused on the need for protests by the Vatican and other religious leaders. Journalists, editors, and authors discussed ways to rouse American public opinion.

In addition to attaining substantial coverage for the rescue issue in the national press and on radio, the conference demonstrated that it was possible to build a broad coalition in support of U.S. rescue action. The nineteen cochairmen of the conference included conservatives such as former president Herbert Hoover (who addressed the delegates by radio) as well as liberals such as American Labor Party leader Dean Alfange, Republican senator Arthur Capper as well as Democratic senator Elbert Thomas, Roosevelt cabinet member Harold Ickes as well as FDR's arch-critic William Randolph Hearst. The speakers on the panels included a broad cross section of prominent journalists, labor leaders, military personnel, and members of Congress, as well as such diverse participants as the presiding bishop of the Episcopal Church and the executive secretary of the NAACP. A coalition of such breadth also posed an implicit political challenge, since it demonstrated to the White House, on the eve of an election year, that rescue was an issue that mattered to a significant number of voters beyond the Jewish community.

Several weeks after Bergson's conference, the major Jewish organizations held a gathering of their own. The American Jewish Conference, which convened in New York City at the end of August, was intended as a display of unity in response to the slaughter of European Jewry and Britain's closure of Palestine to all but a handful of Jewish refugees. The rescue issue was not originally listed as a separate item on the conference's agenda, but, in response to criticism from grassroots activists and the Jewish press, a committee on rescue was added at the last moment.

Dr. Wise, preferring an accommodationist approach toward the British and hoping to keep the anti-Zionist American Jewish Committee from quitting the conference, made no reference to Jewish statehood in his keynote address. This irked activist-minded delegates, including some from Wise's own AJCongress, who gave their time slot to Dr. Abba Hillel Silver, the Cleveland Zionist leader known for his more forthright positions. Silver's electrifying appeal for Jewish statehood "swept the conference like a hurricane," as one delegate put it. "There was repeated and stormy applause, the delegates rising to their feet in a remarkable ovation." A Palestine homeland resolution passed by 498 to 4—an overwhelming vote of American Jewish support for Silver's line and, in effect, a repudiation of Wise's political strategy. Elevated to cochairmanship of the American Zionist Emergency Council alongside Wise, Silver set to work transforming American Zionism into a vigorous activist movement. He mobilized both grassroots Jews and pro-Zionist Christians to hold rallies, write letters to public officials, and lobby Congress and the White House to support Jewish statehood. To the extent that their efforts for Palestine also called attention to the plight of the Jews in Europe, which they almost always did, it could be argued that Silver's work also increased the pressure for a U.S. response to the Holocaust.

Yet, in two important respects, the campaigns for Zionism and rescue did not intersect. First, Silver's ascent triggered a struggle with Wise that continued for nearly two years, with Silver at one point being forced out of the Zionist leadership for some eight months. This internal Zionist battle sapped the energies of both men and their supporters and diverted considerable attention from larger issues such as the Nazi genocide. Second, some members of Congress who were sympathetic to rescue were uncomfortable taking a stand on Palestine because it meant criticizing an American ally, England, in the midst of a war. On Capitol Hill, legislators heard from Zionist leaders, who presented Palestine as the solution for the refugee problem, as well as from Bergson activists who sought to downplay Palestine and focus on immediate rescue needs and temporary refugee shelters wherever they could be established.

To further dramatize the need for rescue action, the Bergson group, working closely with the Vaad ha-Hatzala, brought more than four hundred rabbis to Washington, DC for a march to the White House on October 6, 1943, three days before Yom Kippur. They were met by Vice President Henry Wallace and congressional leaders, to whom they presented a petition pleading for U.S. rescue action. But their hoped-for audience with the president did not materialize; FDR was busy with other matters, they were told. In fact, the president had nothing on his schedule that afternoon but had been urged to avoid the rabbis by his adviser Samuel Rosenman and Dr. Wise, who were embarrassed by the protesters and feared the march might provoke antisemitism. Roosevelt avoided the rabbis by leaving the White House through a rear exit, but he could not avoid the controversy. "Rabbis Report 'Cold Welcome' at the White House," declared the headline of a report in the *Washington Times-Herald*. A columnist for one Jewish newspaper angrily asked, "Would a similar delegation of 500 Catholic priests have been thus treated?" The editors of another Jewish newspaper, the *Forverts*

(Forward), reported that the episode had affected the president's previously high level of support in the Jewish community: "In open comment it is voiced that Roosevelt has betrayed the Jews," he wrote.

The march publicized the plight of the Jews and speeded up introduction of a Bergson-initiated congressional resolution calling for the creation of a government agency to rescue refugees. It was quickly approved by the Senate Foreign Relations Committee. In the House of Representatives, however, the resolution ran into obstacles created by Representative Sol Bloom, chairman of the Committee on International Affairs. A Jewish congressman who was a staunch supporter of the administration's refugee policy and had served on the U.S. delegation to Bermuda, Bloom insisted on holding formal hearings on the resolution and invited a wide range of witnesses. Rabbi Wise, in his testimony, criticized the resolution as "inadequate" because it did not refer to Palestine, while Bergson supporters testified that they had deliberately left Palestine out of the resolution to avoid a controversy over the issue. But the Palestine problem was quickly overshadowed when the State Department's Breckinridge Long gave wildly misleading testimony about the number of refugees who had already been admitted into the United States. Long's misrepresentations sparked widespread media coverage and denunciations from Jewish organizations and members of Congress.

Meanwhile, senior aides to Treasury secretary Henry Morgenthau Jr. discovered that State Department officials had been blocking transmission of Holocaust-related information to the United States and intentionally obstructing opportunities to rescue Jews from Hitler. On Christmas Day 1943 Treasury staffer Josiah DuBois drew up a stinging eighteen-page report documenting the State Department's actions, entitled, "Report to the Secretary on the Acquiescence of This Government in the Murder of the Jews." DuBois and his colleagues presented the report to Morgenthau and urged him to go to the president.

With the rescue issue reaching the boiling point on Capitol Hill and in the press, Morgenthau had the leverage he needed with the president. On January 16, 1944, Morgenthau brought the "Acquiescence" report to FDR, determined to convince Roosevelt that "you have either got to move very fast, or the Congress of the United States will do it for you." Ten months before election day, the last thing FDR wanted was a public scandal over the refugee issue. Within days Roosevelt did what the congressional resolution sought—he issued an executive order creating the War Refugee Board.

The War Refugee Board was given minimal government funding. Yet, with funds contributed primarily by Jewish groups and a staff composed largely of the same Treasury Department officials who helped lobby for the board's creation, it energetically employed unorthodox means of rescue. It moved Jews out of dangerous zones, pressured the Hungarian authorities to end deportations to Auschwitz, and sheltered Jews in places such as Budapest, where Swedish diplomat Raoul Wallenberg saved lives with the funds and assistance of the board. It also persuaded Roosevelt to admit one token group of 982 refugees outside the quota system—"a bargain-counter flourish in humanitarianism," the journalist I. F. Stone called it. Historians estimate that the War Refugee Board's efforts played a major role in saving about 200,000 Jews and 20,000 non-Jews. The board's work demolished the Roosevelt administration's long-standing claim that there was no way to rescue Jews except by winning the war.[38]

Shortly after the German occupation of Hungary in the spring of 1944, the War Refugee Board learned of preparations for the mass deportation of Hungarian Jews to the gas chambers at Auschwitz. At about the same time, it also received the first detailed information about the mass murder process, including specific geographical descriptions of the camp's layout provided by two escapees. This information, combined with the Allies' recently attained control of the skies over Europe, made it possible for the first time to seriously consider using Allied air power to interfere with the Nazi genocide.

In June the board received appeals from Jewish leaders in Europe, forwarded by the American Orthodox group Agudath Israel, asking the U.S. to bomb the railroad lines from Hungary to Poland that were being used for the deportations. War Refugee Board director John Pehle forwarded the appeals to Assistant Secretary of War John McCloy. In a note to his assistant, McCloy instructed him to "kill" Pehle's request by rejecting the bombing proposal as "impracticable" on the grounds that it would require "considerable diversion" of planes that were needed for the war effort.

During the months to follow, the War Refugee Board received requests to bomb the camps themselves, rather than just the railways, from the World Jewish Congress, the Bergson group, and other Jewish individuals and organizations. Such requests for U.S. military intervention generally fell along distinct sociological lines. Those who advocated asking for such intervention typically were Orthodox, or Yiddish-speaking, or recent immigrants, or maximalist Zionists. They felt less American than many other American Jews and consequently felt less vulnerable to the risk of being called unpatriotic. By contrast, those who were the most Americanized were the most concerned at the prospect of their loyalty being questioned and, therefore, were more hesitant to ask for special military action to aid Jews in Europe. They considered themselves fully acclimated Americans and were not inclined to take steps they feared might risk that status.

Each time War Refugee Board director Pehle presented a bombing request to the War Department, it was rejected on the grounds that "a study" had already been conducted finding it not militarily feasible. In fact, however, no such study had been done. The War Department had already secretly decided, back in February 1944, that as a matter of principle it would never use military resources "for the purposes of rescuing victims of enemy oppression." During the summer and autumn of 1944, U.S. and British bombers repeatedly struck German synthetic oil factories just miles from the gas chambers. Roosevelt also ordered U.S. bombers to airlift arms and supplies to Polish Home Army members rebelling against the Nazis in Warsaw that year, despite the likelihood that aircraft would be lost and that many of the containers would end up in the hands of the Germans rather than the Polish fighters. Polish Americans were viewed by the administration as potential swing votes in the 1944 presidential election. But Jewish voters were perceived, correctly, as being virtually in FDR's pocket; more than 90 percent of them had voted for Roosevelt in 1936 and 1940. This diminished the Jewish community's ability to influence policy regarding European Jewry or Palestine.

The American Jewish community was psychologically unprepared for the Hitler persecutions, and its leaders did not easily rise to the new challenge. Many precedents existed for seeking U.S. intervention on behalf of Jews mistreated abroad, but American Jews had never faced anything remotely resembling the barbarism of the Nazis, nor had they ever had to do so in the midst of an economic depression and widespread isolationism and nativism. Jewish fears of provoking antisemitism further contributed to the American Jewish failure of will. During the 1930s leaders of major Jewish organizations hesitated to press their demands lest they be accused of dragging America into war; during the 1940s, when America was in the war, they feared antisemites would accuse them of undermining the war effort. In the case of Stephen Wise, passionate attachment to President Roosevelt's policies clouded his political judgment and inhibited a vigorous response to the Nazi genocide. Jewish leaders genuinely agonized over the suffering of European Jewry, yet they found it difficult to shake off business-as-usual attitudes and modes of political action that were more suited to an earlier era. Nor were they able to rise above religious, political, and personal rivalries, which sapped their energies and undermined their effectiveness in the public arena.

The periodic flare-up of grassroots dissatisfaction and dissident activism offers a glimpse of what might have been. The Jewish Theological Seminary students showed that it was possible to mobilize the community by creatively using traditional religious mechanisms to address a contemporary crisis. Grassroots Jews were deeply troubled by the persecution of their brethren and ready to take action, but they lacked leadership. The rabbis who marched in Washington demonstrated that it was possible, even in wartime, for Jews to demonstrate in the streets of the nation's capital without repercussions; but theirs was the only such demonstration in Washington during the Holocaust.

The Bergson activists were the most effective of the dissidents because of their innovative tactics—the use of newspaper advertisements and theatrical productions to get their message to a broad audience, the recruiting of celebrities to draw attention to their cause, the building of coalitions with disparate political, social, and religious groups, and, especially, the intensive lobbying of Congress in order to bypass the State Department and directly influence White House policy, that is, by bringing about the establishment of the War Refugee Board. Had the board been established just a year earlier, many more lives would have been saved. Few in number, badly underfinanced, and sometimes hampered by the mainstream leadership, the Jewish activists of the 1940s accomplished much despite the odds and the obstacles. Their achievements stand out as bright spots on the record of American Jewish responses to Nazism and the Holocaust.

NOTES

1. Wise to Mack, April 15, 1933, October 18, 1933, and October 20, 1933, in Carl Hermann Voss, ed., *Stephen S. Wise: Servant of the People—Selected Letters* (Philadelphia, 1970), 184, 195–96.

2. Laurel Leff and Rafael Medoff, "New Documents Shed More Light on FDR's Holocaust Failure," *American Jewish World*, April 30, 2004, 5.

3. *Jewish Telegraphic Agency Daily News Bulletin*, March 14, 1933; *New York Times*, May 15, 1933.

4. Wise to Gottheil, April 17, 1933, box 947, Stephen S. Wise papers, American Jewish Archives, Cincinnati.

5. Moshe Gottlieb, "The Anti-Nazi Boycott Movement in the American Jewish Community, 1933–1941," 442, Ph.D. diss., Brandeis University, 1968.

6. Richard Breitman and Alan M. Kraut, *American Refugee Policy and European Jewry, 1933–1945* (Bloomington, 1987), 32.

7. David S. Wyman, *Paper Walls: America and the Refugee Crisis, 1938–1941* (Amherst, 1968), 173, and *The Abandonment of the Jews: America and the Holocaust, 1941–1945* (New York, 1984), 6.

8. Bat-Ami Zucker, "Frances Perkins and the German-Jewish Refugees, 1933–1940," *American Jewish History* 89 (2001).

9. Wise to Nathan, September 17, 1940, cited in Voss, *Stephen S. Wise*, 242.

10. Rafael Medoff, *The Deafening Silence: American Jewish Leaders and the Holocaust* (New York, 1987), 68; Gerald S. Berman, "Reaction to the Resettlement of World War II Refugees in Alaska," *Jewish Social Studies* (Summer-Fall 1982): 271–82.

11. Medoff, *The Deafening Silence*, 53.

12. Jerzy Tomaszewski, "Stephen S. Wise's Meeting with the Polish Ambassador in Washington, 1 April 1938," *Gal-Ed* 11 (1989): 103–15.

13. Allon Gal, *David Ben-Gurion and the American Alignment for a Jewish State* (Bloomington, 1991), 40, 50–53.

14. Wise to Friedenwald, October 12, 1936, and Wise to Neumann, October 13, 1936, in Voss, *Stephen S. Wise*, 216–17; Melvin I. Urofsky, *A Voice That Spoke for Justice: The Life and Times of Stephen S. Wise* (Albany, 1982), 284.

15. Wyman, *Paper Walls*, 73.

16. Rosenman to FDR, December 5, 1938, personal correspondence, Franklin D. Roosevelt papers, Franklin and Eleanor Roosevelt Library, Hyde Park, New York.

17. Henry L. Feingold, *The Politics of Rescue* (New Brunswick, NJ, 1979), 50; Wyman, *Paper Walls*, 97; Judith Tydor Baumel, *Unfulfilled Promise: Rescue and Resettlement of Jewish Refugee Children in the United States, 1934–1945* (Juneau, 1990), 145.

18. V. O. Key Jr., *Public Opinion and American Democracy* (New York, 1961), 277.

19. "Washington Sees Similarity Between Lindbergh's and Berlin's Anti-Jewish Propaganda," *Jewish Telegraphic Agency Daily News Bulletin*, September 14, 1941, 1.

20. Yehuda Bauer, *My Brother's Keeper: A History of the American Jewish Joint Distribution Committee, 1929–1939* (Philadelphia, 1974), *American Jewry and the Holocaust: The American Jewish Joint Distribution Committee, 1939–1945* (Detroit, 1981).

21. Efraim Zuroff, *The Response of Orthodox Jewry in the United States to the Holocaust* (New York, 2000).

22. Bauer, *American Jewry and the Holocaust*, 35.

23. Wyman, *The Abandonment of the Jews*, 75.

24. Wise to Niles, December 9, 1942, SSW-AJA.

25. David S. Wyman and Rafael Medoff, *A Race Against Death: Peter Bergson, America, and the Holocaust* (New York, 2002).

26. Henry L. Feingold, *Bearing Witness: How America and Its Jews Responded to the Holocaust* (Syracuse, 1995), 82.

27. Joint Emergency Committee minutes, March 15, 1943, box 8, American Jewish Commitee papers, YIVO.

28. Noah Golinkin, Jerome Lipnick, and N. [*sic*] Bertram Sachs, "Retribution Is Not Enough," *Reconstructionist* 9 (March 5, 1943): 19–21.

29. "Digest of the Speeches Delivered at the Interseminary Conference," *The Challenge*, March 1943, Noah Golinkin papers, David S. Wyman Institute for Holocaust Studies, Washington, DC.

30. Synagogue Council of America Minutes, March 10, 1943, Synagogue Council of America papers, American Jewish Historical Society.

31. "We Turn to Our Spiritual Leaders for Guidance" (editorial), *Jewish Tribune* (Passaic, NJ), April 29, 1943.

32. Opher to Goldstein, May 7, 1943, Synagogue Council of America papers, American Jewish Historical Society; The European Committee of the Jewish Theological Seminary, "A Program of Action," Noah Golinkin papers, David S. Wyman Institute for Holocaust Studies, Washington, DC.

33. Robert W. Ross, *So It Was True: The American Protestant Press and the Nazi Persecution of the Jews* (Minneapolis, 1980), 182–83.

34. For examples, see Rafael Medoff, "'Retribution Is Not Enough': The 1943 Campaign by Jewish Students to Raise American Public Awareness of the Nazi Genocide," *Holocaust and Genocide Studies* 11.2 (Fall 1997): notes 51, 52, and 53.

35. "Bermuda Conferees Agree to Another Conference," *Independent Jewish Press Service*, April 30, 1943, 3; "Failure in Bermuda" (editorial), *Opinion*, May 1943, 4.

36. Wise to Goldmann, April 23, 1943, SSW, box 1001, AJA; "Jewish Labor Committee Brands Joint Emergency Body as 'Do-Nothing,'" *Independent Jewish Press Service*, August 23, 1943, 1; Joint Emergency Committee minutes, November 5, 1943, box 8, American Jewish Commitee papers, YIVO.

37. Ben Hecht, *A Child of the Century* (New York, 1954), 565; Wyman and Medoff, *A Race Against Death*, 65–69, 241, note 16.

38. Wyman, *The Abandonment of the Jews*, 66, 285.

13

HOLOCAUST CONSCIOUSNESS AND
AMERICAN JEWISH POLITICS

MICHAEL E. STAUB

How has American Jews' sense of the meaning and implications of the Holocaust changed from the end of World War II to the present? It is a deceptively simple question. In the fields of American literature and popular culture, extensive scholarship has focused on representations of the Holocaust (including on television and in film).[1] Others have charted the impact of the Holocaust on theological debates.[2] But the role of Holocaust consciousness in American Jewish politics—and particularly the political battles over the Holocaust's meaning *within* the American Jewish community—has received far less attention. And what little scrutiny there has been—for example, in general overviews of American Jewish history—often assumes that the implications of the Holocaust for American Jewish politics were obvious.

For instance, there has been a long-standing misapprehension that the main lesson learned from the Holocaust for American Jews was that never again could (or should) they allow themselves to experience powerlessness. Yet those who contend that a rejection of Jewish powerlessness has been the sole "lesson" of the Holocaust for American Jewry do so at the expense of the historical record. In truth, this lesson—with all its attendant political ramifications with respect to the state of Israel and the nature of Zionism—did not emerge until the later 1960s. Indeed, one of my main objectives in this essay is to demonstrate the richness and complexity of earlier conflicts—now forgotten—over the Holocaust's potential lessons.

Furthermore, and although many scholars have assumed that the genocide of European Jewry was largely repressed in mainstream American as well as American Jewish consciousness in the first fifteen postwar years, more recent studies suggest that the United States Army's liberation of concentration camps, the Nuremberg trials, and widely read survivor memoirs (like those by Viktor Frankl and Bruno Bettelheim) made the singularity of the mass murder of European Jewry well known to the wider American public.[3] As Lawrence Baron has observed in his summary of the debate about the emergence of Holocaust consciousness in the United States, "though the term 'Holocaust' did not become common in American parlance until the 1960s, a sense of what it denoted had become widespread in the fifteen years after World War II." Baron is adamant that scholars (like American historian Peter Novick) who insist the Holocaust only entered public consciousness in the 1960s (and then did so for instrumental political reasons, like encouraging American Jewish support for Israel) have downplayed and selectively interpreted the existing evidence. Baron is committed to rescuing from historical forgetfulness "the less ethnocentric role the Jewish tragedy played in American and American Jewish consciousness between 1945 and 1960."[4]

Other Jewish studies scholars have advanced comparable arguments. Stuart Svonkin richly documents how Jewish professionals active in the intergroup relations agencies like the American Jewish Committee, American Jewish Congress, and Anti-Defamation League "were profoundly influenced by the cataclysmic events of the 1930s and 1940s" and that "the Holocaust, as it eventually came to be known, was arguably the touchstone of their identities as Jews."[5] And, in his study of the Holocaust on American television, Jeffrey Shandler notes: "Although generally characterized as a period of American Jewish silence on the Holocaust, the immediate postwar years saw a considerable amount of activity in response to this as-yet-unnamed subject: pioneering historical scholarship, the writing of the first of hundreds of personal and communal memoirs, the establishment of the earliest memorials."[6]

Anecdotally, American Jews who lived through this period have mutually contradictory memories. Some declare that the mass murder of European Jewry was never discussed in their synagogue, their Hebrew School, or their family. Others—from both secular and religious backgrounds—testify to the importance of their awareness of this cataclysm for their own early Jewish identification and/or their socialization as activists on behalf of antiracist causes in the United States. Clearly, there were regional and individual differences that explain the varieties of memories. But even if we agree that the number of American Jews debating the potential ramifications of the genocide of European Jewry for the United States context was initially small, it is nonetheless important to take the arguments they advanced seriously. This is so not least because once Holocaust consciousness emerged in the mid-1960s in the forms with which we are more familiar today, those who articulated its contours were already engaged in an argument with prior versions of Holocaust consciousness that insisted the main lesson of the Holocaust for the American context was the urgent need to combat bigotry in all its forms—and antiblack racism in particular.

In sum, then, far from being silent—either out of horror at the magnitude of the Nazi crimes or out of respectful sensitivity toward the trauma of survivors—Jewish commentators of a variety of political persuasions already in the 1940s, 1950s, and early 1960s made analogies to the mass murder of European Jewry when debating domestic political issues or explaining its purported "lessons" for America. This habit of drawing lessons may, in hindsight, seem insensitive. In recent decades we have become more attuned to the Holocaust's grim specificities and the inappropriateness of facile comparisons (even as facile comparisons continue to proliferate widely among both Jews and non-Jews with a broad array of political agendas). Many thoughtful commentators now insist that lesson making of all kinds is a dishonor to the dead, and they emphasize that the essential meaninglessness of the Holocaust is one of the most important things to grasp about it. Yet this notion that it might be indecent to engage in comparisons was not initially understood.

After the horrifying revelations of 1945, the Nazi genocide of European Jews was invoked almost at once in debates over American Jewish politics. Already, by the mid-1960s, assumptions about the lessons of Nazism for political life in the United States had gone through at least three distinct stages. Political commentary (especially in the Jewish press) made frequent reference to Nazism and the mass murder of European Jewry, particularly in the context of the African American civil rights movement.

In the first stage of drawing lessons from the genocide of European Jewry for the United States context, both left-wing (that is, pro-communist) and liberal (pro-Democratic) American Jews continued—as they had done already during World War II—to elaborate analogies between German Nazism and American antiblack racism. These Jews often identified directly with African Americans. In a racist and antisemitic environment—according to the prevailing logic—in helping blacks Jews were also helping themselves. Although the cold war undermined that particular analogy as un-American, and a new analogy between Nazism and Stalinism grew in its place, by the late 1950s a second form of Holocaust consciousness had emerged. Inspired by the Reform rabbis' movement for "prophetic Judaism," and led by committed Zionists within the American Jewish Congress, antiracist activists began to argue that, if they did not help blacks, American Jews would be no better than the gentile German and Polish bystanders who had done nothing to prevent the Holocaust. This line of reasoning came to full flowering in the early 1960s, which also saw the beginnings of a third (more particularist and to us now more familiar) strand of argumentation: one that identified the most important lesson of the Holocaust as the need for Jews—within the United States and around the world—to protect themselves and fight for their own survival.

The remainder of this essay takes the story of Holocaust consciousness in American political life through the tumultuous 1960s to the present day. It lingers a while in the mid to late 1960s and 1970s because that era's reconfigurations of Jewish identity had such a lasting influence. It was in those years that many of the current views on the lessons of the Holocaust and the proper way to honor the memory of the dead were first advanced. In the later 1960s and through the 1970s, for instance, the turn toward a more survivalist interpretation of Jewish identity was especially evident in discussions of American Jewry's relationship to Israel and in debates over Jewish reproductive levels. Further Holocaust lessons were identified and contested in this context. The right-wing Jewish Defense League, formed in 1968 during the height of the New Left student rebellions, became influential far beyond its modest numbers. The JDL slogan "Never Again" became shorthand for the idea that henceforth Jews refused to be on the receiving end of violence, but also that violence could now, however regretfully, be embraced as a necessary component of Jewish pride. Realpolitik replaced idealism. At the same time, in reaction to both the sexual revolution and Jewish involvement in African American civil rights and anti–Vietnam War activism, Orthodox leaders grew increasingly outspoken, especially on the subject of Jewish fertility rates. They, too, became influential far beyond the numbers of their adherents. Orthodox leaders developed the argument—which in the 1970s was taken up by Jews across the religious and ideological spectrum—that a key lesson of the Holocaust was the need for Jewish women to bear more children.

The 1970s through the 1980s also saw the dissemination of Holocaust consciousness to a wider American public, with all the attendant paradoxes of success. On the one hand, these decades experienced the beginnings of what has since become an even more dramatic growth in rigorous scholarship on the Holocaust and a growing institutionalization of Holocaust consciousness in university classrooms and in museums and memorials across the United States.[7] A proliferation of filmic and literary representations made the Holocaust a resonant and iconic touchstone in the popular imagination. On the other hand, even as the reality and intensity of Jewish victimization was made more palpable for viewers and readers, various forms of backlash and exploitation also flourished. Holocaust denial became big news and had enormous political influence, both nationally and internationally.[8] More subtle but also pernicious arguments that Jews were capitalizing on the suffering of their forebears circulated as well. Other groups who felt victimized sought to model their own claims for restitution or even just recognition on what they perceived as Jewish accomplishments in these areas. Yet others—whether the arguments were advanced with antisemitic malice or in earnest anguish—argued that Jewish emphasis on the past of the Holocaust diverted attention from Israeli treatment of the Palestinians.[9] Many also contended that emphasis on the horrors of the Holocaust detracted from more affirmative dedication to faith, community, and Jewish identity. And meanwhile, for far too many

Jews and gentiles alike, Holocaust consciousness was filled more with saccharine pieties than with challenging reflection.[10]

The collapse of the Soviet Union and the end of the cold war made vast new archives of evidence on the details of the Holocaust available to scholars, and in the 1990s both scholarly knowledge and general awareness of the Holocaust advanced exponentially over what was known and understood a generation earlier. From the vantage point of the very beginning of the twenty-first century, it seemed clear that the Holocaust was the central defining event of the twentieth century.[11] Yet the rightward shift of American national politics since September 11, 2001, and even more since the invasion of Iraq in 2003 and the reelection of George W. Bush in 2004, has changed not only the political calculus of American Jews but also the ways the Holocaust's import for the evolving present can be understood.

ANALOGIZING ANTIBLACK AND ANTI-JEWISH RACISM

In the aftermath of the Second World War, the Nazi genocide of European Jewry became a topic for discussion in American Jewish political life almost at once. Commentators agreed that the Nazi genocide was a logical reference point from which to draw conclusions about contemporary social issues in the United States. Leading Jewish liberal periodicals in the immediate postwar era were especially receptive to the analogy between German fascism and American racism.

Directly in the wake of Adolf Hitler's rise to power, Nazi treatment of Jews was already in 1933 described in the African American press as "Jim Crow for Jews Now," while Hitler was described as the "master Ku Kluxer of Germany."[12] Conversely, in the wake of the war, African American periodicals like the *Afro-American* and the *Crisis* (the National Association for the Advancement of Colored People's organ) labeled race laws in the American South "Southern Schrecklichkeit [Southern Horrors]" and suggested that antiblack mob violence resembled "Storm Trooper Fascism."[13] Furthermore, the *Crisis* argued that the "notorious Nazi Nuremberg racial decrees aimed at the Jews were patterned on Dixie's 'techniques of racial oppression.'"[14] Given the extensive involvement of Jews in NAACP projects, these analogies were clearly being developed with Jewish awareness and approval.

Yet these comparisons were openly advanced in explicitly Jewish venues in the immediate postwar years as well. Early postwar Jewish commentary, for instance, did not hesitate to draw direct lessons from "a Nazi extermination program" in order "to explain a southern lynching"—as Leo Pfeffer, a prominent lawyer on the staff of the American Jewish Congress's Commission on Law and Social Action, put it in the pages of the Labor Zionist publication *Jewish Frontier*. Pfeffer wrote in 1946 that "as Hitler well knew, [a lie] will be believed, no matter how big it is, if only it is repeated often enough." So too the "continued repetition of the fairy tale that Negro blood is different from and inferior to Caucasian has caused millions of uneducated or partially educated poor whites to consider Negroes an intermediate species between simian and human." In the same way, ordinary German citizens had

> participated or acquiesced in mass murder of Jews because for years they had been exposed to the lie that the Jews were their enemy and that all would be well when Jewish blood would flow. Race libels do not usually have immediate recognizable results, but their cumulative effect when compared with defamation of individuals is as atomic fission to the explosion of a fire-cracker.[15]

The new journal *Commentary*, sponsored by the American Jewish Committee, also repeatedly invoked a Nazi analogy to dramatize its disapproval of racial discrimination in the U.S., especially in housing and employment practices. A 1947 essay in *Commentary* entitled "Homes for Aryans Only" put a distinctly American spin on the possible lessons of Nazism. The author argued that a libertarian tradition did not give American property owners a legal right to refuse to sell their homes to "non-Caucasians" (including Jews). Rhetorically linking the emancipation of slaves with the liberation of European Jewry, the author wrote, "Eighty years after Gettysburg, and two years after Hitler, the proposition that all men are created equal is again being whittled down, and in the area perhaps most crucial for a future democratic America—the area of our neighborhood life."[16]

For at least a few years the Nazi genocide became a relevant reference point for making sense of American racial (and racist) realities. These analogies were not only taken to be inoffensive to most American Jews; they were widely understood to reflect common sense. It was a double standard, many felt, for the United States *not* to turn its full attention to the eradication of white racism at home after German fascism had been defeated abroad.

With the rise of the cold war, however, nearly every element of American society—including many American Jewish individuals and organizations—endorsed the anticommunist consensus. In prior years many Jewish liberals (along with leftists and left-wing sympathizers) had proclaimed American white racism and German Nazism comparable evils. By 1949 this analogy had virtually vanished—ridiculed as the product of "Communist-fabricated hysteria." Only those few sympathetic to communism continued to press the antiracist linkage, and they were declared anti-American because their rhetoric "furnished new grist for the Kremlin propaganda mill."[17] In 1948 New York University philosopher Sidney Hook had already spelled out a new analogy: it was Soviet communism that most resembled Nazism.[18]

Increasing numbers of Jewish commentators suggested that Jews made the best and most loyal cold war Americans precisely because their suffering at the hands of Nazism had taught them to abhor the excesses of totalitarianism. Fear that Jews might be tarred with the anticommunist brush was great. Suspected Jewish communists and communist sympathizers were expelled from every major American Jewish organization. Many Jews abandoned their active roles in left-wing causes. Analogies between Nazism and American racism grew far less acceptable among Jewish liberals. The vast majority of Jewish intellectuals and leaders retreated wholesale from making pronouncements that could possibly be interpreted as anti-American or pro-communist. Civil rights continued to be supported, but far more cautiously.

References to Nazi crimes in American Jewish discourse began to drop off dramatically. It was only at the end of the 1950s and increasingly in the early 1960s that the Holocaust and its relationship to American politics began to resurface. However, it did so in competing and mutually irreconcilable forms.

BYSTANDER ANXIETY

On August 28, 1963, at the March on Washington rally, Rabbi Joachim Prinz, president of the American Jewish Congress, gave a brief address titled "The Issue Is Silence." At Prinz's side stood Martin Luther King Jr., who was to deliver his "I Have a Dream" speech that same afternoon. The crowd that late summer day numbered two hundred thousand. Prinz spoke of his years as a rabbi in prewar Berlin, an intimate witness to the advance of Nazism.[19] Standing before the Lincoln Memorial, his speech revitalized the link between German antisemitism and American racism that had been all but erased during the cold war. Elaborating on why American Jews struggled for racial justice after Auschwitz, Prinz offered a Holocaust lesson not available in the 1940s:

> When I was the rabbi of the Jewish community in Berlin under the Hitler regime, I learned . . . that bigotry and hatred are not the most urgent problem. The most urgent, the most disgraceful, the most shameful and the most tragic problem is silence.
>
> A great people which had created a great civilization had become a nation of silent onlookers. They remained silent in the face of hate, in the face of brutality and in the face of mass murder. America must not become a nation of onlookers. America must not remain silent. Not merely black America, but all of America. It must speak up and act, from the President down to the humblest of us, and not for the sake of the Negro, not for the sake of the black community, but for the sake of the image, the idea and the aspiration of America itself.[20]

A rabbi attending the March on Washington told *Hadassah Magazine* that Prinz's speech mirrored his own feelings: "Had this march taken place in the 1930s in Germany, there might never have been the mass murder of Jews. The conscience of the Christians in Germany might have been awakened as our consciences are being awakened today."[21] Thus Prinz had formulated a kind of Holocaust analogizing that might best be called "bystander anxiety." If American Jews failed to put themselves at risk to work on behalf of African Americans, then they would be behaving no better than German citizens had under Nazism.

Bystander anxiety had already begun to find expression in rabbinic and other Jewish circles. In 1958 Rabbi Jacob M. Rothschild of Atlanta had asked, regarding civil rights activism: "How can we condemn the millions who stood by under Hitler, or honor those few who chose to live by their ideals, when we refuse to make a similar choice now that the dilemma is our own?"[22] In 1962, in an indicative turn of phrase, gentiles who had rescued Jews from the Holocaust were honored as "Freedom Riders."[23] Rabbi Richard Rubenstein, a year later, describing a discussion at the convention of the Conservative movement's Rabbinical Assembly (concerning the proposed establishment of an institute "to document altruistic deeds done by non-Jews to save Jews during the Hitler holocaust"), reported the following exchange:

> The proposal touched an understandably sore nerve. In the midst of the debate, one rabbi queried why we were concentrating our energies on what had happened twenty years ago [during the Holocaust]. . . . Then, almost as an afterthought, the rabbi asked whether the Rabbinical Assembly was doing the right thing by meeting together rather than adjourning to Birmingham, Alabama, to aid Dr. Martin Luther King and his followers in their struggle for human rights.[24]

These were far from isolated cases. Increasingly, rabbis who saw social justice concerns as integral to their faith found, in the Holocaust, a reference point underscoring the righteousness of antiracist activism. The years 1963–64 would witness the flourishing of this line of argumentation. It did not, however, go unchallenged.

JEWISH SURVIVAL

A competing (and implicitly less liberal) political expression of Holocaust consciousness came to prominence also in the early 1960s. It stressed the urgent need for American Jews to focus on their own communal survival. Interestingly, this opposite perspective was also formulated in the context of civil rights activism.

At the start of the 1960s a number of prominent American Jewish leaders expressed irritation at the community's ardent involvement in civil rights and liberal causes. In 1960 Milton Himmelfarb accused the American Jewish Congress of being more concerned with civil rights than with Jewish religion, education, or culture.[25] That same year *Midstream* editor Shlomo Katz wondered aloud whether civil rights activism wasn't simply a fad wherein students engaged in cathartic, social guilt-releasing bouts of group therapy. Protesting segregation seemed just to be a "fashion" and a "salve for the conscience."[26] Also that year both Himmelfarb and the new *Commentary* editor, Norman Podhoretz, accused American Jewish liberals of inadequate consciousness about the enormity of the Nazi genocide.[27] Meanwhile, Rabbi Emil Fackenheim lamented the inability of young Jews to express what was repugnant about Nazism; he proclaimed "liberal Judaism . . . a contradiction in terms."[28]

In 1963 and 1964 the attacks on Jews involved in African American civil rights activism became more fervent. In his now famous essay, "My Negro Problem—and Ours," Podhoretz confessed to "twisted feelings about Negroes." But he also expressed annoyance at white liberals who, in his view, "romanticize Negroes and pander to them [or] who lend themselves . . . to cunning and contemptuous exploitation by Negroes they employ or try to befriend." Podhoretz expressed condescension toward African Americans even as he also invoked Auschwitz:

> Did the Jews have to survive so that 6 million innocent people should one day be burned in the ovens at Auschwitz? It is a terrible question and no one, not God himself, could ever answer it to my satisfaction. And when I think about the Negroes in America and about the image of integration as a state in which the Negroes would take their rightful place as another of the protected minorities in a pluralistic society, I wonder whether they really believe in their hearts that such a state can actually be attained, and if so *why* they should wish to survive as a distinct group. I think I know why the Jews once wished to survive (though I am less certain as to why we still do): they not only believed that God had given them no choice, but they were tied to a memory of past glory and a dream of imminent redemption. What does the American Negro have that might correspond to this? His past is a stigma, his color is a stigma, and his vision of the future is the hope of erasing the stigma by making color irrelevant, by making it disappear as a fact of consciousness.[29]

Less iconoclastically, but with similar effect, an increasing number of Jewish commentators argued that Holocaust consciousness should cause Jews to withdraw from involvement in civil rights activism and/or criticized African Americans and black culture. They also began to make the argument that Jews who stayed involved in civil rights activism were self-hating.

In seeking to revise the proper meaning of Holocaust consciousness, for example, Abraham G.. Duker attacked Jewish civil rights activists. Duker was an
editor of *Jewish Social Studies* and a professor of history at Yeshiva University.
Speaking at a conference on black-Jewish relations, Duker acknowledged the legitimacy "of this intensive interest in the Negro struggle on the part of so many
Jews. . . . [It] stems from the Jewish tradition of social justice (usually called 'prophetic' tradition)." However, Duker stressed the necessity of taking into account
the consequences of such interest—for "in many cases Jewish communal involvement in integration [has come] at the cost of neglecting . . . Jewish survival."
Blacks were turning on Jews, Duker suggested, because of their own "disappointments with the pace of integration." The Jewish community's very survival was at
risk, he said, if Jews did not recognize how black "demands on [them] are sometimes veiled with threats [and] are remindful of prolegomena to quotas, robberies,
confiscations and pogroms." And Duker explicitly compared demands for the
"Negroization" of Harlem stores to German "Aryanization" propaganda.[30]

Warning that "genocidal Negro extremists have been given respectability and
recognition," he analogized: "That is what happened to anti-Semites in Germany,
and the world is still paying for it." Duker was no less harsh on Jews advocating
the rights of blacks, calling this a "masochistic approach to their own people."
Through an extended chain of associations, he brought together Holocaust imagery with Jewish involvement in civil rights:

> The gas chambers and crematoria have proved at least to one generation the
> bankruptcy of assimilation in Europe. Nevertheless, the pressures of accul-
> turation, Jewish deculturation and thereby de-Judaization have been in-
> creasing, with hedonism and deracination as their most visible hallmarks.
> Departure from the community through intermarriage and indifference
> follows. . . . In the United States escapism from Jewishness has also found
> expression in the integrationist movement. I know of cases of escapist iden-
> tification of Jews with the integration struggle to the extent of extreme *jü-
> discher Selbsthass* [Jewish self-hatred] and active anti-Semitism.[31]

Marie Syrkin, editor of the *Jewish Frontier*, offered another influential example
of this new Holocaust consciousness coupled with disdain for blacks. In "Can
Minorities Oppose 'De Facto' Segregation?" Syrkin gave several reasons why a
civil rights push for desegregation "is not only self-depreciating but deflects energy from more meaningful demands." She made overt reference to her post-
Holocaust Jewish identity in the essay:

> Any point of view which runs counter in any significant respect to the cur-
> rent Negro civil rights program is bound to be suspect. For this reason I
> preface my comments with the statement that I am impelled to write not as

a white liberal, though I believe the label fits, but as a member of a minority which knows more about systematic discrimination and violent persecution than any group in history. In the immediate as well as historic experience of Jews, a ghetto is not a metaphor; it is a concrete entity with walls, storm-troopers and no exit save the gas chamber. And wherever Jews have lived, varying gradations of bias and social exclusion have been their daily diet. I offer these credentials to indicate Jewish expertise in what it means to be a suffering minority. However brilliant his individual success, Auschwitz is in the consciousness of the modern Jew, reinforcing historic memories of catastrophe.

Syrkin warned that black activists should not pursue strategies likely to result in the "resentment of groups formerly in agreement with Negro goals." Careful not to advocate or prescribe civil rights policy, Syrkin claimed only to document actual events and real obstacles facing the struggle for racial equality. Her analogies and examples, nonetheless, revealed a wholly negative view of integration efforts. Calling for full integration, she wrote, amounted to a societal reductio ad absurdum. She likened it to "discover[ing] that most of my fellow passengers on some bus routes or subway trains happened to be Jews. Would I then be justified in protesting *de facto* segregation on my bus?" No more, she concluded, than she should "be expected to travel to Harlem in the interests of integrated dining."[32]

Syrkin also introduced the theme of self-hate in her essay. History, she claimed, had taught the Jewish people how a minority survives. "Self-respecting" Jews knew survival could—and should—mean a desirable degree of voluntary communal separateness. Only "self-hating Jews" would ever view de facto segregation of the Jewish community "as oppressive. . . . Except for avowed assimilationists, Jews have never made complete integration a goal."[33]

A subsequent exchange of views about black-Jewish relations printed in *Midstream* in 1966 included more such comments. Akin to Duker's analogy between "Negroization" and "Aryanization," Lucy Dawidowicz, for instance, compared African American militancy to Nazism. It was "hard to distinguish Black Power from Black Shirts," she observed. Furthermore, Jews involved in Students for a Democratic Society, the Student Nonviolent Coordinating Committee (SNCC), and the Congress of Racial Equality (CORE) were "alienated" from their own heritage, "spitting in the wells from which they drank."[34]

A new set of associations and arguments was evolving. Blacks were not like Jews; blacks, especially when militant, were like Nazis. Jews who worked on behalf of blacks were self-hating and seeking to escape their Jewishness. And the Holocaust's lesson was that Jewish survival should be paramount. Jews who continued to adhere to liberalism, the new theory went, must not be very proud of their heritage. This cluster of beliefs was in dramatic contrast with earlier interpretations of Holocaust consciousness, which had urged Jews to identify with other oppressed minorities and refuse to be bystanders to injustice.

This trend did not go uncontested. Shad Polier and Justine Wise Polier, for instance, challenged Podhoretz directly in an essay titled "Fear Turned to Hatred." Podhoretz had mocked masochistic whites "who romanticize Negroes and pander to them." The Poliers called the *Commentary* editor's vision of Jewishness "woefully insensitive" to the broader context of black lives and "suffused with self-pity" and "infantile self-appreciation": "One cannot but wonder whether the doubt later expressed by Podhoretz concerning the value of Jewish survival does not stem from a preference, conscious or unconscious, to be part of the powerful white *goyim* who could oppress, rather than to be part of any minority which might suffer oppression." Was it Podhoretz, the Poliers implied, who might really be the self-hating Jew? They were particularly aghast at Podhoretz's invocation of "the ovens of Auschwitz" for the purposes of criticizing black efforts to survive as a group. With these remarks, "the writer reveals his own moral bankruptcy," the Poliers said. "The concept of loving oneself not in terms of narcissism but in terms of self-respect and the ideal of loving one's neighbor and the stranger, the great themes of Judeo-Christian ethics, are to be cast aside," they asserted. Seeing in Podhoretz's writing an "admission of self-contempt," the Poliers concluded it was precisely the "great heritage" of commitment to the ideal of "human brotherhood [that had] made the survival of the Jewish people meaningful to Jews as men, and to those lands in which the Jews have lived."[35]

Tensions grew in the years that followed, when not just Jewish liberalism but the very meaning of Jewish survival would become the subject of overt and extended controversy. The Six-Day War between Israel and the Arab nations marked a turning point in American Jewish politics. But as the intense debates over American race relations so decisively show, this seeming turning point of 1967 also needs to be understood as the culmination of an extended conflict that had been brewing for quite some time. Within the United States the Israeli victory over the Arab nations in 1967 consolidated agendas and arguments whose foundations had long ago been laid. In the wake of Israel's victory, these ongoing debates only became more combative.

JEWISH PRIDE

Many American Jews interpreted the Six-Day War as a second potential Holocaust; some even viewed Israel's victory as divinely ordained. Even those put off by a religious interpretation felt something profoundly redemptive about the war's outcome. Podhoretz wrote of the tremendous catharsis felt by most American Jews after the Six-Day War, which would "reinforce a thousand fold a new determination we had already tasted as a saving sweetener to the bitter sensation of isolation and vulnerability." The emotional American Jewish response to Israel's military victory, he added, "represented the recovery, after a long and uncertain convalescence, of the Jewish remnant from the grievous and nearly fatal psychic and spiritual wounds it [had] suffered at the hands of the Nazis."[36]

Dawidowicz summarized the dominant post–Six-Day War mood as "a new kind of pride in being Jewish, in the aura that radiated from General Moshe Dayan, his ruggedness, vigor, determination. Many Jews took pride in the changed image of the Jew, no longer seen as victim or the historic typification of a persecuted people." American Jews, whose strongest political identification had been with the civil rights and anti–Vietnam War movements, "discovered the importance of being Jewish." Indicative of this ardent newfound Jewish pride—and its links to the Holocaust—was the following letter to the *Village Voice*:

> I think it must have been this way for many of my generation, that the Israeli-Arab collision was a moment of truth. For the first time in my grown-up life, I really understood what an enemy was. For the first time, I knew what it was to be us against the killers.
>
> Us. Two weeks ago, Israel was they; now Israel is we. I will not intellectualize it. . . . I will never kid myself that we are only the things we choose to be. Roots count.
>
> And I will never again claim to be a pacifist; I will never again say that, if I had been an adult during World War II, I might have been for non-intervention, or, if a man, been a conscientious objector. I have lost the purity of the un-tested.[37]

Certainly some American Jews continued to voice dissenting perspectives. In the immediate aftermath of the Six-Day War, for instance, left-wing commentator I. F. Stone observed that "Israel's swift and brilliant military victory only makes its reconciliation with the Arabs more urgent." He called upon the world Jewish community, which had undertaken a "huge financial effort to aid Israel" in a time of war, now to use those funds for "a constructive and human cause." This meant that Israel should, Stone wrote, "find new homes for the Arab refugees, some within Israel, some outside it, all with compensation for their lost lands and properties."

> It was a moral tragedy—to which no Jew worthy of our best Prophetic tradition could be insensitive—that a kindred people was made homeless in the task of finding new homes for the remnants of the Hitler holocaust. Now is the time to right that wrong, to show magnanimity in victory, and to lay the foundations of a new order in the Middle East in which Israeli and Arab can live in peace. . . . The first step toward reconciliation is to

recognize that Arab bitterness has real and deep roots. The refugees lost their farms, their villages, their offices, their cities and their country. It is human to prefer not to look at the truth, but only in facing the problem in all its three dimensional frightful reality is there any hope of solving it without new tragedy.[38]

Yet Stone's interpretation of the Six-Day War—especially his reading of the Holocaust and its lessons—was not widely shared.

The new commitment to Jewish pride and Jewish power gained momentum from diverse quarters. Among the most important new advocates of Jewish pride were groups of radical Zionist youth who, inspired by and in emulation of Black Power, argued that proper Holocaust consciousness meant identifying with Israel as a Third World nation. (The Radical Zionist Alliance was founded at Camp Ramah in Massachusetts in February 1970; Jewish students from seventy-five campuses in the United States, Canada, and Israel had gathered there.) In rejecting their parents' assimilationist strategies, and turning against "Bagels & Lox Judaism," the younger generation also sought to make public the psychic damage caused by antisemitism. Young Jewish activists labeled Jewish establishment leaders "Uncle Jakes" (a nod to black militants, who referred to their more accommodationist elders as "Uncle Toms"); they launched more than two dozen campus journals across North America dedicated to exploring Jewish identity; they demanded, through protest actions, far more attention to Jewish education within the United States; and they urged American Jews to make aliyah, i.e., to emigrate to Israel (and did so themselves). Cartoonist Jerry (now Yaakov) Kirschen joked about it in his strip: "Calling All Zionists: Will all the ZIONISTS please stand up? WRONG! 'Cause if you're still here in Amerika [sic] . . . you ain't no Zionist! . . . you're a shmuck."[39]

JEWISH POWER

Further commitment to Jewish pride and power came from the right-wing Jewish Defense League (JDL), born in 1968. Although some retrospective accounts consider the Jewish Defense League a marginal organization, its impact on the terms of debate among American Jews was profound. And, more significantly, according to a poll taken in the late 1960s, one in four American Jews supported the JDL. Another survey by the American Jewish Congress found one in three of that moderate group's membership supported Rabbi Meir Kahane's organization.

Kahane made the Jewish capacity for self-defense central to his message. He urged each Jewish man to stop being a "Nice Irving."[40] He warned Jews to stop being "patsies."[41] In "A Small Voice," Kahane's regular column for the Brooklyn-based Orthodox *Jewish Press*, he wrote:

Vandals attack a Yeshiva—let that Yeshiva attack the vandals. Should a gang bloody a Jew, let a Jewish group go looking for the gang. This is the way of pride—not evil pride, but the pride of nation, of kinship. . . . There are those who will protest: This is not the Jewish way. And yet since when has it been a *mitzvah* [good deed] to be punished and beaten? Since when is it a *kiddush hashem* [blessing] . . . ? It is not a *kiddush hashem*, it is quite the opposite. It is a disgrace to the pride of our people, our G-d.[42]

Kahane was a central figure in the reconfiguration of Holocaust consciousness among American Jews. The JDL's philosophy blamed an inability to confront the legacy of the Holocaust for all the Jewish community's problems. The spiritual sickness of American Jewish identity lay precisely in a reflexive inability to defend itself against aggression, according to JDL and other radical Zionist thinking. Along with the slogan "Never Again," JDL advocated that all Jews learn martial arts and that all Jewish children join rifle associations.[43]

The Holocaust was also a crucial reference point in the group's most controversial recruitment tool: a large *New York Times* advertisement that appeared in June 1969. Prompted by SNCC leader James Forman's decision to read aloud a demand for reparations for slavery at New York City's leading white Christian churches and at Temple Emanu-El, the ad showed several JDL toughs, armed with baseball bats and lead pipes, gathering to defend the synagogue. The ad's caption asked: "Is This Any Way for Nice Jewish Boys to Behave?" The answer followed:

Maybe. Maybe there are times when there is no other way to get across to the extremist that the Jew is not quite the patsy some think he is.

Maybe there is only one way to get across a clear response to people who threaten seizure of synagogues and extortion of money. Maybe nice Jewish boys do not always get through to people who threaten to carry teachers out in pine boxes and to burn down merchants' stores.

Maybe some people and organizations are too nice. Maybe in times of crisis Jewish boys should not be that nice. Maybe—just maybe—nice people build their road to Auschwitz.[44]

In this way the JDL resuscitated the popular and profoundly problematic theory that Jews had been passive under Nazi persecution. Indeed, one of the most striking aspects of Holocaust consciousness in the late 1960s and early 1970s was the exacerbation, rather than the rejection, of the myth that Jews in Europe's ghettos and death camps had gone "like lambs to the slaughter." This stereotype—strongly endorsed in Bruno Bettelheim's *The Informed Heart* (1960) and Hannah Arendt's *Eichmann in Jerusalem* (1963)—was eloquently refuted in the course of the 1960s by Podhoretz, Alexander Donat, and others. Jewish power advocates chose, however, to reinforce the "passive Jew" myth at this moment to advance their cause both in Israel and the United States.

Rabbi Richard Rubenstein's public declarations of the utter necessity of embracing Jewish power took on special significance, for he spoke both as a former civil rights activist and a leading post-Holocaust theologian. By the late 1960s Rubenstein had articulated an openly macho interpretation of Holocaust consciousness. He considered it a chronic misinterpretation to regard antisemitism as something belonging to "the category of emotional abnormality." He argued that "there may be something altogether predictable and even normal about the antipathy often expressed towards Jews."[45] To place antisemitism on the shelf with abnormality was to minimize how it continued to saturate the world, something Jews did at their own great peril. Only Zionists, Rubenstein told a conference in Rehovoth, Israel, had correctly understood antisemitism—and had responded to it by seeking to create a Jewish national homeland.

One consequence of Jewish nationhood was that Jews had to learn new skills and deploy new methods to defend their state.

> In a word, the re-entry of the Jewish community into the realms of nationhood and territory meant a re-entry into the domain of the intelligent use of violence. For two thousand years, the Jewish community had been the passive recipient of aggression. Immense transformations were required in order that the Jewish community attempt to survive in the world of naked power and violence. Secular society's messianic promise had failed. It was succeeded by tribal nationalism to some degree everywhere in the world.[46]

Without power, especially in a world that respected little else, Jews emasculated themselves. The "realities of naked power" were phenomena that Israelis recognized all too well, Rubenstein noted. Sadly, Jews in the Diaspora, imbued with a self-destructive "Jewish messianic optimism," had come to consider powerlessness itself as "a special virtue." But to accept a self-abnegating view toward power "after the gas chambers" was a risk of tremendous proportions, for "powerlessness can mean that the lives and the honor of one's women, one's children and one's person are subject to the good graces of others." In Rubenstein's view, "After the European Holocaust, the entailments of powerlessness should have proven so degrading and frightening that no Jews with a measure of inner dignity would ever want to be placed in that position again."[47]

Rabbi Steven S. Schwarzschild, however, drew a different lesson from the Holocaust. A refugee from Nazism, Schwarzschild felt Rubenstein's perspective defamed the memory of Holocaust victims. "That's not security," he said. "That's insecurity. That's not self-assertiveness and pride in one's identity; that's pathology."[48] Entering the realm of statehood and power, Schwarzschild opined, seemed to be accompanied by a disturbing "transvaluation of all Jewish values." "The problem of our Jewish generation and of our children," Schwarzschild continued, "is whether we can live with the ethics and politics of the persecuted, having, in some ways, ceased to be the persecuted. I implore you and me and all of us not to prove Nietzsche to have been right—that morality is the rationalization of the weak." Schwarzschild insisted that he was "as committed as anybody on earth to the sanctity of every inch of the Holy Land."[49] But he was disturbed to find Jews starting to behave like "men of the new Fascism [rather than] the men of spirit that the Jewish people have always been." To Schwarzschild, Zionism "has to do not so much with survival as with the opportunity to test and incarnate Jewish values on the soil of Israel."[50] However, the space for combining a commitment to Israel's safety with left-wing causes was narrowing. Critiques of Israeli militarism became unacceptable in the American Jewish community and were met with immediate rebuke.

Increasingly, also in the domestic context, during the 1970s concern about the biological survival of Jews began to displace earlier debates about the content of Jewish values. For example, Bill Novak, editor of the Jewish countercultural journal *Response*, in 1971 expressed both the overarching trends of the time and his own hesitations about those trends when he stated:

> Several years ago, during the civil rights movement, there were those who said disdainfully, "nobody helped us" and "let them pull themselves up by their bootstraps like we did." These reckless comparisons are being repeated now in new forms, as if we must give the world tit for tat, as if there were no special obligations, no sense of destiny, or of mission, that Jews have always possessed. And as long as we are here, it is our duty to make life in America better for all people; and this needn't be at the expense of ourselves. For we must assert it loudly: Mere existence, for Jews, *even in the wake of Hitler*, is simply not enough.[51]

POPULATION PANIC

In the course of the 1970s, one further wrinkle entered the debate over what lessons American Jews should draw from the Holocaust. Much attention within the Jewish community focused, at this time, on the future prospects of the Jewish family and the supposed need for Jewish women to have more babies. A corollary to this new argument asserted that the most appropriate response to the Holocaust was to challenge and oppose aspects of the sexual revolution.

Some Orthodox leaders did not hesitate to invoke the Holocaust in making a case against abortion. Among the most influential was Rabbi Walter S. Wurzburger, first vice president of the Rabbinical Council of America. In 1973, speaking at a conference sponsored by the Federation of Jewish Philanthropies of New York, Wurzburger opined that "having lost one-third of our population in the Holocaust and lacking sufficient population to settle the land of Israel, the Jewish community does not reproduce itself adequately."[52] By early 1976 he expressly condemned Reform Jewish leaders' pro-choice stance as "insensitive to the injurious effects on Jewish survival which permissive abortion represents." He added, "It is particularly reprehensible for Jewish groups to promote abortion in light of the fact that the Jews have not yet replaced the Holocaust losses and in light of the fact that Israel needs more population desperately and yet has an alarming rate of abortion."[53] Along related lines, already in 1974 Orthodox Rabbi Sol Roth, president of the New York Board of Rabbis, identified the low American Jewish birth rate of the previous three decades as a "Holocaust-size loss."[54] In 1975 Rabbi Norman Lamm, president of Yeshiva University, noted that although world population control was a "moral imperative," the Jewish situation required special consideration. "Jews are a disappearing species," he argued, "and should be treated no worse than the kangaroo and the bald eagle." Lamm recommended that each married Jewish woman have four or five children.[55]

Nevertheless, most American Jews continued to support birth control and abortion rights and to embrace many aspects of the sexual revolution. A broadening range of advocates, both male and female, from across the denominations expressed vocal dismay that Jewish women were not heeding the call for more children. Jewish leaders counseled families to have four children or more; to do otherwise would be to risk allowing Hitler a posthumous victory. Concern was no longer confined to Orthodox circles. In 1971 a Reform rabbi told the *Jewish Post and Opinion* that, up to the year 2000, "each Jewish family should have at least four children." If Jewish families had only two children, he calculated, the community would, in effect, be "fixing our numbers at the level established by Adolf Hitler."[56] And in 1974 an essay in the *Reconstructionist* (titled "Are the Jews Committing Jewish Genocide?") argued that the "all-time low" fertility rate, among Jews, while "not the result of local pogroms, massive extermination campaigns by Nazis or Communists, or even intermarriage, [could have the same] ultimate effects [as these] within only one or two generations."[57] Even the typically liberal-minded Central Conference of American Rabbis (Reform) released a statement after its annual convention in 1977 officially urging Jewish families "to have at least two or three children" because "there are simply not enough of us to be assured of survival in succeeding generations."[58]

One of the few to examine critically the strategies of pro-fertility advocates was *Lilith* contributor Shirley Frank. In her 1977 critique of the Jewish fertility debates, Frank quoted from a 1961 *Commentary* article by Milton Himmelfarb. He had posed the following moral dilemma: "Where does a Jew's obligation lie? Should he absent himself from paternity awhile, for the good of the human race? Or should he be of good courage, and play the man for the people?" One wonders, Frank noted archly, "what 'play the man' means in this context. It seems clear, however, that the man is making decisions about his paternity quite as if he were a self-fertilizing flower." Challenging rhetoric that constantly associated "the present downward trend in population growth . . . with the Holocaust—as if those who are failing to reproduce in sufficient numbers are somehow collaborating with Hitler," Frank also countered: "The fact remains that we cannot replace the Holocaust victims, and any attempt to equate the unborn with Jews who were murdered is an insult to the martyrs' memories—for surely we define those 6 million Jewish lives in terms more significant than their numbers alone." Moreover, she noted, "those who urge women to breed more babies for the sake of increasing the Jewish population are strangely, indeed, shockingly, echoing Hitler's exhortation of German women to breed more babies for the Fatherland."[59]

In earlier years neoconservative intellectuals (such as Nathan Glazer and Robert Alter) had castigated Jewish liberals and leftists for applying the term genocide too loosely to the abusive treatment of African Americans. Now Frank was at pains to point out that Jewish pro-fertility activists were themselves using the term very loosely and using it with "abandon to describe what we are supposedly doing to ourselves." It was not by chance, Frank thought, that the campaign to raise Jewish numbers gained momentum just as the community felt the first tentative stirrings of a Jewish feminist movement. Could it really be only coincidence, she wondered, that, as Jewish women began to demand a greater role in both communal and religious life, a chorus of men were "loudly hitting the old 'barefoot-and-pregnant' motif as if our very lives depended on it?"[60]

REJECTING VICTIMHOOD

While the anxiety over low birthrates has continued to be voiced in American Jewish circles in the decades since the 1970s, there has been another major development in the evolution of Holocaust consciousness and its relationship to American Jewish political culture. Interestingly, it represents a dramatic reversal of attitudes. In the 1960s and 1970s many formerly liberal American Jews sought to redefine their political views through a stronger identification with the victims of the Holocaust; the 1980s and 1990s, however, witnessed a move away from such redefinitions.

By 1998 historian Edward Shapiro noted a significant backlash against "American Jews' image of themselves as impotent victims." Indeed, for Shapiro, "the sense of the Jew as victim helps explain why radical Jews support other groups also perceived to be victims—such as Palestinians, grape pickers and garment workers in Central America." This was a striking turnabout. In the 1960s and 1970s progressive Jews had been accused of inadequate sensitivity to the lessons of the Holocaust; two decades later they were taken to task for an obliviousness to "the joys of Jewishness" precisely because they focused so intently on the Holo-caust. "One of the challenges facing American Jewry," Shapiro was arguing in the late 1990s, citing Alan Dershowitz: "'is to move the Jewish state of mind be-yond its past obsession with victimization, pain and problems and point it in a new, more positive direction, capable of thriving in an open society.'"[61]

In the last few years, then, the perceived problem with progressive Jews has been that they have too *much* rather than too *little* Holocaust consciousness. Per-haps unsurprisingly, Shapiro was disdainful of Jewish feminists' defense of abor-tion rights and identified the low Jewish birthrate and intermarriage rates as the great moral challenges facing American Jews. His essay—and it was symptomatic of much wider trends—constituted an unabashed call on Jews to drop their old commitments to liberalism and civil liberties and to bring their politics more in line with their rising economic and social status.

Recent reports suggest that an intensification of a long-standing rightward drift of the American Jewish community has indeed been occurring. Throughout the 1980s and 1990s American Jewish commentators delighted in repeating the old Milton Himmelfarb axiom: Jews have the social status of Episcopalians, but they vote like Puerto Ricans. Yet a 2003 study by sociologist Steven M. Cohen, reported in the *Forward*, noted that "American Jews may be poised on the edge of a historic shift to the right in their political views," and "younger Jews are far more willing than their elders to identify as Republicans and to approve of President [George W.] Bush."[62] Indeed, in the 2004 presidential election, 25 percent voted for Bush. And while the percentage of Jews voting Republican in 2006 appeared by some accounts to have declined, a decisive trend toward greater conservatism among younger Jewish voters remains.

In this newly configured political landscape, gestures to the Holocaust have cer-tainly not disappeared and continue to be used to make political points about the evolving present. In an article on President Bush's visit to Auschwitz during a one-day trip to Poland in June 2003, the *New York Times* reported that although "never one to linger at sightseeing," Bush nonetheless "took in the camps, the barracks, the gas chambers and the scenes of torture in about an hour and a half." And subsequently the president inscribed in the Auschwitz guest book the words "Never forget." Still, reporters traveling with the president's entourage were informed that this tour of Auschwitz had "a diplomatic" purpose—a "sear-ing indictment of modern France and Germany" because those nations refused to join the American-led coalition against Saddam Hussein in Iraq. As the article noted, the message of statements by both Bush and national security adviser

Condoleeza Rice was that parallels between Hussein and Hitler "were obvious" and those nations that failed to back the American invasion of Iraq had "made a huge historical mistake."[63]

What we are seeing in the present, then, is a mix and match of contradictory gestures. When Holocaust consciousness would seem to advance a conservative agenda, conservatives (both Jews and non-Jews) embrace it. When Holocaust consciousness would seem to impede such an agenda, they reject it. At the same time, those who see different lessons in Nazism—who worry about the consequences of "preemptive war," the erosion of civil liberties, or the dismantling of international institutions—are energetically rebuffed. (Classically, for instance, *New York Times* staff writer James Traub in June 2003—after the war in Iraq had been formally declared concluded—referred to liberals who worried about these kinds of echoes as nothing more than "Weimar Whiners.")[64]

The ease with which this kind of rhetoric can now be disseminated suggests not only that clear memories of Nazism and the Holocaust are fading but that the memory of earlier postwar debates over the Holocaust's potential lessons for the American context have been lost as well. This loss of historical knowledge about the complexities of earlier American Jewish conflicts over the potential lessons of the Holocaust has serious consequences in the present. In particular, it significantly constrains the ability of younger generations of American Jews to imagine a passionate and serious debate over what should constitute Jewish values for the future.

NOTES

1. For example, see Gary Weissmann, *Fantasies of Witnessing: Postwar Efforts to Experience the Holocaust* (Ithaca, 2004); Jeffrey Shandler, *While America Watches: Televising the Holocaust* (New York, 1999); Yosefa Loshitzky, ed., *Spielberg's Holocaust: Critical Perspectives on Schindler's List* (Bloomington, 1997); Alan L. Berger, *Children of Job: American Second-Generation Witnesses to the Holocaust* (Binghamton, 1997), and *Crisis and Covenant: The Holocaust in American Jewish Fiction* (Binghamton, 1985); and Lawrence Langer, *The Holocaust and the Literary Imagination* (New Haven, 1975).

2. For example, see Dan Cohn-Sherbok, ed., *Holocaust Theology: A Reader* (New York, 2002); and Michael Berenbaum and John Roth, eds., *Holocaust: Religious and Philosophical Implications* (New York, 1989).

3. See Viktor E. Frankl, *From Death-Camp to Existentialism* (Boston, 1959); and Bruno Bettelheim, *The Informed Heart* (Glencoe, 1960).

4. Lawrence Baron, "The Holocaust and American Public Memory, 1945–1960," *Holocaust and Genocide Studies* 17 (Spring 2003): 63, 79.

5. Stuart Svonkin, *Jews Against Prejudice: American Jews and the Fight for Civil Liberties* (New York, 1997), 17.

6. Shandler, *While America Watches*, 46–47.

7. See Edward Linenthal, *Preserving Memory: The Struggle to Create America's Holocaust Museum* (New York, 1995); and Anita Weiner, *Expanding Historical Consciousness: The Development of the Holocaust Educational Foundation* (Skokie, 2002).

8. See Deborah Lipstadt, *Denying the Holocaust: The Growing Assault on Truth and Memory* (New York, 1993); and D. D. Guttenplan, *The Holocaust on Trial* (New York, 2001).

9. See the discussions in Marc H. Ellis, "Jew vs. Jew: On the Jewish Civil War and the New Prophetic," in Tony Kushner and Alisa Solomon, eds., *Wrestling with Zion: Progressive Jewish-American Responses to the Israeli-Palestinian Conflict* (New York, 2003); Tony Judt, "Goodbye to All That?" *Nation*, January 3, 2005; and Judith Butler, *Precarious Life: The Powers of Mourning and Violence* (New York, 2004).

10. See Philip Gourevitch, "Behold Now Behemoth: The Holocaust Memorial Museum—One More American Theme Park," *Harper's*, July 1, 1993, 55–62; Tim Cole, *Selling the Holocaust from Auschwitz to Schindler: How History Is Bought, Packaged, and Sold* (New York, 1999); and Peter Novick, *The Holocaust in American Life* (New York, 1999).

11. See Omer Bartov, "The Holocaust as Leitmotif of the Twentieth Century," in Dagmar Herzog, ed., *Lessons and Legacies VII: The Holocaust in International Perspective* (Evanston, IL, 2006).

12. See Lunabelle Wedlock, *The Reaction of Negro Publications and Organizations to German Anti-Semitism* (Washington, DC, 1942), 91, 105.

13. See "Southern Schrecklichkeit," *Crisis* 53 (September 1946): 276, and "Terror in Tennessee," *Crisis* 52 (April 1946): 105.

14. "Editorial Roundup," *Crisis* 53 (September 1946): 291.

15. Leo Pfeffer, "Defenses Against Group Defamation," *Jewish Frontier* 13 (February 1946): 6.

16. Charles Abrams, "Homes for Aryans Only," *Commentary* 3 (May 1947): 421.

17. "The Peekskill Riots [Editorial]," *Crisis* 56 (October 1949): 265.

18. See Sidney Hook, "Why Democracy Is Better," *Commentary* 5 (March 1948): 203–4.

19. Before his expulsion by the Gestapo, Prinz had been (in the words of one Berlin congregant) "something unheard of in Germany of that period—an ardent, devout and militant Zionist [who] resolutely and unflinchingly [spoke out] against the rising tide of National Socialism." Prinz had even "urged the immediate emigration of Jews from Germany to Palestine, unmasked the shallowness of assimilation, and appealed, again and again, for identification of German Jewry with the eternal fountainhead of the Jewish people and with the upbuilding of its ancient homeland." See Max Nussbaum, "Dr. Prinz at 60," *Congress Weekly* 29 (June 25, 1962): 5–6.

20. Joachim Prinz, " 'America Must Not Remain Silent . . . ,' " reprinted in Michael E. Staub, ed., *The Jewish 1960s: An American Sourcebook* (Waltham, MA, 2004), 90–91.

21. Ruth Gruber Michaels, "March on Washington: The Enemy Is Silence," *Hadassah Magazine* 44 (September 1963): 40.

22. Melissa Fay Greene, *The Temple Bombing* (Reading, MA, 1996), 189.

23. "The Embattled Minority [Editorial]," *Reconstructionist* 28 (June 2, 1962): 4.

24. Richard L. Rubenstein, "The Rabbis Visit Birmingham," *Reconstructionist* 29 (May 31, 1963): 5.

25. Milton Himmelfarb, "In the Community," *Commentary* 30 (August 1960): 160.

26. Shlomo Katz, "Notes in Midstream: Negroes and We," *Midstream* 6 (Spring 1960): 33.

27. See Himmelfarb, "In the Community," 158–59; and Norman Podhoretz, "The Issue: May 1960," *Commentary* 29 (May 1960): a.

28. Emil L. Fackenheim, "The Dilemma of Liberal Judaism," *Commentary* 30 (October 1960): 301.

29. Norman Podhoretz, "My Negro Problem—and Ours," *Commentary* 35 (February 1963): 93–101.

30. Abraham G. Duker, "On Negro-Jewish Relations—a Contribution to a Discussion," *Jewish Social Studies* 27 (January 1965): 20–29.

31. Ibid.

32. Marie Syrkin, "Can Minorities Oppose 'De Facto' Segregation?" *Jewish Frontier* 31 (September 1964): 6–9, 11–12.

33. Ibid., 7, 9–10. Syrkin also pointedly asked: "A minority may justly oppose the quality of housing, schooling or job opportunities available to it, but with what grace can it object to a preponderance of its own people?"

34. Lucy S. Dawidowicz, "Negro-Jewish Relations in America: A Symposium," *Midstream* 12 (December 1966): 13–17.

35. Justine Wise Polier and Shad Polier, "Fear Turned to Hatred," *Congress Bi-Weekly* 30 (February 18, 1963): 5–7.

36. Norman Podhoretz, "A Certain Anxiety," *Commentary* 52 (August 1971): 6.

37. Lucy S. Dawidowicz, "American Public Opinion," in Morris Fine and Milton Himmelfarb, eds., *American Jewish Year Book 1968* (New York, 1968), 205, 211.

38. I. F. Stone, "The Harder Battle and the Nobler Victory," *I. F. Stone's Weekly* 15 (June 12, 1967): 1–2.

39. Jerry Kirschen, "And Now . . . the Pig City Follies," *Hakahal* 1 (March-April 1972): 7.

40. Yossi Klein Halevi, *Memoirs of a Jewish Extremist: An American Story* (Boston, 1995), 79.

41. *The Jewish Defense League: Principles and Philosophies* (New York, n.d.), 275.

42. Meir Kahane, "A Small Voice," *Jewish Press* (July 26, 1968): 36.

43. Through its "Every Jew a .22" campaign, the JDL offered, for a nominal fee, a rifle together with a *siddur* (prayer book) and *yarmulke* (skullcap) to any Jew requesting it. See Michael E. Staub, *Torn at the Roots: The Crisis of Jewish Liberalism in Postwar America* (New York, 2002), 227.

44. "Is This Any Way for Nice Jewish Boys to Behave? [Advertisement]," *New York Times* (June 24, 1969): 31.

45. Richard L. Rubenstein, "Imperatives of Survival," *Congress Bi-Weekly* 36 (February 24, 1969): 33–34.

46. Ibid.

47. Ibid., 37.

48. Steven S. Schwarzschild, "Discussion," *Congress Bi-Weekly* 36 (February 24, 1969): 40.

49. Steven S. Schwarzschild, "On the Theology of Jewish Survival," *CCAR Journal* 63 (October 1968): 2–21.

50. Schwarzschild, "Discussion," 41.

51. Bill Novak, "The Failure of Jewish Radicalism," in Jack Nusan Porter and Peter Dreier, eds., *Jewish Radicalism: A Selected Anthology* (New York, 1973), 309.

52. Walter S. Wurzburger, "Not Rated as 'Necessary Evil,' but 'Swinging Society' Is Out!" *Jewish Week and American Examiner* (June 7–13, 1973): 19.

53. Quoted in "Rabbi Denounces Jews Who Misstate Judaism's 'Abhorrence of Abortion,'" *Jewish Week* (January 29–February 4, 1976): 2.

54. Irving Spiegel, "Rabbi Deplores Small Families," *New York Times* (January 24, 1974): 40.

55. Quoted in "The Disappearing Jews," *Time* (July 14, 1975): 39.

56. Quoted in "Rabbi Recommends 4-Children Family," *Jewish Post and Opinion* (February 19, 1971): 3.

57. H. J. Roberts, "Are the Jews Committing Jewish Genocide?" *Jewish Digest* 20 (March 1975): 37–42.

58. Cited in Shirley Frank, "The Population Panic," *Lilith* 1 (Fall-Winter 1977/78): 13.

59. Ibid., 15–16.

60. Ibid., 16–17. The pro-fertility rhetoric "depresses and disgusts me," Frank concluded, "not so much because I am a feminist, but because I am a Jew. I am deeply ashamed at the idea of Judaism sinking to a level where we are scrounging around for every warm body we can get."

61. Edward S. Shapiro, "Liberal Politics and American Jewish Identity," *Judaism* 47 (Fall 1998): 431–35.

62. Steven M. Cohen, "Survey Sees Historic Shift to the Right," *Forward* (January 17, 2003), http://www.forward.com/issues/2003/03.01.17/news1.html.

63. David E. Sanger, "Witness to Auschwitz Evil, Bush Draws a Lesson," *New York Times* (June 1, 2003): 14.

64. James Traub, "Weimar Whiners," *New York Times Magazine* (June 1, 2003): 11.

14

WHAT IS AMERICAN JEWISH CULTURE?

JEFFREY SHANDLER

The Jewish community's emerging cultural patterns are, to a large extent, the same as those of the general American community in terms of language, leisure time activities, demographic developments . . . even of stereotypes in thinking, including religious concepts as well.

—ABRAHAM DUKER, CA. 1950

It is a new fact of modern Jewish history that it is possible to regard Jewish culture separately from other aspects of Jewish association and activity.

—JUDAH SHAPIRO, 1964

Jewish culture in America no longer possessed its earlier assurance and vigor; they lived with whatever remnants of their youthful experience they could salvage . . . to which they clung partly because it reminded them of all that was gone.

—IRVING HOWE, 1976

Is there an American Jewish culture? The question is nearly imponderable because each of its component terms is so clearly problematic.

—ROBERT ALTER, 1982

An American Jewish subculture often looks parched in the light of an American culture which Jews have done so much to energize.

—STEPHEN WHITFIELD, 1992

When American Jews abandon religion in favor of culture, they disappear.

—ELLIOTT ABRAMS, 1997

Investment in Jewish culture will be investment in the Jewish future.

—GARY TOBIN, 2002

In the six decades since the end of World War II, much ink has been spilled trying to characterize, analyze, or simply define American Jewish culture. Once discussed much less extensively or publicly, it has become an ongoing topic among American Jews in both scholarly and popular writing. This extensive public discussion reveals that conceptualizing American Jewish culture is anything but a straightforward or self-evident enterprise. What prompted this rise in attention to American Jewish culture after the war, and why, at the same time, has this proved to be a problematic subject—so much so that some even question the possibility of its existence?

In order to study this topic, we must first consider the dynamic range of possibilities of what has been considered American Jewish culture—as well as what it has been understood as not being. This examination entails differences over time, across a range of ideological convictions, and, in academic writing, among various scholarly disciplines, including both the humanities and the social sciences. Undertaking this analysis provides an informed basis for further study of American Jewish culture; moreover, it calls attention to the discussion of American Jewish culture as a topic of interest on its own. As communal leader Judah Shapiro noted, debating "the meaning of Jewish culture . . . is itself an aspect of Jewish culture, as are the multiple views and definitions of that term."[1]

WHAT DO WE MEAN BY *CULTURE?*

A primary concern in analyzing the discussion of American Jewish culture is the challenging nature of the terms involved. The epigraphs opening this essay evince an array of assumptions of what American Jewish culture might be. Its distinctiveness, scope, and quality are questioned; the value of American Jewish culture for its constituents spans the spectrum from serving as their downfall (Abrams) to providing their salvation (Tobin). Moreover, literary scholar Robert Alter suggests that the meaning of each of the three words that comprise this term is uncertain.[2] While the words *American* and *Jewish* raise questions of defining group membership (What is an American? Who is a Jew?), the word *culture* poses a different order of challenge.

The social and cultural historian Raymond Williams notes that culture "is one of the two or three most complicated words in the English language," in part because the term is employed with distinctive meanings in several different areas of study. Williams argues that "it is the range and overlap of meanings [of the term *culture*] that is significant," for they indicate "a complex argument about the relations between general human development and a particular way of life." That is, the various meanings of the term suggest a need to investigate assumed relationships between the notion of culture as a process of nurturing human beings generally (culture as "cultivating," one of its oldest meanings) and culture as the distinctive way of life of a particular group of people (a nation, local region, ethnic group, religious community, generation, social class, etc.). This investigation also calls attention to the relations between both of these notions of culture and "the works and practices of art and intelligence"—books, statues, folksongs, movies, and the like—that are often referred to as examples of culture.[3]

As in general discourse, the term *culture* covers a wide range of meanings in discussions of American Jewish life.[4] Of particular interest here are their variations in scope. On one hand, culture is sometimes understood narrowly as a particular set of "works and practices," especially those associated with the arts: painting, music, theater, film, broadcasting, literature, and so on. Sometimes this inventory is expanded to include other activities associated with leisure—sports, games, travel, cooking, hobbies, and so on. This broad spectrum suggests that culture is not something fixed and uniform, but elective and multivalent. In this formulation the term is sometimes qualified further—for example, by creating a hierarchy of "*high*" or *elite culture* vs. "*low*" or *popular culture*. Sociologist Norman Friedman distinguishes American Jewish popular culture as "those ordinary consumption/leisure products and activities . . . that are experienced by many, if not most, American Jews," including "Jewish food, media Jewishness, and basic Yiddish," from a "Jewish elite culture" that is "rooted in the ideals and activities of traditional Judaism."[5]

On the other hand, the term *culture* can be applied much more expansively, embracing a comprehensive array of activities, creations, and beliefs. In such uses of the term, culture often references a paradigm, understood not merely as an accumulation of works and practices, but as what is sometimes termed a *cultural pattern*, in which common structures of meaning link diverse cultural phenomena. In the early post–World War II years historian Abraham Duker, for example, called for a "psycho-cultural approach" to examining contemporary life in order to determine the nature of "Jewish culture patterns in America," arguing that the study of "culture trends" is "a legitimate branch of the history of mores and religious belief."[6] Note that Duker implicitly situates culture within the larger category of religion. Others configure this relationship differently, either subsuming religion within culture as the overarching rubric or treating religion as something separate from (implicitly secular) culture.

Related to this understanding of culture are the terms *subculture, counterculture,* or *alternative culture,* which juxtapose one set of cultural patterns against another, implicitly *normative* or *mainstream culture*. Discussions of Jewish culture sometimes position it as a subculture or alternative culture in relation to a larger entity, such as a mainstream Western or American culture; in other instances Jewish culture is itself seen as having both a mainstream and alternative cultures or subcultures within it.[7]

Yet another use of the term *culture* that has particular implications for the community at hand is the relatively recent use of *cultural Jew* to distinguish—and to characterize—a type of Jewish identity and practice in relation to one defined as religious. The term *cultural Jew* does not merely supersede *secular Jew*, which was more widely used earlier in the twentieth century. Then, more so than now, *secular Jew* usually identified someone committed to a non- or antireligious and frequently politically progressive Jewish ideology, its realization often centered on ethnic or national markers, such as Yiddish or Modern Hebrew. The notion of *cultural Jew* implies different definitional criteria for Jewishness—and for understanding culture as a definitional practice—in the contemporary American context. As the National Foundation for Jewish Culture has recently observed, in its discussion of "the emergence of a Jewish cultural identity," some Jews consider engagement with "culture—including film festivals, klezmer concerts, and fiction—[to be] their sole form of identification" as Jews.[8]

HOW MIGHT WE CONSIDER THE RELATION BETWEEN IDENTITY AND CULTURE?

Considering the multiple meanings of the term *culture* calls attention to the interrelation of the phenomena characterized as culture (be they works of art, leisure activites, or religious customs) with the notion of culture as a community's definitional system or shared views of the nature of the world. In the particular case at hand, the issue of identity concerns two terms—American and Jewish—and their own interrelation.[9] The challenge posed by juxtaposing these two identities can be seen straightaway in the different ways that this interrelation is termed: *American Jewish* versus *Jewish American*, sometimes hyphenated, other times not.[10] Rather than attempting to resolve the questions that these different terms suggest (is someone who claims these two identities a Jew who lives in America, an American who practices Judaism or considers him- or herself ethnically Jewish? and so on), it proves more valuable to consider the implications of the interrelation of these identities with regard to the possibilities of American Jewish culture.

FIRST, WHAT IS THE PLACE OF AMERICANNESS IN JEWISH CULTURE?

From our present vantage it is perhaps difficult to recall that, before World War II, many Jews thought of the Jewish community in America as a cultural frontier rather than a center. For all its size and growing importance in the public affairs of world Jewry, America was then generally considered—even by many American Jews—as extrinsic in relation to the centuries-old Jewish communities of Europe, North Africa, and the Middle East. While there had been a small Jewish population in America for nearly three hundred years, most of the Jews in the United States in the early decades of the twentieth century were a recent presence, being either immigrants or their children, and these Jews largely defined the community's public profile. Typically, they understood their Jewishness primarily in terms of the Jewish life in the Old World homes that they or their parents had left behind.[11]

Moreover, Jewish life in America was widely regarded by both this immigrant community and its Old World counterparts as suspect. It was a common notion that Jews in America, at best, led a weaker version of a more thoroughly informed and "authentic" Jewish existence than did their European cohorts—and, at worst, simply ceased to be Jews altogether. In the decades between the start of mass immigration from eastern Europe in the 1880s and the end of World War II, Jews' discussions of their own culture in America typically conceptualized this subject in negative terms. In contrast to the enthusiasm many voiced with regard to political freedoms and economic opportunities that the United States offered, observers generally characterized Jewish life in America as relatively limited with regard to traditional religious practice and largely devoid of modern high-cultural aspirations.

A noteworthy early example is Rabbi Moses Weinberger's *Jews and Judaism in New York*, published in Hebrew in 1887, which warns religious Jews in eastern Europe considering immigration to America that to do so is to enter a culturally impoverished milieu. "Instead of soaring high on the wings of poetry and song, or burrowing deeply into the world of culture, investigating and enriching scholarship, language, and literature," he writes, even immigrant Jewish intellectuals "delve relentlessly into the practical world. . . . They sink up to their necks in a torrent of present-day banalities and material possessions, just like all the rest of their Jewish brethren in this city and land."[12] Indeed, at times outsiders scrutinizing the community seem to have been more ready to see America's immigrant Jewish culture as a distinctive and worthy entity in itself. Author Hutchins Hapgood, for example, celebrated the protean fervor of the immigrant Jewish life he observed on his visits to New York's Lower East Side at the turn of the twentieth century in his book, *The Spirit of the Ghetto*.[13]

So ingrained were Jewish notions of the cultural inferiority of life in America that Jewish observers on both sides of the Altantic frequently characterized venues in which Jewish culture seemed to flourish especially well on American soil during the early decades of the twentieth century as evanescent phenomena and, ultimately, heavily indebted to their counterparts on the other side of the Atlantic Ocean. This was true even for America's vibrant Yiddish culture—literature, press, political activism, theater, and song—which, in some respects (notably theater and press), flourished more readily, at first, in America than in eastern Europe. Indeed, the dynamics of American Yiddish culture and of its valuation are instructive for assessing the study of American Jewish culture more broadly.

Thus American Yiddish culture during the period of mass immigration offers some views that challenge prevailing sentiments, which dismissed the value of America's Jewish culture. Yiddish folklorist Y. L. Cahan, for example, considered its turn-of-the-century immigrant community a remarkable resource for his studies, reportedly claiming that "here folklore can be scooped up in handfuls."[14] While Cahan's interest was in documenting Old World folkways remembered by older immigrants, rather than American Jewish culture per se, socialist leader Chaim Zhitlowsky exhorted fellow immigrants to exploit the unprecedented opportunities provided by life in America to forge a new secular Jewish culture centered on the Yiddish language and progressive, internationalist politics.[15]

The period between the two world wars, concomitant with the end of mass immigration from Europe to America, marked a watershed in American Jewish life, as the children of immigrants came of age. In the wake of immigration defining so much of American Jewish life, new discourses emerged. In particular, the tension between realizing material success and social integration on one hand and a dissolution of an Old World Jewish distinctiveness, morally as well as culturally, on the other hand, emerged as the defining trope of key works of American Jewish culture, including major works of fiction (e.g., Abraham Cahan's 1917 novel *The Rise of David Levinsky*) and film (the Warner Bros. 1927 feature *The Jazz Singer*).[16] This trope has continued to inform more recent scholarly assessments of the interwar years, even as some challenge its assumptions. Historian Deborah Dash Moore argues that the interwar period is marked by the emergence of an American Jewish "at-homeness" that fostered "a renascent Jewish culture," especially in New York City.[17] Other scholars have characterized American Jewish culture of this period as informed by a sense of profound insecurity, especially during the 1930s, when the bedrock of economic advancement that America offered was abruptly shaken. Historian Beth Wenger writes, "The Great Depression punctuated the maturation of the first mass generation of Jews born in the United States. Occurring precisely at a time when immigrant patterns were giving way to new formulations of Jewish community and culture, the Depression years set in motion Jewish patterns that would last for generations."[18]

American Yiddish culture evinces signal shifts during the interwar years that resonate with these assessments of the period. In the 1920s and 1930s Yiddish culture witnessed the advent of important new forms—notably radio and "talking" pictures—as more established forms (literature, press, theater) reach unprecedented levels of accomplishment.[19] At the same time, however, American Yiddish culture became more self-conscious, reflecting a growing awareness that its creation and consumption relied less and less on native speakers of Yiddish for whom the language served as their primary vernacular. Concern as to how future generations of American Jews would engage with Yiddish was increasingly evident— whether in the appearance of English sections of Yiddish newspapers, in the bilingual format of much of Yiddish radio programming, or in the advent of *shules*, secular afternoon and weekend schools where children learn to read, write, and speak Yiddish.[20] Nevertheless, the notion of Yiddish culture as a set of practices created in Yiddish for speakers of the language, and that embody a collective identity, remained largely self-evident.

This growing sense of cultural uncertainty resonated with pioneering works by American Jewish social scientists on the nature of Jewish life in the modern world, which are more remarkable, perhaps, for what they did *not* say about Jews rather than what they did. During the early decades of the twentieth century, Franz Boas, the doyen of American anthropology, all but erased Jews as a subject of study within this field. He situated Jews beyond the scope of cultural anthropology, which was to be concerned solely with preliterate, "primitive" peoples. Boas only studied Jews in his anthropometric work on immigrants, striving to demonstrate that Jews were not genetically homogeneous, in response to prevailing notions that they were a distinct—and, in the view of some, an inferior—race.[21] In 1927 anthropologist Melville Herskovits posed the question "When is a Jew a Jew?" After dismissing the possibility that Jews could be accurately defined as a common race, nation, speech community, religion, culture, or worldview, he concluded that only the most nominal of definitions holds true: "A Jew is a person who calls himself a Jew, or who is called Jewish by others."[22] In other words, the meaning of the word *Jew* was, in effect, arbitrary. Shortly after World War II, Herskovits revisited the issue and again concluded that perhaps "no word . . . means more things to more people than does the word 'Jew.'"[23]

Herskovits's claim notwithstanding, World War II profoundly transformed the way American Jews understood their stature in the world. Following the devastations of the Holocaust, Jews in America suddenly found themselves the world's largest, most prosperous, and—compared to their fellow Jews throughout postwar Europe and Asia—the most continuous and stable Jewish community. This was, however, a qualified preeminence, achieved by default. As historian Oscar Janowsky wrote in 1964:

> In numbers, wealth, and influence, American Jewry has attained a stature unequalled in any land of the Diaspora during two millennia. The mantle of leadership has fallen to America's Jews as the European communities succumbed to war, revolution and Nazi savagery. America has become the center of Diaspora Jewry, and even Israel depends in long measure upon its assistance. The world's Jews, however, look to their American brethren for financial aid and to a lesser extent for political influence and managerial skill. Cultural leadership is neither proffered nor invited. Indeed, American Jewry is disdained as culturally barren.[24]

Other signal changes complicated American Jewry's new stature. Despite the newness of the State of Israel, it quickly emerged as a contrasting model to American possibilities for Jewish existence politically, socially, and culturally. At the same time, the profile of American Jewry was changing rapidly, marked by swift embourgeoisement, migration from urban enclaves to suburbs, and the rise of American-born Jews as the majority of the nation's Jewish population. Given all these developments, it is not surprising that long-held assumptions about what might define an American Jew's sense of self were called into question in the early postwar era. Indeed, for many members of the American Jewish community at the time, living with questions about identity "in a state of useful discontent was," according to literary critic Irving Howe, "perhaps what it . . . meant to be a Jew."[25]

SECOND, WHAT IS THE PLACE OF JEWISHNESS IN AMERICAN CULTURE?

The mythic image of Jews in America has a centuries-old history and has at times been only tangentially related to actual Jewish life there. During the colonial era, for example, Puritans envisioned their settlement on this continent as the initiation of a "new Zion" in which they emulated the ancient Israelites. Informed in part by this myth, Jews have occasionally contended that their presence in America is somehow exemplary. Philosopher Horace Kallen, for example, maintained in 1915 that east European Jewish immigrants occupied an exceptional place among their contemporaries in the United States, since they came

> far more with the attitude of the earliest settlers than any of the other peoples; for they more than any other present-day immigrant group are in flight from persecution and disaster; in search of economic opportunity, liberty of conscience, civic rights. . . . Among them, as among the Puritans, the Pennsylvania Germans, the French of Louisiana, self-consciousness and like-mindedness are intense and articulate. . . . The Jews, in the mass, have thus far looked to America as their home land.[26]

At the same time, the presence of Jews in America, like that of other ethnic, religious, and racial minorities, has long figured in the nation's popular culture in terms of archetypes, often portrayed to comic effect in humor, the press, and stage performances. These images, especially unflattering stereotypes of Jewish peddlers and merchants, flourished in the United States in the mid-nineteenth century following the arrival of tens of thousands of Jews from German lands.[27] Even as the American Jewish public profile grew exponentially with the arrival of hundreds of thousands from eastern Europe beginning in the 1880s, these representations would continue to inform notions of how Jews figured in American culture for generations to come.

While at the turn of the twentieth century some outside observers of immigrant Jews considered that they, along with other recent arrivals to the United States, enriched the nation's culture, such beneficent views were overshadowed in the years following World War I by much more outspoken American nativists' critiques. Taking a dim view of recent immigrants generally, some nativists viewed the growing presence of Jews in the United States as a destructive force that threatened the integrity of American culture. Most infamously, the industrialist Henry Ford labeled Jews the nation's "foremost problem" and assailed their pernicious influence on a wide array of American cultural life, including music, theater, film, and sports.[28]

When responding to such attacks in national forums during the interwar years, American Jews tended not to defend their distinctive contributions to the nation's culture or to vaunt the creation of a unique Jewish culture in the United States. Rather, they more readily insisted on the Americanness of their lives and cultural undertakings. Integration into an American mainstream did not merely serve as a major theme of American Jewish literature, drama, and film in the early twentieth century (at least those works created in English; different cultural sensibilities informed American works in Yiddish and other Jewish languages). Indeed, integration became a paradigm of American Jewish daily life—for some, the equivalent of a creed. "Most of the children of the immigrants had decisively turned their backs on the old ways of their parents," historian Haym Soloveitchik writes of the American Jewish community of this time. "Many had even attended faithfully the chapel of Acceptance, over whose portals they saw inscribed '*Incognito Ergo Sum*,'"—a phrase Soloveitchik recalls from his college days—"which, like most mottoes, was both a summons and a promise."[29]

For some American social scientists writing during the interwar years, Jews figured as exemplary figures of cultural encounters with modernity. Sociologist Louis Wirth's study of the ghetto, first published in 1928, characterizes it not merely as a phenomenon of Jewish social history, ranging from the first restricted Jewish residential area established in Venice in the sixteenth century to the voluntary urban ethnic enclaves of Chicago, New York, and other contemporary American cities. Wirth also regarded the ghetto as a paradigm of societal behavior defined by prolonged social isolation and, ultimately, as a state of mind, epitomized by Jewish experience. To study the ghetto, then, was to determine "the extent to which isolation has shaped the character of the Jew and the nature of his social life" and to apply this insight to a universal condition of modern life, "akin to the type of isolation of the person who feels lonely though in the midst of the crowd."[30]

In his 1937 study of the "marginal man," sociologist Everett Stonequist cited Diaspora Jewry as the prototype of this phenomenon of modern society: "The marginal man . . . is one whom fate has condemned to live in two societies and in two, not merely different but antagonistic, cultures." As cultural hybrids, Stonequist argued, Jews struggle between the lure of a societal mainstream and their own distinctive, traditional way of life. "The American environment is a baffling one for the Jew. He may establish contacts . . . which lead him strongly in the direction of assimilation. But he is also likely to encounter sharp anti-Semitism. . . . The divergent currents of American life produce their counterpart in his psychic life." At the same time, Stonequist positioned the Jew, as marginal man, in a strategic role in cosmopolitan society: "The marginal man is the key-personality in the contacts of cultures. It is in his mind that the cultures come together, conflict, and eventually work out some kind of mutual adjustment at interpenetration." Indeed, this "position of the Jew . . . becomes a theme of biography and a source of literature."[31]

For both Wirth and Stonequist, American Jews serve as paradigmatic figures of modern experience. But though their situation positions them strategically in society, their hybridity is ultimately understood as a problematic, unresolvable conflict. Unlike many of their neighbors, these scholars suggest, Jews are never fully at home anywhere. In response to these models of incompatibility and marginality, some American Jews called for a reexamination of how they might conceptualize their existence more constructively. Most notably, the founder of Reconstructionist Judaism, Rabbi Mordecai Kaplan, argued that Judaism be viewed not simply as a religion but as a civilization, which he defined as an "accumulation of knowledge, skills, tools, arts, literatures, laws, religions and philosophies," comprising "a complete and self-contained entity." For Kaplan, Jewish life in America was not inherently conflicted. Rather, as he maintained in his landmark 1934 book, *Judaism as a Civilization*, America offered Jews complementary opportunities: "Nothing less than a vigorous participation in the development of American life will content [the Jew]. But it is necessary to make clear that loyalty to American ideals does not call for the suppression of the Jew's deep-seated desire to retain the individuality of his Jewish life."[32]

Just as World War II transformed notions of America's place in Jewish life, the war also proved a watershed in the discussion of Jews' place in American culture. In the postwar American public sphere the profile of Jews was suddenly much higher, as the Nazi persecution of European Jewry and the founding of the State of Israel made headlines repeatedly. Domestic anti-Semitism emerged as a subject of public discussion, thanks to the efforts of organizations dedicated to combating this and other prejudices, and extended to works of popular fiction, film, and broadcasting.[33] Most popular of these were two Hollywood feature films, *Crossfire* and *Gentleman's Agreement*, both released in 1947, which addressed American prejudice against Jews through dramas based on popular novels in the established cinematic genres of film noir and romantic intrigue, respectively.[34]

Moreover, Jewish scholars positioned Jews as paradigmatic figures of contemporary American life in new ways. Theologian Will Herberg, for example, characterized the dynamics of American life over the course of the first half of the twentieth century in terms of a "triple melting pot" of Protestants, Catholics, and Jews. Writing in 1955, Herberg argued that the progeny of various immigrant communities in the United States shed their forebears' ethnic, national, and linguistic identities to become part of a national culture defined by religious pluralism.[35] While Herberg's configuration builds on prewar models of Judeo-Christian ecumenism, it situates Jews, albeit tacitly, as the archetypal minority in Christian America. Jews' acceptance by others as an American religious community thus proves the national commitment to the common bond of religiosity, which includes respect for the freedom of worship. At the same time, however, Herberg conceptualized Jewishness solely in terms of religion, arguing that an ethnic Jewish identity was a transitional phase of immigrants and their children, superseded by members of the third generation, who identified nationally as Americans and religiously as Jews. According to Herberg's model, the fulfillment of American Jewish culture is integration into a national cultural mainstream.

While the discussions of American Jewish culture during the first half of the twentieth century are wide ranging, they share common concerns, if often implicitly. First, there is a prevailing notion that the interrelation of Americanness and Jewishness, however each of these identities may be conceived, is distinctly problematic. In particular, Jews frequently characterized the attractions that life in America proffers—especially its freedoms, its individualism, and its expansive, protean opportunities—as a challenge to Jewish well-being. Typically, the dynamic of Jewish life in the United States, often termed *Americanization*, was understood as a unidirectional path away from a distinct, comprehensive Old World Jewish existence and toward complete assimilation into an American mainstream. More than one mid-twentieth-century observer of American Jewish life described this as a process of "deculturation"—that is, as a loss, rather than transformation, of culture.[36] Conversely, some Jews and non-Jews alike questioned the possibility of Jews being fully at home in America; for some non-Jewish observers the Jewish presence in America was clearly less than welcome.

A second, related concern is the possible intractability of Jewishness, newly problematized by Jews' encounter with modernity. During the first half of the twentieth century Jews in America experienced unprecedented opportunities to transform what it means to be Jewish, as individuals and as communities—including possibilities to reinvent themselves as something other than Jews. At the same time, a powerful new discourse of Jewishness as a biologically determined attribute raised questions about whether Jewish reinvention or assimilation could entail any actual alteration of an ineluctable racial identity.

HOW DOES CULTURE FIGURE IN POSTWAR DISCUSSIONS OF AMERICAN JEWISH LIFE?

Despite the fact that American Jewish culture was typically either characterized in negative terms or went unmentioned altogether before World War II, culture soon became an important category for discussing Jewish life in America in the postwar era. Moreover, culture emerged as an important new category of American Jewish endeavor, increasingly characterized as a mode of definitional behavior for many

American Jews that is equal to—and sometimes superseding—religiosity, political affiliation, language, or ethnicity. The advent of this new discourse coincides with, and to some extent correlates to, signal changes within the American community: new opportunities, new paradigms, and new concerns.

NEW OPPORTUNITIES

Among the array of innovations in American Jewish life in the early postwar years are the emergence of new public venues for creating and discussing Jewish culture, many of them new undertakings by established Jewish communal institutions. For example, the decade following World War II witnessed the debuts of a spate of American Jewish periodicals, including *Commentary, Congress Weekly,* and *Judaism.*[37] Of particular interest is the monthly journal *Commentary,* which made its debut in 1945. Published by the American Jewish Committee, *Commentary* regularly featured essays on Jewish cultural phenomena in the United States, ranging widely from literature, theater, and film to popular television programs, humorists, and foodways, as well as a series of ethnographic portraits of local Jewish life, "From the American Scene."[38] During the mid-1940s the Jewish Theological Seminary initiated two large-scale cultural projects—the opening of The Jewish Museum in the former Warburg mansion on Manhattan's Fifth Avenue and the production of the ecumenical radio (and, later, television) series *The Eternal Light* in conjunction with NBC. Both these undertakings explored connections between art and religion, doing so prominently in the public eye.[39] In Los Angeles the establishment of innovative institutions of higher Jewish learning— the University of Judaism and the Brandeis Institute—helped forge a new vision of Jewishness that emphasized an affective experience of community over traditional forms of worship and study; here, too, the arts came to be regarded as essential to facilitating what Deborah Dash Moore has termed a "spiritual recreation," which was inspired in part by Mordecai Kaplan's notion of Judaism as a civilization.[40]

Other new opportunities arose beyond the efforts of American Jewish institutions. Of paramount importance, perhaps, was the large-scale matriculation of Jews at American institutions of higher learning in the postwar era, thanks to the GI Bill and the rapid entry of Jews into the nation's middle class as well as universities' abandonment of restrictive admissions quotas. The burgeoning number of American Jews who attended college in the post–World War II era created a new kind of widely shared cultural literacy, informed by the scope and sensibilities of liberal arts curricula. Within the academy an intelligentsia flourished that was "more secular, more liberal, and more Jewish than any comparable professional and cultural cohort in the United States." The presence of these "free-thinking Jews," historian David Hollinger argues, made a strategic contribution to American intellectual culture during the early postwar decades.[41]

Among these scholars, special attention has been paid to cohorts of Jewish intellectuals associated with campuses in New York City. Their ranks included Sidney Hook, Meyer Schapiro, Lionel Trilling, followed by Clement Greenberg, Richard Hofstadter, Harold Rosenberg, and then Daniel Bell, Nathan Glazer, Irving Howe, among others. Typically they were east European immigrants' children who came of age before World War II and subsequently became leading voices in national discussions of literature, art, politics, and the study of contemporary society.[42]

In the mid-twentieth century—to say nothing of the period before—the study of American Jewish history, literature, society, or culture received little attention in the university.[43] However, the academy did provide American Jews with a forum in which to consider the place of American Jewish experience within the rubric of the liberal arts, eventually realized as the field of Jewish studies as we know it today. Irving Howe's career offers a telling example. After beginning as a scholar of American literature, he turned his attention to Yiddish literature and culture, collaborating on a series of anthologies of Yiddish prose, poetry, and essays—beginning with A *Treasury of Yiddish Stories*, published in 1954—and writing *World of Our Fathers*, a landmark history of immigrant Jewish culture in New York City, published in 1976.[44]

NEW PARADIGMS

The postwar advent of new opportunities for making and discussing American Jewish culture coincided with fundamental changes in how American Jews defined their community. Sociologist Nathan Glazer characterized this as a paradigm shift from ethnic to religious identity—what he termed a move from Jewishness (i.e., Jews understood as an ethnic group—or, as Glazer termed it, "secular culture and quasi-national feeling") to Judaism (Jews defined as a religious community).[45] This paradigm shift has telling implications. Situating Jews as a religious community locates them within a social category widely recognized in America as legitimate and, moreover, as private. Freedom of worship was a readily acknowledged American value (hailed by President Franklin Roosevelt as one of the four freedoms that Americans were defending during World War II), in contrast to the more problematic notion of freedom of ethnic expression. During the early years of the cold war in particular, Jews' religiosity was called upon to signify their loyalty to the United States, especially as individual American Jews repeatedly made headlines when they were accused of being agents for the Soviet Union (most prominently in the case of the "atom spies" Ethel and Julius Rosenberg).[46] At the same time, the American concept of religiosity as a private pursuit has erased Jewishness a category in certain rubrics—notably among ethnic, national, political, and especially racial identities; in doing so, this paradigm shift has altered notions of what might possibly constitute Jewish culture.[47]

Moreover, the paradigm of religion conceptualizes being Jewish as voluntary (following the Christian model of religious identity as a personal, elective confession of faith). The rubric of religion thus distances Jewishness not only from the intractable model of race but also from notions of Jewish identity as a birthright, a collective covenantal identity, or an ethnicity "by descent." On one hand, this development has opened up the possibilities of realizing Jewishness in the American context to various invented identities (ethnicity "by consent," in Werner Sollors's terms) and self-styled practices, thereby embracing discontinuity as a force that energizes, rather than undermines, culture. In recent decades this has been especially evident in the flourishing of an array of feminist and queer Jewish writings and cultural practices, including innovations in worship and ritual.[47] On the other hand, such changes destabilize long-standing notions of what reliably, inevitably signifies or constitutes Jewishness.[48]

This paradigm shift in American Jewish self-definition was concomitant with and, to some extent, tied to signal changes in geography. Before World War II the social geography of American Jews vis-à-vis the rest of world Jewry was articulated primarily in terms of its status as a New World community in relation to the European (and, to a lesser extent, North African and Middle Eastern) Old World. After the war this geographic model was replaced by the juxtaposition of the Diaspora, now centered in the United States, in relation to the new State of Israel. American Jewry's internal geography was also being remapped. Jewish urban enclaves, epitomized by neighborhoods in New York City and other major cities, were attenuated by outward migration to the suburbs. No longer brought together by close settlement and a considerable, often informally constituted public life—on the street, in parks, shops, schoolyards, and so on—postwar Jewish communities increasingly organized around new institutions. In addition to synagogues and Jewish community centers, new, more formally organized social networks were established, especially philanthropies.[49]

Concomitant with this geographical shift was the decline of immigrant Jewish culture, much of it rooted in the use of Yiddish. The number of Yiddish newspapers and other periodicals, published works of literature and literary criticism, radio programs and theater performances diminished sharply during the first postwar decades; Yiddish film disappeared altogether. More than simply the result of a pervasive shift away from maintaining Yiddish as a Jewish vernacular, this decline indicates a profound shift in American Jewish sense of self, in which having a distinct language of daily life (even a scorned language, as Yiddish often was) no longer plays a defining role. At the same time, the esteem of immigrant culture has risen among scholars of Jewish life. Largely disparaged or neglected by the academy when this culture flourished in the first half of the twentieth century, American Yiddish culture, especially its literature, has been championed in an array of analyses.[50] Moreover, the paradigms of immigrant culture have been reassessed, vaunted as a distinct form of cultural creativity defined by the immigrants' experience negotiating between Old World and New World ways of life.[51]

Indeed, American Jews have assigned their bygone immigrant culture new value as heritage. Heritage culture has taken a wide range of forms, including new interest in Yiddish language, in particular through a series of books in English about Yiddish and its Old World culture, especially klezmer, the traditional instrumental music of east European Jewry.[52] Similar treatment has been accorded immigrant Jewish neighborhoods, above all Manhattan's Lower East Side, which has emerged as a popular center of American Jewish tourism. In addition to local institutions dedicated to commemorating immigrant Jewish experience—notably, the Lower East Side Tenement Museum and the restoration of the Eldridge Street Synagogue, an architectural landmark, built in 1886—the neighborhood is regularly visited by sightseers on any of a variety of walking tours.[53]

The model of heritage has been used to position other aspects of the Jewish past as touchstones of American Jewish culture in the past half-century. Most remarkable is the emergence of the Holocaust as a locus of heritage, which entails conceptualizing the mass murder of European Jewry as a defining event in American Jewish cultural life. The notion of the Holocaust as Jewish heritage has given rise to an extensive array of cultural practices, exemplified by the construction in the 1990s of the Museum of Jewish Heritage: A Living Memorial to the Holocaust in lower Manhattan.[54] This notion also informs the discourse of Holocaust remembrance in the United States, where many children of Jewish Holocaust survivors describe themselves as "second-generation survivors"—the term situating survivors' experience of Nazi persecution as a legacy inherited by their children.[55]

The reification of the Holocaust as Jewish heritage is conjoined with other transformations, notably the prominent place the State of Israel occupies in American Jewish culture. In 1981 Judaic studies scholar Jacob Neusner noted that many American Jews share a "vision of reality beginning in death, 'the Holocaust,' and completed by resurrection or rebirth, 'Israel.'" Neusner argues that, although the Holocaust and the establishment of Israel took place "far from America's shore and remote from American Jews' everyday experience, [these events] constitute the generative myth by which the generality of American Jews make sense of themselves and decide what to do with that part of themselves set aside for 'being Jewish.'"[56] Jonathan Woocher, a Jewish community activist, terms the cultural practices that conceptualize and enact this myth the *civil religion* of American Jews, an "ideology of the American Jewish polity" realized in non-religious communal organizations and their cultural practices, which center to a considerable extent on philanthropy.[57]

NEW CONCERNS

To some extent, issues that American Jews may regard as unprecedented in the post–World War II era are, in fact, iterations of concerns raised during the first half of the twentieth century, if not earlier. Whether articulated as questions of demographic continuity (often centered on the issue of intermarriage) or socio-cultural assimilation, the uncertain future of American Jewry has remained a frequent trope.[58] Similarly, concerns about internal strife within the American Jewish community endure as a subject of discussion, although the particular issues dividing the community change with time.[60]

These debates, which inform notions of what constitutes American Jewish culture, recur during the postwar era as American public culture generally witnesses major shifts in the discussion of cultural difference and hybridity. Like other communities in America—ethnic groups, racial minorities, sexualities, disabilities—Jews are increasingly content to enact their difference and to be seen as different in the public sphere. The possibilities of Jewishness as part of a hybrid identity—as a result not merely of the interaction with an American mainstream culture, but of intimate engagement with other religions and ethnicities—has similarly expanded, at least for some American Jews. This is seen most readily in changing responses to interfaith marriages among some sectors of the American Jewish community. Whereas earlier generations almost uniformly regarded Jewish-Christian intermarriage solely as a loss for the Jewish community, there are now both organized movements and individual convictions that view intermarriage as an opportunity for new kinds of engagement with Jewishness. Similarly, the sizable involvement of American Jews with Buddhism and other non-Western religions has engendered new understandings of the possibilities of Jewish spiritual culture.[59]

If a new concern has in fact emerged in the postwar era, it may be over how one might realize one's Jewishness, given, on one hand, the seemingly limitless spectrum of possibilities that American freedom and prosperity afford and, on the other hand, a sense that once automatic ways of being Jewish are lost. Haym Soloveitchik, writing about the religious culture of American Orthodox Jewry, characterizes this new concern as a pervasive sense that traditional mimetic means of transmitting practices and mores—"imbibed from parents and friends, and patterned on conduct regularly observed in home and street, synagogue and school"—are no longer available and have given way to a text-based transmission of knowledge and practice. Now, Soloveitchik argues, "traditional conduct, no matter how venerable, how elementary, or how closely remembered, yields to the demands of theoretical knowledge. Established practice can no longer hold its own against the demands of the written word."[60] This sense that there has been a fundamental shift in how culture is transmitted—and, as a consequence, how it is conceptualized and even recognized as culture—can be observed more broadly in American Jewish life (even as traditional mimesis continues to inform many

Jews' cultural practices). Consider, for example, much of contemporary Yiddish culture in the United States, where engagements with Yiddish have increasingly become something other than vernacular. This includes dozens of college courses and cultural festivals and is perhaps epitomized by the success of the National Yiddish Book Center (NYBC). Established in 1980 in Amherst, Massachusetts, as a repository for abandoned Yiddish books, which young students of the language were having difficulty finding, the NYBC now sponsors a wide array of activities that celebrate Yiddish (and, more generally, Jewish) culture—doing so primarily in English. Not only do American Jews acquire Yiddish less often as a "native" language, but their engagement with it is increasingly deliberate and self-conscious.[61] At the same time, this signal shift in Yiddish culture has opened up possibilities for engagement with the language for those who did not grow up with Yiddish—including a noteworthy number of non-Jews, who learn Yiddish for a variety of reasons.

HOW, THEN, MIGHT WE STUDY AMERICAN JEWISH CULTURE?

In conjunction with these new opportunities, paradigms, and concerns, culture has assumed new prominence as a resource for examining and realizing American Jewish life. The subject has been addressed in a growing corpus of monographs, essays, exhibitions, documentary films, courses, reports, surveys, and philanthropic endeavors by the press, institutions of higher education, Jewish communal organizations, and public cultural institutions. From our current perspective, there is ample material on this topic.[64]

And yet, almost fifty years ago the sociolinguist Joshua Fishman wondered why, if there were apparently so many American Jews who were social scientists, so few of them had devoted their careers to the study of American Jewry.[62] In the ensuing decades the scholarship on American Jewish experience has grown considerably, taken up by historians, literary scholars, sociologists, anthropologists, folklorists, psychologists, linguists, and others. Of special note, in light of Fishman's observation, is the rise of what anthropologist Sol Tax termed the "in-culture" study of American Jewry—that is, the study of American Jews by members of this population.[63] The special self-reflexive nature of studying "one's own people" has since been given considerable attention by American Jewish anthropologists, beginning in 1978 with the publication of *Number Our Days*, Barbara Myerhoff's landmark study of aging among American Jewish immigrants in Venice, California.[64] Indeed, Fishman anticipated the advent of such scholarship, noting that, by the late 1970s, "almost every adult member of [the American Jewish] community will be American-born and more than two-thirds will be college graduates. In such a community the social sciences will be an integral part of every adult's intellectual nourishment."[65] Under such circumstances the study of American Jewry, encountered in the course of college studies, has had the potential to become a formative experience not merely for an intellectual elite, but for a large portion of the community at large. Consequently, the study of "one's own people" has become a defining cultural undertaking, especially as part of forging an independent sense of self for young adult American Jews as they come of age and begin life independent of parents in the course of undergraduate studies.[66]

The wide range of topics and approaches to the contemporary study of American Jewish culture offers lessons in the possibilities of scholarly engagement with the subject at hand. For example, the considerable number of studies of synagogue culture by historians, sociologists, anthropologists, ethnomusicologists, art historians, and others demonstrates the distinctions among various disciplinary approaches.[67] Reading across the spectrum of work in this field provides important instruction in the value of interdisciplinary scholarship. Indeed, some of the most thoughtful studies of American Jewish culture are by scholars looking beyond their usual purview—such as historian Arthur Goren's work on rites of American Jewish public culture, including Zionist pageants and funerals of famous figures, literary scholar David Roskies's analysis of the iconography of the Workmen's Circle "Honor Row" in the Old Mount Carmel Cemetery in Queens, New York, where many luminaries of Yiddish culture have been interred, or historian Alan Steinweis's examination of contemporary Holocaust remembrance by diverse communities in Nebraska.[68] Other scholars have contributed to the study of American Jewish culture by working across the boundaries between the academy and institutions of public culture. Jenna Joselit, for example, has made equally important contributions to the study of American Jewish social and cultural history in her work as a scholar and as a curator of exhibitions.[69]

The study of culture can examine particular phenomena and practices as points of entry into larger discussions of scholarly interest. A case in point is the klezmer "revival" of the past thirty years, which has generated a considerable body of literature. In addition to the central work of ethnomusicologists, there are both scholarly and popular publications by authors in a variety of fields. Moreover, there is a significant body of writing on the topic by some of the musicians themselves, including popular histories, artists' manifestos, and dissertations.[70] These texts demonstrate how analysis of the performance, reproduction, and consumption of klezmer reveals much about American Jewish life beyond the sphere of music, addressing issues of ethnicity, spirituality, cultural literacy, and communal practice. Klezmer also offers important insights into the role of American Jewish culture abroad, as musicians from the United States and their recordings travel to Latin America, Europe, Israel, and Australia. And, as the klezmer scene has proved to be an important venue for non-Jewish involvement in the production and consumption of Jewish culture, the study of these developments has raised important questions about the relation of identity and culture.

Among the wide range of possibilities within American Jewish culture, certain topics have attracted greater attention from both scholars and other writers. Contemplating scholars' focus on particular topics can in itself offer valuable insight into American Jewish culture and its study. Consider, for example, the extensive literature on American Hasidim, written by journalists as well as historians and social scientists.[71] Since all these authors scrutinize the community from a distance (while they are almost all Jews, none are Hasidim themselves), their work demonstrates the complex, powerful role that American Hasidim play for other Jews in this country as objects of cultural reflection. (In this regard, their scholarship is worth comparing to the literature on European Hasidim written during the first half of the twentieth century.) As Holocaust remembrance has proliferated in America in a wide array of cultural practices—including literature, memoir, historiography, drama, film, broadcasting, exhibition, fine art, music, ritual, monuments, pedagogy—it has also generated an extensive body of public debate and academic study.[72] So extensive is this discourse that it has helped situate Holocaust remembrance as the quintessential case study of cultural works of memory generally.

One of the most extensively examined topics in the study of American Jewish culture—the connections between Jews and American popular entertainment, especially film but also theater, broadcasting, comedy, and other activities—demonstrates the challenges that arise in this field with regard to conceptualizing the relationship between identity and culture. Some studies address this challenge forthrightly, especially as an issue of historical interest, often focusing on issues of stereotyping and antisemitism.[73] Often, however, the problem is subsumed within the rubrics of these studies. In the case of American Jews and film, studies tend to be organized by means of a particular criterion: the Jewishness of the producers or distributors of films, the Jewish content of films, variously identified in terms of character types, images, or themes, or, less often, Jewish audiences.[74] Studies of American television not only are similarly organized around the scrutiny of Jewish content on screen but also sometimes link the evaluation of broadcasts with the authors' concerns for accurate or inspiring representations.[75]

Such approaches impose problematic expectations on popular culture to serve as either a documentary or an edifying presence; moreover, they run the risk of essentializing Jewish identity and drawing facile connections among creators, subjects, and audiences of media works in an effort to define cultural phenomena as "Jewish." At their most extreme, studies of American Jewish entertainment culture propose totalizing schemes that link the Jewishness of artists, characters, themes, and even consumers in a tautological relationship.[76] The motivation to claim Jewish cultural property is of interest in itself—Wherefore the desire to see Hollywood films, comic books, or Broadway musicals as Jewish inventions?—and is worthy of scholarly scrutiny for what it reveals about the sensibilities of American Jews with regard to the interrelation of identity and culture.

As folklorist Elliott Oring has observed about the study of Jewish humor, such issues may be more effectively approached not as phenomena but as concepts. In doing so, one escapes the unresolvable challenge posed when asking, What makes this Jewish? by asking instead, What do people think makes this Jewish? Oring argues that "there is no particular concern that these conceptualizations can be demonstrated as matters of fact—it is the orientation itself that defines the subject matter."[77] In this spirit, it can be more informative to study the connections between Jews and American popular entertainment culture as a concept realized in public discussion. As film critic J. Hoberman and I have written elsewhere,

> The discourse about American Jews and entertainment media, far from being at the periphery, is at the heart of the matter. The topic . . . has not been called into existence by something inherent in Jews or in the American entertainment industry. Rather, it arises from the public observation of the connections made between this community and that component of American culture. . . . Therefore, it is essential to scrutinize the nature of its discourse and to treat the discussion as a cultural phenomenon in itself.[78]

The self-reflexive nature of much of the scholarship on American Jewish culture can be found in other works—notably documentary films and works of contemporary art—that are of interest both as interrogations of American Jewish culture and as examples of it themselves. Since the mid-1970s, dozens of documentary filmmakers have turned their attention to some aspect of American Jewish life, as part of a much more extensive burgeoning of personal filmmaking and videography in America. Many of their films—including works by Alan Berliner (*Intimate Stranger, Nobody's Business, The Sweetest Sound*), Marlene Booth (*Yidl in the Middle*), Gregg Bordowitz (*Fast Trip Long Drop*), Michelle Citron (*Daughter Rite*), Menachem Daum (*Hiding and Seeking*), Sandi DuBowski (*Tom Boychick*), Pearl Gluck (*Divan*), Judith Helfand (*A Healthy Baby Girl*), Alisa Lebow and Cynthia Madansky (*Treyf*), Marian Marzinski (*Shtetl*)—are explicitly self-reflexive, using the medium as a vehicle for autobiography of some kind, often set in the context of family or community relations.[79]

Contemporary American Jewish artists—including Eleanor Antin, Ken Aptekar, Ross Bleckner, Nan Goldin, Deborah Kass, Cary Leibowitz, Rhonda Lieberman, Beverly Naidus, Elaine Reichek, Tom Sachs, Ilene Segalove, Albert Winn—have similarly deployed painting, sculpture, photography, video art, installation art, and other media to explore various aspects of their lives as American Jews, devoting their attention especially to issues of gender, sexuality, and family life. These artists' and filmmakers' works have been drawn into the public discourse of American Jewish culture through exhibitions in Jewish museums (notably "Too Jewish? Challenging Traditional Identities," organized by The Jewish

Museum, New York, in 1996) and through the dozens of Jewish film festivals now held annually across the United States, including major festivals in San Francisco (the oldest such festival, established in 1980), Boston, New York, and Washington, DC. The fact that a sizable number of people attending these festivals analogize the experience to attending synagogue or explain that, for them, the Jewish film festival has replaced congregational worship testifies to larger shifts in notions of what, for some American Jews, constitutes Jewish cultural literacy and sites of Jewish communion.[80]

As a sign of the growing awareness of the importance of these venues, scholars are currently joining with Jewish communal organizations to study the place of culture in American Jewish life. Noting that, in the 1990 National Jewish Population Study, a majority of respondents "identified themselves as Jewish by 'culture,'" the Institute for Jewish and Community Research in San Francisco issued a study by demographer Gary Tobin of Jewish culture in the Bay Area in 2002. By examining what the region's Jews mean by culture and how they engage with it, the report is meant to help leaders of the organized Jewish community "better plan and support the creative evolution of Jewish life" through cultural activity, which is characterized as "a key strategy for strengthening Jewish identity and participation."[81]

The study of American Jewish culture will always be in process, as new arenas of cultural activity (for example, the Internet) and new approaches to thinking about culture emerge. The challenges faced by scholars of this subject today are markedly different than what they were six decades ago. No longer is there a debate as to whether there is something worthy of scrutiny here, nor is the value of its study in the academy an unanswered question. Instead there are new challenges. Paradigms of what constitutes Jewish culture or Jewishness more generally are once more undergoing signal shifts, as are notions of what constitutes identity and cultural literacy in America generally. The new value invested in culture as a locus of Jewish experience calls for scrutiny, and the self-awareness that informs so much of American Jewish culture needs to be recognized as one of its distinctive characteristics; this, too, needs to be examined. Scholars' increasing implication in how American Jews discuss and practice what they regard as their culture warrants the attention of the academy and practitioners of American Jewish culture alike. Finally, there is the challenge of remaining open to all the possibilities of what American Jewish culture might be as the nation's Jews turn with greater frequency and variety to culture, in its various meanings, as a site of self-definition.

NOTES

My thanks to Barbara Kirshenblatt-Gimblett for her assistance and inspiration in preparing this essay.

1. Judah J. Shapiro, "Jewish Culture: Transplanted and Indigenous," in Oscar I. Janwosky, ed., *The American Jew: A Reappraisal* (Philadelphia, 1964), 374.

2. Elliott Abrams, "Can Jews Survive?" *National Review,* May 19, 1997, 38; Gary A. Tobin, "A Study of Jewish Culture in the Bay Area" (San Francisco, 2002); Robert Alter, "The Jew Who Didn't Get Away: On the Possibility of an American Jewish Culture," *Judaism* 31 (Summer 1982): 274. See also Harold Bloom, "A Speculation Upon American Jewish Culture," *Judaism* 31 (Summer 1982): 266–73.

3. Raymond Williams, *Keywords: A Vocabulary of Culture and Society,* rev. ed. (New York, 1983), 87, 91.

4. See, e.g., the discussion in Stephen J. Whitfield, *In Search of American Jewish Culture* (Hanover, 1999), 1–6.

5. Norman, L. Friedman, "Jewish Popular Culture in Contemporary America," *Judaism* 24.3 (Summer 1975): 265, 263.

6. Abraham G. Duker, "Emerging Culture Patterns in American Jewish Life: The Psycho-Cultural Approach to the Study of Jewish Life in America," in Abraham J. Karp, ed., *The Jewish Experience in America; At Home in America: Selected Studies from the Publications of the American Jewish Historical Society,* 5 vols. (Waltham, Mass, 1969), 5:383–84. Duker's essay is a reworking of research and writing done in the late 1940s, see 382, note 1.

7. See, e.g., Paul Buhle's assessment of the "underground," "subversive" nature of American Jewish popular culture in *From the Lower East Side to Hollywood: Jews in American Popular Culture* (New York, 2004); or Riv-Ellen Prell's analysis of how American Jews have responded to notions of otherness in America, especially with regard to gender stereotyping, in *Fighting to Become Americans: Jews, Gender, and the Anxiety of Assimilation* (Boston, 1999).

8. "The Emergence of a Jewish Cultural Identity," *Jewish Culture News* (Spring 2003): 1–2.

9. The term *identity* is also one whose meaning is complex and requires scholarly interrogation. See, e.g., Stuart Hall and Paul du Gay, eds., *Questions of Cultural Identity* (London, 1996), especially Hall's introductory essay, "Who Needs Identity?"

10. See Berel Lang, "Hyphenated Jews and the Anxiety of Identity," *Jewish Social Studies* 12.1 (Fall 2005): 1–15.

11. See, e.g., Rebecca Kobrin, "Rewriting the Diaspora: Images of Eastern Europe in the Bialystok Landsmanshaft Press, 1921-45," *Jewish Social Studies* 12.3 (Spring/Summer 2006): 1-38.

12. Jonathan D. Sarna, ed. and trans., *People Walk on Their Heads: Moses Weinberger's Jews and Judaism in New York* (New York, 1982), 61.

13. Hutchins Hapgood, *The Spirit of the Ghetto: Studies of the Jewish Quarter of New York* (New York, 1902).

14. As cited in Barbara Kirshenblatt-Gimblett, "The Folk Culture of Jewish Immigrant Communities: Research Paradigms and Directions," in Moses Rischin, ed., *The Jews of North America* (Detroit, 1987), 82.

15. See Tony Michels, *A Fire in Their Hearts: Yiddish Socialists in New York* (Cambridge, 2005).

16. On *The Rise of David Levinsky*, see Jules Chametzky's introduction to Abraham Cahan, *The Rise of David Levinsky* (New York, 1993 [1917]), vii–xxv; David Engel, "The Discrepancies of the Modern: Reevaluating Abraham Cahan's *The Rise of David Levinsky*," *Modern Jewish Studies Annual* 3 (1979): 68–91; Esther Romaine, "Eros and Americanization: David Levinsky and the Etiquette of Race," in Jack Kugelmass, ed., *Key Texts in American Jewish Culture* (New Brunswick, NJ, 2003), 25–45. On *The Jazz Singer*, see J. Hoberman and Jeffrey Shandler, *Entertaining America: Jews, Movies, and Broadcasting* (Princeton, 2003), 77–92; Michael Rogin, "Blackface, White Noise: The Jewish Jazz Singer Finds His Voice," *Critical Inquiry* 18.3 (1992): 417–53; Mark Slobin, "Some Intersections of Jews, Music and Theater," in Sarah Blacher Cohen, ed., *From Hester Street to Hollywood: The Jewish-American Stage and Screen* (Bloomington, 1983), 29–43.

17. Deborah Dash Moore, *At Home in America: Second-Generation New York Jews* (New York, 1981), 233.

18. Beth S. Wenger, *New York Jews and the Great Depression: Uncertain Promise* (New Haven, 1996), 5. For a discussion of the cultural uncertainty of small-town American Jews during the period before World War II, see Eva Morawska, *Insecure Prosperity: Small-Town Jews in Industrial America, 1890–1940* (Princeton, 1996).

19. On Yiddish radio, see Ari Y. Kelman, "Station Identification: The Culture of Yiddish Radio in New York," Ph.D. diss., New York University, 2003; on Yiddish film, see J. Hoberman, *Bridge of Light: Yiddish Film Between Two Worlds* (New York, 1991).

20. See Jeffrey Shandler, "Beyond the Mother Tongue: Learning the Meaning of Yiddish in America," in *Jewish Social Studies* 6.3 (Spring/Summer 2000): 97–123.

21. See Leonard B. Glick, "Types Distinct from Our Own: Franz Boas on Jewish Identity and Assimilation," *American Anthropologist* 84 (1982): 545–65; Gelya Frank, "Jews, Multiculturalism, and Boasian Anthropology," *American Anthropologist* 99.4 (1997): 731–45. See also the discussion of Boas in Barbara Kirshenblatt-Gimblett, "Imagining Europe: The Popular Arts of American Jewish Ethnography," in Deborah Dash Moore and S. Ilan Troen, eds., *Divergent Jewish Cultures: Israel and America* (New Haven, 2001), 155–91.

22. Melville Herskovits, "When Is a Jew a Jew?" *Modern Quarterly* 4.2 (June–September 1927): 117.

23. Melville Herskovits, "Who Are the Jews?" in Louis Finkelstein, ed., *The Jews: Their History, Culture, and Religion* (Philadelphia, 1949), 2:1168.

24. Oscar I. Janowsky, "The Image of the American Jewish Community," in Oscar I. Janowsky, ed., *The American Jew: A Reappraisal* (Philadelphia, 1964), 394.

25. Irving Howe, *World of Our Fathers: The Journey of the East European Jews to America and the Life They Found and Made* (New York, 1976), 642.

26. Horace M. Kallen, "Democracy Versus the Melting-Pot: A Study of American Nationality," in Werner Sollors, ed., *Theories of Ethnicity: A Classical Reader* (New York, 1996), 71; originally published in the *Nation* 100.2590 (February 18, 1915), 190–94, 100.2591 (February 25, 1915), 217–20.

27. See Rudolf Glanz, *The Jew in Early American Wit and Graphic Humor* (New York, 1973).

28. See Neil Baldwin, *Henry Ford and the Jews: The Mass Production of Hate* (New York, 2001). See also Leonard Dinnerstein, *Antisemitism in America* (New York, 1994).

29. Haym Soloveitchik, "Rupture and Reconstruction: The Transformation of Contemporary Orthodoxy," *Tradition* 28.4 (1994): 79.

30. Louis Wirth, *The Ghetto* (Chicago, 1956 [1928]), 9, 287. Compare Wirth's conceptualization of the ghetto as a sociocultural paradigm with Max Weinreich, "The Reality of Jewishness Versus the Ghetto Myth: The Sociolinguistic Roots of Yiddish," in *To Honor Roman Jakobson: Essays on the Occasion of His Seventieth Birthday* (The Hague, 1967), 2199–2211.

31. Everett V. Stonequist, *The Marginal Man: A Study in Personality and Culture Conflict* (New York, 1961[1937]), xv, 129, 221, 138. Stonequist's study elaborated on earlier work by sociologist Robert E. Park; see his "Human Migration and the Marginal Man," *American Journal of Sociology* 33.6 (May 1928): 881–93.

32. Mordecai M. Kaplan, *Judaism as a Civilization: Toward a Reconstruction of American Jewish Life* (New York, 1934), 179, 293. Kaplan acknowledged that his notion of Judaism as a civilization was indebted, in part, to the Semiticist Israel Friedlander's formulation of Judaism as a culture; see 180. See also Mel Scult, "Americanism and Judaism in the Thought of Mordecai M. Kaplan," in Robert M. Seltzer and Norman J. Cohen, eds., *The Americanization of the Jews* (New York, 1995), 339–54.

33. See Stuart Svonkin, *Jews Against Prejudice: American Jews and the Fight for Civil Liberties* (New York, 1997).

34. See Donald Weber, "The Limits of Empathy: Hollywood's Imagining of Jews Circa 1947," in Jack Kugelmass, ed., *Key Texts in American Jewish Life* (New Brunswick, NJ, 2003), 91–104.

35. Will Herberg, *Protestant—Catholic—Jew: An Essay in American Religious Sociology* (Garden City, NY, 1955). See also David G. Dalin, "Will Herberg's Path from Marxism to Judaism: A Case Study in the Transformation of Jewish Belief," in Seltzer and Cohen, *The Americanization of the Jews*, 119–32.

36. See, e.g., Duker, "Emerging Culture Patterns in American Jewish Life," 384; Shapiro, "Jewish Culture," 378.

37. On American Jewish publishing before World War II, see Jonathan D. Sarna, "Jewish Culture Comes to America," *Jewish Studies* 42 (2003/2004): 45–57.

38. On *Commentary*, see, e.g., Nathan Abrams, "'America Is Home': *Commentary* Magazine and the Refocusing of the Community of Memory, 1945–60," *Jewish Culture and History* 3.1 (2000): 45–74; Ruth R. Wisse, "The Maturing of *Commentary* and of the Jewish Intellectual," *Jewish Social Studies* 3.2 (1997): 29–41; Steven Zipperstein, "*Commentary* and American Jewish Culture in the 1940s and 1950s," *Jewish Social Studies* 3.2 (1997): 18–28; Milton S. Katz, "*Commentary* and the American Jewish Intellectual Experience," *Journal of American Culture* 3.1 (1980): 155–66.

39. On *The Eternal Light*, see Jeffrey Shandler and Elihu Katz, "Broadcasting American Judaism: The Radio and Television Department of the Jewish Theological Seminary," in Jack Wertheimer, ed., *Tradition Renewed: A History of the Jewish Theological Seminary* (New York, 1997), 363–401; on the Jewish Museum, see Julie Miller

and Richard I. Cohen, "A Collision of Cultures: The Jewish Museum and JTS, 1904–1971," in Wertheimer, *Tradition Renewed*, 309–61.

40. See Deborah Dash Moore, *To the Golden Cities: Pursuing the American Jewish Dream in Miami and L.A.* (New York, 1994), chapter 5.

41. David A. Hollinger, *Science, Jews, and Secular Culture: Studies in Mid-Twentieth-Century American Intellectual History* (Princeton, 1996), 3.

42. See, e.g., Alexander Bloom, *Prodigal Sons: The New York Intellectuals and Their World* (New York: 1986); Terry Cooney, *The Rise of the New York Intellectuals:* Partisan Review *and Its Circles, 1934–1945* (New York, 1985).

43. The American Jewish encounter with university culture has become a subject of inquiry in itself; see Dan A. Oren, *Joining the Club: A History of Jews and Yale* (New Haven, 1985).

44. See Gerald Sorin, *Irving Howe: A Life of Passionate Dissent* (New York, 2002).

45. Nathan Glazer, *American Judaism*, rev. ed. (Chicago, 1989 [1957]), 108.

46. Remembrance of the Rosenbergs after their execution in 1953 became a noteworthy locus of American Jewish culture. See Deborah Dash Moore, "Reconsidering the Rosenbergs: Symbol and Substance in Second-Generation American Jewish Consciousness," *Journal of American Ethnic History* 8.1 (Fall 1988): 21–37.

47. See, e.g., Karen Brodkin, *How Jews Became White Folks and What That Says About Race in America* (New Brunswick, NJ, 1998); Eric L. Goldstein, *The Price of Whiteness: Jews, Race, and American Identity* (Princeton: 2006); Matthew Jacobson, *Whiteness of a Different Color: European Immigrants and the Alchemy of Race* (Cambridge, 1998).

48. See, e.g., See Evelyn Torton Beck, ed., *Nice Jewish Girls: A Lesbian Anthology* (Watertown, MA, 1982); Miriam Peskowitz and Laura Levitt, eds., *Judaism Since Gender* (New York, 1997); David Shneer and Caryn Aviv, *Queer Jews* (New York, 2002).

49. See Werner Sollors, *Beyond Ethnicity: Consent and Descent in American Culture* (New York, 1986).

50. See, e.g., Albert I. Gordon, *Jews in Suburbia* (Boston, 1959); Marshall Sklare and Joseph Greenblum, *Jewish Identity on the Suburban Frontier* (Chicago, 1979).

51. On American Yiddish literature, see, e.g., Benjamin and Barbara Harshav, *American Yiddish Poetry: A Bilingual Anthology* (Berkeley, 1986); Ruth R. Wisse, *A Little Love in Big Manhattan: Two Yiddish Poets* (Cambridge, 1988); on Yiddish theater and music, see, e.g., Joel Berkowitz, *Shakespeare on the American Yiddish Stage* (Iowa City, 2002); Edna Nahshon, *Yiddish Proletarian Theatre: The Art and Politics of the ARTEF, 1925–1940* (Westport, CT, 1998); Mark Slobin, *Tenement Songs: The Popular Music of the Jewish Immigrants* (Urbana, Ill., 1982).

52. See Kirshenblatt-Gimblett, "The Folk Culture of Jewish Immigrant Communities," 79–94.

53. Key popular books in English about Yiddish include Leo Rosten, *The Joys of Yiddish* (New York, 1968); Maurice Samuel, *In Praise of Yiddish* (Chicago, 1971); and Michael Wex, *Born to Kvetsh: Yiddish Language and Culture in All of Its Moods* (New York, 2005).

54. See Hasia Diner, Jeffrey Shandler, and Beth S. Wenger, eds., *Remembering the Lower East Side: American Jewish Reflections* (Bloomington, 2000), especially Jack

Kugelmass, "Turfing the Slum: New York City's Tenement Museum and the Politics of Heritage," 179–211, and Seth Kamil, "Tripping Down Memory Lane: Walking Tours on the Jewish Lower East Side," 226–40. On the concept of heritage, see David Lowenthal, *The Heritage Crusade and the Spoils of History* (Cambridge, 1988); Barbara Kirshenblatt-Gimblett, *Destination Culture: Tourism, Museums, and Heritage* (Berkeley, 1998).

55. See Rochelle G. Saidel, *Never Too Late to Remember: The Politics Behind New York City's Holocaust Museum* (New York, 1996); for a discussion of the museum, see Jeffrey Shandler, "Heritage and Holocaust on Display: New York City's Museum of Jewish Heritage—A Living Memorial to the Holocaust," *Public Historian* 22.1 (1999): 73–86.

56. See Aaron Hass, *In the Shadow of the Holocaust: The Second Generation* (Ithaca, 1990); Melvin Jules Bukiet, *Nothing Makes You Free: Writings by Descendants of Jewish Holocaust Survivors* (New York, 2002).

57. Jacob Neusner, *Stranger at Home: "The Holocaust," Zionism, and American Judaism* (Chicago, 1981), 1.

58. Jonathan S. Woocher, *Sacred Survival: The Civil Religion of American Jews* (Bloomington, 1986), 20. Woocher's work is, of course, indebted to Rousseau via Robert Bellah's conceptualization of American civil religion: see Robert N. Bellah, "Civil Religion in America," *Daedalus* (Winter 1967): 1–21.

59. For a historical critique of the assimilation model, see Jonathan D. Sarna, "New Paradigms for the Study of American Jewish Life," *Contemporary Jewry* 24 (2003/2004): 157–69; see also Riv-Ellen Prell's response to Sarna, 170–75.

60. See, e.g., Jack Wertheimer, *A People Divided: Judaism in Contemporary America* (New York, 1993); Samuel G. Freedman, *Jew Versus Jew: The Struggle for the Soul of American Jewry* (New York, 2000).

61. On intermarriage, see, e.g., Egon Mayer, *Love and Tradition: Marriage Between Jews and Christians* (New York, 1985); on Jews and Buddhism, see, e.g., Roger Kamenetz, *The Jew in the Lotus: A Poet's Rediscovery of Jewish Identity in Buddhist India* (New York, 1994).

62. Soloveitchik, "Rupture and Reconstruction," 66, 69. On this issue, see also Menachem Friedman, "Life Tradition and Book Tradition in the Development of Ultraorthodox Judaism," in Harvey E. Goldberg, ed., *Judaism Viewed from Within and from Without: Anthropological Studies* (Albany, 1987), 235–56.

63. See Jeffrey Shandler, *Adventures in Yiddishland: Postvernacular Language and Culture* (Berkeley, 2005). Modern Hebrew culture in America follows a different trajectory, shaped largely by the Zionist movement and American Jewish relations with the state of Israel. See Alan L. Mintz, ed., *Hebrew in America: Perspectives and Prospects* (Detroit, 1992).

64. For example, a search run on March 31, 2005, of RAMBI Index of Articles on Jewish Studies (http://jnul.huji.ac.il/rambi/) for entries with the keywords "American," "Jewish," and "Culture" yields a list of 161 items published between 1967 and 2004, of which 152 entires were published in 1980 or later.

65. Joshua A. Fishman, "American Jewry as a Field of Social Science Research," *YIVO Annual for Jewish Social Science* 12 (1958/1959): 70f.

66. Sol Tax, "Jewish Life in the United States: Perspectives from Anthropology," in *Jewish Life in the United States: Perspectives from the Social Sciences* (New York, 1981), 297.

67. See Barbara Myerhoff, *Number Our Days* (New York, 1978).

68. Fishman, "American Jewry as a Field of Social Science Research," 101.

69. On the self-reflexive study of American Jewry, see Jack Kugelmass, ed., *Between Two Worlds: Ethnographic Essays on American Jewry* (Ithaca, 1988).

70. See, e.g, Samuel C. Heilman, *Synagogue Life: A Study in Symbolic Interaction* (Chicago, 1976); David Kaufman, *Shul with a Pool: The "Synagogue-Center" in American Jewish History* (Hanover, 1999); Joseph A, Levine, *Synagogue Music in America* (Crown Point, IN, 1988); Riv-Ellen Prell, *Prayer and Community: The Havurah in American Judaism* (Detroit, 1989); Moshe Shokeid, *A Gay Synagogue in New York* (New York, 1995); Henry Stolzman, *Faith, Spirit, and Identity: Synagogue Architecture in America* (Woodbridge, 2004); Jack Wertheimer, ed., *The American Synagogue: A Sanctuary Transformed* (Cambridge, 1987).

71. Arthur A. Goren, *The Politics and Public Culture of American Jews* (Bloomington, 1999); David G. Roskies, "A Revolution Set in Stone: The Art of Burial," in *The Jewish Search for a Usable Past* (Bloomington, 1999), 120–45; Alan E. Steinweis, "Reflections on the Holocaust from Nebraska," in Hilene Flanzbaum, ed., *The Americanization of the Holocaust* (Baltimore, 1999), 167–80.

72. See, e.g., Susan L. Braunstein and Jenna Weissman Joselit, eds., *Getting Comfortable in New York: The American Jewish Home, 1880–1950* (New York, 1990), and Jenna Weissman Joselit, *The Wonders of America: Reinventing Jewish Culture, 1880–1950* (New York, 1994).

73. See Steve Rogovoy, *The Essential Klezmer: A Music Lover's Guide to Jewish Roots and Soul Music, form the Old World to the Jazz Age to the Downtown Avant-Garde* (Chapel Hill, 2000); Henry Sapoznik, *Klezmer! Jewish Music from Old World to Our World* (New York, 1999); Mark Slobin, *Fiddler on the Move: Exploring the Klezmer World* (New York, 2000); Ruth Ellen Gruber, *Virtually Jewish: Reinventing Jewish Culture in Europe* (Berkeley, 2002), part 4: Klezmer in the Wilderness. Doctoral dissertations on klezmer by *klezmorim* include Hankus Netzky, "Klezmer in Twentieth-Century Philadelphia," Ph.D. diss., Wesleyan University, 2004; Joel Rubin, "The Art of the Klezmer: Improvisation and Ornamentation in the Commercial Recordings of New York Clarinettists Naftule Brandwein and Dave Tarras, 1922–1929," Ph.D. diss., London: City University, 2001.

74. See Janet S. Belcove-Shalin, ed., *New World Hasidim: Ethnographic Studies of Hasidic Jews in America* (Albany, 1995); Robert Eisenberg, *Boychiks in the Hood: Travels in the Hasidic Underground* (New York, 1995); Sue Fishkoff: *The Rebbe's Army: Inside the World of Chabad-Lubavitch* (New York, 2003); Lis Harris, *Holy Days: The World of a Hasidic Family* (New York, 1985); George Kranzler, *Hasidic Williamsburg: A Contemporary American Hasidic Community* (Northvale, NJ, 1995); Jerome R. Mintz, *Hasidic People: A Place in the New World* (Cambridge, 1992); Solomon Poll, *The Hasidic Community of Williamsburg* (New York, 1962).

75. See, e.g., Matthew Baigell, *Jewish-American Artists and the Holocaust* (New Brunswick, NJ, 1997); Dorothy Bilik, *Immigrant Survivors: Post-Holocaust*

Consciousness in Recent Jewish American Fiction (Middletown, 1985); Judith E. Doneson, *The Holocaust in American Film* (Philadelphia, 1987); Hilene Flanzbaum, ed., *Americanization of the Holocaust* (Baltimore, 1999); Annette Insdorf, *Indelible Shadows: Film and the Holocaust* (New York, 1983); S. Lillian Kremer, *Witness Through the Imagination: Jewish-American Holocaust Literature* (Detroit, 1989); Edward T. Linenthal, *Preserving Memory: The Struggle to Create America's Holocaust Museum* (New York, 1995); Peter Novick, *The Holocaust in American Life* (New York, 1999); Jeffrey Shandler, *While America Watches: Televising the Holocaust* (New York, 1999); James E. Young, *The Texture of Memory: Holocaust Memorials and Meaning* (New Haven, 1993); Barbie Zelizer, ed., *Visual Culture and the Holocaust* (New Brunswick, NJ, 2001).

76. E.g., Steven Carr, *Hollywood and Anti-Semitism: A Cultural History Up to World War II* (Cambridge, 2000); Harley Erdman, *Staging the Jew: The Performance of an American Ethnicity, 1860–1920* (New Brunswick, NJ, 1997).

77. See, e.g., Omer Bartov, *The "Jew" in Cinema: From the Golem to Don't Touch My Holocaust* (Bloomington, 2005); David Desser and Lester D. Friedman, *American-Jewish Filmmakers: Traditions and Trends* (Chicago, 1993); Patricia Erens, *The Jew in American Cinema* (Bloomington, 1984); Lester D. Friedman, *Hollywood's Image of the Jew* (New York, 1982); Andrew Heinze, *Adapting to Abundance: Jewish Immigrants, Mass Consumption, and the Search for American Identity* (New York, 1990); Judith Thissen, "Jewish Immigrant Audiences in New York City, 1905–1914," in Melvyn Stokes and Richard Maltby, eds., *American Movie Audiences: From the Turn of the Century to the Early Sound Era* (London, 1999), 15–28.

78. See Vincent Brook, *Something Ain't Kosher Here: The Rise of the "Jewish" Sitcom* (New Brunswick, NJ, 2003); Elliot B. Gertel, *Over the Top Judaism: Precedents and Trends in the Depiction of Jewish Beliefs and Observances in Film and Television* (Lanham, MD, 2003); Jonathan and Judith Pearl, *The Chosen Image: Television's Portrayal of Jewish Themes and Characters* (Jefferson, NC, 1999); David Zurawick, *The Jews of Prime Time* (Lebanon, NH, 2003).

79. See, e.g, Neal Gabler, *An Empire of Their Own: How the Jews Invented Hollywood* (New York, 1988); Andrea Most, *Making Americans: Jews and the Broadway Musical* (Cambridge, 2004).

80. Elliott Oring, "The People of the Joke: On the Conceptualization of a Jewish Humor," *Western Folklore* 42 (1983): 262.

81. Hoberman and Shandler, *Entertaining America*, 12.

82. On this phenomenon in general, see Faye Ginsburg, "The Parallax Effect: Jewish Ethnographic Film," *Jewish Folklore and Ethnology Review* 10.1 (1988): 16–17. On Alan Berliner, see Efrén Cuevas and Carlos Muguiro, eds., *El hombre sin la cámara: El cine de Alan Berliner/The Man Without the Movie Camera: The Cinema of Alan Berliner* (Madrid, 2002).

83. Norman L. Kleeblatt, ed., *Too Jewish? Challenging Traditional Identities* (New Brunswick, NJ, 1996); On Jewish film festivals, see Mikel J. Koven, "'You Don't Have to Be Filmish': The Toronto Jewish Film Festival," *Ethnologies* 21.1 (2003): 115–32.

84. Gary A. Tobin, "A Study of Jewish Culture in the Bay Area" (San Francisco, 2002), 5, preface [unpaginated]. For other recent assessments of the place of culture in

the lives of American Jews, focusing on younger Jews who are "unaffiliated" with a synagogue or other established Jewish organization, see also Steven M. Cohen and Ari Y. Kelman, *Cultural Events and Jewish Identities: Young Adults in New York* (New York: National Foundation for Jewish Culture/UJA-Federation of New York, 2005); Anna Greenberg, "*Grande Soy Vanilla Latte with Cinnamon, No Foam . . .*": *Jewish Identity and Community in a Time of Unlimited Choices* ([New York]: Reboot, [2006?]).

15

RITES OF CITIZENSHIP

Jewish Celebrations of the Nation

BETH S. WENGER

As the nation celebrated the centennial in July of 1876, the Union of American Hebrew Congregations gathered in Washington, DC for its third annual convention. To mark the occasion, the delegates scheduled a break from conference business and traveled to George Washington's grave site in Mount Vernon.[1] The pilgrimage began as they boarded the ship where a flag welcomed the party with the Hebrew words *shalom aleichem*. The group disembarked to musical accompaniment and listened to speeches praising Washington's heroic deeds and passionate commitment to liberty and democracy. Like many others who made the pilgrimage to the site, the Jewish visitors planted a tree at Washington's grave to symbolize "the gratitude which they owe to him and his compatriots."[2] In his remarks, Rabbi Isaac Mayer Wise, the architect of the Reform movement, noted the irony of this Jewish pilgrimage. Why, he asked rhetorically, "are the representatives of the Union of American Hebrew Congregations, the admirers of Moses and the prophets, assembled at the sepulcher of George Washington?" Answering his own question, Wise explained that Washington had "fulfilled in the holy cause of humanity that which Moses has written." Both men, according to Wise, had offered a sacred message of liberty, justice, and equality. Both had set the stage for the best course of human history: "Moses, the son of Amram, and George Washington are the two poles of the axis about which the history of mankind revolves."[3] In a rhetorical flourish that employed the most ubiquitous themes in American Jewish life, Wise neatly paralleled biblical history and American history, setting the fates of Jews and Americans on the same path.

In American Jewish history no theme resounds as loudly or as consistently as the symbiosis between Judaism and American democracy. In books, communal celebrations, and a variety of public proclamations, American Jews championed the essential compatibility of Jewish and American values, consciously constructing perhaps the most fundamental axiom of American Jewish life. Anyone with a passing knowledge of American Jewish history, or of immigrant history for that matter, will recognize the familiar refrains of minority groups declaring their belonging in America through the rhetoric of compatibility. The cultural landscape of America became defined, in part, by immigrant and minority groups proclaiming the similarity, even syncretism, between their traditions and values and the American ideals of liberty, equality, and democracy. Yet the pervasiveness of such rhetoric should not suggest that the recasting of immigrant identity in American terms was an automatic or unconscious process or that all immigrant groups engaged in that process in the same way. Even within the Jewish community different political and social groups articulated distinct ideas about why Jews and Jewish culture could so easily find a place in American society—though almost all agreed on the fundamental principle. Jews proclaimed faith in America confidently and repeatedly, often as much in hope as with certitude. As they publicly celebrated American holidays and heroes, Jews in the United States reinvented their collective past, crafting a new script about Jewish history uniquely tailored to the needs and desires of Jews in America.

Participating in national celebrations provided Jews the opportunity to declare their allegiance to the United States while also expressing their vision of what the nation should be. Jews seized public moments as occasions to write themselves into the narratives of American history and to make themselves and their culture pivotal actors in the creation of the nation. During these moments, they outlined the parameters of a country that made room for Jews and Judaism and also assessed their own progress in America. When they honored American heroes and joined in national observances, Jews conjured and performed versions of American history and sketched a Jewish place within it.

Jewish celebrations of national holidays became occasions for public retellings of a variety of idealized historical narratives about both America and the Jews. As moments of reflection, national observances provided the opportunity to rehearse the long historical journey of the Jewish people, complete with a new coda about the American epoch. In these narratives references to Europe, whether stated or unstated, provided the backdrop for the American Jewish story, constructing a pole of difference that highlighted Jewish experience in the United States. At the same time, these accounts of Jewish history paid homage to America's self-definition as a nation built by immigrants, offering freedom and opportunity to all its citizens. During public moments of national celebration,

Jews often constructed a shared history with America, rooted in a mutual biblical heritage, as both Jews and Americans identified the "Old Testament" as the foundation of their cultures. Using biblical metaphors and images of the "Promised Land" as ideological touch points, Jews claimed a natural affinity between their culture and that of their adopted homeland. In a circuitous fashion, as Jews embraced the freedoms and collective mythology of America as a new promised land, their ability to do so became a proof text of that very definition of America. This does not mean that public celebrations were always harmonious, unequivocal endorsements of the currents within American society and culture. Indeed, these occasions often contained hotly contested moments, providing opportunities for Jews to critique the state of affairs in the United States. Even when this occurred, it remained in a context that positioned Jewish and American culture in an intimate dialogue, with Jews standing at center stage in the drama of American history.

In their historical accounts and celebrations of the nation, Jews situated themselves at the very beginning of the national story, standing alongside Christopher Columbus at the discovery of the New World. When the United States celebrated the four hundredth anniversary of Columbus's landing, Jews joined in the festivities. Although many Jewish leaders believed that Jews should not celebrate the occasion as a separate group but rather join with other Americans in their observances, Jews did mark the event, particularly in synagogues.[4] Across the country, rabbis preached sermons on the subject and read special prayers in synagogues that had been decorated with American flags for the occasion. According to one rabbi, Jews had good reason to give thanks for Columbus, for he had "founded a haven of repose for our noble race . . . he discovered a country for wandering Israel."[5] But Jews did more than express gratitude. Through the years, dozens of children's stories and popular histories recounted the story of Luis de Torres, the converted Jew who sailed with Columbus as his interpreter as well as the supposedly several other men of Jewish descent, Marranos or conversos, who made the voyage. Most of these stories originated from the scholarship of Meyer Kayserling, who authored a work on the connections between Jews and Columbus sponsored by the American Jewish Historical Society in the 1890s. The elite founders of the society were eager to offer "proof" of the role of Jews in Columbus's voyage, believing that it might actually reduce antisemitism. Kayserling obliged them, uncovering many previously unknown interactions between Jews and Columbus, although exaggerating certain findings.[6] Kayserling's work had little effect in diminishing antisemitism, but it had widespread impact within the Jewish community, finding its way into scores of popular books, speeches, and sermons. On Columbus Day, 1918, Rabbi Jacob Stolz relied on Kayserling when he proclaimed, "there was never a time when white people were on American soil in anticipation of Jews."[7]

By the 1930s a host of shaky scholarship even raised the possibility that Columbus himself was Jewish, born of Marrano parents.[8] One popular history titled *Jewish Pioneers in America* tackled the issue by first citing the supposed proof of his Jewishness and then asserting that "whether Columbus was a Jew is uncertain. But there is no doubt of the fact that he was materially assisted in his venture by a number of influential Jews."[9] The author then recounts the Jewish mapmakers, astronomers, advocates, and financial backers from Spain who made Columbus's journey possible. Some of the stories about Jewish involvement with Columbus were indeed historically accurate, based on Kayserling's findings, but historical accuracy was not really the point in these narratives. The purpose was to place Jews integrally within the discovery and founding of America. "Jews witnessed the dawn of American history," this same history book proclaimed, emphasizing that Jews were present at the very moment that the New World was born.[10] Moreover, the discovery of America opened a new chapter in Jewish history. "Sad, indeed, was the plight of the Jews that year [1492]," declared one speaker in 1930, "and yet in the same year came the discovery of America. Is it not true that God had again shown Israel, in its hour of need, the Promised Land?"[11] Some children's books claimed that the Marranos who sailed with Columbus had embarked on a distinctly Jewish mission: "the Marranos," one popular storybook explained, "were seeking a haven for the oppressed Jews."[12] Assessing the meaning of the discovery of the New World for Jews, one of the earliest American Jewish history textbooks concluded that "it is our pride that Jews had much to do with that discovery which, without their foreseeing it, finally won for them a new refuge, a home for a far larger Jewish community than medieval Spain had ever boasted."[13] In these popular retellings, Jewish history and American history were interwoven, providing a way for Jews to tell their own ethnic story intimately tied to the broader canvass of American history.

The founding myths of the United States made room for Jews to insert themselves as integral players in the creation of the nation. To be sure, when the Puritans declared America the New Israel, they envisioned no place for Jews. But Jewish rhetoric generally ignored the Christian triumphalism of the Puritans and focused instead on shared devotion to Hebrew Scriptures. Jewish narratives regularly stressed the essential compatibility of biblical teachings and American democracy. Reform Jews were the first and most vociferous in insisting that the nation's spiritual and legal roots lay in the Hebrew Bible. In the inaugural issue of the *American Israelite*, Isaac Mayer Wise proclaimed that "the principles of the constitution of the United States are copied from the words of Moses and the Prophets."[14] This kind of rhetoric was most pervasive in Reform circles, but rabbis from all three major denominations echoed the same themes. According to one Conservative rabbi, Puritanism "was, in essence, the rebirth of the Hebrew spirit in the Christian conscience."[15] Even the president of the Orthodox Yeshiva

University insisted that there was no "serious conflict between our spiritual heritage and the American way of life, which is itself rooted in Hebraic spiritual values."[16] By insisting that American democracy, as Kaufmann Kohler proclaimed, "found its classical expression in Israel's holy writings," Jews claimed a founding role in the creation of the nation, not only placing themselves at the birth of the country but also taking credit for inventing its fundamental principles.[17]

At stake in these "foundation myths," as one historian has called them, was an assertion about Jewish belonging in America.[18] The claim that "we were here from the beginning" and "our values (rooted in the Bible) are identical to your values (of American liberty and democracy)" allowed Jews to tell their own story about America, a story that placed Jewish contributions at the center. These filiopietistic pronouncements were indeed self-serving, but they expressed an ideal vision of America that promised a secure place for Jews while also laying the groundwork for a harmonious relationship between Jews and Christians rooted in shared devotion to Scripture.

Thanksgiving Day was an especially popular occasion for promoting the shared biblical heritage of Christians and Jews. In the nineteenth century, when Thanksgiving was regularly celebrated in churches and synagogues, Jews availed themselves of the chance to join "one day at least in the year in even religious communion with our fellow-citizens."[19] Thanksgiving became a time for Jews to advertise their commonalities with other Americans and to stake a claim to a mutual metahistory rooted in the Bible. At special synagogue services the singing of the national anthem and other patriotic hymns accompanied traditional psalms and prayers.[20] Rabbis not only preached their own Thanksgiving sermons during these holiday services but often invited Christian clergy to speak from their pulpits in what became public performances of common ground. In 1879, Henry Bellows, minister at New York's First Congregational Church, told the congregation gathered at Temple Emanu-El that "no people . . . has had a beginning or an early history, so like the Hebrews as the American people; and the old claim of being 'a chosen people' has always been somewhat self-appropriated by our countrymen."[21] Both Jewish and Christian clergy were fond of drawing parallels between ancient Hebrews and early Americans. One popular instruction manual for the celebration Jewish holidays declared that

> the Pilgrim Fathers were greatly influenced by Jewish teachings in the Bible. We need but examine their first names—Gamaliel, Ezekiel, Samuel, and the like—to realize how deep this influence was. Many of the laws made by them, as well as the form of government planned, were inspired by the Torah, for they read and studied the Old Testament no less than the New Testament. They sang many of the Psalms on the first Thanksgiving. Jews may truly say, therefore, that they were represented, in spirit if not in body, on that memorable day.[22]

Such claims represent a cultural transitive property of equality (if our texts were present, and recited by the Pilgrims, then by extension we were present at the foundational moment of the nation and actually virtual Pilgrims ourselves). One Jewish author even went so far as to argue the formula in reverse. Bestowing honorary Jewish status on the Puritans, a 1920s publication insisted that they so closely paralleled the Hebrews that "culturally they were Jews as much as non-Jews can possibly be."[23]

But behind all the flowery rhetoric that accompanied the celebration of Thanksgiving also lay a recurring Jewish critique of American government. Especially in the nineteenth century, government officials from the president to governors often issued Thanksgiving proclamations that contained references to Christianity or calls to worship in churches. Year after year, Jews assailed this practice even as they extolled the virtues of America. Speaking from the pulpit in 1868, Marcus Jastrow informed his Philadelphia congregation that

> the Governor of the State has ignored the character of his office, and the character of the Constitution of the United States, by making his own particular belief the basis of a proclamation to the commonwealth, thus intimating that he wishes only such united with him in thanksgiving for the country's happiness and greatness, who may profess certain Dogmas similar to his own, and that he considers all other inhabitants under his jurisdiction unworthy to shout before their God, to serve Him with joy, to come before His presence with triumphal song, when the *country* celebrates a day of *national* importance.[24]

More than thirty-five years later, the *American Israelite* leveled the same charges. "The people know when Thanksgiving Day falls and what is the proper way of observing it," the newspaper told its readers. "The official proclamations are needless and smack too much of a union of Church and State to be to the *Israelite's* liking."[25] These sharp critiques became standard fare at Thanksgiving, included alongside all the rhetoric about the glories of America, as Jews used the occasion not only to celebrate the nation with other Americans but also to define the parameters of the America they desired.

Jews fought desperately to preserve the nonsectarian nature of Thanksgiving, in part, because as long as it remained religiously neutral, Jews could regard it as sacred on their own terms, as an occasion to join equally in the celebration. Religious leaders often drew parallels with the Jewish holiday of Succot, which usually fell about a month before Thanksgiving on the calendar and could be regarded as a loosely similar celebration. "The idea of a harvest festival," explained one Jewish educator, "is not new to the Jewish people. . . . There is good reason to believe that the Puritans modeled Thanksgiving Day after the Jewish Festival of Succot."[26] Another Jewish textbook declared matter-of-factly that "the Pilgrim Fathers, when they kept their first Thanksgiving Day in America, no doubt received the idea from their Hebrew bibles which they knew so well."[27] This logic transformed Thanksgiving into an American holiday that had been essentially created by the Jews, affording Jewish culture a foundational role in the nation. Other attempts to find analogies to Jewish tradition forged a link to Passover, a domestic-centered Jewish holiday that also revolved around a traditional meal. Some Zionists even linked Thanksgiving to the Jewish national effort, explaining that "when Jews are tilling the soil once again in Palestine, it is natural that on Thanksgiving Day we should compare the American pioneers with the HALUT-ZIM who are rebuilding the Jewish Homeland."[28]

The American Jewish encounter with Thanksgiving required finding familiar terms to embrace the new holiday. In her memoir, social worker Elizabeth Stern recalls her immigrant father bringing home a turkey for the first time, which her mother compared to the more familiar duck or chicken traditionally eaten by Jews on holidays. Stern's turn-of-the-century Jewish family celebrated Thanksgiving by setting the table with a white cloth and listening to her father recount lessons from the Talmud, creating a Jewish version of the newly discovered American holiday.[29] Immigrant Jewish families gradually incorporated the secular ritual into their regular observances and often drew parallels between themselves and the Pilgrims. Anzia Yezierska's 1923, semifictional "America and I" recounted her first encounter with the Thanksgiving story: "I began to read American history. I found from the first pages that America started with a band of Courageous Pilgrims. They had left their native country as I had left mine. They had crossed an unknown ocean and landed in an unknown country, as I." Although the early frustrations of immigrant life frequently left Yezierska disappointed with the realities of the American experience, she ultimately found the seeds of hope, discovering that "it was the glory of America that it was not yet finished. And I, the last comer, had her share to give, small or great, to the making of America, like those Pilgrims who came in the Mayflower."[30] By envisioning themselves as modern-day Pilgrims, Jews found a way to insert themselves in the foundation narratives of America.

Similar patterns prevailed when Jews celebrated Independence Day. Once again, Jewish and Christian clergy often joined together to observe this civic holiday. In addressing the interdenominational gathering at the Bunker Hill Monument in 1935, Rabbi Morris Gutstein of Newport's Touro Synagogue insisted that the Declaration of Independence merited "inclusion in the great Literatures of Religion" and should be celebrated by both Jews and Christians as, in his words, "the American Song of Redemption."[31] In most July 4 celebrations, Jews told (at least) two narratives; the first positioned them within an American story and the second recounted the longer epoch of Jewish history. Within American history Jews appeared as the ideological progenitors of American democracy through their role as the People of the Book. Standing on board the SS *Leviathan*, Rabbi Emanuel Hertz of Washington Heights described the nation's founders as setting out "with the Bible under their arm and the Declaration of Independence in their heart."[32] In this formulation, as in so many others, the Jews, as originators of monotheism and the Old Testament, became spiritual founders of the nation. When they turned to the narration of Jewish history, American Jews wrote a new ending to the story, culminating in the United States. On July 4, 1918, both American and blue and white flags adorned the streets outside Brownsville's Stone Avenue Talmud Torah. After a parade through the neighborhood, the schoolchildren staged a pageant in three acts: the first began with the Jews of Egypt being liberated by Moses, the next scene depicted the suffering of the Jews of Spain and Russia (conflating, quite egregiously, centuries of Jewish life into a single epoch of persecution), and the final act culminated with immigrant Jews being welcomed to the shores of America.[33] This story, which notably also begins with biblical history, brings Jewish history to a new climax on American soil. At the same time, Independence Day, as recounted in these celebrations, commemorated the freedoms granted both *by* Jews and *to* Jews. In a deft slight of hand, Jews had rendered themselves simultaneously the originators of an American culture that had been their gift through the Bible and the recipients of that gift as European immigrants, searching to plot a new course in Jewish history. In sum, Jews were celebrating the freedoms of American democracy they had helped to create in the first place. The logic behind such arguments may have been circular and convoluted at times, but it reflects the multiple, and somewhat sophisticated, recasting that took place in the simplest fourth of July celebrations staged by Jewish communities across the United States.

Not all Jews shared such a celebratory tone on Independence Day. July 4 editorials in the socialist *Jewish Daily Forward* regularly scoffed at the notion that all Americans enjoyed equality and used the occasion to claim that only the socialist vision reflected the true intent of the Declaration of Independence.[34] The typical rhetorical formula employed by the *Forward* was to celebrate the vision promoted by America's founders and then to outline how those ideals had been betrayed. Often peppering the critique with allusions to biblical texts and traditions, one 1910 editorial from the *Forward* declared that "the American Declaration of Independence is the world's first true declaration of freedom for an entire nation. . . . Can you find any "Torah" as precious as this?"[35] The editorial then proceeded to enumerate the many ways that America had failed to live up to the principles of its founding through continued class oppression, explaining, with more than a hint of sarcasm, that, "to commemorate this precious 'Torah,' all Americans devote one holy day every year. How thoroughly suffused with the idea of freedom, equality, and justice the Americans must be [so we used to believe]! . . . But oh what a disappointment! The world's worst tyrants celebrate on the 4th of July . . . , the most merciless oppressors."[36] Socialist accounts, like most that emerged from the Jewish left, generally leveled the sharpest critiques and were the least likely to paint the Jewish relationship to America as unequivocally harmonious. Still, like other Jews in the United States, Jewish socialists used the July 4 holiday to put forward their own reading of both Jewish and American history and to assert their particular ideological positions.

Moreover, socialists were hardly the only members of the Jewish community who took advantage of national holidays as occasions to condemn the direction of their adopted homeland. In 1924, when the United States instituted its most restrictive immigration quotas, newspaper editorials across the ideological spectrum of the Jewish press issued bitter denunciations of the new immigration policies. The Communist *Freiheit* (*Liberty*), not surprisingly, published a vitriolic commentary that assailed July 4 as "a holiday for the burial of ideals." The article began with a short history of the Declaration of Independence and proceeded to attack those Americans who had made a mockery of its principles. Calling the nation's leaders "oppressors," "bloodsuckers," and "leeches," the Communist paper insisted the ideals that had once inspired the country's founding had been buried "so deep in the earth that no resurrection will ever revive them."[37] The liberal, more literary Yiddish daily, the *Day* (*Der Tog*) showed greater restraint in its language, but no less disdain for the restrictionist climate that had overtaken the nation. Its editorial contained a stirring tribute to the ways that the United States had created a new definition of citizenship. By breaking with Old World notions that made race and ancestry the sole criteria for citizenship, the *Day*'s editors argued, America had created a country in which principle alone ruled, and thus the fledgling country had asserted not only national but also spiritual independence from its European predecessors. The essay concluded with a quiet warning about the dangerous possibility that on this particular fourth of July America's commitment to independence and to a new national self-definition appeared increasingly precarious.[38] Even the conservative, Orthodox newspaper, the *Jewish Daily News* (*Yiddishes Tageblatt*) railed against the anti-immigrant turn in American culture in 1924. In an article addressed to Uncle Sam by his adopted nephew ("a nephew by choice"), the author explained:

> We selected you, dear Uncle Sam, because we were tired of old world ideals, such as they were, of old world jealousies and hatreds, of the old world spirit of destruction. We came here because we felt that here under your guidance, there might be developed a new civilization based on the broadest humanity. Here there would be an end to the religious prejudices and racial animosities which have made of the old World a slaughterhouse.
>
> We gave more than lip-worship to you. We gave you ourselves and our children so that this country might live as an exemplar to the rest of mankind.
>
> Is our faith to prove an illusion? Are our hopes to be dashed to the ground, shattered beyond repair?[39]

While both tempers and fears were running particularly high during Independence Day celebrations in 1924, the nature of Jewish public responses reflected an enduring pattern. Jewish celebrations of national holidays regularly contained references to Europe, measuring the progress of America (sometimes favorably, sometimes not so favorably) against an Old World precedent. Jews, like other immigrant groups, repeatedly gauged the mood of their adopted homeland in terms of their collective European experience and assessed the degree of improvement or regression. At the same time, Jews appeared in their own renditions of the American story as the most ardent believers in American principles, steadfastly clinging to those ideals, even, as in 1924, when they claimed that the rest of the nation was steering off course. Across the religious, political, and ideological spectrum of the community, Jews found national holidays most useful occasions to project their own image of America and assert an idealized version of the Jewish role within it.

The celebration of presidential holidays also elicited many American Jewish festivities, as Jews demonstrated a particular affinity for honoring George Washington and Abraham Lincoln, reinventing their legacies and legends to suit Jewish communal needs. The figure of George Washington looms large in both Jewish public celebrations and private reminiscences. In her immigrant memoir, Mary Antin wrote adoringly of her first encounters with the legend of Washington. "I could not pronounce the name of George Washington without a pause," she recalled. "Never had I prayed, never had I chanted the songs of David, never had I called upon the Most Holy, in such utter reverence and worship as I repeated the simple sentences of my child's story of the patriot."[40] As the nation's first president, George Washington occupied the opening chapter of the early education of most Jewish immigrants. In the metahistory of American Jews, Washington claimed a similar position, providing a foundation story that cemented the relationship between Jews and the nation. At the Mount Vernon tree-planting ceremony in 1876, one of the key elements of the celebration was the public reading of correspondence between George Washington and several Jewish congregations, particularly his famous 1790 reply to the Newport community in which he assured Jews that the United States gave "to bigotry no sanction, to persecution no assistance." In a pattern of self-definition typical within American Jewish culture, Jews themselves helped to author the guarantee they held so sacred. It was Newport's Jews who first composed the infamous phrase "to bigotry no sanction" in their letter welcoming the president, and Washington repeated these words verbatim in his reply.[41] Washington had delivered similar assurances to many minority groups in America, as he calculated how best to balance group rights in the new nation.[42] But American Jews turned Washington's words into a founding charter of their rights as citizens in the United States—a charter they themselves had crafted. Washington's pledge took on a virtual sanctity among American Jews, who treated it not only as a guarantee of their rights but also as a sacred American Jewish text.

American Jews unfailingly cited Washington's words when the nation celebrated the centennial of his inauguration in 1889, the bicentennial of his birth in 1932, and each year on Presidents' Day. The observance of the 1889 centennial fell during Passover and New York's "chief rabbi" Jacob Joseph composed a special prayer to be recited in synagogues that were decorated in red, white, and blue for the occasion. In New York, Jews who bought ten pounds of matza received a free picture of the first president with their purchase. The newspaper the *American Hebrew* marked the centennial by printing an illustration by Arthur Meyer depicting that year's observance of Passover in American Jewish homes. In the upper-right corner a picture of George Washington hangs on the family's wall, positioned to welcome the prophet Elijah. Washington's picture stands facing a portrait of Moses holding the Ten Commandments, symbolically linking the two icons who offered Jews freedom from oppression.[43]

In 1932, when the nation observed the two hundredth anniversary of Washington's birth, Jews not only joined in the festivities but also took pride that a Jewish congressman, Sol Bloom, was directing this public American celebration. Bloom, who had worked in theater, real estate, and had designed the Midway Plaisance at the Chicago World's Fair before becoming a congressman, set out to "bring George Washington to the people."[44] Rather than holding a single event in one venue, Bloom organized the celebrations on a state level with the intent to have every community in the United States commemorate the occasion.[45] The press took note that the director of the bicentennial was Jewish. One reporter observed:

> To no member of the Society of Mayflower Descendants, to no Boston Brahmin, to no Virginia aristocrat, to the occupant of no history chair at Harvard, Yale or Princeton, to no Son of the American Revolution or husband of a Militant Daughter, but to a man of alien race . . . [a Polish Jew] . . . has come, by a strange turn of fate, the active directorship of the greatest patriotic show ever put on.[46]

The Jewish press chronicled Bloom's contributions to the national celebration, even as the community organized its own events.[47] Rabbis throughout the country preached sermons to mark the occasion, and Bloom gathered their texts together with those of Christian clergy in a commemorative volume.[48] The Jewish National Fund urged American Jews to celebrate the bicentennial by planting a tree in the George Washington Forest in Palestine, newly created by the JNF as "a living memorial to George Washington."[49] Throughout their celebrations of the first president, Jews took the opportunity not only to emphasize their enduring patriotism but also to quote repeatedly Washington's famous promise to them.

The phrase "to bigotry no sanction, to persecution no assistance" became a collective mantra within the American Jewish community, summarizing the promise that Jews believed Washington had extended to them and encapsulating Jewish expectations of America.

Nowhere is the Washington "guarantee" more celebrated than in Newport, Rhode Island, where the local Jewish community takes particular pride in its role as recipient of Washington's letter. First only on special occasions and then every year shortly after the Touro Synagogue was designated a national historic site in 1946, the Jews of Newport have sponsored a public reading of the exchange of letters.[50] Each August for more than fifty years, Newport's Jewish community has rehearsed the words of Washington in an annual ritual, repeating and affirming America's promise of religious freedom and equality to Jews. Invited speakers each year relate the principles of Washington to the issues of the day; civil rights was a recurrent theme through the 1960s, giving way to language about diversity by the 1990s.[51] Members of the community often dress in colonial costume as part of the performance. In 1990, on the two hundredth anniversary of the letter, Jews joined with other Newport residents in a full-scale reenactment of Washington's first visit, with "George Washington" arriving in costume at the Touro Synagogue greeted by the rabbi and the congregation. On this occasion the actor Ed Asner performed the reading of the letter together with a descendant of Moses Seixas, the author of the original.[52] Even as the annual letter reading has become a tourist attraction in recent years, it continues to serve an important public function for the Jews of Newport—a Jewish declaration about the promise of America that the community sees fit to reiterate.

The letter itself was placed on the Freedom Train in 1947, the only item relating to Jews in the collection. Designed to rekindle the spirit of citizenship after World War II, the Freedom Train was a touring exhibit of documents and memorabilia relating to American history that traveled the United States for more than a year. Decorated in red, white, and blue, the seven-car train attracted more than three and a half million visitors as it made its way through 322 cities, demonstrating the virtues of democracy and liberty to the American public.[53] Newport Jews were pleased that the letter received such prominence. But the letter that the community regarded as its sacred document would never be returned to the city. In the intervening years, Morris Morgenstern, an immigrant Jew who earned success in real estate, purchased the letter from a descendant of Moses Seixas for a reputed ten thousand dollars.[54] Members of the Touro Synagogue tried in vain for years to claim the legal right to the letter and to convince Morgenstern to deposit it for permanent display in the congregation.[55] Although Morgenstern brought the letter to Newport for the celebration of the American Jewish tercentenary in 1954, he chose to deposit it in Washington, DC, at B'nai B'rith's Klutznick National Museum. Morgenstern clearly regarded the letter as a sacred document. Applying a commodified meaning to the freedoms of America, he remarked that

"nowhere but in the United States could an immigrant like himself obtain possession of such a document."[56] The Jews of Newport would have to settle for selling
replicas of the Washington letter in the Touro Synagogue gift shop and for having
the synagogue—along with the famous quote—honored in a 1982 stamp from the
United States Postal Service, issued on the 250th anniversary of Washington's
birth.[57]

The only United States president to receive as much attention in Jewish communities as George Washington was Abraham Lincoln. On Presidents' Day, of
course, American Jews celebrated the two together. The Union of American Hebrew Congregations suggested that Jews observe the holiday with a pageant staged
in their synagogues. According to the pageant script, the Statue of Liberty stands
perched in the choir loft, while the characters of Washington and Lincoln remind
the audience of the freedoms they helped bring to America. The Statue of Liberty
welcomes the character of the immigrant Jew to the United States, who then recites Elias Lieberman's poem, "I Am an American."[58] Such theatrical reenact-
ments took place throughout the Jewish community, linking the nation's great
presidents to the saga of Jewish immigration. In one Jewish history pageant,
staged in Milwaukee, Wisconsin, Abraham Lincoln once again stands beside the
Statue of Liberty with an outstretched arm to immigrant Jews. Playing the role of
the Statue of Liberty in this particular 1919 pageant was none other than a young
Golda Meir.[59]

If George Washington represented the guarantor of religious freedom, Abraham Lincoln stood as the Great Emancipator and Jews were fond of comparing
him to Moses. "Across the stretch of two worlds lit up by lesser lights, there are reflected those two perpetual flaming statues of Liberty—Moses and Lincoln," Rabbi
Joseph Silverman told his congregation, forging a historical link between the two
figures that spanned the centuries. Silverman insisted that Moses's message of
freedom had been born in ancient Israel but had fully matured in the American
context. "The sun of freedom that rose in the East 3,000 years ago," he explained,
"has encircled the globe and set itself firmly upon the horizon of the West."[60]
Reflecting on the Jewish relationship to Moses, one Jewish author reckoned:

> We like to think that he was inspired by the teachings of the Old Testament.
> For surely the family would not have named him Abraham if the Bible had
> not been a sacred book to them. Lincoln himself read and studied the Holy
> Scriptures many times, and he must have known well the story of the en-
> slavement of the Hebrews in Egypt and how they freed themselves under
> the leadership of Moses.[61]

Through such rhetorical strategies, Jews not only linked Moses and Lincoln, biblical history and American history, but also used the celebration of Lincoln as

paradigm suggests the gradual diminution of ethnic heritage over the course of the twentieth century, as nationalist frameworks came to dominate ethnic celebrations.[67] It is certainly the case that during the era of mass migration progressives and reformers demonstrated a keen interest in exploiting national holidays in order to Americanize immigrants, using the occasions to instill patriotism and build a national consensus among ethnic newcomers. For example, groups devoted to the Americanization of immigrants, such as the Committee for Immigrants in America and the League of Foreign Born Citizens, marshaled their energies to declare July 4, 1915, as Americanization Day. The outbreak of World War I combined with the presence of thousands of newly arrived immigrants convinced many reformers that Independence Day presented a useful occasion to rally new immigrants in a united celebration and guide them toward good citizenship.[68] Despite the often coercive attempts to impose national allegiance on new immigrants and to indoctrinate them with American ideals, ethnic groups tended to articulate their own narrative strategies when they participated in such occasions; their celebrations were replete with references to the glories of America, but they also positioned American patriotism within a broader historical framework rooted in particular ethnic experiences. Jewish national celebrations certainly revealed a pervasive need to demonstrate national loyalty, yet they also testified to the ways that Jews interpreted the meanings of American citizenship. During Americanization Day on July 4, 1915, Jewish social worker and reformer Lillian Wald reminded immigrants at the Henry Street settlement of the importance of their participation in the celebration. But she interpreted the holiday as more than simply the opportunity for Jews to prove their patriotism and become part of the nation. Rather, she placed the meaning of Independence Day in a Jewish context, explaining that the holiday resonated in the hearts and minds of Jewish immigrants "because there are so many among us who have known persecution and wrong, who have made great sacrifices for ideals, who have come to America believing that here could be realized our highest ideals."[69] In this account the United States remains the bastion of freedom that reformers intended to portray on this day, but within the Jewish celebration the significance of America became defined only against the backdrop of a larger Jewish experience, shaped by a European past and self-definition as immigrants. For all the Americanization efforts of reformers, ethnic celebrations suggest that Jews, like other new immigrants, seldom disentangled their loyalty to America from the longer historical understanding that informed their cultures. To the contrary, Jews worked to incorporate the devotion to America within an ethnic narrative, especially during moments of national celebration. As one Chicago Jewish newspaper explained to its readers in 1918, the July 4 holiday offered "a most welcome opportunity . . . to display their patriotism for America," but nonetheless it remained imperative for the community to "celebrate this occasion as Jews."[70]

For Jews national holiday celebrations were moments for expressing national allegiance, and very often a certain defensive posture pervaded the occasions, as Jews worked to demonstrate that they were loyal American citizens. But, in keeping with historian Mary Ryan's observation that the public has always been a "space where society's members . . . mounted debates rather than established consensus,"[71] the patriotic expressions of American Jews suggest an even more complex process at work. Jews used national holidays not only to demonstrate their loyalty to American ideals but also to put forward their vision of American civil religion—one that made room for the inclusion of Jews within a largely Christian culture. These celebrations represented occasions for imparting lessons of civic virtue to immigrant groups. But Jews, like other American minorities, also seized these moments to deliver their particular perspectives on American civic ideals to the public. The messages articulated were hardly uniform or monolithic; during a single national holiday a cacophony of Jewish voices could be heard outlining a range of programs for both the Jewish and American people. National holidays provided an opportunity for Jewish groups not only to rehearse their own history but also to define their place in America and often to define America itself. Against the backdrop of American national celebrations, Jews sketched their collective self-portrait and created a space for themselves within America's evolving civic culture.

NOTES

1. Union of American Hebrew Congregations, Proceedings of the Third Annual Session of the Council, Washington, DC, July 1876, 264–76.

2. Ibid., 276.

3. Ibid., 275.

4. For a variety of opinions about why Jews should not celebrate the occasion as Jews, apart from other national celebrations, see *The American Hebrew Almanac for 5650, September 1889 to September 1890* (Cincinnati and Chicago, 1890), 62–63.

5. Rabbi Alexander Kohut, quoted in Jonathan D. Sarna, "The Mythical Jewish Columbus and the History of America's Jews," in Bryan L. LeBeau and Menachem Mor, eds., *Religion in the Age of Exploration* (Omaha, 1996), 82.

6. Moritz Kayserling, *Christopher Columbus and the Participation of the Jews in the Spanish and Portuguese Discoveries* (New York, 1968 [1894]); Jonathan Sarna discusses Kayserling's work in detail in "The Mythical Jewish Columbus," 83–86.

7. Jacob Stolz cited in Sarna, "The Mythical Jewish Columbus," 85.

8. Jonathan Sarna discusses this at length in "The Mythical Jewish Columbus," 86–92.

9. Anita Libman Lebeson, *Jewish Pioneers in America, 1492–1848* (New York, 1931), 13.

10. Ibid., 17.

11. Max Goldberg, The Contribution of the Chosen Race to Civic Progress in America: An Address Delivered Under the Auspices of the Essex Institute on February 10,

1930, at Academy Hall, Salem Massachusetts, 1–2; also cited in Orm Øverland, *Immigrant Minds, American Identities: Making the United States Home, 1870–1930* (Urbana, 2000), 63.

12. Rose G. Lurie, *The Great March: Post-Biblical Jewish Stories*, book 2 (Cincinnati, 1939), 6.

13. Lee J. Levinger, *A History of the Jews in the United States* (New York, 1930), 27.

14. Isaac Mayer Wise, "The Fourth of July: An Address Delivered in the Synagogue of K.K. Benai Yeshurun," *Israelite*, July 15, 1854, 3.

15. Abraham A. Neuman, *Relation of the Hebrew Scriptures to American Institutions* (New York, 1939), 6.

16. Rabbi Samuel Belkin cited in Jerold S. Auerbach, *Rabbis and Lawyers: The Journey from the Torah to the Constitution* (Bloomington, 1990), 19 and 211, note 37.

17. Kaufmann Kohler, "The Tocsin Call of Liberty and Democracy," in *A Living Faith* (Cincinnati, 1948), 113–14.

18. Øverland, *Immigrant Minds, American Identities*, 19.

19. *American Hebrew* 41.5 (December 6, 1889): 124; Michael Kammen, *Mystic Chords of Memory: The Transformation of Tradition in American Culture* (New York, 1991), 205.

20. *American Hebrew* 52.3 (November 18, 1892): 83–84.

21. Henry W. Bellows, *Religious Toleration: A Discourse* (New York, 1880), 9.

22. Ben M. Edidin, *Jewish Holidays and Festivals* (New York, 1940), 214.

23. George Cohen, *The Jews in the Making of America* (Boston, 1924), 49.

24. Rev. Dr. Marcus Jastrow, "Sermon Delivered in the Synagogue, Rodeph Shalom, Juliana Street, on Thanksgiving Day" (Philadelphia, 1868), 5.

25. *American Israelite*, November 24, 1904, 4.

26. Edidin, *Jewish Holidays and Festivals*, 214.

27. Elma Ehrlich Levinger, *In Many Lands: Stories of How the Scattered Jews Kept Their Festivals* (New York, 1923), 34.

28. Ibid.

29. Elizabeth G. Stern, *My Mother and I* (New York, 1917), 108–9. Historian Andrew Heinze has noted the ways that holiday celebrations contributed to the process of Jewish acculturation in America. His account, which emphasizes consumerism and advertising, also stresses the commingling of American and Jewish systems of meaning. Andrew R. Heinze, *Adapting to Abundance: Jewish Immigrants, Mass Consumption, and the Search for American Identity* (New York, 1990).

30. Anzia Yezierska, "America and I," in Alice Kessler-Harris, ed., *The Open Cage: An Anzia Yezierska Collection* (New York, 1979), 32–33.

31. Rabbi Morris A. Gutstein, "The Declaration of Independence, the American Song of Redemption," July 4, 1935, 1, American Jewish Historical Society, New York.

32. Emanuel Hertz, "The Significance of the Declaration of Independence," July 4, 1929, American Jewish Historical Society.

33. *Jewish Child*, July 12, 1918, 1.

34. See, for example, *Jewish Daily Forward*, July 4, 1902, July 4, 1910, 4. Eli Lederhendler makes this point in his *Jewish Responses to Modernity: New Voices in America and Eastern Europe* (New York, 1994), 135–36.

35. *Jewish Daily Forward*, July 4, 1910, 4, as cited in Lederhendler, *Jewish Responses to Modernity*.

36. Ibid.

37. *Freiheit*, July 4, 1924.

38. *Der Tog*, July 4, 1924.

39. *Yiddishes Tageblatt*, July 4, 1924.

40. Mary Antin, *The Promised Land: The Autobiography of a Russian Immigrant* (Princeton, 1969 [1912]), 223.

41. Lewis Abraham, "Correspondence Between Washington and Jewish Citizens," *Proceedings of the American Jewish Historical Society* 3 (1895): 91–92.

42. Barry Schwartz, *George Washington: The Making of an American Symbol* (New York, 1987), 85–87.

43. David Geffen, ed., *American Heritage Haggadah: The Passover Experience*, trans. Moshe Kohn (Jerusalem, 1992), 19; Jonathan D. Sarna, "The Cult of Synthesis in American Jewish Culture," *Jewish Social Studies* 5.1/2 (Fall 1998/Winter 1999), 61.

44. Oliver McKee Jr., "Super-Salesman of Patriotism: Sol Bloom, Promoter of Washington's Bicentennial," *Outlook and Independent*, February 3, 1932, 140.

45. "George Washington Bicentennial Celebration," George Washington Bicentennial Commission Records, RG 148, Verda Woods File, box 3, National Archives, College Park, MD.

46. McKee, "Super-Salesman of Patriotism," 139.

47. See, for example, *American Hebrew* February 19, 1932, 362–63.

48. *Sermons on George Washington* (Washington, DC, ca. 1932). A copy of the volume is contained in George Washington Bicentennial Commission Records, RG 148, William Tyler Page File, box 5, National Archives.

49. *American Hebrew*, March 4, 1932, 401.

50. Society of Friends of Touro Synagogue, statement of history and purpose, Society of Friends of Touro Archives, Newport, Rhode Island. The annual programs sponsored by the Society of Friends began in 1948.

51. See, for example, *Newport Daily News*, August 23, 1948, 16, August 29, 1949, 14, September 16, 1963, 1, August 20, 1990, C1–2.

52. Program schedule, 200th Anniversary, George Washington letter, August 17–19, 1990, Society of Friends of Touro Archives; Society of Friends of Touro Synagogue *Update* 2.1 (March 1990).

53. American Heritage Foundation, "Documents and Memorabilia of the American Heritage Carried on the Freedom Train," pamphlet, Sterling Memorial Library, Yale University, New Haven; Stuart J. Little, "The Freedom Train: Citizenship and Postwar Political Culture, 1946–1949," *American Studies* 34.1 (Spring 1993): 35–37.

54. *Newport Daily News*, August 24, 1954, 16.

55. Minutes of Congregation Jeshuat Israel Touro Synagogue, January 15, 1950, June 6, 1950, September 10, 1950, Society of Friends of Touro Synagogue Archives.

56. *Newport Daily News* August 24, 1954, 16.

57. Society of Friends of Touro Synagogue, statement of history and purpose, Society of Friends of Touro Archives.

58. "Proclaim Liberty Throughout the Land: A Pageant on Freedom in Celebration of the Birthdays of Washington and Lincoln," in Nathan Brilliant and Libbie Braverman, *Religious Pageants for the Jewish School* (Cincinnati, 1941), 64–74.

59. Barry Schwartz, *Abraham Lincoln and the Forge of National Identity* (Chicago, 2000), 196–97.

60. Rabbi Joseph Silverman, "Value of Lincoln's Example," in Emanuel Hertz, ed., *Abraham Lincoln: The Tribute of the Synagogue* (New York, 1927), 650; see also Emanuel Hertz, "Abraham Lincoln—Seer," ibid., 568–69.

61. Edidin, *Jewish Holidays and Festivals*, 215.

62. Ritual for the Centennial Celebration of Pres. Abraham Lincoln, Arranged and Adopted by the Lincoln Celebration Committee of the Chicago Hebrew Institute, 1909, American Jewish Historical Society.

63. Howard Johnson, Irving Bibo, and Lou Klein, "(Don't Be Ashamed of) The Name of Abraham" (New York, 1925), sheet music.

64. Rabbi Alexander Lyons, "Lincoln: His Source of Power," in Hertz, *Abraham Lincoln*, 617.

65. Description of activities of various organizations, Lincoln Sesquicentennial Commission, RG 148, box 1, folder "Books-Plays," National Archives.

66. "B'nai B'rith Citizenship Year—1958–1959," Lincoln Sesquicentennial Commission, RG 148, box 9, folder "J," National Archives.

67. John Bodnar, *Remaking America: Public Memory, Commemoration, and Patriotism in the Twentieth Century* (Princeton, 1992), 41–77.

68. Ellen M. Litwicki, *America's Public Holidays, 1865–1920* (Washington, 2000), 223–26; see also William H. Cohn, "A National Celebration: The Fourth of July in American History," *Cultures* 3.1 (1976): 141–56.

69. Lillian Wald, cited in Litwicki, *America's Public Holidays*, 225.

70. *Sunday Jewish Courier*, June 23, 1918, cited in Litwicki, *America's Public Holidays*, 236.

71. Mary Ryan, *Civic Wars: Democracy and Public Life in the American City During the Nineteenth Century* (Berkeley, 1997), 4.

16

A BRIGHT NEW CONSTELLATION

Feminism and American Judaism

PAMELA S. NADELL

It is high time . . . to compel man by the might of right to give woman her political, legal and social rights.

—ERNESTINE ROSE TO THE NATIONAL WOMAN'S RIGHTS CONVENTION
IN WORCESTER, MASSACHUSETTS, OCTOBER 15, 1851

For three thousand years, one-half the Jewish people have been excluded from full participation in Jewish communal life. We call for an end to the second-class status of women in Jewish life.

—EZRAT NASHIM, MARCH 1972

More than a century passed between Polish Jewish immigrant Ernestine Rose's demand of woman's rights for all and the call for women's full participation in Jewish life issued by the feminist, college-educated, Jewishly learned women of Ezrat Nashim. In the interim America's Jewish women had benefited from the new opportunities opened up by the nineteenth-century woman's rights movement and by the waves of American feminism that followed.

The woman's rights movement, one of the great reform movements of the nineteenth century, was launched in the summer of 1848 at Seneca Falls, New York, where some three hundred women and men proclaimed: "We hold these truths to be self-evident: that all men and women are created equal."[1] At the heart of the movement that emerged from this first convention lay the call for woman suffrage. Three years later Ernestine Rose, speaking at the second National Woman's Rights Convention, called upon her adopted nation "to remove the legal shackles from woman . . . to enable woman to deposit her vote." In Poland, at the age of sixteen, Rose, refusing to marry the man her father proposed, sued her father to keep the inheritance he intended to give away as her dowry. In the United States she became the only Jewish woman well known as a suffragette. Yet hers was never the only Jewish voice raised for woman suffrage.[2] In the 1910s East European immigrant Jewish women campaigned on the streets of New York's Lower East Side to compel their fathers and brothers, husbands and sons to grant them the right to vote.[3]

As the woman's rights movement gained momentum, it spurred middle-class American women to uncover interstices, new spaces for female organization and activism, which lay between the private spaces of their homes and the public worlds of business, politics, and society that belonged to their men. America's Jewish women too came to play new roles in their Jewish communities. In 1893 at the World's Columbian Exposition in Chicago, some, meeting as the Congress of Jewish Women, founded the National Council of Jewish Women, the first nationwide American Jewish women's club.[4] In the decades to follow, as other new associations emerged, armies of Jewish women massed to support their synagogues through sisterhood, to promote Zionism through Hadassah, the Women's Zionist Organization of America, and to protect immigrant girls from the perils of "white slavery" through the NCJW.[5] They appeared in the 1910s and 1920s, just as the woman's rights movement gave way to the "new language of Feminism."[6]

As historian Nancy Cott has shown, this first wave of American feminism, which was then spelled with a capital F, signaled the end of the nineteenth-century woman's rights movement. Those advocating the advancement of woman in society had first spoken in the singular, symbolizing "the unity of the female sex . . . propos[ing] that all women have one cause, one movement." But feminism fractured that "singular *woman*" even as it proposed revolutionizing "all the relations of the sexes." Feminists demanded full citizenship, and that meant the freedom to choose work regardless of sex or marriage, to earn equal wages for that work, to experience "psychic freedom and spiritual autonomy," to enjoy sexual liberation, and to proclaim the independence of wives. None of these specific demands was new. Each "had been made at some time, piecemeal, by women before." Yet, feminists differed from their predecessors: their intensity as they simultaneously espoused multiple feminist goals was new. Moreover, feminists embraced women's heterogeneity, "the internal diversity and lack of consensus among women themselves." Finally, they exhibited a "characteristic doubleness," seeking "to achieve sexual equality while making room for sexual difference." These became the "constellation Feminism," and feminists transformed its "formlessness, that lack of certain boundaries, that potential to encompass opposites, into virtues." To connect the points of that constellation, feminists struggled "to find language, organization, and goals adequate to the paradoxical situation of modern women." As they did, not surprisingly, they met hostility and resistance as well as enthusiasm.[7]

Understanding that from its inception feminism was fraught with paradox and heterogeneity, open to different ways of speaking and organizing, and met by both enthusiasm and hostility, provides a framework for viewing the constellation that emerged when feminism confronted Judaism during the second wave of American feminism. The establishment, in 1961, of President John F. Kennedy's Commission on the Status of Women "implicitly recognized the existence of gender-based discrimination in American society."[8] When, in 1963, the Jewish housewife and journalist Betty Friedan published *The Feminine Mystique*, she chronicled the discontent of her generation of female college graduates confined to suburban homes she called "comfortable concentration camps."[9] Congress paved the way for women to act on that discontent as it passed the Equal Pay Act of 1963 and Title VII of the 1964 Civil Rights Act, which banned discrimination in employment on the basis of sex as well as race. After the Equal Employment Opportunity Commission showed little interest in enforcing Title VII when it came to female complaints of job discrimination, the National Organization for Women came into existence to pressure the government to secure equal rights for all. Its 1966 birth heralded the arrival of the second wave of American feminism.[10] The women of Ezrat Nashim who, in 1972, called for change in Jewish life, rode its crest.[11]

Whether they knew it then or not—and one of them, historian Paula Hyman, was already asking "Why had we been deprived of our heroines?"[12]—they were not the first to connect feminism to Judaism. Although before the mid-1960s American feminism had never coalesced into a single movement or mobilized the masses, historians have uncovered those who advanced feminist goals long before the second wave burst forth. In fact, women's history reveals numerous feminist projects "sparked again and again" by lone individuals and small groups who, often as not, rejected the feminist label.[13] Scholar Susan Hartmann calls these women "lively characters," key players pushing from within their establishment settings to raise feminist consciousness.[14] Although United States women's historians largely ignore Judaism's encounter with feminism before the early 1970s, lively feminist characters, making their way across American Jewish history, stood as harbingers of what would become Jewish feminism.

They surface in the challenges raised by the women who would have been rabbis if they could have been rabbis. In 1921, seventeen-year-old Martha Neumark, a student at Reform Judaism's Hebrew Union College, asked the college for a High Holiday pulpit assignment. She wanted, on the coming holy Days of Awe, to lead a small community in prayer just as her male classmates would. That request, demonstrating that Neumark indeed saw herself on the way to becoming a rabbi, launched a two-year-long debate in the world of Reform Judaism. Would its leaders, who had already sanctioned so many other transformations of traditional praxis, cross the gender divide and ordain women? In the end the College's Board of Governors voted against women's ordination, and Martha Neumark never became a rabbi. But Neumark well understood that the discussion about "the admission of women as rabbis is merely another phase of the woman question" that emerges "each time that a woman threatens to break up man's monopoly." Decades later, in 1964, just as the second wave of American feminism burst forth, she would trumpet once again that at last "the time is ripe" for women to become rabbis.[15]

Another lively character appeared at what is widely regarded as the first American bat mitzvah. In 1922 Jewish Theological Seminary professor Mordecai M. Kaplan called his eldest daughter Judith, then aged twelve and half, to read a portion of the Torah—from a printed book, not from the sacred handwritten scroll—on Sabbath morning. Years later Judith Kaplan Eisenstein recalled both the "excitement" and the "disturbance" evoked by this gender shift, although those most disturbed seemed to be her grandmothers who had tried to convince their son and son-in-law not to do this "terrible thing." In fact, this first bat mitzvah failed to cause "the kind of sensation" that Mordecai M. Kaplan's other radical changes would.[16] But, even if it did not provoke furor,[17] bat mitzvah surely indicated a meeting between feminism and Judaism. In fact, later that summer, as Reform rabbis debated whether or not Martha Neumark could be ordained, one favoring women's ordination reported that "the rabbi of an Orthodox congregation had a bar mitzva of girls," and this proved that "the other wing of Judaism is also making progress."[18]

Moreover, Judith Kaplan Eisenstein remembered a deliberate connection between feminism and Judaism back then. After the woman's suffrage amendment passed when she was eleven, she recalled "a conscious feminism in our household."[19] A year or so later, she joined a Hebrew-speaking girls club. Chosen to represent the club in a contest, she gave a long speech on "women's place in the synagogue," arguing that "women should be allowed to read from the Torah which they weren't yet . . . and all sorts of things." Later her uncle, who had heard her speak, pulled her aside to warn: "You know it's all very well for you to say what you think in some places, but you must remember that you represent your father and you will get him into trouble if you start these terrible things."[20]

To these two harbingers of the "terrible things" unleashed by the meetings of Judaism with feminism before the second wave erupted, others could be added. They date back to the founding of the National Council of Jewish Women, and they also include the women who tried after Martha Neumark to become rabbis; the women's organizations determined to write women into Jewish history at the tercentenary of American Jewish life in 1954; the mothers and fathers who sent their daughters to Hebrew School rather than to Sunday School, the daughters who wanted to go, and the rabbis who taught them there; those who celebrated their bat mitzvah in the 1950s and earlier; and the *rebbetzin* whose aliyah during High Holiday services in the mid-1950s drove hundreds of shocked congregants out of the service.[21] These events demonstrate feminism reverberating in American Judaism across the twentieth century smoothing the way for the wave that would later crash on its shores.

In the early 1970s, as the second wave of American feminism surged, an emerging Jewish feminism surfaced. It began, as Anne Lapidus Lerner, then an instructor in modern Hebrew literature at the Jewish Theological Seminary, described in 1976, "as a series of isolated questionings in the shadow of the women's movement."[22] These isolated questions were articulated amidst the euphoria sweeping American Jewry in the wake of Israel's victory in the 1967 Six-Day War. They sprang out of the Jewish "counterculture," out of the intimate study and worship communities of the *havurah* movement as young Jewish activists created alternatives to the established and establishment synagogues in which they had been raised and whose spiritual aridity they decried.

The first Jewish feminists of the late 1960s and early 1970s included college and graduate students who found themselves "torn in two." Their feminism promised them intellectual and spiritual equality with their male peers, but their Judaism relegated them to second-class status within the walls of their synagogues, within the corpus of Jewish law (*halakhah*).[23] They also included those who sprang up from among the ranks of Jewish communal leaders, who, deeply influenced by the "remarkable re-burgeoning of the Women's Movement," wanted to bring its message to bear upon American Jewish life.[24] Together they began to form the constellation that would outline Jewish feminism.

Signs of light emanating from this constellation appeared even before Ezrat Nashim issued its "call for an end to the second-class status of women in Jewish life." By the late 1960s the women's movement was spinning off in a dizzying array of new directions. Feminists turned their attention to a host of legal, political, and social inequities. They demanded an end to job ads labeled "Help Wanted—Male." They marched to legalize abortion. They coined the slogan "Sisterhood Is Powerful," and they meant it. Women's liberation, which celebrated female difference, burst forth, and with it came the first consciousness-raising groups: small, intimate circles of female friends decrying sexism sprang up on college campuses, in suburban backyards, and in middle-class urban apartments.[25] A "great media blitz," well underway by 1970, broadcast "stories all year long on the new women's movement."[26]

Some of them revealed American religion wrestling with the feminist critique. Headlines blazoned "Women's 'Lib' on the March in the Churches," as the National Organization for Women created an ecumenical task force on women and religion, and churches, like the United Methodist and United Presbyterian, established their own task forces. Protestant denominations, which had not before ordained women, began to do so. Together they presented a picture of feminism storming the bastion of American religion.[27] Some of the stories revealed the first meetings between second-wave feminism and American Judaism. *Time* and *Newsweek* reported that Hebrew Union College rabbinical student Sally J. Priesand planned to become "Rabbi Sally."[28] The *New York Times* discovered Hilda Abrevaya, the first woman cantor in the United States.[29] The Jewish student press featured stories connecting the feminist critique to America's Jews and their Judaism.[30] Against this background, the women of Ezrat Nashim coalesced.

Its founders, members of the alternative religious fellowship, the New York Havurah, were deeply committed to Jewish tradition. But they were also drawn to the women's movement. Martha Ackelsberg had participated in a consciousness-raising group; then graduate student Paula Hyman had helped organize the women's caucus of Columbia University's history department. When, in the fall of 1971, they and six other women began meeting, they constituted but one of the many study groups linked to the New York Havurah. Deeply disturbed by Judaism's bias in favor of men's learning and prayer, they set out to explore the social and historical forces that had shaped women's roles in Judaism. It took but a single event to "transform this informal consciousness-raising group into a band of activists." When leaders of the Jewish counterculture insisted that a national conference that they were planning be open only to men, the women of Ezrat Nashim exploded in anger. Moving beyond their private consciousness-raising, they went public. In January 1972 they prepared a position paper titled "Jewish Women Call for Change." It demanded that women become full members of their synagogues, that they count in the prayer quorum (minyan) of ten—traditionally ten men—needed for worship, that they become synagogue and Jewish communal leaders, that they have the right to serve as witnesses and to initiate divorce, roles Jewish law prohibited to them, and that they attend rabbinical and cantorial schools. Although Ezrat Nashim's first target, presenting their demands at the annual meeting of Conservative Judaism's rabbis in March 1972, was the Conservative movement, their "Call for Change" and the accompanying publicity they received in the national press brought Jewish feminism out into the open.[31]

Ezrat Nashim's demands resonated among American Jewish women and men whose consciousnesses had already been raised by the second wave of American feminism. Its members were deluged with requests to share their message widely. They spoke to synagogues, Jewish communal organizations, student groups, and the national and Jewish presses. They also helped plan the first National Jewish Women's Conference, held in New York City in February 1973.

That first conference drew together over five hundred women from all across the United States. Their varying interests and concerns exposed the sweep of the constellation Jewish feminism. Like the second wave of American feminism of which it was a part, Jewish feminism was decentralized. It emerged wherever women connected feminism to Judaism and their Jewish lives and communities. Its adherents never embraced a single address.[32] They espoused diverse feminist aims. Like the first glimmers of American feminism, Jewish feminism too came to be characterized by multiple feminist goals, an internal diversity often fractured along denominational lines that demonstrated feminist and Jewish difference, and the desire to achieve sexual equality while allowing for gender difference. Jewish feminism would seek to transform gender relations affecting the intimate lives of Jewish women, men, and their families; their synagogues and American Judaism's denominations; and the network of agencies, welfare funds, advocacy groups, and community centers that sustain American Jewry.

The first National Jewish Women's Conference paved the way. It shed light on the issues that would become the constellation Jewish feminism, which would include Jewish women's socialization and their roles within the family, their status within Jewish law, within the state of Israel, and within Jewish communal life, their places within Jewish communal politics and the synagogue, and their access to religious texts and learning. Topics that would spark enormous Jewish feminist creativity in the years to come—developing new religious rituals to acknowledge significant moments in women's lives, which Jewish tradition ignored, uncovering in the past "feminist" role models, revisioning Judaism's androcentric God and prayer, mining Jewish history and culture to create Jewish women's studies, opening up space for lesbians—already appear in the constellation.

Those who would become noted pioneering Jewish feminists, like Judith Plaskow and the Orthodox feminist advocate Blu Greenberg, addressed the first National Jewish Women's Conference. There Plaskow, whose 1990 *Standing Again at Sinai: Judaism from a Feminist Perspective* is one of the cardinal texts of Jewish feminism, "explored both the sexism of the Jewish tradition" and the contradictions she sensed "between Judaism and feminism as alternative communities."[33] But the real "stars of the show," according to one observer, were New York congresswomen Bella Abzug and Elizabeth Holtzman. Their presence underscored the diversity of Jewish feminists. They included those committed to Jewish religious observance and to the body of Jewish law who were deeply disturbed by its gendered bias. These religious Jewish feminists stood next to those for whom Judaism was but a single strand of their lives, who, like Abzug and Holtzman (and, of course, Friedan), were prominent second-wave feminists. They expected feminism to transform all of American society. That it would also transform American Jewish life was, for them, a happy by-product of that wider fundamental revolution. So Abzug stood with those at the conference to proclaim: "Today we are writing a different kind of history. Your being here is the history of the future."[34]

As the conference ended, the delegates launched several projects reflecting their diversity and their different aims. They planned to encourage Jewish consciousness-raising and study groups, to found an abortion-counseling service for Jewish women, and to spread Jewish feminism through a speakers' bureau and publications.[35] Soon the issues raised by this first National Jewish Women's Conference—and the other conferences and publications that followed in the mid-1970s, including the emergence of *Lilith*, the first Jewish feminist magazine in 1976[36]—reached the women who had long found outlets for their communal activism through the national Jewish women's organizations.[37]

What then are the major points of the constellation Jewish feminism? For many Jewish feminists, transformation of their roles within the synagogue sat atop their feminist agenda. For those affiliated with the liberal denominations of American Judaism, with the Reform, Conservative, and Reconstructionist movements in Jewish life, this meant reconfiguring the synagogue as an egalitarian institution. In time this came to mean, for some, women wearing the prayer shawls and head coverings traditionally worn only by men,[38] women counting toward the quorum of ten necessary for a complete prayer service,[39] women learning Hebrew and the liturgical skills they had never acquired as girls and celebrating, as adults, a bat mitzvah, women taking on new roles in their synagogues, like reading regularly from the Torah, women elected synagogue presidents,[40] and, most visibly and dramatically, women becoming rabbis.

The history of women's quest for rabbinic ordination dates back to the late nineteenth century when the debate over woman's right to be a rabbi emerged as part of a larger debate about American women's access to all the learned professions. If women wanted to become doctors, lawyers, and ministers, then professions that largely excluded them, why should they also not want to be rabbis? Yet, despite a series of challengers and engagement of the question for nearly a century, it took the collision of second-wave feminism with American Judaism to propel women into the rabbinate. In 1972 in Reform Judaism, in 1974 in Reconstructionist Judaism, and in 1985 in Conservative Judaism the first women rabbis emerged.[41] Eventually, the presence of hundreds of female rabbis would further the feminist agenda in American Jewish life.

Not surprisingly, the constellation Jewish feminism also includes within its orbit Orthodox Judaism. In fact, Orthodoxy has created its own small bright feminist constellation. The "spiritual mother" of Orthodox feminism is Blu Greenberg, author of *On Women and Judaism: A View from Tradition*. Greenberg gave the opening address at the 1973 National Jewish Women's Conference (although conference organizers first thought to invite her husband, distinguished scholar and communal activist Rabbi Yitz Greenberg!), and she came to lead the charge on feminist challenges to Orthodoxy, daring to ask "Will there be Orthodox women rabbis?" Convinced that "where there's a rabbinic will, there's a *halakhic* way," she asserted that if rabbis wanted to solve the plight of women chained by Jewish matrimonial law to marriages that were no longer tenable, they could. (Under Jewish law only men can initiate divorce; if a couple obtains a civil divorce but the husband refuses to give his wife a Jewish divorce, the woman cannot remarry as an Orthodox Jew.) In 1997 Greenberg gave the keynote at the International Conference on Feminism and Orthodoxy and founded the Jewish Orthodox Feminist Alliance (JOFA).[42] Its Web site reveals feminism's impact on Orthodoxy. JOFA suggests "possible trajectories for women being ordained as rabbis," advocates ritual innovation by highlighting wedding ceremonies transformed "within the framework of *halakha* in order to make them more inclusive of women, in general, and the bride, in particular," and includes a section on "challenges to the community" that covers body image, domestic and sexual abuse, and lesbians.[43]

Signs of feminism's redefining women's roles in the Orthodox world proliferate. Orthodox parents celebrate a daughter's bat mitzvah, adopting the innovation that permits adolescent Jewish girls to mark a rite of passage to maturity just as their brothers do in their bar mitzvah, although the Orthodox bat mitzvah service is not identical with that of the bar mitzvah.[44] A "learning revolution" has transformed what Jewish girls learn in Orthodox educational settings and has come to include for many a year of post–high school study of religious texts in women's educational settings in Israel. There women scholars have won the right to become advisers in religious courts and to represent women—and men—in divorce and custody cases. In America Orthodox women gather in women's prayer groups. By choosing to pray in a single-sex setting, they may take on ritual roles not open to them when men are present. In New York a few Orthodox synagogues pioneered a new position of congregational intern to permit learned women to teach and to counsel members, customarily rabbis' duties. Not surprisingly, a few Orthodox women have even studied for rabbinical ordination.[45] Thus all the movements of American Judaism fall within the constellation Jewish feminism.

Another sign of feminist transformation is ritual invention. As feminists turned a critical lens upon Judaism, they realized, despite its array of blessings and religious ceremonies, that few affirmed the great moments in women's lives. From birth, Judaism treats girls and boys differently. Feminists have sought to unite Judaism to the occasions, great and small, that rest at the core of women's lives and are so often intimately linked to the feminine, to the female body.

Not surprisingly then, some of the first feminist ritual innovations focused on the newborn. Baby girls are traditionally welcomed into the community with relatively little fanfare, especially when compared to the powerful ceremony of circumcision required for boys on the eighth day after their birth. Hence early feminist ritual creativity offered new ceremonies that would give "as much ceremonial importance to a girl's birth as to a boy's."[46]

In this arena of ritual creativity female rabbis have stood out. They came to take the lead as they realized just how little the tradition they had mastered met their own spiritual needs, especially around "invisible life passages."[47] Hence an astonishing array of prayers, readings, and ceremonies dot the constellation Jewish feminism. They include prayers for going to the *mikveh* (the ritual bath) to be said on the evening the couple wishes to conceive,[48] for the first months of pregnancy and for entering the ninth month, for the onset of labor, for a Caesarean birth, and for nursing for the first time. New rituals sustain those grieving infertility, suffering stillbirth, seeking medical intervention, and turning to adoption. Ceremonies mark the onset of menses and the completion of menopause, offer solace after rape, affirm remaining single, and acknowledge marital separation.[49] This remarkable creativity suggests that no event or personal milestone in the female life cycle has remained untouched by feminist spiritual innovation.

Feminists have not only sought to sanctify the private, they have also turned their attention to public rituals and celebrations, creating new venues for communal feminist spirituality. They reclaimed Rosh Chodesh, Judaism's marking of each new month in its lunar calendar, as a women's holiday, inventing "ceremonies which draw upon the similarity between women's cycles and the moon's cycles, the capacity of both women and the moon to physically wax and wane, ebb and flow, give birth, die, and be reborn."[50] They reappropriated *mikveh*, the pool in which observant married women immerse for the ritual purification required to resume sexual relations following their proscription during and immediately after menstruation. This reappropriation transforms *mikveh* into a space for women to celebrate Rosh Chodesh, to mark a milestone, or to bring closure to a crisis.[51] Feminists have imagined public ceremonies for "croning," honoring women who have reached the age of sixty, the age of wisdom. Some have formed feminist spirituality groups. Their retreats and gatherings over the years have offered spaces for ritual invention and liturgical creativity.[52]

Of the public communal feminist spiritual innovations, the one that has reached most widely is the women's seder. The foremother of these seders took place in New York in 1976. Over the years it included well-known second-wave feminists: politician Bella Abzug, *Ms.* magazine editor Gloria Steinem, feminist psychologist Phyllis Chesler. Rewriting the Haggadah, the traditional text recited in the home on the eve of Passover, the women's seder "regendered the players. The rabbis of old became the wise women connected to them; the questions of the four sons were put into the mouths of the four daughters." The feminist seder incorporates a broad critique of gender relations in American society and within Judaism. It asks: "Why have our Mothers on this night been bitter?" answering: "Because . . . they did the serving but not the conducting. They read of their fathers but not of their mothers." It recovers those mothers, telling of "the legacy of Miriam," and naming women from the Jewish past, especially learned women who have become role models for contemporary Jewish women.[53] By the end of the twentieth century women's seders had sprung up in Jewish communities all across the United States.[54]

Undergirding women's new visibility within the synagogue and their enhanced ritual choices are the first explorations in Jewish feminist theology. Even as feminist theologians, among them Judith Plaskow and Rachel Adler, author of *Engendering Judaism*, critique Judaism's androcentricity, its obliteration of the voices and perspectives of women, they work from within the body of Jewish tradition seeking avenues to the theological, legal, and liturgical transformations essential to redress the wrongs of women's exclusion. For example, these theologians, and feminist liturgists like Marcia Falk, grapple with "the problems of engendering the language with which we speak to and about God." They know, as Rachel Adler writes, that real inclusion can occur only when women cease to be invisible as women. . . . When congregations pray only prayers written exclusively by men for men, prayers that invoke forefathers but never foremothers, prayers that address the God whose image both women and men are said to bear in exclusively masculine forms and metaphors, prayers that express only the hopes of men, prayers that confess only the sins of men, then women are both invisible and silent.

She concludes: effecting "real inclusion" will "engender a world that Jewish women build together with Jewish men, a *nomos* we inhabit where we co/habit justly and generously."[55]

The feminist theologians' critique forms part of the growing canon of Jewish women's and gender studies. At the first National Jewish Women's Conference, one woman mused, "We have the ideas, we have the potential to make history quite specifically as Jewish women; but we need the textbooks, the equipment, the basic technical skills, with which to explore our past and create our future."[56] When the Association for Jewish Studies, the professional organization of Jewish studies scholars emerged in 1969, no woman was among its founders. However, since then, as women's and gender studies have found a home in the academy, a generation of feminist Jewish studies scholars have become the first women in Jewish history to have acquired "the basic technical skills" needed to explore Jewish civilization from a feminist perspective. Some fields within Jewish studies, notably modern Jewish history, Jewish literatures, and the social sciences, have been more amenable than others to the integration of this new feminist scholarship.[57] Nevertheless, today no discipline concerned with Jewish studies—Bible, rabbinics, history, sociology, anthropology, literature, philosophy, film studies, and performance studies—remains untouched by this work.[58] Jewish feminists have embraced this scholarship and its scholars who, following in the footsteps of the women of Ezrat Nashim, lecture widely throughout the American Jewish community, sharing their insights with America's Jewish women and men.

Scholars are not the only writers energized by Jewish feminism. Its constellation encompasses an explosion of feminist literary creativity. In *The Women's Torah Commentary* female rabbis from across the denominations interject women into almost every one of the fifty-four weekly Torah portions. They discover female characters unnamed in the text, like Naamah, Noah's wife, and use the laws of kashrut to comment upon Jewish women cooking holiday foods and to raise concerns about anorexia.[59] This creativity includes *midrashim*, imaginative recreations of the biblical text, like Anita Diamant's wildly successful *The Red Tent*. Here Diamant imagines Jacob's daughter Dinah whispering the stories of her father's wives.[60] Each month as they bled, they retreated to the red tent where "they traded secrets like bracelets" and handed them down to Dinah, their only surviving daughter.[61] Feminist writers of serious fiction also riff upon Jewish tradition, as Cynthia Ozick does in *The Puttermesser Papers*, where her protagonist Ruth Put- termesser creates a female golem (a character out of Jewish folklore, a human fig- ure made of clay) who gets her elected mayor of New York.[62]

Another point in the constellation Jewish feminism illuminates transforma- tions affecting marriage and the Jewish family. Jewish tradition celebrates both. The rabbis taught: "A man who does not have a wife lives without joy, without blessing, and without goodness"[63] and "Who brings no children into the world is like a murderer."[64] A point of contention between Jewish feminists and many second-wave feminists was the latter's depiction of the nuclear family as the source of women's oppression. Jewish feminists, by and large, continued to uphold the centrality of marriage and family to Jewish life.[65] At the first National Jewish Women's Conference they largely ignored notions then on the feminist agenda such as "radical role changes within the family" and shifting child-rearing "from the Jewish Mother to the day care center, in kibbutz fashion."[66] Yet, by the begin- ning of the twenty-first century, American Jewish families had indeed been af- fected by shifts resulting from second-wave feminism and the transformations of postindustrial American society. A quarter of all Jewish adults surveyed in 2000–1 was single and had never married. Twenty-six percent of Jewish women aged forty to forty-four were childless.[67] These statistics point to the wide diversity of con- temporary Jewish family configurations, and these families have come to include lesbians.

At the first National Jewish Feminist Conference "a staged invasion by a group of gay Jewish women who felt that they had been excluded by virtue of their lesbi- anism" launched this issue into the constellation Jewish feminism.[68] Evelyn Tor- ten Beck's 1982 *Nice Jewish Girls: A Lesbian Anthology* was but the first of a number of important books to expose the painful dichotomy of lesbian Jewish identity: that these women feel marginalized as lesbians in the Jewish world and as Jews in their lesbian communities.[69] Since then other works have focused at- tention on specific groups of Jewish lesbians. In *Lesbian Rabbis: The First Genera- tion* the authors write of the ramifications of revealing their sexuality to their teachers and congregants and of choosing whether or not to limit their work to leading one of the few gay and lesbian synagogues that now exist.[70] The 2001 film *Trembling Before G-d* depicts the despair of Orthodox gays and lesbians rejected by their religious communities.[71] Asserting their right to remain fully within Jew- ish tradition, Jewish lesbians have stood under the chuppah, the canopy that hov- ers over the couple in a traditional Jewish wedding.[72]

Perhaps the most widely known of the feminist transformations associated with lesbianism is the addition of an orange to the seder plate. In the mid-1980s the distinguished scholar Susannah Heschel, editor of the pioneering collection *On Being a Jewish Feminist*,[73] added an orange to her family's seder plate (the platter of ritual foods essential for conducting the Passover seder) and asked all present to "eat it as a gesture of solidarity with Jewish lesbians and gay men, and others who are marginalized within the Jewish community."[74]

Even as the constellation Jewish feminism encompasses feminist denominational diversity, private and communal ritual and liturgical innovation, feminist scholarly and literary creativity, and new configurations of the Jewish family, it also includes within its borders transformations in the so-called secular Jewish world, among the network of national and local advocacy, welfare, and communal agencies that constitute a major aspect of American Jewish society. In 1972 Jacqueline K. Levine, then president of the Women's Division of the American Jewish Congress and a vice president of the Council of Jewish Federations and Welfare Funds, told the Council's General Assembly: "Women are stating, in clear and resounding cadences, that they will no longer be second-class citizens." Pointing to the gross gender imbalance in Jewish communal leadership, she challenged her peers to restructure Jewish communal life to fully include its women as leaders.[75]

A 2005 study found some, but insufficient, change.[76] In the intervening years some Jewish communal organizations, like the American Jewish Congress, which had long maintained separate women's divisions, disbanded them in favor of integrating the sexes. Still others, like B'nai B'rith, saw its women's division secede rather than face integration.[77] At the turn of the twenty-first century the Jewish women's associations founded more than a century ago, like synagogue sisterhoods and Hadassah, continued to offer women rich and varied opportunities for voluntarism and professional work, but their agendas—training women to lead religious services,[78] opening a Washington Action Office that lobbies to end violence against women—had brought them within the constellation Jewish feminism.

Yet outside of the women's organizations women's progress in advancing as volunteer and professional Jewish leaders was checkered. A 2005 study by Ma'yan: The Jewish Women's Project concluded: "Jewish organizations continue to limit women's access to power in all areas of Jewish communal life."[79] It observed that, despite incremental change, women seeking to advance in Jewish life hit a glass ceiling that runs over all Jewish institutions—synagogues, communal agencies, and schools.[80]

If feminists have been disappointed in their failure to transform the Jewish community to the extent they envisioned when the constellation Jewish feminism burst forth, they have also been deeply disturbed and, in fact, shocked by anti-Judaism and antisemitism in the women's movement in the 1970s and 1980s. Christian feminists have blamed Judaism for inventing patriarchy, the source of women's oppression. They imagined that before ancient Hebrew civilization emerged, that "the goddess reigned in matriarchal glory." They have charged that Jesus meant to restore egalitarianism, but that he was thwarted by lingering Jewish patriarchal influences.[81] Jewish feminists were deeply disturbed by these theological charges, which perpetuate in a new feminist guise Christianity's anti-Judaism. But the antisemitism of the international women's movement shocked those who thought that their solidarity with feminists precluded their being singled out as Jews.

Jewish women were prominent second-wave feminists.[82] In the early years of the women's movement many of them subordinated their Jewish identities to their feminism. Yet in time they came to discover that the women's movement not only dismissed their Jewishness as a legitimate category of difference, while embracing so many other kinds of distinction, but that it also spouted antisemitism.[83] Political attacks upon Israel at international women's conferences sponsored by the United Nations in Mexico City in 1975 and in Copenhagen in 1980 revealed its depths. Said one who attended the Copenhagen conference: "I heard people say that Gloria Steinem, Betty Friedan, and Bella Abzug all being Jewish gives the American Women's Movement a bad name. I heard, 'The only good Jew is a dead Jew.' I heard, 'The only way to rid the world of Zionism is to kill all the Jews.'" Shaken by this "anti-Semitism that was overt, wild and irrational,"[84] some Jewish feminists reconsidered their Jewish affinities even as they tried to compel the women's movement to grapple with its anti-Jewish animus.

In the nearly four decades since it has come into view, the constellation Jewish feminism has shone brightly. In fact, it is difficult to imagine American Jewish life stripped of feminist influence. Wherever one looks in the Jewish community, the constellation Jewish feminism is visible. It can been sighted from the pulpit where female rabbis preach, from classrooms where girls learn Talmud, from homes as couples gather family and friends to bring their infant daughters into the covenant of the Jewish people. It is present in Jewish communal boardrooms each time leaders deliberately seek out women for inclusion, in college classrooms where Jewish feminist scholars teach, and in Jewish community center day care programs. Its light illuminates synagogue sanctuaries as Jews pray that God blessed Abraham, Isaac, and Jacob, Sarah, Rebekah, Leah, and Rachel.

The brightness of the constellation Jewish feminism was reflected during a celebration of 350 years of American Jewish women's activism in Washington, DC in fall 2004. Of the twenty-two women honored that evening,[85] all had lived lives and had careers scarcely imaginable before second-wave feminism, and most did so within the orbit of the constellation Jewish feminism. They included creators of religious Jewish feminism: Rabbi Sally Priesand, the first woman rabbi, Orthodox writer Blu Greenberg, songwriter Debbie Friedman, whose celebration of Miriam's dancing with timbrels has become a staple of the women's seder,[86] and *Ms.* magazine editor Letty Cottin Pogrebin, who had turned away from Judaism when, as a teen, she was told that her prayers did not count toward the quorum needed to mourn her mother, but who found antisemitism in the women's movement driving her back to Judaism.[87] Female Jewish communal leaders were there, like Shoshana Cardin, whose long list of "firsts" includes being the first woman to head the Conference of Presidents of Major American Jewish Organizations. Jewish studies professor Deborah Lipstadt was honored for battling Holocaust denier David Irving in a British courtroom, but also for contributions to Jewish feminism, such as what happened when "Deborah Made Ten" (the number needed for a minyan).[88] Not surprisingly, that evening, others stood out, just as had Abzug and Holtzman at the first National Jewish Women's Conference. This time the politicians were Vermont's first Jewish governor Madeline Kunin and Congresswomen Shelley Berkley and Nita Lowey. Surely, the brightest star in the constellation that evening was Supreme Court Justice Ruth Bader Ginsburg. Justice Ginsburg made her mark as a lawyer battling sex discrimination, and she credited anti-Jewish discrimination in this country with sensitizing her to all forms of discrimination.[89]

If Jewish feminism has not achieved all that it set out to do and some of its stars, especially the one shining light on the women's movement, have at times flickered, it has, nevertheless, as this celebration proved, in a few short decades transformed American Jewish life. At the beginning of the twenty-first century the constellation Jewish feminism was fixed in the firmament hovering over American Jewry.

NOTES

1. "Declaration of Sentiments and Resolutions, Seneca Falls, 1848," in Miriam Schneir, ed., *Feminism: The Essential Historical Writings* (New York, 1972), 77.

2. Ernestine Rose's speech to the National Woman's Rights Convention in Worcester, Massachusetts, October 15, 1851; http://www.brandeis.edu/centers/wsrc/Ernestine_Rose_Website/1851speech.html; accessed January 20, 2005. On Rose see Carol A. Kolmerten, *The American Life of Ernestine L. Rose* (Syracuse, 1999).

3. Elinor Lerner, "Jewish Involvement in the New York City Woman Suffrage Movement," *American Jewish History* 71 (June 1981): 442–61.

4. On the Congress and the founding of the NCJW, see Deborah Grand Golomb, "The 1893 Congress of Jewish Women: Evolution or Revolution in American Jewish Women's History?" *American Jewish History* 70 (September 1980): 52–67; Faith Rogow, *Gone to Another Meeting: The National Council of Jewish Women, 1893–1993* (Tuscaloosa, 1993); Pamela S. Nadell, *Women Who Would Be Rabbis: A History of Women's Ordination, 1889–1985* (Boston, 1998), 31–40.

5. On women's organizations in these years, see Anne Firor Scott, *Natural Allies: Women's Associations in American History* (Urbana, 1991). On the national denominational sisterhood bodies, see Pamela S. Nadell and Rita J. Simon, "Ladies of the Sisterhood: Women in the American Reform Synagogue, 1900–1930," in Maurie Sacks, ed., *Active Voices: Women in Jewish Culture* (Urbana, 1995), 63–75; Jenna Weissman Joselit, "The Jewish Priestess and Ritual: The Sacred Life of American Orthodox Women," in Pamela S. Nadell, ed., *American Jewish Women's History: A Reader* (New York, 2003),

153–74. On Hadassah see Joyce Antler, "Zion in Our Hearts: Henrietta Szold and the American Jewish Women's Movement," ibid., 129–49.

6. Nancy F. Cott, *The Grounding of Modern Feminism* (New Haven, 1987), 4.

7. Ibid., quotations, 3–4, 8–10, 49, 283.

8. Leila J. Rupp and Verta Taylor, *Survival in the Doldrums: The American Women's Rights Movement, 1945 to the 1960s* (New York, 1987), 166.

9. Kirsten Lise Fermaglich, "'The Comfortable Concentration Camp': The Significance of Nazi Imagery in Betty Friedan's *The Feminine Mystique* (1963)," *American Jewish History* 91.2 (2003): 205–32.

10. Many have discussed the emergence of the second wave of American feminism; see, among others, William H. Chafe, *The Paradox of Change: American Women in the Twentieth Century* (New York, 1991); Ruth Rosen, *The World Split Open: How the Modern Women's Movement Changed American* (New York, 2000).

11. "Ezrat Nashim: Jewish Women Call for a Change," 1972; rpt. in Jacob Rader Marcus, ed., *The American Jewish Woman: A Documentary History* (New York, 1981), 894–96.

12. Charlotte Baum, Paula Hyman, and Sonya Michel, *The Jewish Woman in America* (New York, 1975, 1976), xii.

13. Cott, *The Grounding of Modern Feminism*, 282.

14. Susan M. Hartmann, *The Other Feminists: Activists in the Liberal Establishment* (New Haven, 1998).

15. On Neumark, see Ellen M. Umansky, "Women in Judaism: From the Reform Movement to Contemporary Jewish Religious Feminism," in Rosemary Ruether and Eleanor McLaughlin, eds., *Women of Spirit: Female Leadership in the Jewish and Christian Traditions* (New York, 1979), 339–42; Nadell, *Women Who Would Be Rabbis*, 62–72, 102–4, Neumark quoted, 104. For her account of her effort to become a rabbi, see Pamela S. Nadell, "Ordaining Women Rabbis," in Colleen McDannell, ed., *Religions of the United States in Practice*, vol. 2 (Princeton, 2001), 389–417, Neumark quoted, 417.

16. Quotations from Ellen Dickstein (Kominers) interview with Judith Kaplan Eisenstein, 1 November 1974; copy of tape in my possession.

17. On the bat mitzvah, see Mel Scult, *Judaism Faces the Twentieth Century: A Biography of Mordecai M. Kaplan* (Detroit, 1993), 301–2.

18. *Central Conference of American Rabbis Yearbook* (1922), 171, quoting Rabbi Stern. No first names appear in the record of the debate. Possibly this refers to Rabbi Harry J. Stern (1897–1984); Kerry M. Olitzky, Lance J. Sussman, and Malcolm H. Stern, eds., *Reform Judaism in America: A Biographical Dictionary and Sourcebook* (Westport, CT: 1993), 205–6.

19. Judith Kaplan Eisenstein, "Looking Back: A Career in Jewish Music," *Reconstructionist* (1987). This quotation comes from the typescript submitted for this article, which was published with significant cuts.

20. Ellen Dickstein (Kominers) interview with Judith Kaplan Eisenstein, November 1, 1974; copy of tape in my possession.

21. Nadell, *Women Who Would Be Rabbis*, chapter 3; Joyce Antler, "Between Culture and Politics: The Emma Lazarus Federation of Jewish Women's Clubs and the Promulgation of Women's History, 1944–1989," in Vicki L. Ruiz and Ellen Carol DuBois, eds.,

Unequal Sisters: A Multicultural Reader in U.S. Women's History, 3d rev. ed. (New York, 2000 [1995]), 519–41; Regina Stein, "The Road to Bat Mitzvah in America," in Pamela S. Nadell and Jonathan D. Sarna, eds., *Women and American Judaism: Historical Perspectives* (Hanover, NH, 2001), 223–34; Deborah Dash Moore, *To the Golden Cities: Pursuing the American Jewish Dream in Miami and L.A.* (New York, 1994), 120–21.

22. Anne Lapidus Lerner, "'Who Hast Not Made Me a Man': The Movement for Equal Rights for Women in American Jewry," *American Jewish Year Book* 77 (1976): 3–38.

23. For other accounts of Jewish feminism's emergence, see, for example, Reena Sigman Friedman, "The Jewish Feminist Movement," in Michael N. Dobkowski, ed., *Jewish American Voluntary Organizations* (New York, 1986), 574–601; Sylvia Barack Fishman, *A Breath of Life: Feminism in the American Jewish Community* (New York, 1993), 1–15. Note that these narratives fail to consider that an old guard, like National Federation of Temple Sisterhoods' executive director Jane Evans and the journalist Trude Weiss-Rosmarin, had been raising feminist issues for decades before the late 1960s. On both Evans and Weiss-Rosmarin's feminism, see Nadell, *Women Who Would Be Rabbis,* 123, 125, 127–29, 131–35.

24. Jacqueline Levine, "The Changing Role of Women in the Jewish Community, 1972," in Jacob Rader Marcus, ed., *The American Jewish Woman: A Documentary History* (New York, 1981), 902–7.

25. For a chronology of these developments, see Rosen, *The World Split Open.*

26. For a chronology of these developments, see ibid., quotation, xxi.

27. Nadell, *Women Who Would Be Rabbis,* 152, 161–62.

28. "Rabbi Sally," *Newsweek,* February 23, 1970, 89; "Women at the Altar," *Time,* November 2, 1970, 71ff.

29. Irving Spiegel, "A First in the States, a Woman Cantor," *New York Times,* May 30, 1971, BQ56.

30. Alan Silverstein, "The Evolution of Ezrat Nashim," *Conservative Judaism* 30 (1975): 41–51, 45–46.

31. This is based on ibid. The "Call for Change" appears in "Jewish Women Call for Change, 1972," in Marcus, *The American Jewish Woman,* 894–96.

32. The short-lived Jewish Feminist Organization, founded in 1974, tried to be that address, but it lasted only two or three years; Friedman, "The Jewish Feminist Movement," 584–87.

33. Ibid., 581–82. Note Judith Plaskow was then known as Judith Plaskow Goldenberg. Quotations from her 1973 address appear in Elisabeth S. Fiorenza, *Changing the Paradigms* (1990, accessed March 16, 2005); http://www.religion-online.org/showarticle .asp?title=439. Judith Plaskow, *Standing Again at Sinai: Judaism from a Feminist Perspective* (San Francisco, 1990).

34. Shirley Frank, "Women—Writing the History of the Future," *Attah* (1973): 4–5.

35. Shirley Frank, "Concrete Results Noted on Journals, Midwest Parley in Fall," *Attah* (1973): 5.

36. See, for example, Elizabeth Koltun, ed., *The Jewish Woman: New Perspectives* (New York, 1976). This began in 1973 as a special issue of the journal *Response.*

37. Friedman, "The Jewish Feminist Movement," 581–83.

38. At the 1973 National Jewish Women's Conference, Rachel Adler excited many not only by wearing tallit (prayer shawl) and tefillin (phylacteries) but also by showing other women how to put them on; Rachel Adler, e-mail communication, May 6, 2005.

39. Irving Spiegel, "Conservative Jews Vote for Women in Minyan," *New York Times,* September 11, 1973, 1.

40. A few women became synagogue presidents before the second wave of feminism burst forth; Nadell, *Women Who Would Be Rabbis,* 129. As a result of Jewish feminism, by 2005, women as synagogue presidents were commonplace everywhere except among the Orthodox. On the first woman to head an Orthodox congregation in Washington, DC, see Paula Amman, "Beth Sholom Breaks Ground: First Local Orthodox Shul to Elect Woman President," *Washington Jewish Week,* April 7 2005, 9.

41. This history is detailed in Nadell, *Women Who Would Be Rabbis.* See also the film *And the Gates Opened: Women in the Rabbinate,* New York: Jewish Theological Seminary of America, 2005.

42. This is based on the sketch of Greenberg in Shuly Rubin Schwartz, "Ambassadors Without Portfolio? The Religious Leadership of Rebbetzins in Late-Twentieth-Century American Jewish Life," in Nadell and Sarna, *Women and American Judaism,* 235–67, 253–60. Greenberg's advocacy for women's ordination is discussed in Nadell, *Women Who Would Be Rabbis,* 215–19. Blu Greenberg, *On Women and Judaism: A View from Tradition* (Philadelphia, 1981).

43. JOFA: *Jewish Orthodox Feminist Alliance* (accessed May 6, 2005); www.jofa.org.

44. Norma Baumel Joseph, "Ritual Law and Praxis: Bat Mitsva Celebrations," *Modern Judaism* 22.3 (2002): 234–60.

45. Laurie Goodstein, "Women Take Active Role to Study Orthodox Judaism," *New York Times,* December 21, 2000, 1ff. She quotes Blu Greenberg. On the "learning revolution," see Rochelle Furstenberg, *The Flourishing of Higher Jewish Learning for Women* (Jerusalem Center for Public Affairs, May 1, 2000; accessed May 9, 2005); http://www .jofa.org/social.php/education/posthighscho. On Orthodox women and ordination, see Laurie Goodstein, "Ordained as Rabbis, Women Tell Secret," *New York Times,* December 21, 2000, A29; Haviva Ner-David, *Life on the Fringes: A Feminist Journey Toward Traditional Rabbinic Ordination* (Needham, MA, 2000).

46. Sandy Eisenberg Sasso, "B'rit B'not Israel: Observations on Women and Reconstructionism," *Response: A Contemporary Jewish Review* 8.2 (Summer 1973): 101–5, quotation, 103.

47. Debra Orenstein, *Lifecycles: Jewish Women on Life Passages and Personal Milestones,* vol. 1 (Woodstock, VT:, 1998), 117. Orenstein lists an array of moments Jewish men and women should honor in their lives. They include first love, first sexual experience, weaning, finding out the biopsy is negative, becoming a grandparent, cooking a grandmother's recipe, and "discovering Jewish feminism"; 119–20.

48. Nina Beth Cardin, *Tears of Sorrow, Seeds of Hope: A Jewish Spiritual Companion for Infertility and Pregnancy Loss* (Woodstock, VT, 1999), 28.

49. Orenstein, *Lifecycles*; Laura Levitt and Sue Ann Wasserman, "Mikvah Ceremony for Laura," in Ellen M. Umansky and Dianne Ashton, eds., *Four Centuries of Jewish Women's Spirituality* (Boston, 1992), 321–26.

50. Lenore Bohm, "The Feminist Theological Enterprise," *CCAR Journal* (Summer 1997): 70–79, 76. A major collection of Rosh Chodesh readings is Penina V. Adelman, *Miriam's Well : Rituals for Jewish Women Around the Year*, 2d ed. (New York, 1990).

51. Elyse Goldstein, "Rabbi Elyse Goldstein," in Francine Zuckerman, ed., *Half the Kingdom: Seven Jewish Feminists* (Montreal, 1992), 71–88, quotations, 82–83.

52. Judith Plaskow, "Spirituality," in Paula Hyman and Deborah Dash Moore, eds., *Jewish Women in America: An Historical Encyclopedia* (New York, 1997), 1302–6.

53. E. M. Broner, *The Telling* (New York, 1993), 1, 193–94. The film *Miriam's Daughters Now* shows a feminist seder, women celebrating *tashlich*, the casting away of sins on the Jewish new year, and a baby naming ceremony; *Miriam's Daughters Now*, New York: Center for Visual History, 1986.

54. Nadine Brozan, "Waiting List Grows as Seders for Women Increase in Popularity," *New York Times*, March 16 1999, B5. There is no standard text for these seders. Reflecting the grassroots nature of this transformation, women in the synagogue and Jewish communal groups sponsoring the seders tend to write their own, borrowing and adapting from various texts that circulate privately.

55. Rachel Adler, *Engendering Judaism: An Inclusive Theology and Ethics* (Boston, 1998), xxvi, 63–64, 212. Her introduction surveys developments in feminist Jewish theology.

56. Frank, "Women—Writing the History of the Future."

57. Paula E. Hyman, "Judaic Studies," in Hyman and Moore, *Jewish Women in America*, 705–9; Lynn Davidman and Shelly Tenenbaum, eds., *Feminist Perspectives on Jewish Studies* (New Haven, 1994).

58. Influential titles include, in Bible, Tikva Frymer-Kensky, *Reading the Women of the Bible: A New Interpretation of Their Stories* (New York, 2002); in rabbinics, Judith Hauptman, *Rereading the Rabbis : A Woman's Voice* (Boulder, 1997); in philosophy, Hava Tirosh-Samuelson, *Women and Gender in Jewish Philosophy*, Jewish Literature, *and Culture* (Bloomington, 2004); in history, Paula Hyman and Deborah Dash Moore, eds., *Jewish Women in America: An Historical Encyclopedia*, 2 vols. (New York, 1997); in sociology, Fishman, *A Breath of Life*; in anthropology, Susan Starr Sered, *Women as Ritual Experts: The Religious Lives of Elderly Jewish Women in Jerusalem* (New York, 1992); in Jewish literatures, Naomi B. Sokoloff, Anne Lapidus Lerner, and Anita Norich, *Gender and Text in Modern Hebrew and Yiddish Literature* (New York, 1992).

59. Elyse Goldstein, ed., *The Women's Torah Commentary: New Insights from Women Rabbis on the Fifty-four Weekly Torah Portions* (Woodstock, VT, 2000).

60. Gen 30:21, Gen. 34:1ff.

61. Anita Diamant, *The Red Tent* (New York, 1997), 2. First published in 1997, *The Red Tent* has gone through multiple reprintings and is available in more than twenty countries; http://www.jwa.org/this_week/week40.html.

62. Cynthia Ozick, *The Puttermesser Papers*, 1st ed. (New York, 1997).

63. Babylonian Talmud, *Yevamot*, 62b.

64. Ibid., 63b.

65. Paula Hyman, "Jewish Feminism Faces the American Women's Movement: Convergence and Divergence," in Nadell, *American Jewish Women's History*, 297–312.

66. Frank, "Women—Writing the History of the Future."

67. Laurence Kotler-Berkowitz, Steven M. Cohen, Jonathon Ament, Vivian Klaff, Frank Mott, Danyelle Peckerman-Neuman, "The National Jewish Population Survey, 2000–1: Strength, Challenge, and Diversity in the American Jewish Population" (New York, 2003), 3–4.

68. Frank, "Women—Writing the History of the Future."

69. Evelyn Torton Beck, *Nice Jewish Girls: A Lesbian Anthology*, rev. ed. (Boston, 1989); Christie Balka and Andy Rose, *Twice Blessed: On Being Lesbian, Gay, and Jewish* (Boston, 1989); Melanie Kaye/Kantrowitz and Irena Klepfisz, *The Tribe of Dina: A Jewish Women's Anthology*, rev. ed. (Boston, 1989). See also the journal *Bridges*.

70. Rebecca Alpert, Sue Levi Elwell, and Shirley Idelson, eds., *Lesbian Rabbis: The First Generation* (New Brunswick, 2001).

71. Sandi Simcha Dubowski, *Trembling Before G-d*, Simcha Leib Productions, 2001.

72. Joe Berkofsky, "San Francisco Simchas? Gay Jews Among Those Lining Up to Wed, Seek 'Equal Rights,'" *Deep South Jewish Voice* 14.4 (2004): 39, 42.

73. Susannah Heschel, *On Being a Jewish Feminist : A Reader* (New York, 1983).

74. Susannah Heschel, *The Origin of the Orange on the Seder Plate* (Miriam's Cup, 2001, accessed May 12, 2005); http://www.miriamscup.com/Heschel_orange.htm. Although this was originally conceived by Susannah Heschel as symbolizing the fruitfulness that would accrue to the Jewish community by fully including gays and lesbians, an alternative story circulated that made this a response to the exclusion of women from the rabbinate. In this widely repeated version a man told Heschel that a woman belongs on the *bima* (the podium in the synagogue) as much as does an orange on the seder plate.

75. Levine, "The Changing Role of Women in the Jewish Community, 1972."

76. Tamara Cohen, Jill Hammer, and Rona Shapiro, *Listen to Her Voice: The Ma'yan Report; Assessing the Experiences of Women in the Jewish Community and Their Relationship to Feminism* (New York, 2005).

77. B'nai B'rith Women became independent in 1990 and is now known as Jewish Women International.

78. Shuly Rubin Schwartz, "Women's League for Conservative Judaism," in Hyman and Moore, *Jewish Women in America*, 1493–97.

79. Cohen, Hammer, and Shapiro, *Listen to Her Voice*, 25.

80. Ibid., 32ff.

81. This is discussed in Hyman, "Jewish Feminism Faces the American Women's Movement," 301–2.; she quotes Judith Plaskow.

82. In addition to those already named, leaders of its radical women's liberation wing, like Shulamith Firestone, also stood out.

83. Letty Cottin Pogrebin, "Anti-Semitism in the Women's Movement: A Jewish Feminist's Disturbing Account," *Ms.* (1982): 145–49. This is also discussed in Hyman, "Jewish Feminism Faces the American Women's Movement," 302; and Fishman, *A Breath of Life*, 9–12.

84. Pogrebin, "Anti-Semitism in the Women's Movement."

85. *Lion of Judah Conference Program* (2004, accessed May 18, 2005); http://www.ujc .org/content_display.html?ArticleID=127866.

86. Debbie Friedman, "Miriam's Song" (ASCAP 1988).

87. Letty Cottin Pogrebin, *Deborah, Golda, and Me: Being Female and Jewish in America* (New York, 1991).

88. Lipstadt tells the story of her libel trial in Deborah E. Lipstadt, *History on Trial: My Day in Court with Holocaust Denier David Irving* (New York, 2005). Deborah E. Lipstadt, "And Deborah Made Ten," in Heschel, *On Being a Jewish Feminist*, 207–9.

89. Malvina Halberstam, "Ruth Bader Ginsburg," in Hyman and Moore, *Jewish Women in America*, 515–20.

17

CONTEMPORARY JEWISH THOUGHT

ALAN T. LEVENSON

If there is one point of agreement among students and practitioners of Jewish theology in North America, it is that not much creative work has been forthcoming over the last two decades.

—ARNOLD EISEN, "JEWISH THEOLOGY IN NORTH AMERICA:
NOTES ON TWO DECADES," *American Jewish Yearbook* (1991): 3–33

The list [of books] goes on and on. The reality all this reflects is that [Robert] Goldy's description of the renewal of Jewish theology in post-World War II America is continuing unabated.

—DAVID ELLENSON, "THE CONTINUED RENEWAL OF NORTH
AMERICAN THEOLOGY," JOURNAL OF REFORM JUDAISM (WINTER 1991): 1–16

What is the reader to conclude from such seemingly incompatible verdicts on the state of Jewish theology, rendered by two prominent and astute observers, looking at similar evidence in exactly the same period? Before adjudicating this matter, some historical and intellectual context for understanding contemporary Jewish thought is essential. It is a truism that ideas do not form in a vacuum, but one cannot overestimate how much events of the last century have shaped the agenda of Jewish thinkers. The Holocaust, the creation of the state of Israel, the successful integration of American Jews, the feminist movement and the recent stirrings in American religion, have driven the discussion. This sensitivity to events results not only from the general rule of environmental impact but also from the fact that participants in Jewish thought are most unlikely to be indifferent to the realities of American Jewry—a small and shrinking element of the general population (around 2 percent in 2000). The fate of Jewry (ethnically defined) and Judaism (religiously defined) are not divisible—that is the central of theme of this volume.

To the extent that theology is limited to considerations of purely "religious" matters, it is clear that much of what we call modern Jewish thought would not fit easily into this rubric.[1] Jewish thinkers, from the beginning of modernity, have been deeply concerned with the nature of actual practice, communal health, political orientation, liturgical reform, and the like. Some, including Ahad Ha'Am and Mordecai Kaplan, approached religion principally from a sociological perspective; the former was an agnostic, the latter was more interested in the functionality of religion than in its propositional "truths." Frequently, these practical concerns emerged from the professional orientation of the thinkers. Until recently, the most influential modern Jewish thinkers (Moses Mendelssohn, Abraham Geiger, Samson Raphael Hirsch, Moses Hess, Theodor Herzl) were not professors, but businessmen, journalists, and, above all, rabbis. Even today, when humanistic disciplines in the academic world have become hospitable to Jewish studies, many notable contributors to the field of Jewish thought work in rabbinical seminaries, medical and legal faculties (Leon Kass and Alan Dershowitz), and even Jewish colleges (Byron Sherwin).

The more than religious nature and professional profile of Jewish thinkers offer two justifications for preferring the term *Jewish thought* to *Jewish theology*, but there are other reasons as well. In an early attempt to locate the source of American Jewry's indifference to theology, Eugene Borowitz, arguably the most influential liberal thinker of the last half-century, doubted that a "systematic" theology could be constructed, despite the need for an overarching interpretation, which Borowitz termed *holism*. The two commentators cited in the epigraph to this essay attempted to locate reasons for this failure. Arnold Eisen included American pragmatism, theology's particularistic/elitist nature, and the lack of qualified practitioners.[2] David Ellenson, while offering a more upbeat assessment, also noted the lack of a pre-Emancipation past "that has denied North American Jewry even a memory of communal life, practice and belief."[3] It seems to the present author that the need for holism, grasping all of Jewry, Judaism and Jewishness in its multifaceted dimensions, is itself a serious impediment. To take in this much of the picture and produce a systematic theology, I maintain, would boggle even a Moses Maimonides.[4]

Let us take post-Holocaust theology as an example of the difficulty of forging a contemporary synthesis.[5] The Holocaust, or Shoah, manifestly concerns more than the age-old question of theodicy addressed by the book of Job and numerous rabbinic texts.[6] The historical magnitude of the murder of European Jewry, as Emil Fackenheim formulated it, constituted an "epoch-making event," which challenged the very "root experience" of Jewish faith. How do we know that Jewish faith—and the Jewish people—have not been fatally wounded by Auschwitz, considering that six million individual Jews, five million non-Jews, and eastern European Jewish culture were exterminated? Fackenheim, the most wide-ranging of the post-Holocaust thinkers, integrates biblical, midrashic, philosophical, historical, anecdotal, and autobiographical evidence in his prolonged response to the Holocaust. The reasons for his catholic approach are varied. These include the existentialist influence of Martin Buber and Franz Rosenzweig, the postmodern sensibility of forcing texts to confront events, and the linchpin in Fackenheim's argument: world Jewry's collective response since 1945, which offers hope that the foundations ("root experiences") of Judaism have not been punctured.[7] Appropriately, Fackenheim speaks of responses rather than so-lutions to the age-old problem of theodicy pressed upon us so urgently by the Holocaust. Although Fackenheim received a rigorous training in philosophy in his native Germany and taught philosophy at the University of Toronto, midrash, with its penetrating but equivocal sense of biblical meaning, strikes him as the best language to grasp the enormity of our contemporary situation.

Do we lighten the load by asking only for Jewish thinkers in place of Jewish theologians? *Jewish thought* is a less rigid term than *Jewish theology*, but it is not amorphous. At the very least, serious Jewish thought would include the following criteria: existential engagement in the fate of the covenantal community known as Jewry, grounding in the Jewish sources, both primary and secondary, awareness of parallel problems and solutions faced and entertained by non-Jewish communi-ties. These criteria may fall short of those for the Jewish theologian, who would be presumed to possess mastery of the modern theological-philosophical corpus and a commitment to striving for system. On the other hand, the term *Jewish thinker* encompasses most of the influential Jewish intellectual figures of modernity, many of contemporary Jewry's most listened to voices, and varied forms of religios-ity that eschew precisely those elements of rigor typical of theology-philosophy. On the whole, then, enlarging the category from theology to thought better cap-tures the Jewish dialogue. Not coincidentally, it helps narrow the gap between the two judgments found at the beginning of this essay. If systematic theology is deemed a desideratum, American Jewry will continue to fall short (Eisen). If in-tellectual ferment is the relevant standard (Ellenson), we seem poised for another half-century of creativity.

WITHIN THE ORGANIZED MOVEMENTS OF AMERICAN JUDAISM

While one could certainly organize such an essay around thematic issues of rec-ognized importance (God-Torah-Israel, for instance), I prefer to begin with a fo-cus on the movements, or branches, of American Judaism.[8] American religion presents a notoriously wild and ill-charted terrain. Nevertheless, 46 percent of American Jews at any given time identify with a synagogue, and an overwhelming percentage of these belong to one of the four principal movements.[9] (A plethora of small, independent rabbinical institutions now exist. This has long been the case within Orthodoxy; it is now true within other varieties of Judaism.) The vast ma-jority of American Jewry's religious leaders (rabbis, cantors, educators) continue to receive their training through the three principal seminaries and the smaller Re-constructionist Rabbinical College. Beyond this immediate influence on the pu-tative religious leaders of the community, the constituent congregations offer the testing ground for ritual changes proposed from above and, often, the impetus for changes generated from below.[10] The movements and their most representative thinkers, therefore, provide a rich array of intellectual positions and a convenient starting point for assessing the timbre of Jewish thought in America.

EUGENE BOROWITZ

The validation of ethnic differences since the 1960s and 1970s, and the beginnings of what is now called multicultural America, changed the direction of Reform Judaism. When judged by liturgy, prayer books, Jewish learning initiatives, declarations of principles, and synagogue aesthetics, Reform Judaism has dramatically moved toward tradition in the quarter-century. Despite this move toward tradition, Reform continues to emphasize personal and congregational autonomy, welcomes intermarried couples more than it did a quarter-century ago, and resolutely champions equality toward gay and/or straight rabbis and cantors. Above all, in its adherence to the highly controversial patrilineal descent decision of 1983 (which breaks with traditional halakhah by tracing Jewish descent from either the father or mother), the trajectory of Reform also seems to be moving away from time-honored Jewish norms. As one observer of American Jewry puts it, Reform seems to "change in both directions."[11] Certainly the era of classical Reform, which prevailed from the mid-nineteenth to mid-twentieth centuries, is over. Classical Reform included a posture of high acculturation to general society, free adaptation of non-Jewish religious forms (mixed seating, organs, choirs), a tepid relationship to Israel, and a conscious distancing from eastern European Jewish customs.[12] All of these classical Reform positions have been abandoned; for Reform, as for American Jewry at large, earlier anxiety about integration has been entirely displaced by anxiety regarding group survival.

One figure has lived through these changes in Reform ideology and helped guide them—Eugene Borowitz, a professor at Hebrew Union College-Jewish Institute of Religion (HUC-JIR). Although American born and educated, the very title of Borowitz's *Liberal Judaism* (1984) signals his intellectual connection to the more moderate European tradition of religious reform.[13] Borowitz has given the name *covenant theology* to his attempts at bringing insights from Buber and Rosenzweig into dialogue with post-Holocaust American-Jewish realities. In *Renewing the Covenant* (1991) Borowitz details the dialectical components of God, Torah, and Israel, arguing the mutual responsibilities of all parties. While Borowitz's language occasionally seems dated (e.g., the picture of American Jews in revolt from religious institutions, the assertions of Israel's "exceptional moral accomplishments"), his arguments have an undeniable moral thrust. And, whereas the ethical remains the heart of his program (e.g., "Why the Prophets Are Important to Liberal Jews" in *Liberal Judaism*), Borowitz stresses the role of ritual as well.

Borowitz's conception found expression not only in the 1976 San Francisco Platform, which he largely authored, but also in the Statement of Principles adopted by the Central Conference of American Rabbis in Pittsburgh in 1999. The city was chosen deliberately: the Pittsburgh Platform of 1885 is considered by all the clearest articulation of classical reform—the most recent Statement of Principles (American Reform produced major position papers in 1869, 1885, 1937, 1976, and 1999) represents a repudiation of its predecessors and a confirmation of Borowitz's desire to point the way toward a Reform Jewish praxis.[14] By praxis Borowitz means nothing less than an identifiably Jewish (though not parochial or exclusivist) lifestyle—a Judaism that is to be practiced by the committed Reform Jew on a regular basis and not only at lifecycle events, High Holidays, and temple Sabbath services. Borowitz makes no claims that Reform rabbis have a right to enforce these standards. The value of personal and congregational autonomy is too dear to American Jews to be seriously challenged and, in any event, the Reform understanding of Torah, revelation, and halakhah could not support such a use of religious authority. Ultimately Borowitz relies on the refusal of Jews to break the links with the Jewish past and its traditions. Despite some who view the Reform validation of both autonomy and the language of commandment as hopelessly in contradiction, this may be the only firm ground for a liberal theologian. But this grounding may be sufficient. As sociologist Nathan Glazer commented many years ago, the most striking fact about American Judaism has been the unwillingness of the majority of its practitioners to abandon it.[15]

NEIL GILMAN

For good and for ill, the defining feature of Conservative Judaism in America has been its status as the movement of the middle—neither Orthodox nor Reform. In the opening years of the twentieth century Solomon Schechter presented this as a virtue: Conservative Judaism represented the Jewish majority, what Schechter called Catholic Israel. Schechter propounded reforms in Judaism that were positive (i.e., unlike Reform, sought to maintain a high degree of continuity with traditional practices), but also historic (i.e., unlike Orthodoxy, accepted the interplay between Judaism and historical developments).[16] Conservative Judaism benefited from this positioning. It emerged in the middle decades of the twentieth century as the natural home for second- and third-generation Jews who sought both thorough acculturation to America and a degree of Jewishness (*Yiddishkeit*) in the synagogue that most Reform congregations did not permit.[17] Another benefit of this moderate position was the ability of the Jewish Theological Seminary, until recently the only training ground for the Conservative rabbinate, to employ teachers of widely differing viewpoints. In the periods before and after the Second

World War II, respectively, Mordecai Kaplan and Abraham Joshua Heschel were the dominant creative forces in American Jewry.[18]

Both Kaplan and Heschel profoundly influenced Neil Gilman, who, by dint of his long tenure at JTS, several excellent books, and role in the crafting of Conservative Judaism's official theological works, may be considered representative of the movement. It is no disparagement of Gilman's originality to say that he splits the difference between his two mentors. Kaplan considered Jewish life from a fundamentally sociological perspective and prioritized belonging, behaving, and believing accordingly. Gilman is more "theological" than Kaplan; the former considers the absence of an articulated system of beliefs an Achilles' heel of modern Jewish communal health. Gilman's *Sacred Fragments* (1990) attempts to steer the modern Jew toward that articulation. Yet Gilman's intellectual touchstones tend to be other philosophers and concepts drawn from the academic study of religion; this is evident in his definitions of myth, mitzvah (i.e., commandment), ritual, and liturgy. Gilman is not, as Heschel was, a practitioner of an inward-tending "depth theology." Unlike Heschel, whose Hasidic background indelibly shaped his theological oeuvre, Gilman works in the rationalist tradition.

In the tradition of Frankel and Schechter, Gilman carves out a large place for the Jewish community to determine what is true and authentic. But Gilman travels farther than these founders of Conservative Judaism in a populist direction. He advises individual Jews to "acknowledge that you have something to say about these questions that has value."[19] Theology, for Gilman, aims precisely at helping individuals and communities deal with their realities. Again true to the tradition of Conservative Judaism, Gilman evinces comfort with integrating both the "facts of history" and the "midrashic method."[20]

Unlike traditionalists and unlike the functionalist Kaplan, Gilman understands mitzvah in mythic terms. How a particular mitzvah mobilizes Jews to collective action, how the performance of a particular mitzvah invokes the covenant, how the mitzvah connects with tradition (history), how the mitzvah is invested with ethical or ritual significance, how a mitzvah is capable of spiritual enrichment, and how mitzvah becomes permanent habit—these are the multifaceted criteria Gilman applies in place of a simple assertion of divine revelation at Sinai.[21] The resulting theology of commandment (with or without a commander) offers fine anthropocentric grounds—not reasons—for those already committed to a life of mitzvot.

Employing the language of *grounds* rather than *reasons*, Gilman explicitly rejects the notion that the Jewish theologian's task is to persuade the skeptic: existential commitment, not reason, is the prerequisite. Unwillingness to live the life of a committed Jew is the failure of the dissenter, not the theologian. This understanding of mitzvah leaves Gilman firmly with the Conservative movement when it comes to the role of halakhah in Jewish life. Gilman asserts, "There is simply no religious authenticity in Judaism outside of a halakhic system—not necessarily

the halakhic system that the traditionalists exalt, but a halakhic system that con-
cretizes our sense of covenantedness as a community to God" (*Sacred Fragments*,
59). Gilman's halakhic system differs not only from that of Orthodoxy, but also
from the approach of Isaac Klein's *A Guide to Jewish Religious Practice*, the semi-
official law code for an earlier generation of Conservative practitioners.[22] A large
gap exists between asserting the need for a structure, or "a halakhic system," and
demanding Jewish adherence to halakhah as a prerequisite for what qualifies as
authentic observance. Gilman's denominational allegiance is less apparent in
later works such The *Death of Death* and *The Way Into Encountering God in Judaism*.[23] These works, clearly responding to resurgent spirituality, artfully stretch the
limits of the rationalist tradition.

NORMAN LAMM

Any discussion of Orthodox thought must acknowledge the great changes taking
place within American Orthodoxy in the last half-century. The arrival from eastern Europe of an Orthodox elite during and after the Holocaust and the subsequent transformations wrought in day schools and synagogue life amount to what
Jeffrey Gurock called the "winnowing" of American Orthodoxy. Until the 1950s
the majority of Orthodox Jews were so out of habit, nostalgia, or social comfort.
The Orthodox leadership in this period centered on Yeshiva University and followed the model of Torah study combined with secular learning pioneered in
Western Europe. Today the majority of Orthodox Jews are so by ideology. The
leadership of American Orthodoxy, which is more dynamic and varied than it was
a generation ago, may be found in many locations, including Lithuanian-style
yeshivot and Hasidic-style courts, both of which reject the combination of Torah
learning and secular study championed by earlier leaders of Yeshiva University
such as Bernard Revel and Samuel Belkin. On a sliding scale of "accommodation" and "resistance" to modernity and surrounding culture, the balance at present has tipped toward the latter. One figure who has resisted the resisters, the
long-time president of Yeshiva University, Norman Lamm, has articulated a powerful vision of modern Orthodoxy.[24]

Lamm, the first American-born president of Yeshiva University, considers his
mentor to be Rav Joseph Soloveitchik, a figure that towered over American Orthodoxy for nearly half a century. Soloveitchik possessed encyclopedic knowledge of
the rabbinic sources and received a doctorate in philosophy from the University of
Berlin in 1932. Soloveitchik embodied the combination of Torah and secular
learning, but his legacy has been disputed by those who revere Soloveitchik the
talmudist only and those who also honor him as the great thinker. Lamm patently
falls into the latter category, arguing in the tradition of Soloveitchik that Orthodox Jews should strive to acquire higher education as a value in itself and not

merely as a practical necessity of the modern work world. Lamm rejects literalist interpretation of the doctrine that the Torah contains all wisdom (sacred and profane) and rejects the attempt to present the formula of Samson Hirsch, "the study of Torah with the ways of the land," as merely a concession to the times. Lamm stresses the importance of moderation in general and to the observant Jew in particular, what the medieval philosopher Maimonides called "the middle way." Sober consideration of each situation, rather than ideology, ought to guide decision making. Typical was Lamm's unhesitating decision in the wake of September 11, 2001, to suspend the normal gender rules of *shmira* (guarding the corpse) in order to let the women of nearby Stern College help fulfill this important mitzvah. Lamm also champions the principle of "community of Israel" even when it conflicts with that of policing the boundaries of Torah observance. As Lamm sees it, the love of Israel may bring Jews back to Torah observance, whereas "triumphalist arrogance" will not. (Many will consider Chabad, or Lubavitch, Hasidism the most visible exemplars of this principle.) Lamm also regards the state of Israel as an unadulterated good—a position rejected by the ultra-Orthodox right on the grounds that the state is run by Western law (i.e., not halakhah) and by democratically elected Jews of wide-ranging religious practices, as opposed to observant Jews chosen by rabbinic sages.

Lamm stands in good company in the world of modern Orthodox thought: Isaac (Yitz) Greenberg has written widely on the Holocaust. David Hartman, who has directed the Shalom Hartman Institute in Jerusalem for many years, was originally a New Yorker and has written many works in English. His emphasis on a sober view of Israel as a harbinger of the messianic era stands firmly in the Maimonidean tradition. Hartman has been an important voice forwarding a Jewish state without religious compulsion and a champion of cultivating relations between Israeli and Diaspora Jewries. Michael Wyschogrod's seminal *The Body of Faith* constituted a particularly bold assertion of the demands of the divine and the inscription of the covenant on the body politic of all Israel. Marc Angell, the late Eliezer Berkovits, Saul Berman, and Blu Greenberg all rate highly as Jewish thinkers. The ultra-Orthodox (*haredi*) world has its own intellectual discussions, which, regrettably, lie beyond the present author's competence.

FEMINISM

Feminism is the single most important creative force in American Judaism today.[25] Any survey of Jewish thought, therefore, ought to address feminism not only as it influences activity within the organized movements of Judaism, new venues of spiritual seeking, and the attraction to syncretistic and alternatives religious expressions but also as a critique and a force on its own. Jewish feminism has transformed all aspects of American Jewish life (see Pamela Nadell's article in this volume).

To narrow my task, I will address the impact of feminism on American Judaism only, not the far larger category of the impact of feminism on American Jewish life at large. Moreover, I will not attempt to discuss the role that gender analysis plays in Jewish academic life.[26] Suffice it to say that gender, like socioeconomic class, has becomes an indispensable tool of scholarship.

Within the landscape of American Judaism, feminism has changed the scenery most dramatically. By the mid-1990s, there were 254 ordained female rabbis in the United States; according to Yale University's Paula Hyman, that number has now passed 400.[27] In counseling and pastoral positions, in Hillel foundations on college and university campuses, and in educational roles, the impact of female rabbis is at least as great as in the pulpit. There are over two hundred female cantors. The ubiquity of *batei* mitzvah ceremonies in three of the four branches of American Judaism—a practice innovated in 1922 by Mordecai Kaplan but largely dormant until the 1970s—has created a generation of Jewish youth whose passage into adulthood is marked in gender-equal terms. In Reform Judaism the counting of women in prayer quorums (*minyanim*), distribution of Torah honors (*aliyot*), Torah reading, delivery of sermons (*divrei torah*), and inclusion in choirs prevails. As the vestiges of classical reform disappear and give way to more participatory services, the prominence of women on the *bima* (the dais where officiants stand) can only increase. Conservative synagogues are still debating some of these issues, but the direction of these debates points toward Reform, not Orthodox, Judaism. Retrospectively, it seems almost quaint that in the nineteenth century liberal congregations debated the appropriateness of seating males and females together. The *mechitzah* (divider), or women's gallery, is found today only in Orthodox congregations. In brief, the *bima* has become an egalitarian site in liberal Judaism. On the *bima* Reform rabbis, male and female, wear the traditional Jewish regalia. In the aisles, too, male and female laity have returned to the donning of *kipot* (head coverings) and *tallitot* (prayer shawls). This return to ritual melds tradition with gender egalitarianism—a quintessentially postmodern development.

The gender revolution in Judaism finds dramatic expression in synagogue changes, but occurs along a much broader front. Formal Jewish education has been equalized, providing women for the first time in Jewish history with access to the sources of Judaism and training in the skills needed to employ those sources. Second, adult education thrived in the last 25 years as in no other period in American Jewry's 350-year history. Testifying to this development are a plethora of programs (Melton, Meah, Elder Hostels), evening classes at universities and seminaries, and the evolution of Hebrew teachers' colleges into centers of adult Jewish education. Jewish women, naturally, are well represented in all these domains. In traditional Judaism the adult male was more familiar with the elite, written texts of the tradition (even learned females often had even more learned husbands and/or fathers). In contemporary Judaism this is no longer the case. The

Jewish mother or grandmother always played an enormous role in conveying Jew-ishness mimetically—this role has now been expanded to the intellectual appre-ciation of Judaism.

That women's roles in Judaism have been transformed in the last generation is beyond dispute, yet feminist thought varies greatly. Differences of upbringing, or-ganizational affiliation, formative training, and intellectual proclivities play a large role in shaping the vision of the Jewish future. A crucial distinction may be made between an *egalitarian* Judaism and a *feminist* Judaism. As Judith Plaskow, a professor at Manhattan College, explained in her seminal essay, "The Right Question Is Theological":

> The Jewish woman's movement of the past decade has been and remains a civil-rights movement rather than a movement for women's liberation. It has been a movement concerned with the images and status of women in Jew-ish religious and communal life, and with halakhic and institutional change. It has been less concerned with analysis of the origins and bases of women's oppression that render change necessary. It has focused on getting women a new piece of the Jewish pie; it has not wanted to bake a new one![28]

Writing a few years later, Plaskow reaffirmed her sense "that while the non-Orthodox community has been willing to accept egalitarianism, it has for the most part, not been willing to confront the deeper issues of liturgical change that emerge from a commitment to exploring women's experiences and perspectives." *Egalitarian Judaism* signifies a Judaism in which men and women are entitled to play an equal role. *Feminist Judaism* denotes a Judaism that not only removes gender-based discrimination but that has also been rethought along the lines of a feminist critique. As Susannah Heschel puts it pungently, "Jewish feminism is not about equality with men. Why should we women want to define ourselves by imi-tating male Jewishness?"

To be sure, women needed a civil rights movement. The gains made in equalizing the status of men and women are crucial: in the case of rabbinic leadership and Jewish education these advances toward egalitarian Judaism are a necessary prerequisite to developing a feminist Judaism. The liberal move-ments were pressured to admit women to the rabbinate and to the *bima* pre-cisely by the changed status of women in American society. A formally egalitarian ethos alone did not generate impetus for changing gender roles un-til the advent of second-stage feminism from the 1960s to the 1970s.[29] The dis-tinction between *egalitarian* and *feminist* goals may not be as sharp as Plaskow suggests. To borrow Plaskow's kitchen metaphor, any cook knows that changing the ingredients of a pie makes for a new pie. It is inevitable (and desirable) that women in traditional male roles—the rabbinate is a good example—cannot help but import female sensibilities and realities into their actions. An *egalitarian* Judaism, in which women fill roles traditionally filled by men without wanting to transform them, may not be a *feminist* Judaism, but it is already a changed Judaism.

What would qualify as examples of *feminist Judaism?* To begin with, women's prayer groups, *minyanim*, and study groups have proliferated across this country, in both liberal and Orthodox circles. Daughter-welcoming services (*shalom bat*), symbolic redemption services (*pidyon ha-bat*) have elevated the importance of the birth of girls—traditionally marked by little more than an honorable mention in synagogue. New Moon (*Rosh Hodesh*) festivals as well as festivals for a variety of life cycle events, many of which appropriate the practices of women in traditional Jewish society, have been reclaimed. Historians such as Chava Weissler have brought to light a wider world of female spirituality than had previously been assumed. Eastern Europe—that most *Jewish* of Jewish civilizations—saw a flowering of women's prayer books, Bibles, and moralizing literature. This literature was composed mainly by men and read mainly by women.

In addition to changes enacted by official Judaism—most strikingly the equalizing the patriarchs and matriarchs by adding the mothers (*emahot*) to the fathers (*avot*) in prayer books. Every year American Jewish women publish feminist Passover Haggadot, Jewish women's Bible commentaries, and modern *midrashim* that consciously put the female experience at the center of the story and thus strive for a *feminist* Judaism. I mentioned before that both men and women in liberal congregations wear *kipot* and *tallitot*. New ritual items, alongside multicolored and delicate *kipot* and *tallitot* often worn by women in synagogues, have created a minor revolution in ritual expression.[30]

Paradoxically, Orthodoxy's insistence on a gender-specific view of religious roles has led to a distinct upsurge of *feminist Judaism*. In place of the *bat mitzvah*, still prohibited by Orthodox law, twelve-year-old girls in modern Orthodox circles nowadays celebrate this life cycle event with Torah talks, festive meals (*seudot*), and, in some modern Orthodox congregations, female-only services. The inability of Orthodox women thus far to become rabbis, has not stopped the proliferation of Orthodox female professors, authors, rabbinic legal aids, etc. Most of these developments are direct responses to the challenge of egalitarianism in America— some are adaptations of Israeli practices, where Orthodoxy is the governmentally approved version of Judaism.

Possibly no topic displays fault lines between feminist thinkers as clearly as those of halakhah (loosely translated—Jewish law). As Rachel Adler explains:

> Whether gender justice is possible within halakhah and whether a feminist Judaism requires a halakhah at all are foundational questions for feminist Jewish theology that have no parallel in Christian feminist theology. A language for critique could not be borrowed from it. Appropriating the terms

and methods of halakhah itself, many feminists concluded, drew them into a game they could not win. In its infancy, Reform Judaism had embarked on a critique of halakhah, but it had simply abandoned this project, so offered few resources for feminist critique. Halakhah became the elephant in the living room. Everyone agreed it was in the way, and no one knew how to get rid of it.[31]

Those who would render halakhah more egalitarian would include such traditionally minded feminists as Cynthia Ozick and Blu Greenberg as well as such maverick Orthodox thinkers as Avi Weiss and the late Eliezer Berkovits. The majority of feminists, however, find this approach inadequate. In an essay published in Susannah Heschel's *On Being a Jewish Feminist* (1983), Judith Plaskow chided Cynthia Ozick and Rachel Adler for presuming that gender inequality in Judaism could be addressed by a recipe of "add women and stir." An *egalitarian* Judaism, in which women participate equally but leave the forms of Judaism unchanged, responds inadequately to a situation where Jewish women have always been players, but in a ballpark built by men. Plaskow correctly identified these issues as theological and challenged the feminist theologian to redefine the three basic terms of Judaism: God, Torah, and Israel.

In *Standing Again at Sinai* (1990), the first classic of Jewish feminist theology, Plaskow responded to her own challenge. Plaskow's discussion of Torah dramatically begins with Exodus 19:15, in which Moshe warns the people: "Be ready for the third day; do not go near a woman." At the critical moment of receiving the Torah, "the people" includes only the men—the women are excluded from the covenant, treated as a possible source of contamination, and silenced. While the words are those of Moses, not God, and while rabbinic tradition itself attempts to correct the absence of women, the Torah's exclusion of women at this crucial juncture is reenacted every year. "The Bible [writes Plaskow] focuses on war, government and the cult, all male spheres."[32]

Plaskow acknowledges that women have made Jewish history as much as men, but the texts of Judaism do not reflect this. The texts were written by men, about men, and for men. In Plaskow's view, the resulting Jewish memory "defines Jewish women out of the Jewish past." The creation of a repaired Jewish memory that includes the world of female experiences must be constructed. Since 1990 feminist historiography has blossomed; a work such as Judith Baskin's edited volume *Jewish Women in Historical Perspective* simply could not have been written twenty years ago. "Historiographical research is crucial to a new understanding of Torah because it helps recover women's religious experiences and relativizes the Torah we have." Yet Plaskow is undoubtedly correct that other forms of expression beside historiography will be needed to extend the borders of Jewish memory to include the female experience.[33] For Plaskow, creative midrash and new liturgies must forge a new Jewish memory.

Plaskow's projected feminist transformation of Torah hangs a major question mark over the role of halakhah. From a feminist perspective, Plaskow identifies three tiers of problems. First, the content of many of the halakhot (family purity laws, ritual worship, Talmud Torah, marriage and divorce) are simply unjust. Second, the fundamental otherness of women is presumed by the halakhah. The Talmud has tractates called "women" and "menstrual purity" but none called "men" or "masturbation." Women are obviously the exception to the norm, defined as the male. Plaskow raises an even broader question: "is law a female form?" Her carefully wrought answer is ambivalent: "Any halakhah that is part of a feminist Judaism would have to look very different from halakhah as it has been. It would be different in not just in its specifics but in its fundamentals. It would begin with the assumption of women's equality and humanity and legislate only on that basis." As Plaskow describes it, a feminist halakah is so unlikely, unnecessary, and artificial that it is difficult to see why any feminist would undertake the task of its reconstruction. But this conclusion largely reflects Plaskow's background as a Reform Jew for whom halakhah has never held as large a place in the definition of Torah, as a liberal who is uncomfortable with the very issue of compulsion implicit in halakhah, and as something of a gender essentialist who accepts the incompatibility of law as a female mode of discourse too uncritically.

In contrast to Plaskow, Rachel Adler is an observant Jew by inclination who lived in an Orthodox community and was married to an Orthodox rabbi. By dint of her rejection of gender-specific Judaism, she is now a liberal Jew by ideology and a professor at HUC-JIR Los Angeles. Adler's 1973 essay "The Jew Who Wasn't There" represents a pointed rejection of an apologetic approach that relied on a "story-oriented" attempt to hold up a few exceptional women as a shield against a critique of the ways in which ordinary women have been excluded. Adler correctly noted that, with respect to women, *aggadah* (lore) treats exceptions; halakhah establishes the norms, and at the injustices of halakhah Adler concentrated her fire. Yet, given the heat of her critique, her postscript was remarkably tepid: "The sort of *piskei halakhah* [legal corrections] requested in the text of this article are genuine decisions based on sources and understanding of the halakhic process made by people who understand and observe the Torah. Rationalizations will not do."[34]

It became clear to Adler that *piskei halakhah*, legal corrections, did not adequately address the following problems: Is halakhah hopelessly enmeshed in a gendered approach? Is halakhah a fundamentally flawed medium for a feminist approach to religion? Does the halakhic process itself, not just specific halakhot, require serious revision? Do "understanding and observance" of the Torah transcend an Orthodox monopoly? Adler's meliorist solution collapsed under the weight of these questions.

Yet Adler ultimately drew different conclusions from Plaskow regarding halakhah. Like the Hebrew poet Chaim Nachman Bialik, who portrayed a lawless

Judaism as prescription for chaos, Adler agrees that a Judaism that is all *aggadah* cannot stand—it must have a communal praxis. In *Engendering Judaism*, published a full quarter-century after "The Jew Who Wasn't There," Adler describes a third way between apologetic and rejection:

> [We must] exercise our own covenantal authority to redefine and refashion halakhah fundamentally so that contemporary Jewish women and men can live it out with integrity. Yet, if we define halakhah not as a closed system of obsolete and unjust rules, but as a way for communities of Jews to generate their Jewish moral visions, that is exactly what we would do.[35]

Adler provides a theoretical underpinning for this project in a chapter titled "Here Comes Skotsl" (Skotsl is a clever heroine in Yiddish folklore). Adler acknowledges that premodern praxis has become incompatible with our postindustrial, democratic, pluralistic, inclusive values. Relying on the legal scholar Robert Cover's insistence that all law relies on an agreed-upon master narrative, we must literally talk our way into the tradition so that we are finally able to inhabit "a single nomos as partners and friends." Thus Adler's view of halakhah includes a healthy dose of aggadah, as we tell our stories in order to change the axioms of halakhah and create a proactive halakhah able to create new forms of Jewish life that capture what Adler calls "our moral visions." Adler's own contribution in this endeavor—an ingenious egalitarian wedding ceremony, which she calls *brit ahuvim* ("a lovers' covenant")—has yet to catch on as a new Jewish custom, but, given the innovative path of American Judaism in the last twenty years, it may. Adler is well aware that belief in the divine underpinnings of halakhah has been abandoned by most liberal Jews, and the Jewish community no longer has the power to compel obedience. Without an attempt a *jurigenesis*, the creation of an engendered praxis in which all committed Jews can partake, Adler sees little hope of avoiding communal anomie. Plaskow and Adler share a vision of *feminist* Judaism, but their visions are not identical, and on at least one major issue—halakhah—in tension.

MODERN JEWISH BIBLE SCHOLARSHIP

"Modern" Bible study connotes the freedom of scholars to challenge the antiquity, authorship, and authority of Scripture. It also implies that academic practitioners will be free from the biases of denominational traditions of Bible-reading: Jewish, Christian, or Muslim. "Jewish" Bible study has been a millennial endeavor, but one conducted mainly in Hebrew, within a Jewish sociological context, and with very different hermeneutic goals than the secular academy. So a thorny question emerges: can Bible scholarship be both modern and Jewish? In practice there are many Jews in the academy who meet the highest professional standards, but also exhibit tendencies resulting from a Jewish education and eth-noreligious background and thereby to cultivate an approach recognized as Jewish by the academy and the marketplace. I will highlight four facets of this emerging field: its apologetic nature, its use of traditional Jewish exegesis, its insistence on the pluriformity of biblical texts, and its commitment to the priority of the redacted text.

An apologetic spirit animates modern Jewish Bible scholarship. In large measure this is a response to the Protestant biases that dominated the field for two centuries. The Jewish Theological Seminary's leader, Solomon Schechter, went so far as to claim that the very purpose of modern Bible scholarship was to deprive Jews of their claim to greatness and challenge their legacy to general civilization.[36] Kaufmann Kohler accepted the methods of the modernist "Higher Critics," who divided the Bible into different authorial sources, but shared Schechter's view that their findings were tainted by antisemitism.[37] Kohler's tenure as president of Hebrew Union College, the Reform movement's seminary, opened the door to critical Bible scholarship, but the subject long remained sequestered from the rank and file.

When the impulse for a Jewish Bible scholarship resumed after the Second World War and the Holocaust, Jews continued their predecessors' battle with the prejudicial scholarship of earlier generations.[38] In *Understanding Genesis* (1966) Nahum Sarna of Brandeis University wrote,

> We have constantly emphasized in this book the importance of difference, and have been at pains to delineate those areas in which Israel parted company with its neighbors. . . . The old mythological motifs were not slavishly borrowed; there is no question here of uncreative imitation. Sometimes, in fact, those [Ancient Near Eastern] motifs seem to have been deliberately used to empty them of their polytheistic content.[39]

Sarna submerges the composite nature of Creation and Flood narratives by expounding the message of the redacted text, contrasting it at every point with Ancient Near Eastern analogues. Even Richard Friedman's popular updating of the source critical method, *Who Wrote the Bible?* concludes, "In a very real way, the Bible is greater than the individuals who wrote it," and "The question is, after all, not only who wrote the Bible, but who reads it." Friedman promises that honest dialogue with the biblical text need not paralyze the reader.[40]

Jon Levenson (Harvard Divinity School) has analyzed the Protestant nature of Old Testament theology and staked out grounds for a Jewish response.[41] In *Sinai and Zion* Levenson wrote that it seems as if Protestant Bible scholars have been looking for new ways to caricature Jewish legalism and to repeat Jesus's curse on the temple.[42] This book's title aptly signals the author's intention to defend the Sinai/law and the Zion/temple as unfairly maligned high points in Ancient

Israelite religion. His work exemplifies the sympathetic treatment accorded to legal and ritual materials once denigrated by Bible scholars. Schechter wanted the
Christian scholarly world to leave Judaism alone. The current generation has a
more ambitious agenda, seeking a fairer appraisal of Judaism. This challenge has
largely succeeded.[43]

Modern biblical scholarship implies a dramatic break with traditional Jewish
approaches to the Bible. How, then, does the modern Jewish Bible scholar relate
to the vast corpus of commentary created by prior generations? In Professor Adele
Berlin's judgment, modern Jewish academicians initially shied away from traditional exegesis, which "made no pretense of being academically objective and religiously neutral."[44] Recently, however, scholars have found the reading skills of
the rabbis useful and its lack of putative "neutrality" less bothersome. The *JPS
Torah Commentary*, which juxtaposes traditional and contemporary scholarship,
offers the lay reader two approaches to the Bible largely sequestered from each
other just a generation ago—a fine example of constructing a *modern Jewish* approach to Torah.

Addressing the interpretive fecundity of Second Temple Judaism, Michael
Fishbane asks:

> Where did all this come from? What preceded the exegetical methods of
> Yose ben Yoezer and Nahum of Gimzo and all their congeners? Jewish tra-
> dition has one answer, modern scholarship suggests another. . . . Neither
> answer seems particularly wrong, nor particularly right. Is it possible that
> the origins of the Jewish exegetical tradition are native and ancient?[45] (*Bib-
> lical Interpretation in Ancient Israel*, 1979)

Fishbane thoroughly proves the point that a diverse, native, and ancient tradition of interpretation existed in Ancient Israel. Implicitly, then, the contemporary
scholar stands in an analogous relationship to the Bible, as did the rabbinic sages.
For Fishbane the biblical texts themselves enjoy a dynamic, interpretative relationship. Fishbane rejects the Protestant quest for the pristine text, refuses to
privilege the original *traditum* over against the subsequent *traditio*. In antiquity
and today, meaning emerges in the encounter between the received tradition and
the interpreter.[46]

The Jewish insistence on textual pluriformity has been fueled by the Protestant quest for a biblical-theological keystone. In *Creation and the Persistence of
Evil* Jon Levenson forwards a theology of human coresponsibility with God, relying heavily on the claim that Genesis 1 does not exhaust the biblical view of creation.[47] Contrary to the impression given by that majestic opening, the Bible is
full of images of God's striving to neutralize, subdue, and channel the forces of
evil. Israel aids God in this necessary divine-human task. In Ancient Israel sacrificial service in the tabernacle and the temple was the principal medium; in the

present the medium of Sabbath observance. Levenson draws a complex picture of creation from material embedded in the Psalter and Wisdom literature, two genres often ignored by Protestant theologians.

Pluriformity in the biblical text implies multiple voices. In *Countertraditions in the Bible* Ilana Pardes rejects Phyllis Trible's famous reading of Genesis 2–3, which insists that centuries of expositors read male superiority into an egalitarian, if not a feminist, text.[48] Drawing on postmodern narrative theory, Pardes hears several contending voices in the biblical texts. Although acknowledging her debt to Mieke Bal, Pardes criticizes Bal's attempt to read the Bible like any other text. Pardes unsympathetically cites Bal's claim, "It [the Bible's message] can be an issue only for those who attribute moral, religious or political authority to these texts, which is precisely the opposite of what I am interested in."[49] Pardes thus carves out a middle ground between Trible's Protestant insistence on finding an unambiguous teaching and Bal's dismissal of the Bible as a text worthy of veneration.

Pardes challenges the traditional Christian "ending" of the Eden cycle, to which Bal also succumbs. Pardes rereads the story in light of Eve's naming speeches in Genesis 3–4. The careful scrutiny of baby-naming formulae, and the awareness that the traditional weekly Torah portion (*parsha*) does not break at Genesis 3 but rather at Genesis 6:8, all constitute elements in her reading that may be considered typically Jewish. The traditional rabbinic interests in genealogy, family dynamics, and procreation—lesser themes in Christian tradition—have not been slavishly adopted; they have been leavened by the application of modern critical perspectives such as gender studies.[50] Pardes takes Eve's role as procreator and hence as cocreator with God seriously, but does not fall into the trap of taking the text as a whole as feminist or gender neutral. Jewish interpreters find "countertraditions" within the Bible they can live with, rather than abandon the canon altogether. The Bible as well as the Talmud preserve minority opinions—you just have to look harder.[51]

Beginning with the German-born Erich Auerbach, many Jews have used a literary approach to tease out meaning in the biblical text. Robert Alter, Meir Sternberg, and Robert Polzin insist that the Bible expresses its religious value through its literary artistry. Alter's ideology includes an apotheosis of "R," a reducing of the existential distance between reader and text, and a dismissive attitude toward the value of reading the component pieces on their own. "Thus, in Speiser's commentary it is not Jacob and Esau, but E, J, and P who become the subject of investigation. In this way the text is held at a distance for inspection, and any voice that might speak from its imagined situation to our actual one is in effect suppressed."[52] Alter, Sternberg, and Polzin reject a scholarly tradition which presumes the more atomistic, the more scientific.

Contemporary Jewish Bible scholarship is more than the application of traditional perspectives in a new context: the enterprise is a significant theological development. Postmodernity has validated the integration of communal commitments, traditional perspectives, and modern methods. That has afforded Jews—only recently welcomed into the secular academy as equals—an opportunity to shape the way in which the Bible is read within the academy and beyond it. The figures mentioned above serve a dual role: as practitioners of their craft and as contributors to a particularistic Jewish attempt to continue to relate to Torah on a plane both spiritually meaningful and intellectual honest. Commentary has long been a primary form of Jewish thought. The attractiveness of the Bible—and midrash—as a point of departure for Jewish reflection may be evidenced not only in figures discussed above but also in the emergence of a school of "textual reasoning," still in its infancy.[53]

The flowering of Jewish Bible scholarship and Jewish feminism invites a brief revisiting of my preference for *thought* over *theology* as a descriptive term. Since Levenson's seminal essay, "Why Jews Are Not Interested in Biblical Theology" (1986), Jewish Bible theology has advanced in Israel and the United States, including such names as Tikvah Frymer Kensky, Marc Brettler, Moshe Goshen-Gottstein, and Moshe Greenberg. Similarly, Plaskow's *Standing Again at Sinai* marked the first synthetic program of Jewish feminism, transcending piecemeal calls for legal, social, and ritual reform. Works by Ellen Umansky, Ellen Frankel, Rita Gross, Laura Levitt, Blu Greenberg, Lori Lefkowitz, Rita Gross, and many others, have considerably furthered the goals enunciated by Plaskow and Adler. Since the above-named figures evidence philosophic rigor and hold prestigious university postings, perhaps theology is the correct term, especially as both disciplines (Jewish feminism and modern Jewish Bible study) emerged in response to universal rather than particularistic Jewish stimuli? That argument notwithstanding, the reader should also bear in mind the influence antisemitism played in accelerating both these disciplines, the identity politics of consciously formulating a Jewish perspective, and the role of the Jewish community (from seminary to synagogue) in translating intellectual innovation into lay praxis and belief. In sum, if the university provides the natural home for the practitioners of these two disciplines, the germinating impulses and arenas of activism of Jewish Bible scholars and Jewish feminists alike are located outside the safety of ivory towers. Once again, it seems to this author that the usual understanding of the term *theology* is not nearly broad enough to encompass these emerging disciplines.

SECULAR, SYNCRETISTIC AND POSTDENOMINATIONAL JUDAISM

The breakdown of traditional Jewish life and the acculturation of Jews into the dominant ideologies of Europe led to widely variegated range of religious beliefs and practices. The breakdown of traditional Jewish life, without a concomitant

abandonment of Jewish identity, also led to secular alternatives to Judaism. Socialism, Zionism, and psychoanalysis substituted for traditional Judaism—with Judaism and Jewishness playing varied roles in each case. America's economic
opportunities shortened the careers of several secular Jewish movements originat-
ing in eastern Europe (including socialist Zionism and a variety of Yiddishist
groups). But figures such as Felix Adler, founder of ethical culture, Sherwin
Wine, founder of humanistic Judaism, and even Mordecai Kaplan (a theist to be
sure, but one who placed Jewish folkways at the center of his theology), displayed
the power of secular conceptions of Judaism. The splintering of religious Judaism
in the eighteenth and nineteenth centuries has been matched (in North America)
by a dissipation of ethnic Jewishness in the late twentieth and early twenty-first
centuries. It is also undeniable that the stability of Jewish identity without religious underpinnings has been challenged by life in a free society. Notwithstanding the emergence of a new spirituality (below), proponents of secular Judaism
have not disappeared. David Ivry, Judith Seid, and Alan Dershowitz have all articulated Jewish agendas with religion either at the periphery or nowhere to be
found.

Another quintessentially modern and American phenomenon is the range
of religions being practiced that combine Judaism and some other system. The
dictionary defines syncretism as "the merging of different religions or religious
traditions, or the absorption of foreign elements into a particular religion. The
term is often employed negatively to refer to the contamination of one religion by
another." Jewish syncretism has accelerated in the openness of the American religious landscape. Who would have anticipated twenty-five years ago that
non-Western religions would not only claim many Jewish adherents but actually
owe much to Jews for bringing it to the wider public? Yet this has happened in the
case of American Buddhism and Hinduism, which number Bernard Glassman,
Baba Ram Dass (né Richard Alpert), Jonathan Omer-Man, and others as its leading spokespersons.[54] At least for Western-born Buddhists (the immigrant Buddhist
community has had little impact on American religious practices), Jews have
played a prominent role. In a strange recapitulation of the end of the nineteenth
century, when figures like Martin Buber embraced Eastern religion as a path to
greater spirituality, the counterculture of the 1960s—itself another site of surro-
gate and syncretistic Jewishness—fueled much of the contemporary interest in
Buddhism. Far from demanding the denial of Jewishness (or Judaism), typical of
medieval confrontations with Christianity and Islam, Eastern religions invite an
acceptance of one's own background as a pathway to individual enlightenment.

Whatever one may think of JUBUs (Jewish Buddhists) or messianic Jews (the
self-designation of Jews for Jesus), their emergence must be reckoned as a surprise
story in modern American Judaism. Judging by the success of popular works
such as Rodger Kamenetz's *The Jew in the Lotus* and *Stalking Elijah*, the exploration of one's own faith through that of others is very attractive. As Generations X

and Y come to maturity, still other permutations seem likely.[55] Should the reader think my appraisal of secular and syncretistic Judaism has descended entirely into the world of "pop" culture, and has no echo among "serious" Jewish thinkers, I cite the following from a professor and former dean at Reconstructionist Rabbinical College:

> When [Arthur] Green suggests that the mystic's insights begins in silence he acknowledges that Judaizing them means giving them voice. Buddhist insight suggests a more powerful role for silence, in prayer and in action. . . .
>
> Our theological differences are vast. Nonetheless, I want room in my Judaism for a great variety of theological perspectives. I want room to explore the meaning of ancient Hebrew Goddess worship; to let its existence seep into my contemporary struggles with a masculine God. I want room for those who are secular to work out their theologies without reference to God.[56]

This position, as well as those carved out by Sandra Lubarsky's *Tolerance and Transformation*, goes beyond a call for interreligious dialogue. Some will think that Alpert and Lubarsky have overstepped the line of Jewish authenticity—others will not.[57] Certainly the erstwhile debate between opponents of religious dialogue (e.g., Soloveitchik) and proponents (e.g., David Novak) has ended, with reality casting the decisive vote. American Jews represent too integrated an element in American life to foreclose such dialogue: the questions are what such dialogue intends to accomplish and how may a Jewish thinker enter into such a dialogue without jeopardizing the integrity of Judaism. "Dabru Emet" ("Speak Truth"), a statement issued by the Institute for Christian and Jewish Studies and signed by many prominent figures, called for a reevaluation of Jewish attitudes toward Christianity. No one could deny that organized Christianity since the 1960s has struggled significantly with its anti-Jewish past. "Dabru Emet" nevertheless provoked considerable controversy within Jewish ranks—testimony to the sensitive history of Jewish-Christian relations, but also to Jewish anxiety about the blurring of boundaries limned above. All agree that a strong postdenominational streak exists within Judaism at present, perhaps best evidenced by the creation of consciously postdenominational rabbinic seminaries.

THE RANGE OF JEWISH SPIRITUALITY

No overview of contemporary Jewish thought would be complete without a glance at its spiritual ferment, clearly related to what some scholars have termed America's Third Great Awakening. In both the Christian and Jewish cases a renewed search for meaning in a relativistic era, a frustration with institutional religion, a quest for community, and a desire to self-actualize one's belief system have propelled this development. For Jews the spiritual quest has also been fueled by the ongoing revolt against the politics of assimilation. An early opponent of assimilation, the great historian-philosopher of Jewish mysticism, Gershom Scholem, devoted his scholarly career to arguing the centrality and richness of the mystical tradition. His students and detractors have played an important role in raising Jewish mysticism from a somewhat neglected area of Jewish studies to a centerpiece.

Mysticism, kabbalah study, and meditation have won many adherents within the Jewish and gentile world. Kabbalah, which started out as an esoteric tradition studied only by a Jewish elite, has become, arguably, the most attractive Jewish material outside the Bible. The success of kabbalah centers, the popularity of red wristbands (a Jewish mystical practice), and Hebrew tatoos may be offered as a case in point. Although the public face of this development is at times faddish, the underlying desire for meaningful and authentic Jewish spirituality impulse has found serious expression.

Arthur Green, author of a slew of important works (e.g., *Devotion and Commandment, Tormented Master,* and *Seek My Face, Speak My Name*), continues the tradition of Martin Buber and Abraham Joshua Heschel as a translator of Hasidic pietism into forms comprehensible to an audience that did not grow up in observant or religious homes. Green combines top-notch academic credentials with a long history of institutional leadership, including the presidency of Reconstructionist Rabbinical College. A professor at Brandeis University, Green is also the dean of Boston Hebrew College's nondenominational rabbinical school. Green's rejection of denominational and disciplinary borders strikes a deep chord, as does his determination to trace his intellectual patrimony back to the eastern European pietists (Abraham Joshua Heschel, Abraham Isaac Kook, Judah Loeb Alter of Ger) rather than the western European rationalists. As Green explained in a widely cited essay, "New Directions in Jewish Theology in America," this latter group emphasizes intuition, inwardness, experience, depth and creation theologies. For Green "prayer is the bridge between the abstract notion of divine speech and the use of human words to speak of God. . . . Theology is dependent upon prayer."[58]

Rabbi Zalman Schachter-Shalomi has had an eclectic career as a university professor, organizer of some of the more important Jewish renewal groups, rebbe (rabbi-mentor) to scores of students whom he has also ordained, and prolific author of *Paradigm Shift, Wrapped in a Holy Flame, From Age-ing to Sage-ing,* and many more. Polish-born and Vienna-educated, Schachter-Shalomi hails from Belzer Hasidim but was trained and ordained by Lubavitch Hasidism. Schachter-Shalomi (known by his disciples and admirers as Reb Zalman) speaks of a paradigm shift in the post-Holocaust era comparable to those of the destruction of the

First and Second Temples. But, rather than embracing an insular Judaism as a response to the Holocaust, Schachter-Shalomi propounds a form of Jewish renewal with emphasis on integrating a love for the diversity of the world, acknowledging the technological nature of contemporary times, and retaining the maximum of spiritual traditions that makes meaning out of this complex. Schachter-Shalomi has used the term *Gaian* as shorthand for the new paradigm. In his pan-universalism and postdenominationalism, though not his mysticism, Schachter-Shalomi resembles the first modern Jewish thinker—Benedict (Baruch) Spinoza.

Lawrence Kushner also carries on the Buberian task of translating Jewish mysticism (especially Hasidism) for acculturated Jews. A product of the Reform movement, Kushner stands worlds away from classical, liberal thought as expounded by somebody like Eugene Borowitz. Beginning in the mid-1970s, Kushner authored a slew of deceptively simple books that unfold the mystical tradition. In *Eyes Remade for Wonder*, Kushner uses the Hebrew alphabet as the prompt for a series of forays, often autobiographical, into the world of the spirit.[59] Green, Schachter-Shalomi, Kushner are only three names of many serious thinkers (including Arthur Waskow, David Wolpe, David Ariel) who seek to restore spirituality to its rightful place in Jewish life. The desire for a spiritual Judaism seems only to increase as those Jews who have committed to reclaim a meaningful Jewish identity find the contemporary alternatives either inadequate (secular Jewishness, increased communal involvement, formal participation in synagogue life) or peripheral to their deepest motivations. As in the cases of feminism and modern Bible scholarship, the new spirituality seems to be at the beginning of its attempted rejuvenation of the Jewish world.

American Jewish thought is indeed wide-ranging and diverse. There seems to be general agreement that the temper of the times discourages systematic Jewish theology, as does the premium placed on individual response and a modesty wholly appropriate to living after the Holocaust. The organized movements remain important sites of translating ideas into practice, but, unlike a century ago, much Jewish thought also takes place in the university. This development has the advantage of greater ideological independence and disciplinary sophistication. If specialized vocabularies and intellectual parochialism at times render academic discussions remote from Jewish laypeople, there appears to be no shortage of rabbis and other teachers to translate the language of the academy into more popular idioms.

It may be true that there have been no replacements for the giants of Jewish thought, from the eighteenth through the early twentieth century. Nevertheless, standing on the shoulders of giants does yield valuable vantage points. Eugene Borowitz's covenantal theology has preserved the dialogical elements of Buber while supporting a Buberian weakness: balancing individual autonomy and communal commitments. Arthur Green, Lawrence Kushner, and Zalman Schachter-Shalomi have furthered the Hasidic-inspired depth theology of Heschel and succeeded in forwarding the dimensions of prayer, mitzvah, meditation, and movement as idioms of Jewish worship. Neil Gilman has continued the Conservative tradition of Catholic Israel and extended the democratic implications of that doctrine in an accessible North American idiom. Norman Lamm may not possess Rav Soloveitchik's towering presence (no Jew does), but exceeds the Rav in political engagement and a willingness to publicly argue for Orthodoxy's commitment to the entire Jewish people. Feminism, a truly revolutionary advance, is still in its youth, and the same may be said about contemporary Jewish biblical studies. In short, contemporary Jewish thought in America represents an area of considerable Jewish creativity, albeit one generally underestimated by experts and laypeople alike.

NOTES

1. The two major genres of classical rabbinic literature are law (*halakhah*) and lore (*aggadah*), not statements of creed, as in the Christian tradition. Whether literal, philosophical, or mystical, commentary, rather than systematic theology, was the principal mode of Jewish expression. Nevertheless, all of the above genres are chock-full of theological views: my avoidance of the term Jewish theology is based on other grounds, explained below.

2. Arnold Eisen, "Jewish Theology in North America: Notes on Two Decades," *American Jewish Yearbook* 91 (1991): 3–33.

3. David Ellenson, "The Continued Renewal of North American Theology," *Journal of Reform Judaism* 38 (Winter 1991): 1–16.

4. On assessing the scope of contemporary Jewish theology, see the comments by Elliot Dorff and Louis Newman, eds., in *Contemporary Jewish Theology: A Reader* (New York, 1999), 1–6.

5. An adequate discussion of post-Holocaust theology is beyond the scope of this essay. Among the more important post-Holocaust theologians are Richard Rubenstein, Emil Fackenheim, Eliezer Berkovits, and Ignaz Maybaum. For a solid overview, see Michael Morgan, *Beyond Auschwitz: Post-Holocaust Jewish Thought in America* (New York, 2001).

6. Whether the Holocaust constitutes a *novum*, a new and unique historical-theological datum, is the subject of considerable discussion. See Steven Katz, *The Holocaust in Historical Context* (New York, 1994); Alan Rosenbaum, *Is the Holocaust Unique? Perspectives on Comparative Genocide* (Boulder, 1996). Eliezer Berkovits, *Faith After the Holocaust*, while agreeing that the Holocaust discredits Western Christendom's claims to progressively increasing humanity, asserts that the problem of human evil in a divinely ordained world (theodicy) has not changed since the first human beings.

7. Emil Fackenheim, *God's Presence in History* (New York, 1970), 85ff.

8. Scholars employ a variety of terms (e.g., *denomination, branch, sector, movement*) to describe the various religious streams of American Judaism.

9. The figure 46 percent for current synagogue membership comes from the National Jewish Population Survey 2000. No doubt, the percentage over the course of the entire life span would be much higher. Arguably, then, the synagogue remains the single most important institution in American Jewish life.

10. On creative religious impulses from within, see Jonathan D. Sarna, *American Judaism in Historical Perspective*, Beilin Lectures 10 (Ann Arbor, 2003).

11. Jack Wertheimer, *A People Divided: Judaism in Contemporary America* (New York, 1993), 93–113.

12. For a deft summary of classical Reform Judaism, see Marc Lee Raphael, *Judaism in America* (New York, 1999), 65–66.

13. Michael Meyer, *Response to Modernity. The Reform Movement in Judaism* (New York, 1988) offers the authoritative portrait of the European and American models of Reform Judaism and their interrelationship.

14. Eugene Borowitz, *Choices in Modern Jewish Thought* (New York, 1983), 288–89, represents an early articulation of covenental theology.

15. "We must begin with something that has not happened; this negative something is the strongest and, potentially, most significant religious reality among American Jews: it is that the Jews have not stopped being Jews." Nathan Glazer, *American Judaism*, 2d ed. (Chicago, 1972), 141.

16. The shift in nomenclature from Zecharias Frankel's *positive-historic Judaism* to Schechter's *Conservative Judaism* took place during Schechter's tenure as head of Jewish Theological Seminary. For the earlier American roots of Conservative Judaism see Moshe Davis, *The Emergence of Conservative Judaism. The Historical School* (Philadelphia, 1963).

17. I am referring to such simple matters as the wearing of head covering and prayer shawls, the use of Hebrew, and the choreography of prayer. Much of this has to do with nostalgic longing and filiopietism rather than ideology—standing for the silent *Amidah* prayer, for instance, had little to do with belief in the content of the eighteen benedictions of that prayer, but much to do with the fact that grandpa stood up at this point in the service.

18. Joseph Soloveitchik (1903–1993), the leading figure in American Orthodoxy for roughly four decades (1940s–1980s), began to exert influence on non-Orthodox Jews with the appearance of his works in English, e.g., *The Lonely Man of Faith* (1964) and *Halakhic Man* (1944, but in English translation 1983).

19. Neil Gilman, *Sacred Fragments: Recovering Theology for the Modern Jew* (Philadelphia, 1990), 278.

20. Ibid., xxiv–xxv.

21. Consistent with the articulation of "Emet v'Emunah: Statement of Principles of Conservative Judaism" (1988), Gilman considers several views of revelation legitimate for the modern Jew.

22. Isaac Klein's *A Guide to Jewish Religious Practice* (New York, 1979), may be described as a Conservative *Shulchan Aruch* (the normative Orthodox law code), as

revised with reference to the demands of modernity, for instance the Conservative decision to permit driving on Shabbat, but only to synagogue.

23. Neil Gilman, *The Death of Death* (Woodstock, VT, 1997) and *The Way Into Encountering God in Judaism* (Woodstock, VT, 2000).

24. Lamm has authored numerous studies on a wide variety of topics including studies of Hasidism and the Lithuanian yeshivot, Jewish marriage, the *Sh'ma* (the primary affirmation of God's sovereignty and a centerpiece of Jewish worship services), and Jewish ethics in a democratic society.

25. Susannah Heschel, "Feminism," writes, "In a sense, the feminist challenge to Judaism today can be compared in magnitude to other major crises in Judaism such as the destruction of the Jerusalem Temple, which necessitated a shift from sacrificial to liturgical worship." In Steven Katz, ed., *Frontiers of Jewish Thought* (Washington, DC, 1992), 65.

26. See Lynn Davidman and Shelly Tenenbaum, eds., *Feminist Perspectives on Jewish Studies* (New Haven, 1994).

27. Paula Hyman, "Jewish Feminism Faces the American Women's Movement," *Frankel Lectures* 6 (Ann Arbor, 1997), 1.

28. Judith Plaskow, "The Right Question Is Theological," in Susannah Heschel, *On Being a Jewish Feminist* (New York, 1983), 223–32.

29. On the development of Jewish feminist thought since the 1970s, see Heschel, *On Being a Jewish Feminist*; Davidman and Tenenbaum, *Feminist Perspectives on Jewish Studies*; Ellen Umansky, "Jewish Feminist Theology," in Eugene Borowitz, *Choices in Modern Jewish Thought*, 2d ed. (West Orange, NJ, 1995); Laura Levitt and Miriam Peskowitz, eds., *Judaism Since Gender* (New York, 1997).

30. Novel ritual items inspired by feminism would include *kos miryam* (miryam's cup), *tapuz devorah* (Deborah's orange on seder plates).

31. Rachel Adler, *Engendering Judaism: An Inclusive Theology and Ethics* (Boston, 1998), xx.

32. Judith Plaskow, *Standing Again at Sinai: Judaism from a Feminist Perspective* (San Francisco, 1990), 20.

33. Plaskow's distinction between history and memory relies heavily on Yosef Yerushalmi's *Zakhor. Jewish History and Jewish Memory* (New York, 1989).

34. Rachel Adler, "The Jew Who Wasn't There," in Heschel, *On Being a Jewish Feminist*, 17.

35. Adler, *Engendering Judaism*, 21.

36. Solomon Schechter, "Higher Criticism-Higher Antisemitism," in *Seminary Addresses and Other Papers* (New York, 1959), 35–39.

37. Kaufmann Kohler, "The Attitude of Christian Scholars Toward Jewish Literature," in *Studies, Addresses and Personal Papers* (New York, 1931).

38. Nahum Sarna, *Exploring Exodus* (New York, 1986) devotes many pages arguing the basic historicity of the Exodus, using the tools of archaeology, and the findings of the Egyptologists. Sarna's *JPS Torah Commentary Genesis-Exodus* reiterates many of his earlier themes: "The present commentary is primarily concerned with the completed edifice and only to a minor extent with the building blocks. It is not based on a coroner's approach, that is, on dissecting a literary corpse," xvi.

39. Sarna, *Understanding Genesis* (New York, 1966), xvii–xviii. The claim that "difference" is more telling than "similarity" may also be found in Joseph Hertz's *The Pentateuch and Haftorahs: Hebrew Text, English Translation and Commentary* (London, 1961), 194, 197, 498, and in the works of earlier scholars such as Abraham Geiger, Heinrich Graetz, and Yehezkel Kaufmann.

40. Friedman contends that each strand of authorship represents a legitimate "take" on reality—the multiple truths to be found in the text and in reality help explain how the Bible has communicated meaning across the generations.

41. Jon D. Levenson, "Why Jews Are Not Interested in Biblical Theology," *Judaic Perspectives on Ancient Israel* (Philadelphia, 1987), 281–307, "The Hebrew Bible, The Old Testament, and Historical Criticism," in *The Future of Biblical Studies* (Atlanta, 1987). Other significant contributors to a Jewish biblical theology would include the late Moshe Goshen Gottstein, Moshe Greenberg, Marc Brettler, Tikva Frymer-Kensky, and Michael Fishbane.

42. Levenson's discussion of the relationship between Jeremiah 7 and Psalm 50 seems driven by his awareness that Protestant theologians took their cues from Israel's own prophets. *Sinai and Zion* (San Francisco, 1985), 165–69, 206–9. On legal and cultic aspects of the Hebrew Bible, the works of Jacob Milgrom, Baruch Levine, and Menachem Haran deserve special mention.

43. To see the impact of a Jewish critique on academic presentations of the Bible by non-Jews, one may: 1. compare the way in which Ezra and Judaism in general is discussed in the first and fourth editions of Bernhard Anderson's standard *Introduction to Old Testament* (Englewood, 1986 [1957]); 2. glance at Alice Bach's introductory comments in *Women in the Bible* (New York, 1999); 3. look at the authors and subjects of the recent New English Bible (NEB) Study Edition. To fully explicate the issue of Jewish influence on modern Bible scholarship would require a separate essay.

44. Adele Berlin, "On the Use of Traditional Jewish Exegesis in the Modern Literary Study of the Bible," in *Tehillah le-Moshe* (Winona Lake, IN, 1997), 173–83.

45. Michael Fishbane, *Biblical Interpretation in Ancient Israel* (Philadelphia, 1979), 19.

46. James Kugel (review of) Michael Fishbane, *Biblical Interpretation in Ancient Israel*, in *Prooftexts* 7 (1987): 269–305.

47. Jon D. Levenson, *Creation and the Persistence of Evil* (San Francisco, 1988).

48. See Nancy Fuchs-Kreimer, "Feminism and Scriptural Interpretation," *Journal of Ecumenical Studies* 20 (1983): 540.

49. Mieke Bal, *Lethal Love* (Bloomington, 1987). See Pardes's discussion of Bal in *Countertraditions in the Bible* (Cambridge, 1992), 26–33.

50. Devora Steinmetz, *From Father to Son* (Louisville, 1991); Naomi Steinberg, *Kinship and Marriage* (Minneapolis, 1993).

51. Ilana Pardes, *Countertraditions in the Bible* (Cambridge, 1992), passim.

52. Robert Alter, *World of Biblical Literature* (New York, 1991), 206.

53. See Peter Ochs, "B'nei Ezra: An Introduction to Textual Reasoning," in Dorff and Newman, *Contemporary Jewish Theology*, 502–14.

54. On Hinduism, see Barbara Holdrege, *Veda and Torah: Transcending the Textuality of Scripture* (Albany, 1996); Hananya Goodman, ed., *Between Jerusalem and Benares*

(Albany, 1994). On Buddhism, see Jacob Teshima, *Zen Buddhism and Hasidism: A Comparative Study* (Latham, MD, 1995).

55. See, for instance, Lisa Schiffman, *Generation J* (San Francisco, 1999).

56. Rebecca Alpert, "Another Perspective on Theological Directions for the Jewish Future," in Dorff and Newman, *Contemporary Jewish Theology*, 495, 497.

57. "Dabru Emet" generated considerable response, some of it critical.

58. Arthur Green, "New Directions in Jewish Theology in America," in Dorff and Newman, *Contemporary Jewish Theology*, 489.

59. Lawrence Kushner, *Honey from the Rock* (San Francisco, 1977); *Eyes Remade for Wonder* (Woodstock, VT, 1998).

18

THERE'S NO SPACE LIKE HOME

The Representation of Jewish American Life in Abraham Cahan,
Anzia Yezierska, Philip Roth, and Cynthia Ozick

LINDA S. RAPHAEL

To understand a culture, one must study its literature. There one finds the cultural memory that pertains to a particular people at a particular time in a particular place and that relates to the world as human beings have always related to the world, in terms of their passions.[1] The passions that philosophers have studied since ancient times find vivid expression in the Hebrew Bible and are abundantly evident in Jewish writing since those ancient days. As in antiquity, when the problem of "Jewish" identity first emerged, there has always been some difficulty in identifying the people. No one doubts that American Jews live in a particular place; however, there is nothing so obvious about who or what are the "Jewish people" in America, especially when one chooses to assign writers and readers to the group.

For example, Mark Shechner opens his excellent comprehensive 1979 essay in *The Harvard Guide to Contemporary American Writing*[2] with a slight disclaimer: It is difficult to "be cogent" about Jewish American writing "at a time when a coherent and identifiable Jewish culture and religion have effectively ceased to exist except in special enclaves" (191). He puts forward several ideas that have influenced the definition of Jewish literature: "Neither 'Jewish writer' nor 'Jewish fiction' is an obvious or self-justifying subdivision of literature, any more than Jewishness itself is now a self-evident cultural identity. . . . 'Jewish fiction' and 'the Jewish novel' are not 'useful as literary categories . . . or national catchalls . . . [however] they do merit a place in social history'" (191). In the years following Shechner's analysis, the explosion of ethnic studies in American academies has motivated an upsurge in the academic study of Jewish American literature. With this phenomenon has come an easy assumption that Jewish American literature is a cohesive subgenre, if not "entirely obvious" or "self-justifying."

Shechner gives a historical context to the category, however, by asserting that three conditions influenced those who became models for later Jewish writers: 1. "the traditional way of life that stressed the rigorous spiritual authority of the Bible, the oral authority of an extensive legal and ethical code, contained in the Talmud and its commentaries," 2. "the democracy of learning," and 3. "successive waves of Hassidic enthusiasm, Enlightenment liberalism, Zionism, trade unionism, and socialism . . . that undermin[ed] the traditional way of stoic pietism, stir[ring] Jews to revolt" (193). Bonnie K. Lyons adds to this account in an essay on Jewish American literature from 1930–1945: "Being Jewish means being part of a chosen people with a sense of uniqueness, purpose, and calling."[3]

In a recent large anthology of the genre, *Jewish American Literature*, the editors assert that "Jewish American" is a better choice than "American Jewish" as it is in keeping with "Mexican American literature," "African American literature," "Asian American literature," and "Native American literature." The group name is subordinated to "American," suggesting that it is the American-ness of the literature that is primary. As the editors note, the identity of the other groups is based on place and nationhood. Taking that fact as a starting point, the editors press further with questions about what is meant by "Jewish people."[4] The issues that concern them are essential in nature. However, because they are the same ones dealt with in many of the essays in this collection, I will not rehearse all the relevant matters. For purposes of this essay, a work is considered to be Jewish American literature if the author was born into a Jewish family or converted to Judaism and if the work concerns Jews in America. Literature written by authors who were born into a Jewish family or who converted to Judaism but have not written about Jewish life is not Jewish American literature, according to these criteria; rather, such works suggest the broad interest of Jews who live and write in America, as they indicate the wide variety in styles and subject matter expressed in the writing of both self-identified and nominally Jewish writers. These works are better placed in American literature than Jewish American literature; to impose on the works of someone born in a Jewish family who does not identify with the Jewish people or someone who does identify as a Jew but does not write about Jews is a move that tends to make the category Jewish American literature too broad and perhaps meaningless.

Philip Roth, in defending his fiction against charges of antisemitism, has made several significant contributions to a definition of Jewish American literature. In a 1960 interview he explained, "the story ["Defender of the Faith"] is by no means about the Jews. It's about individuals who happen to be Jewish."[5] When asked about his caustic representations of Jewish suburban life, he responded, "I can't deny I have feelings of anger and censure as a human being and a Jew although I would say this is not particularly a Jewish problem, but an American problem" (2). These early responses to questions about his fiction support Roth's continuing assertions that he writes about Jews because that is what he knows. Such a claim—that that is all they know—would not be true for some writers who happen to be Jewish. While Roth's explanations may appear to be simple, and in some sense are, they go very deep in terms of what it means to write fiction about a particular group—and they put limits on what we as readers can or should expect. They are not, after all, historians, theologians, or sociologists. Like all serious writers, they are people with a moral conscience and a powerful imagination—influenced in some ways by being Jews.

While the mood in contemporary literary theory is particularly hospitable to the concept of ethnic writing as a significant category (in fact, some literary theorists as well as English department offerings have little interest in any categories that do not represent people "on the margins"), such was not always the case. As in many areas, Jews favored in literature a place among the mainstream of the American way of life. Shechner declares that the American writers who had gained the most attention at that time, Hawthorne, Poe, Emerson, Thoreau, and Whitman, developed styles and themes that would surely appeal to writers in revolution—from the profound representation of the inner life in Hawthorne, the short story and psychological thriller of Poe, the resistance against an anxiety of influence in Emerson, to the social rebellion of Thoreau, and the stylistic and social code breaking of Whitman.

In a consideration of ethnic literature, Thomas Friedman has asked, "What is American Literature if not regional literature, a narrow focus that broadens into a national vision?" Thus one may read Jewish American literature with an eye to what American literature is; that is, the regional and ethnic literatures are not on the margins, but they are what make American literature. Similarly, Diane Matza warns against trying to pin down an ethnic literature.[6] Yet, if we consider the American Jewish experience to be the experience of a culture, perhaps more than one culture, then we may find in Jewish American literature the particular memories of a group of people. While those whom we call members of this group are often only loosely connected to one another, in their literature may be discerned signs of those connections. They are connected by their feelings of insider/outsider, their ambivalence about their practice of religion, and their desire to live out the American dream.

PLACE AND SPACE

If one wanted to study the effects of place on a group of people, the Jews would be an ideal group to take up because they have lived in so many diverse places. Since the Middle Ages, Jews have been lucky, or most times unlucky, according to their place of birth. The luckiest Jews, at least until the establishment of the state of Israel, have been the Jews of America. The freedom to worship was never contested, and the vestiges of antisemitism, expressed nationally in immigration restrictions and university quotas in the first half of the century, all but disappeared by the mid-twentieth century (when Jews became "white folks").[7] Within a half-century of the arrival of the greatest number of Jewish immigrants to the country, Jews were gaining admission to elite universities, entering professions, establishing businesses, and figuring as prominent members on the political and cultural landscape.

Nonetheless, one can read in place and space representations of the difficulties Jews have faced in America, difficulties not always different from those of non-Jews who were living in America for a century or more or from other immigrant or ethnic groups. American literature in general has frequently depicted America as a place of unlimited space—the frontiers figure prominently, whether they are geographic or intellectual. At the same time, American literature challenges the dearly held belief that the possibilities for success in America are limitless.

Just as William Dean Howells used the conventions of literary realism to create fictional depictions of New England middle-class life, so early twentieth-century Jewish immigrant writers found the conventions of the genre compatible with the representation of Jewish families in America. However, neither critics nor readers always thought of *representation*, with the many nuances of what we mean when we say that something is re-presented in an artistic form. American realism, building on the psychologically profound fiction of great American writers such as Nathaniel Hawthorne and Henry James, and the socially provocative novel *Huckleberry Finn*, provided late nineteenth- and early twentieth-century Jewish American writers with a tradition they incorporated into the Yiddish culture they brought with them. When naturalism and social determinism appeared on the literary scene in the works of Stephen Crane, Kate Chopin, Theodore Dreiser, and, later, Edith Wharton, there developed an even greater natural affinity between immigrants and literary forms. One might argue that the presence of an increasing number of immigrants in America stimulated the forms—Jacob Riis photographed the physical conditions common to immigrant life, and writers recreated similar circumstances in fiction. Although such an absolute belief in the "truth" of representation has not defined the sole response to realism, it has been only in the last few decades that the "truth" of representation and the differing positions from which readers approach texts have become matters central to thinking about fiction

The significance of place in fictional representations cannot be overstated. No matter how universal the theme of a work of fiction, its setting is particular (unlike many poems and essays, for example). Even a writer such as Henry James who set much of his fiction in England and Europe, and who took up permanent residence in the former, was overwhelmingly interested in revealing aspects of American character in the foreign settings he chose. He discovered angles from which to view the significance of place—how Americans developed certain characteristics in their own place—and then acted them out in other locations, England or Europe. Thus even an American writer who set his stories elsewhere testified to the significance of place (America as the place where character was developed, England and Europe the places where the American character is tested and revealed).

Whereas *place* in this essay refers to the location of a work (America in general and a specific location in the country in particular), *space* refers to the precise setting of scenes, including the physical space itself and the characters who inhabit that space. Jewish American writers have not followed Henry James's example in terms of leaving America to write about it, but they have brought the experiences—the traditions, the fears, and even the horrors—of other places to their writing. Representations of Jewish American life in literature suggest that place, the nations where Jews formerly lived as well as their American homeland, and space, the homes, workplaces, and meeting places of Jews and their non-Jewish compatriots, have varying and complex significance in Jewish life. The Jewish American texts discussed in this chapter take America as their location; they follow a common, though not absolute, tendency of fictional works to center on the domestic space.

Abraham Cahan's novella *Yekl* (1893) exemplifies a fiction writer's use of domestic relations to exemplify conflicts in immigrant Jewish American life. Cahan employs the home both metaphorically and realistically in this story of Yekl, the immigrant antihero who mistakes American assimilation for happiness. However, when the translation of the novel from Yiddish to English made it possible for Cahan's work to be taken up by the non-Jewish literary community (Howells in particular), it was regarded as a work only about life in America.[8] The predisposition to take fictional representations as "real" hardly led readers or critics to deconstruct the text. The comments of one critic, who compared *Yekl* to Crane's *Maggie, a Girl of the Streets* in 1896 (*Pittsburgh Bulletin*), imply the straightforward analysis to which Cahan's work might be subjected:

> There is much that is painful in his [Cahan's] story, as there is much that is dreadful in Mr. Crane's work, but both of these writers persuade us that they have told the truth, and that as such conditions have made the people they deal with, we see their people. If we have any quarrel with the result, we cannot blame the authors, who have done their duty as artists and for the moment have drawn aside the thick veil of ignorance which parts the comfortable few from the uncomfortable many in their city . . . . Mr. Cahan, without being less serious than [Mr. Crane] is essentially humorous.[9]

Indeed, many humorous incidents flavor the novel. In the opening page of the novel Jake delivers the following exposition to his fellow Jewish immigrant employees in the cloak shop:

> When I was in Boston, he went on, with a contemptuous mien intended for the *American metropolis, I knew a feller,* so he was a *preticly* friend of John Shullivan's. He is a Christian, that feller is, and yet the two of us lived like brothers. May I be unable to move from this spot if we did not. How, then, would you have it? Like here, in New York, where the Jews are a lot of greenhornsh and can not speak a word of English? Over there every Jew speaks English like a stream.[10]

Another amusing incident that is characteristic of the humor in the novel, while at the same time revealing Yekl's antipathy toward Gitl as a symbol of the Old World, occurs when Yekl criticizes his wife for saying "fentzer": "Can't ya say veenda?" Yekl demands.[11] Although *Yekl* testifies to Cahan's wit, the novel is scarcely only humorous. The author's commitment to verisimilitude in terms of the plight of a transnational Jew could not have been expressed without a sense of the tragic aspects of human character.

However, the truth *Yekl* conveys may be far more complex than early critics believed. Recently the critic Matthew Frye Jacobson, for example, shed light on the complexity of place in *Yekl* in terms of authorial intention and reader response:

> *Yekl* in Yiddish is engaged in transnational debates regarding the essence of Jewish character, its basis, nature, and its possibilities. Debates occasioned by a complex of crises known at the time as the Jewish question, the historic convergence in the 1890s of horrific pogroms in the east, to which Jews were vulnerable because they had not assimilated at all and antisemitic uprisings around the Dreyfus affair in the West to which Jews were so vulnerable because they had not assimilated so thoroughly raised questions about Jews' collective destiny.[12]

The "transnational debates" to which Jacobson refers are engaged by the immigrant couple in their domestic space.

Jake, as he is called by American friends, first arrived on American soil in Boston. As his diatribe quoted above indicates, he had not felt himself to be as enclosed there with other Jews, in a ghetto atmosphere, as he does in the present narrative time, in New York City. In Boston he had been interested in the great American pastime, sports, but in New York he has taken up dancing because, in the isolating ghetto community, he finds few English speakers with whom to enjoy his interest. As a sports enthusiast, he was able to keep his domestic life in place—sports did not challenge his loyalty to Gitl and Yossele, to whom he sent regular payments from which Gitl would be able to save enough to make the trip to America. The New York ghetto life kept him far more separate from English speakers; thus his interest in sports waned, and he took up the nonverbal social activity that brought him into the company of women, specifically one woman, Mamie. Ironically, when he spoke English, "broken" though his is, more frequently, he was mentally loyal to Gitl and Yossele; when he returned to a Yiddish-speaking community, he grew more distant (of course, time accounted for his disaffection as well). This complex interplay of language and culture articulates the tension between the immigrant's experience of success—at the minimal but significant level of language—and his fears of failure. When he feels good about his progress in American society, he can hold his domestic life in an imagined positive place; when he identifies himself as a "greenhorn," they become a primary reminder of his "otherness." As part of a "charming tale" that he is "neither willing to banish from his memory nor able to reconcile with the actualities of his American present,"[13] Jake's family brings to his mind and heart a painful ambivalence.

As soon as the anxious greenhorn catches a glimpse of his small family, who have just completed their tedious journey across the Atlantic, "his heart sinks at his wife's uncouth and un-American appearance" (28). Yekl's vicious attitude toward Gitl finds many outlets, which the narrator presents from both his and her viewpoints:

> His presence terrified her, and at the same time it melted her soul in a fire, torturing yet sweet, which impelled her at one moment to throw herself upon him and scratch out his eyes, and at another to prostrate herself at his feet and kiss them in a flood of tears.
>
> Jake, on the other hand, eyed Gitl quite frequently, with a kind of malicious curiosity. Her general Americanized make up, and, above all, that broad-brimmed, rather fussy, hat of hers, nettled him. It seemed to defy him, and as if devised for that express purpose. Every time she and her adviser caught his eye, a feeling of devouring hate for both would rise in his heart. He was panting to see his son; and, while he was thoroughly alive to the impossibility of making a child the witness of a divorce scene between father and mother, yet, in his fury, he interpreted their failure to bring Joey with them as another piece of malice. (64)

The presentation of consciousness exemplified here—both Yekl's and Gitl's—attests to Cahan's interest in giving voice to both sides of the assimilation question. As Jacobson puts it, Yekl embodies the "racialized view of immutable yiddishkayt that has a second dimension."[14] This other dimension, the distinction between masculinity and femininity, finds expression in Gitl's fears concerning her husband's insistence that she look and behave like an American woman. One might guess that Yekl would have been pleased that Gitl took advice from another woman as she tries to accommodate his desires. Yet what he desires is to have more control over his environment. Gitl's makeup and hat and her adviser nettle him because they further his tendency to objectify her—to see her metonymically (the hat and makeup equal the person) and to use condensation (her adviser equals Gitl). In this way he creates what is for him an enabling psychodrama. The space of the home substitutes for the world outside.

When Gitl's attempts to Americanize in her own way trigger Yekl's rejection, it is evident that he cannot negotiate with Gitl or with the New World. Rather, his insecurity favors total immersion. Gitl's attachment to identifying markers (wearing a wig, for example) make it easier for him to fall into Mamie's arms, since her easy ways and apparent success in America not only take him from the marriage bed but also release him from the traditions that he regards as the only obstacles to his success. Yet, when Yekl and Gitl divorce, neither one experiences immediate happiness:

> If he could now have seen Gitl in her paroxysm of anguish, his heart would perhaps have swelled with a sense of his triumph, and Mamie would have appeared to him the embodiment of his future happiness. Instead of this he beheld her, Bernstein, Yoselé, and Mrs. Kavarsky celebrating their victory and bandying jokes at his expense. Their future seemed bright with joy, while his own loomed dark and impenetrable. What if he should now dash into Gitl's apartments and, declaring his authority as husband, father, and lord of the house, fiercely eject the strangers, take Yoselé in his arms, and sternly command Gitl to mind her household duties? (68)

Ultimately, the novel figures the home ambivalently—a space where one longs to find acceptance and support, but where one must offer it in order to find it. The frustrated immigrant, no longer at home with old ways or assured in new customs or language, cannot proffer the love he does not feel. The "violent lurch" that describes both the streetcar's movement and Yekl's "heart"(68), forming the final image of the novel, places Yekl outside the home, connected to an uncaring outside world. Both a part of the naturalist novel and the transnational representation of Jewish life, *Yekl* articulates anguish in domestic life that challenges the nostalgic viewpoint from which individuals and groups sometimes regard the past.

Anzia Yezierska provides an equally complex view of home as place in *The Bread Givers*. Sara Smolinsky, the first-person narrator, has five sisters, who, along with their mother, endure mistreatment at the hands of the father and husband, Reb Smolinsky. Trained in Jewish religious thought and observance, he rightly thinks of himself in one sense as an accomplished man. Nonetheless, he is constantly frustrated by his powerlessness in New York, where Talmudic learning cannot compete with business acumen. His struggle against his increasingly negative self-image and anger exacerbate his frustration because he has nothing to fight against except his family, who might have offered him solace if he were not so rigid in his traditional behavior. He tyrannizes his wife—whom he calls "Woman"—and daughters and sometimes his neighbors. Sara comments: "Of course we all knew that if God had given Mother a son, Father would have permitted a man child to share with him his best room in the house. A boy could say prayers after father's death. God didn't listen to women" (9). Yezierska's novel is unabashedly feminist, although the ending compromises the strong feminist tone—perhaps because this is a work of realism.

Like Jane Austen's Mr. Bennett, Reb Smolinsky has many daughters to see married. Rich sons-in-law would not only secure his daughters' futures, but would bring him honor by association. His doggedness results in unhappy situations—he does not gain wealth or prestige through his daughters' marriages, and they do not find the satisfaction they might have had he not denied them even a shred of autonomy.

First, Reb Smolinsky, attached to the wages the admirable and gentle Bessie earns, demands that her prospective fiancé, Berel Bernstein, pay for the wedding and set him up in business. Mr. Bernstein, willing to forgo a dowry, finds this reprehensible, but still desires to marry Bessie, who will not go to him without her father's consent. Next Mashah falls in love with a piano player, Jacob Novak; although his family is wealthy, Reb Smolinsky's disapproves of his profession. He tricks Jacob into staying away from his home, but Jacob figures out the deception and returns to beg Mashah's forgiveness. When he plays the piano, Reb Smolinsky demands that he leave their home because he has played on the Sabbath. Fania's suitor, Morris Lipkin, is a poor poet and hardly stands a chance with Reb Smolinsky, who succeeds in humiliating him enough that he gives up his claims on Fania. Having successfully ended three romances, Reb Smolinsky sets about arranging three marriages, each of which causes misery.

Although her father's actions infuriate Sara, she cannot influence him for the better. However, the author creates an event that punishes him: he takes the money he received from Bessie's marriage to buy a grocery store that has been stocked with fake goods. Reb Smolinsky is both tyrannical and foolish. The reader surely gives a sigh of relief when Sara leaves her home in both a literal and figurative sense. She would have lived with either Bessie or Mashah, but neither enjoys the sort of domestic tranquillity that would welcome a guest. Sara avoids reliving the scenes of her father's tyranny in her sisters' homes by renting a small dirty room for which she pays with her earnings at a laundry. In the evenings Sara takes classes and studies. While Sara imitates her father's commitment to learning, she may have derived strength from her mother's devotion. In a touching scene Mrs. Smolinsky comes to take care of Sara when she learns that her daughter is ill. Bringing food and comfort, she symbolizes the fulfillment of domestic love. The most positive scene of domestic support in the novel occurs in a small rented room.

Yet working and studying present such great challenges for Sara that she almost capitulates to her father's values by accepting the attention of the acquisitive Max Goldstein. When she recognizes his money-oriented interests, she rejects him, an act that causes her father, upon hearing of it, to disown her. The imaginary place that she has inherited from him, the place of learning, provides her with enough stimulation to continue her efforts to earn a college degree, despite the lack of material or emotional support. For Reb Smolinsky, the value of learning functions as a place—he continues the tradition of Jews in which not land but learning creates a people. Thus, while Reb Smolinsky's learning ties him to the lands where Jews have lived and written in the past, Sara's learning earns her a place in America. Orthodox Jewish women, who do not partake of the commandments for learning, traditionally have made learning possible and meaningful for men. This significant though subordinate role, demonstrated in *Yekl* in Gitl's relationship with Bernstein, is not specifically shown in *The Bread Givers* because Reb Smolinsky devalues his wife and daughters. However, without them he has nothing: in the context of this subordination of the women and elevation of the self, he finds his identity.

The intricate domestic dynamics that result from the nexus of orthodox Jewish custom and assimilation return to the novel when Sara, having achieved her dream of becoming a teacher, meets Hugo Seelig, a Jew, who is principal of the school where she teaches. While the narrative emphasizes the conflict between a woman's desire for autonomy and her aspirations to marry, it simultaneously creates a longing for a positive love relationship amidst all the failed engagements and unhappy marriages. Hugo Seelig incorporates American success and the possibility of continuing Jewish learning without the trappings of immigrant status. On first meeting Sara, Hugo corrects her speech—putting his hands on her throat in a potentially erotic move, he instructs her on how to move her throat to pronounce a word. In a novel in which the first-person narrator occasionally uses nonstandard English, the emphasis on correct pronunciation is slightly ironic. Yet this is only one way that language functions as an indicator of hierarchical or insider/outsider relations.[15]

One evening, after Sara and Hugo have become engaged, they come upon Sara's father on the street. He has turned into an almost unrecognizable beggar now that her mother is dead and he has divorced a second wife, who would not tolerate his abusive ways. Sara embraces her father, who is in no position to refuse her offer of a renewed relationship. He and Hugo develop a rapport based on Hugo's desire to learn Hebrew. While Sara is not as fine an English speaker as Hugo, she will be left out completely when he learns Hebrew because Hebrew is a language only for men. Yiddish, which women speak, is not Sara's language, nor will it be the language of Jewish American women in the years that follow Yezierska's writing. Jewish learning would continue for a long time to be the province of Jewish males, as it is of Hugo and Reb Smolinsky. The males will be connected through this ancient language to the Jewish people and to the many places they have lived, while Jewish women would, in decreasing numbers, keep a "Jewish home" by following food laws and domestic rituals of the Sabbath and holy days. Because Sara will not be the one learning Hebrew, she may remain subordinate in some sense—in her home—just as she has been subordinate to Hugo outside the home.

The home serves in one respect as the place where the lives of immigrants' daughters pay a high price for being female. Their father denies them the learning he values, he pushes them into undesirable marriages and fails to offer comfort or help when his actions wreak havoc on their lives. However, the daughters do return to their mother at various times—when she dies, they are reunited briefly in the home. The hierarchy established in the home by the commitment to the learning transmitted through Hebrew language paradoxically supports the hierarchies of male/female that women faced in America, while the commitment to this ancient language and its traditions sometimes creates estrangement from the world outside. The home validates the outside world as it keeps it out.

The "cost" of success for Jake in *Yekl: A Tale of the New York Ghetto*, as well as for Sara in *The Bread Givers*, introduces a theme that will dominate Jewish writing in twentieth-century America. Philip Roth has explored the terms of success in his fiction with increasing sophistication, and perhaps pessimism, over the years. His fictional accounts of Jewish life begin at just about the time Jews become "white folks." That is, Jews are no longer counted as a distinct minority group, nor are Italians. They are put into the white category when American politics and culture instantiate the critical distinction between blacks and all other Americans. The eponymous story in the collection *Goodbye, Columbus* registers the entry of large numbers of Jews into upper-middle-class American life while it scrutinizes the distinctions between the newly rich Jews and their less fortunate coreligionists. In a 1959 review William Peden noted, "there is blood here and vigor, love and hate, irony and compassion."[16] Indeed, these characteristics of fiction define Roth's entire oeuvre.

In *Goodbye, Columbus*, a novella in which the incredible number and acuity of realistic details alone give a stunning picture of mid-fifties middle- and upper-middle-class Jewish life in New Jersey, the home is the site of both the niggling mannerisms of the previous generation and the dissolution of family relations due to geographical mobility. Neil Klugman's parents have moved to Phoenix, leaving him to the care of his Aunt Gladys and Uncle Max; that is, Neil has graduated from college and is working as a librarian, but either his income or custom places him in his relatives' modest home, where their habits come from a world that is not unknown but still distinctly foreign to Neil. His aunt coaxes him to eat food he does not enjoy, while in his girlfriend Brenda Patimkin's home he finds food temptations not only at the table but kept in surplus amounts in the basement. Unaccustomed to the phantasmagoric selection of delicacies with which the basement refrigerator is stocked, Neil stuffs his pockets with cherries from the bushels he discovers. At the same time, he is aware of the Patimkins' ample liquor supply— a variety and quantity unknown in most Jewish American homes.

Place—in the form of his aunt and uncle's home—signifies what Neil wants to give up or transcend: the mediocrity and stagnation of the average Jewish working-class life. Yet he is as disconcerted by the Patimkins' markers of affluence as he is attracted to the newness. As he drives out of Newark to the cool breezes of Short Hills, a suburb Aunt Gladys says no "real Jews" live in (41), Neil imagines Aunt Gladys and Uncle Max "sharing a Mounds Bar in the cindery darkness of their alley, on beach chairs, each cool breeze sweet to them as the promise of afterlife" (6).[17] His nostalgia for a life he simultaneously rejects offers a glimpse into what becomes a more common phenomenon, especially in the later part of the century when Jewish Americans, in acknowledging the devastating consequences of the Holocaust, long for a European life many never knew or romanticized before.

Neil's encounters with a young black boy who frequents the library to study a book of Gauguin paintings symbolize the longing Neil ambivalently shares with the boy to transcend his present place for more exotic and beautiful landscapes. One day a man asks Neil to find this same book for him. Neil tells the man that the book is checked out so that the boy will not be disappointed when he comes to read it. When the man returns another time, Neil decides that the better plan would be for the boy to check out the book. The boy, barely understanding what that would entail, finally tells Neil that if he took the book to his home it would be destroyed. Neil, as obtuse about the boy's circumstances as the Patimkins are about his own, suggests that he keep the book hidden in a desk at his home. The boy's home would be no more receptive to the Gauguin book than is Neil's home to the idea of the Patimkins' home. The scenes with the African American youth obviously register racially based differences in American life, but the Patimkins' lifestyle as compared to Neil's Newark existence discloses more subtle class distinctions that inform Jewish society in America.

Roth portrays the Patimkins with great wit and insight into Jewish American life. Mrs. Patimkin pays attention to whether a Jew is Orthodox, Conservative, or Reform (though she says "reformed"), declares her allegiance to Jewish institutions—synagogues and women's organizations—and in one especially hilarious scene misunderstands Neil's question about whether she knows Martin Buber to be a question about a local resident: "Is he orthodox or conservative?" she asks. Mr. Patimkin, who owns Patimkin Kitchen and Bathroom Sinks, does not score points for his intellect, according to his daughter Brenda, though he wins her affection. All the Patimkins are athletically inclined: Mrs. Patimkin had been an accomplished tennis player; Mr. Patimkin plays golf and coaches his younger daughter, Julie, in the sport. Ron, the oldest child, played sports at

Ohio State University and would apparently have liked to become a gym teacher. That desire is easily squelched as he is eased into a role at Patimkin Sink when he becomes engaged. Brenda has won many medals for horseback riding and is now a competitive tennis player and good swimmer. Sports are limited to the country club, though a lot of time at home is spent practicing a sport. Athletics are not a profession for the Patimkins or their social equals; rather the pursuit of the "good life" includes sports because they signal that one has leisure time and money. While blacks learned to play basketball in part because of two aspects of their circumstances, the lack of space in the urban setting and little money to spare made a sport that required only a small court and no equipment save a net a good choice, Americans who had physical space and money could play golf and tennis and could swim, ideally at country clubs. Restricted from membership at clubs all around the country, Jews built their own country clubs. As well as playing sports at the country club, the Patimkins finance a lavish wedding at the club, hire servants, and consume the best material goods American society has to offer.

The story of the Patimkin family has generally been read in terms of Neil's attraction and repulsion to it. In that story, and not outside of Neil's awareness, is the poignant story of Brenda. She is not only pivotal in the story in terms of what it means for someone like Neil Klugman to become involved with a rich and beautiful college-age woman, but in terms of what her place in the family reveals about American life through the lens of a Jewish family. It is not unusual that a fictional daughter marks the place where cultural ways are most glaringly revealed. Beginning with Lot's daughters, who are sacrificed by their father to men demanding sexual favors so that he might save his male guests, who otherwise would have been surrendered to the men, daughters are both loved and offered on the marketplace by their fathers. One after another, Jane Austen's novels retell the story of daughters who need to marry. Seldom do they have a mother to emulate or one who protects them; the marriages always seem enviable, but they serve the fathers' purposes as much as they fulfill the daughters' desires (this is glaringly obvious in the case of the daughters who are not the heroines of the novels). Henry James's fictional daughters are placed unabashedly by their fathers on the market, and, when they are unsuccessful, they rarely get pity from a father figure. Daughters are the site of political and psychological recklessness in much late twentieth-century fiction, including Roth's *American Pastoral*. Mrs. Patimkin expresses contempt for her daughter because, Brenda tells Neil, "She is jealous. It's so corny, I'm ashamed to say it" (19). Neil had already regarded her in a way that recalls Snow White's stepmother:

> I did not like Mrs. Patimkin, though she was surely the handsomest of all of us at the table. She was disastrously polite to me, and with her purple eyes, dark hair, and large persuasive frame, she gave me the feeling of some

captive beauty, some wild princess who has been tamed and made the servant to the king's daughter—who was Brenda. (15)

Brenda explains that her mother had "had the best back-hand in New Jersey" (18)
and that she, Brenda, has been intrigued by photographs in which her mother's
exceptional beauty is evident. When she mentions the photos to her mother and
suggests that they have one blown up so that she can have it at school, her mother
chastens her with the claim that they have better things to do with their money.
Money is an issue between the mother and daughter; Mrs. Patimkin chides
Brenda for shopping at Bonwit Teller, insisting that Orbach's is good enough.
Brenda considers her father to have barrels of money and can think of no reason
not to spend it. As Neil muses, Brenda's "life . . . consisted to a large part of cor-
nering the market on fabrics that felt soft to the skin" (18–19).

What is at stake is no less than the survival of each woman's identity—Mrs.
Patimkin's has already been painfully altered and Brenda's is in jeopardy of heading in the same downward direction. When Neil asks Brenda how she thinks her
sister Julie, ten years her junior, will fare, Brenda quips that she will probably do
better than herself. Julie, who was introduced in the narrative in the act of hitting
golf balls in the yard with her father, while, Neil conjectures, other children her
age are out playing with one another, represents the possibility that a female child
might not be sacrificed to the needs of the parents, but she functions more to
emphasize Brenda's already determined future. Brenda may be right, but she suggests at another point that in a few years Julie will be as despised by her mother as
Brenda.

Since Mrs. Patimkin is still beautiful, and since she can afford many luxuries,
and she could probably still play tennis, even if not at her youthful level, one wonders why she is jealous of her daughter. Roth has crafted the story too carefully for
her to be dismissed as simply a cantankerous woman. Several contradictions in
her attitudes and assertions lend insight into her character. Mrs. Patimkin considers herself to be Orthodox, while her husband is Conservative. Although she
keeps a kosher home, when she interrogates Neil one has the sense that her activities in Hadassah constitute the whole of her religious affiliation. In terms of her
values, according to Brenda, she acts as if the family still lives in Newark, but she
disapproves of Neil in part because he does in fact live in Newark and has a modest job. She has a maid, but she resents Brenda's failure to take part in any
housework. Mrs. Patimkin is ambivalent, ambivalent as a Jew and ambivalent as
an American woman. Although she tells Neil that Brenda had been an excellent
Hebrew School student and regrets her daughter's loss of interest in Judaism, she
apparently has offered only a kosher kitchen and her own membership in Hadassah as incentives toward Brenda's continuing religious study.

Mrs. Patimkin's day precedes the time when adult Jewish education began to
flourish all over the country, when women who had not had a bat mitzvah studied

and became adult b'nai mitzvah, and when women became presidents of synagogues, not just presidents of sisterhoods. Had she wanted to pursue a different life
in the secular world, Mrs. Patimkin would have had few opportunities for work
that suited a woman in the upper middle class. Some women may have wished for
different lives for their daughters, and those women may have had the where-
withal to steer their offspring in new directions. Such women rarely appear in
fiction; rather, female fictional protagonists are remarkably free of mothers. Mrs.
Patimkin offers a highly realistic insight into the place of Jewish women of the
1950s who enjoyed material and social ascent. They showcased the gains their
husband had made. Who would people the country clubs on weekdays, decorate
and maintain the increasingly lavish homes, or entertain guests, if not they? If
women's liberation had not arrived, neither had men's, and the husbands were
unlikely to find pleasure in domestic duties. Nor could the hardworking man advertise on his own the leisure that increasing incomes made possible. It was the
women, in high heels and skirts even in their homes, who made this new leisure
evident. Post–World War II society depended on the consumer wife, while new
notions of privacy in America provided a model for aspiring Jewish women.[18]

Brenda was probably right, and Roth therefore prophetic, as he has been in
other places,[19] when she predicted that Julie would be better off than she. During
the 1970s life changed for American middle-class women, and Jewish women,
who often held college degrees, entered the workforce, returned to universities to
graduate programs, went to professional schools, started businesses, kept their
maiden names, headed organizations—in numbers previously unknown and
seemingly unthought of. Why would Mrs. Patimkin not have considered Brenda
an ally in the world of women whose lives were constricted by the demands of
consumer culture? While Roth does not flesh out the reasons for Mrs. Patimkin's
aversion to Bonwit Teller and preference for the bargains found at Orbach's, the
narrative makes evident that she identifies herself in some ways with her old life in
Newark. Brenda exemplifies a rejection of a disappearing lifestyle her mother cannot recapture and has not replaced to her satisfaction. She has no advice to offer
Brenda on how to create a different sort of existence; at the same time, the manner in which Brenda mirrors the life she is now living repels her.

The disheartening relationship between Brenda and her mother helps to explain an odd passage in the narrative when Brenda tells Neil that her father had
shown her three hundred dollars he hid for her in the attic in case anything happened. The only things Brenda needs to be protected from are her mother's wrath
and her future as a woman just like her mother. The relationship between the
Patimkins is not fully developed; however, when Neil thinks that Mrs. Patimkin,
a "wild princess," has become the servant to the king's daughter, his thoughts suggest that Mrs. Patimkin has lost her place as first woman in the house. She no
longer exhibits the best backhand but now occupies herself with keeping the castle. Money won't protect Brenda from her mother's wrath, of course, and, once

Mr. Patimkin has given his daughters lessons in sports, he has nothing else to offer but money. The intersection of Jewish interests and the new abundance of American middle- and upper-middle-class life find expression in *Goodbye, Columbus*—with great humor—from the opening scene at a country club where rich Jews wile their time away to the lavish wedding of Brenda's brother, Ron.

Newark, New Jersey figures as well in Roth's *American Pastoral* (1998), a novel that, among other things, investigates the motivations and consequences of Jewish Americans' economic and social mobility with the insight of a writer who has developed an unflinching critique of American life in the second half of the twentieth century. The critic Timothy Parrish writes, "with his work in the 1990s it has become obvious that Roth—in Cynthia Ozick's words—'is being catapulted along a fascinating trajectory' which is culminating in an expression of Jewish identity that no one—not Irving Howe or Philip Roth—could have imagined thirty years ago."[20] It almost seems as if, once Roth's characters are let loose from the confines of their Jewish neighborhood in Newark, they are set on self-destructive paths. This is not to say that Newark offered an idyllic life in Roth's fiction, but that the economic and social achievements Americans make as they climb up an invisible ladder brings new risks. Along with various social and personal areas of angst, *Goodbye, Columbus* anticipates the father/daughter relationship in *American Pastoral*—a relationship that transgresses boundaries that did not come into play in the earlier work. The protagonist, Seymour Levov, known as the Swede because of his fair hair, complexion, and blue eyes, is haunted by the memory of the kiss that he and his eleven-year-old daughter shared on a hot summer day, the last of many days they had spent together in their beach cottage. "Daddy, kiss me the way you k-k-kiss umumumother"(89), Merry, who could not overcome her habitual stuttering, had requested. "Sun-drunk" from a morning playing in the sand and surf with Merry, the Swede had looked down and had seen "the red bee bite that was her nipple" (89). Perhaps in an effort to stifle an erotic response to what he saw, the Swede retorted with a brief but brutal, "N-n-no" and demanded that she fix her suit strap.

Yet, perhaps because he was as stunned as was Merry at his mimicry, the Swede signals both their potential erotic attachment to one another and the shame that this attachment and his criticism as well cause: "Just as he had decided that he and she could find their way back from their summer romance" (90), punctuated by occasions when Merry ran through the room with only a towel to fetch a dry swimsuit, yelling "Nobody look" (89) and walked in on him in the bathroom, "He lost his vaunted sense of proportion, drew her to him with one arm, and kissed her stammering mouth with the passion that she had been asking him for all month long while knowing only obscurely what she was asking for" (91). When Merry's life turns toward tragedy—she throws a bomb at the local post office, killing the town doctor as the act of a 1960s radical whose stuttering is symbolic of her inability to articulate, or probably to comprehend beyond an elementary level, the national problems that bring mayhem to that decade of American life—the Swede wonders, "What did he do to her that was so wrong? The kiss? That kiss? So beastly?"[21] Seymour's response recognizes one sort of transgression, but avoids the other, the boundary-crossing of a Jew into a gentile community where his daughter disrupts the tranquillity of the bucolic and homogeneous town with an assault that transcends the repressed violence that characterizes her home life.[22]

One of the remarkable things about the kiss and all that follows is that Roth presents this as a quintessential scene of Jewish American life. That is, the narrator, Zuckerman, "dreams" the life of the Swede, the older brother of his friend Jerry. The Swede was handsome, great at sports, and, not surprisingly, popular. Nathan Zuckerman had idolized him. In 1985, when the Swede was fifty-eight and Nathan fifty-three, they accidentally met at a Mets game. Ten years later the Swede wrote to Nathan asking him to meet to discuss a tribute he wanted to write in honor of his father, who had died the year before. Still intrigued by his youthful idol, Zuckerman met with him, but the matter of the tribute never came up. A few months later, Zuckerman encountered Jerry at their forty-fifth high school reunion and mentioned the meeting, only to be told the shocking news that the Swede had died.

Using some precise details about Seymour's life, Zuckerman recounts what "must have been" the life of the Swede, his wife, his daughter, and his parents. Just as the immigrant Lou Levov's great financial success as a glove manufacturer rehearses a common success story of Jewish immigrants in the mid-twentieth century, so Seymour's inheritance of the business and move away from Newark to a conspicuously non-Jewish area in the countryside of New Jersey and Jerry's success as a physician provide realistic images of Jewish American life in the second half of the twentieth century.

The middle-class Newark home where the Swede and Jerry grew up fails to provide a model that either son chooses to replicate exactly. Although Jerry does not play a central role in the novel, his flamboyant spending, boastful manner, and multiple divorces reflect in an exaggerated way a change in the demeanor of American physicians in the booming years of the second half of the century. Seymour's marriage is consistent with a new American trend as well—an increase in interfaith marriages. Thinking back to *Goodbye, Columbus*, one can construct some general ideas about the changing values that influence Jewish Americans. Taking the success of his father's business to new heights, Seymour uses his wealth and gentile wife, the former "Miss New Jersey" in the Miss America Pageant, to gain entry, if only on the margins, into the gentile world. Marshall Bruce Gentry claims that "the simplest of the major charges against Swede is that he accepts the injustices of capitalism."[23] Yet, as Sandra Kumamoto Stanley notes, "What the Swede never understands is how his pastoral vision of America could give birth to Merry's anger."[24] Both of these observations lend credence to the idea that daughters suffer at the hands of fathers who are driven by the dictates of success in a capitalist world. The Jew who envisions the pastoral world as a part of the American dream that is open to all and is founded on material accomplishments recalls Yekl and Reb Smolinsky as much as he evokes images of Horatio Alger or, alternatively, Jay Gatsby.

Seymour's father, Lou, decides to tolerate his son's marriage to a non-Jew if she declares that she does not believe in Christ. For Merry, matters are more difficult. Her parents' indecisive approach to religious affiliation leaves her to her own devices, which involve her in attaching herself first to the religion of one parent and then to the religion of the other. Her identity is further confused by her mother's beauty, which she has not inherited. The most significant and well-remembered accomplishment of her mother's life was becoming Miss New Jersey in 1949—an award that, though it had been won by one Jewish woman (Bess Myerson, in 1945), was hardly the province of Jewish females then or stuttering and overweight women at any time. When Merry expresses interest in Christianity, the material symbols work to threaten her Jewish grandparents. Since Merry cannot inherit what her mother had in the larger society, she might have welcomed support for what she could get from her father—Judaism. Seymour's parents are loving grandparents; the reader might fantasize a meaningful Jewish existence for Merry. However, Roth rarely creates situations that are enhanced by religious activity. Rather, he charts in the case of Merry the experience of perhaps many children, offspring of religiously unaffiliated intermarried couples, who want to have similar experiences to their friends. They may long for some religious life—perhaps only because children want to be like their friends as much as possible. In any case, whichever way Merry turns, she is thwarted. She embodies the anger that the youth of the 1960s expressed, although she cannot articulate her frustrations adequately. Her stuttering figures as a metaphor for her identity—a nonfluent American girl who cannot find a place where she can speak her piece.

The representation of the senior Levovs offers a nostalgic longing for a Jewish American life that could not be continued into the late twentieth century. Lou's satisfaction as an immigrant made good would have been all Yekl could have imagined; his success, however, sets a new bar for his sons. If American success concerned fewer socioeconomic expectations and more nonmaterial gains, Lou's sons would have found plenty to work toward. While the entire novel is a creative discourse against American superficiality, prejudice, and ego-driven existence, particular scenes function to give a succinct view of such: an early scene in Newark that makes clear the misery in American life that has resulted from the division of a society into black and white (a division that profits the Jews), Dawn's beauty contest trophy and later search for beauty through plastic surgery as a response to her daughter's disappearance, and the final scene, a dinner party during which Seymour realizes that Dawn is having an affair with a neighbor, whose membership in the community is sanctioned by generations of American citizenship, and where Lou Levov is stabbed in the cheek by a disgruntled woman to whom he attempts to give sympathetic advice.

Lou's paternalism and his wife's domestically oriented life find challenges in late twentieth-century America. Feminist and race issues altered the landscape of American life; women and people of color rightly envied the place of white men. In the complicated changes that have taken place and not taken place, the criteria for success in America have not changed. When Seymour wonders, "What could have wounded Merry?" he refers to the sort of psychic wound that regularly features in contemporary fiction. The "wound" is something to which one returns—Merry cannot overcome her wound; Philip Roth returns again and again to the wounds that people suffer when either they or those close to them mindlessly follow the dictates of society. Those dictates may be the American work ethic, a puritanical view of life, an endless need for material consumption, or a growing rootlessness.

The story that Zuckerman dreams resonates with American readers because it describes so many aspects of American life. Yet the comments that Zuckerman makes early in the novel speak to Roth's postmodern interest in epistemology:

> You fight your superficiality, your shallowness, so as to try to come at people without unreal expectation, without an overload of bias or hope or arrogance, as untanklike as can be, sans cannon and machine guns and steel plaint half foot thick . . . and yet you never fail to do them wrong. . . . You get them wrong when you meet them, while you're anticipating meeting them; you get them wrong while you're with them, and then you go home to tell somebody else about the meeting and you get them all wrong again. . . . The fact remains that getting people right is not what living is all about anyway. It's getting them wrong that is living, getting them wrong and wrong and wrong, and then, on careful reconsideration, getting them wrong again. (35)

This is pretty disappointing news, especially when Zuckerman adds that writers, more than others, get people wrong. After all, don't we read novels to get it right? On the one hand, Roth creates a realistic portrait of Jewish American and American life; on the other hand, he acknowledges that no one is transparent and that our best attempts to understand others will fail to some extent. He, however, does not get it wrong when it comes to representing American society.

Many Jewish Americans writers have made the Holocaust the subject of their writing. Among those writers are nonsurvivors as well as survivors. Emily Budick argues that for Roth "speaking or writing the word Holocaust is the American Jew's inheritance and destiny; though how that destiny will be voiced will not be for any one writer (Jewish or non-Jewish) to decide."[25] Cynthia Ozick recalls the image of the wandering Jew in *The Shawl*, originally published as two stories, "The Shawl" (1980) and "Rosa" (1983), in the *New Yorker*. In the first story a young Jewish woman of about twenty-four, her baby of about a year, and her fourteen-year-old niece are on a march. It becomes clear by the second page with the reference to the yellow star they were made to wear that the march is to a concentration or death camp. Homeless and unprotected, persecuted, they signify the most horrific happening to Jewish life, the ultimate representation of homelessness. The baby Magda "flopped on with her little pencil legs scribbling this way and that, in search of the shawl; the pencil legs faltered where the light began."[26] Magda's "pencil legs," referred to several times, anticipate the role that the act of writing plays in the text. After Magda is killed—she runs on her thin legs to reach the shawl that Stella has taken from her and is shot by a guard—Rosa is fully articulate only when she writes, and she is comforted, though the comfort is meager, only by her writing. Her attachment to the shawl, on the other hand, indicates her silence: when she witnesses Magda's fall "from her flight against the electrified fence . . . she took Magda's shawl and filed her worn mouth with it, stuffed it in and stuffed it in, until she was swallowing up the wolf's screech and tasting the cinnamon and almond depth of Magda's saliva; and Rosa drank Magda's shawl until it dried"(10).

The powerful depiction of Rosa in "The Shawl" as knowing more about what would happen in the barracks—that Magda would be killed—than would have been possible illustrates a problem in holocaust fiction. The philosopher Berel Lang, who has written extensively about the Holocaust, argues that "'The Shawl' (along with several other texts he cites) exemplifies a particular sort of misrepresentation:

> [All these] include an overlay which not only assumes knowledge in the audience of the intent and outcome of the Holocaust, but, more significantly, projects into the consciousness of the individual characters depicted and so into the plot as a whole . . . the recognition of a cataclysm that goes beyond their own immediate condition, however dire that is. And *this*, it seems clear, *is* a misrepresentation—a serious one, as it combines both "technical" or historical and "narrative" and even "moral" misrepresentation. For . . . it was virtually never "*the Holocaust*" that its victims experienced. And this means that so far as the fullness of that event is made part of the consciousness or agency of figures depicted in Holocaust-representation, that representation becomes a *mis*representation at the level of the genre, a form of overdetermination which although understandable in origin, is yet a distortion.[27]

While the inclusion here of Lang's noteworthy contention is not intended to undermine the effect of this analysis of *The Shawl*, it points to two issues that are relevant here. First, the fact that some writers cannot imagine that what they know about the Holocaust was not known to those who experienced its effects, from the early days of the Nazi round-ups on, suggests that the ubiquity of the

Holocaust in the writing of Jews (what Roth refers to) has had just this effect of rewriting history. Second, like all fictional texts, holocaust fiction tells as much (sometimes more) about the time during which the fiction was written as it does about the time during which the fiction is set. As suggested above, *Yekl* expresses the transnational concern of Jewish identity; *American Pastoral* reflects the concern with Jewish assimilation at the end of the twentieth century, even though much of the novel takes place decades earlier.

Following this brief barely seven-full-page story, the story "Rosa" takes place in Miami, Florida, home to a whole host of Jewish retirees. Rosa Lublin has demolished her store in New York, where she had specialized in antique mirrors, which symbolize the continual reflection of her past life into her present consciousness. Her home is now a single room in a hotel where "instead of maid service there was a dumbwaiter on a shrieking pulley."[28] The silence of the dumbwaiter and the shrieking of the pulley suggest both Rosa's silence and her shrieking—the shawl in the mouth and out of the mouth.[29] The silence that Rosa meets from a world that does not want to listen is the subject of one of her letters to Magda—sometimes she writes to Stella, who has been her financial support since she smashed the store, and sometimes to Magda. To the first she writes in English, though her English is "crude"; to Magda she writes in a "brittle most excellent literary Polish" (14).

The most significant encounter Rosa has in Miami is with Persky, who comes from Poland. Their initial meeting, in a laundromat, results in a lasting friendship because Persky is determined to make Rosa his friend. He tells her of his past: he was a button manufacturer (Rosa loses a button on her dress; he would like to keep her "buttoned up"—not closed off, but "together"); his wife is mentally ill and institutionalized; he supports his son, who has a Ph.D. in philosophy, and he has two daughters who married successful businessmen. His story is fairly enough representative of the life of a Jew who came from Poland, as he did, in 1920. The very fact of contingency—of the sheer luck but enormous consequence of geography—finds expression in the meeting of these two people. As Berel Lang argues, "geography is not destiny—but neither is it an historical irrelevance."[30] Never after the Holocaust could American Jews whose families had immigrated anytime before World War II take lightly that significant personal fact. In Rosa's words to Mr. Persky, "My Warsaw isn't your Warsaw" (19). His America is not her America either: Persky is at home; Rosa feels herself to be homeless. She thinks:

Home. Where, Where? (38)

The single-line paragraph follows Rosa's reading of a letter from James W. Tree, a professor of social pathology, who has been "amass[ing] survivor data as rather a considerable specialty" (36). Suggesting the possibilities of "acute cerebral damage, derangement, disorientation, premature senility . . . hormonal changes, parasites, anemia, thready pulse, hyperventilation,"Dr. Tree asks Rosa to join his study "by means of an in-depth interview in [her] home" (38). The narrative expresses the superiority of writing over interviewing—that is, Rosa's writing over Tree's interviewing—but writing is not sentimentalized:

> What a curiosity it was to hold a pen—nothing but a small pointed stick, after all, oozing its hieroglyphic puddles: a pen that speaks, miraculously, Polish. A lock removed from the tongue. An immersion into the living language: all at once this cleanliness, this capacity, this power to make a history, to tell, to explain. To retrieve, to reprieve!
>   To lie. (44)

Rosa inscribes the untraceable, creating a life for Magda and an imaginary world for herself, but she knows that her act is "to lie."

Although Magda's "pencil legs scribbling this way and that" represent a writing of one history of the Jews, Rosa's continual writing expresses Ozick's brilliant articulation of the silence, despair, and delusion of a Jew who is not only without a home but whose home and culture have been destroyed. Rosa responds in kind by destroying her store and by rejecting the Jews whom she observes in Miami. The Jewish women she scrutinizes but refuses to acknowledge are "old socialists: idealists. The Human race was all they cared for" (16). Her reaction to the women, in particular, mirrors the cynicism about Jews who "make it in America" reflected in any number of Jewish American writers:

> They recited meals they used to cook in their old lives. Mainly the women thought about their hair. They went to hairdressers and came out into the brilliant day with plantlike crowns the color of zinnias. Sea-green paint on the eyelids. One could pity them: they were in love with rumors of their grandchildren, Katie at Bryn Mawr, Jeff at Princeton. To the grandchildren Florida was a slum, to Rosa it was a zoo. (17)

Rosa mocks the women in part out of jealousy, indicated in her rumination, "She had no one but her cold niece in Queens, New York" (17). She envies them not only their successful grandchildren but their at-home existence in America. The Jews' ability to become more American than non-Jewish Americans finds expression in Jewish jokes and Jewish fiction. In Woody Allen's story "No Kaddish for Weinstein,"[31] the protagonist is described as having "suffered injustices and persecutions because of his religion, mostly from his parents. True, the old man was a member of the synagogue, and his mother, too, but they could never accept the fact that their son was Jewish. 'How did it happen,' his father asked?" (206). This reversal of the proverbial worry of children that their parents may be different than other folk expresses a particular social phenomenon of the 1950s—the assimilationist desires of some Jews that were allowed freer expression than they had been heretofore. The parents' membership in a synagogue follows a typical move of Jews from a Yiddish immigrant identity of "Jew" to "Judaism." American Jews are represented as consuming as many material goods as any Americans, but they are also shown to progress professionally and economically. In many cases Jews are shown to have lost the imaginary place that characterized the early fiction, as Weinstein's father's query so aptly represents.

The Shawl expresses a longing for an imaginary place that is attenuated, though not entirely gone. The retired Jewish men Rosa observes read Yiddish newspapers, and the women cook recipes handed down through the generations. Rosa's Jewish world has disappeared. The entire world of European Jewry, hundreds of synagogues, hundreds of thousands of homes, and millions of books, have been destroyed, and, most important, the Nazis exterminated six million people. Rosa's envy for other women's motherhood—their children and their grandchildren—finds clear expression when she thinks that the philosophers talk about the meaning of life—but that the meaning of life is motherhood: "Motherhood—I've always known this—is a profound distraction from philosophy, and all philosophy is rooted in suffering over the passage of time. I mean the *fact* of motherhood, the physiological fact. . . . To pass on a whole genetic system" (41). The end of Rosa's motherhood, the death of Magda, symbolizes the end of centuries of Jewish European life. In the final lines of the narrative, Rosa accepts Persky into her life. To acknowledge Persky, who embraces life, despite personal disappointments, Rosa must let go of Magda, the reminder of death. This positive end must be seen in the light or perhaps the darkness of the end of her line, representing the end of the line of six million people. Sara Horowitz, using a term coined by the poet Paul Celan, explains that second-generation writers, "those who were not there (such as Cynthia Ozick), bear witness for the witness."[32]

In some ways a postscript to "The Shawl," Roth's *The Plot Against America* refigures the destruction of European Jewry into the dilemma of American Jewry. The novel revises history to have Lindberg defeat Roosevelt for a third term as president, acknowledging in this alteration of American events the lasting connection among Jews worldwide. Like the Jews in Europe, the Jews in America are removed from their homes, the safe places that American Jews have come to feel are inviolable.

The first-person fictional account of the experience of the Roth family (all the names are the same as those of Philip's family) includes divisions as well as integrity within the family. Philip's older brother, Sandy, at first refuses to believe that Lindbergh's administration will oppress the Jews. Philip's older cousin, who lost his leg in battle, gets into a fist fight with Philip's father over their differing political views. The violence of their fight recalls the violence that intrudes into the narrative of *American Pastoral* (Merry bombing the post office).[33]

The freedoms cherished in American society have been challenged on many fronts; in this novel their assured nature is called into question in the Jewish American home. Once again, Philip Roth represents through the experience of Jews in America some of the most significant cultural and political events in the country. In *The Dying Animal*, published in the spring of 2001, two lovers refer to Osama Bin Laden's expected attempt to blow up an American site at the turn of the twentieth century. Focusing on home as the place where the experiences of the outside world have their most intense expression, his narratives have dramatic and realistic coherence.

This essay began with the claim that "to understand a culture, one must study its literature." In the first extended example of Jewish literature, Cahan's *Yekl*, the transnational concerns of Jews figure significantly into the representation of Jewish life in America. Late twentieth- and early twenty-first century fiction, by writers from all over the world, takes up global matters, suggesting that any "culture" is inextricably linked to larger world, not only national, matters. Ozick's *The Shawl* is just one instance of the impact of worldwide events on the subject matter of fiction. Roth's uncanny mention of a terrorist event in a novel published just before September 11, 2001, anticipates the global concern with terrorism expressed in much recent fiction.[34] Yet the space of the home retains its privileged position in even fiction that incorporates global and/or transnational events and concerns. In Jewish American fiction as well as other fiction, the dynamics of family life and intimate relationships offer insight into the particular desires, habits, and experiences of individual groups, inscribing the diverse and changing experiences of the group.

NOTES

1. Philip Fisher discusses literature and the passions in *The Vehement Passions* (New Haven, 2002), introduction.

2. Mark Shechner, "Jewish Writers," in Daniel Hoffman, ed., *The Harvard Guide to Contemporary American Writing* (Cambridge, 1979), 191–239.

3. Bonnie K. Lyons, "American Jewish Fiction Since 1945," in Lewis Fried et al., eds., *Handbook of Jewish American Literature: An Analytical Guide to Topics, Themes, and Sources* (Westport, CT, 1988), 61–89.

4. Jules Chametzky et al., eds., *Jewish American Literature: A Norton Anthology* (New York: Norton, 2001), 1–16.

5. "The NBA Winner Talks Back, Martha McGregor/1960," in George J. Searles, ed., *Conversations with Philip Roth* (Jackson, MI, 1992), 1.

6. Thomas Friedman, from a talk given at Utica College in April 1985, also printed in Utica College Occasional Papers, an in-house publication. Quoted in Diane Matza, ed., *Sephardic-American Voices: Two Hundred Years of a Literary Legacy* (Hanover, 1997), 1.

7. Karen Brodkin discusses the American phenomenon of race in the 1950s in *How Jews Became White Folks and What That Says About Race in America* (New Brunswick, NJ, 1998).

8. Contemporary readers of Jewish American fiction are likely to know the works of Abraham Cahan, *Yekl: A Tale of the New York Ghetto* (New York, 1896) and *The Rise of David Levinsky* (1917), in particular, and Anzia Yezierska; although *Hungry Hearts* (1920) and *The Children of Loneliness* (1923) are less well-known than *The Bread Givers* (New York, 1925). James Oppenheim (1882–1932), an American-born Jew, grew up in a middle-class home in New York. Working as a teacher and a social worker in the slums of the Lower East Side, he reflected in his writings on his experience as assistant director of Hudson Guild Settlement and later the Hebrew Technical School for girls. His works include *Dr. Rast* (1909), *The Nine-Tenths* (1911), and *Pay Envelopes* (1911). Arthur Bullard (1870–1929) studied social conditions of the early twentieth century, worked in social service as a member of the University Settlement in New York, and later as a probation office that represented the Prison Association of New York. He traveled to Africa, the Middle East, the Balkans, and Central Europe and wrote about these experiences. His novel *The Fugitive* (1904) incorporates many of the experiences of his travels, but in one section deals exclusively with Jewish life in America. His sensitivity to the rigors of life incumbent on immigrant laborers is evident in *Comrade Yetta* (1913), a novel he dedicated "to organized workers."

9. *Pittsburgh Bulletin*, August 8, 1896, quoted in Richard Weatherford, *Stephen Crane: The Critical Heritage* (New York, 1973), 46–47.

10. Cahan, *Yekl*, 3–4.

11. Ibid., 33.

12. Jules Chametzky, *From the Ghetto: The Fiction of Abraham Cahan* (Amherst, 1977). Matthew Frye Jacobson, "The Quintessence of the Jew: Polemics of Nationalism and Peoplehood in Turn-of-the-Century Yiddish Fiction," in Werner Sollors, ed., *Multilingual America: Transnationalism, Ethnicity, and the Languages of American Literature* (New York, 1998), 103–11. According to Jacobson, *Yekl* is much like the works of Leon Kobrin, Jacob Gordin, Bernard Goren and the poetry of Morris Winchevsky, Abraham Liessen, and Morris Rosenfeld. These were generated in social and political contexts in which Yiddish thinkers on both sides of Atlantic were absorbed with the question of Jewish identity itself and its relation to other ethnic religious racial or national groups on the world scene (104). On Cahan, see also Sanford E. Marovitz, *Abraham Cahan* (New York, 1996).

13. Cahan, *Yekl*, 22.

14. Jacobson, "The Quintessence of the Jew," 106.

15. Hana Wirth-Nesher writes that the courtship scene between Hugo and Sara "intertwines desire for English and sexual desire as the body is roused to produce consonants without debasing traces of other languages." "Language as Homeland in Jewish-American Literature," in David Biale et al., ed., *Insider/Outsider* (Berkeley, 1998), 212–30.

16. "In a Limbo Between Past and Present," *New York Times*, May 17, 1959. 4.

17. Philip Roth, "Goodbye, Columbus," in *Goodbye, Columbus* (New York, 1959), 1–136.

18. Elaine Tyler May, *Homeward Bound: American Families in the Cold War Era* (New York, 1988).

19. E.g. , Philip Roth's *The Dying Animal* (Boston, 2001).

20. Timothy Parrish, "The End of Identity: Philip Roth's *American Pastoral*," *Shofar* September 1, 2000, 84–99. Cynthia Ozick quoted in Elaine M. Kauvar, "An Interview with Cynthia Ozick," *Contemporary Literature* 34.3 (1993): 373.

21. Roth, *American Pastoral*, 92.

22. Marshall Bruce Gentry writes that "Philip Roth's *American Pastoral* contains a feminist subversion of its dominant male voices: the protagonist Swede Levov, the narrator Nathan Zuckerman, even author Roth. While reviews treat Swede as a good man punished for his virtues, the novel's women refute his reputation as the world's nicest guy. Swede's major faults are that he accepts the injustices of capitalism, that he never genuinely loves women, and that he does not think for himself. In creating ambiguity about his stance toward Swede, Roth may be admitting he has built a house of fiction that causes women to become bombmakers." "Newark Maid Feminism in Philip Roth's *American Pastoral*," *Shofar*, September 1, 2000, 74–83. Although I cannot specifically take up Gentry's intriguing claims about Roth's feminism here, the essay offers a fascinating way to consider the novel.

23. Ibid., 78.

24. Sandra Jumamoto Stanley, "Mourning the 'Greatest Generation': Myth and History in Philip Roth's *American Pastoral*," *Twentieth Century Literature* 51.1 (March 2005): 1–24.

25. Emily Budick, "Acknowledging the Holocaust," in Ephraim Sicher, ed., *Breaking Crystal* (Urbana, 1998), 329–43.

26. Cynthia Ozick, *The Shawl* (New York, 1990), 7.

27. Berel Lang, "Representation and Misrepresentation: On or about the Holocaust," presented at the Representations of the Holocaust in Literature and Film II: Consultation at the College of William and Mary, April 2006. Quoted with permission of the author.

28. Ozick, *The Shawl*, 15.

29. Michael G. Levine offers a psychoanalytic analysis of Rosa's silence and of other aspects of the novella in "'Toward an Addressable You': Ozick's *The Shawl* and the Mouth of the Witness," in Marianne Hirsch and Irene Kacandes, eds., *Teaching the Representation of the Holocaust* (New York, 2004), 396–411.

30. Berel Lang, "Act and Idea in the Nazi Genocide," in *Judaism* 53.3–4 (Summer/Fall 2004): 253–59.

31. The story is in Woody Allen, *Without Feathers* (New York, 1972), 205–11.

32. Sara Horowitz, "Auto/Biography and Fiction After Auschwitz," in Sicher, *Breaking Crystal*, 276–94.

33. Roth's *The Human Stain* (Boston, 2001) includes several violent scenes, centered on the amorous relationship between the protagonist, a professor born to a black family who passes as a "white" Jew, and a woman who cleans houses and milks dairy cows and her Vietnam veteran partner. On Roth see also Derek Parker Royal, ed., *Philip Roth: New Perspectives on an American Author* (Westport, CT, 2005); and Mark Shechner, *Up Society's Ass, Copper: Rereading Philip Roth* (Madison, 2003).

34. The following examples of highly esteemed fiction that incorporates global matters into plot and character are only a few on a list of many: Michael Chabon, *The Yiddish Policeman's Union* (2007), Don DeLilo, *Falling Man* (2007), John Updike, *The Terrorist* (2006), Ian McEwan, *Saturday* ([2005] which was regarded to be predictive of the terrorist events in London in July, 2005), Hari Kunzru, *Transmission* (2004), Azar Nafasi, *Teaching Lolita in Tehran* (2003), Kazuo Ishiguro, *When We Were Orphans* (2003) and *The Unconsoled* (1999), Zadie Smith, *White Teeth* (2000), and Jose Saramago, *Blindness* (1995).

CONTRIBUTORS

Dianne Ashton is professor of religion studies and director of the American studies program at Rowan University. She is the coeditor of *Four Centuries of Jewish Women's Spirituality* (with Ellen M. Umansky) and is currently working with Umansky on a second edition of that work. She writes widely on the lives of Jewish women in America, looking particularly at nineteenth-century Jewish life. Her books on American Jews include *Rebecca Gratz: Women and Judaism in Antebellum America* and *Jewish Life in Pennsylvania*. She is a past fellow of the Gilder Lehrman Institute for American History and the American Jewish Archives and recipient of grants from the National Endowment for the Humanities and the Hadassah Brandeis Institute for her upcoming work on Hanukkah in America.

Mark K. Bauman earned masters degrees from Lehigh University and the University of Chicago as well as a Ph.D. from Emory. He retired as a professor of history in 2002 from Atlanta Metropolitan College. His dissertation on Southern Methodist bishop Warren Candler won the Jesse Lee Prize from the Methodist Commission on Archives and History and was published in 1981. Consequently he has written a biography of Atlanta rabbi Harry Epstein, coedited *Quiet Voices: Southern Rabbis and Black Civil Rights*, edited *Dixie Diaspora: An Anthology of Southern Jewish History*, and published over forty-five articles in anthologies and historical journals dealing with America ethnic, religious, and minority history. His most recent articles on southern Jewry appeared in *COMPASS*, Corrie E. Norman and Don S. Armentrout, eds., *Religion in the Contemporary South*, and Glenn Feldman, ed., *Politics and Religion in the White South*. He also served as editor of the journal of the Georgia Association of Historians, guest edited three special issues of *American Jewish History*, and is founding and current editor of *Southern Jewish History*. Bauman is a past president of the G.A.H., recipient of its 2002 Distinguished Service Award, and past vice president of the Southern Jewish Historical Society. Recipient of Starkoff and Director's Fellowships from the American Jewish Archives in Cincinnati, he was also a Mason Fellow in the department of religious studies, College of William and Mary (Spring 2005) where he taught Judaism in America.

Kimmy Caplan teaches modern Jewish history at the department of Jewish history, Bar-Ilan University, Israel. His fields of scholarly interest include American Jewish religious history, Jewish preaching in the nineteenth and twentieth centuries, Jewish Orthodoxy and ultra-Orthodoxy. He is the author of *Orthodoxy in the New World* and *The Internal Popular Discourse in Israeli Haredi Society*, and coedited with Emmanuel Sivan a volume entitled *Israeli Haredim: Integration Without Assimilation?* (all in Hebrew). In addition, he has published articles on various aspects of the aforementioned topics.

Eli Faber is professor of history at John Jay College of Criminal Justice and at the Graduate Center, both of the City University of New York. He is the author of *A Time for Planting: The First Migration, 1654–1820*, the first volume of the five-volume work entitled *The Jewish People in America*, as well as of *Jews, Slaves, and the Slave Trade: Setting the Record Straight*. He edited *American Jewish History*, the journal of the American Jewish Historical Society, for the period 2001–2006.

Eric L. Goldstein received his Ph.D. in history from the University of Michigan (2000) and is currently associate professor of history and Jewish studies at Emory University, where he also directs the graduate program in Jewish studies. He is the author of *The Price of Whiteness: Jews, Race and American Identity*, which explores what it has meant to be Jewish in a nation defined by the categories of black and white. He has written and lectured widely on topics including American Zionism, Yiddish culture in America, American Jewish women, Southern Jewish history, and black-Jewish relations. He is currently at work on a study of popular Yiddish print culture in the United States during the late nineteenth and early twentieth centuries and the connection between reading and identity among Eastern European Jewish immigrants. He is the editor of the quarterly academic journal *American Jewish History*.

Jeffrey S. Gurock is Libby M. Klaperman Professor of Jewish History at Yeshiva University. He is a former associate editor of *American Jewish History* and has been a chair of the Academic Council of the American Jewish Historical Society. His most recent work is *Judaism's Encounter With American Sports*.

Jenna Weissman Joselit is a professor of American studies and modern Judaic studies at Princeton University where she specializes in the history of daily life in nineteenth- and twentieth-century America and its relationship to religion and ethnicity. The author, among other books, of *The Wonders of America: Reinventing Jewish Culture, 1880-1950*, which received the National Jewish Book Award in History, and *A Perfect Fit: Clothes, Character, and the Promise of America*, she is also a longtime columnist for the *Forward* newspaper as well as a frequent contributor to the *New Republic* and TNR

Online. Currently at work on a book about America's fascination with the Ten Commandments, Joselit will be a visiting scholar at the Library of Congress's Kluge Center in 2007.

Melissa R. Klapper earned her B.A. from Goucher College and her Ph.D. from Rutgers University. She is currently associate professor of history at Rowan University. Her research focuses on the intersections of gender, ethnicity, and youth. Dr. Klapper has published *Jewish Girls Coming of Age in America, 1860–1920* and *Small Strangers: The Experiences of Immigrant Children in America, 1880–1925*.

Alan Levenson has a B.A. and an M.A. from Brown University and a Ph. D. from Ohio State University. He teaches courses in Jewish history, modern Jewish thought, and Bible. His essays on German Jewry, modern Jewish thought, and pedagogy have appeared in a variety of journals. He has received fellowships from Tel Aviv University, the American Council of Learned Societies, the German Academic Exchange Program (DAAD), and the Lucius Littauer Foundation. His book *Modern Jewish Thinkers: An Introduction* has recently been reissued in paperback. He is currently at work on another popular work that stems from his teaching at Siegal College, *Reading the Bible Through Jewish Eyes: The Story of Joseph*.

Rafael Medoff is founding director of the David S. Wyman Institute for Holocaust Studies, which focuses on issues related to America's response to the Holocaust (www.WymanInstitute.org). He has served as associate editor of the scholarly journal *American Jewish History* and is the author of seven books about the Holocaust, Zionism, and the history of American Jewry, the most recent of which is *A Race Against Death: Peter Bergson, America, and the Holocaust* (coauthored with David S. Wyman). His textbook, *Jewish Americans and Political Participation*, was named an Outstanding Academic Title of 2003 by the American Library Association's *Choice* magazine. He has also authored numerous essays for scholarly journals, and has contributed to the *Encyclopedia Judaica* and other reference books. Dr. Medoff has taught Jewish history at Ohio State Unversity, Purchase College of the State University of New York, and elsewhere.

Pamela S. Nadell is the Patrick Clendenen Professor of History and director of the Jewish studies program at American University. She is the author or editor of five books, including *Women Who Would Be Rabbis: A History of Women's Ordination, 1889–1985*.

Riv-Ellen Prell is professor of American studies at the University of Minnesota, and teaches in Jewish studies as well as in the department of gender, sexuality and women. She is the author of *Fighting to Become Americans: Jews, Gender, and the Anxiety of Assimilation, Prayer and Community: The Havurah in American Judaism*, coeditor of *Interpreting Women's Lives: Personal Narrative and Feminist Theory*, and editor of *Women Remaking American Judaism*.

Linda Raphael, M.A., Ph.D., is associate clinical professor of psychiatry and behavioral sciences and director of medical humanities at the George Washington University School of Medicine, Washington, DC. She is the author of *Narrative Skepticism: Moral Agency and Representations of Consciousness in Fiction* and coedited (with Marc Lee Raphael) *When Night Fell: An Anthology of Holocaust Short Stories*.

Marc Lee Raphael is the Nathan and Sophia Gumenick Professor of Judaic Studies, professor of religious studies, chair of the department of religious studies, and director of the program in Judaic studies at the College of William and Mary. He is the author of many books about Jews and Judaism in the United States, including *Judaism in America*. He is currently writing a history of the synagogue in America.

Jeffrey Shandler is an associate professor in the department of Jewish studies at Rutgers University. He is the author of *Adventures in Yiddishland: Postvernacular Language and Culture, While America Watches: Televising the Holocaust,* and *Entertaining America: Jews, Movies, and Broadcasting* (with J. Hoberman), among other titles.

Michael E. Staub teaches English and American studies at Baruch College, City University of New York. He is the author of numerous articles and reviews; these have appeared in *American Quarterly, Shofar, Radical History Review, Journal of American History,* the *Nation, American Jewish History, Tikkun,* and elsewhere. He is also a contributor to several anthologies, including *Wrestling with Zion: Progressive Jewish-American Responses to the Israeli-Palestinian Conflict,* edited by Tony Kushner and Alisa Solomon. He has published four books, including *The Jewish 1960s: An American Sourcebook* and *Torn at the Roots: The Crisis of Jewish Liberalism in Postwar America.* Among his current research interests is an examination of the role played by liberal commentators like Thomas L. Friedman in rallying popular support for Operation Iraqi Freedom and the invasion of Iraq in 2003.

William Toll teaches American Jewish history as an adjunct professor at the University of Oregon in Eugene. His books include *The Making of an Ethnic Middle Class, Portland Jewry Over Four Generations, Women, Men, and Ethnicity: Essays on the Structure and Thought of American Jewry,* and *Commerce, Climate, and Community, A History of Portland and Its People* (ohs.org/education/oregonhistory/narratives). He is currently completing, with Ava Kahn and Ellen Eisenberg, a history of Jews in the American West.

Beth S. Wenger is the Katz Family Term Chair in American Jewish History and associate professor of history at the University of Pennsylvania. She is the author of *New York Jews and the Great Depression: Uncertain Promise* and *The Jewish Americans: Three Centuries of Jewish Voices in America.* Wenger is also coeditor of *Remembering the Lower East Side: American Jewish Reflections* and *"Holy Land:" Place, Past, and Future in American Jewish Culture.* Her current book project is tentatively titled *History Lessons: The Invention of American Jewish Heritage.*

Stephen J. Whitfield holds the Max Richter Chair in American Civilization at Brandeis University. He is the author of eight books, including *In Search of American Jewish Culture,* and is the editor, most recently, of *A Companion to Twentieth-Century America.* He has written mostly on the intersection of politics and ideas in twentieth-century America and on American Jewish history.

INDEX

Abraham (Biblical), 38
Abram, Morris, 279
Abrams, Elliott, 336, 338
Abzug, Bella, 156, 391
academic quotas, 3, 13, 147–148, 289n39, 348, 436. *See also* higher education
acculturation, 69, 209, 238n3, 267, 292, 382n9; as accommodation, 114; versus assimilation, 205, 263. *See also* Americanization
Ackelsberg, Martha, 389
Ackerman, Walter, 214n28, 216n61
Adler, Cyrus, 66, 94, 95
Adler, Jacob, 80
Adler, Rachel: *Engendering Judaism*, 394–395, 419, 423; on Jewish law and gender equality, 416–417; "The Jew Who Wasn't There," 418–419
adult education, 414. *See also* education
Adventure in Freedom (Handlin), 1
affluence: Jewish attainment of, 13, 142, 145, 146, 251, 343; mercantile and professional skills gained by Jews, 29,

73, 145, 235; social life and, 248; stereotypes of, 50; upward mobility, 77, 115–116, 144–145, 266–267. *See also* poverty
African Americans, racism towards, 131, 152, 317–319. *See also* Black-Jewish relations; civil rights movement
Afro-American (journal), 317
aggadah (Jewish lore), 418, 428n1
Agudat Harabanim. *See* Union of Orthodox Jewish Congregations of America
Agudath Israel of America, 182
Aguilar, Grace, *The Spirit of Judaism*, 58
Ahavath Achim, 102
Aish HaTorah, 204
"AJCommittee". *See* American Jewish Committee
"AJCongress". *See* American Jewish Congress
Alfange, Dean, 305
Allen, Frederick Lewis, *Only Yesterday*, 258